Public Library San Francisco

Classified English Prose Fiction

Public Library San Francisco

Classified English Prose Fiction

ISBN/EAN: 9783744694902

Printed in Europe, USA, Canada, Australia, Japan

Cover: Foto ©Thomas Meinert / pixelio.de

More available books at **www.hansebooks.com**

San Francisco Free Public Library.

CLASSIFIED

English Prose Fiction,

INCLUDING

Translations and Juvenile Works

WITH

Notes and Index to Subject-references.

No. 6, 1891.

SAN FRANCISCO:

H. S. Crocker Company, Stationers and Printers.

1891.

PREFACE.

In re-cataloguing the fiction department of this library it was thought best to attempt to push a little further toward complete execution the aim of the Class List of English Prose Fiction (sixth edition, 1877), issued by the Public Library of Boston. As the work progressed the scope enlarged, so that the present volume reaches, perhaps, beyond the limit heretofore attained in like endeavors. It is hoped that this classified and annotated catalogue will not only enable the reader to find the novel desired, but draw the attention to substantial matter in other departments of the library which, without it, might pass, in too many instances, unexamined, not to say undiscovered. It is hoped, too, that this is a step toward bringing the library into closer relationship with the schools, and lastly, that our patrons will find herein a handy reference work for general use, at least until such time as the mass of material scattered through the library shall be arranged and made thoroughly accessible. A special effort has been made to enter authors' names with all the fullness and accuracy possible, the real name, when known, being followed by the pseudonym in brackets.

EXPLANATIONS.

The class number 808 indicates a book for young people.
For subjects with reference notes see index, pp. 301–306.

In conformity with the recommendations of the American Library Association, the more common masculine and feminine fore-names have been abbreviated by means of a colon or two periods placed after the initial, *viz.*:

MASCULINE.		FEMININE.	
A:	Augustus	A..	Anna
B:	Benjamin	B..	Beatrice
C:	Charles	C..	Charlotte
D:	David	D..	Delia
E:	Edward	E..	Elizabeth
F:	Frederick	F..	Frances
G:	George	G..	Grace
H:	Henry	H..	Helen
I:	Isaac	I..	Isabella
J:	John	J..	Jane
K:	Karl	K..	Katharine, Kate
L:	Louis	L..	Louisa
M:	Mark	M..	Mary
N:	Nicholas	N..	Nancy
O:	Otto	O..	Olivia
P:	Peter	P..	Pauline
R:	Richard	R..	Rebecca
S:	Samuel	S..	Sarah
T:	Thomas	T..	Theresa
		U..	Ursula
		V..	Victoria
W:	William	W..	Wilhelmina
		Z..	Zenobia

A single star at the left of the shelf-number signifies that the book can be taken home only by permission of the Librarian; two stars signify that the book cannot go out of the Library.

This publication is a section of the intended general catalogue.

JOHN VANCE CHENEY,
Librarian.

San Francisco, August 1, 1891.

REGULATIONS.

(Reprint of Borrower's Hand-Book issued February, 1888.)

OPEN DAYS AND HOURS.

The Library will be open every day from 9 A. M. to 9 P. M., except Sundays, legal holidays, and the evenings before Christmas and New Year's. On Sundays it will be open from 1 to 5 P. M.

It may, however, be closed at any time by action of the Trustees.

WHO MAY BECOME BORROWERS.

All residents of the City and County of San Francisco, twelve years of age and over, and all non-resident tax-payers of said city and county, may become borrowers.

HOW TO BECOME BORROWERS.

Apply at the Library for an application (*Form No. 25*), fill it out according to directions thereon, and return it.

Call again after two or more days, and, if the application be approved, a *card* will be issued which entitles the owner to full privileges of the Library for the period of two years from the date of issue.

HOW TO DRAW A BOOK.

FOR HOME USE.—Fill out one of the *buff* blanks, provided for this purpose, with the name and address, *as on the borrower's card*, together with the shelf number of the desired book, as found in the Catalogue ; then hand in at the Delivery Desk both the buff slip and card.

FOR USE IN THE LIBRARY.—Fill out a *pink* blank and hand in the slip only. If the book be delivered, hand in the door check.

RULES CONCERNING BOOKS.

THERE ARE THREE CLASSES OF BOOKS.

I. Books issued simply on presentation of card, or slip and door check, for use either at home or in the Library.

II. Books issued on card, or slip and door check, by permission of the Librarian.

III. Books issued on slip and door check only, and not to be taken out of the Library. Among these are : books of reference, books restricted by terms of gift, books not easily replaced, books deemed unsuitable for general circulation, unbound periodicals, and periodicals dating back more than five years. Books with purely medical contents will be issued only to adults, to medical students, and to physicians. The Librarian will exercise his discretion in granting the use of any books of the classes named in this paragraph. An appeal from his decision will always lie to the Trustees.

THE NUMBER OF BOOKS THAT MAY BE DRAWN AT ONE TIME.

Only one book at a time may be obtained for either home or Library use. An exception will be made when a single volume is of little service without others of the set to which it belongs.

HOW LONG A BOOK MAY BE RETAINED.

Books may be retained two weeks, if no other limit be set at the time of drawing, and may be renewed for the same period either by personal application or by letter; after which they cannot be again issued to the same borrower until they shall have been at least one day in the Library.

Books in the hands of borrowers are, however, always subject to recall for Library purposes.

Books must be returned at the expiration of the time for which they are issued, all days to be counted except the day of issue. If a book becomes due on a closed day the time will be extended to the next open day.

FINE FOR BOOKS OVERDUE.

A fine of five cents will be imposed for each day that a book is overdue. Borrowers refusing to pay such fines will be denied the privileges of the Library.

FORBIDDEN.

I. Borrowers are forbidden to lend Library books, or to exchange them with other borrowers. Each book must be kept in the personal custody of the borrower, and returned on the card on which it was drawn.

II. Marking, writing in, or in any way defacing any Library book, pamphlet or paper, is strictly forbidden, and will subject the offender to the penalties of the law.

PENAL CODE.

Section 623 of the Penal Code reads:—

"And every person who maliciously cuts, tears, defaces, breaks or injures any book, map, chart, picture, engraving, statue, coin, medal, apparatus, or other work of literature, art or mechanics, or object of curiosity, deposited in any public library, gallery, museum, collection, fair or exhibition, is guilty of felony."

The Trustees offer a reward of Fifty Dollars for the detection and conviction of any person mutilating any book, periodical, pamphlet or journal belonging to the Library.

Borrowers finding any book or periodical defaced or mutilated are required to report the fact to the Librarian before taking the book from the Library.

LOSS OR INJURY.

If a book belonging to a set be lost or injured, the book must be replaced, or the set paid for by the borrower.

Borrowers refusing to comply with this regulation will be denied the privileges of the library, besides being held legally responsible.

RULES CONCERNING CARDS.

NOT TRANSFERABLE.

Cards may be transferred for the use of members of the owner's household only. When an infringement of this rule is detected, the card will be taken up.

CHANGE OF RESIDENCE.

Notice of change of residence of borrower or guarantor must be given immediately to the Secretary of the Library. Neglect to give this notice will subject the borrower to a forfeiture of privileges.

SURRENDER OF CARDS.

Cards must be surrendered at the Library when the holders cease to be residents or tax-payers of San Francisco.

LOST CARDS—DUPLICATE CARDS—TRIPLICATE CARDS.

If a borrower's card be lost, a duplicate may be issued upon a new application, indorsed by the same or another guarantor, two weeks after filing the application. If a duplicate card be lost, three months must elapse after notice to the Secretary and filing of new application, before a triplicate card can be issued.

Borrower's cards found in books or elsewhere must be returned to the Secretary.

Cards may be canceled at any time by the Secretary or Librarian.

LIABILITY OF THE GUARANTOR.

A guarantor is understood to guarantee the card issued on the application signed by him, and he is liable on his guaranty for all uses made of the card guaranteed, *until its return and cancellation*. If a book is not returned, or a fine not paid within ten days after due, the guarantor will be called upon to pay such fine or the value of such book.

MISCELLANEOUS.

THE DOOR CHECK.

Visitors, whether they have borrower's cards or not, must take a check from the door-keeper when they come in, and return it when they go out. *This door check must be kept*, and not laid down on the tables or elsewhere in the Library.

COMPLAINTS.

Complaints about the service of the Library must be made to the Librarian immediately after the occurrence of cause of complaint ; and, if in writing, must be signed with the writer's name and address.

Complaints against the management of the Library, or the conduct of any employé thereof, must be reduced to writing and submitted to the Trustees through their Secretary, who will place them before the Board at the earliest opportunity.

NO ADMITTANCE TO THE BOOK SHELVES.

No person other than an officer or employé will be admitted to the shelves or behind the Library railing unless by permission of the Trustees, or when invited by the Secretary or by the Librarian.

WRITING WITH INK.

All writing in the reading-room must be done with a pencil. The use of ink is forbidden.

ABUSE OF LIBRARY PRIVILEGES.

When, in the judgment of the Librarian, a violation of any of the rules of the Library demands summary action, he may cause the offender to be at once ejected, and excluded from the Library until such time as the Trustees may have opportunity to give final decision.

GIFTS.

The Trustees will gladly accept, for the Library, gifts of books and pamphlets of every description that may be of public interest.

On notice to the Librarian, packages in the city will be sent for.

Contributors living at a distance may forward at the expense of the Library.

English Fiction.

A., J. Y., *pseud.* See Akerman, J: Yonge.
"A man's a man for a' that." 823.1277
"Abandoned." Verne, J. 823.5784
Abbé Constantin, L'. Halévy, L. 823.3845
Same. 823.4563; *in* 823.6690
Abbé Tigrane. Fabre, F. 823.4136
Abbot, The. Scott, *Sir* W. 823.1391
Same. in 823.4803; *in* 823.5159; *in* 823.6027
Abbott, Edwin Abbott. [*A square.*] Flatland:
a romance of many dimensions. 823.4902
Abbott, Jacob. American history. 8 vols.
  v. 1. Aboriginal America. 973.690
  v. 2. Discovery of America. 973.691
  v. 3. The southern colonies. 973.692
  v. 4. The northern colonies. 973.693
  v. 5. Wars of the colonies. 973.694
  v. 6. Revolt of the colonies. 973.695
  v. 7. War of the revolution. 973.696
  v. 8. Washington. 973.697
—— Harper's story b'ks. 12 vols. 808.580-91
—— Marco Paul ser. 6 vols. 808.719-24
  v. 1. In New York. 808.719
  v. 2. On Erie canal. 808.720
  v. 3. In the forests of Maine. 808.721
  v. 4. In Vermont. 808.722
  v. 5. In Boston. 808.723
  v. 6. At the Springfield armory. 808.724
—— Rollo ser. 14 vols. 808.903-16
—— Rollo's tour in Europe. 10 vols.
                 808.917-26
—— Science for the young; or, the funda-
mental principles of modern philosophy
explained and illustrated. 4 vols.
  v. 1. Heat. 808.716
  v. 2. Light. 808.798
  v. 3. Water and land. 808.715
  v. 4. Force. 808.1105
Abbott, J: Stephen Cabot. American pioneers
and patriots.
  Boone, Daniel. 808.542
  Columbus, Christopher. 808.538
  Crockett, D: 808.541
  Franklin, B: 808.797
  Jones, J: P. Life . . . of. 808.546
  Kidd, *Capt.* W: 808.540
  La Salle, Chevalier de, and his companions.
             808.1050
  Standish, Miles. 808.545
  Stuyvesant, P: 808.547
  Washington, G: 808.543
Abdalla, History of. Weber, H.
            p. 593, *in* ** 823.6232
Abdallah. Laboulaye, E. R. L. 823.4100
Abel Allnutt. Morier, J. * 823.6180
Ablest man in the world, The. 28 pp.
Mitchell, E: P. p. 45, *in* 823.4711
Aboard the Mavis. Markham, R: 808.1866
Aboriginal America. Abbott, J. 973.690
About, Edmond François Valentin (1828-
1885). The king of the mountains. Tr. by
M., L. Booth. 823.6976
—— The man with the broken ear. Tr. by
H: Holt. 823.3436
—— *Same.* 823.6804
—— The notary's nose. Tr. by H: Holt.
             823.6836
—— Rouge et noir: a tale of Baden-Baden.
Tr. by E. R. 823.6282
—— The story of an honest man. 823.6051
  Note.—For his life and writings, *see* Appletons'
journal, v. 3. p. 664. ** 51.053.—Mazade, C. de. Les
idées libérales. (*Rev. d. Mondes.* 2e pér. v. 22.)
p. 727, *in* ** 54.255.—Men of the third republic.
923.1165.—Montégut, E. Les romans d'A. (*Rev. d.
d. Mondes.* 2e pér. v. 22.) p. 987, *in* ** 54.227.—Sat-
urday rev., v. 59. p. 110, ** 52.484¹.
  See also Poole's Index (to 1882). p. 2, *in* ** 50.1;—
Same. Jan. 1, 1882-Jan. 1, 1887. p. 1, *in* ** 50.1².

English Fiction. *Contin.*

About giants and other wonder people.
Smithson, I., *and* Barnes, G: F. 808.1598
About money and other things. Craik, *Mrs.*
D. M. (M.) 823.5518
Abram Van Zandt, the man in the picture.
Lowell, R. T. S. p. 11, *in* 823.1019
Absentee, The. Edgeworth, M. ** 823.4655
Abyssinia. See also Africa, note.
—— Dalton, W: The tiger prince; or, ad-
ventures in the wilds of Abyssinia. 808.870
—— Hawkesworth, J: Almoran and Ham-
et: an oriental tale. (Life in Abyssinia.)
(Barbauld, *Mrs.* A. L. (A.), *ed. The British
novelists*, v. 26.) p. 135, *in* ** 823.2087
—— Johnson, S: History of Rasselas, prince
of Abyssinia. (Life in Abyssinia.) 823.903
  Note.—See Table décennale du "Tour du
monde." 1860-1870. p. 1, *in* ** 913.138¹.—Wilkins,
Col. H. St. Reconnoitring in Abyssinia (1867-8).
916.129.—Winstanley, W. A visit to Abyssinia.
2 vols. 1881. 916.191-2.
  See also Catalogues of this Library.
    No. 2. 1880. p. 2.   No. 4, 1884, p. 1.
    No. 3, 1882, p. 1.   No. 5, 1888, p. 1.
  See also Poole's Index (to 1882). p. 3, *in* ** 50.1;—
Same. Jan. 1, 1882-Jan. 1, 1887. p. 1, *in* ** 50.1².
Acadia. See Nova Scotia.
Accomplished gentleman. Sturgis, J. 823.1535
Same. 823.5445
Achilles Tatius. The loves of Clitopho and
Leucippe. (Greek romances. Tr. by Rev.
R. Smith.) p. 349, *in* 823.2134
Achsah. Round, W: M. F. 823.1371
Across the chasm. Magruder, J. 823.5607
Adam, *Uncle, pseud.* See Wetterbergh, Carl
Anton.
Adam, *Mme.* Edmond. See Adam, *Mme.* Ju-
liette (Lamber).
Adam, *Mme.* Juliette (Lamber). A fascinat-
ing woman. (Laide.) 823.4527
Adam and Eve. Parr, *Mrs.* L. (T.) 823.6092
Adam Bede. Cross, *Mrs.* M.. A.(E.) 823.996
Adam Dickson. Mason, T: 823.7187
Adam Graeme of Mossgray, Memoirs and res-
olutions of. Oliphant, *Mrs.* M. O. (W.)
                   in 823.5089
Adams, Francis Colburn. Siege of Washing-
ton, D. C., written . . . for little people.
                   808.1700
Adams, Herbert Cadwallader. Charlie Luck-
en at school and college. 823.6333
—— Perils in the Transvaal and Zululand.
                   808.1618
—— Schoolboy honour: a tale of Halminster
college. 808.1608
—— School-days at Kingscourt: a tale of
1803. 808.1567
—— Who was Philip? a tale of public school
life. 808.1609
Adams, J: S. Town and country. 823.2
Adams, J: T. The lost hunter: a tale of early
times. 823.4291
Adams, M.. An honorable surrender.
                   823.4494
Adams, Nehemiah. The sable cloud: a south-
ern tale with northern comments.
                   823.6980
Adams, W: H: Davenport. The forest, the
jungle and the prairie; or, scenes with the
trapper and the hunter in many lands.
                   808.131

English Fiction. *Contin.*
Adventures of Oliver Twist. Dickens, C: J: H. 823.5300
Same. 823.5334; 823.6352; 823.6935
Adventures of Peregrine Pickle. Smollett, T. G: 823.1472
Adventures of Philip. Thackeray, W: M. 823.1571
Same. 2 vols. 823.5002-3
Adventures of Prince Lazybones, and other stories. Hays, *Mrs.* H.. 808.1355
Adventures of Reuben Davidger. Greenwood, J. 823.6018
Adventures of Rob Roy. Grant, J. 823.647
Adventures of Roderick Random. Smollett, T. G: 823.1473
Adventures of Telemachus. Fénelon, F. de S. de la M. 823.6211
Adventures of three Englishmen and three Russians in southern Africa. Verne, J. 823.6973
Adventures of Ulysses, The. Lamb, C: *in* 823.5562

Aerial voyages.
—— Ballantyne, R. M. Up in the clouds; or, balloon voyages. 808.1281
—— — *Same.* (*In his* Tales of adventure.) *in* 808.1268
—— Verne, J. Five weeks in a balloon. 823.6924
—— — The mysterious island. 823.5784
Note.—For recent accounts, *see* Bibliography. Mansfield, C: B. Aerial navigation. (Books consulted, pp. 493-496.) 533.8.—L'aérostation pendant le siége de Paris. (*Rev. d. d. Mondes.* 2e pér. v. 90.) p. 612, *in* ** 54.295.—Glaisher, J., *ed.* Travels in the air, by Glaisher, Flammarion, de Fonvielle, and Tissandier. * 533. 11.—Pettigrew, J. B. Various modes of flight in relation to aeronautics. 9 pp. (*Smithsonian Rep.*, 1867.) p.325, *in*** 500.22.—Turnor, C. II. Astra castra. Experiments and adventures in the atmosphere. 1865. * 533.12.
See also "Aeronautics" *in* Catalogues of this Library. No. 2, 1880, p. 3.
See also under "Aerouautics" *in* Poole's Index (to 1882). p. 8, *in* ** 50.1;—*Same.* Jan. 1, 1882-Jan. 1, 1887. p. 3, *in* ** 50. 1².
Afghan knife, The. Sterndale, R. A. 823.6468

Afghanistan.
—— Grant, J. Colville of 'The Guards.' 823.5681
—— — Duke of Albany's Own Highlanders. 823.4796
—— — *Same.* 823.5679
—— — Only an ensign: a tale of the retreat from Cabul. 823.643
—— Henty, G: A. For name and fame; or, through Afghan passes. 808.1472
—— Longfellow, H: W. Poems of places. p. 261, *in* 821.228
Note.—See Bibliography. Boston Pub. Lib. *Bulletin*, v. 4. pp. 34-5, *in* ** 17.135.—Rodenbough, T. F. Afghanistan and the Anglo-Russian dispute. 1885. (Authorities, pp. 131-133.) 958.10.—McCarthy, J. H. England under Gladstone, 1880-1885. *in* 942.1294.—Malleson, Col. G. B. History of Afghanistan (to 1878). Map. 958.11.—Yule, Col. Article "Afghanistan" in Encyclop. Britann., v. 1. ** 12.18.
See also Catalogues of this Library.
No. 3, 1882 p. 2. No. 5, 1888, p. 2.
No. 4, 1884, p. 2.
See also Poole's Index (to 1882). pp. 9-10, *in* ** 50.1;—*Same.* Jan. 1, 1882-Jan. 1, 1887. p. 3, *in* ** 50.1².
Afloat and ashore. Cooper, J. F. 823.289

English Fiction. *Contin.*
Afloat in the forest. Reid, *Capt.* T: M. 808.436
Afraja. Mügge, T. 823.6809
Africa. *See also notes* under Abyssinia.—Algeria.—Carthage.—Egypt.—Madagascar.—Mauritius.—Zululand.
—— Ballantyne, R. M. Hunting the lions; or, the land of the negro. 808.1286
—— — *Same.* (*In his* Tales of adventure.) *in* 808.1268
—— Du Chaillu, P. B. My Apingi kingdom; with life in the great Sahara, and sketches of the chase of the ostrich, hyena, &c. 808.691
—— — Stories of the gorilla country. 808.799
—— Haggard, H: R. Allan Quatermain. 823.7154
—— — Allan's wife. 823.6987
—— — Maiwa's revenge. 823.5530
—— Knox, T: W. Boy travellers in the far East. Pt. 5. 808.1839
—— — Boy travellers on the Congo. 808.1843
—— Marryat, *Capt.* F: The mission; or, scenes in Africa. 808.775
—— — *Same.* 808.1500
—— Ober, F: A. The Knockabout Club in north Africa. 808.1924
—— Wentworth, W. Kibboo Ganey; or, the lost chief of the copper mountain. 808.1537

Africa, *Central.*
—— Belot, A. The black Venus: a tale of the dark continent. (Sequel to Thirst for the unknown.) 823.5793
—— Haggard, H: R. King Solomon's mines. 823.7157
—— McCabe, J. D. Our young folks in Africa. Adventures in Algeria, and in south central Africa. 808.1874
—— Mayo, W: S. Kaloolah; or, journeyings to the Diébel Kumri: an autobiography of Jonathan Romer. 823.1144
—— Stanley, H: M. My Kalulu, prince, king and slave. 808.1420
Soudanese war.
—— Ballantyne, R. M. Blue lights; or, hot work in the Soudan. 823.6622
—— Grant, J. Playing with fire. 823.6523
Africa, *Eastern. See also* Abyssinia.—Egypt.
—— Cameron, V. H: L. Adventures of Herbert Massey in eastern Africa. 808.1433
Slavery.
—— Ballantyne, R. M. Black ivory: a tale of adventure among the slavers of east Africa. 808.453
—— — Gorilla hunters: a tale of the wilds of Africa. 808.211
Africa, *Northern. See also* Egypt.—Carthage.
—— Dumas, A. D. Tales of Algeria. 916.95
—— Kingston, W: H: G. Saved from the sea; or, the loss of the "Viper" and the adventures of her crew in the great Sahara. 808.349
—— Mayo, W: S. The Berber; or, the mountaineer of the Atlas: a tale of Morocco. 823.1143
—— Reid, *Capt.* T: M. The boy slaves. 808.422

English Fiction. *Contin.*
Africa, *Southern. See also* Zululand.
—— Ballantyne, R. M. Settler and savage.
808.206
—— —— Six months at the Cape. 808.1550
—— Bleek, W. H. I. Reynard the Fox in
south Africa. * 899.15
—— Fenn, G: M. Off to the wilds.
808.1183
—— — *Same.* 808.1496
—— Frith, H: Hunting of the "Hydra;"
or, the phantom pirate. 808.1495
—— Haggard, H: R. Jess. 823.5074
—— — *Same.* 823.5075; 823.6591; 823.7156
—— Henty, G: A. By sheer pluck: a tale of
the Ashanti war. 808.1486
—— Hogg, J. Singular letter from southern
Africa. 13 pp. (*In* Tales from Blackwood,
v. 5.) *in* ** 823.6651
—— Reid, *Capt.* T: M. Bush-boys. 808.756
—— — Giraffe hunters. 808.432
—— — The vee-boers. 808.1463
—— — The young yägers. 808.1466
—— Sheldon, L. V. An I. D. B. in south
Africa. 823.6580
—— Verne, J. Adventures of three Eng-
lishmen and three Russians in southern
Africa. 823.6973
Diamond fields of.—Reade, C: A simpleton.
823.1983
Africa, *Western.*
—— Collingwood, H. The Congo rovers: a
story of the slave squadroon. 808.1706
—— Du Chaillu, P. B. The country of the
dwarfs. 808.693
—— — Lost in the jungle. 808.692
—— — Wild life under the equator. 808.694
—— Gilman, J. B. The drifting island; or,
the slave-hunters of the Congo. 808.1689
—— Henty, G: A. By sheer pluck.
808.1486
—— Homer, A. N. Red ruin: a tale of
west African river life. 823.7212

Note.—For historical narratives (early travelers),
see Le Vaillant, F. **1780-85.** (Interior, via Cape of
Good Hope.)—Park, Mungo. **1795-07.** (Interior.)
in 823.5026.—Barrow, *Sir* J: **1797-98.** (Interior
Southern.)—Latrobe, C. J. **1815-16.** (Southern.)—
Lyon, *Capt.* G. F. **1818-20.** (Northern.)
For recent travels and explorations, *see* [Denham,
Maj. D., *and* Clapperton, *Capt.* H. **1822-24.**
(North and Central.)—Clapperton, **1828.** (Soccatoo.)
—Barth, H. **1849-55.** (North and Central.)].—
Buel, J. W. Heroes of the dark continent, and how
Stanley found Emin Pasha. 1889. 916.177.—Du
Chaillu, P. B. Explorations in equatorial Africa.
1871. 916.45.—Emin Pasha (Dr. Schnitzer) in cen-
tral Africa: being a collection of his letters and
journals. Ed. by Prof. G. Schweinfurth, *and others.*
1889. 923.1875.—Keltie, J.S., *ed.* The story of Emin's
rescue as told in Stanley's letters. 1890. 816.47.—
Little, H: W. Henry M. Stanley: his life, travels
and explorations. 1890. 923.1974.—Livingstone,
Dr. D: Mission travels and researches in south
Africa. (1857.) 916.54;—Narrative of an expedition
to the Zambesi. 1858-1864. 916.44;—Last journals in
central Africa. (1865-73.) 966.1;—*Same.* 916.49;—
Personal life of, being unpublished journals, correspondence, etc. Ed. by Blaikie. 920.220.—Mackenzie, J: Austral Africa: losing it or ruling it.
2 vols. 1887. 968.3-4.—Schweinfurth, *Dr.* G. A.
Heart of Africa. 2 vols. 916.21-2.—Stanley, H: M.
How I found Livingstone. (1872.) 916.176.—Through
the dark continent. 2 vols. (1878.) 916.47-8;—The
Congo, and the founding of its free state. 1885.
2 vols. 916.164-5;—In darkest Africa. 2 vols. 1890.
* 916.184-5.—Taylor, B. The lake regions of cen-

English Fiction. *Contin.*
Africa, *Western.* *Contin.*
Note. Contin.
tral Africa. 1885. 916.182.—Taylor, G: L. The new
Africa: its discovery and destiny. 56 pp. 1888.
916.179.—Ward, H. Life among the Congo savages.
(Human sacrifices.) (*Scribner's mag.*, Feb. 1890.)
pp. 135-56, *in* * 51.5102⁵.—Wauters, A. J. Stanley's
Emin Pasha expedition. Maps. 1890. 916.178.
See also Catalogues of this Library.
No. 2, 1880, p. 4. No. 4, 1884, pp. 2-3.
No. 3, 1882, p. 2. No. 5, 1888, p. 2.
See also Poole's Index (to 1882). pp. 10-13, *in* **
50.1;—*Same.* Jan. 1,1882-Jan. 1,1887. p. 4, *in* ** 50.1².
See also Index to Consular reports. 1880-1885;
1886-1889. 2 vols. (U. S. Pub. Docs. *Dept. of State.*)
** 350.5496¹⁻².

After dark, and other stories. Collins, W: W.
823.249
After many days. Tiernan, *Mrs.* F. C. (F.)
823.5928
After shipwreck. Owen, *Mrs.* J. A.
823.6945
After the ball. 12 pp. Opie, *Mrs.* A. (A.)
p. 363, *in* 823.6136
After-dinner stories. Balzac, H. de. 823.5587
Afterglow. Lathrop, G: P. 823.1996
Against heavy odds. Boyesen, H.H. 808.1703
Against the stream. Charles, *Mrs.* E.. (R.)
823.202
Agamenticus. Tenney, E. P. 823.1549
Agatha Page. Henderson, I: 823.5750
Agatha's husband. Craik, *Mrs.* D. M. (M.)
823.5832
Age of chivalry. Bulfinch, T: 823.6313
Agincourt. James, G: P. R. ** 823.6716
Agnes. Oliphant, *Mrs.* M. O. (W.)
823.5030
Agnes Hilton. Hoffman, M.. I. 823.769
Agnes of Sorrento. Stowe, *Mrs.* H. E.. (B.)
823.2038
Agnes Sorel. James, G: P. R. 823.5058
Same. 823.5059
Agnes Surriage. Bynner, E. L. 823.7169
Agnew, Cora. Peerless Cathleen: an Eng-
lish society story. 823.4
Aguilar, Grace. The days of Bruce: a story
from Scottish history. 2 vols. (in 1).
823.5398
—— *Same.* 2 vols. 823.5-6
—— Home influence. 823.7
—— Home scenes and heart studies. 823.8
—— The mother's recompense: a sequel to
Home influence. 823.9
—— The vale of cedars; or, the martyr.
823.10
—— Woman's friendship. 823.11
Ahsahgunushk Numamahtahseng. 91 pp.
Herbert, H: W: p. 309, *in* 823.4253
Aïdé, Hamilton. Carr of Carrlyon. 2 vols.
(in 1). 823.2368
—— Introduced to society. *in* 823.5145
—— *Same.* *in* 823.5187
—— A nine-days' wonder. 823.5828
—— Penruddocke. 823.5823
Aikin, J:, *and* Barbauld, *Mrs.* A.. Letitia
(Aikin). Evenings at home; or, the juve-
nile budget opened. 808.1664
Aimard, Gustave. The gold-seekers: a tale
of California. Ed. by Percy B. St. John.
(*And*) The treasure of pearls: a romance
of adventures in California. 823.7008

English Fiction. *Contin.*
Aims and obstacles. James, G: P. R.
in 823.6247
Ainslie, Herbert, *pseud.* See Maitland, E.
Ainsworth, W: Harrison (1805-1882). Auriol;
or, the elixir of life. (*Also*) A night's
adventure in Rome (1830). 823.27
—— Beau Nash ; or, Bath in the eighteenth
century. 823.5790
—— Boscobel; or, the royal oak: a tale of
the year 1651. 823.5601
—— Cardinal Pole; or, the days of Philip and
Mary. 823.5606
—— The constable of the tower. 823.5605
—— Crichton. 823.16
—— The flitch of bacon; or, the custom of
Dunmow: a tale of English home. 823.17
—— Guy Fawkes; or, the gunpowder treason.
823.18
—— Jack Sheppard. 823.19
—— James the Second. 823.20
—— John Law, the projector. 823.5602
—— The Lancashire witches : a romance of
Pendle forest. 823.21
—— The leaguer of Lathom: a tale of the
civil war in Lancashire. 823.5603
—— Life and adventures of Mervyn Clith-
eroe. 823.22
—— The Lord Mayor of London; or, city life
in the last century. 823.5604
—— Mervyn Clitheroe, Life . . . of. 823.22
—— The miser's daughter: a tale. 823.23
—— The mysteries of the court of Queen
Anne. 823.5912
—— A night's adventure in Rome. (*With*
his Auriol.) in 823.27
—— Old St. Paul's: a tale of the plague and
the fire. 823.24
—— *Same.* * 823.6014
—— Ovingdean Grange: a tale of the south
downs. 823.25
—— Rookwood: a romance. (With memoir
and biog. sketch of A.) 823.26
—— *Same.* 823.5625
—— Saint James's; or, the court of Queen
Anne. 823.28
—— The spendthrift: a tale. 823.29
—— The Star-chamber: an historical ro-
mance. 823.30
—— Tower of London. 823.5825
—— Windsor Castle. 823.32
Note.—For his life and writings, *see* Appletons'
journ., v. 8. pp. 152-54, *in* ** 51.958.—Stephen's
Dict. of national biog., v. 1. ** 920.330¹.
"Airy fairy Lilian." Hungerford, *Mrs.* M.
823.740
Akerman, J: Yonge. (*A.*, *J: Y.*) Tales of
other days. 823.1
Contents:—The magic phial; or, an evening at
Delft.—Tale of the civil wars.—Friar Rush.—Ghys-
brecht, the free-lance.—The three suitors.—The
fifth of November.—A tale of the low countries.—
Trial by battle.—The castle of Stauffenberg.—The
brothers.—Roger Clevelly.—Haviland Hall.
Alarcón, Pedro Antonio de. Black eyes.
12 pp. Tr. by Mrs. F.. C. Henderson. (*In*
Henderson, *Mrs.* F.. C., *Dunderviksborg*
. . .) p. 175, *in* 823.6534
—— The tall woman. Tr. by Rollo Ogden.
34 pp. (*In* Modern ghosts.)
p. 79, *in* 823.7349

English Fiction. *Contin.*
Alaska. Allen, W. B. The Red Mountain of
· Alaska. 808.1912
Note.—See Badlam, A. The wonders of Alaska.
1890. 9177.620.—Bibliography. Bancroft, H. H.
History of the Pacific states. v. 28: Alaska.
(1730-1885. Authorities quoted, pp. xxiii-xxxviii.)
* 970.97.—Elliott, H: W. Our arctic province,
Alaska and the Seal islands. 1887. 9177.608.—
Murphy, T: G. History of Alaska. (From the
Alaska Times.) 977.161.
See also Catalogues of this Library.
No. 2, 1880, p. 5. No. 4, 1884, p. 4.
No. 3, 1882, p. 3. No. 5, 1888, p. 3.
See also Poole's Index (to 1882). p. 18, *in* ** 59.1;—
Same. Jan. 1, 1882-Jan. 1, 1887. p. 6, *in* ** 50.1³.
See also Catalogue of govt. pubs. of the U. S.
(1774-1881). p. 1246, *in* ** 15.202
Alba's dream and other stories. 823.5816
Contents:—Alba's dream.—A message.—How
Percy Bingham caught his trout.—The legend of
Friar's Rock.—The wild rose of St. Regis.—Jane's
vocation.—A sweet revenge.—The Wolf-tower.—
Juliette.—A silent courtship.—The little chapel at
Monamullin.
Albert, M.. A hidden terror. 823.4983
Albert Lunel. 3 vols. (in 1). Brougham,
Lord H: P: ** 823.6685
Same. 3 vols. 823.6441-3
Albert Travers, Fortunes of. Berrington,
B. S. 823.7197
Albrecht. Bates, A. 823.6951
Alcestis. Cornish, *Mrs.* —. 823.806
Alcock, Deborah. The czar: a tale of the
time of the first Napoleon. 823.5909
—— Geneviève: a story of old France.
823.7196
—— The Spanish brothers: a tale of the six-
teenth century. 823.1184
—— *Same.* 823.5910
—— Under the southern cross: a tale of the
new world. 823.1183
Alcott, L.. May. A garland for girls.
808.1462
Contents:—May flowers.—An ivy spray and ladies'
slippers. — Pansies. — Water-lilies. — Poppies and
wheat.— Little button-rose.— Mountain-laurel and
maidenhair.
—— Independence: a centennial love story.
(*With her* Silver pitchers.) *in* 823.34
—— Modern Mephistopheles. 823.1997
—— Moods. 823.33
—— *Same.* 823.4295
—— Silver pitchers. (*And*) Independence: a
centennial love story. 823.34
Contents:—Silver pitchers.—Anna's whim.—Trans-
cendental wild oats.—The romance of a summer
day.—My rococo watch.—By the river.—Letty's
tramp.—Scarlet stockings.—Independence: a cen-
tennial love story.
—— Work: a story of experience. 823.35
Alcove, The. Abbott, J. *in* 808.587
Alden, *Mrs.* I.. (McDonald). [*Pansy.*] The
Chautauqua girls at home. 808.1511
—— The hall in the Grove. 808.1512
Alderbrook. Judson, *Mrs.* E. (C.) 823.908
Aldrich, T: Bailey. Marjorie Daw and other
people. 823.6926
Contents:—Marjorie Daw.—A Rivermouth ro-
mance.—Quite so.—A young desperado.—Miss
Mehetable's son.—A struggle for life.—The friend
of my youth.—Mademoiselle Olympe Zabriski.—
Père Antoine's date-palm.
—— Marjorie Daw and other stories. 823.36
Contents:—Marjorie Daw.—Miss Mehetabel's son.
—Our new neighbors at Ponkapog.—A midnight
fantasy.—Mademoiselle Olympe Zabriski.—A strug-
gle for life.—Père Antoine's date-palm.—Quite so.—
A Rivermouth romance.—The little violinist.

English Fiction. *Contin.*
America. *Contin.*
—— Brinton, D. G. The myths of the new
world. 1876. 291.19
—— Butterworth, H. Young folks' history
of America. 970.67
—— Longfellow, H: W. Poems of places.
3 vols. 821.206-7; 821.210
—— Schele de Vere, M. R. B. The romance
of American history. 1872. 970.30
—— Wright, H. C. Children's stories in
American history. 808.1695
Note.—See Ford, P. L. **Bibliography,** catalogues, and reference lists on America. (*Lib. Jour.*,
v. 13. pp. 37-40.) *in ** 19.24⁵.—* Watson, P. B. **Bibliography** of the pre-Columbian discoveries of
America. 38 pp. (*Lib. Jour.*, v. 6. 1881.) p. 227,
*in ** 19.21.—*Maps of America, 1540-1600. (Bost. Pub.
Lib. *Bulletin*, No. 41, pp. 205-7.) *in ** 17.135.—*Winsor, J., *ed.* Narrative and critical history of America.
8 vols. 1889. * 970.127¹⁻⁸. (Critical notes on
sources of information and accounts of the cartography of the country follow many chapters.) v. 1.
contains the following bibliographical notes by the
editor: Americana in libraries and bibliographies;
Early descriptions of America and collective accounts of the early voyages thereto; The progress of
opinion respecting the origin and antiquity of man
in America; Bibliography of aboriginal America;
Comprehensive treatises on American antiquities;
Bibliographical notes on the industries and
trade of the American aborigines, on American
linguistics, on the myths and religions of America;
Archæological museums and periodicals. *970.127¹.
For antiquities of America, *see* Publications of
the Smithsonian Institution.
See also Catalogues of this Library.
   No. 2, 1880, pp. 7, 8.   No. 4, 1884, pp. 6, 7.
   No. 3, 1882, pp. 4, 5.   No. 5, 1888, pp. 5, 6.
American, The. James, H:, *jr.* 823.883
American baron, The. De Mille, J. 823.5844
American coin. By the author of "Aristocracy." 823.7236
American girl's home book of work and play.
Campbell, *Mrs.* H.. (S.) 808.1313
American history. 8 vols. Abbott, J.
  973.690-97
American history, Stories of. Dodge, N. S.
  808.1675
American Humane Educational Society. *See*
Animals, *note.*
American literature. *See* Literature.
American notes. Dickens, C: J. H.
  p. 601, *in* 823.4968
Same. 823.5331
American penman, An. Hawthorne, J. C.
  823.5444
American pioneers and patriots. *See* Abbott,
J: S. C.
American politician, An. Crawford, F. M.
  823.4873
Améro, Constant, *joint author.* *See* Tissot, V:
Ames, Lucia True. Memoirs of a millionaire.
  823.6556
Amicis, Edmondo de. Cuore: an Italian
schoolboy's journal. Tr. by I. F. Hapgood.
  808.1657
Amid the corn. By the author of "The evening and the morning." 3 vols. 823.1987-9
  v. 1. The Christmas party.
  v. 2. The Whitsuntide visit.
  v. 3. The bridegroom and the bride.
Amis and Amiloun. Weber, H: W:
  p. 367, *in* * 821.1240
Among the hills. Poynter, E. F.. 823.1857
Among the pines. Gilmore, J. R. 823.608

English Fiction. *Contin.*
Among the Turks. Cameron, V. H: L.
  808.1585
Amongst machines. Lukin, J. 808.620
Amorassan. Lewis, M. G. p. 107, *in* 823.4275
Amos Kilbright. Stockton, F. R: 823.5764
Amulet, The. Conscience, H.
  p. 157, *in* 823.5707
Anaconda, The. 56 pp. Lewis, M. G.
  p. 49, *in* 823.4275
Anastatius. 3 vols. Hope, T: * 823.2057-9
Ancient régime, The. 3 vols. James, G: P. R.
  * 823.6403-5
Anderdon, W: H: Antoine de Bonneval: a
tale of Paris in the days of St. Vincent de
Paul. 823.39
Andersen, Hans Christian. (1805-1875.)
Danish fairy legends and tales. Tr. by
Caroline Peachey. 808.771
*Contents:—*The wild swans.—The ugly duckling.—
The little mermaid.—The storks.—The nightingale.
—Little Ida's flowers.—The swineherd.—Ole Luckōie; or, the dustman.—The daisy.—The buckwheat.
—The emperor's new clothes.—The real princess.—
The top and the ball.—The garden of Paradise.—
The fir-tree.—Mother Elder.—Elfin-mount.—The
snow-queen.—Holger the Dane.—Tommelise.—Great
Claus and little Claus.—The constant tin soldier.
—The naughty boy.—The angel.—The clogs of fortune.—The shepherdess and the chimney-sweeper.
—The tinder-box.—The red shoes.—The fellow-travellers.—The leaping-match.—The rose-elf.—The
flying-trunk.—The old street lamp.—The little
match girl.—The neighbours.—The bell.—The
darning-needle.—Little Tuk.—The shadow.—The
old house.—The flax.—The drop of water.—The
happy family.—The false collar.—Story of a mother.
—The history of the year.—The world's fairest
rose.—A picture from the castle ramparts.—"Quite
true."—The swans' nest.—Good humour.—Grief of
heart.—"Everything in its place."—The nisse at
the grocer's.—A thousand years hence.—Under the
willow-tree.—A vision of the last day.
—— The improvisatore (life in Italy). Tr.
by M.. Howitt. 823.4223
—— The man from Paradise (poem). 7 pp.
(*In* Bushby, *Mrs.* —, *tr.* The Danes,
. . . v. 1.) p. 305, *in* 823.6444
—— Morten Lange. A Christmas story.
10 pp. (*In* Bushby, *Mrs.* —, *tr.* The
Danes . . . v. 1.) p. 199, *in* 823.6444
—— Fairy tales. (Complete collection.) Tr.
by Mrs. H. B. Paull. 808.1928
—— The goloshes of fortune, and other
stories. Tr. by H. W. Dulcken. 808.600
*Contents:—*The goloshes of fortune.—The old street
lamp.—The elf-hill.—The loveliest rose in the world.
—The swineherd.—Something.—The buckwheat.—
The rose-elf.
—— O. T.: a Danish romance. 823.6788
—— The old church bell, and other stories.
Tr. by H. W. Dulcken. 808.605
*Contents:—*The old church bell.—A story from the
sand-dunes.—The last dream of the old oak tree.—
The Psyche.—My boots.
—— Only a fiddler: a Danish romance.
  823.4219
—— The sand-hills of Jutland (and other
stories). 823.4182
*Contents:—*The sand-hills of Jutland.—The mud-king's daughter.—The quickest runners.—The bell's
hollow.—Soup made of a sausage-stick.—The neck
of a bottle.—The old bachelor's nightcap.—Something.—The old oak tree's last dream.—The wind
relates the story of Waldemar Daae and his daughters.—The girl who trod upon bread.—Olé, the
watchman of the tower.—Anne Lisbeth; or, the
apparition of the beach.—Children's prattle.—A
row of pearls.—The pen and the inkstand.—The
child in the grave.—Charming.

English Fiction. *Contin.*

Andersen, Hans Christian. *Contin.*

— Stories. 57 pp. (*In* Scudder, H. E., *comp.* The *children's book*.)
p. 154, *in* 808.1882

— Stories for the household. 808.1323

— The two baronesses. 823.4006

— *Same.* 823.6635

*Note.—*For life and writings *see* **Andersen, H. C.** Story of my life. 18;6. 928.83.—Brandes, G. (*In his* Eminent authors of the 19th cent.) 1886. p. 61, *in* 809.67.
See also **Poole's Index** (to 1882). p. 37, ** 50.1.

Andersonville violets. Collingwood, H. W. 823.7320

Andreas Hofer. Mundt, *Mrs.* C. (M.) 823.6265

Andreds-weald. Crake, *Rev.* A. D. 823.5654

Andrews, Fanny [*Elzey Hay*]. A mere adventurer. 823.5842

Andrews, J.. The seven little sisters who live on the round ball that floats in the air. 808.1428

Angel of the bells, The. Du Boisgobey, F. 823.5097

Angèle's fortune. Theuriet, A. 823.5550

Animals. *See also* Hunting.— Natural history, *note.*

— Church, E. R. Home-animals. 808.1597

— Kingston, W: H: G. Stories of the sagacity of animals. Cats and dogs. 596.106

— — The horse and other animals. 808.1445

— Newton, *Rev.* R: Bible animals and the lessons taught by them. 808.1722

— Sewell, A.. Black Beauty: his grooms and companions. Ed. by the American Humane Education Society. 808.1697

— Tolstoï, *Count* L. N. Tales from zoölogy. 14 pp. (*In his* The long exile, *etc.*)
p. 187, *in* 808.1348

— Wood, J: G: Routledge's picture book of animals. 808.1883

Note.—See **Baker, Sir S: W.** Wild beasts and their ways. Illus. 1890. 590.126.—**Barnum, P. T.** The wild beasts, birds and reptiles of the world. 1889. *590.117.—**Beaugrand, C:** The walks abroad of two young naturalists. 590.114.—**Bibliography.** *In* Lindsay, W. L. Mind in the lower animals in health and disease. v. 2. 1879. pp. 399-418, *in* 590.41. —**Broderip, W. J:** Zoölogical recreations. 1862. 590.26.—**Buckland, F. T.** Curiosities of natural hist. 4 series. 1868-73. D 4.62-5.—**Buckley, A. B.** Life and her children: glimpses of animal life. 1881. 590.67;—The winners in life's race. 1883. 596.39.—**Gould, C:** Mythical monsters. 1886. * 590.104.—**Hehn, V.** The wanderings of plants and animals from their first home. 1888. 580.87.— **Holder, C. F.** The ivory king: the elephant and its allies. 1886. 599.107;—Living lights: account of phosphorescent animals and vegetables. 1887. 590.106;—A strange company, wonder-wings, mullingongs, colossi, etc. Illus. 1888. 590.118.—**Ingersoll, E.,** *and others.* Habits of animals. 1882. 590.-115.—**Lankester, E. R.** Uses of animals to man. 636.33.—**Lee, Mrs. R.** Anecdotes of the habits and instincts of birds, reptiles and fishes. 1876. 590.34. —**Menault, E.** Wonders of animal instinct. 158.2. —**Oswald, F. L.** Zoölogical sketches. 1883. 596. 38.—**Simmonds, P. L.** Dictionary of useful animals and their product. 590.97.—**Smith, H. A.** Animals, birds and fishes. 1887. * 590.107.—**Wilson, A.** Facts and fictions of zoölogy. (*Humboldt Lib.*, No. 29.) 1882. *in* 824.327.—**Wood, J. G.** Strange dwellings. 1872. D 4.67;—Trespassers. D 4.70.
See also **Natural history.—Zoölogy in Catalogues** of this Library.

No. 2, 1880, p. 163; 256.   No. 4, 1884, p. 198; 324.
No. 3, 1882, p. 130; 209.   No. 5, 1888, p. 263; 391.

English Fiction. *Contin.*

Anna Karénina. Tolstoï, *Count* L. N. 823.5241

Annals of a baby. Stebbins, *Mrs.* S.. (B.) 823.4529

Annals of a quiet neighbourhood. MacDonald, G: 823.1061

Annals of a sportsman. Turgenef, I. S. 823.4910

Annals of the parish. Galt, J: 823.4191

Annan water. Buchanan, R. W: 823.5116

Anne. Woolson, C. F. 823.4468

Anne Furness. Trollope, *Mrs.* E.. E. (T.) 823.6002

Anne Judge, spinster. 3 vols. Robinson, F: W: 823.4128-30

Anne of Geierstein. Scott, *Sir* W. 823.1392

Same. p. 291, *in* ** 823.6033

Anne Séverin. Craven, *Mme.* P. (de la F.) 823.6842

Annie Kilburn. Howells, W: D. 823.5541

Annouchka. Turgenef, I. S. 823.4901

Another's crime. Hawthorne, J. C. 823.5752

Anson, W. S. W., *ed.* Epics and romances of the middle ages. Adapted from the work of Dr. W. Wagner by M. W. MacDowall. 823.6146

Anstey, F., *pseud.* *See* Guthrie, F: Anstey.

Antarctic regions. *See also* Arctic regions, *note.*

— Poe, E. A. Narrative of A. Gordon Pym. (*With his* The prose tales.)
in 823.1921

Note.—See **Bibliography.** Chavanne, J., *and others.* Die Litteratur über die polar-Regionen der Erde. 1878. * 16.214.—Enderby. Discoveries in the Antarctic ocean. 1833. (Roy. Geog. Soc. *Journal,* v. 3.) p. 105, *in* ** 910.3.—**Hartwig, G.** The polar world (popular). 1881. 919.112.—**Laugel, A.** Le pôle austral et les expéditions antarctiques. (*Rev. d. d. Mondes.* 2e pér. v. 1.) p. 802, *in* ** 54.206.— **Weddell, J.** Voyage towards the south pole. (1822-24.) ** 9191.25.—**Wilkes, C:** U. S. exploring expedition. 1838-42. v. 1. p. 133; v. 2. p. 281, *in* ** 910.70-1.

Anteros. Lawrence, G: A. 823.954

Antipodes, Zigzag journeys in the. Butterworth, H. 808.1815

Antiquary, The. Scott, *Sir* W. 823.1393

Same. ** 823.6024

Antoine de Bonneval. Anderdon, W: H. 823.39

Antoinette. 2 vols. Blyth, M. P. 823.7206-7

Antoinette. Ohnet, G. 823.6676

Antonia. Dudevant, *Mme.* A. L. A. (D.) 823.6790

Antonina. Collins, W: W. 823.250

Antonio di Carara. A Paduan tale. 79 pp. (*In* Tales from Blackwood, v. 10.)
in ** 823.6656

Antony Brade. Lowell, R. T. S. 823.1018

Aphrodite. Eckstein, E. 823.6981

Apologue, An. 11 pp. Shorthouse, J. H:
p. 307, *in* 823.5438

Apostate. The. Daudet, E. 823.6501

April day, An. Jephson, P. P. *in* 823.4993

April hopes. Howells, W: D. 823.5522

Apuleius, Lucius, *Madaurensis.* Works of Apuleius: comprising the Metamorphoses; or, golden ass.—The God of Socrates.—The Florida. (*And*) His defence; or, a discourse on magic. New tr. Added, A metrical

English Fiction. *Contin.*
Apuleius, Lucius, *Madaurensis.* *Contin.*
  version of Cupid and Psyche. (*And*) Mrs.
  Tighe's Psyche: a poem in six cantos.
  (Bohn's lib.) 1888.   823.2116
Arabella Stuart. (Time of James I. of Eng-
  land.) 3 vols. James, G: P. R.
               * 823.6406-8
Arabesques. Greenough, *Mrs.* S.. D.
                   823.665
Arabia, *etc.*
—— Church, A. J: Stories of the magicians.
  Thalaba and the magicians of the Dom-
  daniel, Rustem and the genii, Kehama and
  his sorceries.   823.5663
—— Clerk, *Mrs.* G., *tr.* 'Ilâm-eu-Nâs.
  Historical tales . . . of the time of the
  early Khalifahs.   823.1836
—— — *Same.*   953.12
—— Ebers, G. Homo sum. (The anchor-
  ite spirit—in the deserts and rocks of the
  Sinaitic peninsula.)   823.4525
—— — *Same.*   823.4063
—— Laboulaye, E. R. L. Abdallah; or, the
  four-leafed shamrock.   833.4100
—— Longfellow, H: W. Poems of places.
              p. 167, 821.228
—— — *Same.*   *in* * 821.231
—— Palgrave, W: G. Alkamah's cave: a
  story of Nejd.   p. 303, *in* 915.365
  Note.—See Crichton, A. History of Arabia, an-
  cient and modern. Map. Illus. 2 vols. 1840. 953.8-9.
  —Doughty, C: M. Travels in Arabia Deserta.
  Map. Illus. 2 vols. 1888. 915.352-3.—Lanar, E:
  W: Arabian society in the middle ages. 1883.
  962.23.—Myers, A. B. R. Life with the Hamram
  Arabs (chiefly sporting). 1876. 915.366.—Ruete,
  Mrs. E. Memoirs of an Arabian princess. 1888.
  923.1953.—Taylor, B. Travels in Arabia. 1887.
  915.354.
    See also **Catalogues** of this Library.
    No. 2. 1880, p. 11.   No. 4, 1884, p. 11.
    No. 3, 1882, p. 8.   No. 5, 1888, p. 21.
    See also **Poole's** Index (to 1882). pp. 49-50, *in*
    ** 50.1;—*Same.* Jan. 1, 1882-Jan. 1, 1887. pp. 17-18,
    in ** 50.1².
Arabian days' entertainments. Hauff, W.
                  823.4327
Arabian entertainments. (*In* Weber,
  H: *Tales of the east,* v. 1.) *in* ** 823.6230
Arabian nights' entertainments: additional
  tales. (*In* Weber, H: *Tales of the east,*
  v. 2.)   p. 725, *in* ** 823.6231
Arabian nights' entertainments. *Same as*
  The thousand and one nights.
Arabian nights' entertainments. *See* Thous-
  and and one nights, *note.*
Arblay, *Mme.* Francisca (Burney) d'. 1752-
  1840. Cecilia; or, memoirs of an heiress.
  3 vols. (Barbauld, *Mrs.* A. L. (A.), *ed.*
  The British novelists, vols. 40-42.)
             ** 823.2101-3
—— Evelina; or, the history of a young
  lady's introduction to the world. 2 vols.
  (in 1).   823.1911
—— *Same.* 2 vols. (Barbauld, *Mrs.* A. L.
  (A.), *ed. The British novelists,* vols. 38-39.)
             ** 823.2099-2100
  Note.—For her life and writings, *see* Macaulay,
  T: B. Misc. essays. p. 728, *in* 824.65.—Stephen,
  L. Dict. of nat. biog., v. 2. ** 920.330².—Woolsey,
  S.. C., *ed.* Diary and letters. 2 vols. 928.363-4.
  See also Poole's Index (to 1882). pp. 50, 51, *in*
  ** 50.1;—*Same.* Jan. 1, 1882-Jan. 1, 1887. p. 18, *in*
  ** 50.1².

English Fiction. *Contin.*
Arbouville, *Mme.* Sophie (de Bazancourt) d'.
  Christine: a Dutch story. Tr. by F: Hard-
  man. 85 pp. (*In* Tales from Black-
  wood, v. 6.)   *in* ** 823.6652
—— The village doctor. 77 pp. (*In* Tales
  from Blackwood, v. 5.)   *in* ** 823.6651
Arcadia, Countess of Pembroke's. Sidney,
  Sir P.   823.6639
Archer, E. M. Betwixt my love and me.
                in 823.5069
Archibald, Malmaison. Hawthorne, J. C.
                823.5684
Archie Lovell. Edwardes, *Mrs.* A.
                in 823.2815
Same.   823.5807
Archipelago on fire, The. Verne, J.
                in 823.5064
Arctic Crusoe. St. John, P. B.   808.374
Arctic regions. *See also notes* under Antarc-
  tic regions;—Eskimos.
—— Ballantyne, R. M. Fast in the ice.
                808.673
—— — *Same.*   808.1284
—— — World of ice; or, the whaling cruise
  of "The Dolphin."   808.265
—— Knox, T: W. Voyage of the "Vivian"
  to the north pole and beyond.   808.1845
—— St. John, P. B. The Arctic Crusoe: a
  tale of the polar sea.   808.374
—— Schwatka, F: The children of the cold.
                808.1673
—— Verne, J. At the north pole.   823.5537
—— — The desert of ice; or, the further
  adventures of Captain Hatteras.   823.6879
—— — The English at the north pole.
                823.6880
—— — The field of ice.   823.4343
—— — The fur country. 2 pts. 823.6881-2
  Note.—See **Bibliography.** Chavanne, J., *and*
  others. Die Litteratur über die polar-Regionen der
  Erde. 1878. ** 15.214.—Hartwig, G: Heroes of the
  Arctic regions, from "The polar world." 1888.
  919.110;—The Polar world: a popular description of
  man and nature in the Arctic and Antartic regions
  of the globe. 1886. 919.121.—Jeannette expedition, 1879-1882. (*Petermann's Mittheilungen,* v. 28.)
  p. 241, *in* ** 910.317.—Lauridsen, P: Vitus Bering:
  the discoverer of Bering strait. (Russian explorations, 1725-1743.) 1889. 9191.89.—Markham, A. H.
  Northward ho! 1879. 9191.93;—A polar recon-
  naissance: being the voyage of the "Isbjörn" in
  1879. 919.118.—Markham, C. R. Life of John
  Davis the navigator, 1550-1605, discoverer of Davis
  strait. 925.94.
    For attempts to discover a North-west passage, *see*
  Allibone's Dict. of authors, v. 1. p. 653, *in* ** 803.6
  See also **Catalogues** of this Library.
    No. 2, 1880, p. 12.   No. 4, 1884, p. 13.
    No. 3, 1882, p. 10.   No. 5, 1888, p. 23.
    See also **Poole's** Index (to 1882). pp. 55-56, *in*
    ** 50.1;—*Same.* From Jan. 1, 1882-Jan. 1, 1887. p. 20,
    in ** 50.1².
    See also **Catalogue** of gov't pubs. of the U. S. to
  March, 1881. ** 15.202.
Arden Court. Graham, B.   *in* 823.5012
Ardis Claverden. Stockton, F. R: 823.7417
Argles, *Mrs.* M., *now* Hungerford, *Mrs.*
  Margaret.
Argonauts of North Liberty. Harte, F. B.
                823.5286
Argyle, A.. The Cecilias; or, the force of
  circumstances.   823.6124
—— Olive Lacey: a tale of the Irish rebellion
  of 1798.   823.41

English Fiction. *Contin.*
Ariadne. Durand, *Mme.* A. M. C. (H.)
823.2326
Ariadne. La Ramée, L. de.   823.1814
Ariosto, Lodovico. Tales from Ariosto. Re-
told for children by A lady.   808.777
Contents.—The story of the Princess Angelica.—
The story of Ginevra.—The story of Ruggiero and
Bradamante.
Aristocracy. (Anon.)   823.7237
Arius, the Libyan. Kouns, N. C.   823.7239
Armadale. Collins, W: W.   823.251
Arminell. Gould, S. Baring-.   823.6577
Armitt, Annie. In shallow waters.
in 823.4975
Armorel of Lyonesse. Besant, W.   823.7163
Armourer of Paris. 83 pp. Smith, A.
p. 333, *in* 823.1449
Army society. Stannard, *Mrs.* H. E. V. (P.)
in 823.5040
Arne. Björnson, B.   823.4218
Same.   823.4364
Arnold, G: Why Thomas was discharged.
25 pp. (*In* Stories by Amer. authors, v. 5.)
p. 142, *in* 823.4706
Arnold's promise. Brame, *Mrs.* C.. M. (L.)
in 823.5123
Around a spring. Droz, A. G.   823.4042
Around the golden deep. Reeder, A. P.
in 823.5343
Around the world in eighty days. Verne, J.
823.3105
Same.   823.6918
Arr, E. H., *pseud.* See Rollins, *Mrs.* Ellen
Chapman (Hobbs).
Arrom, *Mrs.* Cécilia (Böhl de Faber). [*Fernan
Caballero.*] La Gaviota–the sea-gull; or,
the lost beauty.   823.6892
—— The old and the new; or, three souls too
good for this world. (*In* Zimmern, H..,
and A. *Half-hours with for. novelists*, v. 2.)
in 823-6614
Art novels. (Art life, æsthetics, etc.)
—— Barnard, C: The soprano: a musical
story.   823.6632
English art.
—— Collins, W: W. Hide-and-seek. 823.257
—— —— Leaves from Leah's diary. (*In his*
After dark and other stories.) *in* 823.249
—— Edwardes, *Mrs.* A. Archie Lovell.
823.5807
—— —— *Same.* (*With her* Leah.)
in 823.2815
—— Fothergill, J. The first violin.
823.586
—— Thackeray, W: M. The Newcomes.
(*Works,* v. 3.)   823.1578
—— —— *Same.* 2 vols.   823.5000-1
German art.
—— Drew, C. Lutaniste of St. Jacobi's.
823.1847
—— Heyse, J. L. P. Children of the world.
3 vols.   823.6455-7
Italian art.
—— Colonna the painter. A tale of Italy
and the arts. (*In* Tales from Blackwood,
v. 1.)   *in ** 823.6647
—— Hawthorne, N. The marble faun. 2 vols.
823.4362-3
—— —— *Same.*   823.6553-4

English Fiction. *Contin.*
Art novels. (Art life, æsthetics, etc.) *Contin.*
Italian art. Contin.
—— Jameson, *Mrs.* A.. Diary of an ennuyée.
914.268
—— Vosmaer, C. The amazon. 823.4804
Note.—See "Fine Arts" in **Catalogues** of this
Library.
No. 2, 1880, p. 83.   No. 4, 1884, p. 104.
No. 3, 1882, p. 71.   No. 5, 1888, p. 139.
Arthur, *King. See* England, *Arthurian era.*
Arthur, Timothy Shay. All's for the best.
823.6975
—— The Latimer family, and other temper-
ance stories.   823.5911
—— The mill and the tavern.   823.5758
—— Orange blossoms: fresh and faded.
823.5688
—— The strike at Tivoli mills; and what came
of it.   823.5622
—— The wife's engagement ring. 823.5757
Arthur. Sue, M. J.   823.6298
Arthur Blaue. Grant, J.   823.618
Arthur Bonnicastle. Holland, J. G. 823.785
Arthur Merton. Porter, D: D.   823.6503
Arthur Mervyn. 2 vols. Brown, C: B.
823.137-8
Same.   823.6201-2
Arthur Monteith. Blackford, *Mrs.* —.
in 823.6584
Arthur O'Leary, Adventures of. Lever, C: J.
823.969
Artiste. Grant, M. M.   823.659
Artist's love, The. Southworth, *Mrs.* E. D.
E. (N.)   823.1475
Artists' wives. Daudet, A.   823.6573
Arundel motto. Hay, M.. C.   823.2790
Same.   823.5080
As Avon flows. Vince, H: S. *in* 823.5084
"As it fell upon a day." 19 pp. Hunger-
ford, *Mrs.* M.   *in* 823.4981
Same.   *in* 823.4982
As it may happen. Davis, R. S.   823.363
As it was written. Harland, H: 823.4914
As 'tis in life. Delpit, A.   823.7250
Asbury twins, The. Clarke, R.. S. 823.234
Ascanio. Dumas, A. D.   823.7161
Ashcliffe Hall. Holt, E. S..   808.1520
Ashmore, Annie. Faithful Margaret. 823.42
Asia. *See also notes* under Afghanistan,—
Asia Minor,—Assyria,—Babylon,—Caucas-
us,—China,—India,—Japan,—Persia,—Tur-
key. (*Also*) Hunting . . . adventures.
—— Dalton, W: Phaulcon the adventurer;
or, the Europeans in the east. 823.6082
—— —— White elephant; or, the hunters of Ava
and the king of the golden foot. 808.872
—— Fenn, G: M. Middy and ensign: a tale
of the Malay peninsula.   808.1222
—— —— *Same.*   823.5740
—— Hearn, L. Stories of Moslem lands.
22 pp. (*In his* Stray leaves . . .)
p. 169, *in* 823.4791
—— Longfellow, H: W. Poems of places.
vols. 1-3. 3 vols.   821.227-9
Asia, *Central.*
—— Geddie, J: Beyond the Himalayas: a
story of travel and adventure in the wilds
of Thibet.   808.1184
—— Ker, D. Lost city.   808.1361

English Fiction. *Contin.*
Asia, *Central.* *Contin.*
—— Lubomirski, *Prince.* Safar-Hadgi ; or, Russ and Turcoman.   823.2330
—— Reid, *Capt.* T: M. Plant hunters; or, adventures among the Himalaya mountains.   808.430
—— — The cliff-climbers. (Sequel to "The plant hunters.")   808.757
—— Secret of the Lamas: a tale of Thibet.   823.7076
Note.—See Curzon, G: N. Russia in central Asia in 1889, and the Anglo-Russian question. 1889. (Bibliography, pp. 440-68.) 914.127.—Lansdell, H. Russian central Asia. 2 vols. 1885. (Bibliography, in v. 2, pp. 654-84.) 915.323-4.—Bibliography. Murray, H. Discoveries and travels in Asia. 3 vols. 1820. (List of authorities, etc., in v. 3, pp. 487-513.) *915.337-9.—Bonvalot, G. Through the heart of Asia over the Pamir to India. 2 vols. 1889. 915.340-1.—Taylor, B. Central Asia. 1889. 915.348. —Wardrop, O. The Kingdom of Georgia. (With bibliography.) 1888. 915.367.
See also **Catalogues** of this Library.
   No. 2, 1880, p. 14.   No. 4, 1884, p. 15.
   No. 3, 1882, p. 11.   No. 5, 1888, p. 25.
See also **Poole's Index** (to 1882).   pp. 67, 68, *in* ** 50.1;—*Same.* Jan. 1, 1882-Jan. 1, 1887. pp. 24, 25, *in* ** 50.1².
Asia Minor. *See also* notes under Arabia.— Assyria.—Persia.—Syria.
—— Eckstein, E. Aphrodite: a romance of ancient Hellas. (551 B. C.)   823.6981
—— Longfellow, H: W. Poems of places.   821.228
Note.—See Storrett, J. R. S. The Wolf expedition, 1884-5. (Archæolog. Inst. of Amer. *Papers, etc.,* v. 3.) * 956.35;—Au epigraphical journey in Asia Minor, 1883-4. *956.34.—Collignon, M. Voyage en Asie-Mineure. (*Rev. d. d. Mondes.* 3e pér. v. 37, p. 150; v. 38, p. 891. ** 54.351, 352.
See also **Catalogues** of this Library. No. 3, 1882, p. 11; No. 4, 1884, p. 15; No. 5, 1888, p. 25.
See also **Poole's Index** (to 1882). p. 68, *in* ** 50.1;—*Same.* Jan. 1, 1882-Jan. 1, 1887. p. 25, *in* ** 50.1².
See also **Index** to Consular reports. 1880-1885; 1886-1889. 2 vols. (U. S. Pub. Docs. *Dept. of State.*) ** 350.5496¹⁻².
Askaros Kassis the Copt. De Leon, E.   823.4048
Aslauga's knight. 42 pp. La Motte-Fouqué, F. H. K: *in* 823.5196
Same.   p. 169, *in* 823.4762
Asmodeus. Le Sage, A. R.   823.6872
Aspasia. 2 vols. Hamerling, R.   823.4312-13
Aspendale. Preston, H. W.   823.1275
Aspern papers. James, H: 823.5780
Asphodel. Maxwell, *Mrs.* M.. E.. (B.)   823.1589
Same.   823.2415; 823.5045
Assunta Howard. Salter, H.   823.5961
Ass'ya. Turgenef, I. S. p. 123, *in* 823.5763
Assyria. *See also* Babylon, *note.*
—— Melville, G: J: W.—Sarchedon. A legend of the great queen. [Semiramis, 13th cent. B. C.] (*With his* Brookes of Bridlemere.)   *in* ** 823.4662
Note.—See **Bibliography.** Ragozin, Z. A. Story of Assyria. (Principal works consulted, pp. xiii-xvi.) 1887. 935.16.—Trübner & Co. Cat. of leading books on Egypt . . . and on Assyria . . . 1881. ** 11.351.—Kaulen, F. Assyrien und Babylonien nach den neuesten Entdeckungen. 1885. 935.13.— Ranke, L. V. Universal history. Ed. by G: W. Prothero. 1885. 909.169.—Rawlinson, G: Five great monarchies. 3 vols. 1873. * 930.33-5.
See also **Catalogues** of this Library.
   No. 2, 1880, p. 14.   No. 5, 1888, p. 25.
   No. 3, 1882, p. 11.

English Fiction. *Contin.*
Assyria. *Contin.*
See also **Poole's Index** (to 1882). p. 69, *in* ** 50.1; —*Same.* Jan. 1, 1882-Jan. 1, 1887. p. 25, *in* ** 50.1¹.
Astor, W: Waldorf. Sforza: a story of Milan.   823.7015
Astronomy. *See also* Moon, *note.*
—— Abbott, J. Rollo's philosophy—sky.   808.910
—— Ball, *Sir* R. S.. Star-land.   808.1602
—— Flammarion, C. . Uranie.   823.7257
Note.—See **Bibliographies.** Chambers, C. F. Handbook of descriptive astronomy. (Bibliography, pp. 850-873.) 1877. * 523-33.—Holden, E. S. On reference catalogues of astronomical papers, etc. 11 pp. (Smithsonian Institution. *Misc. coll.,* v. 20.) 1881. p. 95, *in* ** 500-160.—Pritchett, H. S. Hand list for student of astronomy. 4 pp. (*St. Louis Pub. Lib.*) *in* ** 16.223.—Proctor, R. A. Article "Astronomy" in Encyclop. Brit., v. 2. (Bibliography, p. 720.) *in* ** 32.272.—Clerke, A. M. Popular hist. of astronomy during the 19th cent. 1885. 520.49.—Dun Echt Observatory: Publications. 3 vols. 1876-85. ** 522.26-8.—Frith, H. Marvels of astronomy. 520.44.—Houzeau, J. C. Fabulous astronomy. 6 pp. (Pop. science, v. 35. June, 1889.) p. 194, *in* * 505.469¹.—Lick Observatory. Publications. v. 1. 1887. ** 522.19.—Lockyer, J. N. Star-gazing. Past and present. 1878. 522.29.— Oliver, J: A. W., *and others.* Astronomy for amateurs. 1888. 522.33.—Parkes, S. H. Unfinished worlds. 1888. 520.50.—Proctor, R. A. Easy star lessons. 522.13;—Expanse of heaven. D 4.34;— Half-hours with the stars. 524.2;—Mysteries of time and space. 520.34;—Myths and marvels of astronomy. 521.4;—New star atlas. 524.1;—Other worlds than ours. 523.6.—Serviss, G. P. Astronomy with an opera glass. 1889. 522.22.—Young, C: A. A text-book of general astronomy. 1888. 522.25.
See also **Catalogues** of this Library.
   No. 2, 1880, pp. 14, 15.   No. 4, 1884, pp. 15, 16.
   No. 3, 1882, pp. 11, 12.   No. 5, 1888, pp. 25, 26.
See also **Poole's Index** (to 1882). pp. 70, 71, *in* ** 50.1;—*Same.* Jan. 1, 1882-Jan. 1, 1887. pp. 26, 27, *in* ** 50.1².
At a high price. Bürstenbinder, E.   823.4991
Same.   823.6704
At an old château. Macquoid, *Mrs.* K.. S.   823.6461
At any cost. Mayo, *Mrs.* L.. (F.) *in* 823.4995
Same.   *in* 823.5202
At bay. Hector, *Mrs.* A. (F.)   823.4839
Same.   823.4981; 823.4982
At fault. Smart, H.   823.7129
At her mercy. Payn, J.   823.5952
At his gates. Oliphant, *Mrs.* M. O. (W.)   823.4831
Same.   823.5018
At last. Kingsley, C: 823.5746
At last. Terhune, *Mrs.* M.. V. (H.) 823.1551
At odds. Tautphœus, J. (M.) *Freiherrin* von.   823.1797
At the councillor's. John, E.   823.2775
At the north pole. Verne, J.   823.5537
At the world's mercy. James, *Mrs.* F. A. (P.)   *in* 823.4993
At war with herself. Brame, *Mrs.* C.. M. (L.)   823.5100
Same.   823.5128
At ye Grene Griffin. Holt, E. S..   823.7102
Athens. Eddy, D. C. Walter in Athens.   808.1651
Atherton, *Mrs.* Gertrude Franklin (Horn). [*Frank Lin.*] Los Cerritos: a romance of the modern time.   823.7006
—— What dreams may come.   823.7359
Atlantic, Rollo on the. Abbott, J.   808.919

English Fiction. *Contin.*

Attaché, The. Haliburton, T: C.   823.687
Attila. James, G: P. R.   823.848
— *Same.*   823.7020
Attorney, The. Irving, J: T.   823.4025
Aubert Dubayet. Gayarré, C: E. A. 823.4624
Auer, Adelheid von, *pseud. See* Cosel, C.. von.
Auerbach, Berthold. Aloys. Tr. by C: T. Brooks.   823.4346
— The axe. 13 pp. (*In* Zimmern, H.., *and* A. *Half-hours with foreign novelists.*) *in* ** 823.6613
— Black Forest village stories. Tr. by C: Goepp.   823.5730
  *Contents:—*The gawk.—The pipe of war.—Manor-House Farmer's Vefela.—Nip-cheeked Tony.—Good government.—The hostile brothers.—Ivo, the gentleman.—Florian and Crescence.—The Lauterbacher.
— Brigitta. Tr. by C. Bell.   823.4045
— The convicts and their children. Tr. by C: T. Brooks.   823.7092
— The foresters.   823.4002
— German tales.   823.7013
  *Contents:—*Christian Gellert's last Christmas.—The step-mother.—Benigna.—Rudolph and Elizabeth.—Erdmutha.
— The "good hour;" or, evening holiday. Tr. by H. W. Dulcken.   823.5626
— Joseph in the snow.   823.4347
— Landolin. Tr. by A. B. Irish. 823.6791
— The little barefoot. Tr. by E. B. Lee.   823.3053
  Issued also as The barefoot maiden.
— Lorley and Reinhard. Tr. by C: T. Brooks.   823.6792
— Master Bieland and his workmen. Tr. by E. Hancock.   823.4590
— *Same.*   823.6629
— On the heights. Tr. by S. A. Stern. 2 vols.   823.5642-3
— Poet and merchant: a picture of life from the times of Moses Mendelssohn. Tr. by C: T. Brooks.   823.6793
— Spinoza. Tr. by E. Nicholson.   823.4576
— The villa on the Rhine; with a biographical sketch of the author by Bayard Taylor. 2 vols.   823.4333-4
  Issued also as Villa Eden : the country house on the Rhine.
— Waldfried: a novel. Tr. by S. A. Stern.   823.6628
— *Same.*   823.6794
  Note.—See article on "Auerbach" in the Nation, v. 41, Aug. 1885. p. 179, *in* ** 51.740.
Aulnay Tower. Teufel, *Mrs.* B. W. (H.)   823.4898
Aulnoy, Marie Catherine (Jumelle de Berneville), *comtesse* d'. Fairy Tales. Tr. by J. R. Planché.   808.1927
Aunoy, *comtesse* d'. *See* Aulnoy, M. C. (J. de B.), *comtesse* d'.
Aunt Margaret. Abbott, J. *in* 808.588
Aunt Patty's scrap-bag. Hentz, *Mrs.* C. L. (W.)   823.751
— *Same.* *in* 823.758
Aunt Rachel. Murray, D: C. *in* 823.5105
Aunt Serena. Teufel, *Mrs.* B. W. (H.)   823.1863
Aurelian. 2 vols. Ware, W: 823.1648-9
Aurifodina. Peck, G: W. ** 823.6717

English Fiction. *Contin.*

Auriol. Ainsworth, W: H.   823.27
Aurora. Tincker, M.. A.   823.4905
Aurora Floyd. Maxwell, *Mrs.* M.. E.. (B.)   *in* 823.5066
— *Same.*   823.5904
Austen, J.. (1775-1817). Emma: a novel.   823.43
— Mansfield Park.   823.44
— Northanger Abbey. (*With her* Pride and prejudice.) *in* 823.5341
— *Same.* (*And*) Persuasion. 823.2012
— Persuasion. *in* 823.47
— *Same.* *in* 823.2012
— Pride and prejudice. (*And*) Northanger Abbey.   823.5341
— Sense and sensibility.   823.5536
— *Same.* (*And*) Persuasion. 823.47
  *Note.—*For her life and writings, *see* Blackwood's mag. v. 86. p. 99, *in* ** 52.184.—Boucher, L. Le roman classique en Angleterre. (*Rev. d. d. Mondes.* 3e pér. 1878. v. 29.) pp. 449-67, *in* ** 54.343.—Forsyth's "Novels and novelists." 820.35.—Harper's monthly, v. 41. p. 225, *in* ** 51.436.—Malden, *Mrs.* S. F. (Life of) Jane Austen. (Fam. women ser.) 1889. 928.695.—Stephen, L. Dict. of nat. biog. v. 2. p. 259, *in* ** 920.320².
Austin, *Mrs.* J.. (Goodwin). Cipher: a romance.   823.5827
— The Desmond hundred.   823.6626
— Dr. Le Baron and his daughters: a story of the old colony.   823.7360
— Mrs. Beauchamp Brown. 823.6625
— Moonfolk: a true account of the home of the fairy tales.   808.396
— A nameless nobleman.   823.5786
— Nantucket scraps : being the experiences of an off-islander, in season and out of season, among a passing people. 823.5674
— The shadow of Moloch mountain.   823.5835
— Standish of Standish : a story of the pilgrims.   823.6543
Austin Elliot. Kingsley, H: 823.937
Austin Friars. Riddell, *Mrs.* C. E. L. (C.)   823.1321
Australasia. Knox, T: W. The boy travelers in Australasia.   808.1842
Australia. *See also note* under Pacific ocean.
— Gordon, W: J: The captain-general: being the story of the attempt of the Dutch to colonize New Holland. 823.7045
— Howitt, W: Boy's adventures in the wilds of Australia.   818.193
— Verne, J. Voyage around the world : Australia.   823.5546
Life and manners.
— Bowman, A. The kangaroo hunters.   808.892
— Farjeon, B: L. The golden land.   808.1711
— — Grif: a story of Australian life.   823.545
— — Joshua Marvel.   823.5860
— Fraser, J. Uncle Piper of Piper's Hill.   823.6370
— Keyser, A. An exile's romance ; or, realities of Australian life. 823.7391
— Kingsley, H: The Hillyars and the Burtons.   823.941
— Recollections of Geoffry Hamlyn.   823.944

English Fiction. *Contin.*
Australia. *Contin.*
Life and manners. *Contin.*
—— Kingston, W: H: G. Twice lost : a story of shipwreck, and of adventure in the wilds of Australia.   808.348
—— Rowcroft, C. The Australian Crusoes.
  823.1373
—— Southlanders, The : expedition to the interior of New Holland.   823.4095
Bush life.
—— Boldrewood, R. Robbery under arms . . . life . . . in the bush and in the gold-fields . . .   823.7168
—— Henty, G: A. A final reckoning.
  808.1476
—— Trollope, A. Harry Heathcote of Gangoil.   823.5889
Mining and convict life.
—— McCarthy, J., *and* Praed, *Mrs.* R. (M. P.) C. The ladies' gallery.   823.7266
—— O'Reilly, J: B. Moondyne : a story from the under-world. 3d ed.   823.1223
—— Reade, C: It is never too late to mend: a matter-of-fact romance.   823.1292

Note.—For explorers of the 19th century before 1870, *see* Sonnenschein's " The best books." p. 216, *in* ** 17.238.
See also **Brassey,** *Lady* A. (A.) The last voyage to . . . Australia in the "Sunbeam." 1889. * 910. 611.—**Cook,** *Capt.* Three voyages round the world. Ed. by C: R. Low. (1st voyage 1768-71 ; 2d voyage, 1772-75 ; 3d voyage, 1776-79.) * 910.264.—**Curr,** E: M. The Australian race. 4 vols. 1886-87. 994.24-27. —**Denton,** S. F. Incidents of a collector's rambles in Australia . . . 1889. 919.116.—**Lumholtz,** C. Among cannibals. 1889. * 919.109.—**Rusden,** G: W: History of Australia. 3 vols. 1883. 994.28-30.— **Willoughby,** H. Australian pictures drawn with pen and pencil. 1886. *9190.49.
See also **Catalogues** of this Library.
  No. 2, 1880, p. 16.   No. 4, 1884, p. 17.
  No. 3, 1882, p. 12.   No. 5, 1888, pp. 26, 27.
See also **Poole's Index** (to 1882). pp. 78, 79, *in* ** 50.1 ;—*Same.* Jan. 1, 1882-Jan. 1, 1887. p. 29, *in* ** 50.1³.
See also Index to **Consular reports,** 1880-1885 ; 1886-1889. 2 vols. (U. S. Pub. Docs. *Dept. of State.*) ** 350.5496¹·⁷.

Australian aunt, The. 51 pp. Hector, *Mrs.* A. (F.)   p. 251, *in* 823.6623
Same.   *in* 823.6694
Australian Crusoes. Rowcroft, C: 823.1373
Austria. *See also* Germany, *note.*
—— Adams, W: T. Sunny shores.
  808.497
—— Longfellow, H: W. Poems of places.
  p. 189, *in* 821.221
—— Vernaleken, T. In the land of marvels: folk-tales from Austria and Bohemia.
  808.1691
—— Wratislaw, A. H. Sixty folk-tales from exclusively Slavonic sources. Tr. with brief introd. and notes. 1890. 823.6946
EIGHTH CENTURY.
Bohemia, A. D. 738. Musæus, J. H. Libussa. (*In* Tales from the German.)
  p. 1, *in* 823.6276
Hungary. (Early times.)
—— Gore, *Mrs.* C. F.. G. (M.) Hungarian tales. 3 vols.   823.6567-9
—— Pulzsky, F. A., *and* T. Tales and traditions of Hungary. 3 vols.   823.5731-3

English Fiction. *Contin.*
Austria. *Contin.*
TWELFTH CENTURY.
Hungary.
—— Koerner, K. T. Zriny, ein Trauerspiel.
  p. 269, *in* 831.42
—— Pulzsky, F. A., *and* T. The baron's daughter. 17 pp. (Contrast of the proud allodial proprietor.) (*In their* Tales . . . of Hungary, v. 1.)   p. 11, *in* 823.5731
—— —— Castle of Zipsen. 20 pp. (Opposition of the knight to the burghers.) (*In their* Tales . . . of Hungary, v. 1.)
  p. 29, *in* 823.5731
—— —— Yanoshik. 12 pp. (The common robber appears as avenger of social injustice.) (*In their* Tales . . . of Hungary, v. 1.)   p. 52, *in* 823.5731
THIRTEENTH CENTURY.
Rudolph von Hapsburg, 1273-1291.
——, drama. Kotzebue, A. A. F. von. (*Theater,* v. 34.)   *in* 832.82
——, poem. Schiller, F. von.   831.54
SEVENTEENTH CENTURY.
Thirty years' war, 1618-1648. *See* Germany, *note.*
Prince Eugene, 1663-1736.
—— Mundt, *Mme.* C. (M.) Prince Eugene and his times.   823.6271
—— Zschokke, H. Der Pascha von Buda.
  p. 231, *in* 833.1038
EIGHTEENTH CENTURY.
Maria Theresa, Queen of Hungary, 1741-1780.
—— Dudevant, *Mme.* A. L. A. (D.) Cousuelo.   823.6214
—— —— *Same.*   823.6885; 823.6703
—— Mundt, *Mme.* C. (M.) Maria Theresa and her fireman. (*With her* The Merchant of Berlin.)   *in* 823.5888
—— Paalzow, *Mrs.* H. (W.) von. The citizen of Prague.   823.6073
Seven years' war, 1756-1763. *See* Germany. Seven years' war.
Hungary. Pulzsky, F. A., *and* T. Jacobins in Hungary. 2 vols. (*In their* Tales . . . of Hungary, vols. 2-3.)   823.5732-3
Joseph II., 1765-1790. Mundt, *Mme.* C. (M.) Joseph II. and his court.   823.6301
NINETEENTH CENTURY.
—— Trollope, A. The last Austrian who left Venice. (1866.)   p. 251, *in* 823.1614
Life and manners.
—— Fogerty, J. Countess Irene.   823.7040
—— Gerard, D. Orthodox.   823.7078
—— Kürschner, L. Erlach Court.   823.6578
—— "O thou, my Austria!"   823.7415
—— Trollope, A: Lotta Schmidt. (Vienna.)
  823.1614
Musical life. See also Musical novels.
—— Haydn's first lesson in music and love. (*In* Robert . . . and other stories.)
  p. 186, *in* 823.5811
—— Haydn's struggle and triumph. (*In* Robert . . and other stories.) p. 196, *in* 823.5811
Galicia.
—— Franzos, K. E. For the right. 823.6551
—— —— The Jews of Barnow. (Jewish life in eastern Galicia.)   823.4474

English Fiction. *Contin.*
Austria. *Contin.*
NINETEENTH CENTURY. *Contin.*
Hungary.
— Bowring, J: Poetry of the Magyars.
                                 * 831.10
—— Jókai, M. A modern Midas. 823.4927
—— Pandour and his princess. 64 pp. (*In*
Tales from Blackwood, v. 9.) *in* ** 823.6655
Tyrol.
—— Hillern, *Mrs.* W. (B.) von. Geier-
Wally: a tale of the Tyrol. 823.6806
—— Immermann, C. Andreas Hofer: play.
                p. 469, *in* 832.87
—— Mundt, *Mme.* C. (M.) Andreas Hofer.
                          823.6265

Note.—See **Bibliography.** Krones, F., *Ritter von Marchland.* Grundriss der österreichischen Geschichte mit besonderer Rüchsicht auf Quellen-und Literaturkunde. 1882. 943.115.—**Brogile,** *Duc* de. Frederick II. and Maria Theresa: 1740-42. 2 vols. 1883. 943.111-12.—**Coxe,** W: History of house of Austria (1218-1792), with contin. of same to revolution of 1848. 4 vols. 943.17-20.—**Gindely,** A. Rudolf II. und seine Zeit. 1600-1612. 2 vols. 1868. 943.124-5.—**Kohlrausch,** F: History of Germany (to 1814). 1856. 943.4.—**Leger,** L. History of Austro-Hungary to 1889. 943.110.—**Maurice,** C. E. The revolutionary movement of 1848-9 in Italy, Austria-Hungary, and Germany. 1887. 943.313.—**Metternich,** *Prince,* Memoirs of, 1773-1835. 4 pts. (in 1). 1881-2. 923.1049.—**Motley,** J: L. Vienna, 1862-1867. (*In his* Correspondence, v. 2.) p. 33, *in* * 928. 673.—**Palacky,** F. Geschichte von Böhmen (to 1526), 10 pts. (in 5 vols.). 1864-7. 943.119-23.—**Wagner,** *Lieut.* A. L. Campaign of Königgrätz (1866). 1889. 943.114.
See also **Catalogues** of this Library.
No. 2, 1880, p. 16.   No. 3, 1882, p. 13.
See also **Poole's Index** (to 1882). pp. 79, 80, *in* ** 50.1;—*Same.* Jan. 1, 1882-Jan. 1, 1887. p. 29, *in* ** 50.1².
See also **Index to Consular reports.** 1880-1885; 1886-1889. 2 vols. (U. S. Pub. Docs. *Dept. of State.*) ** 350.5496¹·².

Author of Beltraffio (and 4 other stories).
James, H:, *Jr.* 823.4894
Author's love, An. Balch, E.. 823.5467
Automaton ear, and other sketches. McLandburgh, F. 823.1076
Avatar. Gautier, T. 823.5737
Aveline, Alfred d', *pseud. See* Hasselt, André-Henri-Constant van.
Avenger, The. 59 pp. De Quincey, T:
                p. 5, *in* 823.1778
Away in the wilderness. Ballantyne, R. M.
                      808.631
Same. *in* 808.1268 ; *in* 808.1279
Axel and Anna. 41 pp. Bremer, F.
                p. 470, *in* 823.2120
Ayesha, the maid of Kars. Morier, J.
                    * 823.6181
Ayrshire legatees. Galt, J: p. 167, *in* 823.4191
Ayrton, Chaplin. Child-life in Japan, and Japanese child-stories. Illus. 808.1871
Aytoun, W: Edmondstoune. The emerald studs. A reminiscence of the circuit. 66 pp. (*In* Tales from Blackwood, v. 6.)
                in ** 823.6652
—— The Glenmutchkin railway. 44 pp. (*In* Tales from Blackwood, v. 1.) *in* ** 823.6647
—— How I became a yeoman. 55 pp. (*In* Tales from Blackwood, v. 2.) *in* ** 823.6648
—— How I stood for the Dreep-daily burghs. 79 pp. (*In* Tales from Blackwood, v. 4.)
                in ** 823.6650

English Fiction. *Contin.*
Aytoun, W: Edmondstoune. *Contin.*
—— How we got possession of the Tuileries. 89 pp. (*In* Tales from Blackwood, v. 5.)
                in ** 823.6651
—— Norman Sinclair. 3 vols. 823.6137-9
—— The surveyor's tale. 48 pp. (*In* Tales from Blackwood, v. 8.) *in* ** 823.6654
Azarian. Spofford, *Mrs.* H. E.. (P.)
                  823.5165
Same. 823.5759
Azeglio, Massimo Taparelli, *marquis* d'. The challenge of Barletta. Tr. by Lady L.. Magenis. 2 vols. (in 1). ** 823.6637
Aztec treasure-house. Janvier, T: A.
                  823.7165
Babiole, the pretty milliner. 2d part. Du Boisgobey, F. *in* 823.5141
Same. *in* 823.5188
Baboe Dalima. Perelaer, T. H. 823.7223
Baby Rue. Clark, *Mrs.* C.. M. 823.1872
Babylon.
—— Crawford, F. M. Zoroaster. (5th cent. B. C.) 823.4886
—— Ward, *Mrs.* E.. S. (P.), *and* Ward, H. D. The master of the magicians. (6th cent. B. C.) 823.7342

Note.—For Babylon and Babylonia *see* **Kaulen,** *Dr.* F. Assyrien und Babylonien. 3. Aufl. (Mit Litteratur, 1620-1885.) 935.13.—**Layard,** A. II. Discoveries among the ruins of Nineveh and Babylon. Map. Illus. 1853. 915.116;—Early adventures in . . . Babylonia. 2 vols. 1887. 916.180-1.—**Rawlinson,** G: Five great monarchies. * 930.33-5.—Records of the past. 6 vols. 930.50-5.—**Smith,** G: Hist. of Babylonia. 939.12.
See also **Poole's Index** (to 1882). p. 84, *in* ** 50.1;—*Same.* Jan. 1, 1882-Jan. 1, 1887. p. 36, *in* ** 50.1².

Bach, Johann Sebastian. Barnard, C: Bach and Beethoven. (*The tone masters,* v. 3.)
                808.1620
Bach, Wilhelm Friedemann. Friedemann Bach. 19 pp. (*In* Robert . . . . . . and other stories.) p. 153, *in* 823.5811
Bachelor of Salamanca. 2 vols. Le Sage, A. R. 823.5735-6
Bachelor of the Albany. Savage, M. W.
                ** 823.4674
Same. 823.4832; 823.4988
Bachelor vicar of Newforth. Roe, *Mrs.* J. H.
                in 823.5108
Bachelor's blunder, A. Norris, W: E:
                in 823.5120
Bachelors' surrender. 823.2397
Back to back. Hale, E: E. *in* 823.5562
Back to the old home. Hay, M.. C.
                in 823.4986
Same. *in* 823.5021; *in* 823.2790
Bad to beat. Smart, H. *in* 823.4985
Same. *in* 823.5020
Baden, *Mrs.* F.. (Henshaw). Stories. (*With* The artist's love, by Mrs. E. D. E. (N.) Southworth.) *in* 823.1475
—— Stories. (*With* The Christmas guest, by Mrs. E. D. E. (N.) Southworth.)
                in 823.1481
—— Stories. (*With* The fatal secret, by Mrs. E. D. E. (N.) Southworth.) *in* 823.1490
—— Stories. (*With* The phantom wedding, by Mrs. E. D. E. (N.) Southworth.)
                in 823.1504

English Fiction. *Contin.*
Baden, *Mrs.* F.. (Henshaw). *Contin.*
—— Stories. (*With* The spectre lover, by Mrs. E. D. E. (N.) Southworth.)
in 823.1508
Baffled conspirators, The. Norris, W: E: 823.7341
Bag of diamonds, The. Fenn, G: M. 823.5591
Bage, Robert. Man as he is not. (*In* Barbauld, *Mrs.* A. L. (A.), *ed.* The British *novelists*, v. 48.) ** 823.2109
Baggesen, Jens. Aguete and the merman (poem). 12 pp. (*In* Bushby, *Mrs.* —., *tr.* The Danes . . . v. 1.)
p. 251, *in* 823.6444
Bagpipers, The. Dudevant, *Mme.* A. L. A. (D.) 823.7027
Bailey, James Montgomery [*Danbury News Man*]. Mr. Phillips' goneness. 823.52
Bailiff's maid. John, E. 823.4060
Baker, *Sir* S: White. Cast up by the sea. 808.338
Same. 823.2301
Baker, W: Mumford [*G: F. Harrington*]. Blessed Saint Certainty. 823.4188
—— Colonel Dunwoddie, millionaire: a story of to-day. (Anon.) 823.6372
—— Inside: a chronicle of secession. 823.5927
—— The making of a man. 823.4900
—— Mose Evans: a simple statement of the singular facts of his case. 823.50
—— The new Timothy. 823.1912
—— The Virginians in Texas: a story for young old folks and old young folks. 823.5923
Balacchi brothers. 25 pp. Davis, *Mrs.* R. B. (H.) p. 120, *in* 823.4702
Balch, E.. An author's love: being the unpublished letters of Prosper Mérimée's "Inconnue." (Anon.) 823.5467
Baldwin, James. Heroes of the olden time. 3 vols.
Story of Roland. 823.5624
Story of Siegfried. 823.5623
Story of the golden age. 823.5515
Balfour, *Mrs.* Clara Lucas (Liddell). The Burnish family. (Anon.) 823.7311
Balfour, D: Stevenson, R. L: Kidnapped: being the adventures of D. in 1751.
in 823.5051
Ball, *Sir* Robert Stawell. Star-land: being talks with young people about the wonders of the heavens. Illus. 808.1602
Ball at Sceaux. Balzac, H. de.
p. 89, *in* 823.4255
Ballantyne, Robert Michael. Away in the wilderness. 808.631
—— *Same.* *in* 808.1279
—— The battery and the boiler; or, adventures in the laying of submarine electric cables. 808.1262
—— The battle and the breeze. (*With his* Wrecked but not ruined.) *in* 808.1265
—— Battles with the sea: being descriptive of our coast-life-saving apparatus. 808.1549
—— The big otter: a tale of the great nor'-west. 808.1531

English Fiction. *Contin.*
Ballantyne, Robert Michael. *Contin.*
—— Black ivory: a tale of adventure among the slavers of east Africa. 808.453
—— Blue lights; or, hot work in the Soudan: a tale of soldier life. 808.6622
—— The cannibal islands; or, Captain Cook's adventures in the south seas. (*With his* Hunting the lions.) *in* 808.1286
—— Chasing the sun; or, rambles in Norway. 808.637
—— *Same.* *in* 808.1281
—— The coral island: a tale of the Pacific ocean. 808.817
—— Deep down: a tale of the Cornish mines. 808.1264
—— *Same.* *in* 808.6692
—— Digging for gold; or, adventures in California. 808.1285
—— Dog Crusoe: a tale of the western prairies. 808.207
—— Dusty diamonds cut and polished: a tale of city-Arab life and adventure. 808.1272
—— Erling the Bold: a tale of the Norse sea-kings. 808.1273
—— Fast in the ice; or, adventures in the polar regions. 808.673
—— *Same.* (*And*) Fighting the whales. 808.1284
—— Fighting the whales. 808.674
—— *Same.* *in* 808.1284
—— Finding his fate. 16 pp. (*In* Twenty novelettes . . .) p. 143, *in* 823.7183
—— Fire brigade ; or, fighting the flames. 808.208
—— The floating light of the Goodwin Sands. 808.209
—— Freaks on the fells. (*Also*) Papers from Norway. 808.213
—— The fugitives; or, the tyrant queen of Madagascar. 823.5636
—— Gascoyne, the sandalwood trader: a tale of the Pacific. 808.210
—— The golden dream; or, adventures in the far west. 808.829
—— Gorilla hunters: a tale of the wilds of Africa. 808.211
—— Hunting the lions; or, the land of the negro. (*And*) The cannibal islands; or, Captain Cook's adventures in the south seas. 808.1286
—— The iron horse: a tale of the Grand National Trunk Railway. 808.1261
—— The life-boat: a tale of our coast heroes. 808.827
—— Lighthouse: being the story of a great fight between man and the sea. 808.267
—— The lonely island; or, the refuge of the mutineers. 808.1263
—— Lost in the forest. (*And*) Away in the wilderness. 808.1279
—— Madman and the pirate. 808.1277
—— Martin Rattler; or, a boy's adventure in the forests of Brazil. 808.263
—— Over the Rocky mountains; or, Wandering Will in the land of the redskins. (*With his* The pioneers.) *in* 808.1280

English Fiction. *Contin.*

Ballantyne, Robert Michael. *Contin.*

—— The pioneers: a tale of the western wilderness. (*And*) Over the Rocky mountains.
808.1280

—— The pirate city: an Algerine tale.
808.1275

—— Post haste: a tale of her majesty's mails.
808.1271

—— The Red Eric; or, the whaler's last cruise.
823.6908

—— The red man's revenge: a tale of the Red river flood. 808.1270

—— Red Rooney. 823.6621

—— Rivers of ice. 808.814

—— Saved by the life-boat. (*With his* Sunk at sea.) *in* 808.1282

—— The settler and the savage: a tale of peace and war in south Africa. 808.206

—— Shifting winds: a story of the sea.
808.212

—— Six months at the Cape. 808.1550

—— Sunk at sea; or, the adventures of Wandering Will in the Pacific. (*And*) Saved by the life-boat. 808.1282

—— Tales of adventure. 808.1268
Contents:—Away in the wilderness.—The pioneers.—Hunting the lions.—Up in the clouds.

—— Tales of adventure on the coast.
808.1269
Contents:—The story of the rock; or, building on the Eddystone.—Wrecked but not ruined.—Saved by the life-boat.—Chasing the sun; or, rambles in Norway.

—— Tales of adventure on the sea.
808.1266
Contents:—Fighting the whales.—Fast in the ice; or, adventures in the Polar regions.—The cannibal islands.—The battle and the breeze.

—— Ungava: a tale of Esquimaux-land.
808.264

—— Up in the clouds ; or, balloon voyages. (*And*) Chasing the sun ; or, rambles in Norway. 808.1281

—— Why I did not become a sailor. (*With his* Freaks on the fells.) 808.213

—— Wild man of the west : a tale of the Rocky mountains. 808.703

—— World of ice; or, adventures . . . in the Polar regions. 808.265

—— Wrecked but not ruined. (*And*) The battle and the breeze. 808.1265

—— The young fur traders. 808.268

Ballroom repentance, A. Edwardes, *Mrs.* A.
823.2785

Ballyblunder : an Irish story. (Anon.)
823.6431

Balsamo. Dumas, A. D. 823.5903

Balsam-seller of Thurotzer, The. Gore, *Mrs.* C. F. G. (M.) p. 1, *in* ** 823.6569

Balzac, Honoré de (1799–1850). After-dinner stories. Tr. by M. Verelst. 823.5587
Contents:—Introduction.—Balzac. (By E. Saltus.) —The Red Inn.—Madame Firmiani.—The "Grande Bretèche."—Madame de Beauséant.

—— The Alkahest; or, the house of Claës. Tr. by K.. P. Wormeley. 823.5208

—— A Breton town. (*In* Zimmern, H.., *and* A. *Half-hours with for. novelists*, v. 2.)
in ** 823.6614

—— Bureaucracy; or, a civil service reformer. Tr. by K.. P. Wormeley. 823.5460

English Fiction. *Contin.*

Balzac, Honoré de. *Contin.*

—— The cat and battledore, and other tales. Tr. by P. Kent. 3 vols. 823.4254-6
Contents:—v. 1. The cat and battledore.—The vendetta.
v. 2. The purse.—The ball at Sceaux.
v. 3. Madame Firmiani.—A double family.
First 4 tales issued also as The vendetta.

—— César Birotteau. 823.5209

—— The country doctor. 823.5149

—— *Same.* 823.5570

—— Cousin Bette. Tr. by K.. P. Wormeley.
823.5510

—— Cousin Pons. Tr. by K.. P. Wormeley.
823.5210

—— A Cretin village. (*Also*) A Breton town. (*In* Zimmern, H.., *and* A. *Half-hours with for. novelists*, v. 2.) *in* ** 823.6614

—— The Duchesse de Langeais; with An episode under the Terror. (*Also*) The illustrious Gaudissart ;—A passion in the desert ; —and The hidden masterpiece. Tr. by K.. P. Wormeley. 823.5211

—— An episode under the Terror. (*With his* Duchesse de Langeais.) *in* 823.5211

—— Eugénie Grandet. 823.3438

—— *Same.* 823.4969

—— Fame and sorrow, *etc.* Tr. by K.. P. Wormeley. 823.7177
Contents:—Fame and sorrow.—Colonel Chabert. —The atheist's mass.—La Grande Bretèche.—The purse.—La Grenadière.

—— The hidden masterpiece. (*With his* Duchesse de Langeais.) *in* 823.5211

—— The illustrious Gaudissart. (*With his* Duchesse de Langeais.) *in* 823.5211

—— Louis Lambert. (Philosophical studies.) Tr. by K.. P. Wormeley. 823.5428
Contents:—Introd. (by G. F. Parsons).—Louis Lambert.—Facino Cane.—Gambara.

—— The magic skin. Tr. by K.. P. Wormeley. 823.5212

—— Modeste Mignon. Tr. by K.. P. Wormeley. 823.6542

—— A passion in the desert. (*With his* Duchesse de Langeais.) *in* 823.5211

—— Père Goriot. 823.4866

—— *Same.* *in* 823.5105

—— Seraphita. (*Also*) Jesus Christ in Flanders. (*And*) The exiles. Tr. by K.. P. Wormeley. 823.7335

—— Shorter stories. Tr. by W: Wilson and the count Stenbock; with a prefatory notice. 823.7353

—— Sons of the soil. Tr. by K.. P. Wormeley. 823.6942

—— The two brothers. Tr. by K.. P. Wormeley. 823.5213

—— The vendetta: tales of love and passion. 823.7118
Contents:—The cat and battledore.—The vendetta.—The purse.—The ball at Sceaux.
Note.—For life and writings, *see* Gautier, T., *and others.* Balzac. 78 pp. (*In their* Famous French authors.) 928.87.—Lerminier, J. L. E. Œuvres complètes de Balzac. 24 pp. (*Rev. d. d. Mondes*, 1847, n. s. v. 18.) p. 193, *in* ** 54.167.—Lilly, W. S. The age of Balzac. 41 pp. (*Contemp. Rev.* v. 37.) p. 1004, *in* ** 52.5387.—Molènes, G. de. Essais d'histoire littéraire. M. de Balzac. 22 pp. (*Rev. d. d. Mondes*, 1842, 4 s. v. 32.) p. 390, *in* ** 54.149.—Novels. 24 pp. (Rev. of *in N. Amer. Rev.* v. 65.) p. 85, *in* ** 51.544.—Poètes et romanciers modernes de la France. M. de Balzac. 19 pp. (*Rev. d. d. Mou-*

English Fiction. *Contin.*
Bedford-Row conspiracy. 42 pp. Thackeray,
W: M. *in* 823.1572
Beechcroft. Yonge, C.. M.. 823.1760
Beecher, *Mrs.* Eunice White (Bullard). From
dawn to daylight; or, the simple story of a
western home. 823.7375
Beecher, H: Ward (1813-1887). Norwood; or,
village life in New England. 823.64
Note.—For life and writings, *see* Abbott, L. H.
W. Beecher: his career, etc. 1883. 922.261.—Annual
Cyclopædia. 1887. p. 60, *in* ** 31.36¹⁰.—Apple-
tons' Cyclopædia of Am. biog., v. 1. ** 920.320.—
Beecher, W: C., *and others.* Biography of Rev. H.
W. Beecher. 1889. 922.321.
See also Poole's Index (to 1882). p. 107, *in* ** 50.1;
—*Same.* Jan. 1, 1882–Jan. 1, 1887. p. 39, *in* ** 50.1².
Bee-man of Orn and other fanciful tales.
Stockton, F. R: 808.1349
Beers, H: Augustin. Split zephyr: an atten-
uated yarn spun by the fates. 53 pp. (*In*
Stories by Amer. authors, v. 8.)
p. 48, *in* 823.4709
Beesly, *Mrs.* —. Stories from the history of
Rome. 2d ed. 808.841
Beethoven, L. van (1770-1827).
—— Barnard, C: Bach and Beethoven. (*The
tone masters*, v. 3.) *in* 808.1621
—— Beethoven. 18 pp. (*In* Crucifix of
Baden, *etc.*) p. 135, *in* 823.5817
—— Sheppard, E.. S. Rumor. 823.6043
Note.—See **Graeme, E.** Beethoven : a memoir.
1887. 927.281.—**Grove, Sir G:** Beethoven's nine
symphonies: analytical essays. 1888. 785.4.—**Hale,
E: E.** Lights of two centuries. * 920.314.—**Mos-
cheles, I.** Life of Beethoven (contains list of his
works. pp. 385-390). 927.51.—**Nohl, L.** Beethoven,
depicted by his contemporaries. 927.181.—**Rudall,
H. A.** Beethoven. (Great musicians.) 927.287.—
Wagner, R. Beethoven. 927.109.
Before the dawn. Dulac, G: 823.5402
Beggar on horseback, A. Payn, J. 823.5988
Same. 823.6057
Begum's daughter, The. Bynner, E. L.
823.6434
Behind blue glasses. Hackländer, H. W.
823.5563
Behind closed doors. Rohlfs, *Mrs.* A.. K.. (G.)
823.7147
Behind the arras. Neville, C. M. 823.5948
Behrens, Bertha [*W. Heimburg*]. Lora :
the major's daughter. Tr. by *Mrs.* J. W.
Davis. 823.6321
Beleaguered city, A. Oliphant, *Mrs.* M. O.
(W.) 823.5640
Belgium. *See* Netherlands.
—— Longfellow, H: W. Poems of places.
p. 127, *in* 821.220
Belinda. 2 vols. Edgeworth, M.
** 823.2110-2111
Same. ** 823.4647-8
Bell, Currer, *pseud. See* Nicholls, *Mrs.* C..
(Brontë).
Bell, *Mrs.* Lenox. Not to be won. 823.4779
Bell, Malcolm. Roanoke of Roanoke Hall.
823.6344
Bell of St. Paul's. Besant, W. 823.6362
Bellamy, C: Joseph. The Breton mills.
823.5700
—— An experiment in marriage. 823.7167
Bellamy, E: Dr. Heidenhoff's process.
823.7361
—— Looking backward 2000-1887. 823.5495

English Fiction. *Contin.*
Bellamy, E: *Contin.*
—— Lost. 20 pp. (*In* Stories by Amer.
authors, v. 7.) p. 47, *in* 823.4708
—— Miss Ludington's sister: a romance of
immortality. 823.7338
—— Six to one. 823.7162
Belle Nivernaise, La, and other stories.
Daudet, A. 823.5252
Bellehood and bondage. Stephens, *Mrs.* A.
S. (W.) 823.1965
Belles and ringers. Smart, H. 823.4030
Bellows-mender of Lyons. 24 pp. (*In* Fa-
mous stories. By De Quincey, and others.)
p. 259, *in* 823.1778
Belot, Adolphe (1829-1890). The black Ve-
nus. (Sequel to The thirst for the un-
known.) Tr. by G: D. Cox. 823.5793
—— Fedora; or, the tragedy in the Rue de la
Paix. Tr. by A. D. H. 823.5727
Issued also as Men are what women make them;
or, the drama of Rue de la Paix.
—— La grande Florine. (Sequel to The
stranglers of Paris.) Tr. by G: D. Cox.
823.2774
—— My good friend. Tr. by E: Wakefield.
823.7005
—— The stranglers of Paris. ("Les étran-
gleurs.") Tr. by G: D. Cox. 823.3498
Belt and spur. Saxon, *Mrs.* E. L., *ed.* 808.1610
Belton estate. Trollope, A. 823.1603
· *Same.* *in* 823.6262
Ben Brace. Chamier, F: 823.197
Benedict, *Mrs.* Anne (Kendrick). My won-
der-story. 808.1900
Benedict, Frank Lee. Frank Worthington's
name. 823.5833
—— Hammer and anvil. 823.69
—— Her friend. 823.65
—— A late remorse. 823.5699
—— Miss Van Kortland. 823.6038
—— My daughter Elinor. 823.5834
—— The price she paid. 823.5673
—— St. Simon's niece. 823.6039
—— *Same.* 823.6131
Ben-Hur. Wallace, L. 823.4860
Benjamin, E. Bedell. Hilda and I: a story of
three loves. 823.2018
Benjamin, Park. The end of New York. 60
pp. (*In* Stories by Amer. authors, v. 5.)
p. 82, *in* 823.4706
Ben-na-groich. 32 pp. (*In* Tales from Black-
wood, v. 7.) *in* ** 823.6653
Bennett, Emerson. Ellen Norbury. 823.70
—— Forest and prairie. 823.71
—— Kate Clarendon. 823.72
—— The orphan's trials. 823.74
—— Viola. 823.77
Bentzon, Thérèse, *pseud. See* Blanc, *Mme.*
Marie Thérèse (de Solms).
Berber, The. Mayo, W: S. 823.1143
Berger, E., *pseud. See* Sheppard, E.. Sara.
Berkeley the banker. Martineau, H.
** 823.6710
Same. Pt. 2. ** 823.6752
Berlin. Lander, S.. W. Berlin. (Spectacles
for young eyes.) 808.98
Bernard Lile. Clemens, J. 823.7100

English Fiction. *Contin.*
Bernhard, Carl, *pseud.* *See* Heiberg, T. C.
Bernthal. Mundt, *Mrs.* C. (M.) 823.5915
Berrington, B. S. The fortunes of Albert
Travers: a tale of the 18th century.
823.7197
Berry, E: Payson. Leah of Jerusalem: a
story of the time of Paul. 823.6396
Bertha's engagement. Stephens, *Mrs.* A. S.
(W.) 823.1962
Bertram family. Charles, *Mrs.* E.. (R.)
823.203
Bertrams, The. Trollope, A. 823.1604
Bertrand de la Croix. (*In* Picken, A., *ed.*
The club-book.) *in* 823.702
Besant, Walter. All sorts and conditions of
men: an impossible story. 823.3719
—— Armorel of Lyonesse. 823.7163
—— The bell of St. Paul's. 823.6362
—— Children of Gibeon. *in* 823.4985
—— *Same.* *in* 823.5020; 823.6962
—— Dorothy Forster. *in* 823.5039
—— For faith and freedom: a novel.
823.5531
—— A glorious fortune. *in* 823.4999
—— Herr Paulus: his rise, his greatness, and
his fall; a novel. 823.5885
—— The holy rose. 823.5135
—— *Same.* *in* 823.5136
—— In luck at last. *in* 823.5141
—— *Same.* *in* 823.5188
—— The inner house. (*With his* Katherine
Regina.) *in* 823.6603
—— Katherine Regina. (*Also*) The inner
house. 823.6603
—— The lament of Dives. 823.7029
—— Let nothing you dismay. 823.6689
—— "Self or bearer." *in* 823.5046
—— To call her mine. *in* 823.4983
—— Uncle Jack. 74 pp. *in* 823.4981
—— *Same.* *in* 823.4999
—— *Same.* (*With* As it fell upon a day. By
Mrs. M. Hungerford.) *in* 823.4982
—— World went very well then. 823.5145
—— *Same.* 823.5187
——, *and* Rice, James. By Celia's arbour: a
tale of Portsmouth town. 823.6113
—— The case of Mr. Lucraft and other tales.
823.6330
Contents:—From the supernatural: The case of
Mr. Lucraft;—The mystery of Joe Morgan;—An
old, old story;—Lady Kitty;—The old four-poster;—
My own experience.—From fairyland: Titania's
farewell.—From fact: On the Goodwin;—Edelweis;
—Love finds the way;—The death of Samuel Pick-
wick;—When the ship comes home.
—— The chaplain of the fleet. 823.6085
—— The golden butterfly. 823.6118
—— My little girl. 823.6213
—— Ready-money Mortiboy. 823.5884
—— The seamy side. 823.6086
—— This son of Vulcan. 823.6191
—— 'Twas in Trafalgar's bay, and other sto-
ries. 823.6084
Contents:—'Twas in Trafalgar's bay.—Shepherds
all and maidens fair.—Such a good man.—Le chien
d'or.
—— With harp and crown. 823.6409
Bessie. Kavanagh, J. 823.5924
Bessie Harrington's venture. Mathews, J. A.
823.1122

English Fiction. *Contin.*
Bessie Lang. Corkran, A. 823.1793
Bessie's fortune. Holmes, *Mrs.* M.. J.. (H.)
823.4848
Bessy Rane. Wood, *Mrs.* E. (P.) 823.6011
Best of husbands. Payn, J. 823.6063
Bethesda. Halstead, L. B. 823.4726
Bethusy-Huc, Valeska *Gräfin* [*Moritz von
Reichenbach*]. The Eichhofs. Tr. by Mrs.
A. L. Wister. 823.4345
Betrothed, The. Manzoni, A. 823.2138
Same. 823.5048; 823.7399
Betrothed, The. Scott, *Sir* W. 823.1394
Same. *in* 823.4803; *in* 823.5328
Same. p. 281, *in* 823.6031
Better times stories. Kirk, *Mrs.* E. W. (O.)
823.5464
Betty's bright idea. 25 pp. Stowe, *Mrs.* H.
E.. (B.) *in* 823.6678
Between the lines. King, *Capt.* C: 823.6544
Between two loves. Brame, *Mrs.* C.. M. (L.)
in 823.5117
Between two sins. Brame, *Mrs.* C.. M.. (L.)
823.5111
Between whiles. Jackson, *Mrs.* H.. M. (F.)
823.5264
Betwixt my love and me. Archer, E. M.
in 823.5069
Beulah. Wilson, *Mrs.* A. J.. (E.) 823.4013
Same. 823.1905
Beyond pardon. Brame, *Mrs.* C.. M. (L.)
823.6605
Beyond recall. Sergeant, A. *in* 823.5128
Beyond the breakers. Owen, R. D. 823.5954
Beyond the gates. Ward, *Mrs.* E.. S. (P.)
823.4620
Beyond the Himalayas. Geddie, J: 808.1184
Bianca. Maturin, E: 823.1123
Biart, Lucien. An involuntary voyage. Tr.
by Mrs. C. Hoey, and Mr. J: Lillie.
823.6837
Bible animals and the lessons taught by them.
Newton, *Rev.* R: 808.1722
Bible stories. Favourite Bible stories.
808.1582
Bickerstaffe, I: (1735-1812?). Macaulay, *Miss*
E. Tales of the drama founded on . . .
the comedies of . . . Bickerstaff. 823.1051
Note.—See **Stephen's** Dictionary of national
biography, v. 5. °° 920.330°.
Bidwell, Jennie. There's nothing in it.
823.2056
Big brother series. *See* Eggleston, G: C.
Big Jack Small. 45 pp. Gally, J. W.
p. 199, *in* 823.4162
Big otter, The. Ballantyne, R. M. 808.1531
Bigly, Cantell A., *pseud.* *See* Peck, G: W.
Bigot, *Mrs.* M.. (Healy). [*Jeanne Mairet.*]
Lakeville. 823.5872
—— Storm-driven. 823.738
Bikelas, D. Loukis Laras. Reminiscences of
a Chiote merchant during the Greek war
of independence. Tr. by J. Gennadius.
823.4198
Same. 823.6115
Biographical stories.
—— Adams, W. Our standard-bearer. (Life
of U. S. Grant.) 808.1555
—— Ames, L. T. Memoirs of a millionaire.
823.6556

English Fiction. *Contin.*
Biographical stories. *Contin.*
—— Barnard, C: The tone masters. 3 vols.
(v. 1: Mozart and Mendelssohn;—v. 2: Handel and Haydn; — v. 3: Bach and Beethoven.) 808.1619-21
—— Brayman, J. O. Daring deeds of American heroes; with biog. sketches. 808.1314
—— Brooks, E. S. Historic girls: stories of girls who have influenced the history of their times. 808.1925
—— Charles, *Mrs.* E.. (R.) Sketches of the women of Christendom. 823.5696
—— Cook, J: E. The youth of Jefferson. (1764.) 823.7421
—— Croffut, W: A: The Vanderbilts and the story of their fortune. 923.2000
—— De Foe, D. Memoirs of Captain Carleton. (*Novels*, v. 2.) p. 273, *in* 823.2123
—— Denison, C: W. The tanner boy. (Life of U. S. Grant.) 808.224
—— Famous boys and famous men. 808.1666
—— Frost, J: Old Hickory. (Life of Gen. A. Jackson.) 808.1715
—— Hawthorne, N. Queen Christina, 1626-89.—Oliver Cromwell, 1599-1658.—B: Franklin, 1706-90.—S: Johnson, 1709-84.— Sir I: Newton, 1642-1727.—B: West, 1738-1820. (*In his* Tales and sketches.) p. 137, *in* 824.414
—— Holt, E. S.. In all time of our tribulation. (Piers Gaveston.) 823.5616
—— Keddie, H. Papers for thoughtful girls, with sketches of some girls' lives. 808.325
—— Parton, J. Captains of industry; or, men of business who did something besides making money. 808.1548
—— Rau, H. Mozart: a biog. romance. 823.7350
—— Shorthouse, J. H. Little schoolmaster Mark: a spiritual romance. (Childhood of H. Jung-Stilling.) 823.5413
—— Thayer, W: M. From farm-house to the White House. (Life of G: Washington.) 808.1727
—— Tulloch, W. W. Story of the life of Queen Victoria. 808.1674
—— Wright, *Mrs.* J. (McN.) (Stories of) Twelve noble men. 808.1540
Note.—For other biographical stories, *see* the name of the person.
For bibliography, *see* **Phillips**, L. B. Dict. of biog. reference; with a classed index of the biographical literature of Europe and America. (Refers to no book published after 1870.) ** 920.282³.— **Thomas**, J. Dict. of biog. and mythology. 1888. ** 920.227.
See also **Catalogues** of this Library.
No. 2, 1880, pp. 24-26. No. 4, 1884, pp. 29-30.
No. 3. 1882, pp. 21-22. No. 5, 1888, pp. 35-36.

Bird, Robert Montgomery. Nick of the woods; or, the jibbenainosay: a tale of Kentucky. 823.79
Birds. Wood, J: G: Routledge's picture book of birds. 808.1884
Birds of prey. Maxwell, *Mrs.* M.. E.. (B.) 823.2403
Same. *in* 823.4987
Birth and education. Schwartz, *Mrs.* M. S. (B.) 823.5808

English Fiction. *Contin.*
Bischoff, Joseph Eduard Konrad. [*K. von Bolanden.*] The trowel or the cross, and other stories and sketches. 823.6275
Contents:—The trowel or the cross.—How George Howard was cured.—A Christmas recognition.—Grace Seymour's mission.—Cain, what hast thou done with thy brother?—The fur trader.— Travels with a valetudinarian.—Laughing Dick Cranstone.—My cousin's introduction.—"For better —for worse."—An English Christmas story.—The cross through love, and love through the cross.— Acoma.
Bishop, W: H: Choy Susan and other stories. 823.5672
Contents:—Choy Susan.—The battle of Bunkerloo. —Deodand.—Braxton's new art.—One of the thirty pieces.—McIntyre's false face.—Miss Calderon's german.
—— Detmold: a romance. 823.5698
—— The golden justice. 823.5785
—— The house of a merchant prince: a novel of New York. 823.4480
—— One of the thirty pieces. 40 pp. (*In* Stories by Amer. authors, v. 1.) p. 81, *in* 823.4702
—— The yellow snake. (*Lippincott's mo. mag.*, July 1888.) 823.6391
Bishop's vagabond, The. 42 pp. French, A. p. 5, *in* 823.4708
Bit o' writin'. Banim, J:, *and* M. 823.53
Bitter atonement, A. Brame, *Mrs.* C.. M. (L.) 823.236
Same. *in* 823.5061
Bitter reckoning. Payn, J. *in* 823.4994
Bitzius, Albert. [*Jeremias Gotthelf.*] Wealth and welfare. 2 vols. 823.6093-4
Bivouac, The. Maxwell, W: H. 823.1127
Björnson, Björnstjerne. Arne. Tr. by Rasmus B. Anderson. 823.4364
—— Arne: a sketch of Norwegian country life. Tr. by A. Plesner and S. Rugeley-Powers. (*Also*) The happy boy: a tale of Norwegian peasant life. Tr. by H. R. G. 823.4218
—— The betrothal. (*Also*) The wedding. (*Extr. from* The bridal march.) (*In* Zimmern, H., *and* A. Half-hours with for. novelists, v. 2.) *in* ** 823.6614
—— The bridal march, and other stories. Tr. by Rasmus B. Anderson. 823.4467
Contents:—The bridal march.—Thrond.—A dangerous wooing.—The bear hunter.—The father.— The eagle's nest.—Blakken.—Fidelity.—A problem of life.
—— Captain Mansana, and other stories. Tr. by R. B. Anderson. 823.4477
Contents:—Captain Mansana.—The railroad and the churchyard.—Dust.
—— The fishing girl. Tr. by A. Plesner and F. Richardson. 823.4224
—— The happy boy: a tale of Norwegian peasant life. Tr. by H. R. G. (*With his* Arne.) *in* 823.4218
—— Magnhild. Tr. by R. B. Anderson. 823.4478
—— Synnöve Solbakken. Tr. by R. B. Anderson. 823.4236
Black, W: The adventure in Thule. (*And*) Marriage of Moira Fergus. (*Also*) Lady Silverdale's sweetheart, and other tales (*viz.*: The maid of Killeena. 44 pp. (*And*) A fight for a wife. 17 pp.). 823.2885
—— A daughter of Heth: a novel. 823.80

English Fiction. *Contin.*

Bliss, W: Root. Colonial times on Buzzard's
  bay. 2d ed. 823.6537
Blithedale romance. Hawthorne, N.
  in 823.733
Blockade of Phalsburg, The. Erckmann, É.,
  and Chatrian, A. 823.6854
Blockade runners. Verne, J. 823.5181
  Same. p. 197, *in* 823.6243; *in* 823.7091
Bloody chasm. De Forest, J: W: 823.1891
Blossom and fruit; or, Madame's ward.
  823.5123
Blossom-bud and her genteel friends. Smith,
  Mrs. J. P. 823.4537
Blow, *Mrs.* M.. W. (Glascock.) Dare.
  823.4299
Blue and the grey ser. *See* Adams, W: T.
Blue banner, The. Cahun, L. 823.6283
Blue bell of Red-Neap. Parr, *Mrs.* L.. (T.)
  823.1231
Blue fairy book. Lang, A., *ed.* 808.1687
Blue lights. Ballantyne, R. M. 823.6622
Bluebeard's keys. 41 pp. Ritchie, *Mrs.* A..
  I.. (T.) 823.5984
Blue-stocking, A. Edwardes, *Mrs.* A.
  823.1906
Blyth, M. P. Antoinette. 2 vols. 823.7206-7
Blythe, J. A. St. J: A lonely life. 823.2355
Bodley grandchildren and their journey in
  Holland. Scudder, H. E. 808.1852
Bodleys afoot. Scudder, H. E. 808.1850
Bodleys on wheels. Scudder, H. E. 808.1849
Bodleys telling stories. Scudder, H. E.
  808.1848
Body and soul. 2 vols. (in 1). Wilkins, *Rev.*
  G: ** 823.6736
Bogle o' the brae. Hogg, J. *in* 823.702
Boisgilbert, Edmund, *pseud. See* Don-
  nelly, Ignatius.
Bolanden, Konrad von, *pseud. See* Bis-
  choff, Joseph Eduard Konrad.
Boldrewood, Rolf. Robbery under arms; a
  story of life and adventure in the bush and
  in the goldfields of Australia. 823.7168
Bölte, Amalie C.. Elise Mariane (*Known as
  Amely*). Mme. de Staël: an historical
  novel. Tr. by T. Johnson. 823.7093
Bölte, Amely. *See* Bölte, Amalie C.. E. M.
Bolton, *Mrs.* S.. (Knowles). Present prob-
  lem. 823.110
Bolton and his friends. Stowe, *Mrs.* H. E.
  (B.) *in* 823.6678
Bonaventure. Cable, G: W. 823.5248
Bondman, The. Caine, H. 823.7034
"Bones and I." Melville, G: J: Whyte-
  823.7271
  Same. *in* ** 823.4660
Boniface, Joseph Xavier. [*X. B. Saintine.*]
  Picciola. 823.6294
  —— *Same.* p. 755, *in* ** 823.6215
  —— The solitary of Juan Fernandez; or, the
  real Robinson Crusoe. Tr. by A. T. Wil-
  bur. 823.6838
Bonne-Marie. Durand, *Mme.* A. M. C. (H.)
  823.6867
Bonner, J: A child's history of Greece. 2 vols.
  808.621-2

  v. 1: B. C. 500–B. C. 456.
  v. 2: B. C. 447–A. D. 1843.

English Fiction. *Contin.*

Bonner, J: *Contin.*
—— A child's history of Rome. 2 vols.
  808.623-4
—— A child's history of the United States.
  3 vols. 808.618-20
  v. 1: A. D. 1500–A. D. 1776.
  v. 2: A. D. 1776–A. D. 1860.
  v. 3: A. D. 1860–A. D. 1865.
Bonnie Prince Charlie. Henty, G: A.
  808.1443
Bonny Kate. Tiernan, *Mrs.* F.. C. (F.)
  823.6360
Bonnybel Vane. Cooke, J: E. 823.5661
Bonnyborough. Whitney, *Mrs.* A. D. (T.)
  823.4883
Book of American explorers. Higginson, T:
  W. 808.298
Book of life, The. Galt, J: *in* 823.702
Book of Scottish story: historical, humorous,
  legendary, and imaginative. Selected from
  the works of standard Scottish authors.
  823.1835
Book of snobs. Thackeray, W: M. 823.1572
  Same. *in* 823.6324
Books and reading:
—— Abbott, L., *ed.* Hints for home reading.
  (Cop. 1883.) 16.212
—— Atkinson, W. P. On the right use of
  books. 1878. 824.4
—— Axon, W. E. A. Books and reading.
  (*Library chronicle*, 1887, v. 4.) ** 19.67⁴
—— Baldwin, J. The book-lover. 4th ed.
  1885. 17.175
—— Best hundred books: containing an arti-
  cle on the choice of books, by J. Ruskin,
  etc. 1886. 374.16
—— Best reading, 4th rev. and enl. ed., con-
  tin. to Aug., 1876, with the addition of
  select lists of the best French, German,
  Spanish and Italian literature. Ed. by F: B.
  Perkins. 1877. * 17.2
—— *Same.* 2d ser. English and American
  publications for the five years ending Dec.
  31, 1881. Ed. by L. E. Jones. (Suppl. to
  4th ed.) 1882. * 17.2²
—— *Same.* 3d ser. For the five years ending Dec. 1, 1886. Ed. by L. E. Jones. 1887.
  * 17.2³
—— Book-lover's Enchiridion. (A. Lang.)
  1883. * 804.4
—— "Books that have helped me." Repr.
  from "The forum." 1888. 16.211
—— Burt, M.. E. Literary landmarks: a
  guide to good reading for young people,
  and teachers' assistant. 1890. 17.258
—— Dibdin, *Rev.* T. F. The library companion. 1824. 17.234
—— Fiction in libraries and the reading of
  children. Papers read at the Boston con-
  ference of the Amer. Library Assoc., 1879.
  (*Lib. jl.*, v. 4, 1879, pp. 316–366.) ** 19.19
—— Green, S. S. The relation of the public
  library to the public schools. (*Lib. jl.*, v.
  5, p. 235.) ** 19.20
—— Harrison, F. The choice of books, and
  other literary pieces. 1886. 824.389
—— Hazard, W. P. The library; or, some
  hints about what to read. 1870. 17.262

English Fiction. *Contin.*
Books and reading: *Contin.*
—— How to read a book in the best way.
67 pp. 16.210
—— Langford, J: A. The praise of books,
as said and sung by English authors.
824.205
—— Legouvé, E. Art of reading. 815.19
—— — Reading as a fine art. (Abr.) 9th ed.
1879. 815.20
—— Leypoldt, F. A reading diary. 1881.
* 16.74
—— —, and Jones, L. E. The books of all
times. 1882. ** 11.143
—— Mathews, W. What shall we read?
(*In his* Men, places and things.) 1888.
p. 335, *in* 824.397
—— Ogle, J. J. Fifty works of reference for
a small reading-room. (*Lib. chronicle,*
1887.) 19.67⁴
—— Parsons, F., *and others.* The world's
best books. 1889. 374.19
—— Poole, R. B. Fiction in libraries. 3 pp.
(*Lib. jl.,* v. 16, 1891, p. 8.) ** 19.24⁵
—— Porter, N. Books and reading; with
app. containing a select catalogue of books.
1881. D 2.19
—— Pryde, D. Highways of literature; or,
what to read and how to read. 1883.
374.15
—— Richardson, C: F. The choice of books.
(1881.) 16.216
—— Sonnenschein, W. S. The best books.
1887. ** 17.238
—— Thwing, C: F. The reading of books:
its pleasures, profits, and perils. 1883.
16.209
—— Van Dyke, J. C. Books, and how to use
them. 1883. 374.14
—— Van Rhyn, G. A. F. What to read and
how to read: a guide to recent English literature. 1875. * 17.1
Authors.
—— A hundred American authors perhaps
worthiest of being read. (*Critic,* July 24,
1886.) ** 51.1426
—— A hundred and twenty-five great authors.
(*Critic,* July 17, 1886.) ** 51.1426
See also Allibone, S. A. Critical dictionary of
English literature and British and American authors. 3 vols. v. 1: A-Lytton;—v. 2: Mab.-Szyrma;—
v. 3: Taafe-Z. (Index.) ** 803.6-8.—Stedman, E.
C., *and* Hutchinson, E. M. Library of American
literature. 11 vols. (Index in v. 11.)
Contents.—v. 1. Early colonial period. 1607-1675.
** 820.122
v. 2. Later colonial period. 1676-1764. ** 820.123
v. 3. Lit. of the revolutionary period. 1765-1787.
** 820.124
v. 4. Lit. of the republic. Pt. 1: 1788-1820. ** 820.125
v. 5. Lit. of the republic. Pt. 2: 1821-1834. ** 820.126
vols. 6-8. Lit. of the republic. Pt. 3: 1835-1860.
** 820.127-9
vols. 9-11. Lit. of the republic. Pt. 4: 1861-1889.
** 820.130-131¹
Annual American catalogue, with full titles
and descriptive notes. 4 vols. 1886-9. ** 15.261-3².
Authors for boys. See
Adams.—Aldrich.—Alger.—Ballantyne.—Blake.—
Brooks.—Butterworth.—Church.—Clemens.—Edgar.
—Fenn.—Fosdick.—Frith.—Hale.—Hawthorne.—
Henty.—Hodgetts.—Hopes.—Hughes.—Hutchesou.
—Kaler.—Kellogg.—Kingston.— Knox.—Lamb.—
Lanier.—Munroe.—Reed.—Reid.—Scott.—Stables.—
Stoddard.—Trowbridge.—Verne, and others.

English Fiction. *Contin.*
Books and reading: *Contin.*
Authors for girls. See
Alcott.—Aulnoy, *Mme.* d'.—Beale. — Browne.—
Catherwood, *Mrs.*—Champney, *Mrs.*—Dickens.—
Dodge, *Mrs.* — Dodgson. — Doudney. — Douglas. —
Ewing.—Harris, *Mrs.*—Hawthorne.—Holmes, *Mrs.*
—Holt.—Irving.—Keddie.—Lamb.— Marshall, *Mrs.*
—Meade.—Perry.— Richards. *Mrs.*—Sewell.— Sher-
wood, *Mrs.* — Swan.— Symington. — Wetherell. —
Whitney, *Mrs.*—Woolsey.—Yonge, and others.
Authors for the little ones. See
Andersen.—Æsop.—Barbauld, *Mrs.*—Bloomfield.
—Burnett, *Mrs.* — Day. — Edgeworth. — Grimm. —
Hawthorne.—Hood.—Hugessen.— Jackson, *Mrs.*—
Kingsley. — Lillie, *Mrs.* — MacDonald. — Meade.—
Molesworth, *Mrs.*—Montgomery.—Moulton, *Mrs.*
—Richards, *Mrs.*—Ruskin.— Scudder. — Trimmer,
Mrs.—Walton, *Mrs.*—Watts, *Dr.*—Wesselhoeft, *Mrs.*
—Wiggin, *Mrs.*—Woolsey, and others.
Books for the young.
—— Best one hundred books for boys. (*The
Critic,* July 17, 1886.) ** 51.1426
—— Books for boys and girls. (*Lib. jl.,* June
1881, v. 6.) p. 182, *in* ** 19.21
—— Books for very little children. (*Lit.
News,* 1886, v. 7.)
pp. 306, 338, *in* * 15.207¹
—— Books for young women. (From the
Christian register. *Publisher's weekly,*
Sept. 21, 1878, v. 14.) p. 369, *in* ** 11.66
—— Burt, M. E. Literary landmarks: a
guide to good reading for young people.
1890. 17.258
—— Harris, A. B. American authors for
young folks. 1887. 820.157
—— Hundred books for boys. (*Lit. news,*
Feb. 1887, v. 8.) p. 51, *in* ** 15.207²
—— Salmon, E. Juvenile literature as it is.
1888. 16.213
—— Sargent, J: F., *comp.* Reading for the
young; classified and annotated catalogue
with alphabetical author-index. 1890.
16.222
—— Smart, J. H. Books and reading for
the young. 1880. 16.215
Boone, Daniel (1735-1820).
—— Abbott, J. S. C. Daniel Boone.
808.542
—— Jones, J. B. Wild western scenes.
823.906
Note.—See Flint, T. Memoir of B. ** 923.419.—
Hartley, C. B. Life of B. 923.416.—Peck, J: M.
Life of D. Boone. (Sparks, J. *Amer. biog.,* s. 2, v.
13.) * 923.1382.
Booth, *Mrs.* Eliza M. J. (Gollan) von.
["*Rita.*"] Daphne. 823.5783
—— Faustine. 823.5779
—— Fragoletta. 823.3888
—— My lady coquette. *in* 823.6691
Bootle's children. Stannard, *Mrs.* H. E. V.
(P.) *in* 823.6607
Boots at the Holly-tree inn. 20 pp. Dickens,
C: J. H. p. 80, *in* 823.5478
Border beagles. Simms, W: G. 823.1427
Border shepherdess, A. Barr, *Mrs.* A. E.
(H.) 823.5225
Borlase, J. S. The king of the conjurors.
823.111
Born coquette, A. Hungerford, *Mrs.* M.
823.7089
Bornemann, *Mrs.* M.. Madame Jane Junk
and Joe. 823.5813

English Fiction. *Contin.*
Boy's adventure in the barons' war, A. Edgar,
  J: G: 808.1909
Boy's adventures in the wilds of Australia.
  Howitt, W: 808.193
Boys' and girls' Herodotus. White, J: S., *ed.*
  808.1880
Boys' and girls' Plutarch. White, J: S., *ed.*
  808.1881
Boy's King Arthur, The. Malory, *Sir* T:
  808.1870
Boys of '76. Coffin, C: C. 808.1857
Boys of the Sierras, The. Montgomery, W.
  808.1877
Boy's own book of indoor games and recrea-
  tions. Stables, G., *and others.* 808.1906
Boy's town, A. Howells, W: D. 808.1718
Boys' useful pastimes. Griffith, R. 808.1645
Boy's workshop, with plans and designs: for
  in-door and out-door work. By a boy and
  his friends. 808.1552
Boz, *pseud.* See Dickens, C: J: H.
Bracebridge Hall. Irving, W. 823.1810
Brachvogel, Albert Emil. Beaumarchais:
  an historical novel. Tr. by T. J. Radford.
  823.6105
Braddon, M.. E.. *See* Maxwell, *Mrs.* M.. E..
  (Braddon).
Bradley, E: [*Cuthbert Bede.*] Adventures
  of Mr. Verdant Green, an Oxford freshman.
  823.117
  Issued also as The dude; or the adventures of
  Verdant Green.
—— Nearer and dearer: a novelette.
  823.4134
Bradshaw, Annie. Crimson stain.
  in 823.5090
  Same. 823.5143
Braga, Teofilo, *joint author. See* Harding,
  Victor Eugenio.
Bragelonne, the son of Athos. Dumas, A. D.
  823.6302
Brakespeare. Lawrence, G: A. 823.956
Brame, *Mrs.* C.. M. (Low). [*Bertha M.
  Clay.*] Arnold's promise. (*With her* The
  earl's error.) *in* 823.5123
—— At war with herself. 823.5100
—— *Same.* 823.5128
—— Between two loves. *in* 823.5117
—— Between two sins. 823.5111
—— Beyond pardon. (*Also*) A golden heart.
  823.6605
—— A bitter atonement. 823.236
—— *Same.* *in* 823.5061
—— Broken wedding-ring. 823.5129
—— Claribel's love story. *in* 823.5017
—— A dark marriage morn. 823.5120
—— A dead heart. (*And*) Lady Gwendo-
  line's dream. *in* 823.5064
—— Dora Thorne. 823.5063
—— The duke's secret. *in* 823.5080
—— The earl's atonement. *in* 823.5088
—— The earl's error. (*And*) Arnold's prom-
  ise. *in* 823.5123
—— Evelyn's folly. 823.5126
—— Fair but false. 823.5099
—— Fair mystery. 823.5042
—— For another's sin. 823.4877
—— *Same.* *in* 823.5079

English Fiction. *Contin.*
Brame, *Mrs.* C.. M. (Low). *Contin.*
—— From gloom to sunlight. *in* 823.5104
—— *Same.* 823.5133
—— A golden dawn. 823.5054
—— A golden heart. (*With her* Beyond par-
  don.) *in* 823.6605
—— A haunted life. *in* 823.5019
—— Her martyrdom. 823.4919
—— *Same.* *in* 823.5103
—— Her mother's sin. *in* 823.5022
—— Her second love. 823.5127
—— Hilary's folly. *in* 823.5019
—— *Same.* 823.5472
—— Hilda. *in* 823.5094
—— In Cupid's net. *in* 823.5064
—— Ingledew House. (*And*) More bitter than
  death. *in* 823.5132
—— Lady Damer's secret. 823.237
—— *Same.* *in* 823.5117
—— Lady Gwendoline's dream. (*With her*
  A dead heart.) *in* 823.5064
—— Lady Hutton's ward. *Same as* Hilda.
—— Letty Leigh. *in* 823.5123
—— Like no other love. *in* 823.5101
—— Love for a day. *in* 823.5054
—— Love's warfare. *in* 823.5106
—— Madolin's lover. *in* 823.5134
—— Marjorie. 2 pts. *in* 823.5140
—— *Same.* 823.5186; 823.5195
—— More bitter than death. (*With her* In-
  gledew House.) *in* 823.5132
—— My sister Kate. 29 pp. *in* 823.4994
—— The mystery of Colde Fell. *in* 823.4992
—— The mystery of the holly-tree: a
  Christmas story. (*With her* On her wed-
  ding morn.) *in* 823.5133
—— On her wedding morn. (*And*) The
  mystery of the holly-tree: a Christmas
  story. *in* 823.5133
—— A passion flower. 823.4772
—— "Prince Charlie's daughter." 823.5076
—— Put asunder. *in* 823.4980
—— A queen amongst women. *in* 823.5080
—— Redeemed by love. *in* 823.5134
—— Repented at leisure. *in* 823.5036
—— Romance of a black veil. 823.5013
—— Set in diamonds. *in* 823.5132
—— The shadow of a sin. *in* 823.5118
—— *Same.* *in* 823.5124
—— The shattered idol. *in* 823.5123
—— Sin of a lifetime. *in* 823.5101
—— The squire's darling. *in* 823.5079
—— Struggle for a ring. (*Also*) Sweet Cym-
  beline. 823.5180
—— Sunshine and roses. 823.5119
—— Sweet Cymbeline. (*With her* Struggle
  for a ring.) *in* 823.5180
—— Thorns and orange blossoms.
  in 823.5076
—— Thrown on the world. 823.5132
—— True Magdalen. *in* 823.5111
—— 'Twixt smile and tear. *in* 823.5124
—— Two kisses. 823.5101
—— Under a shadow. 823.5137
—— An unnatural bondage. (*And*) That beau-
  tiful lady. *in* 823.5035
—— Wedded and parted. *in* 823.5099
—— Which loved him best? 823.5115

English Fiction. *Contin.*
Brame, *Mrs.* C.. M. (Low). *Contin.*
—— Wife in name only.　　　　823.5099
—— The wife's secret.　　　*in* 823.5099
—— A woman's error.　　　　823.5118
—— A woman's temptation.　*in* 823.5126
—— A woman's war.　　　　823.5134
—— The world between them.　*in* 823.5137
—— *Same*.　　　　　　　　823.4768
Bramleighs of Bishop's Folly. Lever, C: J.
　　　　　　　　　　　　　823.972
Branksome Dene. Walmsley, H. M. 823.1669
Brant and Red Jacket. Eggleston, E:, *and*
　Seelye, *Mrs.* L. (E).　　　　808.767
Brave lady, A. Craik, *Mrs.* D. M. (M.) 823.324
Bravest of the brave, The. Henty, G: A.
　　　　　　　　　　　　　808.1473
Bravo, The. Cooper, J. F.　　823.290
Braxtons Bar. Daggett, R. M.　823.4528
Brayman, James O., *ed.* Daring deeds of
　American heroes, with biographical sketch-
　es.　　　　　　　　　　　808.1314
Brazil. See also South America, note.
—— Ballantyne, R. M. Martin Rattler; or,
　a boy's adventure in the forests of Brazil.
　　　　　　　　　　　　　808.263
　Note.—See **Adalbert,** *Prince.* Travels in . . .
　Brazil . . . 2 vols. 918.32-33.—**Agassiz,** *Prof., and*
　Mrs. L: Journey in Brazil. 1879. 918.15.—Win-
　sor, J. Narr. and crit. hist. of America. 8 vols.
　(Bibliography, v. 8, pp. 349-358.) *See* vols. 1, 2, 8.
　* 970.127, 127*³, 127*⁵.—**Ewbank,** T: Life in Brazil.
　(1845-6.) 1856. 918.11.—**Fletcher,** J. C., *and* Kidder,
　D. P. Brazil and the Brazilians. Port. Maps. Illus.
　1868. 918.28.—**Muthall,** M. G. Brazil, past and
　present. (*Contemp. rev.*, v. 57. 1890.) pp. 103-11, *in*
　* 52.5402².—**Smith,** H. H. Brazil: the Amazons
　and the coast. Map. Illus. 1879. 918.16.—Southey,
　R. History of Brazil. 3 vols. 1810-19. 981.8-10.
　See also **Catalogues** of this Library.
　　No. 2, 1880, p. 31.　　No. 4, 1884, p. 37.
　　No. 3, 1882, p. 26.　　No. 5, 1888, p. 41.
　See also **Poole's** Index (to 1882). p. 158, *in* **
　50. 1³—*Same.* Jan. 1, 1882-Jan. 1, 1887. p. 55, *in* ** 50.1³.
　See also **Index** to Consular reports. 1880-1885;
　1886-1889. 2 vols. (U. S. Pub. Docs. *Dept. of State.*)
　** 350.5496¹⁻².
　See also **Royal** Geog. Soc. journal. 46 vols.
　1831-1876. ** 910.1-46.
Bread-and-cheese and kisses. 76 pp. Far-
　jeon, B: L.　　　　　　*in* 823.6125
Bread upon the waters. Craik, *Mrs.* D. M.
　(M.)　　　　　　　　　823.325
—— *Same.*　　　*in* 823.330; *in* 823.5508
Bread-winners, The. Hay, J: 823.4692
Breaking a butterfly. Lawrence, G: A.
　　　　　　　　　　　　　823.958
Bred in the bone. Payn, J.　823.6052
Bremer, Fredrika. (1801-1865.) Brothers and
　sisters: a tale of domestic life. 823.6107
—— Father and daughter: a portraiture from
　the life.　　　　　　　　823.2174
—— The four sisters: a tale of social and do-
　mestic life in Sweden.　823.1919
　Issued also as Hertha.
—— The home; or, family joys and family
　cares.　　　　　　　　823.2173
—— The midnight sun: a pilgrimage.
　　　　　　　　　　　in 823.5023
—— *Same.*　　　　　　　823.6109
—— The neighbors: a story of every-day
　life.　　　　　　　　　823.2175
—— *Same.* (And other stories, *viz.:* Hopes.
　—The twins.—Tralinnau: a sketch from
　the olden time.)　　　823.2117

English Fiction. *Contin.*
Bremer, Fredrika. (1801-1865.) *Contin.*
—— New sketches of every-day life: A diary;
　together with Strife and peace.　823.6108
—— The parsonage of Mora.　823.6106
　Issued also as Life in Dalecarlia.
—— The president's daughters.　823.2118
—— *Same.* Part 2: Nina.　823.6129
—— Works. Tr. by Mrs. M.. Howitt. 4th
　ed.　　　　　　　　　823.2120
　Contents:—A diary.—The solitary.—The com-
　forter.—A letter about suppers.—The H—— family.
　—Axel and Anna; or, correspondence between two
　lovers.
—— *Same.* (*viz.:*) The home; or, life in
　Sweden. And Strife and peace. 823.2119
　Note.—See **Bremer,** C.. Life, letters and post-
　humous works (sketches and poems) of F. Bremer.
　928.84.
Brenda Yorke. Hay, M.. C.　*in* 823.2472
Same.　　　　　　　　*in* 823.4998
Bresciani, *Rev.* A., *S. J.* Mathilda of Can-
　ossa, and Yoland of Groningen. Tr. by
　A.. T. Sadlier.　　　　823.1904
—— Ubaldo and Irene: a historical romance.
　Tr. by A.. T. Sadlier. 2 vols. 823.6888-9
Bressant. Hawthorne, J. C.　823.722
Breton maiden, A. By A French lady. 3
　vols.　　　　　　　　823.7208-10
Breton mills, The. Bellamy, C: J. 823.5700
Brian Fitz-Count. Crake, *Rev.* A. D.
　　　　　　　　　　　823.5657
Bric-a-brac stories. Harrison, *Mrs.* C. (C.)
　　　　　　　　　　　808.1685
Bricks without straw. Tourgée, A. W.
　　　　　　　　　　　823.2312
Bridal eve, The. Southworth, *Mrs.* E. D. E.
　(N.)　　　　　　　　823.1477
Bridal march, and other stories. Björnson, B.
　　　　　　　　　　　823.4467
Bridal of Borthwick. Moir, D: M. *in* 823.702
Bride of Lammermoor. Scott, *Sir* W.
　　　　　　　　　　　823.1396
　Same.　　　　　823.4437; 823.4803
　Same.　　　*in* 823.5326; *in* 823.5337
　Same.　　　*in* 823.5797; ** 823.6026
　Same.　　　　　　　** 823.6724
Bride of Landeck, The. James, G: P. R.
　　　　　　　　　　　in 823.5562
Bride of Monte-Cristo. Sequel to "Count of
　Monte Cristo."　　　*in* 823.5104
Bride of the Nile, The. 2 vols. Ebers, G. M.
　　　　　　　　　　　823.5738-9
Bridegroom of Barna. 78 pp. (*In* Tales
　from Blackwood, v. 12.)　*in* ** 823.6658
Bride's fate, The. Southworth, *Mrs.* E. D.
　E. (N.)　　　　　　823.1479
Bridges, *Mrs. Col.* [*Mrs. Forrester.*] Al-
　though he was a lord, and other tales.
　　　　　　　　　　　in 823.5049
　Same.　　　　　　*in* 823.5075
—— Diana Carew; or, for a woman's sake.
　　　　　　　　　　　823.583
—— *Same.*　　　　　*in* 823.5016
—— Dolores.　　　　*in* 823.2451
—— *Same.*　　　　　*in* 823.5118
—— Fair women.　　*in* 823.4990
—— *Same.* (*Also*) My hero. *in* 823.3157
—— From Olympus to Hades. *in* 823.5034
—— I have lived and loved.　823.3757
—— *Same.*　　　　　　823.5082

English Fiction.
Bridges, *Mrs. Col.* [*Mrs. Forrester.*] *Contin.*
—— June. *in* 823.4986
—— *Same.* *in* 823.5021
—— Mignon. 823.584
—— My hero. (*With her* Fair women.)
  in 823.3157
—— My lord and my lady. 823.3945
—— Omnia vanitas · a tale of society.
  in 823.4986
—— *Same.* *in* 823.5021
—— Once again. 823.5040
—— Rhona. 823.3513
—— *Same.* *in* 823.5120
—— Roy and Viola. 823.4053
—— *Same.* 823.585
—— Viva: a novel. 823.585
—— *Same.* *in* 823.4996; *in* 823.5422
—— A young man's fancy, and other tales.
(*Also*) From Olympus to Hades.
  823.3064
Briery Creek. Martineau, H. *in* ** 823.6713
Brig and the lugger, The. Walmsley, H. M.
  p. 75, *in* 823.1670
Brigade commander. De Forest, J: W:
  823.4709
Brigadier Frederick. Erckmann, E., *and*
Chatrian, P. A. 823.6103
Bright, *Mrs.* Matilda A. [*Lyndon.*] Margaret: a story of life in a prairie home.
  823.1248
Same. 823.2047
Bright days in the old plantation time.
Banks, M.. R. 808.1192
Bright star of life. Farjeon, B: L.
  in 823.6587
Same. 823.7122
Brigitta. Auerbach, B. 823.4045
Brink, *Mrs.* Marie [di Sebregondi] ten. Not
in their set; or, in different circles of society. Tr. by MS. 823.7111
Brinvilliers, Marie Marguerite (d'Aubray),
marquise de. Smith, A. Marchioness of
Brinvilliers, the poisoner of the seventeenth
century: a romance of old Paris. 823.1450
British Columbia. *See also* British North
America.
—— Butterworth, H. Zigzag journeys in the
great northwest; or, a trip to the American
Switzerland. 808.1915
British North America. *See also* notes under
Hudson Bay,—Nova Scotia,—United States.
—— Ballantyne, R. M. Away in the wilderness. 808.631
—— —— Young fur-traders. 808.268
Note.—See **History** of the British dominions in
North America, 1497-1763. Map. 1773. * 9171.22.—
Murray, II. Historical and descriptive account of
British America. 2 vols. 1840. 971.4-5.
See also **Catalogues** of this Library, under America, *British.*
No. 2, 1880, p. 8. No. 4, 1884, p. 7.
No. 3, 1882, p. 5. No. 5, 1888 (Brit. Amer.), p. 42.
British Columbia.
—— Ballantyne, R. M. The red man's revenge: a tale of the Red river flood.
  808.1270
—— —— Wild man of the west: a tale of the
Rocky mountains. 808.703
Note.—See **Bibliography.** Bancroft, H. H.
Works, v. 32. History of British Columbia, 1792-
1887. (Authorities quoted, pp. xiii-xxxi.) * 970.96.—

English Fiction. *Contin.*
British North America. *Contin.*
British Columbia. Contin.
Note. Contin.
Winsor, J. Narrative and critical history of
America. v. 8: Later history of British . . . America. 1889. * 970.127².
See also **Catalogues** of this Library. No. 2,
1880, p. 32.
See also **Poole's** Index (to 1882). ** 50.1;—*Same.*
Jan. 1, 1882-Jan. 1, 1887. ** 50.1².
See also Index to **Consular reports.** 1880-1885;
1886-1889. 2 vols. (U. S. Pub. Docs. *Dept. of State.*)
** 350.5496¹⁻².
Canada.
—— Catherwood, *Mrs.* M.. (H.) Romance
of Dollard. (Canada, 1660.) 823.6555
—— —— Story of Tonty. (1678.) 823.6994
—— Henty, G: A. With Wolfe in Canada.
(1759.) 808.1477
—— Kirby, W: Chien d'Or: a legend of Quebec. (1798.) 823.950
—— —— Golden Dog. (*Same as* Chien d'Or.)
  823.7051
—— Marryat, *Capt.* F: Settlers in Canada.
  823.1118
—— *Same:* written for young people.
  808.776
Note.—See **Bryce**, G: Canada from 1763-1867.
(Winsor, J., *ed. Narr. . . . hist. of Amer.*, v. 8.)
p. 131-190, *in* ** 970.127².—**Hart**, C. E. The fall of
New France, 1755-1760. 1888. ** 972.27.—**MacMullen**, J: History of Canada. 2d ed. 1869. 972.4.—
Parkman, F., *jr.* History of the conspiracy of
Pontiac, and the war of the North American tribes
against the English colonies after the conquest of
Canada. Map. 1851. 973.318.—**Winsor**, J. General documentary sources of Canadian history. (*In
his* Narr . . . hist. of Amer., v. 4.) 1884. (*See* Index, v. 8.) p. 366, *in* * 970.127².
See also **Catalogues** of this Library.
No. 2, 1880, pp. 39, 40. No. 4, 1884, p. 51.
No. 3, 1882, p. 34. No. 5, 1888, p. 51.
See also **Poole's** Index (to 1882). pp. 192-5, *in* **
50.1;—*Same.* Jan. 1, 1882-Jan. 1, 1887. pp. 65-66, *in*
** 50.1².
See also Index to **Consular reports.** 1880-1885;
1886-1889. 2 vols. (U. S. Pub. Docs. *Dept. of State.*)
** 350.5496¹⁻².
Labrador. Stephens, C: A. Left on Labrador. 808.240
Note.—See **Hind**, H: Y. Explorations in the interior of the Labrador peninsula. Map. Illus. 2
vols. 1863. 9171.4-5.—**Stearns**, W. A. Labrador, its
peoples, industries, natural history. 1884. 971.9.—
Winsor, J. Narr. and critical hist. of America. 8
vols. 1887-9. (*See* Index, v. 8.) * 970.127-127².
See also **Poole's** Index (to 1882). p. 715, *in* ** 50.1;
—*Same.* Jan. 1, 1882-Jan. 1, 1887. p. 245, *in* ** 50.1².
Newfoundland. Lowell, R. T. S. New priest
in Conception bay. 2 vols. 823.2308-9
Note.—See Winsor, J. Newfoundland (with bibliography). (*Narr. and critical hist. of America.*) vols. 3, 4, 8. * 970.127²⁻⁴.*.—**Pedley**, C. History of Newfoundland to 1860. 1863. 971.11.
See also **Poole's** Index (to 1882). pp. 910, 911, *in*
** 50.1;—*Same.* Jan. 1, 1882-Jan. 1, 1887. pp. 310,
311, *in* ** 50.1².
British novelists, with an essay . . . by Mrs.
Barbauld. 50 vols. ** 823.2062-2111
Brittany and La Vendée. Souvestre, É.
  823.6878
Brock, *Mrs.* F.. E.. Georgina (Baynes) Carey-
Charity Helstone. 823.120
—— Children at home. 823.121
—— Home memories. 823.4325
—— The rectory and the manor: a tale.
  823.124
—— Working and waiting. 823.4337
Broken columns. Dixon, *Rev.* J. 823.215

English Fiction. *Contin.*

Brown, Theron. [*Park Ludlow.*] The red-shanty boys; or, pictures of New-England school life thirty years ago. 808.1617

Browne, C: Farrar. [*Artemus Ward.*] Moses, the sassy. 7 pp. (*In* Half-hours with great story tellers.) p. 46, *in* 823.5478

Brownies and bogles. Guiney, L. I.
808.1599

Brownings, The. Fuller, J.. G. 808.1580

Brownlows. Oliphant, *Mrs.* M. O. (W.)
823.5949

Brownson, Orestes A: The spirit-rapper: an autobiography. 823.1867

Brueton's bayou. Habberton, J: 823.6634

Bruin: the grand bear hunt. Reid, *Capt.* T: M. 808.426

Bruner, J.. W. Free prisoners: a story of California life. 823.4384

Bruno. Abbott, J. 808.580

Brush, *Mrs.* Christine (Chaplin). Colonel's opera cloak. 823.1999

Bryan, *Mrs.* M.. (Edwards). Manch.
823.143

Bryda. Field, *Mrs.* E. M. 823.7041

Brydges, *Sir* S: Egerton. Hall of Hellingsley. 3 vols. 823.146-8

—— Tragic tales. 2 vols. * 823.144-5
v. 1. Coningsby.
v. 2. Coningsby.—Lord Brockenhurst.

Buchanan, *Mrs.* Harriett (Jay). The dark colleen: a love story. 823.893

—— A marriage of convenience. 823.5060

Buchanan, Robert Williams. Annan Water.
823.5116

—— God and the man. *in* 823.5039

—— *Same.* (*Also*) The martyrdom of Madeline. 823.6600

—— The heir of Linne. (*With his* Stormy waters.) *in* 823.6594

—— The martyrdom of Madeline. (*With his* God and the man.) *in* 823.6600

—— The master of the mine. *in* 823.5138

—— Matt: a tale of a caravan. 93 pp.
823.5141

—— *Same.* 823.5188

—— The shadow of the sword. 823.4166

—— Stormy waters: a story of to-day.
823.7009

—— *Same.* (*Also*) The heir of Linne.
823.6594

—— That winter night; or, love's victory.
823.5015

Buchholz family, The. 2 vols. Stinde, J.
823.5220-1

Buffets. Doe, C: H: 823.6100

Bulfinch, T: The age of chivalry; or, legends of King Arthur.—"King Arthur and his knights."—"The Mabinogeon."—"The Crusades."—"Robin Hood," etc. Ed. by E: E. Hale. 823.6313

—— Legends of Charlemagne; or, romance of the middle ages. 823.150

Bulgaria. Wratislaw, A. H., *tr.* Bulgarian stories. (*In his* Sixty folk-tales, etc.) 1890. p. 175, *in* 823.6946

Bulldog and butterfly. Murray, D: C.
in 823.5131

Bulwer, E: G: Earle Lytton. *See* Lytton.

English Fiction. *Contin.*

Bunce, J: Thackeray. Fairy tales: their origin and meaning, with some account of dwellers in fairyland. 823.4509

Bunce, Oliver Bell. Romance of the revolution: being true stories of the adventures . . . of the days of '76. (Anon.)
823.157

Bungener, Laurence L: Félix. Preacher and the king; or, Bourdaloue in the court of Louis XIV. 823.1875

—— Priest and the Huguenot; or, persecutions in the age of Louis XV. 2 vols.
823.4064-5

Bunner, H: Cuyler. Love in old cloathes. 17 pp. (*In* Stories by Amer. authors, v. 4.)
p. 40, *in* 823.4705

—— A woman of honor. 823.4595

——, *joint author. See* Matthews, James Brander.

Bunyan, J: The pilgrim's progress. 823.2647

Same. (*In* Lib. of famous fiction, *etc.*)
p. 12, *in* ** 823.6215

Burbury, *Mrs.* E. J. "The trust." 24 pp. (*With* Fortunes of the Colville family. By F. E. Smedley.) p. 310, *in* 823.1443

Burch, Harriette E. Stella Rae; or, the yoke of love. 823.6393

Burdett, C: Margaret Moncrieffe; the first love of Aaron Burr: a romance of the revolution. With letters of Colonel Burr to "Kate" and "Eliza," and from "Leonora," *etc.* 823.2061
Issued also as The beautiful spy.

Bureaucracy. Balzac, H. de. 823.5460

Burgomaster's family. Walrée, *Mrs.* E. C. W. (G.) van. 823.6272

Burgomaster's wife, The. Ebers, G. M.
823.4311

Burke, *Sir* Bernard. *See* Burke, *Sir* J: B.

Burke, *Sir* J: Bernard. Family romance; or, episodes in the domestic annals of the aristocracy. 823.152

Burlesques. Thackeray, W: M. 823.5010

Burnand, Francis Cowley. Happy-Thought Hall. 823.153

—— More happy thoughts, &c., &c.
823.154

—— My health. 823.155

—— My time and what I've done with it: an autobiography. Compiled from the diary, *etc.*, of Cecil Colvin, son of Sir John Colvin, Bart. 823.156

Burnett, *Mrs.* F.. Eliza (Hodgson). A fair barbarian. 823.4151

—— Haworth's. 823.158

—— Jarl's daughter, and other novelettes.
823.5633

Contents:—Jarl's daughter.—The men who loved Elizabeth.—Wanted, a young person.—Miss Vernon's choice.

—— Kathleen. 823.5631
Issued also as Kathleen mavourneen.

—— Lindsay's luck. 823.5632

—— Louisiana. 823.1917

—— Miss Crespigny. 823.5473

—— Miss Defarge. (*With* Brueton's bayou. By J: Habberton.) p. 123, *in* 823.6634

—— Pretty Polly Pemberton. 823.1833

—— The pretty sister of José. 823.7033

English Fiction. *Contin.*
Burnett, *Mrs. F..* Eliza (Hodgson). *Contin.*
—— A quiet life.   823.5630
—— Story of the Latin quarter.   30 pp.   (*In*
Stories by Amer. authors, v. 3.)
p. 30, *in* 823.4704
—— Surly Tim, and other stories.   823.5362
Contents.—Surly Tim, a Lancashire story.—"Le monsieur de la petite dame."—Smethurstses.—One day at Arle.—Esmeralda.—Mère Giraud's little daughter.—Lodusky.—"Seth."
—— That lass o' Lowrie's.   823.159
—— Through one administration.   823.4579
—— Vagabondia: a love story.   823.4697
Issued also as Dolly.
Burney, *Miss* Francisca.   *See* Arblay, *Mme.*
Francisca (Burney) d'.
Burnham, *Mrs.* Clara Louise (Root).   [*Edith Douglas.*]   The mistress of Beech Knoll.
823.6993
—— Next door.   823.6953
—— Young maids and old.   823.5458
Burnish family, The.   Balfour, *Mrs.* C. L.
(L.)   823.7311
Burnt million, The.   Payn, J.   823.7088
Bürstenbinder, E.. [*E. Werner.*]   At a high
price.   Tr. by M.. S. Smith.   823.6704
Issued also as No surrender.
—— *Same.*   Tr. by C. Tyrrell.   823.4991
—— Banned and blessed.   Tr. by Mrs. A. L.
Wister.   823.4614
—— "Good luck"!   (Glück auf.)   Tr. by F..
A. Shaw.   823.6264
Issued also as Success and how he won it.
—— Raymond's atonement.   Tr. by C. Tyr-
rell.   823.4995
—— *Same.*   823.5202
—— Saint Michael.   Tr. by Mrs. A. L. Wis-
ter.   823.5762
—— Vineta, the phantom city.   Tr. by F..
A. Shaw.   823.6796
Issued also as Under a charm.
Burton, J: Bloundelle-   The silent shore.
in 823.5044
Burton, R: Francis, *ed.*   Vikram and the
vampire; or, tales of Hindu devilry.
823.4154
Büsching, Johann Gustav Gottlieb.   Popular
traditions.   22 pp.   (*In* Roscoe, T: *The German novelists*, v. 2).
p. 213, *in* ** 823.6827
Bush-boys, The.   Reid, *Capt.* T: M.
808.756
Bushby, *Mrs.* —, *tr.*   The Danes sketched by
themselves.   A series of popular stories by
the best Danish authors.   3 vols.
823.6444-6
Busken-Huet.   *See* Huet, C. B.
But a Philistine.   Townsend, V. F..   823.4752
But yet a woman.   Hardy, A. S.   823.4496
Same.   823.4618
Butler, *Lady* Rachel.   Jessie Cameron: a
Highland story.   823.7319
Butler, S: Erewhon; or, over the range.
* 823.1856
Butt, B.. May.   Geraldine Hawthorne.
823.4570
—— Miss Molly.   823.161
Butterworth, Hezekiah.   Young folks' his-
tory of America.   970.67
—— Young folks' history of Boston.   974.143

English Fiction. *Contin.*
Butterworth, Hezekiah.   *Contin.*
—— A zigzag journey in the sunny south; or,
wonder tales of early American history.
808.1819
—— Zigzag journeys in Acadia and New
France: a summer's journey . . . through
. . . the early French settlements of
America.   808.1811
—— Zigzag journeys in classic lands; or,
Tommy Toby's trip to Mount Parnassus.
808.1816
—— Zigzag journeys in Europe.   808.1820
—— Zigzag journeys in India; or, the anti-
podes of the far east: a collection of
Zenänä tales.   808.1817
—— Zigzag journeys in northern lands: the
Rhine to the Arctic.   808.1814
—— Zigzag journeys in the antipodes.
808.1815
—— Zigzag journeys in the British Isles; or,
vacation rambles in historic lands.
808.1813
—— Zigzag journeys in the great northwest;
or, a trip to the American Switzerland.
808.1915
—— Zigzag journeys in the Levant, with a
Talmudist story-teller: a spring trip . . .
through Egypt and the Holy Land.   808.1812
—— Zigzag journeys in the Occident: the
Atlantic to the Pacific.   808.1810
—— Zigzag journeys in the Orient: the Adri-
atic to the Baltic.   808.1818
Button's inn.   Tourgée, A. W.   823.5295
By a way she knew not.   Robertson, M. M.
823.7087
By and by.   Maitland, E: 823.1079
Same.   823.2354
By Celia's arbour.   Besant, W., *and* Rice, J.
823.6113
By his own might.   Hillern, *Mrs.* W. (B.)
von.   823.7095
By pike and dyke.   Henty, G: A.   808.1588
By proxy.   Payn, J.   823.6059
By sheer pluck.   Henty, G: A.   808.1486
By shore and sedge.   Harte, F. B.   823.4876
By still waters.   Mayo, *Mrs.* I.. (F.)
823.1135
By the gate of the sea.   Murray, D: C.
823.5038
By the Tiber.   Tincker, M.. A.   823.4152
By woman's wit.   Hector, *Mrs.* A.. (F.)
in 823.5017
Bynner, Edwin Lasseter.   Agnes Surriage.
823.7169
—— The begum's daughter.   823.6434
—— Damen's ghost.   (Anon.)   823.1841
—— Nimport.   823.4034
—— Tritons.   823.4033
—— , *joint author.*   *See* Hale, L. P.
Byrnes, *Inspector* T: F.   Hawthorne, J. C.   An
American penman.   823.5444
—— — Another's crime.   823.5752
—— — The great bank robbery.   823.5446
—— — Section 558; or, the fatal letter.
823.5269
—— — A tragic mystery.   823.5400
Caballero, Fernan, *pseud.*   *See* Arrom, *Mrs.*
Cécilia (Böhl de Faber).

English Fiction. *Contin.*
Cabin on the prairie. Pearson, C: H.
   808.1654
Cable, G: Washington. Bonaventure; a prose
pastoral of Acadian Louisiana. 823.5248
—— Dr. Sevier. 823.4863
—— The Grandissimes: a story of creole
life. 823.2442
—— Madame Delphine. 823.1895
—— Old creole days. 823.162
—— *Same.*, (New ed.) 823.5247
—— Strange true stories of Louisiana.
   823.6317
Caddell, Cecilia M.. Nellie Netterville; or,
one of the transplanted: a tale. 823.163
—— Wild times : a tale of the days of Queen
Elizabeth. 823.164
Caddy, *Mrs.* (—). Adrian Bright. *in* 823.5041
Cadell, *Mrs.* H. M. *See* Cadell, *Mrs.* Jessie.
Cadell, *Mrs.* Jessie. Ida Craven. 823.165
Cædwalla. Cowper, F. 823.7123
Cady, *Mrs.* H. N. A history of New Eng-
land in words of one syllable. Illus.
   808.1901
Caged lion. Youge, C.. M.. 823.1761
Cahun, Léon. The adventures of Captain
Mago; or, a Phœnician expedition. B. C.
1000. 823.6392
—— The blue banner; or, the adventures of
a Mussulman, a Christian and a pagan, in
the time of the crusades and Mongol con-
quest. Tr. by W. C. Sandars. 823.6283
Caine, Hall. The bondman: a new saga.
   823.7034
—— The deemster. 823.5448
—— A son of Hagar: a romance of our time.
   823.5519
Caird, *Mrs.* Mona (Alison). For money or
for love. 31 pp. (*In* Twenty novelettes
. . .) p. 253, *in* 823.7184
—— The wing of of Azrael. 823.7199
Cakes and ale. Jerrold, D. W: *in* 823.4828
Calbot's rival. 80 pp. Hawthorne, J. C.
 p. 148, *in* 823.5507
Calderon, the courtier. Lytton, E: G: E. L.
Bulwer- *in* 823.1035
Same. *in* 823.5957
Caleb Krinkle. Coffin, C: C. 823.244
Caleb Williams, Adventures of. Godwin,
W: 823.613
Same. 823.6263
California. *See also* United States: *Colonial
period,—Life and manners,—Post-revolu-
tionary period,—Western States.*
—— Marryat, *Capt.* F: Travels . . . of
Monsieur Violet in California . . . 823.1104
—— Sill, E: R. The hermitage, and later
poems. 821.1326
—— Wentworth, M., *ed.* Poetry of the Pa-
cific. 821.424
Origin of the State. Hale, E: E. Queen of
California. 46 pp. (*With his* His level
best.) p. 235, *in* 823.681
LIFE AND MANNERS.
In early days.
—— Aimard, G. The gold seekers. (*Also*)
The treasure of pearls. 823.7008
—— Daggett, R. M. Braxton's Bar: tale of
pioneer life in California. 823.4528

English Fiction. *Contin.*
California. *Contin.*
LIFE AND MANNERS. *Contin.*
In early days. Contin.
—— Grey, W: A picture of pioneer times in
California: anecdotes, stories, etc. 977.82
—— Harte, F. B. Argonauts of North Lib-
erty. 823.5286
—— By shore and sedge. (*viz:* An apos-
tle of the tules.—Sarah Walker.—A ship
of '49.) 823.4876
—— Devil's Ford. (*With his* A million-
aire of Rough-and-Ready.)
 p. 169, *in* 823.5152
—— — Gabriel Conroy. 823.712
—— — *Same.* 823.6216
—— — Luck of Roaring Camp, and other
sketches. 823.713
—— — A millionaire of Rough-and-Ready.
   823.5152
—— — On the frontier. 823.4792
—— — Tales of the Argonauts. (*In his*
Luck of Roaring Camp . . .)
 p. 329, *in* 823.4322
—— — A ward of the Golden Gate.
   823.7382
—— Montgomery, W. Boys of the Sierras
. . . California in '49. 808.1877
—— Munroe, K. Golden days of '49.
   823.6318
—— Spurr, G: G. The land of gold: a tale
of '49. 823.4336
Irish colony. Jessop, G: H. Gerald Ffreuch's
friends. 823.6574
Political aspect. Collins, R. U. (?) John
Halsey, the anti-monopolist. 823.4827
Sporting life.
—— Van Dyke, T. S. Flirtation Camp.
   823.7137
—— — Rifle, rod and gun in California.
   823.4157
Stage robbing. Harte, F. B. Snow-bound at
Eagle's. 823.5280
In general.
—— American coin. By the author of "Aris-
tocracy." 823.7236
—— Atherton, *Mrs.* G. F. (H.) Los Cerritos:
a romance of the modern time. 823.7006
—— Ballantyne, R. M. Digging for gold.
   808.1285
—— — The golden dream. 808.829
—— Bruner, J.. W. Free prisoners.
   823.4384
—— Clark, F: T. In the valley of Havilah.
   823.7245
—— Fitzgerald, O. P. California sketches.
   9177.486
—— Harte, F. B. A drift from Redwood
Camp. 43 pp. (*With his* A Phyllis of the
Sierras.) p. 173, *in* 823.5281
—— — Flip: a California romance. (*Also*)
Found at Blazing Star. 823.4492
—— — Heritage of Dedlow Marsh, and other
tales. 823.6911
—— — Maruja. 823.5282
—— — A Phyllis of the Sierras. 823.5281
—— — The story of a mine. 823.2041
—— Henty, G: A. Captain Bayley's heir.
   808.1475

English Fiction. *Contin.*
California. *Contin.*
LIFE AND MANNERS. *Contin.*
In general. *Contin.*

—— Jessop, G: H. Judge Lynch: a romance of the California vineyards.   823.6528
—— Legif, L. Jim Skaggs of Skaggsville: a Sierran sketch.   823.4357
—— Loyal, C., *pseud.* The squatter and the don.   823.4813
—— Miller, C. H. First fam'lies of the Sierras.   823.1159
—— Powers, S. California saved. 14 pp. (*With his* Muskingum legends.)   p. 340, *in* 823.4145
—— Royce, J. Feud of Oakfield creek.   823.6506
—— Shuck, O. T. The California scrap-book: prose and poetry, tales, etc.   829.233
—— Stevenson, R. L.: The Silverado squatters.   808.1344
—— Verne, J. Godfrey Morgan: a Californian mystery.   823.4608
—— Wiggin, *Mrs.* K.. D. (S.) A summer in a cañon.   823.6189
—— Winthrop, T. John Brent.   823.1725
See also poems by F. B. Harte (821.146); C. H. Miller (821.1314); E: Pollock (821.499); C: W. Stoddard (821.499), and others.
See also United States, American life and character. *Western.*

Yosemite.
—— Toland, *Mrs.* M. B. M. Tisáyac of the Yosemite. Illus.   * 821.1339
—— Yelverton, *Mrs.* M. T. (L.) Zanita.   * 823.1759

Note.—See Bryant, W: C. Picturesque America. v. 1. p. 465, *in* ** 9173.423.—Le Conte, J. Rough notes of a Yosemite camping trip. (*Overland mo.*, 2d ser., v. 6, 1885.) pp. 414, 493, *in* * 51.887.—Whitney, J. D. Yosemite guide-book. 1870. 9177.48.
See also Catalogues of this Library.
No. 4, 1884, p. 323.   No. 5, 1888, p. 391.
Note.—For miscel. works on California, *see* Anderson, W. Mineral springs and health resorts of California. 1890. 615.40.—Avery, B: P. Californian pictures in prose and verse. 1878. 9177.47.—Bancroft, H. H. History of California. 6 vols. 1542-1859. (*Works*, vols. 18-23). * 970.82-7;— Popular tribunals. v. 2. (*Works*, v. 37.) * 970.997.—Bartlett, J: R. Personal narrative of explorations . . . in . . . California. v. 2. 9173.105.—Bancroft, H. H. California pastoral. 1888. (Bibliography, pp. 751-792.) 977.176.—Bidwell, Gen. J: The first emigrant train to California. 24 pp. (*Century mag.*, v. 41, 1890.) p. 106, *in* * 51.1196²;—Life in California before the gold discovery. 20 pp. (*Century mag.*, v. 41, 1890.) p. 163, *in* * 51.1196².—Browne, J. R. The coast rangers of California. (*Harper's mag.*, v. 23; pp. 306, 593; v. 24; pp. 1, 283) *in* * 51.359-60.—Dana, R: H., *Jr. In his* Two years before the mast. 9177.127.—Davis, W: H. Sixty years in California. 1889. 977.165.—Delessert, B: Les mines d'or de la Californie. 16 pp. (*Rev. d. d. Mondes*, 1849, n. pér. v. 1.) p. 485, *in* ** 54.174.—Dillon, P. La Californie dans les derniers mois de 1849. 27 pp. (*Rev. d. d. Mondes*, 1850, n. pér. v. 5.) p. 193, *in* ** 54.179.—Fitch, G: H. How California came into the union. 17 pp. (*Cent. mag.*, v. 40, 1890.) p. 775, *in* * 51.1196².—Fremont, *Capt.* J. C. Report of the exploring expedition to . . . Oregon and northern California in 1843-44. * 9173.109.—Hittell, J: S. Resources of California. 6th ed. 9177.42.—Hittell, T. H: History of California. vols. 1-2. (To admission, Sept. 9, 1850.) 9772.108-9.—King, C: Mountaineering in the Sierra Nevada. * 9177.49;—Same. 9177.123.—Nordhoff, C: California: for health, pleasure and residence. 9177.50.—Rowell, J: C. List of printed maps of California. (*In* Univ. of Calif. Lib. bulletin, No. 9, 1887.) * 910.629;—*See also* "California." (*In* Contents: index, v. 1. *Lib. of the Univ. of Calif.*) pp. 71-4, *in* ** 19.134.—Royce, J. California

English Fiction. *Contin.*
California. *Contin.*
Note. *Contin.*
from the conquest in 1846 to the second vigilance committee in San Francisco. (Amer. commonwealths.) 1886. 977.163.—Van Dyke, T. S. Millionaires of a day: an inside history of the great southern California "boom." 1890. 9177.626.—Warner, C: D. The heart of the desert. 21 pp.;—The outlook in southern California. 19 pp.;—The winter of our content. 22 pp. (*Harper's mag.*, v. 82.) pp. 392, 189, 58, *in* * 51A.16⁷.—Winsor, J. *In his* Narrative and critical history of America. 8 vols. (*See* Index, v. 8.) * 970.127-127⁵.
See also Catalogues of this Library.
No. 2, 1880, p. 37.   No. 4, 1884, p. 48.
No. 3, 1882, p. 31.   No. 5, 1888, p. 45.
See also Poole's Index (to 1882). p. 186, *in* ** 50.1;—Same. Jan. 1, 1882-Jan. 1, 1887. p. 64, *in* ** 50.1².
See also Catalogue of govt. pubs. of the U. S. (1774-1881).   ** 15.202

SAN FRANCISCO.
—— Clark, J. F. Society in search of truth; or, stock-gambling in San Francisco.   823.4512
—— Harte, F. B. Captain Jim's friend;—"A knight-errant of the foot-hills;"—A secret of Telegraph hill. (*With his* The heritage of Dedlow Marsh.)   *in* 823.6911
Note.—See Lloyd, B. E. Lights and shades in San Francisco. 1876. * 9177.6.—Moses, *Prof.* B. The establishment of municipal government in San Francisco. 83 pp. (*In* Johns Hopkins Univ. studies, etc., v. 7.) 1889. *in* 973.582¹.—Soulé, F., *and others.* The annals of San Francisco. 1855. * 977.25.—Winsor, J. Narr. and crit. hist. of America, v. 8. pp. 211-12, 261, *in* * 970.127⁵.
See also Catalogues of this Library.
No. 2, 1880, pp. 201-2.   No. 4, 1884, pp. 257-8.
No. 3, 1882, pp. 168-9.   No. 5, 1888, pp. 310-11.
See also Poole's Index (to 1882). pp. 1148-9, *in* ** 50.1;—Same. Jan. 1, 1882-Jan. 1, 1887. p. 385, *in* ** 50.1².

Called Back. Fargus, F: J: 823.4913
Same.   *in* 823.5094
Called to account. Cudlip, *Mrs.* A. H. (T.)   823.4775
Callista. Newman, J: H: 823.1188
Cambridge series of English classics. Blaisdell, A. F., *ed.* Readings from the Waverley novels.   808.1667
Cameron, *Mrs.* H. Lovett. A life's mistake.   823.5369
Cameron, Verney H: Lovett. Adventures of Herbert Massey in eastern Africa.   808.1433
—— Among the Turks.   808.1585
Cameron pride. Holmes, *Mrs.* M.. J.. (H.)   823.786
Cameronians, The. Grant, J.   823.4799
Camille. Dumas, A., *the younger.*   823.5567
Note.—See also The "Demi-monde;" a satire on society. Tr. by Mrs. E. G. Squier. 822.1080.
Camiola. McCarthy, J.   *in* 823.5098
Camors. Feuillet, O.   823.7160
Camp on the Severn. Crake, A. D.   823.7096
Campaner Thal. Richter, J. P. F.   823.6818
Campbell, Archibald. Captain MacDonald's daughter.   823.5249
Campbell, *Sir* Gilbert. Dark stories from the sunny south; or, legends of the Mediterranean.   823.7242
—— Mysteries of the unseen; or, supernatural stories of English life.   823.7243
—— Wild and weird; or, remarkable stories of Russian life.   823.7244

English Fiction. *Contin.*

Campbell, *Mrs.* H.. (Stuart). The American girl's home book of work and play.
808.1313
—— Roger Berkeley's probation. 823.5250
—— Unto the third and fourth generation; a study. 823.1909
Campbell-Praed, *Mrs.* —. *See* Praed, *Mrs.* Rosa (Murray-Prior) Campbell-
Camping out. Stephens, C: A. 808.241
Camping-out series. *See* Stephens, C: A.
Camps and quarters. Forbes, A., and others.
823.6281
Can you forgive her? Trollope, A. 823.1605
Canada. Butterworth, H. Zigzag journeys in Acadia and New France. 808.1811
Cancelled will, The. Dupuy, E. A. 823.491
Cannibal islands. Ballantyne, R. M.
in 808.1266
Same. *in* 808.1284
Cannon, C: James. [*Grandfather Greenway,*] Ravellings from the web of life. 823.166
Canolles. Cooke, J: E. 823.7099
Canon's ward, The. Payn, J. 823.6588
Canterbury tales. 2 vols. Lee, H. 823.966-7
Canterbury tales. Lee, S. 823.968
Canvassing. Banim, J;, *ed.*
p. 209, *in* 823.59
Cape Cod folks. Greene, *Mrs.* S.. P. (McL).
823.1849
Capsadel, L.., *pseud. See* Hammond, *Mrs.*—.
Captain Bayley's heir. Henty, G: A.
808.1475
Captain Blake, Adventures of. Maxwell, W: H. 823.1124
Captain Dangerous, The strange adventures of. Sala, G: A: *in* 823.5026
Captain Fracasse. Gautier, T. 823.6883
Captain Jack, the scout. McKnight, C:
823.1075
Same. 823.4335; 823.1139
Captain McDonald's daughter. Campbell, A.
823.5249
Captain Mago, The adventures of. Cahun, L. 823.6392
Captain Mansana, and other stories. Björnson, B. 823.4477
Captain of the guard. Grant, J. 823.621
Captain of the Janizaries. Ludlow, J. M.
823.7022
Captain of the Polestar, and other tales. Doyle, A. C. 823.6410
Captain of the Wight. Cowper, F. 823.5697
Captain Sam. Eggleston, G: C. 808.1057
Captain Singleton, Life . . . of. DeFoe, D.
823.2122
Captain-general, The. Gordon, W: J:
823.7045
Captain's daughter. Pushkin, A. S.
823.5023
Same. *in* 823.4196
Captains of industry. Parton, J. 808.1548
Cardinal Pole. Ainsworth, W: H. 823.5606
Cardinal sin, A. Fargus, F: J: 823.4924
Same. *in* 823.5125
Cardinal's daughter. Warfield, *Mrs.* C. A. (W.) 823.1654
Cards for four. 26 pp. Eckstein, E.
p. 243, *in* 823.6534

English Fiction. *Contin.*

Carette, *Madame* (—) (Bouvet). Recollections of the court of the Tuileries. Tr. by E.. P. Train. 823.5669
Carey, J. H., *tr.* The Marannos: a tale of the inquisition, during the reign of Ferdinand and Isabella. 823.6123
Carey, Rosa Nouchette. Barbara Heathcote's trial. 823.4829
—— Heriot's choice. 823.7362
—— Nellie's memories. 2 vols. (in 1).
823.2594
—— Queenie's whim. 2 vols. (in 1). 823.3376
—— *Same.* 823.4815
—— Wooed and married. 823.2993
Carey-Brock, *Mrs. See* Brock, *Mrs.* F.. E.. G. (Baynes) Carey-
Carità. Oliphant, *Mrs.* M. O. (W.) 823.6356
Carl and Jocko. Abbott, J. 808.599
Carlén, *Mrs.* Emilia (Schmidt). 1807-. The brothers' bet; or, within six weeks.
823.6447
—— The guardian. 3 vols. 823.7229-31
—— The smugglers. (*In* Zimmern, H.., *and* A. *Half-hours with foreign novelists.*)
in 823.6613
Carlén, *Mrs.* Flygare. *See* Carlén, *Mrs.* Emilia (Schmidt).
Carleton, *pseud. See* Coffin, C: C.
Carleton, *Capt.* L. C. Mysterious hunter.
in 823.5141
Same. *in* 823.5188
Carleton, W: Barney Branagan. (*With his* The clarionet.) *in* 823.169
—— The black baronet; or, the chronicles of Ballytrain. 823.167
—— The black prophet: a tale of Irish famine. 823.168
—— The clarionet; The dead boxer; and, Barney Branagan. 823.169
—— The dead boxer. (*With his* The clarionet.) *in* 823.169
—— The emigrants of Ahadarra. 823.170
—— The evil eye; or, the black spectre: a romance. 823.171
—— Fardorougha, the miser; or, the convicts of Lisnamona. 823.172
—— Half hours with Irish authors.
in 823.1073
Contents: — The Donagh. — Larry McFarland's wake.
—— Jane Sinclair; or, the fawn of Springvale (and other stories). 823.173
—— *Same;* Neal Malone, and other tales.
823.5517
—— Neal Malone. 30 pp. (*In* Johnson, R., *ed. Little classics,* v. 5.) p. 188, *in* 829.128
—— The poor scholar, and other tales of Irish life. 2 vols. (in 1). 823.174
—— The tithe-proctor: a novel. 823.175
—— Traits and stories of the Irish peasantry. (1st and 2d ser.) 823.7363
—— *Same.* 2 vols. 823.5819-20
—— *Same.* 4th ed. 5 vols. ** 823.6641-5
Contents:—v. 1. Ned M'Keown.—The three tasks; or, the little house under the hill.—Shane Fadh's wedding.—Larry M'Farland's wake.—The battle of the factions. ** 823.6641
v. 2. The party fight and funeral.— The hedge school, and the abduction of Mat Kavanagh.—The station. ** 823.6642

English Fiction. *Contin.*
Caxton, Pisistratus, *pseud.* *See* Lytton, E:
  G: Earle Lytton Bulwer-
Caxtons, The. Lytton, E: G: E. L. Bulwer-
                      823.1023
  Same.   823.6217
Cecil Castlemaine's gage, and other stories.
  La Ramée, L. de.   823.1817
Cecil Dreeme. Winthrop, T.   823.1723
Cecilia. 3 vols. Arblay, *Mme.* F. (B.) d'.
                  ** 823.2101-3
Cecilias, The. Argyle, A..   823.6124
Cecil's tryst. Payn, J.   823.6053
Cecily. Dixon, *Mrs.*   808.1210
Central America. Knox, T: W. Boy travel-
  lers in Mexico . . . with a description of
  the republics of Central America and of
  the Nicaragua canal.   808.1803
—— Simms, W: G. The damsel of Darien.
  2 vols. (in 1).   ** 823.6729
—— Warburton, E. B. G: Darien. (Buccaneers.) 3 vols.   823.2048-50
   Note.—See Allen, B. Sketch of eastern coast of
  C. A. (*In* Roy. Geog. Soc. jl., v. 11, 1841. pp. 76-89,
  in ** 910.11.—Bibliography. Bancroft, H. H. History of Central America. V. 1, 1501-1530; v. 2, 1530-
  1800; v. 3, 1801-1887. (Authorities quoted, v. 1, pp.
  xxv-lxxii.) (*Works*, vols. 6-8.) 1882-7. * 970.70-2.—
  Chambers's papers for the people, No. 13. v. 3. *in*
  829.36.—Charney, D. The ancient cities of the
  new world. 1888. * 9178.59.—Fitzroy, R. On the
  great isthmus of C. A. (*In* Roy. Geog. Soc. jl., v.
  20, 1851.) pp. 161-189, *in* ** 910.20.—Froebel, J.
  Seven years' travel in C. A. 1859. 9179-37.—Scher-
  zer, C. Travels in C. A. 2 vols. 1857. 9179.10-11.—
  Squier, E. G: Waikna. 1855. 9176.5.—Viollet-
  le-Duc. Cités et ruines Américaines. 1863. 970.51.
  —Wells, W. V. Historical sketch of C. A. 1502-
  1857. (*In his* Explor. in Honduras.) p. 449, *in*
  9179.18;—Same. 978.53.—Winsor, J. Mexico and
  Central America (with critical essay on the sources
  of information). (*Narr. . . . hist. of Amer.*, v. 1,
  pp. 133-208.) * 970.127[1].
    See also America, Central, *in* Catalogue of this
  Library. No. 2, 1880, p. 8.
    See also Poole's Index (to 1882). p. 212, *in* ** 50.1;
  —Same. Jan. 1, 1882-Jan. 1, 1887. p. 73, *in* ** 50.1[3].
    See also Index to Consular reports. 1880-1885;
  1886-1889. 2 vols. (U. S. Pub. Docs. *Dept. of State.*)
  ** 350.5496[1-3].
Century of gossip. Nash, W. G. 823.1181
Cerise. Melville, G: J; Whyte- 823.1151
  Same.   *in* ** 823.4667; 823.7273
Cerritos, Los. Atherton, *Mrs.* G. F. (H.)
                     823.7006
Cervantes Saavedra, Miguel de. Adventures
  of Don Quixote and his squire Sancho
  Panza. Tr. by C: Jarvis.   823.6897
  Same.   823.6896
—— Don Quixote of La Mancha. Tr. by Mot-
  teux. With notes, life and writings of
  Cervantes, by J: G. Lockhart. 4 vols.
                823.6899-902
—— *Same.*   823.5235-8
—— The exemplary novels of C.: to which
  are added El buscapié; or, the serpent.
  (*And*) La Tia fingida; or, the pretended
  aunt. Tr. by W. K. Kelly. Port. (Bohn's.)
                    823.6898
   Contents:—The Lady Cornelia.—Rinconete and
  Cortadillo; or, Peter of the corner and the little
  cutter.—The licentiate Vidriera; or, Doctor Glass-
  case.—The deceitful marriage.—Dialogue between
  Scipio and Berganza, dogs of Hospital of the Res-
  urrection . . . commonly called the dogs of Ma-
  hudes.—The little gipsy girl.—The generous lover.
  —The Spanish-English lady.—The force of blood.—
  The jealous Estramaduran.—The illustrious scul-
  lery-maid.—The two damsels.—The serpent.—The
  pretended aunt.

English Fiction. *Contin.*
Cervantes Saavedra, Miguel de. *Contin.*
—— Galatea : a pastoral romance. Tr. by
  G. W. J. Gyll.   823.2121
—— The wanderings of Persiles and Sigis-
  munda: a northern story. (Tr. by L. D. S.)
  Port.   823.6903
César Birotteau. Balzac, H. de. 823.5209
Cesarine Dietrich. Dudevant, *Mme.* A. L. A.
  (D.)   823.6295
Césette. Pouvillon, É.   823.4484
Ceylon. Knox, T: W. The boy travellers in
  the far east. Pt. 3: Adventures of two
  youths in a journey to Ceylon and India.
                    808.1837
—— Nordhoff, C: Ceylon. (*In his* Stories
  of the island world.) p. 151, *in* 808.165
Chainbearer, The. Cooper, J. F. 823.291
Chaldean magician, The. Eckstein, E.
                    823.7125
Challenge of Barletta. 2 vols. (in 1). Azeglio,
  M. T. d'.   ** 823.6637
Chamberlain, Nathan H: The sphynx in
  Aubrey parish.   823.7140
Chamberlain, Parthene B. Mistress of the
  house.   823.195
Chambers, Julius. [*Felix Somers.*] A mad
  world and its inhabitants.   823.196
Chamier, *Capt.* F: Ben Brace; the last of
  Nelson's Agamemnons.   823.197
—— The saucy Arethusa.   823.6347
—— Tom Bowling: a tale of the sea.
                    823.6348
Chamisso, Adalbert von. *See* Chamisso de
  Boncourt, L: C: A.
Chamisso de Boncourt, L: C: Adélaïde
  (*called* Adalbert). Peter Schlemihl. Tr.
  by Sir J: Bowring. 3d ed.   * 823.4344
Chamois-hunter, The. Souvestre, É.
                    823.5941
Champney, *Mrs.* E.. (Williams). The heart-
  break cameo. 22 pp. (*In* Stories by
  Amer. authors, v. 6.) p. 94, *in* 823.4707
—— Three Vassar girls abroad: rambles . . .
  through France and Spain . . . 808.1821
—— Three Vassar girls at home: a holiday
  trip . . . through the south and west.
                    808.1825
—— Three Vassar girls in England. 808.1824
—— Three Vassar girls in France: a story of
  the siege of Paris.   808.1826
—— Three Vassar girls in Italy. 808.1828
—— Three Vassar girls in Russia and Tur-
  key.   808.1823
—— Three Vassar girls in South America.
                    808.1822
—— Three Vassar girls in Switzerland.
                    808.1919
—— Three Vassar girls on the Rhine.
                    808.1827
—— Witch Winnie. The story of a "King's
  Daughter."   808.1913
Chance acquaintance, A. Howells, W: D.
                    823.828
Chance child. 51 pp. Mayo, *Mrs.* I.. (F.)
                    823.4050
Chances and changes. 2 vols. (in 1). Strutt,
  E..   ** 823.6767
Chandos. La Ramée, L. de.   823.1818

English Fiction. *Contin.*
Changed brides, The. Southworth, *Mrs.* E.
D. E. (N.) 823.1480
Chanler, *Mrs.* Amélie (Rives). A brother to
dragons, and other old-time tales.
823.5384
Channings, The. Wood, *Mrs.* E. (P.)
823.6388
Chantry House. Yonge, C.. M.. *in* 823.3347
Chantry priest of Barnet. Church, A. J:
823.5293
Chaplain of the fleet. Besant, W., *and* Rice,
J. 823.6085
Chaplain's craze, The. Fenn, G: M.
823.5595
Chaplet of pearls, The. Yonge, C.. M..
823.1762
Same. 823.6004; 823.6096
Chaplin, Heman White. [*C. H. White.*] Eli.
38 pp. (*In* Stories by Amer. authors, v.
9.) p. 55, *in* 823.4710
—— Five hundred dollars, and other stories
of New England life. 2d ed. 823.6937
—— The village convict. 25 pp. (*In* Stories
by Amer. authors, v. 6.) p. 5, *in* 823.4707
Character sketches. 30 pp. Thackeray, W:
M. *in* 823.1572
Charity Helstone. Brock, *Mrs.* F.. E.. G.
(B.) Carey. 823.120
Charlemagne cycle of romances, The.
—— Ariosto, L. Orlando furioso; with notes
by W. S. Rose. 2 vols. 1858. 851.1–2
—— Bulfinch, T: Legends of Charlemagne.
823.150
—— Cox, *Sir* G: W., *and* Jones, E. H. Ro-
land. (*In their* Romances of the middle
ages.) p. 202, *in* 940.54
—— Early Eng. Text Soc. Publications. The
Eng. Charlemagne romances. 11 pts. (Ex-
tra ser., Nos. 34–41; 43–5.) ** 806.2³⁴⁻⁴¹,⁴³⁵
—— Lockhart, J. G., *tr.* Spanish ballads.
821.854
—— Théroude (*attributed to*). The song of
Roland. Tr. by J: O'Hagan. 821.1286
—— Wieland, C. M. Oberon. Ein roman-
tisches Heldengedicht. (*Werke*, v. 1.)
831.44
Note.—See article "Roland, Legend of," in En-
cyclop. Brit., v. 20. p. 641, *in* ** 32.290.
Charlemont. Simms, W: G. 823.1428
Charles, *Mrs.* E.. (Rundle). Against the
stream : the story of a heroic age in Eng-
land. 823.202
—— The Bertram family. 823.203
—— The black ship : with other allegories
and parables. 808.1490
—— Chronicles of the Schönberg-Cotta fam-
ily. 823.204
—— Conquering and to conquer. 823.205
—— The cripple of Antioch, and other
scenes from the Christian life in early
times. 823.5577
Contents:—The cripple of Antioch.—The false
Christ : a tale of the second fall of Jerusalem.—
Wayside notes in the days of Chrysostom.
—— Diary of Kitty Trevylyan : a story of
the times of Whitefield and the Wesleys.
823.206
—— The Draytons and the Davenants : a
story of the civil wars. 823.207

English Fiction. *Contin.*
Charles, *Mrs.* E.. (Rundle). *Contin.*
—— The early dawn ; or, sketches of Christian life in England in the olden time.
823.208
Contents:—Lights and shadows of the early
dawn.—The two martyrs of Verulam.—Annals of
an Anglo-Saxon family through three generations.
—Saxon schools and homes.—Saxon minsters and
missions.—Alfred the truth-teller.—Saxon and Nor-
man.—A story of the Lollards.—Annals of an
abbey.
—— Joan the maid, deliverer of France and
England : a story of the fifteenth century.
823.209
—— Lapsed, but not lost. 823.2158
—— The martyrs of Spain, and The libera-
tors of Holland. 823.6598
—— On both sides of the sea : a story of the
Commonwealth and the Restoration. A
sequel to 'The Draytons and the Davenants.' 823.210
—— Sketches of the women of Christendom.
823.5696
Contents:—The first woman.—The women of the
Gospels.—The women of the Acts of the Apostles.—
The women of the early church.—The Christian
women of Rome in the fourth century.—The Chris-
tian women of the middle ages.—Christian women
of modern times.—The women of the army of suc-
cor.
—— The victory of the vanquished : a story
of the first century. 823.211
—— Winifred Bertram and the world she
lived in. 823.212
Charles Auchester. Sheppard, E.. S..
823.5960
Same. 3 vols. ** 823.6233-5
Charles Dickens parlor album of illustrations.
823.1799
Charles Lever. Gresley, *Rev.* W:
** 823.6772
Charles O'Malley. Lever, C: J. 823.973
Charles Tyrrell. 2 vols. (in 1.) James, G: P.
R. 823.850
Charley Kingston's aunt. Oliver, P. 823.7407
Charlie Lucken at school and college.
Adams, H. C. 823.6333
Charlotte Ackerman. Müller, O: 823.6812
Charlotte Temple. Rowson, *Mrs.* S. (H.)
823.5022
Charlotte's inheritance. Maxwell, *Mrs.* M..
E.. (B.) *in* 823.2403
Same. *in* 823.5048
Charmed sea, The. Martineau, H.
in ** 823.6710
Same. ** 823.6751
Charming widow, A. Macquoid, *Mrs.* K.. S.
823.7398
Chasing the sun. Ballantyne, R. M.
808.637
Same. *in* 808.1269; *in* 808.1281
Chasseur d'Afrique. Walmsley, H. M.
823.1670
Château d'Or. Holmes, *Mrs.* M.. J.. (H.)
823.4846
Château Frissac. Sikes, *Mrs.* O. (L.)
823.6116
Château Morville. Tr. by E. R. 823.6877
Chatelain, *Mme.* Clara (de Pontigny) de.
The Dalecarlian conjuror's day-book.
** 823.6608

English Fiction. *Contin.*
Chatrian, Pierre Alexander, *joint author.* See Erckmann, Émile.
Chatsworth. Patmore, P: G: 823.6074
Chatterjee, Bankim Chandra. The poison tree: a tale of Hindu life in Bengal. Tr. by M. S. Knight.   823.4936
Chautauqua girls at home. Alden, *Mrs.* I.. (McD.)   808.1511
Cheaterie packman, The. Ritchie, L.
                                    in 823.702
Checco: a tale of Perugia. Macquoid, *Mrs.* K.. S.   *in* 823.1622
Chelsea householder, A. Lawless, *Hon.* E.
                                    823.4592
Cheney, *Mrs.* C. Emma. Young folks' history of the civil war.   973.689
Cheney, *Mrs.* Ednah Dow (Littlehale). Nora's return: a sequel to "The doll's house" of Henry Ibsen.   823.7322
Cheney, J: Vance. The old doctor: a romance of Queer village.   823.5177
Cherbuliez, Victor. Count Kostia. Tr. by O. D. Ashley.   823.6840
—— L'idée de Jean Têterol. (*In* Zimmern, H.., *and* A. *Half-hours with foreign novelists*).   *in* 823.6613
—— Jean Têterol's idea.   823.2331
—— Meta Holdenis.   823.2318
—— *Same.*   823.2378
—— Prosper. Tr. by C. Benson.   823.6841
—— The romance of an honest woman.
                                    823.7119
—— Saints and sinners. (Noirs et rouges.) Tr. by M.. N. Sherwood.   823.6435
—— *Same.* (*Also*) The lawyer's secret; (*and*) The mystery at Fernwood. By Mrs. M.. E.. (B.) Maxwell.   823.6384
—— Samuel Brohl and Company.   823.2322
—— *Same.*   *in* 823.6688
Cherry and Violet. Rathbone, *Mrs.* M.. A. (M.)   823.1093
Chesebro', C. The foe in the household.
                                    823.6245
Chesney, C: Cornwallis. [*A volunteer.*] The battle of Dorking; or, reminiscences of a volunteer. By an eye witness, in 1925.
                                    823.5649
—— The fall of England? The battle of Dorking: reminiscences of a volunteer.
                                    823.4015
Chevalier de Maison Rouge, The. Dumas, A. D.   823.3108
Same.   823.6522
Chevaliers of France. Herbert, H: W:
                                    823.4253
Chicot, the jester. Dumas, A. D.   823.4611
Same.   823.6514
Chien d'Or, Le. Besant, W., *and* Rice, J.
                                    in 823.3138
Chien d'Or. Kirby, W: 823.950
Child, *Mrs.* Lydia Maria (Francis). Philothea: a Grecian romance.   823.7084
Child and woman. Helm, C.   823.6805
Child of the century, A. Wheelwright, J: T.
                                    823.5430
Child of the revolution, A. Roberts, M.
                                    in 823.5033
Child wife, The. Reid, *Capt.* T: M. 823.6334

English Fiction. *Contin.*
Childhood, boyhood, youth. Tolstoï, *Count* L. N.   823.6366
Childhood's memories. 12 pp. Stannard, *Mrs.* H. E. V. (P.)   *in* 823.5076
Child-life in Italy. Watson, E. H. 808.1684
Child-life in Japan, and Japanese child-stories. Ayrton, C.   808.1871
Child-pictures from Dickens.   808.1914
Children at home. Brock, *Mrs.* F.. E.. G. (B.) Carey-   823.121
Children of Gibeon. Besant, W. *in* 823.4985
Same.   *in* 823.5020 ; 823.6962
Children of the abbey. Roche, R. M.
                                    823.1354
Children of the cold. Schwatka, F:
                                    808.1673
Children of the New Forest. Marryat, *Capt.* F: 823.1095
Children of the world. 3 vols. (in 1). Heyse, J. L. P.   ** 823.6633
Same. 3 vols.   823.6455-7
Children of to-morrow. Sharp, W: 823.7295
Children's book, The. Scudder, H. E., *comp.*   808.1882
Children's book of poetry. Coates, H: T., *comp.*   808.1868
Children's stories in American history. Wright, H. C.   808.1581
Same.   808.1695
Children's stories in English literature. Wright, H. C.   808.1533
Children's stories of American progress. Wright, H. C.   808.1696
Children's stories of the great scientists. Wright, H. C.   808.1644
Child's history of England, A. Dickens, C: J. H.   808.686
Same.   *in* 823.5334
Child's history of Greece. 2 vols. Bonner, J: 808.621-2
Child's history of Rome, A. 2 vols. Bonner, J: 808.623-4
Child's history of the United States, A. 3 vols. Bonner, J: 808.618-20
Child's own book, and treasury of fairy stories.   808.1028
China. Dalton, W: Wolf boy of China.
                                    808.871
—— Davis, J. A. Chinese slave-girl . . . woman's life in China.   808.836
—— Gueullette, T: S. Chinese tales. 80 pp. (*In* Weber, H: *Tales of the east,* v. 3.)
                          p. 335, *in* ** 823.6232
—— Hwa Tsien Ki. The flowery scroll: a Chinese novel.   823.1837
—— Knox, J: W. The boy travellers in the far east. Pt. 1.   808.1835
—— Lander, S.. W. Spectacles for young eyes: Pekin.   808.101
—— Longfellow, H: W. Poems of places.
                          p. 191, *in* 821.229
—— Sealy, T: Chinese legends.   828.81
—— Verne, J. Adventures of a Chinaman in China.   823.5178
—— — Tribulations of a Chinaman in China.
                                    823.4342
Note.—See The Chinese in America. (Bibliography.) [Bost. Pub. Lib. *Bulletin,* No. 51. v. 4. p. 143.] *in* ** 17.135.—Möllendorff, P. G., *and* O. F.

English Fiction. *Contin.*

China. *Contin.*

Note. Contin.

von. Manual of Chinese **bibliography**. 1876. **
15.275.—**Boulger**, D. C. History of China. 3 vols.
1881-4. 951.33-5.—**Culin**, S. Chinese secret societies
in the U. S. 5 pp. (*Journ. of Amer. folk-lore*, v. 3.)
1890. p. 44, *in* 291.81³.—**Davis**, J: F. The Chinese:
a general description of China and its inhabitants.
2 vols. (*Lib. of entertain. knowledge.*) 1836. 951.4-5.
—**Doolittle**, J. Social life of the Chinese. 1876.
915.136.—**Farwell**, W. B. Why the Chinese must be
excluded. 8 pp. (*The forum*, v. 6, 1888-9.) p. 196, *in*
* 51.4701⁴.—**Gray**, J. H. China: history of the laws,
manners and customs of the people. 2 vols. 1878.
915.174-5.—**Hübner**, J. A., *Baron* von. Ramble
round the world. 910.59.—**James**, H. E. M. The
long White Mountain; or, a journey in Manchuria.
1888. 915.369.—**Margary**, A: R. Journey from
Shanghae to Bhamo and back to Mamoyne. 2d ed.
1876. 915.166.—**Mayers**, W: F. The Chinese government. 1886. 323.15.—**Mendoza**, J. G. de. History of China. (*Hakluyt Soc.*, 1853.) 2 vols. **
951.7-8.—**Pinkerton's** voyages . . . v. 7. 1811. **
913.15.—**Ross**, J: The Manchus; or, the reigning
dynasty of China: their rise and progress. 1880.
951.32.—**Taylor**, B. India, China and Japan.
915.41.—**Thomson**, J. Straits of Malacca, Indo-
China and China. 1875. 915.69.—**Universal history.** v.18. ** 909.48.—Modern part of an **universal
history.** v. 7. ** 909.55.—**Williams**, S. W. The
middle kingdom. 2 vols. 1883. * 951.29-30.
See also **Catalogues** of this Library.

No. 2, 1880, p. 45.   No. 4, 1884, p. 59.
No. 3, 1882, p. 37.   No. 5, 1888, p. 57.

See also **Poole's** Index (to 1882). pp. 231-236, *in* **
50.1;—*Same.* Jan. 1, 1882-Jan. 1, 1887. pp. 78-80, *in* **
50.1².

See also Index to **Consular reports**, 1880-1885;
1886-1889. 2 vols. (U. S. Pub. Docs. *Dept. of State.*)
** 350.5496⁻².

See also "**Chinese Question**" in Catalogues of
this Library.

No. 3, 1882, p. 38.   No. 4, 1884, p. 59.

Chinese slave girl. Davis, J. A.   808.836

Chinese tales. 80 pp. Gueullette, T: S.
   p. 335, *in* ** 823.6232

Chita. Hearn, L.   823.7141

Choy Susan. Bishop, W: H: 823.5672

Chris. Norris, W: E: 823.5594

Chris and Otho. Smith, *Mrs.* J. P.
   823.1464

Christian's mistake. Craik, *Mrs.* D. M. (M.)
   823.326

Christie Johnstone. Reade, C: *in* 823.5420
Same.   823.7410
Same, and other stories. Reade, C:
   823.1285

Christina, *Queen of Sweden.* (1632-1654.)
—— Hawthorne, N. Biographical stories. 11
pp. (*In his* Tales and sketches.)
   p. 203, *in* 824.414
Note.—See **Barine**, A. Christine de Suède.
(*Rev. d. d. Mondes.* 3d pér 1888. v. 89.) p. 783,
in * 54.399³.—**Collins**, W: W. A queen's revenge.
17 pp. (*In his* My miscellanies.) p. 42, *in* 824.18.—
Jameson, *Mrs.* A. M. Female sovereigns. v. 2.
p. 1, *in* 923.933.—**Ranke**, L. von. Hist. of the popes.
v. 2. p. 351, *in* 282.56.—**Woodhead**, H. H. Memoirs of
Christina. 2 vols. 1863. 923.2048-9.

Christine. Curtis, L. J.   823.4640

Christmas books. Dickens, C: J: H. 823.394
Same.   823.5307; 823.5333; 823.5557
Christmas books. Thackeray, W: M.
   823.1574

Christmas eve and Christmas day. Hale, E:
E.   823.680

Christmas guest, The. Southworth, *Mrs.* E.
D. E. (N.)   823.1481

Christmas stories. Dickens, C: J: H. 823.395
Same. *in* 823.5321; 823.5332; *in* 823.5555

English Fiction. *Contin.*

Christmas stories (New). Dickens, C: J: H.
   in 823.426

Christmas stories. Holmes, *Mrs.* M..J.. (H.)
   823.4850

Christmas wreck, and other stories. Stockton, F. R: 823.5219

Christopher, and other stories. Barr, *Mrs.* A.
E. (H.)   823.5418

Christopher Tadpole, Struggles . . . of . .
Smith, A.   823.1448

Christowell. Blackmore, R: D.   823.3916
Same.   823.4941

Christy Carew. McNabb, *Mrs.* M.. (L.)
   823.3119

Chronicles of Dustypore. Cunningham, H.
S.   823.4190
Same.   823.4375

Chronicles of the Canongate. Scott, *Sir* W.
v. 2.   p. 171, *in* 823.1394
Same.   *in* 823.1412; 823.4826
Same.   823.5160; p. 311, *in* ** 823.6032

Chronicles of the Schönberg-Cotta family.
Charles, *Mrs.* E.. (R.)   823.204

Chrysal. 4 vols. (in 2). Johnston, C:
   823.7364-5
Same. 4 vols.   823.4518-21

Chrysostom, Wayside notes in the days of.
Charles, *Mrs.* E.. (R.)
   p. 219, *in* 823.5577

Chubbuck, Emily. *See* Judson, *Mrs.* Emily
(Chubbuck).

Chuck Purdy. Stoddard, W: O.   808.1726

Church, Alfred J: The chantry priest of
Barnet: a tale of the two Roses. 823.5293
—— The count of the Saxon shore; or, the
villa in vectis : tale of the departure of the
Romans from Britain.   823.5292
—— Stories from Homer.   808.1131
Contents.—The Iliad.—The Odyssey.
—— Stories from Livy.   808.1545
For contents, *see* Livius Patavius, Titus.
—— Stories from the Greek tragedians.
   808.1378
Contents:—The story of the love of Alcestis.—The
story of the vengeance of Medea.—The story of the
death of Hercules.—The story of the seven chiefs
against Thebes.—The story of Antigone.—The story
of Iphigenia in Aulis.—The story of Philoctetes; or,
the bow of Hercules.—The story of the death of
Agamemnon.—The story of Electra; or, the return
of Orestes.—The story of the Furies; or, the loosing
of Orestes.—The story of Iphigenia among the Tau-
rians.—The story of the Persians; or, the battle of
Salamis.—The story of Ion.
—— *Same.*   823.4155
—— Stories from Virgil.   808.1413
For contents, *see* Virgilius.
—— Stories of the east from Herodotus.
   808.1546
—— Stories of the magicians. Thalaba and
the magicians of the Domdaniel, Rustem
and the genii, Kehama and his sorceries.
   823.5663
—— The story of the Persian war from Herodotus.   823.5671
—— Three Greek children: a story of home
in old time.   808.1705
—— To the lions: a tale of the early Christians.   823.6545
——, *and* Seeley, Richmond. The hammer:
a story of the Maccabean times. 823.6940

English Fiction. *Contin.*
Church, *Mrs.* Ella (Rodman). Home-animals. 808.1597
—— Little neighbors at Elmridge. 808.1633
Church, *Mrs.* Florence (Marryat) Ross- *See* Lean, *Mrs.* F. (M.)
Churton, H:, *pseud. See* Tourgée, Albion Winegar.
Cigarette-maker's romance. Crawford, F. M. 823.7334
Cinnamon and pearls. Martineau, H. *in* ** 823.6712
Cinq-Mars. Vigny, A.-V., *comte de.* 823.1873
Same. 2 vols. ** 823.6311-12
Cipher. Austin, J.. G. 823.5827
Circuit rider. Eggleston, E: 823.520
Citizen Bonaparte. 1794-1815. Erckmann, É., *and* Chatrian, P. A. 823.6862
Same. *in* 823.7253
Citizen of Prague. Paalzou, *Mrs.* H. (W.) von. 823.6073
Citoyenne Jacqueline. Keddie, H. 823.923
City and suburb. Riddell, *Mrs.* C.. E. L. (C.) 823.1322
City boys in the woods. Wells, H: P. 808.1802
City in the sea. Saxon, E. L., *comp.* 823.7173
Civil-service reform. By Major Simpleton. 823.4593
Clack, *Mrs.* Louise. Our refugee household. 823.1852
Claire. By the author of "Vida." 823.6399
Clandestine marriage. Dupuy, E. A. 823.492
Clara Howard. Brown, C: B. *in* 823.141
Same. p. 285, *in* ** 823.6205
Clara Vaughan. Blackmore, R: D. 823.2517
Same. 823.4950
Clare Avery. Holt, E. S.. 808.1523
Claretie, Jules. Monsieur le ministre: a romance in real life. Tr. by J: Stirling. 823.4321
Claribel's love story. Brame, *Mrs.* C.. M. (L.) 823.5017
Clarionet, The. 82 pp. Carleton, W: 823.169
Clarissa. Richardson, S: 823.1316
Same. 5 vols. ** 823.6164-8
Same. 8 vols. ** 823.2062-9
Clark, C: Heber. [*Max Adeler.*] The fate of young Chubb. 5 pp. (*In* Half-hours with great story tellers.) p. 75, *in* 823.5478
Clark, *Mrs.* C.. (Moon). [*C: M. Clay.*] Baby Rue [her adventures and misadventures, her friends and her enemies]. 823.1872
Clark, F: Thickstun. In the valley of Havilah. 823.7245
Clark, H. H. Joe Bently, naval cadet. 823.7035
Clark, J. F. The society in search of truth; or, stock gambling in San Francisco. 823.4512
Clarke, C: Three courses and a dessert; comprising three sets of tales, West country, Irish, and legal; and a melange. With fifty illustrations by G: Cruikshank. 823.352

English Fiction. *Contin.*
Clarke, *Mrs.* M.. V.. (Novello) Cowden- The girlhood of Shakespeare's heroines: in a series of tales. 2 vols. 823.5821-2
—— A rambling story. 823.4110
—— Yarns of an old mariner. 823.233
Same. 823.4248
Clarke, R.. Sophia. [*Sophie May.*] The Asbury twins. 823.234
—— The doctor's daughter. 823.235
—— Our Helen. 823.1915
Classic tales: comprising Johnson's Rasselas.—Goldsmith's Vicar of Wakefield.— Swift's Gulliver's travels.—Sterne's Sentimental journey. 823.4489
Claude, M.. S. Twilight thoughts: stories for children and child-lovers. Ed. by M.. L. Avery, with a preface by M. Arnold. 808.1467
Claude Stocq. Reybaud, *Mrs.* H. E. F. (A.) *in* 823.812
Claudia. Douglas, A. M. 823.476
Clavers, *Mrs.* M.., *pseud. See* Kirkland, *Mrs.* C. M. (S.)
Clay, Bertha M., *pseud. See* Brame, *Mrs.* C.. M. (Low).
Clay, C: M., *pseud. See* Clark, *Mrs.* C.. (Moon).
Clay, H: Life of Henry Clay, the statesman and the patriot. 808.792
Claytor, Graham. Pleasant Waters: a story of southern life and character. 823.7170
Cleland, Robert. Barbara Allan, the provost's daughter. 823.6992
Clemens, Jeremiah. Bernard Lile: an historical romance embracing the periods of the Texas revolution and the Mexican war. 823.7100
Clemens, S: Langhorne. [*Mark Twain.*] A Connecticut Yankee in King Arthur's court. 823.6141
—— The prince and the pauper: a tale for young people of all ages. 823.6133
—— The stolen white elephant, etc. 823.6978
   Contents:— The stolen white elephant.—Some rambling notes of an idle excursion.—The facts concerning the recent carnival of crime in Connecticut.—About magnanimous-incident literature. —Punch, brothers, punch.—A curious experience.— The great revolution in Pitcairn.—Mrs. McWilliams and the lightning.—On the decay of the art of lying. —The canvasser's tale.—An encounter with an interviewer.—Paris notes.—Legend of Sagenfeld, in Germany.—Speech on the babies.—Speech on the weather.—Concerning the American language.— Rogers.—The loves of Alonzo Fitz Clarence and Rosannah Ethelton.
——, *and* Warner, C: Dudley. The gilded age: a tale of to-day. 823.5809
Clergyman's tale:—Pembroke. Lee, S. p. 11 *in* 823.968
Clerk, *Mrs.* Alice M., *tr.* 'Ilâm-en-Nâs: historical tales and anecdotes of the times of the early Khalifahs. Tr. from the Arabic. 823.1836
Clerk, *Mrs.* Godfrey. *See* Clerk, *Mrs.* Alice M.
Clever woman of the family, The. Yonge, C.. M.. 823.1763
Cleverdale mystery, The. Wilkins, W. A. 823.4485

English Fiction. *Contin.*
Collins, W: Wilkie. *Contin.*
—— Basil: a novel. 823.252
—— Blind love. 823.7247
—— The dead secret: a novel. 823.5826
—— The evil genius: a domestic story.
823.5647
—— The frozen deep, and other tales.
823.256
Contents:—The frozen deep.—The dream woman.
—John Jago's ghost; or, the dead alive.
—— The ghost's touch. 43 pp. (*And*) Percy
and the prophet. 73 pp. *in* 823.6686
—— The guilty river: a novel. 823.5646
—— Hide-and-seek; or, the mystery of Mary
Grice. 823.257
—— "I say no;" or, the love-letter answered.
823.4788
—— The law and the lady: a novel. 823.258
—— The legacy of Cain. (*Also*) My lady's
money: an episode in the life of a young
girl. 823.3563
—— Love's random shot, and other stories.
in 823.6696
Contents:—Love's random shot.—The dream
woman.—John Jago's ghost.
—— Man and wife. 823.259
—— The moonstone. 823.260
—— My lady's money: an episode in the life
of a young girl. (*With his* The legacy of
Cain.) *in* 823.3563
—— The new Magdalen. 823.262
—— No name. 823.263
—— Percy and the prophet. 73 pp. (*With
his* The ghost's touch.) *in* 823.6686
—— Poor Miss Finch. 823.264
—— Queen of hearts. 823.265
—— A rogue's life: from his birth to his mar-
riage. 823.266
—— The two destinies. 823.267
—— The woman in white. 823.268
Colomb, *Mme.* (—). Uncle Chesterton's heir.
Tr. by H: Frith. 823.6913
Colombo, Cristoforo. (1446 *or* 7–1506.) Ab-
bott, J: S. C. Life of Columbus. 808.538
—— Barlow, J. The Columbiad: a poem.
821.22
—— Cooper, J. F. Mercedes of Castile.
(First voy. of Columbus.) 823.300
—— Humphrey, F.. A. Adventures of early
discoverers. 808.1905
Note.—See **Anderson**, R. B. America not dis-
covered by Columbus. 1877. 970.33.—**Biblio-
graphical** account of voyages. (*Hist. mag.*, 1861, v.
5.) pp. 33–38, *in* ** 973.522.—**Irving**, W. Life of Co-
lumbus. 3 vols. 923.207–9.—**Parton**, J. The real
merits of Columbus. (*In his* Triumphs of enter-
prise.) 1874. pp. 511–531, *in* 920.245.—**Winsor**, J.
Columbus and his discoveries. (Narr . . . hist. of
Amer. ii, 1–92.) * 970.127².
See also **Catalogues** of this Library.
No. 2, 1880, p. 51.   No. 5, 1888, p. 62.
No. 3, 1882, p. 43.
See also **Poole's** Index (to 1882). p. 280, *in* ** 50.1;
—*Same.* Jan. 1, 1882–Jan. 1, 1887. p. 94, *in* ** 50.1².
See also **Encyclop.** Britann. *Index.* p. 106, *in* **
32.27P.
Colonel Dunwoddie, millionaire. Baker, W:
M. 823.6372
Colonel Enderby's wife. Harrison, *Mrs.* R.
G. (K.) 823.4830
Same. *in* 823.4973
Colonel Jack, Life of. De Foe, D.
in 823.2122

English Fiction. *Contin.*
Colonel Quaritch, *V. C.* Haggard, H: R.
823.5529
Colonel's daughter, The. King, *Capt.* C:
823.7392
Colonel's opera cloak. Brush, *Mrs.* C. (C.)
823.1999
Colonial days. Markham, R: 808.1865
Colonial times of Buzzard's bay. Bliss, W:
R. 823.6537
Colonna the painter: a tale of Italy and the
arts. (*In* Tales from Blackwood, v. 1.)
in ** 823.6647
Colquhoun, M. J. Primus in Indis. 823.5065
Colston, E: (1636–1721.) Marshall, *Mrs.* E.
(M.) In Colston's days: a story of old Bris-
tol. 823.5774
Columbus, Christopher. *See* Colombo, Cris-
toforo.
Colville of 'the Guards.' Grant, J. 823.5681
Same. 823.6525
Cometh up as a flower. Broughton, R.
823.132
Same. *in* 823.2338
Coming race. Lytton, E: G: E. L. Bulwer-
823.1024
Same. 823.5863; 823.5975
Comins, Lizzie B. [*Laura Caxton.*] The
Hartwell farm. 823.2359
—— Marion Berkley: a story for girls.
823.270
Commodore Junk. Fenn, G: M. *in* 823.6698
Commonplace, and other short stories. Ros-
setti, C. G. 823.1370
Comyn, L. N. Elena: an Italian tale.
823.272
Con Cregan, The confessions of. Lever, C:
J. 823.974
Con O'Regan. Sadlier, *Mrs.* M.. A. (M.)
823.1378
Condemned door, The. Du Boisgobey, F.
in 823.5086
Condensed novels. Harte, F. B. 823.711
Confederate chieftains. Sadlier, *Mrs.* M.. A.
(M.) 823.1377
Confession. Simms, W: G. 823.1429
Confessions of a clarionet player, and other
tales. Erckmann, É., *and* Chatrian, P. A.
823.6855
Confessions of a Thug. Taylor, M. 823.4276
Same. 3 vols. * 823.4629–31
Confessions of an odd-tempered man. 19 pp.
Opie, *Mrs.* A. (A.) p. 394, *in* 823.6136
Confessions of Claud. Fawcett, E. 823.5743
Confessions of Con Cregan. Lever, C: J.
823.974
Confessions of Harry Lorrequer. Lever, C: J.
** 823.6221
Confidence. James, H:, *Jr.* 823.1928
Conformists, The. Banim, J:
p. 234, *in* 823.56
Congo. Abbott, J. 808.591
Congo river. *See* Kongo river.
Congo rovers, The. Collingwood, H.
808.1706
Coningsby. 2 vols. Brydges, *Sir* S: E.
* 823.144–5
Coningsby. Disraeli, B: 823.459
Same. *in* 823.3002

English Fiction. *Contin.*

Cooley, *Mrs.* Alice (Kingsbury). Ho! for Elf-land! 808.1027

Cooley, W: Forbes. Emmanuel: the story of the Messiah. 823.6575

Cooper, James Fenimore. (1789–1851.) Afloat and ashore: a tale. 823.289

—— The bravo: a tale. 823.290

—— The chainbearer; or, the Littlepage manuscripts. 823.291

—— The crater; or, Vulcan's peak: a tale of the Pacific. 823.292

—— The deerslayer; or, the first war-path: a tale. 823.293

—— Eve Effingham; or, home: a sequel to "Homeward bound." ** 823.6259
Issued also as Home as found.

—— The headsman; or, the Abbaye des Vignerons: a tale. 823.294

—— The Heidenmauer; or, the Benedictines: a legend of the Rhine. 823.295

—— Home as found. Sequel to "Homeward bound." 823.296

—— Homeward bound; or, the chase: a tale of the sea. 823.297

—— Jack Tier; or, the Florida reef. 823.298

—— The last of the Mohicans; or, a narrative of 1757. 823.320

—— Leatherstocking tales (should be read in the following order):

The deerslayer (1841).	823.293
Last of the Mohicans (1826).	823.320
The pathfinder (1840).	823.304
The pioneers (1822).	823.306
The prairie (1826).	823.307

The dates are the years when the books were finished.

—— Lionel Lincoln; or, the leaguer of Boston. 823.299

—— Lucy Hardinge. *Same as* Miles Wallingford.

—— Mercedes of Castile; or, the voyage to Cathay. 823.300

—— Miles Wallingford. Sequel to Afloat and ashore. 823.301
Issued also as Lucy Hardinge.

—— The monikins. 823.302

—— The oak openings; or, the bee-hunter. 823.303

—— The pathfinder; or, the inland sea. 823.304

—— The pilot: a tale of the sea. 823.305

—— The pioneers; or, the sources of the Susquehanna: a descriptive tale. 823.306

—— The prairie: a tale. 823.307

—— Precaution: a novel. 823.308

—— The Red Rover. 823.309

—— The redskins; or, Indian and Injin: being the conclusion of the Littlepage manuscripts. 823.310

—— Rose Budd. *Same as* Jack Tier. 823.298

—— Satanstoe; or, the Littlepage manuscripts: a tale of the colony. 823.311

—— The sea lions; or, the lost sealers. 823.312

—— The spy: a tale of the neutral ground. 823.319

—— Stories of the prairie, and other adventures of the border. 808.1127

—— The two admirals: a tale. 823.313

English Fiction. *Contin.*

Cooper, James Fenimore. *Contin.*

—— The Water-Witch; or, the skimmer of the seas: a tale. 823.314

—— The ways of the hour: a tale. 823.315

—— The wept of Wish-Ton-Wish. 823.316
Issued also as The borderers.

—— The Wing-and-Wing; or, le Feu-Follet: a tale. 823.317
Issued also as Jack-o'-Lantern.

—— *Same.* 823.6173

—— Wyandotté; or, the hutted knoll: a tale. 823.318

Note.—For his life and writings, *see* Bryant, W: C. Orations and addresses. p. 43, *in* 825.12.—Griswold, R. W. Prose writers of America. p.263, *in* * 829.110.—Hillard, G. S. (*In* Atlantic monthly, v.9. 1862.) p. 52, *in* ** 51.9.—Homes of American authors. 1853. pp. 179-215, *in* ** 917.37.—Longacre *and* Herring. National portrait gallery, v. 1. *in* ** 923.1597.—Lounsbury, T. R. J. F. Cooper. 1883. (Warner, C: D. *Amer. men of letters.*) 928.656.—North American review, v. 89. 1859. p.289, *in* ** 51.568.—Poe, E. A. J. F. Cooper. 12 pp. (*Works*, v. 2.) p. 389, *in* 829.219.—Sainte-Beuve, C. A. Fenimore Cooper. (*In his* Premiers lundis, v. 1.) 824.443.—Sumner, C. Letter to Rev. R. W. Griswold. 2 pp. (*Works*, v. 3.) p. 43, 329.58. *See also* Poole's Index (to 1882). p. 298, *in* ** 50.1;—*Same.* Jan. 1, 1882-Jan. 1, 1887. p. 101, *in* ** 50.1*.

Cooper, *Mrs.* K.. (Saunders). The haunted crust. 34 pp. (*In* Johnson, R., *ed.* *Little classics*, v. 5.) p. 51, *in* 829.128

—— The High Mills. 823.6087

Cooper, S: Williams. Three days: a midsummer love-story. 823.7000

Coquette's conquest, A. King, R: A. 823.5062

Coral island, The. Ballantyne, R. M. 808.817

Coral pin, The. 2 pts. Du Boisgobey, F. 823.5093

Corbett, Julian. The fall of Asgard: a novel. 823.5648

—— For God and gold. 823.5650

—— *Same.* 823.6907

—— Kophetua the Thirteenth. 823.6910

Cord and creese. De Mille, J. 823.6349

Corea. *See* Korea.

Corinne. Staël-Holstien, A. L. G. (N.), *baronne* de. 823.4258

Same. 823.6261; 823.6297

Corkran, Alice. Bessie Lang. 823.1793

Cornet of horse. Henty, G: A. 808.1574

Cornish, *Mrs.* (—). Alcestis. (Anon.) 823.806

Corse de Leon. James, G: P. R. 823.853

Cosel, C.. von. [*Adelheid von Auer.*] It is the fashion. 823.6789

Cossacks, The. Tolstoï, *Count* L. N. 823.1871

Cottin, *Mme.* Sophie (Ristaud). Elizabeth; or, the exiles of Siberia. 823.4965

—— *Same.* p. 701, *in* ** 823.6215

—— Matilda, princess of England: a romance of the crusades. Tr. by J. W. Raum. 2 vols. 823.5652-3

—— The Saracen; or, Matilda and Malek Adhel: a crusade romance, with an historical introd. by J. Michaud. 4 vols. (in 2). 823.2364-5

Coulson, G: James Atkinson. The Clifton picture. 823.5930

English Fiction. *Contin.*
Craik, *Mrs.* Dinah Maria (Mulock). *Contin.*
—— Christian's mistake. 823.326
—— Hannah. 823.328
—— The head of the family: a novel.
823.329
—— A hero.—Bread upon the waters.—Alice
Learmont. 823.330
—— *Same.* 823.5508
—— His little mother, and other tales and
sketches. 823.3294
—— In a house-boat. (*With her* Miss
Tommy.) *in* 823.4805
—— Is it true? Tales curious and wonderful.
808.114
—— John Halifax, Gentleman. 823.331
—— King Arthur: not a love story.
in 823.4978
—— *Same. in* 823.4984; 823.5056; 823.5389
—— The laurel bush: an old-fashioned love-
story. 823.332
—— A life for a life. 823.334
—— Miss Tommy: a mediæval romance;
and, In a house-boat: a journal. 823.4805
—— Mistress and maid: a household story.
823.335
—— *Same.* 823.6263
—— My mother and I: a love story.
823.336
—— A noble life. 823.4285
—— The Ogilvies: a novel. 823.337
—— Olive. 823.338
—— The Rosicrucian. 32 pp. (*In* John-
son, R., *ed. Little classics,* v. 7.)
p. 83, *in* 829.130
—— Studies from life. 823.339
—— Two marriages (*viz.:* John Bowerbank's
wife.—Parson Garland's daughter).
823.340
—— The unkind word: and other stories.
823.341
—— Will Denbigh, nobleman. 823.2003
—— The woman's kingdom: a love story.
823.342
—— Young Mrs. Jardine: a novel. 823.343
Crake, *Rev.* A. D. Alfgar the Dane; or, the
second chronicle of Æscendune: a tale of
the days of Edmund Ironside. 6th ed.
823.5655
—— The Andreds-weald; or, the house of
Michelham: a tale of the Norman conquest.
2d ed. 823.5654
—— Brian Fitz-Count: a story of Wallingford
Castle and Dorchester Abbey. 823.5657
—— The camp on the Severn: a tale of the
tenth persecution in Britain. 823.7096
—— The doomed city; or, the last days of
Durocina: a tale of the Anglo-Saxon con-
quest of Britain and the mission of Augus-
tine. 823.7120
—— Edwy the fair; or, the first chronicle of
Æscendune: a tale of the days of Saint
Dunstan. 823.5656
—— Fairleigh Hall: a tale of Oxfordshire
during the great rebellion. 823.7098
—— The house of Walderne: a tale of the
cloister and the forest in the days of the
Barons' wars. 823.5658

English Fiction. *Contin.*
Crake, *Rev.* A. D. *Contin.*
—— The last abbot of Glastonbury: a tale of
the dissolution of the monasteries.
823.7097
—— Stories from old English history.
808.1625
Contents:—The fall of Anderida.—Edwin of
Northumbria.—The childhood of Offa.—The battle
of Benson.—The hapless love of Ethelbert.—The
avenger of blood.—Saint Kenelm, the little king.—
Ragnar Lodbrog.—Edmund the martyr.—The burn-
ing of Croyland Abbey.—Alfred in Athelney.—Edgar
and Elfrida.
—— The victor's laurel; a tale of school-life
during the tenth persecution in Italy.
823.7121
Crane, A.. Moncure. *See* Seemüller, *Mrs.*
A.. M. (Crane.)
Cranford. Gaskell, *Mrs.* E.. C. (S.) 823.600
Same. 823.5033
Crater, The. Cooper, J. F. 823.292
Craven, *Mme.* A: *See* Craven, *Mme.* P.. (de
la Ferronays.)
Craven, *Mme.* P.. (de la Ferronays). Anne
Séverin. 823.6842
—— Fleurange. Tr. by M. M. R. 823.6843
—— A sister's story. Tr. by E. Bowles.
823.6844
—— The veil withdrawn. ("Le mot de
l'enigme.") 823.6284
Crawford, Francis Marion. An American
politician. 823.4873
—— A cigarette-maker's romance. 823.7334
—— Doctor Claudius. 823.4851
—— Greifenstein. 823.5455
—— Marzio's crucifix. 823.5231
—— Mr. Isaacs: a tale of modern India.
823.4471
—— Paul Patoff. 823.5230
—— Roman singer. 823.4737
—— Sant' Ilario. (Sequel to Saracinesca.)
823.6548
—— Saracinesca. 823.4970
—— A tale of a lonely parish. 823.4921
—— To leeward. 823.4634
—— With the immortals. 2 vols. (in 1).
823.5542
—— Zoroaster. 823.4886
Crawfurd, Oswald J: F: The world we live in.
823.4793
Crayon, Geoffrey, Gent., *pseud. See* Irving,
Washington.
Crayon miscellany. No. 3. Irving, W.
** 823.6739
Craze of Christian Engelhart. Darnell, H:
F. 823.7001
Same. 823.7037
Creighton, Louise. Stories from English his-
tory. 808.1181
Crew of the "Dolphin." Smith, H.
823.1455
Crew of the "Sam Weller." Habberton, J:
823.7401
Crichton. Ainsworth, W: H. 823.16
Crime and punishment. Dostoyevsky, F. M.
823.5476
Crime of Christmas-day. Hunter, H., *and*
White, W. *in* 823.5084
Crime of Henry Vane. Stimson, F: J.
823.4758

English Fiction. *Contin.*
Crusades. Cahun, L. The blue banner.
823.6283
—— Collin de Plancy, J. Légendes des croisades. * 291.14
—— Henty, G: A. The boy knight who won his spurs fighting with King Richard of England. 808.1491
—— Holt, E. S.. Lady Sybil's choice.
823.808
—— La Motte Fouqué, F. H. K: *Baron* de. Thiodolf the Icelander. 823.6866
First, 1096–1099. (Jerusalem taken and Godfrey de Bouillon made king.)
—— Kotzebue, A. F. F. v. Die Kreuzfahrer. (*Theater*, v. 32.) * 832.81
—— Scott, *Sir* W. Count Robert of Paris.
823.1781
—— *Same.* *in* 823.5328; *in* 823.6034
—— Tasso. Jerusalem delivered. Tr. by Wiffen. 3 vols. 851.12–14
Note.—See **Raumer, F:von.** Der erste Kreuzzug, with English notes by W. Wagner. 1878. 940.89.
Second, 1142–1148. (Promoted by St. Bernard. Led by Louis VII. of France and Emperor Conrad of Germany.)
Third, 1148–1188. (Emperor Frederick I. [Barbarossa], joined by Richard I. of England and Philip II. of France. Fruitless victories of Richard I.)
—— Cottin, *Mme.* S. (R.) Matilda, princess of England. 2 vols. 823.5652–3
—— —— The Saracen; or, Matilda and Malek Adhel. 4 vols. (in 2). * 823.2364–5
—— Scott, *Sir* W. The talisman. 823.1412
—— *Same.* *in* 823.6031
—— *Same.* (*With his* Ivanhoe.) 823.5160
Note.—See also **Archer, T. A.,** *comp.* The crusades of Richard I. 1189–92. 1889. 942.1386.—**Lamb,** *Lady* C. Richard I. (*In her* Warrior kings, *etc.*) p. 67, *in* 923.1418.
Fourth, 1195–1198. (Set on foot by the Knights of St. John (1193), seconded by Pope Celestine III.)
Note.—See **Pears, E.** The fall of Constantinople. 1886. 940.174.
Fifth, 1198–1204. (Instigated by Pope Innocent. Baldwin takes Constantinople, 1203.)
Sixth, 1200–1215. (50,000 children engage in the crusade and perish. Jerusalem surrendered to Frederick II.)
Seventh, 1242–1245. [Louis IX. (St. Louis) captured and his army destroyed.]
Eighth, 1270–1291. (Death of Louis IX.)
—— Yonge, C. M.. The prince and the page.
808.1504
Note.—See **Bibliography.** Sybel, H. von. History and literature of the crusades. 1861. * 16.224—**Cox,** G: W: Crusades. 940.65.—**Gibbon, E:** History of the decline and fall of the Roman empire. vols. 4–5. 937.11–12.—**James,** G: P. R. History of chivalry. 392.5.—**Keightley,** T: The crusaders: scenes, events and characters. 1852. 940.87.—**Michaud,** J. F. History of the crusades. 3 vols. 1855. 940.5–7.—**Milman,** H. H. Latin Christianity. vols. 4–8. (*See* Index, v.8.) 270.45–8.—**Oakeley,** F: Influence of the crusades on art and literature. (*In* Oxf. prize essays, v. 4) pp. 155–184. *in* 824.314.—**Palgrave,** *Sir* F. Origin and intent of the crusades.—Robert the crusader. (*In his* Hist. of Normandy, *etc.*, v. 4.) *in* 942.492.—**Itchard** *of Devizes.* Chronicle concerning the deeds of Richard I. 78 pp. *in* ** 942.1320.
See also **Poole's** Index (to 1882). p. 321, *in* ** 50.1; —*Same.* Jan. 1, 1882–Jan. 1, 1887. p. 109, *in* ** 50.1².

English Fiction. *Contin.*
Crusoe in New York, and other tales. Hale, E: E. 823.4330
Crust and the cake. Mayo, *Mrs.* I. (F.)
823.1137
Cry of blood, The. 2 pts. Du Boisgobey, F.
in 823.5078
Cryptogram, The. De Mille, J. 823.5851
Cryptogram, The. Verne, J. 823.4491
Same. 823.6310
Cuba. See Spain.
Cudjo's cave. Trowbridge, J: T. 823.1635
Cudlip, *Mrs.* Annie Hall (Thomas). Called to account. 823.4775
—— Denis Donne. *in* 823.6213
—— Jenifer. 823.4999
—— No alternative. 823.1583
—— No medium. 823.5012
—— On guard. (*With her* Played out.)
in 823.6246
—— A passion in tatters. *in* 823.6263
—— Played out. (*Also*) On guard. 823.6246
—— Walter Goring. 823.1584
Cudlip, *Mrs.* Pender. See Cudlip, *Mrs.* A. H. (Thomas).
Cumberland, R: (1732–1811.) Macaulay, *Miss* E. Tales of the drama founded on . . . the comedies of . . . Cumberland . . .
823.1051
Note.—For his life and writings, *see* **Edinburgh** review, v. 8. April, 1806. p. 107, *in* ** 52.373.—**Foster,** J. Cumberland. 11 pp. (*Crit. essays*, v. 2.) p. 52, *in* 824.117.—**Notes and queries,** 5th ser., v. 11. p. 504, *in* ** 52.678¹.—**Scott,** *Sir* W. Cumberland. 40 pp. (*Misc. works*, v. 3.) p. 191, *in* 920.366.—**Stephen,** L. Dict. of nat. biog., v. 13. ** 923.12¹³.
Cumberland, Stuart C. The rabbi's spell: a Russo-Jewish romance. *in* 823.5097
Cumming, *Lt.-Col.* W. Gordon. Wild men and wild beasts: or, scenes in camp and jungle. 823.6581
Cummins, Maria Susanna. El Fureidîs.
823.354
—— The lamplighter. (Anon.) 823.356
—— Mabel Vaughan. 823.357
Cunningham, Allan. Gowden Gibbie. (Picken, A., *ed. The club-book,* v. 2.)
in 823.702
—— The haunted ships. 22 pp. (Johnson, R., *ed. Little classics,* v. 8.)
p. 128, *in* 829.131
—— The king of the peak. 24 pp. (Johnson, R., *ed. Little classics,* v. 7.)
p. 206, *in* 829.130
—— Lord Roldan. 2 vols. (in 1). 823.5667
Cunningham, H. S. Chronicles of Dustypore: a tale of modern Anglo-Indian society. 823.4190
Same. 823.4375
Cuore: an Italian schoolboy's journal. Amicis, E. de. 808.1657
Cupid and the sphinx. McClellan, *Mrs.* H. (H.) 823.1059
Cupid on crutches. Wood, A. B. 823.1647
Cupples, G: The green hand: adventures of a naval lieutenant. 808.345
Curate and the rector. Strutt, *Mrs.* E..
823.1372
Curate in charge. Oliphant, *Mrs.* M. O. (W.)
823.5950

English Fiction. *Contin.*

Curly: an actor's story. Coleman, J:
823.5062
Curran, J: Elliott. Miss Francis Merley.
823.6957
Curse of Carne's Hold, The. Henty, G: A.
823.7048
Curse of Clifton. Southworth, *Mrs.* E. D. E.
(N.) 823.1483
Curse of Everleigh. Pierce, *Mrs.* H.. C.
823.1261
Curse of gold, The. Stephens, *Mrs.* A. S.
(W.) 823.1964
Curse of Koshiu. Wingfield, L. 823.7192
Curse of the village, The. Conscience, H.
p. 169, *in* 823.5705
Curtis, G: W: My châteaux. 22 pp. (John-
son, R., *ed.* *Little classics*, v. 4.)
p. 160, *in* 829.127
—— Prue and I. 823.358
—— Trumps: a novel. 823.359
Curtis, Laura J. Christine; or, woman's
trials and triumphs. 823.4640
Cut by the county. Maxwell, *Mrs.* M.. E..
(B.) *in* 823.5108
Cuthbertson, *Misses.* Forest of Montalbano.
4 vols. ** 823.6783-6
Cutler, *Mrs.* M.. C. Philip; or, what may
have been: a story of the first century.
823.7248
Cynic fortune. Murray, D: C. *in* 823.5131
Cyrilla. Tautphoeus, J. (M.) *Freiherrin*
von. 823.6439
Czar, The. Alcock, D. 823.5909
Daddy Darwin's dove-cote. 28 pp. Ewing,
Mrs. J. H. (G.) *in* 823.5090
Daddy Jake, the runaway. 56 pp. Harris,
J. C. * 808.1808
Daggett, Rollin Mallory. Braxton's Bar: a
tale of pioneer life in California. 823.4528
Dahlgren, *Mrs.* Madeleine (Vinton). Lights
and shadows of a life. 823.5666
Dahn, Felix. Felicitas. Tr. by M.. J. Saf-
ford. 823.5728
Daisy. 2 vols. (in 1). Warner, S.
823.1674
Daisy Burns. Kavanagh, J. 823.912
Daisy chain, The. Yonge, C.. M..
823.1764
Daisy Thornton. Holmes, *Mrs.* M.. J.. (H.)
823.788
Dalbroom folks, The. 2 vols. Smith, J.
823.6397-8
Dalecarlian conjurer's day-book, The. Chate-
lain, *Mme.* C. (de P.) de. ** 823.6608
Dalton, W: Phaulcon the adventurer; or, the
Europeans in the east: a romantic biog-
raphy. 823.6082
—— Tiger prince; or, adventures in the wilds
of Abyssinia. 808.870
—— White elephant; or, the hunters of Ava
and the king of the Golden Foot. 808.872
—— The wolf boy of China. 808.871
Issued also as John Chinaman.
Daltons, The. Lever, C: J. 823.976
Same. 823.6341
Same. 2 vols. 823.5716-17
Damant, M.. Peggy Thornhill: a tale of the
Irish rebellion. 823.7171

English Fiction. *Contin.*

Damascus. *See also* Syria, *note.*
—— Eddy, D. C. Walter in Damascus.
808.1649
Dame Durden—little woman. Dickens, C: J:
H. 808.1569
Damen's ghost. Bynner, E. L. 823.1841
Damon, Sophie M. Old New-England days:
a story of true life. 823.5379
Damsel of Darien, The. 2 vols. (in 1).
Simms, W: G. ** 823.6729
Danes, The, sketched by themselves. Stories
. . . tr. by Mrs. Bushby. 3 vols.
823.6444-6
Daniel, J. W. The girl in checks; or, the
mystery of the mountain cabin. 823.7249
Daniel Deronda. 2 vols. Cross, *Mrs.* M.. A.
(E.) 823.997-8
Danish fairy legends and tales. Andersen,
H. C. 808.771
Danites in the Sierras. Miller, C. H.
823.4204
Daphne. Booth, *Mrs.* E. M. J. (G.) vou.
823.5783
Dare. Blow, *Mrs.* M.. W. (G.). 823.4299
Darien. 3 vols. Warburton, E. B. G:
823.2048-50
Daring deeds of American heroes. Brayman,
J. O., *ed.* 808.1314
Daring deeds of the old heroes of the revolu-
tion. Watson, H: C. 808.387
Daring fiction, A. 42 pp. Boyesen, H. H.
p. 112, *in* 823.4711
Dark colleen, The. Buchanan, *Mrs.* H. (J.)
823.893
Dark days. Fargus, F: J: 823.4817
Same. 823.4915; *in* 823.5106
Dark house, The. Fenn, G: M. *in* 823.5046
Dark inheritance, A. 99 pp. Hay, M.. C.
in 823.6694
Dark marriage morn, A. Brame, *Mrs.* C.. M.
(L.) 823.5120
Dark marriage morn, A. Marston, O.
823.4771
Dark stories from the sunny south. Camp-
bell, *Sir* G. 823.7242
Darkness and daylight. Holmes, *Mrs.* M..
J.. (H.) 823.789
Darnell, H: Faulkner. The craze of Chris-
tian Engelhart. 823.7001
Same. 823.7037
Darragh, J. T:, *C. C. S., pseud. See* Hale,
E: Everett.
Darrell, Joyce. Winifred Power. *in* 823.5073
Darryll Gap. Townsend, V. F.. 823.1595
Dasent, *Sir* G: Webbe. Popular tales from
the Norse. With an introductory essay on
the origin and diffusion of popular tales.
3d ed. 808.1801
—— The story of Gisli the outlaw: from the
Icelandic. Illus. 823.6448
Daudet, Alphonse. (1840—.) Artists' wives.
Tr. by L. Ensor. 823.6573
    Contents:—Prologue.—Madame Heurtebise.—The
credo of love.—The Transteverina.—A couple of
singers.—A misunderstanding.—Assault with vio-
lence.—Bohemia at home.—Fragments of a
woman's letter found in the rue Notre-Dame-des-
Champs.—A great man's widow.—The deceiver.—
The comtesse Irma.—The confidences of an acad-
emic coat.

English Fiction. *Contin.*
Daudet, Alphonse. *Contin.*
—— La Belle Nivernaise: the story of an old boat and her crew, and other stories. (Tr. by R. Routledge.) Illus. by Montégut.
823.5252
Contents:—La Belle Nivernaise.—The fig and the idler.—My first dress coat.—The three low masses. —The new master.
—— L'évangéliste: a Parisian novel. Tr. by M.. N. Sherwood. 823.5566
—— The immortal; or, one of the "forty." (*L'immortel.*) Tr. by A. W. and M. de G. Verrall. 823.7012
—— Indret.—The vice. (*And*) The machines. (*Extr. from* Jack.) (Zimmern, H.., *and* A. *Half-hours with foreign novelists.*)
in ** 823.6613
—— Jack. Tr. by L. Ensor. 823.6566
—— *Same.* Tr. by M.. N. Sherwood.
in 823.2827; 823.6845
—— The little good-for-nothing. Tr. by M.. N. Sherwood. 823.6846
—— The nabob. Tr. by L. H. Hooper.
823.3189
—— *Same.* 823.6884
—— Numa Roumestan. Tr. by V. Champlin. 823.4289
—— *Same.* 823.5664
—— The partners; or, Fromont, Jr., and Risler, Sr. (*Fromont jeune et Risler aîné.*)
823.5580
Issued also as Sidonie.
—— Port Tarascon: the last adventures of the illustrious Tartarin. Tr. by H: James.
823.6449
—— Robert Helmont: diary of a recluse, 1870–1871. Tr. by L. Ensor. Illus. by Picard and Montégut. 823.6331
—— Sappho: Parisian manners. * 823.5423
—— Sidonie. (*Fromont jeune et Risler aîné.*) Tr. by M.. N. Sherwood. 823.6922
—— *Same.* (*Also*) Jack. Tr. by M.. N. Sherwood. 823.2827
—— Stories of Provence. 823.4958
Contents:—Introduction.—Maître Cornille's secret —The pope's mule.—Mr. Seguin's goat.—The old couple.—The Reverend Father Gaucher's elixir.— The woman of Arles.—Ballads in prose.—The curé of Cucugnan.—The light-house at the Sanguinaires. —The wreck of the "Sémillante."—Legend of the man with gold brains.—Bixiou's pocket-book.—The poet Mistral.—The two inns.—At Millanah.—Homesickness.
—— Tartarin of Tarascon, traveller, "Turk" and lion-hunter. Illus. by Montégut, and others. 823.5253
—— Tartarin on the Alps. Illus. by Rossi, and others. Tr. by H: Frith. 823.5347
—— Wives of men of genius. Tr. by E: Wakefield. 823.6340
Issued also as Artists' wives.
Note. — For life and writings, *see* **James,** H: Partial portraits. p. 195, *in* 824.390.—**Mauris,** M. French men of letters. p. 219, *in* 928.179.—**Montégut,** E. Nouveaus romanciers. 28 pp. (*Rev. d. d. Mondes,* 1876, 3e pér. v. 18.) p. 605, *in* * 54.332. *See also* Poole's Index (to 1882). p. 334, *in* * 50.1; —*Same.* Jan. 1, 1882–Jan. 1, 1887. p. 112, *in* ** 50.1°.
Daudet, Ernest. The apostate. 823.6501
Daughter of an empress, The. Mundt, *Mrs.* C. (M.) 823.5800
Daughter of Bohemia, A. Tiernau, *Mrs.* F.. C. (F.) 823.6359

English Fiction. *Contin.*
Daughter of Eve, A. Kirk, *Mrs.* E. W. (O.)
823.5397
Daughter of Fife, A. Barr, *Mrs.* A. E. (H.)
823.5414
Daughter of Heth. Black, W: 823.80
Daughter of night, The. Fullom, S. W.
823.5926
Daughter of silence. Fawcett, E. 823.5621
Daughter of the Philistines. Boyesen, H. H.
823.4542
Same. 823.5621
Daughter of the stars, and other tales. Fargus, F: J: *in* 823.5094
Daughters of Eve. Meritt, P. 823.7056
Davault's mills. Jones, C: H: 823.904
Davenport Dunn. Lever, C: J. 823.977
Same. 2 vols. 823.5710–11
David Copperfield. Dickens, C: J: H.
823.400
Same. 2 vols. 823.5311–12; 823.6350–51
David Elginbrod. MacDonald, G: 823.1062
David Lloyd's last will. Smith, H.
823.1456
Davidson, Ellis A. The boy joiner and model maker: containing practical instructions for making numerous articles for use and ornament, mechanical toys, models, etc.; with descriptions of various tools and the method of using them. 808.1867
Davis, J. A. The Chinese slave-girl: a story of woman's life in China. 808.836
Davis, L. Clarke. A stranded ship: a story of sea and shore. 823.360
Davis, *Mrs.* R.. Blaine (Harding). Balacchi brothers. 25 pp. (*In* Stories by Amer. authors, v. 1.) p. 120, *in* 823.4702
—— The captain's story. 20 pp. (Johnson, R., *ed.* Little classics, v. 2.)
p. 187, *in* 829.125
—— A faded leaf of history. 20 pp. (Johnson, R., *ed.* Little classics, v. 10.)
p. 201, *in* 829.133
—— John Andross. 823.361
—— Margret Howth: a story of to-day.
823.4257
—— Waiting for the verdict. 823.5857
Davis, Robert S. [*Trebor.*] As it may happen: a story of American life and character. 823.363
Dawes, Rufus. Nix's mate: an historical romance of America. 2 vols. (in 1).
** 823.6236
Dawn. Haggard, H: R. *in* 823.5072
Same. 823.7155
Day, *Rev.* Lal Behari. Folk-tales of Bengal.
808.1694
Day and night stories. Sullivan, T: R.
823.7026
Day of fate, A. Roe, *Rev.* E: P. 823.2341
Day will come, The. Maxwell, *Mrs.* M.. E.. (B.) 823.7198
Days of Bruce. 2 vols. (in 1). Aguilar, G.
823.5398
Same. 2 vols. 823.5-6
Days of my life, The. Oliphant, *Mrs.* M. O. (W.) 823.5027
Days of yore. 2 vols. Keddie, H.
823.924-5

English Fiction. *Contin.*
Dethroned heiress, The. Depuy, E. A.
823.493
Detlef, K:, *pseud. See* Bauer, Klara.
Detmold. Bishop, W: H: 823.5698
De Vere. Ward, R. P.   823.4054
Devereux. Lytton, E: G: E. L. Bulwer-
823.1025
Same. 2 vols.   ** 823.6257-8
Devil-puzzlers, and other sketches. Perkins,
F: B.   823.4500
Devil's chain, The. Jenkins, E: 823.899
Devil's Ford. Harte, F. B.
p. 169, *in* 823.5152
Devil's ward, The. 13 pp. Mackay, W:
in 823.5084
Same.   *in* 823.5089
Devon boys. Fenn, G: M.   808.1713
Dialect tales. McDowall, *Mrs.* K.. S. (B.)
823.6121
Dialogues. Abbott, J. Dialogues for the
amusement and instruction of young per-
sons. (*In his* Harper's story books, v. 8.)
in 808.587
Note.—See also Catalogues of this Library.
No. 3, 1882, p. 52.   No. 4, 1884, p. 80.
Diamond button, The. North, B.   823.6956
Diamond cut diamond. Trollope, T: A.
in 823.5073
Diamond necklace.
Note.—See Carlyle, T: The diamond necklace.
(*In his* Crit. and miscel. essays, v. 3.) p. 1, *in* 824.401.
—Vizetelly, H. The story of the diamond neck-
lace. 944.424.
Diana. Warner, S.   823.1675
Diana Carew. Bridges, *Mrs. Col.* —.
823.583
Same.   *in* 823.5016
Diana, Lady Lyle. 3 vols. Dixon, W: H.
823.4555-7
Diana of the cross ways. Meredith, G:
in 823.5060
Diana's livery. McGlasson, E. W.   823.7397
Diane Coryval.   823.4673
Diary, A. Bremer, F.   823.2120
Same.   p. 9, *in* 823.6108
Diary of a superfluous man. 68 pp. Turge-
nef, I. S.   p. 63, *in* 823.4740
Diary of a woman. Feuillet, O.   823.4234
Diary of an old doctor. Maitland, J. A.
823.1082
Diary of Kitty Trevylyan. Charles, *Mrs.* E..
(R.)   823.206
Diary on the continent. Marryat, *Capt.* F:
in 823.1107
Diavolo. 2 pts. Maxwell, *Mrs.* M.. E.. (B.)
in 823.5119
Dick Netherby. Walford, *Mrs.* L. B. (C.)
823.4320
Dick o' the fens. Fenn, G: M.   808.1444
Dick Onslow among the redskins, Adventures
of. Kingston, W: H: G.   808.1554
Dick Rodney. Grant, J.   823.624
Dick Sand. Verne, J.   *in* 823.5129
Same.   *in* 823.2855; 823.6300
Dick, the door-boy. 39 pp. Greene, H.
p. 191, *in* 808.1357
Dickens, C: J: Huffam. [*Boz.*] (1812-1870.)
Additional Christmas stories. (*With his*
The uncommercial traveller. *in* 823.5321

English Fiction. *Contin.*
Dickens, C: J: Huffam. [*Boz.*] *Contin.*
—— The adventures of Oliver Twist.
823.5300
—— *Same.*   823.6352
—— Barnaby Rudge: a tale of the riots of
'eighty.   823.5551
—— *Same.* (*And*) Hard times.   823.5336
—— *Same.* 2 vols.   823.5303-4
—— *Same.* (*And*) Mystery of Edwin Drood.
823.384
—— *Same.* (*And*) Sketches. Pt. 2. 4 vols.
(in 1).   823.385
Contents:— Barnaby Rudge. — Sketches. Pt. 2,
(*viz.:* Characters: The dancing academy.—Shabby-
genteel people. — Making a night of it. — The
prisoners' van.—Tales: The boarding-house.—Mr.
Minns and his cousin.—Sentiment.—The Tuggs's
at Ramsgate.—Horatio Sparkins.—The black veil.
—The steam excursion.—The great Winglebury
duel.—Mrs. Joseph Porter.—A passage in the life of
Mr. Watkins Tottle.—The Bloomsbury christening.
—The drunkard's death.)
—— Bleak House.   823.390
—— *Same.* 2 vols.   823.5313-14
—— Boots at the Holly-Tree inn. 20 pp.
(*In* Half-hours with great story tellers.)
p. 80, *in* 823.5478
—— Child-pictures from Dickens. 808.1914
Contents:— Little Nell.—The marchioness.—Paul
and Florence.—The fat boy.—Tiny Tim.—Smike.—
Oliver Twist.
—— A child's dream of a star. 4 pp. (John-
son, R., *ed. Little classics,* v. 10.)
p. 223, *in* 829.133
—— A child's history of England. (*Also*) A
holiday romance, and other pieces, (*viz.:*
George Silverman's explanation.—Sketches
of young couples.)   808.686
—— *Same.*   942.1259
—— Chops, the dwarf. 16 pp. (Johnson, R.,
ed. Little classics, v. 2.)
p. 118, *in* 829.125
—— Christmas books.   823.5307
Contents:— Introd. — Christmas carol. — The
chimes.—The cricket on the hearth.—Battle of life.
—The haunted man.
—— *Same.* (*Also*) A tale of two cities.
(*And*) A message from the sea.   823.5557
—— *Same.* (*Also*) The uncommercial trav-
eller.   823.5333
Contents:— Christmas books, (*viz.:* The seven
poor travellers. — The Holly Tree. — The wreck of
the Golden Mary.—The perils of certain English
prisoners.—Going into society.—The haunted house.
—A message from the sea.—Tom Tiddler's ground.
—Somebody's luggage.—Mrs. Lirriper's lodgings.—
Mrs. Lirriper's legacy.—Doctor Marigold.—Two
ghost stories.—Mugby Junction.)—The uncommer-
cial traveller.—*Also* (No thoroughfare. By Dickens,
C: J: H., *and* Collins, W: W.)
—— *Same.* (*And*) Reprinted pieces.
823.394
*Contents:—*Christmas stories, (*viz.:* A Christmas
carol.—The chimes.—The cricket on the hearth.—
The battle of life.)
Additional Christmas stories, (*viz.:* The haunted
man.—Somebody's luggage.—Mrs. Lirriper's lodgings.—Mrs. Lirriper's legacy.—Doctor Marigold.—
Two ghost stories.—The boy at Mugby.—The seven
poor travellers.)
Reprinted pieces, (*viz.:* The long voyage.—The
begging-letter writer.—A child's dream of a star.—
Our English watering-place.—Our French watering-place.—Bill-sticking.—"Births. Mrs. Meek, of
a son."—Lying awake.—Poor relation's story.
—The child's story.—The school-boy's story.—Nobody's story.—The ghost of art.—Out of town.—Out
of the season.—A poor man's tale of a patent.—The

English Fiction. *Contin.*
Dickens, C: J: Huffam. [*Boz.*] *Contin.*
—— Christmas books. (*And*) Reprinted pieces. *Contin.*
  Contents. Contin.
  noble savage.—A flight.—The detective police.—
  Three "detective" anecdotes.—On duty with In-
  spector Field.—Down with the tide.—A walk in a
  workhouse.—Prince Bull: a fairy tale.—A plated
  article.—Our honorable friend.—Our school.—Our
  friend.—Our vestry.—Our bore.—A monument of
  French folly.—A Christmas tree.) .
—— A Christmas carol. 44 pp. (Johnson, R., *ed.* *Little classics*, v. 5.)
               p. 7, *in* 829.128
—— Christmas stories. (*Also*) Great expectations.   823.5332
  Contents:—Christmas stories, (*viz.:* A Christmas
  carol.—The chimes.—The cricket on the hearth.—
  The battle of life.— The haunted man.)—Great
  expectations.
—— *Same.* (*Also*) Pictures from Italy, and American notes. 4 vols. (in 1). 823.395
—— David Copperfield, Personal history of. 2 vols.   823.5311-12
—— *Same.* .   823.5559-60; 823.6350-51
—— Dickens' Little folks.   808.1569
  Contents:— Dame Durden—little woman, from
  Bleak House.—Smike, from Nicholas Nickleby.—
  The two daughters, from Martin Chuzzlewit.
—— *Same.*   808.1570
  Contents:—Florence Dombey, from Dombey and
  Son.—Oliver, and the Jew Fagin, from Oliver Twist.
  —The boy Joe and Samuel Weller, from Pickwick
  papers.
—— *Same.*   808.1571
  Contents:—Little Nell, from The old curiosity shop.
  —Dolly Varden, the little coquette, from Barnaby
  Rudge.—Tiny Tim ; Dot and the fairy cricket, from
  the Christmas stories.
—— Dombey and Son.   823.406
—— *Same.*   823.5849
—— *Same.* 2 vols.   823.5308-9
—— Great expectations.   823.409
—— *Same.*   823.5318
—— *Same.* (*Also*) Pictures from Italy. (*And*) American notes.   823.4968
—— Hard times.   *in* 823.414
—— *Same.*   *in* 823.5304; *in* 823.5336
—— *Same.* (*And*) Reprinted pieces. 823.4750
  Contents:—Hard times.—Reprinted pieces, (*viz.:*
  Child's story.—Detective police.—Down with the
  tide.—A flight.—Ghost of art.— Lying awake.—
  Monument of French folly.— Noble savage.— No-
  body's story.— On duty with Inspector Field.—
  Our bore.—Our honorable friend.—Our school.—
  Our vestry.—Out of the season.—Out of town.—
  Plated article.—Poor man's tale of a patent.—Poor
  relation's story.—Prince Bull.—School-boy's story.
  —Three detective anecdotes.—Walk in a workhouse.)
—— *Same.* 2 vols.   823.411-12
  vols. 1-2.—Hard times.
  v. 2.—Reprinted pieces.
—— A holiday romance, and other pieces. (*With his* A child's history of England.)
               in 808.686
—— *Same.*   *in* 942.1259
—— The life and adventures of Martin Chuzzlewit. 2 vols. (in 1). 823.424
—— *Same.*   823.5848
—— *Same.* 2 vols.   823.5305-6
—— Life and adventures of Nicholas Nickleby. 2 vols. 823.437-7½
—— *Same.*   823.5298-9
—— *Same.* 4 vols.   823.433-6
—— Little Dorrit.   823.419
—— *Same.* 2 vols.   823.5315-16

English Fiction. *Contin.*
Dickens, C: J: Huffam. [*Boz.*] *Contin.*
—— Martin Chuzzlewit, Life and adventures of. 2 vols. (in 1).   823.424
—— *Same.*   823.5848
—— *Same.* 2 vols.   823.5305-6
—— *Same.* 4 vols.   823.420-423
—— Master Humphrey's clock. 823.425
—— *Same.*   *in* 823.5554
—— Miscellanies. (*With his* Old curiosity shop.)   *in* 823.5554
  For contents, *see forward under* Old curiosity shop.
—— Mudfog papers.   823.4046
  Contents:—Public life of Mr. Tulrumble, once
  mayor of Mudfog.—Full report of the first meeting
  of the Mudfog Association for the Advancement
  of Everything.—The pantomime of life.—Some
  particulars concerning a lion.—Mr. Robert Bolton,
  the "gentleman connected with the press."
—— Mystery of Edwin Drood.   823.384
—— *Same.*   *in* 823.432
—— *Same,* and other stories. 823.5323
  Contents:— Mystery of Edwin Drood.— Master
  Humphrey's clock. — Hunted down.— A message
  from the sea. — Full report of the first meeting of
  the Mudfog Assoc. for the Advancement of Every-
  thing.
—— *Same,* and other stories. (*With his* Pictures from Italy . . .) *in* 823.5331
—— *Same.* (*Also*) Pt. II, by T: P. James.
              823.6122
—— New Christmas stories. (*With his* The uncommercial traveller.) *in* 823.426
—— Nicholas Nickleby.   823.5553
—— *Same.* 2 vols.   823.437-7½
—— *Same.*   823.5298-9
—— *Same.* 4 vols.   823.433-6
—— Old curiosity shop.—Master Humphrey's clock.—(*And*) Miscellanies. 823.5554
  Contents:— Old Curiosity Shop.— Master Hum-
  phrey's clock.—Miscellanies, (*viz.:* On duty with
  Inspector Field.—Down with the tide.—A walk in
  a workhouse.—Prince Bull: a fairy tale.—A plated
  article.—Our honorable friend.—Our school.—Our
  vestry.—Our bore.—Hunted down.—Mudfog Association: First meeting.—Mudfog Association: Second
  meeting.—The Holly-Tree inn.—A Christmas tree.)
—— *Same.* (*And*) Reprinted pieces. 2 vols. (in 1).   823.6585
  Contents: — Old curiosity shop. — Master Humphrey's clock. — Miscellanies. — Reprinted pieces,
  (*viz.:* The long voyage. — The begging-letter
  writer.—A child's dream of a star.—Our English
  watering-place.—Our French watering-place.—Bill-
  sticking.—"Births. Mrs. Meek, of a son."—Child's
  story.—Detective police.—Down with the tide.—A
  flight.—Ghost of art.—Lying awake.—Monument of
  French folly.—Noble savage.—Nobody's story.—On
  duty with Inspector Field.—Our bore.—Our honorable friend.—Our school.—Our vestry.—Out of the
  season.—Out of town.—Plated article.—Poor man's
  tale of a patent.—Poor relation's story.—Prince
  Bull.—School-boy's story.—Three "detective" anecdotes.—Walk in a workhouse.—A Christmas tree.)
—— *Same.* 2 vols.   823.5301-2
—— Oliver Twist. 2 vols. (in 1).
              ** 823.5300
—— *Same.*   823.6352 ; 823.6756
—— *Same.* (*And*) A child's history of England.   823.5334
—— *Same.* (*And*) Great expectations. 4 vols. (in 1).   823.6935
—— *Same.* (*Also*) Uncommercial traveller. (*And*) Short Christmas stories, (*viz.:* Some-body's luggage.—Mrs. Lirriper's lodgings. —Mrs. Lirriper's legacy.—Doctor Marigold. —Two ghost stories.)   823.5555

English Fiction. *Contin.*
Dickens, C: J: Huffam. [*Boz.*] *Contin.*
— Our mutual friend. 2 vols. (in 1).
823.1858
— *Same.* 823.5171; 823.5552
— *Same.* 2 vols. 823.6342-3
— *Same.* 823.5319-20
— *Same.* 4 vols. 823.427-30
— The personal history of David Copper-
field. 2 vols. 823.5559-60
— *Same.* 823.6350-51
— Pickwick club, Posthumous papers of
the. 823.5173
— *Same.* 823.5556; 823.5677
— *Same.* 2 vols. 823.449-9²
— *Same.* 823.5296-7
— Pickwick papers. 4 vols. 823.445-8
— Pictures from Italy, and American
notes for general circulation. (*Also*) Mys-
tery of Edwin Drood, and other stories,(*viz.:*
Master Humphrey's clock.—Hunted down.
—Holiday romance.—George Silverman's
explanation.) 823.5331
— Posthumous papers of the Pickwick
club. 823.5173
— *Same.* 823.5556; 823.5677
— *Same.* 2 vols. 823.449-9²
— Readings condensed by himself. 823.1832
Contents:—A Christmas carol.—Bardell and Pick-
wick.—David Copperfield.—Mr. Bob Sawyer's
party.—Story of Little Dombey.—Nicholas Nick-
leby (at the Yorkshire school).—Boots at the Holly-
Tree inn.—Dr.Marigold.—Nicholas Nickleby.—[Short
reading.]—Mrs. Gamp.
— Reprinted pieces. (*With his* Christmas
books.) *in* 823.394
— *Same.* (*With his* Hard Times.)
in 823.4750
— *Same.* (*With his* Old curiosity shop.)
in 823.6585
— *Same.* *in* 823.5302
— *Same.* (*With his* A tale of two cities.)
in 823.414
— *Same.* (*Also*) Sketches by Boz illustra-
tive of every-day life and every-day people.
v. I. 823.4957
— Short Christmas stories. (*With his*
Oliver Twist.) *in* 823.5555
For contents, *see before under* Oliver Twist.
— The signal-man. 19 pp. (Johnson, R.,
ed. Little classics, v. 8.)
p. 109, *in* 829.131
— Sketches by Boz. 823.5324
Contents:—Seven sketches from our parish.—
Scenes.—Characters.—Tales.
— *Same.* *in* 823.4957
— *Same.* Pt. 2. (*With his* Barnaby
Rudge.) *in* 823.385
For contents, *see before under* Barnaby Rudge.
— Tale of two cities. 823.5317
— *Same.* Hard times for these times.
(*Also*) Reprinted pieces. 823.414
— Uncommercial traveller. (*With his*
Oliver Twist.) *in* 823.5555
— *Same,* and additional Christmas stories.
823.5321
— *Same.* (*And*) New Christmas stories.
(*Also*) Master Humphrey's clock.—Gen-
eral index of characters and their appear-
ances, familiar sayings from Dickens's
works. 823.426

English Fiction. *Contin.*
Dickens, C: J: Huffam. [*Boz.*] *Contin.*
—, *and* Collins, W: W. No thoroughfare.
in 823.6689
— *Same.* p. 470, *in* 823.5333
—, *and others.* Christmas stories. 823.452
Contents:—The haunted house.—A message from
the sea.—Tom Tiddler's ground.

— The Charles Dickens parlor album of
illustrations [selected]; chronologically
arranged . . . with a table of contents, including the artists' names. 823.1799
Contents:—Sketches by Boz.—The Pickwick
papers.—Oliver Twist.—Nicholas Nickleby.—Old
curiosity shop.—Barnaby Rudge.—Christmas stories.—Martin Chuzzlewit.—Dombey and Son.—
David Copperfield.—Bleak House.—Little Dorrit.—
Tale of two cities.—Our mutual friend.
— Pierce, G. A., *and* Wheeler, W. A. The
Dickens dictionary: a key to the characters
and principal incidents in the tales of
Charles Dickens. 823.5325
Note.—For his life and writings, *see* Bagehot, W.
Literary studies. 40 pp. (*Works*,v.2.) p. 239,*in* 814.23.
—Bibliography. Johnson,C.P. Hints to collectors
of original editions of the works of Charles Dickens.
1885. ** 10.10.—Brunetière, E. Revue littéraire.
11 pp. (*Rev.d.d.Mondes*, 3e pér., v. 92. 1888.) p.695,
in * 54.399³.—Dickens, C: Letters, 1833-1870. 3
vols. 1879-81. 826.7-8-8a.—Drake, S: A. Our
great benefactors. p. 102, *in* * 920.312.—Fields, J.
T. Dickens. 126 pp. (*In his* Yesterdays with
authors.) p. 125, *in* 928.76.—Forster, J: Life of
Charles Dickens. 3 vols. 1872-4. 928.50-2.—Hale,
E: E. Lights of two centuries. 1887. p. 269, *in* *
920.314.—Horne, R. H. (*In his* New spirit of the
age. 1844.) p. 9, *in* 928.77.—Jeaffreson, J: C.
Charles Dickens. 32 pp. (*In his* Novels, *etc.*, v. 2.)
p. 303, *in* 820.187.—Foe, E. A. C: Dickens. 17 pp.
(*Select works.*) p. 600, *in* 829.406.—Ward, A. W:
(Memoir of Charles) Dickens. 1882. 928.422.—
Whipple, E. P. The genius of D. (*In his* Success
. . .) 1877. p. 250, *in* 829.272;—Novels and novel-
ists. C: Dickens. (*In his* Literature . . .) 1871.
p. 42, *in* 829.275.
See also references in Allibone's Dictionary. v. 1.
** 803.6.—Index to Harper's monthly. ** 51.475.—
Poole's Index (to 1882). pp. 349-51, *in* ** 50.1;—
Same. Jan. 1, 1882-Jan. 1, 1887. p. 118,*in* ** 50.1².
—Stephen, L. Dict. of nat. biog., v. 15. ** 920.-
330¹ᵃ.—Taine, H. A. Eng. lit., v. 3. 820.58,—
Thomas. Lippincott's Dictionary. ** 920.1.
Dickens, M.. Angela. A mist of error.
823.7228
Dickens' Little folks. *See* Dickens, C: J: H.
Dickins, F. Victor, *tr.* The old bamboo-
hewer's story: the earliest of the Japanese
romances, written in the tenth century.
With analytical notes and vocabulary.
Illus. * 823.6430
Dickory Cronke. De Foe, D. *in* 823.2123
Dick's wanderings. Sturgis, J. R.
in 823.6700
Did she love him? Grant, J. 823.625
Digby Grand. Melville, G: J: Whyte-
** 823.4671
Same. 823.7275
Digging for gold. Ballantyne, R. M.
808.1285
Dikes and ditches. Adams, W: T. 808.488
Dillwyn, E. A. Jill and Jack. 823.6909
Dimitri Roudine. Turgenef, I. S. 823.7066
Dingelstedt, Franz, *Freiherr* von. The ama-
zon. Tr. by J. M. Hart. 823.6825
Dinna forget. Stannard, *Mrs.* H. E. V. (P.)
823.7068
Dinner-party. 48 pp. Eddy, J:
p. 92, *in* 823 4703

English Fiction. *Contin.*

Diothas, The. Thiusen, I. 823.4596
Discarded daughter, The. Southworth, *Mrs.*
E. D. E. (N.) 823.1485
Discoveries. Hale, E: E. Stories of discovery, told by discoverers. 808.1369
Disk, The. Robinson, E: A., *and* Wall, G: A. 823.4727
Disowned, The. Lytton, E: G: E. L. Bulwer- 823.1026
Same. 823.6337
Disraeli, B:, *Earl of Beaconsfield.* (1804–1881.) Alroy. (*Also*) Ixion in heaven.— The infernal marriage. (*And*) Popanilla. 823.458
—— Coningsby; or, the new generation. 823.459
—— *Same.* *in* 823.3002
—— Contarini Fleming: a psychological autobiography. 2 vols. ** 823.6737–8
—— *Same.* (*With his* Endymion.) *in* 823.2314
—— *Same.* (*And*) The rise of Iskander. 823.460
—— Endymion. 823.2313
—— *Same.* 823.6157
—— *Same.* (*Also*) Contarini Fleming. 823.2314
—— Henrietta Temple: a love story. 823.461
—— *Same.* *in* 823.3002
—— The infernal marriage. (*With his* Alroy.) *in* 823.458
—— Ixion in heaven. (*With his* Alroy.) *in* 823.458
—— Lothair. 823.464
—— *Same.* (*Also*) The young duke. 823.2751
—— Miriam Alroy. (*Also*) Henrietta Temple. (*And*) Coningsby. 823.3002
—— Novels and tales. v. 6. Venetia. 823.469
—— Popanilla. (*With his* Alroy.) *in* 823.458
—— The rise of Iskander. (*With his* Contarini Fleming.) *in* 823.460
—— *Same.* 98 pp. (Johnson, R., *ed. Little classics,* v. 6.) p. 137, *in* 829.129
—— Sybil; or, the two nations. 823.466
—— *Same.* (*Also*) Venetia. 823.3230
—— Tancred; or, the new crusade. 823.467
—— Venetia. 823.469
—— *Same.* (*With his* Sybil.) *in* 823.3230
—— Vivian Gray. 2 vols. (in 1). 823.470
—— The young duke. 2 vols. (in 1). 823.468
—— *Same.* *in* 823.2751
Note.—For his life and writings, *see* Bagehot, W. Mr. Disraeli as a member of the House of Commons. 5 pp. (*Works,* v. 3.) p. 446, 814.24.—**Bibliography.** (*In* Lit. world, Apr. 23, 1881.) ** 805.660.—**Cucheval-Clarigny,** A. Lord Beaconsfield et son temps. 112 pp. (*Rev. d. d. Mondes,* 1879. v. 35.) pp. 481, 787; v. 36, p. 129, *in* ** 54.349–50.—Life of the Right Honorable Benjamin Disraeli . . . 14 pp. 1878. 923.786.—**Froude,** J. A. Lord Beaconsfield. 1890. 923.2017.—**Greg,** W. R. The great twin brethren. 12 pp. (*In his* Miscel. essays.) p. 149, *in* 824.284.—**Higginson,** T: W. Disraeli. 36 pp. (*In his* English statesmen.) p. 35, *in* 923.90.—**Jeaffreson,** J: C. The Right Hon. Benjamin Disraeli. 42 pp. (*In his* Novels, *etc.,* v. 2.) p. 221, *in* 820.187.—Political adventures of Lord Beaconsfield. 923.62.—Shep-

---

English Fiction. *Contin.*

Disraeli, B:, *Earl of Beaconsfield.* *Contin.*
Note. Contin.
hard, W: Benjamin Disraeli, Lord Beaconsfield. 79 pp. (*In his* Pen pictures, *etc.*) 1884. p. 87, *in* 820.158.—Smiles, S: Brief biographies. 1877. p. 222, *in* 923.841.—Stephen, L. Dict. of nat. biog. v. 15. p. 101, *in* ** 920.330[12];—Mr. Disraeli's novels. 49 pp. (*In his* Hours in a lib., 2d. ser.) p. 344, *in* 824.320.—Towle, G: M. Beaconsfield. 30 pp. (*In his* Certain men of mark.) 1880. p. 95, *in* 923.777. *See also* Poole's Index (to 1882). pp. 354–5, *in* ** 50.1;—*Same.* Jan. 1, 1882–Jan. 1, 1887. p. 119, *in* ** 50.1².

Dissolving views. Lang, *Mrs.* A. 823.5049
Same. 823.5050
Disturbing element, The. Yonge, C.. M.. 823.5637
Dita. Majendie, *Lady* M. E.. 823.1089
Same. 823.5037
Divided lives. Fawcett, E. 823.5573
Dixon, *Mrs.* (—.) [*Emma Leslie.*] Cecily: a tale of the English reformation. 808.1210
—— Elfreda: a sequel to Leofwine. 808.1207
—— Leofwine the Saxon: a story of hopes and struggles. 808.1209
—— Walter: a tale of the times of Wesley. 808.1187
Dixon, *Rev.* J. Broken columns. (Anon.) 823.215
Dixon, W: Hepworth. Diana, Lady Lyle. 3d ed. 3 vols. 823.4555–7
—— Ruby Grey. 3 vols. 823.4552–4
Djambek the Georgian. Suttner, A. G. von. 823.7049
Dmitri. Bain, F. W. 823.7355
Doctor Basilius. Dumas, A. D. 823.7346
Doctor Breen's practice. Howells, W: D. 823.4279
Dr. Caldwell. Roe, E: R. 823.7412
Doctor Claudius. Crawford, F. M. 823.4851
Doctor Glennie's daughter. Farjeon, B: L. 823.7373
Dr. Goethe's courtship. S., V. 823.4249
Doctor Grimshawe's secret. Hawthorne, N. 823.4551
Dr. Heidenhoff's process. Bellamy, E: 823.7361
Doctor Hildreth. White, A. L. 823.1940
Doctor Jacob. Edwards, M. B. Betham- 823.4099
Same. 823.5055; *in* 823.5068
Doctor Johns. 2 vols. Mitchell, D. G. 823.1161–2
Dr. Le Baron and his daughters. Austin, *Mrs.* J.. (G.) 823.7360
Dr. Rameau. Ohnet, G. 823.7075
Dr. Sevier. Cable, G: W. 823.4863
Doctor Thorne. Trollope, A. 823.1607
Same. *in* 823.6262
Doctor Vandyke. Cooke, J: E. 823.5830
Dr. Wainwright's patient. Yates, E. H. 823.5890
Doctor Zay. Ward, *Mrs.* E.. S. (P.) 823.4487
Doctor's daughter. Clarke, R.. S. 823.235
Doctor's wife. Maxwell, *Mrs.* M.. E.. (B.) 823.2408
Same. 823.4977
Documents in the case. 50 pp. Matthews, J. B., *and* Bunner, H: C. p. 31, *in* 823.4702
Dodd, *Mrs.* Anna Bowman (Blake). Glorinda: a story. 823.5456

English Fiction. *Contin.*
Dodd family abroad. Lever, C: J. 823.979
 Same. 2 vols. 823.5718-19
Dodge, M.. Abigail. [*Gail Hamilton.*] First
 love is best: a sentimental sketch. 823.694
—— Gala-days. 823.1794
  Contents:—Gala days.—A call to my country-
  women.—A spasm of sense.—Camilla's concert.—
  Cheri.—Side-glances at Harvard class-day.—Suc-
  cess in life.—Happiest days.
Dodge, *Mrs.* M.. E.. (Mapes). Hans Brinker:
 a story of life in Holland. 808.1417
—— Theophilus, and others. 823.4075
—— *Same.* 823.5665
Dodge, N. S. Stories of American history.
  808.1675
Dodgson, *Rev.* C: Lutwidge. [*Lewis Carroll.*]
 Alice's adventures in Wonderland.
  808.688
—— Sylvie and Bruno. 808.1553
—— A tangled tale. 823.4925
—— Through the looking-glass, and what
 Alice found there. 808.687
Doe, C: II: Buffets. 823.6100
Dog Crusoe. Ballantyne, R. M. 808.207
Dog fiend, The. Marryat, *Capt.* F: 823.1096
 Same. ** 823.6674
Doing and dreaming. Mayo, *Mrs.* I.. (F.)
  823.1139
Doings of the Bodley family in town and
 country. Scudder, H. E. 808.1855
Dole, Nathan Haskell. Young folks' history
 of Russia. 947.46
Dollars and cents. Warner, A.. B. 823.1672
Dolliver romance. Hawthorne, N. *in* 823.727
 Same, and other pieces. 823.4083
Dolly Varden, the little coquette. Dickens,
 C: J: H. *in* 808.1571
Dolores. Bridges, *Mrs. Col.* —. 823.2451
 Same. *in* 823.5118
Dombey and Son. Dickens, C: J: H.
  823.406
 Same. 823.5849
 Same. 2 vols. 823.5308-9
Don Gesualdo. La Ramée, L. de.
  p. 217, *in* 823.5747
Don John. Ingelow, J. 823.3426
Don Quixote, Adventures of. Cervantes
 Saavedra, M. de. 823.6896
 Same. 823.6897
 Same. 4 vols. 823.5235-8; 823.6899-902
Donal Grant. MacDonald, G: *in* 823.5043
Donnelly, Ignatius. [*Edmund Boisgilbert.*]
 Cæsar's column: a story of the twentieth
 century. 823.6432
Donnet, *Mme.* Léonie. The notary's daugh-
 ter. Tr. by Lady G. Fullerton. 823.6912
Donovan. Bayly, A. E. 823.6968
Doom! 85 pp. McCarthy, J. H. *in* 823.5105
Doomed city. Crake, A. D. 823.7120
Dora Deane. Holmes, *Mrs.* M.. J.. (H.)
  823.790
Dora Thorne. Brame, *Mrs.* C.. M. (L.)
  823.5063
Doris's fortune. James, *Mrs.* F. A. (P.)
  in 823.5015
Dorothea; or, a ray of the new light. 3 vols.
 (Anon.) ** 823.6725-7
Dorothy Forster. Besant, W. *in* 823.5039
Dorothy Fox. Parr, *Mrs.* L.. (T.) 823.5942

English Fiction. *Contin.*
Dorothy's venture. Hay, M.. C. 823.3146
 Same. 823.5063
Dorothy's vocation. Green, E. E. 823.7377
Dorr, *Mrs.* Julia Caroline (Ripley). Sibyl
 Huntington. 823.472
Dorsey, *Mrs.* A.. (Hauson). Conscience: an
 American Catholic tale. 2 vols. (in 1).
  823.473
—— The oriental pearl; or, the Catholic emi-
 grants. 823.474
—— Tangled paths. 823.475
Dostoyevsky, Feódor Mikhailovitch. Crime
 and punishment: a Russian realistic novel.
  823.5476
Dot and the fairy cricket. Dickens, C: J: H.
  808.1571
Double family,. A. Balzac, H. de.
  p. 59, *in* 823.4256
Double story, A. MacDonald, G: 823.1063
Double wedding. Warfield, *Mrs.* C. A. (W.)
  823.1655
Double wedding at Dunderviksborg.
 Zedritz, K: E: p. 31, *in* 823.6534
Doubleday, T: The murderer's last night.
 22 pp. (*In* Tales from Blackwood, v. 7.)
  in ** 823.6653
Doubleday's children. Cook, D. 823.1805
Doubly false. Stephens, *Mrs.* A. S. (W.)
  823.1966
Doubtful gentleman, A, *pseud.* *See* Paulding,
 James Kirke.
Doudney, S.. Miss Tweed's ghost story. 10
 pp. (*In* Twenty novelettes . . .)
  p. 205, *in* 823.7183
—— Prudence Winterburn. 808.1631
Douglas, Amanda Minnie. Claudia.
  823.476
—— Hope mills; or, between friend and
 sweetheart. 823.479
—— Home nook; or, the crown of duty.
  823.478
—— In trust; or, Dr. Bertrand's household.
  823.480
—— Lost in a great city. 823.4164
—— Lucia: her problem. 823.481
—— Nelly Kinnard's kingdom. 823.482
—— The old woman who lived in a shoe.
  823.4501
 Issued also as There's no place like home.
—— Out of the wreck; or, was it a victory?
  823.4871
—— Seven daughters. 823.483
—— Stephen Dane. 823.484
—— Sydnie Adriance; or, trying the world.
  823.485
—— Whom Kathie married. 823.4502
Douglas, Edith, *pseud.* *See* Burnham, *Mrs.*
 C. L. (Root).
Douglas, Marian, *pseud.* *See* Robinson, *Mrs.*
 A. D. (G.)
Douglas Duane. Fawcett, E. *in* 823.5571
Douglass, *Mrs.* R. Dun. A romance at the
 antipodes. 823.7038
Dove in the eagle's nest. Yonge, C.. M..
  823.1765
Down south. Adams, W: T. 808.893
Down the ravine. Murfree, M.. N. 808.1343
Down the Rhine. Adams, W: T. 808.489

English Fiction. *Contin.*
Down the west branch. Farrar, C: A. J.
    808.1731
Down-easters, The. Neal, J: ** 823.6237-8
Downward path, The. Gaboriau, E.
    823.5907
 Same.   823.6174
Dowson, *Prof.* J:, *tr.* Ikhwánu-s Safá; or, brothers iu purity. From the Hindustáni.
    * 823.1854
Doyle, A. Conan. The captain of the Pole-star, and other tales. 823.6410
Dragomonov, Michael. [*Stepniak.*] A female Nihilist. 823.6188
Dragon and the raven, The. Henty, G: A.
    808.1480
Dragon of the north. Oswald, E. J.
    823.7086
Dragon's teeth. Queiros, E. de. 823.5471
Drake, *Sir* Francis. (1540-1596.)
—— Corbett, J. For God aud gold. (Drake's 3d voyage.) 823.5650
—— *Same.*   823.6907
—— Henty, G: A. Under Drake's flag.
    808.1487
—— Towle, G: M. Drake, the sea-king of Devon. 808.1144
 Note.—For his life and voyages, *see* **Barrow,** *Sir* J. Life, voyages, and exploits of Drake. 1864. 910.630. — **Johnson,** S: Sir F. Drake. 25 pp. (*Works.*) p.466, *in* 829.123.—**Leng,** R. Sir F. Drake's service against the Spaniards. 1587. (*Camden Soc.,* No. 87.) *in* * 942.1057.—**Lodge,** E. Portraits. v. 2. p. 237, *in* * 920.186.—**Stillman,** J. D. B. Did Drake discover San Francisco bay? 6 pp. (*Overl'd mo.,* v. 1. 1868.) p. 332, *in* ** 51.200.—**Winsor,** J. Narr. and crit. hist. of America. 8 vols. (*See* Index, v. 8.) * 970.127-127*.
 See also **Poole's** Index (to 1882). pp. 362, *in* ** 50.1;—*Same.* Jan. 1, 1882-Jan. 1, 1887. p. 122, *in* ** 50.1*.
Drake, the sea-king of Devon. Towle, G: M.
    808.1144
Drawn game, A. King, R: A. 823.4833
 Same,   *in* 823.5062
Drayton. Shreve, T: H. 823.4266
Draytons and Davenants. Charles, *Mrs.* E.. (R.)   823.207
Dreadful temptation, A. Miller, *Mrs.* A. McV.   823.7057
Dream and a forgetting, A. Hawthorne, J. C.   823.5443
Dream children. Scudder, H. E. 808.1560
Dream life. Mitchell, D. G. 823.5290
Dreamer, A. Wylde, K.. 823.4043
Dreamer of dreams, A. Nicholson, J. S.
    823.5501
Dred. Stowe, *Mrs.* H. E.. (B.) 823.1526
Drew, Catherine. Lutaniste of St. Jacobi's.
    823.1847
Drift from Redwood Camp. 43 pp. Harte, F. B. p. 173, *in* 823.5281
Drift from two shores. Harte, F. B.
    823.5285
Drifting island, The. Gilman, J: B.
    808.1689
Drifting round the world. Hall, *Capt.* C: W.
    808.1869
Drift-wood. Longfellow, H: W.
    in 823.1010
Driven back to Eden. Roe, E: P. 823.4859
Driver Dallas. Stannard, *Mrs.* H. E. V. (P.)
    823.6680

English Fiction. *Contin.*
"Dropped from the clouds." Verne, J.
    823.5784
Droz, Antoine Gustave. Around a spriug. Tr. by MS. 823.4042
Droz, Gustave. *See* Droz, Antoine Gustave.
Drysdale, W: The princess of Montserrat: a strange narrative of adventure and peril ou land and sea. 823.7321
Dubois, C: Madame Agnes. 823.6285
Du Boisgobey, Fortuné. The angel of the bells. (*L'auge du bourdon.*) Tr. by L. E. Kendall. 823.5097
—— Babiole, the pretty milliner. 2d pt.
    in 823.5141
—— *Same.*   *in* 823.5188
—— Cash on delivery. (*Rubis sur l'ongle.*)
    in 823.5135
—— *Same.*   *in* 823.5136
—— Closed door. 823.5092
—— Condemned door. (*Porte close.*)
    in 823.5086
—— The consequences of a duel: a Parisian romance. Tr. by A. D. Hall. 823.5098
—— The coral pin. Tr. by C. A. Merighi. 2 pts.   823.5093
—— The cry of blood. Tr. by L. E. Kendall. 2 pts. *in* 823.5078
—— The lost casket. Tr. from "La main coupée," by S. Lee. 823.4149
 Issued also as The severed hand.
—— The lottery ticket. 823.5095
—— The Matapan affair. Tr. by L. E. Kendall. 2 pts. (in 1). 823.6595
—— The mystery of an omnibus. *in* 823.6702
—— Old age of Monsieur Lecoq. Tr. by F. E. Garnett. 2 pts. (in 1). 823.3226
—— Piedouche, a French detective. (*Le coup d'œil de M. Piedouche.*) 823.5094
—— The pretty jailer. 2 pts. (in 1).
    in 823.5025
—— The prima donna's husband.
    in 823.5126
—— The red band: the adventures of a young girl during the siege of Paris. 2 pts.
    in 823.5130
—— The sculptor's daughter. (*Margot la balafrée.*) Tr. by L. E. Kendall. 2 pts. (in 1). *in* 823.5025
—— Sealed lips. 823.5096
—— The severed hand. (*La main coupée.*) 2 pts. (iu 1). 823.3393
—— Zig-zag, the clown; or, the steel gaunt-lets. *in* 823.5069
Du Bois-Melly, C: The history of Nicolas Muss: an episode of the massacre of St. Bartholomew. 823.6570
Du Chaillu, Paul Belloni. Country of the dwarfs. 808.693
—— Lost in the jungle: narrated for young people. 808.692
—— My Apingi kingdom: with life in the great Sahara, and sketches of the chase of the ostrich, hyena, etc. 808.691
—— Stories of the gorilla country: narrated for young people. 808.799
—— Wild life under the equator: narrated for young people. 808.694
Duchess, The, *pseud. See* Hungerford, *Mrs.* Margaret.

English Fiction. *Contin.*
Duchess Frances. 2 vols. Keddie, H.
    823.7226–7
Duchess of Rosemary lane. Farjeon, B: L.
    823.5865
Duchesse de Langeais. Balzac, H. de.
    823.5211
Ducie diamonds, The. Blatherwick, C.
    in 823.5091
Dudevant, *Mme.* Amantine Lucile Aurore
  (Dupin). [*G: Sand.*] (1804–76.) Antonia.
  Tr. by V. Vaughan.   823.6790
—— The bagpipers. Tr. by K.. P. Worme-
  ley.   823.7027
—— Cesarine Dietrich. Tr. by E: Stanwood.
    823.6295
—— Consuelo.   823.6214
—— *Same.* Tr. by F. Robinson.   823.6703
—— *Same.*   823.6885
—— The countess of Rudolstadt: sequel to
  "Consuelo."   823.7090
—— *Same.* Tr. by F. Robinson.   823.6921
—— Fanchon the cricket; or, "La petite
  fadette."   823.6847
  Issued also as Little Fadette; *and* Fadette.
—— First and true love; or, the days and
  times of Monsieur Antoine.   823.6296
—— Indiana. With a biog. of George Sand,
  and tr. by G: W. Richards.   823.6848
—— Jealousy; or, Teverino. With a biog. of
  George Sand, and tr. by O. S. Leland.
    823.6849
—— The marriage. 10 pp. (*Also*) The
  cabbage. 13 pp. (*Extr. from* La mare au
  diable.) (Zimmern, H.., *and* A. *Half-
  hours with foreign novelists.*)
    in ** 823.6613
—— Mauprat. Tr. by V. Vaughan.   823.6850
—— The miller of Angibault. Tr. by M.. E.
  Dewey.   823.6851
—— Monsieur Sylvestre. Tr. by F. G:
  Shaw.   823.6914
—— My sister Jeannie. Tr. by S. R.
  Crocker.   823.6852
—— Princess Nourmahal. Tr. by L. Van-
  derpoole.   823.5534
—— The snow man. Tr. by V. Vaughan.
    823.6853
—— Spiridion.   ** 823.6640
—— The tower of Percemont.   823.2317

Note.—For her life and writings, *see* Arnold, M.
Mixed essays, *etc.* 1883. p. 236, *in* 824.407.—Caro,
(—.) George Sand. (*Rev. d. d. Mondes,* 1887.) 3e pér.
v. 83. p. 572, *in* ** 54.398.—Dudevant, *Mme.* A. L.
A. (D.) Histoire de ma vie. 4 vols. (in 2). 928.530–1.
—Gautier, T., *and others.* Famous French authors.
p. 85, *in* 928.87.—Haussonville, G. P. O. C., *vicomte* d'. George Sand. 100 pp. (*Rev. d. d. Mondes,* 1878.) 3e pér. v. 25, p. 729; v. 26, pp. 5, 332, *in*
** 54.339–40.—Sainte-Beuve, C. A. George Sand.
(*In his* Premiers lundis, v. 2.) 824.444.—Thackeray, W: M. Madam Sand and the new apoca-
lypse. 24 pp. (*In his* Paris sketch book.) p. 172, *in*
914.131.—Thomas, B. (Life of) George Sand. 928.
658.—Underwood, S. A. Heroines of free-thought.
p. 117, *in* 922.234.
  See also Poole's Index (to 1882) pp. 369, 370, *in*
** 50.1;—*Same.* Jan. 1, 1882–Jan. 1, 1887. p. 125, *in*
** 50.1³.

Dudley Carleon. Maxwell, *Mrs.* M.. E.. (B.)
    in 823.4991
Duellists, The. A tale of the "Thirty years'
  war." 28 pp. (*In* Tales from Blackwood,
  v. 10.)   *in* ** 823.6656

English Fiction. *Contin.*
Duke of Albany's Own Highlanders. Grant,
  J.   823.4796
—— *Same.*   823.5679
Duke of Monmouth. Griffin, G.   823.672
Duke's dilemma, The. 52 pp. (*In* Tales
  from Blackwood, v. 4.)   *in* ** 823.6650
Duke's motto. The. 96 pp. Féval, P. H. C.
    * 823.6223
Duke's secret, The. Brame, *Mrs.* C.. M. (L.)
    in 823.5080
Dulac, G: Before the dawn: a story of Paris
  and the Jacquerie.   823.5402
Dulcie Carlyon. Grant, J.   823.6526
Dumas, Alexandre, *the younger.* (1824 —.)
  Camille. ("*La dame aux camelias.*")
    823.5567

Note.—For his life and writings, *see* Matthews,
J. B. Alex. Dumas, fils. 26 pp. (*In his* French
dramatists of the 19th cent.) p. 136, *in* 824.39.—
Mauris, M. French men of letters. p. 151, *in*
928.179.—Scherer, E. Les préfaces de M. A. Dumas,
fils. 17 pp. (*Études* . . . v. 4.) p. 305, *in* 844.35.
  See also Poole's Index (to 1882). p. 371, *in* **
50.1;—*Same.* Jan. 1, 1882–Jan. 1, 1887. p. 125, *in* **
50.1³.

Dumas, Alexandre Davy. (1803–1870.) Ad-
  ventures of a marquis.   823.5883
—— *Ascanio: an historical romance.
    823.7161
—— *Beau Tancrede; or, the marriage ver-
  dict.   *in* 823.5063
  Issued also as The marriage verdict;—The young
  chevalier.
—— *Same.* (*Also*) The three guardsmen.
    823.3229
—— The black tulip.   823.6450
—— Bragelonne, the son of Athos; or, "ten
  years later": being the conclusion of
  "Twenty years after."   823.6302
—— The chevalier de Maison Rouge: a tale
  of the reign of terror.   823.3108
—— *Same.*   823.6522
—— Chicot the jester. (Sequel to Marguer-
  ite de Valois.)   823.4611
  Issued also as Diana of Meridor.
—— *Same.*   823.6514
—— La comtesse de Charny. (Same as
  Countess of Charny. Last pt. Andrée de
  Tavernay.)
—— The conscript. (*Conscience l'innocent.*)
    823.6923
—— The conspirators.   823.3164
  Issued also as Chevalier d'Harmental.
—— *Same.*   823.6516
—— *Count of Monte-Cristo. 2 vols. (in 1).
    823.6303
—— *Same.*   823.6508
—— Countess de Charny. (Sequel to Tak-
  ing the Bastile.)   823.3099
—— *Same.*   823.6521
—— Diana of Meridor. (Same as Chicot the
  jester.)
—— Doctor Basilius.   823.7346
—— Felina de Chambure. The female fiend.
    823.5880
—— Forty-five guardsmen. (Sequel to Chicot
  the jester.)   823.5538
—— *Same.*   823.6515
—— *The half brothers.   823.7085
  Issued also as The iron hand.
—— The horrors of Paris: a sequel to "The
  Mohicans of Paris."   823.6228

English Fiction. *Contin.*
Dumas, Alexandre Davy. *Contin.*
—— Ingenue. 823.3243
—— The iron mask. Tr. by T: Williams.
823.5803
—— Isabel of Bavaria. 823.3161
—— Joseph Balsamo: a novel. 823.5903
Issued also as Memoirs of a physician.
—— Louisa; or, the adventures of a French milliner. Tr. by G. Griswold. 823.5881
—— Louise La Vallière. 823.5802
—— Love and liberty: a thrilling narrative of the French revolution of 1792. 823.6915
—— Madame de Chamblay. 823.5879
—— The man with five wives. 823.5882
—— *Marguerite de Valois. 823.5183
Issued also as Margaret of Navarre.
—— *Same.* 823.6513
—— The memoirs of a physician. 823.6518
—— Memoirs of a physician ser.:
1: The memoirs of a physician.—2: The queen's necklace.—3: Six years later.—4: The countess of Charny.—5: Andrée de Taverney.—6: The chevalier de Maison-Rouge.
—— The Mohicans of Paris. 823.6353
Contin. and conclusion Salvator.
—— Nanon; or, women's war. 823.7348
—— Pauline; or, buried alive. 823.5565
Issued also as Buried alive.
—— Queen's necklace. (Sequel to Memoirs of a physician.) 823.3481
—— *Same.* 823.6519
—— Regent's daughter. (Sequel to The conspirators.) 823.2739
—— *Same.* 823.6517
—— Six years later: being the "third series" of "The memoirs of a physician." 823.6286
Issued also as Taking the Bastile.
—— Taking the Bastile: a sequel to The Queen's necklace. 823.6520
—— *The three guardsmen. *in* 823.3229
Issued also as The three musketeers.
—— *Same.* *in* 823.5088; 823.6930
—— The three guardsmen ser.:
1: The three guardsmen.—2: Twenty years after.—3: Bragelonne, the son of Athos.—4: The iron mask.—5: Louise de La Vallière.
—— *The three musketeers. (Being the first of the d'Artagnan romances.) 823.6509
—— *Twenty years after. (Sequel to The three musketeers.) 823.2748
—— *Same.* *in* 823.5077; 823.6500; 823.6510
—— The twin captains. 823.5564
Issued also as Twin lieutenants.
—— *The two Dianas. 823.7347
—— Vicomte de Bragelonne: being the completion of "The three musketeers," and "Twenty years after." 2 vols. 823.6511-12
—— The watchmaker. 823.2448
—— The young chevalier. (Sylvandire.)
Same as The marriage verdict.—Beau Tancred.
Note.—[star] Authorship questioned. *See* Quérard's Supercheries littéraires dévoilées, v. 1. pp. 1086-1118, *in* ** 14.8.
*Note.—*For his life and writings, *see* **Bibliography.** Lorenz, O. Catalogue général de la Librarie française. vols. 2. 5. 9. ** 15.32.35.38¹.—**Castelar,** E. Alexander Dumas. (*In his* Life of Lord Byron . . .) p. 207, *in* 928.337.—**Dumas,** A. D. Mes memoires. 10 vols. (in 5). 1850-2. 928.532-6.—**Fitzgerald,** P. Life and adventures of Dumas. 2 vols. 1873. 928.88-9.—**Gautier,** T., *and others.* Famous French authors. 1879. p. 264, *in* 928.67.—**Hayward,** A. Alexander Dumas. (*In his* Selected essays, v. 1.) p. 393, *in* 824.252.—

English Fiction. *Contin.*
Dumas, Alexandre Davy. *Contin.*
Note. Contin.
Matthews, J. B. Dumas. 32 pp. (*In his* French dramatists of the 19th cent.) p. 46, *in* 824.39.—
Romand, H. Poètes et romanciers modernes de la France. 35 pp. (*Rev. d. d. Mondes.* 1834. 3e pér. v. 1.) p. 129, *in* ** 54.114.—**Sainte-Beuve,** C. A. Dumas. (*In his* Premiers lundis, v. 2.) 824.444.
See also **Poole's** Index (to 1882). p. 371, *in* ** 50.1;—*Same.* Jan. 1, 1882-Jan. 1, 1887. p. 125, *in* ** 50.1².
Dun, The. Edgeworth, M. *in* 823.506
Same. p. 295, *in* 823.7427
Duncan Campbell, Life . . . of. De Foe, D.
823.2125
Dunderviksborg and other tales. Henderson, *Mrs.* F.. C. 823.6534
Dunlap, Walter D. [*Sylvanus Cobb, Jr.*] The painter of Parma: an Italian story of love, mystery and adventure. 823.7011
Dunlap, W: Thirty years ago; or, the memoirs of a water drinker. 2 vols. 823.487-8
Dunning, C.. *See* Wood, C.. Dunning.
Dupree, Frank. Married by proxy. 823.7251
Dupuy, Eliza Ann. All for love; or, the outlaw's bride. 823.490
—— The cancelled will. 823.491
—— The clandestine marriage. 823.492
—— The dethroned heiress. 823.493
—— The Huguenot exiles; or, the times of Louis XIV.: a historical novel. 823.489
—— Michael Rudolph. 823.4284
—— A new way to win a fortune. 823.499
—— Was he guilty? 823.501
Issued also as How he did it.
—— Who shall be victor? A sequel to "The cancelled will." 823.502
—— Why did he marry her? 823.503
Durand, *Mme.* Alice Marie Céleste (Henry). [*H: Gréville.*] Aline. Tr. by W: G. Temple. 823.7046
—— Ariadne. 823.2326
—— Bonne-Marie: a tale of Normandy and Paris. Tr. by M.. N. Sherwood. 823.6867
—— Guy's marriage. Tr. by M.. N. Sherwood. 823.4610
—— Mam'zelle Eugénie. 823.4934
—— Markof, the Russian violinist. Tr. by H.. Stanley. 823.6920
—— Pretty little countess Zina. Tr. by M.. N. Sherwood. 823.7101
—— The princess Oghérof. Tr. by M.. N. Sherwood. 823.4035
—— Sylvie's betrothed. Tr. by M.. N. Sherwood. 823.4526
—— Trials of Raïssa. (*Les épreuves de Raïssa.*) Tr. by M.. N. Sherwood. 823.4001
—— Xénie's inheritance. Tr. by L. E. Kendall. 823.4209
Durward, Mostyn. For better, for worse.
823.4773
Dusantes, The. Stockton, F. R: 823.6192
Dust. Hawthorne, J. C. 823.4742
Dusty diamonds. Ballantyne, R. M.
808.1272
Dutchman's fireside. 2 vols. (in 1). Paulding, J. K. 823.7014
Dutheil, Eugenie. [*Mme. Eugénie de La Rochere.*] The castle of Roussillon; or, Quercy in the sixteenth century. Tr. by Mrs. J. Sadlier. 823.6871

English Fiction. *Contin.*

Dwarfs. Smithson, I., *and* Barnes, G: F. About giants and other wonder people.
808.1598
Dynamiter, The. Stevenson, R. L:, *and* Stevenson, *Mrs.* F. Van de G. 823.5078
Dynevor terrace. Yonge, C.. M.. 823.1766
Earl Hubert's daughter. Holt, E. S..
808.1525
Earl of Mayfield. 823.1253
Earle, Anne Richardson. Her great ambition. 823.7339
Earl's atonement, The. Brame, *Mrs.* C.. M. (L.) *in* 823.5088
Earl's error, The. Brame, *Mrs.* C.. M. (L.)
in 823.5123
Earl's promise, The. Riddell, *Mrs.* C.. E. L. (C.) 823.1323
Early dawn, The. Charles, *Mrs.* E.. (R.)
823.208
Early lessons. Edgeworth, M. 808.292
Early western life. Rideout, *Mrs.* J. B.
808.1596
Earnest trifler. Sprague, M.. A. 823.2005
Earth trembled, The. Roe, E: P. 823.5270
East Angels. Woolson, C. F. 823.4966
East Lynne. Wood, *Mrs.* E. (P.) 823.1731
Eastern tales, by many story tellers. Valentine, *Mrs.* —, *ed.* 808.389
Eavesdropper, The. 69 pp. Payn, J.
in 823.6691
Ebb-tide. Tiernan, *Mrs.* F.. C. (F.)
823.6226
Eberhardt, (—.) Popular traditions. 34 pp. (Roscoe, T: *The German novelists,* v. 2.)
p. 179, *in* ** 823.6827
Ebers, Georg Moritz. The bride of the Nile. Tr. by C. Bell. 2 vols. 823.5738-9
—— The burgomaster's wife. Tr. by M.. J. Safford. 823.4311
—— An Egyptian princess. Tr. by E. S. Buchheim. 823.3258
Issued also as Daughter of an Egyptian king.
—— *Same.* Tr. by E. Grove. 2 vols.
823.2347-8
—— The emperor. Tr. by C. Bell. 2 vols.
823.4202-3
—— Gred of Nuremberg: a romance of the 15th century. Tr. by E. V. Conder.
823.7039
—— Homo sum. Tr. by C. Bell. 823.4063
—— *Same.* 823.4525
—— Joshua: a tale of Biblical times. Tr. by M.. J. Safford. 823.6698
—— Margery (Gred.): a tale of old Nuremberg. Tr. by C. Bell. 2 vols. 823.6571-2
Issued also as Gred of Nuremberg.
—— A question. Tr. by M.. J. Safford.
823.4200
—— Serapis. Tr. by C. Bell. 823.4926
—— *Same.* Tr. by M.. S. Smith. 823.5088
—— The sisters. Tr. by C. Bell. 823.2578
—— Uarda: a romance of ancient Egypt. Tr. by C. Bell. 2 vols. 823.2161-2
—— A word only a word. 823.7452
Echo of passion, An. Lathrop, G: P.
823.5364
Eckstein, Ernst. Aphrodite: a romance of ancient Hellas. Tr. by M.. J. Safford.
823.6981

English Fiction. *Contin.*

Eckstein, Ernst. *Contin.*
—— Cards for four. 26 pp. Tr. by Mrs. F.. C. Henderson. (Henderson, *Mrs.* F.. C. *Dunderviksborg* . . .) 1881.
p. 243, *in* 823.6534
—— The Chaldean magician: an adventure in Rome in the reign of the emperor Diocletian. Tr. by M.. J. Safford. 823.7125
—— Nero: a romance. Tr. by C. Bell and M.. J. Safford. 2 vols. 823.7150-1
—— Prusias: a romance of ancient Rome under the Republic. Tr. by C. Bell. 2 vols.
823.4731-2
—— Quintus Claudius: a romance of imperial Rome. Tr. by C. Bell. 2 vols.
823.6982-3
Eddy, Daniel Clarke. Walter's tour in the east. 6 vols. 808.1646-51
v. 1. Walter in Egypt. 808.1646
v. 2. Walter in Jerusalem. 808.1647
v. 3. Walter in Samaria. 808.1648
v. 4. Walter in Damascus. 808.1649
v. 5. Walter in Constantinople. 808.1650
v. 6. Walter in Athens. 808.1651
Eddy, J: A dinner-party. 48 pp. (*In* Stories by Amer. authors, v. 2.)
p. 92, *in* 823.4703
Eden, *Hon.* Emily. The semi-detached house. Ed. by Lady M. T: Lewis.
823.4183
Edgar, J: G: A boy's adventures in the barons' wars. 808.1909
—— Cavaliers and Roundheads. 808.1483
—— History for boys ; or, annals of the nations of modern Europe. 808.800
—— *Same.* 808.803
—— Sea kings and naval heroes: a book for boys. 808.802
—— Wars of the Roses. 808.801
Edgar Huntly. Brown, C: B. 823.139
Same. 823.6203
Edgeworth, Maria. (1767-1849.) Belinda. 2 vols. (Barbauld, *Mrs.* A. L. (A.), *ed. The British novelists,* vols. 49-50.)
** 823.2110-2111
v. 1. Belinda.
v. 2. Belinda, *concluded.*—The modern Griselda.
—— Early lessons. — Parents' assistant. — Frank. — Rosamond. — Harry and Lucy. Re-ed. and rev. by Mrs. Valentine. 808.292
—— The modern Griselda. (*With her* Belinda.) 82 pp. (Barbauld, *Mrs.* A. L. (A.), *ed. The British novelists,* v. 50.)
p. 245, *in* 823.2111
—— Murad, the unlucky. 45 pp. (Johnson, R., *ed. Little classics,* v. 12.)
p. 83, *in* 823.135
—— Tales and miscellaneous pieces. 14 vols.
** 823.4646-59
Contents:—v. 1. Castle Rackrent.—Essay on Irish bulls.—Modern Griselda. * 823.4646
vols. 2-3. Belinda. * 823.4647-8
v. 4. Essay on self-justification.—Leonora.—Letters of Julia and Caroline, etc. * 823.4649
v. 5. Lame Jervas.—Limerick gloves.—Lottery.—Manufacturers.—Murad the unlucky.—Out of debt out of danger.—Rosanna.—The will.
* 823.4650
v. 6. Contrast.—Dramas. (*viz.:* Love and law;—Rose, thistle and shamrock.)—Grateful negro;—To-morrow. * 823.4651
v. 7. Almeria.—Ennui. * 823.4652
v. 8. The dun.—Madame de Fleury.—Manœuvring.
* 823.4653

English Fiction. *Contin.*
 Edgeworth, Maria. *Contin.*
—— Tales and miscellaneous pieces. *Contin.*
  Contents. Contin.
  v. 9. Emilie de Coulanges.—Vivian.   * 823.4654
  v. 10. The absentee.   * 823.4655
  vols. 11–12 Patronage.   * 823.4656–7
  v. 13. Harrington.—Ormond.   * 823.4658
  v. 14. Ormond, *concluded.*   * 823.4659
—— Tales and novels. 18 vols.   823.7422–39
  Contents:—v. 1. Castle Rackrent.—Essay on Irish
  bulls.—Essay on . . . self-justification.   823.7422
  vols. 2–3. Moral tales. 2 vols. (*viz.:* v. 1: Forester.
  —The Prussian vase.—The good aunt. v. 2: An-
  gelina; or, l'amie inconnue.—The good French
  governess.—Mademoiselle Panache.—The knap-
  sack.)   823.7423–4
  vols. 4–5. Popular tales. 2 vols. (*viz.:* v. 1: Lame
  Jervas.—The will.—The Limerick gloves.—Out of
  debt out of danger.—The lottery.—Rosanna. v.
  2: Murad, the unlucky.—The manufacturers.—
  The contrast.—The grateful negro.—To-morrow.)
     823.7425–6
  vols. 6–10. Tales of fashionable life. 5 vols. (*viz.:*
  v. 1: Ennui.—The dun. v. 2: Manœuvring.—Almeria. v. 3: Vivian. vols. 4–5: The absentee.
  v. 5: (*Also*) Madame de Fleury.—Emilie de Coulanges.—Modern Griselda.)   823.7427–31
  vols. 11–12. Belinda. 2 vols.   823.7432–33
  v. 13. Leonora.—Letters on various subjects.
     823.7434
  vols. 14–16. Patronage. 3 vols. v. 3: (*Also*) Comic
  dramas. (*viz.:* Love and law;—The rose, thistle
  and shamrock.)   823.7435–37
  v. 17. Harrington.—Thoughts on bores.   823.7438
  v. 18. Ormond.   823.7439
—— Tales of fashionable life, (*viz.*): Ennui;
—Emilie de Coulanges.   823.505
—— *Same,* (*viz.*): Manœuvring;—Madame
de Fleury;—The dun.   823.506
—— *Same,* (*viz.*): Vivian;—Almeria.   823.507
  Note.—For her life and writings, *see* **Drake,** S:
  A. Our great benefactors. 1884. p. 69, *in* * 920.312.
  —**Hayward,** A. Maria Edgeworth: her life and
  writings. 57 pp. (*Biog. . . . and crit. essays,* v. 1.)
  p. 130, *in* 824.220.—**Jeaffreson,** J: C. Maria Edgeworth. 8 pp. (*In his Novels, etc.,* v. 2.) p. 7, *in*
  820.187.—**Oliphant,** *Mrs.* M. O. (W.) Maria Edgeworth. (*In her* Lit. hist. of Eng.) 1883. p. 325, *in*
  820.89.—**Oliver,** G. A. A study of Maria Edgeworth. 1882. 928.399.—**Stephen,** L. Dictionary of
  national biography, v. 16. p. 380, *in* ** 920.330¹³.—
  Zimmern, H.. (Life of) Maria Edgeworth. (Fam.
  women ser.) 1884. 928.662.
  See also references in **Allibone's** Dict. of Eng.
  lit., v. 1. p. 542, *in* ** 803.6.
  See also **Poole's** Index (to 1882). p. 338, *in* **
  50.1;—*Same.* Jan. 1, 1882–Jan. 1, 1887. p. 130, *in* **
  50.1².
Edina. Wood, *Mrs.* E. (P.)   823.6361
Edith Lyle. Holmes, *Mrs.* M.. J.. (H.)
     823.791
Edith Mortimer. Parsons, *Mrs.* G. (H.)
     823.1234
Editor's tales, An. Trollope, A.   823.1616
Edmond Dantes. Sequel to the Count of
Monte-Cristo.   823.6120
Edna Browning. Holmes, *Mrs.* M.. J.. (H.)
     823.792
Edward. 2 vols. Moore, J: 823.6462–63
 Same. 4 vols.   ** 823.6768–71
Edwardes, *Mrs.* Annie. Archie Lovell: a
love story.   *in* 823.2815
—— *Same.*   823.5807
—— A ball-room repentance.—Vivian the
beauty. (*And*) A point of honor.   823.2785
—— A ball-room repentance.
  Issued also as At the eleventh hour.
—— A blue-stocking.   823.1906
—— Jet: her face or her fortune?   823.2905
—— Leah: a woman of fashion.   823.6376
—— *Same.* (*Also*) Archie Lovell.   823.2815

English Fiction. *Contin.*
 Edwardes, *Mrs.* Annie. *Contin.*
—— Ought we to visit her?   823.5869
—— *Same.* (*Also*) Philip Earnscliffe.
     823.3233
—— Pearl-powder.   823.7372
—— Philip Earnscliffe. (*With her* Ought we
to visit her?)   *in* 823.3233
—— A point of honor.   823.514
—— *Same.*   *in* 823.2785
—— Steven Lawrence: a love story.
     823.5806
—— Susan Fielding: a love story.   823.5856
—— A vagabond heroine.   823.517
—— *Same.*   *in* 823.6694
—— Vivian the beauty.   *in* 823.2785
—— *Same.*   823.4354
Edwards, Amelia Blandford. The four-fifteen
express. 38 pp. (Johnson, R., *ed. Little
classics,* v. 8.)   p. 71, *in* 823.6325
—— Hand and glove.   *in* 823.2522
—— *Same.*   823.4385
—— Miss Carew.   823.5086
—— *Same.* (*Also*) My brother's wife. (*And*)
Hand and glove.   823.2522
—— My brother's wife. (*With her* Miss
Carew.)   *in* 823.2522
Edwards, Bruce. Rachel Noble's experience.
     823.7073
Edwards, C: Di Vasari: a tale of Florence.
95 pp. (*In* Tales from Blackwood, v. 8.)
     in ** 823.6654
Edwards, Harry Stillwell. Two runaways,
and other stories.   823.6325
Edwards, H: Sutherland. Case of Reuben
Malachi.   *in* 823.5074
Edwards, Matilda Barbara Betham- Doctor
Jacob.   823.4099
—— *Same.*   *in* 823.5055; *in* 823.5068
—— Flower of doom, and other stories.
     in 823.5108
—— Love and mirage: an out-of-door ro-
mance. (Anon.)   *in* 823.5036
—— The Sylvestres; or, the outcasts.
     823.519
—— *Same.*   823.5846
Edwin Brothertoft. Winthrop, T.   823.1724
Edwy the fair. Crake, *Rev.* A. D.   823.5656
Effie Ogilvie. Oliphant, *Mrs.* M. O. (W.)
     in 823.5131
Eggleston, E: The circuit rider: a tale of
heroic age.   823.520
—— The end of the world: a love story.
     823.521
—— The Graysons: a story of Illinois.
     823.5516
—— The hoosier school-master: a novel.
     823.522
—— The mystery of Metropolisville. 823.523
—— Queer stories for boys and girls.
     808.1418
—— Roxy.   823.4029
——, *and* Seelye, *Mrs.* Lillie (Eggleston).
Famous American Indians.
  Brant and Red Jacket.   808.767
  Montezuma and the conquest of Mexico.   808.826
  Tecumseh and the Shawnee prophet.   808.1589
Eggleston, G: Cary. Big brother series:
Captain Sam; or, the boy scouts of 1814.
     808.1057

English Fiction. *Contin.*
Eggleston, G: Cary. *Contin.*
—— Strange stories from history for young people.   808.1432
—— The wreck of the Red Bird: a story of the Carolina coast.   808.1142
Eglantine. Stephenson, *Mrs. E.* (T.)
     823.5989
Egoist, The. Meredith, G: 823.2264
Same.   823.6620
Same. 3 vols.   823.4369-71
Egypt, Ancient.
—— Gautier, T. The romance of a mummy.
     823.4544
—— Hearn, L. Book of Thoth: from an Egyptian papyrus. 14 pp. (*In his* Stray leaves . . .)   p. 19, *in* 823.4791
—— Henty, G: A. The cat of Bubastes. (Time of Thotmes III.)   808.1605
—— Melville, G: J: Whyte- Sarchedon : a legend of the great queen. (B. C. 2000.)
     in ** 823.4662
—— Walloth, W. The king's treasure house. (B. C. 2000.)   823.6986
—— Ingraham, J. H. The pillar of fire; or, Israel in bondage. (B. C. 1491.)   249.13
—— Ebers, G. M. Uarda: a romance of ancient Egypt. 2 vols. (B. C. 1489. Rameses II.)   823.2161-2
—— — Joshua: a tale of Biblical times. (B. C. 1391?)   823.6998
—— — Egyptian princess. (B. C. 526.)
     823.3258
—— — *Same.* 2 vols.   823.2347-8
—— — The sisters. (B. C. 160.)   823.2578
First century, A. D. Croly, G: Salathiel. 3 vols.   823.345-7
Second century, A. D. Ebers, G. M. The emperor. 2 vols. (Roman dominion and early Christianity.)   823.4202-3
Third century, A. D. Moore, T: The epicurean. (Worship of Isis.)   187.2
Fourth century, A. D.
—— Ebers, G. M. Homo sum.   823.4063
—— — Serapis. (Edict of Theodosius against paganism.)   823.4926
—— — *Same.*   823.5088
Fifth century, A. D. Kingsley, C: Hypatia. (Neo-Platonism.)   823.933
Seventh century, A. D. Ebers, G. M. Bride of the Nile. 2 vols.   823.5738-9
Eleventh century, A. D. Disraeli, B: Alroy.
     823.458
Note.—See **Belzoni, G. B.** Narrative of . . . recent discoveries . . . in Egypt and Nubia. v. 1: Text. v. 2: Plates. 2 vols. 1820. ** 962.28-9.—**Bibliography.** Bibliotheca Ægyptiaca and supplement. 2 vols. (in 1). * 16.53;—Trübner & Co. Catalogue of leading books on Egypt and Egyptology . . . 1881. ** 11.351.—**Brugsch-bey,** H: Geographische Inschriften altägyptischer Denkmäler. 3 vols. 1857-60. ** 932.56-8;—History of Egypt under the Pharaohs. 2 vols. 932.13-14.—**Bunsen,** C. C. J. Egypt's place in universal history. 5 vols. 1854-67. * 962.3-7.—**Duncker,** M. Hist. of antiquity. 6 vols. (*See* v. 1.) * 930.145-50.—**Egypt Exploration Fund.** Publications. 6 vols. 1885-1888. ** 932.52-52°.—**Herodotus.** Hist.; ed. by Rawlinson. 4 vols. * 930.36-9.—**Lanoye,** F. de. Rameses the great; or, Egypt 3300 years ago. 1875. 931.1.—**Maspero,** G. C. C: Egyptian archæology. Illus. 932.60.—**Rawlinson.** C. C. History of ancient Egypt. 2 vols. 912.62-3;—Story of ancient Egypt (story of the nations). 1890. 932.55.—**Wil-**

English Fiction. *Contin.*
Egypt, Ancient. *Contin.*
Note. Contin.
kinson, *Sir* J. G. Manners and customs of the ancient Egyptians. 2d ed. 3 vols. 1878. * 932.23-5;—Popular account of the ancient Egyptians. 2 vols. 1874. 932.2-3.
See also **Catalogues** of this Library.
     No. 2, 1880, p. 69.   No. 4, 1884, p. 90.
     No. 3, 1882, p. 59.   No. 5, 1888, pp. 97, 98.
See also **Encyclop. Britann.** Index. p. 144, *in* ** 32.27F.
Egypt, Modern.
—— Butterworth, H. Zigzag journeys in the Levant, with a Talmudist story-teller . . . trip through Egypt.   808.1812
—— De Leon, E. Askaros Kassis the Copt.
     823.4048
—— Eddy, D. C. Walter in Egypt.
     808.1646
—— Fletcher, J. C. Kismet.   823.4301
—— Grant, J. The Royal Highlanders; or, the Black Watch in Egypt.   823.6530
—— Hale, E: E., *and* Hale, S. A family flight over Egypt . . .   808.1829
—— Knox, T: The boy travellers in the far east. Pt 4.   808.1838
—— Palgrave, W: G. Hermann Agha: an eastern narrative. (Egypt, 1762-1773.)
     823.1229
Note.—See **Bibliography.** Bowen, J. E. Conflict of East and West in Egypt. (*Polit. sci. quar.,* 1886, v. 1.) (Books and periodicals consulted, pp. 676-677.) pp. 295, 449, 636, *in* 320.132².—**Gleichen, Count,** (—). With the Camel Corps up the Nile. (1884-85.) 1889. 916.19o.—**Gordon,** *Gen.* C. J. Journals at Khartoum. (Ed. from MSS. by Hake.) 1885. 916.166.—**Jerrold,** W: B., *ed.* The Belgium of the east. 916.194.—**Lane,** E: W. . . . Manners and customs of the modern Egyptians. (1825-1835.) 2 vols. 916.24-5.—**Murray,** J: Handbook for travellers in lower and upper Egypt. 1888. * 9102.3.—**Royle,** C: The Egyptian campaigns, 1882-1885, and events which led to them. 2 vols. 1886. 962.26-7.—**Wallace,** D. M. Egypt and the Egyptian question. 1883. 962.21.—**Waters,** *Mrs.* C. (E.) (Hist. of) Egypt. 1881. 932.53.—**Wilson,** *Sir* C. W. From Korti to Khartum (to relieve Gordon). 1885. 916.193.
See also **Bartlett,** S. C. From Egypt to Palestine. 1879. 914.180.—**Field,** H: M. From Egypt to Japan. 1877. 910.120.—**Gionnie,** J. S. S. Pilgrim memories. 1875. 915.54.—**Martineau,** H. Eastern life: present and past. 1848. 915.113;—*Same.* 962. 10.—**Taylor,** I: Leaves from an Egyptian notebook. 1888. 916.196.
Pyramids.
See **Seiss,** J. A. Miracle in stone. 4th ed. 1877. 916.32.—**Smyth,** P. Our inheritance in the great pyramid. 4th ed. 1880. 932.8.
See also **Catalogues** of this Library.
     No. 2, 1880, pp. 69, 70.   No. 4, 1884, p. 90.
     No. 3, 1882, p. 59.   No. 5, 1888, pp. 97, 98.
See also **Poole's Index** (to 1882). pp. 394-7, *in* ** 50.1;—*Same.* Jan. 1, 1882-Jan. 1, 1887. pp. 133-5, *in* ** 50.1².
See also **Index to Consular reports.** 1880-1885; 1886-1889. 2 vols. (U. S. Pub. Docs. *Dept. of State.*) ** 350.5496¹⁻³.
See also **Index to Harper's monthly.** pp. 173-4, *in* ** 51.475.
See also **Rowell,** J. C. Contents-index. (*Lib. of Univ. of Cal.*) ** 19.134.
Egyptian princess, An. Ebers, G. M.
     823.3258
Same. 2 vols.   823.2347-8
Eichhofs, The. Bethusy-Huc, V. *Gräfin.*
     823.4345
Eight hundred leagues on the Amazon. (Pt. 1 of The giant raft.) Verne, J.   823.4350
Same.   823.6310
"89. Henry, E.   823.5441

English Fiction. *Contin.*
Eiloart, *Mrs.* C. J. G. *See* Eiloart, *Mrs.* E..
Eiloart, *Mrs.* E.. Some of our girls.
823.5091
Eisenbach. Picken, A. p. 119, *in* 823.702
El Fureidîs. Cummins, M. S. 823.354
Elbon, Barbara, *pseud. See* Halstead, Leonora B.
Elect lady, The. MacDonald, G: 823.5409
Elective affinities. Göthe, J. W. von.
823.6801
Elena. Comyn, L. N. 823.272
Eleventh commandment, The. Barrili, A. G.
823.4508
Elfred. Abbott, J. *in* 808.585
Elfreda. Dixon, *Mrs.* (—.) 808.1207
Eli. 38 pp. Chaplin, H. W.
p. 55, *in* 823.4710
Eliot, G:, *pseud. See* Cross, *Mrs.* M.. Ann. (Evans).
Elizabeth. Cottin, *Mme.* S. (R.) 823.4965
Same. p. 701, *in* ** 823.6215
Elizabethines, The. 38 pp. Gore, *Mrs.* C. F.. G. (M.) p. 189, *in* ** 823.6568
· Elizabeth's fortune. Thomas, B. 823.4998
Ella of Garveloch. Martineau, H.
in ** 823.6707
Ellen Middleton. Fullerton, *Lady* G. C.. (L. G.) 823.593
Ellen Norbury. Bennett, E. 823.70
Ellie. 26 pp. Shorthouse, J. H:
p. 281, *in* 823.5438
Ellinwood, March. A year at Poplar Row.
823.524
Elliot, F.. The Italians: a novel. 823.526
—— The red cardinal. *in* 823.5060
—— Romance of old court-life in France.
823.6050
Elliott, *Mrs.* Maud (Howe). The San Rosario ranch. 823.4751
Elliott, S. B. The Felmeres: a novel.
823.525
Ellis, *Mrs.* S.. (Stickney.) Family secrets; or, hints to those who would make home happy. 3 vols. 823.527-9
—— Hearts and homes; or, social distinction. 3 vols. 823.530-2
—— Home; or, the iron rule: a domestic story. 823.4101
—— Pique: a tale of the English aristocracy. (Anon.) 823.4633
Elsa. Hogbin, *Rev.* A. C. 823.780
Elsie Venner. Holmes, O. W. 823.804
Elsie's children. Finley, M. 823.559
Elsie's motherhood. Finley, M. 823.560
Elsie's widowhood. Finley, M. 823.4644
Elster's folly. Wood, *Mrs.* E. (P.) 823.6008
Elves, The. 7 pp. Tieck, L. 823.6328
Emerald gems: a chaplet of Irish fireside tales, historic, domestic and legendary.
823.1190
Emery, *Mrs.* F.. B. Queens. 823.533
Emery, M. S. Every-day business; notes on its practical details: arranged for young people. 808.1586
Emery, S.. A. Three generations. 823.5858
Emigrants of Ahadarra. Carleton, W:
823.170

English Fiction. *Contin.*
Emilie de Coulanges. 70 pp. Edgeworth, M.
p. 171, *in* 823.505
Same. p. 295, *in* ** 823.4654
Same. p. 143, *in* 823.7431
Emma. Abbott, J. *in* 808.581
Emma. Austen, J.. 823.43
Emmanuel. Cooley, W: F. 823.6575
Emperor, The. 2 vols. Ebers, G. M.
823.4202-3
Empress Josephine. Mundt, *Mrs.* C. (M.)
823.6266
Empty heart. Terhune, *Mrs.* M.. V. (H.)
823.1552
Enchanted moccasins and other legends of the American Indians. Matthews, C. 808.1856
Enchanter Faustus and Queen Elizabeth. 12 pp. (*In* Tales from Blackwood, v. 2.)
in ** 823.6648
Enchanting and enchanted. Hackländer, F. W. 808.1493
End of New York. 60 pp. Benjamin, P.
p. 82, *in* 823.4706
End of the world. Eggleston, E: 823.521
Endymion. Disraeli, B: 823.2313
Same. 823.2314; 823.6157
Engel, *Dr.* M. E. Popular tales. 29 pp. (Roscoe, T: *The German novelists,* v. 4.)
p. 346, *in* ** 823.6829
Engineer, The. Abbott, J. 808.586
England. *See also* London.
—— Abbott, J. Story of English history, from the earliest periods to the American revolution. (*Harper's story books,* v. 5.)
808.584
—— —— Vernon; or, conversations about old times in England. (*Harper's story books,* v. 9.) *in* 808.588
—— Adams, W: T. Red Cross; or, Young America in England and Wales. 808.493
· —— Bell, R., *ed.* Early ballads: illustrative of history, traditions and customs. 821.471
—— Butterworth, H. Zigzag journeys in the British Isles. 808.1813
—— Champney, *Mrs.* E.. (W.) Three Vassar girls in England. 808.1824
—— Crake, A. D. Stories from old English history. 808.1625
For contents, *see* Crake, A. D.
—— Creighton, L. Stories from English history. 808.1181
—— Cunningham, A. Traditional tales of the English . . . peasantry. 2 vols.
* 291.52-3
—— Dickens, C: J: H. A child's history of England. *in* 808.686
—— *Same.* *in* 823.5334
—— Ellis, G: Specimens of early English metrical romances. 821.130
—— Hunt, R., *ed.* Popular romances of the west of England; or, the drolls, traditions and superstitions of old Cornwall. 2 vols.
828.47-47[1]
—— Knox, *Mrs.* I. (C.) Little folks' history of England. 808.616
—— Knox, T: W. The boy travellers in Great Britain and Ireland. 808.1930
—— Neele, H: Romance of history: England. 823.1182

English Fiction. *Contin.*
England, *Contin.*
—— Percy, S. Tales of the kings and queens of England: stories of camps and battlefields, wars and victories. 808.1603
—— Scudder, H. E. English Bodley family.
808.1853
—— Strickland, A. Tales from English history for children. 808.293
For contents, *see* Strickland, A.
—— Towle, G: M. Young people's history of England. 942.1310
—— Yonge, C.. M.. Young folks' history of England. 808.794
MYTHICAL. Swinburne, A. C: Locrine: a tragedy. 822.1071
Note.—For the early period, *see* **Dawkins,** *Prof.* W. B. Early man in Britain. 1880. 571.9.—**Elton,** C: I. Origins of English history. 942.1363.—**Geikie,** J. Prehistoric Europe: a geological sketch. 1881. 81.6.—**Geoffrey** *of* **Monmouth.** British history. (*In* Six old Eng. chronicles.) p. 87, *in* 942.139.—**Keary,** C. F. Dawn of history. 1878. 504.13.—**Rhys,** J: Celtic Britain. 1884. 942.1321.—**Scarth,** H: M. Early Britain: Roman Britain. 942.1361.—**Wright,** T: The Celt, the Roman and the Saxon. 1875. 942.197.
ROMAN PERIOD, B. C. 55–A. D. 409.
ROMAN.
—— Beaumont *and* Fletcher. Bonduca; trag.
in ** 822.898
—— Church, A. J: Count of the Saxon shore; or, the villa in vectis: tale of departure of the Romans from Britain.
823.5292
—— Shakespeare, W: Cymbeline. B. C. 4.
822.651
Note.— For other editions, *see under* **Shakespeare** *in* Catalogues of this Library.
No. 2, 1880, p. 207. No. 4, 1884, p. 265.
No. 3, 1882, p. 173. No. 5, 1888, pp. 317–318.
—— Tupper, M. F. King Veric. (*With* Smedley, F. E: *Fortunes of the Colville family.*) p. 239, *in* 823.1443
Note.—Britain abandoned by the Romans, A. D. 410.
EARLY CHRISTIANS.
—— Charles, *Mrs.* E.. (R.) Early dawn.
823.208
—— Crake, A. D. Camp on the Severn: a tale of the tenth persecution in Britain. (303–313.) 823.7096
—— Holt, E. S.. Imogen: a story of the mission of Augustine. 823.5725
—— Smith, A. Edwin of Deira (poem).
821.371
Note.—See **Bede.** Ecclesiastical history of England. 274.2.—**Cæsar's** Commentaries. (Books iv and v.) *in* 937.51.—**Elton,** C: I. Origins of English history. 942.1363.—**Gildas** (*the Wise*) Works. 942. 139.—**Guest,** E. Origines Celticæ. (B. C. 150–A. D. 577.) 2 vols. 1883. 942.1306–7.—**Pearson,** C: H. Early and middle ages of England. 942.1227.—**Scarth,** H: M. Roman Britain. 942.1361.—**Tacitus's** Agricola and other annals. 2 vols. 937.14–15. —**Vine,** F. T. Cæsar in Kent. 1887. 942.1395.—**Wright,** T: The Celt, the Roman and the Saxon. 942.197.
BRITONS AND SAXONS, A. D. 410–1066.
—— Crake, A. D. Doomed city; or, the last days of Durocina . . . Anglo-Saxon conquest . . . and mission of Augustine.
823.7120
—— Ireland, S: W: H. Vortigern: hist. play.
822.1105
—— Milman, H. H. Samor. (*Poetical works,* v. 2.) p. 1, *in* 821.1328

English Fiction. *Contin.*
England, *Contin.*
BRITONS AND SAXONS, A. D. 410–1066.
Contin.
ARTHURIAN ERA.
—— Arthur: his life, etc., in English verse.
(*Early Eng. Text Soc.*, v. 1.) ** 806.1
—— Baillie, J. Ethwald; trag. (*Works.*)
in 822.897
—— Bulfinch, T: Age of chivalry; or, legends of King Arthur. 823.6313
—— Chaucer, G. The wif of Bathes tale.
p. 157, *in* 821.87
—— Dryden, J: King Arthur; opera.
p. 363, *in* 822.140
—— Geoffrey the Knight: a tale of chivalry of the days of King Arthur. * 823.5192
—— Lafon, J. B. Jaufry the knight and the fair Brunissende. 823.6104
—— Lytton, E: G: E. L. Bulwer- King Arthur; poem. p. 201, *in* 821.246
—— —— *Same.* With notes. 821.722
—— Malory, *Sir* T: Boy's King Arthur . . . history of King Arthur and his knights of the Round Table. 808.1870
—— —— History of King Arthur and his knights of the Round Table. 3 vols.
* 823.6615–17
—— —— La mort d'Arthure. 3 vols.
** 823.6773–5
—— Merlin: or early history of King Arthur. (*Early Eng. Text Soc.*, vols.3–4.)
** 806.1³⁻⁴
—— Morte Arthure; poem. (*Early Eng. Text Soc.*, v. 2.) ** 806.1²
—— Scott, *Sir* W. The bridal of Triermain. (*Poetical works.*) p. 379, *in* 821.355
—— —— Sir Tristrem. (*Poetical works.*)
p. 574, *in* 821.355
—— Tennyson, *Lord.* Idylls of the King. 1879. 821.631
—— Wordsworth, W: The Egyptian maid (poem). p. 281, *in* 821.441
ST. AUGUSTINE, A. D. 597. Holt, E. S.. Imogen. 823.5725
ISLE OF WIGHT, 7th century, A. D. Cowper, F. Cædwalla. 823.7123
DANISH WARS.
—— Crake, A. D. Alfgar the Dane; or, the second chronicles of Æscendune: a tale of the days of Edmund Ironsides. 823.5655
—— Hughes, T: . Scouring of the White Horse. 823.836
ALFRED THE GREAT, 871–901.
—— Henty, G: A. The dragon and the raven. 808.1480
—— Knowles, J. S. Alfred the great; play.
p. 176, *in* 822.147
SAXON LIFE. Dixon, *Mrs.* (—.) Leofwine the Saxon. 808.1209
HAROLD II., 1066. Tennyson, *Lord.* Harold; drama. 822.285
Note.—See **Allen,** C: G. Anglo-Saxon Britain. 942.1322.—**Armitage,** *Mrs.* E. S. Childhood of the English nation. (chaps. I.–IX.) 1877. 942.216.—**Bede's** Ecclesiastical history of England. (to A. D. 731.) 1875. 274.2.—**Church,** A. J: The story of early Britain. 1890. 942.1283.—**Church,** R: W: Beginning of the middle ages. 940.64. **Creasy,** *Sir* E: S. History of England. (to 1480.) 2 vols. 942.1327–8. **Elton,** C: I. Origins of English history.

English Fiction. *Contin.*
England. *Contin.*
BRITONS AND SAXONS, A. D. 410–1066.
Contin.

Note. Contin.
1882. 942.1363.—**Freeman**, E: A. Historical essays.
(1st ser.) 1875. 904.16;—History of the Norman
conquest. (vols 1 and 2.) 1873. 942.107–8;—Old English history. 1881. 942.448;—Origin of the English
nation. 942.1421.—**Geoffrey** *of Monmouth.* British
history (to A. D. 688). 1848. p. 87, *in* 942.139.—**Gildas** (*the Wise*). Works. (Roman conquest to 560.) 942.
139.—**Green**, J: R: Conquest of England. (758–1071.)
942.1371;—The making of England. 1882. 942.837.—
Lappenberg, J. M. England under the Anglo-
Saxon kings. 2 vols. (B. C. 54–A. D. 1066.) 942.
1276–7;—Geschichte von England. v. 1: to 1066. 1842.
1428.—**Pauli**, *Dr.* R. Life of Alfred. 1878. 920.194.—
Pearson, C: H: History of England during the
early and middle ages. 2 vols. 1861. 942.1227;—
Historical maps of England during the first thirteen
centuries. 942.1417.—**Powell**, F. Y. Early England, to the conquest. 942.325.—**Stubbs**, W. Constitutional history of England. 3 vols. 1880. 942.
451–3.—**Taine**, H. A. History of English literature.
3 vols. 1876. 820.56–8.—**Yonge**, C. M.. Cameos of
English history. (Cameos I.–V.) 1868. 942.179.
See also **Catalogues** of this Library.
No. 2, 1880, pp. 72–4, 97. No. 4, 1884, pp. 94–5, 120–1.
No. 3, 1882, pp. 61–2, 83–4. No. 5, 1888, pp. 100–1, 187–9.

NORMAN PERIOD, 1066–1154.
WILLIAM THE CONQUEROR, 1066–1087.
—— Crake, A. D. Andreds-weald; or, the
house of Michelham. 823.5654
—— —— Brian Fitz-Count: a story of Walling-
ford Castle and Dorchester Abbey. 823.5657
—— Cumberland, R: Battle of Hastings;
trag. *in* * 822.6
—— Kingsley, C: Hereward the Wake "Last
of the English." 823.932
—— —— Same. 823.6422
—— Lytton, E: G: E. L. Bulwer- Harold,
the last of the Saxon kings. 823.6000
Note.—See **Armitage**, E. S. Childhood of the
English nation. 1877. 914.216.—**Bede's** Anglo-
Saxon chronicle. 1875. *in* 274.2.—**Bruce**, J: C.
Bayeux tapestry elucidated. 1854. * 942.1373.—
Church, R: W: (Life of) Saint Anselm. (1034–
1109.) 922.341.—**Cobbe**, T: History of the Norman
kings. (515–1129.) 1869. 942.1326.—**Creighton**, L.
England a continental power. 942.291.—**Freeman**,
E: A. History of William Rufus. 2 vols. 1882.
942.969–70;—Norman conquest. (5 vols. and index.)
6 vols. 1873–9. 942.107–11¹;—Short history of the
Norman conquest. 3d ed. 942.1324.—**Henry** *of
Huntingdon.* History of the English. (A. D. 55–
A. D. 1155.) 1879. 942.653.—**Jewett**, S.. O. The
story of the Normans. (Story of the nations.) 1890.
942.1387.—**Johnson**, A. H. Normans in Europe.
1870. 940.55.—**Lappenberg**, J: M. Geschichte von
England. (to 1154.) 2 vols. 942.1428–9.—**Michel**, F.
X. Chroniques anglo-normandes. (Poems and
legends.) 3 vols. 1836–40. * 841.66–8.—**Ordericus
Vitalis**. Ecclesiastical history. 4 vols. 1856. 942.
359–62.—**Roger** *de Hovedon.* Chronicle. (732–1201.)
2 vols. 1880. 942.367–8.—**Rule**, M. Life and times
of Saint Anselm. (1034–1109.) 2 vols. 922.344–5.—
Stubbs, W: Constitutional history of England. 3
vols. 1880. 942.451–3.—**Taine**, H. A. History
of English literature. 3 vols. 1876. 820.56–8.—
Thierry, A. Conquest of England. 2 vols. 1875.
942.378–378A.—**Wace**, R. Roman de Rou. (to A. D.
1106.) * 942.1372.—**William** *of Malmesbury.* Chronicle. (to A. D. 1142.) 1876. 942.71;—De gestis pontificum Anglorum. 1870. 942.617.—**Wright**, T:, *ed.*
The Anglo-Latin satirical poets and epigrammatists
of the 12th century. 2 vols. * 942.633–4.—**Yonge**, C..
M.. Cameos of Eng. hist. (Cameos vi–xviii.) 942.179.
See also **Froude**, J. A. Life and times of Thomas
Becket. (*In* Nineteenth century, v. 2, 1877.) (Answered by Mr. **Freeman** *in* Contemporary rev., v.
31. 1878.) p. 821, *in* ** 52.5381.
See also **Catalogues** of this Library.
No. 2, 1880, pp. 72–4, 97. No. 4, 1884, pp. 94–5, 120–1.
No. 3, 1882, pp. 61–2, 83–4. No. 5, 1888, pp. 100–1, 187–9.

English Fiction. *Contin.*
England. *Contin.*
ANGEVIN PERIOD, A. D. 1154–1399.
HENRY II., 1154–1189.
—— Dixon, *Mrs.* (—.) Elfreda: a sequel to
Leofwine. 808.1207
—— Hull, T. Henry the Second; drama.
p. 366, *in* ** 822.104
CRUSADES. *See also under* Crusades, p. 48.
—— Scott, *Sir* W. The betrothed (prep-
arations for the 3d crusade). 823.1394
—— —— Same. (*With his* Count Robert of
Paris.) *in* 823.5328
RICHARD CŒUR DE LION, 1189–1199.
—— Scott, *Sir* W. Ivanhoe. 823.1401
—— —— Same. 823.5160; ** 823.6026
—— —— Talisman. 823.1412
—— —— Same. 823.5160; ** 823.6031
JOHN, 1199–1216.
—— Scott, *Sir* W. Ivanhoe. 823.1401
—— —— Same. 823.5160; ** 823.6026
—— Shakespeare, W: King John. 822.652
Note.—For other editions, *see under* Shake-
speare *in* Catalogue of this Library. No. 5, 1888, p.
85.
Barons' war.
—— Crake, A. D. House of Walderne.
823.5658
—— Edgar, J: G: Boy's adventure in the
barons' war. 808.1909
—— Stewart, E.. M. Heir of Rougemain.
(*In her* Cloister legends.)
p. 11, *in* 823.1519
EDWARD I., 1272–1307.
—— Holt, E. S.. In all times of our tribula-
tion: the story of Piers Gaveston (mur-
dered in 1312). 823.5616
—— Peele, G: Edward I.; drama.
p. 371, *in* 822.120
EDWARD II., 1307–1327. Marlowe, C. Ed-
ward II.; drama. p. 179, *in* 822.122
EDWARD III., 1327–1377.
—— Chaucer, G. Canterbury tales. 821.87
—— —— Same. Annotated . . . by J: Saun-
ders. 821.1248
—— Henty, G: A. St. George for England:
a tale of Cressy and Poitiers. 808.1479
—— Herbert, H: W. Eustache de St. Pierre;
or, the surrender of Calays. (1347.) 8 pp.
(*In his* The chevaliers of France.)
p. 107, *in* 823.4253
—— Holt, E. S.. The well in the desert.
823.5768
—— Planché, J. R. William with the ring.
(Siege of Calais; poem.) 821.807
Edward, the Black Prince. Shirley, W. Ed-
ward, the Black Prince; drama. *in* * 822.9
—— —— Same. * 822.84
RICHARD II., 1377–1399. Shakespeare, W:
King Richard II. 822.273
Note.—For other editions, *see under* Shake-
speare *in* Catalogues of this Library.
No. 2, 1880, p. 207. No. 4, 1884, p. 265.
No. 3, 1882, p. 173. No. 5, 1888, p. 86.

—— Holt, E. S.. Lord mayor: a tale of
London in 1384. 823.7104
Isabella of France. Holt, E. S.. In convent
walls: story of the Dispensers. 823.5608

English Fiction. *Contin.*
England. *Contin.*
ANGEVIN PERIOD, **A.D.** 1154-1399. *Contin.*
RICHARD II., 1377-1399. *Contin.*
Robin Hood.
—— James, G: P. R. Forest days. 823.6377
—— Jonson, B. Sad shepherd; drama.
            p. 490, *in* 822.121
—— Scott, *Sir* W. Ivanhoe. 823.1401
—— — *Same.* 823.5160; *in* ** 823.6026
Note.—See **Ashley,** W: J. Edward III. and his wars, 1327-1360. (Authorities, pp. 188-91.) 942.1403.—**Besant,** W., *and* Rice J. Sir Richard Whittington, Lord Mayor of London. 1881. 923.2008.—**Charles,** E. Vie de Roger Bacon. 923.2043.—**Creighton,** L. Life of Edward, the black prince. (1330-1381.) 1877. 923.2006;—Life of Simon de Montfort. 923.443.—**Froissart,** *Sir* J: Chronicles. (Edward II. to coronation of Henry IV.) 2 vols. 940. 13-14.—**Gairdner,** J., *and* Spedding, J. The Lollards. (*In their* Studies in Eng. hist.) 1881. 942. 925.—**Hall,** H. Court life under the Plantagenets. (Reign of Henry II.) 1890. *942.1297.—**Hutton,** *Rev.* W. H. The misrule of Henry III. (1236-1251.) 1887. 942.1402;—Simon de Montfort and his cause. (1251-1266.) 942.1425.—**Lanier,** S. Boy's Froissart. 1879. 940.15.—**Lechler,** G. V. Life of Wiclif. 922. 320.—**Longman,** W: Life and times of Edward III. (1327-1377.) 2 vols. 1869. 942.1356-7.—**Matthew Paris.** Chronicle. (1235-1257.) 3 vols. 942.372-6.—**Maurice,** C. E. Lives of English popular leaders: Tyler, Ball and Oldcastle. 920.379;—Stephen Langton. 923.2013.—**Norgate,** K. England under the Angevin kings. 2 vols. 1887. 942.1295-6.—**Pauli,** R. Geschichte von England. (1154-1399.) 2 vols. 942.1430-1;—Pictures of old England. 1861. 942.1413; —(Memoir of) Simon de Montfort. 1876. 923.1105.—**Pearson,** C: H. Middle ages of England. 1861. 942.1227;—English history . . . in the 14th century. 1875. 942.124;—**Prothero,** G: W. Life of Simon de Montfort. 1877. 923.1057.—**Richard** of Devizes. Chronicle. (1189-1192.) 1841. 942.1320.—**Rogers,** J. E. T. John Wiklif. (*In his* Hist. gleanings, 2d ser.) 1870. 923.966.—**Rowley,** J. Rise of the people. (1215-1485.) 942.307.—**Seebohm,** F. The black death and its place in English history. 24 pp. (*Fortnightly rev.,* v. 2. 1865.) pp. 149, 268, *in* ** 52. 1181.—**Stubbs,** W: Learning and literature at the court of Henry II. (1154-1189.) (Lectures vi and vii. *In his* Seventeen lectures, *etc.*) 940.172;—Constitutional history of England. 3 vols. 1880. 942. 451-3;—Early Plantagenets. 1876. 942.323.—**Taine,** H. A. History of English literature. 3 vols. 1876. 820.56-8.—**Walsingham.** Historia brevis. (1272-1422.) (no translation yet.) ** 942.1416.—**Warburton,** W. Edward III. 1876. 942.324.—**Wright,** T; *ed.* Political poems and songs rel. to Eng. hist. (1327-1483.) 2 vols. * 942.522-3.
See also **Catalogues** of this Library.
     No. 2, 1880, pp. 72-74, 97.
     No. 3, 1882, pp. 61-62, 83-84.
     No. 4, 1884, pp. 94-95, 120-121.
     No. 5, 1888, pp. 100-101, 187-189.

LATER PLANTAGENETS (Houses of Lancaster and York), 1399-1485.
HENRY IV., 1399-1413.
—— Shakespeare, W: Henry IV. 2 pts.
            in 822.254
*Note.—*For other editions, *see under* Shakespeare *in* Catalogues of this Library.
     No. 2, 1880, p. 207.   No. 4, 1884, p. 265.
     No. 3, 1882, p. 173.   No. 5, 1888, p. 318.
LOLLARDS.
—— Holt, E. S.. The wild rose of Langley: a story of the court of England in the olden time. 808.1528
HENRY V., 1413-1422.
—— Reeve, C. Old English baron: a Gothic story. ** 823.2083
—— Shakespeare, W: Henry V. 822.72
*Note.—*For other editions, *see under* Shakespeare *in* Catalogues of this Library.
     No. 2, 1880, p. 207.   No. 4, 1884, p. 265.
     No. 3, 1882, p. 173.   No. 5, 1888, p. 318.

English Fiction. *Contin.*
England. *Contin.*
LATER PLANTAGENETS (Houses of Lancaster and York), 1399-1485. *Contin.*
HENRY V., 1413-1422. *Contin.*
—— Yonge, C.. M.. The caged lion.
            823.1761
HENRY VI., 1422-1461.
—— Shakespeare, W: Henry VI. 822.651
*Note.—*For other editions, *see under* Shakespeare *in* Catalogues of this Library.
     No. 2, 1880, p. 207.   No. 4, 1884, p. 265.
     No. 3, 1882, p. 173.   No. 5, 1888, p. 318.
—— Strutt, J. Queenhoo-Hall: a romance. 4 vols. * 823.4675-8
EDWARD IV., 1461-1483.
—— Evenings at Haddon Hall. 823.2151
—— Heywood, T. King Edward IV.; play. 2 pts. *in* 822.177
EDWARD V., 1483-1483 (murdered in the tower by Richard III.?).
RICHARD III., 1483-1485.
—— James, G: P. R. The woodman. 823.882
—— Shakespeare, W: Richard III.
            in 822.651
*Note.—*For other editions, *see under* Shakespeare *in* Catalogues of this Library.
     No. 2, 1880, p. 207.   No. 4, 1884, p. 265.
     No. 3, 1882, p. 173.   No. 5, 1888, p. 318.
WAR IN FRANCE.
—— Charles, *Mrs.* E.. (R.) Joan, the maid deliverer of France and England. 823.209
—— James, G: P. R. Agincourt. ** 823.6716
WARS OF THE ROSES, 1455-1485.
—— Church, A. J: Chantry priest of Barnet: a tale of the two Roses. 823.5293
—— Edgar, J: G: Wars of the Roses. 808.801
—— Heseltine, W: Last of the Plantagenets. 823.1813
—— Holt, E. S.. At ye Greue Griffin; or, Mrs. Treadwell's cook. 823.7102
—— — Red and white. 808.1518
—— Lytton, E: G: E. L. Bulwer- Last of the barons. 823.5933
—— Stevenson R. L: The black arrow.
            823.5246
Note.—See **Besant,** W., *and* Rice, J. Life of Sir Richard Whittington. 1881. 923.1183.—**Brougham,** H: P., *Baron.* England and France under the house of Lancaster. 1852. (Attributed also to Sir W: Courthope.) 942.1329.—**Fortescue,** *Sir* J: Governance of England. 1885. 340.155.—**Gairdner,** J. History of Richard III. 1878. 923.2019;—The houses of Lancaster and York. 1875. 942.318.—**Hall,** E: Chronicle: history of England during the reign of Henry IV. to Henry VIII. (1399-1547.) 1809. 942. 1378.—**Kirk,** J: F. Charles the Bold. 3 vols. 1864-68. 923.137-9.—**Knight,** C. Life of William Caxton. 1877. 928.294.—**Legge,** A. O. The unpopular king: Richard III. 2 vols. 942.1414-15.—**More,** Sir T: Edward V. and Richard III. (*In* Kennett, W. *Hist. of England,* v. 1.) p. 481, *in* ** 942.1418.—**Paston letters.** Ed. by J. Gairdner. (1422-1509.) 3 vols. 1872-5. v. 1, 1422-1461; v. 2, 1461-1471; v. 3, 1471-1509. 942.926-8.—**Pauli,** C. R. Geschichte von England. (v. 3: 1399-1509.) 942.1432.—**Rowley,** J. Rise of the people. (1215-1485.) 942.307.—**Stevenson,** *Rev.* J., *ed.* Letters illust. of the wars of the English in France. (1422-1461.) (*Gt. Brit. Rolls. chron.*) 3 vols. * 942.1404-6.—**Strickland,** A. Margaret of Anjou. (*In her* Queens of England, v. 1.) p. 534, *in* 920.198.—**Stubbs,** W. Constitutional history of England. 3 vols. 1880. 942.451-3.—**Taine,** H. A. English literature. 3 vols. 1876. 820.56-8.—**Towle,** G: M. History of Henry V. 942.1366.—**Walsingham,** T: Historia brevis. (1272-1422.) ** 942.1416.—**Wright,** T; *ed.* Political poems and songs rel. to Eng. hist. 1327-1483.) 2 vols. * 942.522-3.

English Fiction. *Contin.*
England. *Contin.*
LATER PLANTAGENETS (Houses of Lancaster and York), 1399-1485. *Contin.*
Note. *Contin.*
See also **Catalogues** of this Library.
No. 2, 1880, pp. 72-74, 97.
No. 3, 1882, pp. 61-62, 83-84.
No. 4, 1884, pp. 94-95, 120-121.
No. 5, 1888, pp. 100-101, 187-189.

TUDOR PERIOD, 1485-1603.
HENRY VII., 1485-1509.
—— Cowper, F. Captain of the Wight: a romance of Carisbrooke Castle in 1488.
823.5697
—— Holt, E. S.. Tangled web: a tale of the fifteenth century. (Perkin Warbeck.)
823.7105
HENRY VIII., 1509-1547.
—— Ainsworth, W: H. Windsor Castle.
823.32
—— —— The Lancashire witches. (Introduction.)
823.21
—— Crake, A. D. Last abbot of Glastonbury: a tale of the dissolution of the monasteries.
823.7097
—— Filleul, M. Pendower. Cornwall in the time of Henry VIII.
823.558
—— Herbert, W: H: Memoirs of Henry VIII. of England, with the fortunes, fates and characters of his six wives. 823.5726
—— Holt, E. S.. Isoult Barry of Wynscote: her diurnal book.
808.1519
—— Lettice Eden: a tale of the last days of Henry VIII.
808.1522
—— Marshall, *Mrs.* E. (M.) Dayspring: story of the time of William Tyndale.
823.5775
—— —— Story of John Marbeck. 823.5578
—— Mundt, *Mrs.* C. (M.) Henry the Eighth and his court.
823.5886
—— Rathbone, *Mrs.* M.. A. (M.) Passages in the life of the faire gospeller, Mistress Anne Askew.
823.4079
—— Reynolds, G: W. M. The necromancer.
823.6339
—— Shakespeare, W: King Henry VIII.
in 822.651
Note.—For other editions, *see under* **Shakespeare** *in* Catalogues of this Library.
No. 2, 1880, p. 207. No. 4, 1884, p. 265.
No. 3, 1882, p. 173. No. 5, 1888, p. 318.
Anne Boleyn. Milman, H:H. Anne Boleyn; poem.
p. 1, *in* 821.1329
Sir Thomas More.
—— M., C. J. Alice Sherwin. 823.1376
—— Sir Thomas More; play. (*In* Amyot, T:, *and others, eds. Suppl. to Dodsley's old plays,* v. 3.)
in ** 822.181
—— Stewart, A. M. Margaret Roper.
823.1894
THE REFORMATION. *See also* Reformation, *note.*
—— Dixon, *Mrs.* (—.) Cecily. 808.1210
—— Robinson, J.. Westminster Abbey.
823.2026
EDWARD VI., 1547-1553.
—— Ainsworth, W: H. The constable of the tower.
823.5605
—— Clemens, S: L. The prince and the pauper.
823.6133

English Fiction. *Contin.*
England. *Contin.*
TUDOR PERIOD, 1485-1603. *Contin.*
LADY JANE GREY, 1553-1553.
—— Ainsworth, W: H. The tower of London.
823.5825
—— Rowe, N. Lady Jane Grey; trag.
in 822.15
MARY, 1553-1558.
—— Ainsworth, W: H. Cardinal Pole.
823.5606
—— Holt, E. S.. All for the best. 808.1516
—— —— For the Master's sake. 808.1514
—— —— The King's daughters. 808.1526
—— —— Robin Tremayne: a tale of the Marian persecution.
823.5724
—— Hugo, V. M., *comte.* Marie Tudor; drama.
in 840.48
—— Tennyson, A., *Lord.* Queen Mary; drama.
822.284
ELIZABETH, 1558-1603.
—— Caddell, C. M.. Wild times. 823.164
—— Holt, E. S.. Joyce Morrell's harvest; or, the annals of Selwick Hall. 823.7103
—— Kingsley, C: Westward ho! 823.935
—— M., C. M. May Lane. (*With* Holt, E. S.. *The well in the desert.*)
p. 185, *in* 823.5768
—— Scott, *Sir* W. Kenilworth. 823.1402
—— —— *Same.* 823.5155; ** 823.6028
—— Wordsworth, W: The white doe of Rylstone (poem).
p. 155, *in* 821.441
Catholics.
—— Boyce, J: The spaewife. ' 823.115
—— —— *Same.* 2 vols. 823.6931-2
—— Caddell, C. M.. Wild times. 823.164
—— Fullerton, *Lady* G. C.. (L. G.) Constance Sherwood: an autobiography of the 16th century.
823.6363
—— Kingston, W: H: G. Three hundred years ago.
808.1615
Spanish Armada.
—— Holt, E. S.. Clare Avery. 808.1523
—— Macaulay, T: B. Armada; poem. (*In his* Essays and poems, v. 3.)
p. 741, *in* 824.69
William Shakespeare.
—— Black, W: Judith Shakespeare.
823.5535
—— Somerset, C. A. Shakespeare's early days; drama. (Lacy's . . . plays . . . , v. 93.)
in 822.753
—— Williams, R. F. Shakespeare and his friends. (*Also*) The secret passion. (*And*) The youth of Shakespeare. ** 823.6260
Sir Francis Drake.
—— Corbett, J. For God and gold. 823.5650
—— Henty, G: A. Under Drake's flag.
808.1487
—— Towle, G: M. Drake, the sea king of Devon.
808.1683
Earl of Essex. Jones, H. Earl of Essex; trag.
in * 822.6
Mary, Queen of Scots. See under Scotland.
Note.—See **Aikin**, *Miss* L. Life of Queen Elizabeth. 2 vols. 1823. ** 923.43-4.—**Bacon**. History of Henry VII. (*Works*, v. xi.) 1869. 01.11.—**Barrows**, *Sir* J: Life of Drake. * 910.630.—**Blunt**, J: II: Reformation of the Church of England. (1514-1547.) 1869. 283.57.—**Brewer**, J:S. Reign of Henry

English Fiction. *Contin.*
England. *Contin.*
TUDOR PERIOD, 1485-1603. *Contin.*
Note. Contin.
VIII. (1509-30.) 2 vols. ** 942.1407-8.—**Brosch,**
M. Geschichte von England. v. 6: 1509-1603.
942.1433.—**Bund,** J. W. W- State trials. v. 1:
Trials for treason. (1327-1660.) 340.162.—**Burton,** J.
H. Queen Mary. (*In his* History of Scotland, v.
4.) (Impartial.) 941.124.—**Creighton,** L. Life of
Sir Walter Ralegh. 1877. 923.442.—**Creighton,**
M. Age of Elizabeth. 1887. 942.1270.—**Demaus,**
R. Life of Hugh Latimer. 922.342.—**Dixon, R: W.**
History of the Church of England. (Impartial.)
(1529-1558.) 4 vols. 1878-81. 283.104-7.—**Edwards,**
E: Life of Sir Walter Ralegh. 2 vols. 1868. 923.
94-5.—**Ewald,** A. C. Stories from the state papers.
1882. 942.867.—**Fisher, G: P.** (Account of) the
Reformation. 1873. 274.28.—**Friedmann, P. Anne**
Boleyn: a chapter of English history. (1527-1536.)
2 vols. 1884. 923.1950-51.—**Froude,** J. A. History
of England. (1529-1588.) 12 vols. 1884. 824.32-34².—
Gairdner, J. Henry the Seventh. 1889. 923.1933.
—**Gairdner,** J., *and* Spedding, J. Studies in English history. 1881. 942.925.—**Geikie, C.** History of
the English Reformation. (Partisan.) 1879. 274.11.
—**Goadby,** E. The England of Shakespeare. 942.
869.—**Hall,** E: Chronicle. (1398-1509.) 1809. **
942.1378.—**Hall,** H. Society in the age of Elizabeth.
942.1370.—**Hallam,** H. Constitutional history of
England. (1485-1760.) 3 vols. 942.41-3.—**Holin-
shed,** R. Chronicles of England, Scotland and Ireland. (to 1577.) 6 vols. 1807-8. ** 942.1379-84.—
Hosack, J: Mary, Queen of Scots and her accusers.
(1542-1587.) 2 vols. 1870-74. 923.2003-4.—**Latimer,**
H. Sermon on the ploughers, 18 Jan. 1549. (Arber,
E. *Reprints*.) 829.13;—Seven sermons before Edward VI. 1549. (Arber, E. *Reprints*.) 829.18.—
Lee, F: G: Reginald Pole, Cardinal Archbishop of
Canterbury: an historical sketch. 1888. * 922.332.—
Lingard, J: History of England. (B. C. 55–A. D.
1689.) (Rom. Catholic.) 10 vols. 942.87-96.—**Macaulay, T: B.** Burleigh and his time. (*In his* Essays, v.
3.) p. 1, *in* 824.135;—Ranke's history of the Popes.
(*In his* Essays, v. 4.) p. 299, *in* 824.135.—**Nicholls,**
J. F. Life of Cabot. 923.2042.—**Seebohm, F.** The
era of the Protestant revolution. 274.13;—**Strickland, A.** Anne Boleyn. (*In her* Queens of England,
v. 2.) p. 176, *in* 920.199;—Catherine of Aragon. (*In
her* Queens of England, v. 2.) p. 97, *in* 920.199;—Elizabeth. (*In her* Queens of England, v. 3.) 920.200;—
Mary. (*In her* Queens of England, v. 2.) p. 475, *in*
920.199.—**Stubbs, W:** Reign of Henry VII. (1485-
1509.) Lectures xv. and xvi. (*In his* Seventeen
lectures, *etc.*) *in* 940.172;—Reign of, and parliament
under Henry VIII. (1509-1547.) Lectures xi and
xii. (*In his* Seventeen lectures, *etc.*) *in* 940.172.—
Taine, H. I. A. English literature. 3 vols. 1876.
820.56-8.—**Thornbury,** G. W. Shakespeare's England. 2 vols. 942.1400-1.—**Towle,** G: W. Ralegh,
his exploits and voyages. 1882. 923.1118.

See also Catalogues of this Library.
No. 2, 1880, pp. 72-4, 97. No. 4, 1884, pp. 94-5, 120-1.
No. 3, 1882, pp. 61-2, 83-4. No. 5, 1888, pp. 100-1, 187-9.

STUART PERIOD, 1603-1714.

JAMES I., 1603-1625. *See* Scotland.
— Ainsworth, W: H. Guy Fawkes; or,
the gunpowder treason. (1605.)   823.18
— — The Lancashire witches.   823.21
— — The star-chamber.   823.30

— Fenn, G: M. Sweet Mace: a Sussex le-
gend of the iron times.   823.7117
— Scott, *Sir* W. Fortunes of Nigel.
                                          823.1398
— — *Same.*   823.5158; ** 823.6029
Arabella Stuart. James, G: P. R. Arabella
Stuart. 3 vols.   * 823.6406-8
CHARLES I., 1625-(beheaded) 1649.
— Ainsworth, W: S. The star-chamber.
                                          823.30
— Cooke, J: E. Her majesty the queen.
                                          823.275

English Fiction. *Contin.*
England. *Contin.*
STUART PERIOD, 1603-1714. *Contin.*
CHARLES I., 1625-1649. *Contin.*
— Crouch, A. T: Q. The splendid spur;
. . . adventures of Mr. John Marvel, a
servant of . . . King Charles I., in . . .
1642-3.   823.7061
— Marshall, *Mrs.* E. (M.) Memories of
troublous times: being the history of Dame
Alicia Chamberlayne of Ravensholme,
Gloucestershire.   823.5772
— — Under Salisbury spire in the days of
George Herbert.   823.7269
— Martineau, H. The Hampdens.
                                          823.7400
— Mitford, M.. R. Charles I.; trag.
                                          in 829.390
— Robinson, J.. Whitehall; or, the days
of Charles the First.   823.1347
Prince Rupert. Melville, G: J: Whyte-
Holmby House.   ** 823.4667
COMMONWEALTH, 1649-1660.
— Ainsworth, W: H. Boscobel; or, the
royal oak: a tale of the year 1651.
                                          823.5601
— — The leaguer of Lathom: a tale of the
civil war of Lancashire.   823.5603
— — Ovingdean Grange: a tale of the
south downs.   823.25
— Akerman, J: Y. A tale of the civil
wars. (*In* Tales of other days.)
                                          p. 10, *in* 823.1
— Charles, *Mrs.* E.. (R.) Draytons and
Davenants.   823.207
— — On both sides of the sea.   823.210
— Crake, A. D. Fairleigh Hall: a tale of
Oxfordshire during the great rebellion.
                                          823.7098
— De Foe, D. Memoirs of a cavalier.
(*Works*, v. 2.)   823.2123
— Edgar, J: G: Cavaliers and Round-
heads; or, stories of the great civil war.
                                          808.1483
— Grant, J. Harry Ogilvie.   823.630
— Henty, G: A. Friends, though divided.
                                          808.1575
— James, G: P. R. The cavalier. (Ends
with the battle of Worcester, 1651.)
                                          823.7107
— — Henry Masterton; or, the adventures
of a young cavalier. 2 vols. (in 1.)
                                          823.864
— — Two scenes from the civil wars. 10
pp. (*In his* The desultory man.)
                                          p. 84, *in* 823.856
— MacDonald, G: St. George and St. Mi-
chael.   823.1068
— Marryat, *Capt.* F: Children of the New
Forest.   823.1095
— Marshall, *Mrs.* E. (M.) Memories of
troublous times: being the history of Dame
Alicia Chamberlayne of Ravensholme,
Gloucestershire.   823.5772
— Marvel, A. On the victory obtained by
Blake; poem. 11 pp. (1657.) (*Fuller
worthies' lib.*) p. 2061, *in* ** 821.1070
— Melville, G: J: Whyte- Holmby House:
a tale of old Northamptonshire. 823.7278

English Fiction. *Contin.*
England. *Contin.*
STUART PERIOD, 1603–1714. *Contin.*
COMMONWEALTH, 1649–1660. *Contin.*
—— Peard, F.. M.. To horse and away.
808.1509
—— Rathbone, *Mrs.* M.. A. (M.) Lady Willoughby. (Diary of the 17th cent.)
823.7394
—— Reid, *Capt.* T: M. No quarter! 823.6336
—— Scott, *Sir* W. Woodstock. 823.1414
—— — *Same.* *in* ** 823.6032
—— Yonge, C.. M.. The pigeon pie: a tale of Roundhead times. 823.1771
—— — Under the storm. *in* 823.6693
Cromwell.
—— Herbert, H: W: Oliver Cromwell; or, England's great protector. 823.765
—— — *Same.* 823.2352; 823.5687
—— Hugo, V. M., *comte.* Cromwell; trag. (*Théâtre*, v. 1.) 840.46
—— Marvel, A. State poems. (*Fuller worthies' lib.*) pp. 161–207. *in* ** 821.1070
See also poems by Dryden, Lowell, Milton and Shelley in their poetical works.
John Milton.
—— Rathbone, *Mrs.* M.. A. (M.) Maiden and married life of Mary Powell, afterwards Mistress Milton. 823.4763
—— Ring, M. John Milton and his time.
823.5964
Also—De Foe, D. Life of Colonel Jack. (*Works*, v. 1.) *in* 823.2122.—Dryden, J: Absolom and Achitophel; poem. (Polit. satire.) p. 46, *in* 821.125.
CHARLES II., 1660–1685.
—— Bayly, A. E. In the golden days.
823.6564
—— Holt, E. S.. Wearyholme. 823.7106
—— James, G: P. R. Russell. 823.877
—— Keddie, H. Duchess Frances. 2 vols.
823.7226–7
—— Marshall, *Mrs.* E. (M.) In the east country, with Sir Thomas Browne.
823.5771
—— — Memories of troublous times: being the history of Dame Alicia Chamberlayne of Ravensholme, Gloucestershire. 823.5772
—— Robinson, J.. Whitefriars. 823.1346
—— Scott, *Sir* W. Peveril of the Peak.
823.1405
—— — *Same.* *in* 823.4803; 823.5329
—— — *Same.* ** 823.6029
Nell Gwynne. Jerrold, D. Nell Gwynne; play. *in* 822.697
Great plague, 1664–5.
—— Ainsworth, W: H. Old Saint Paul's: a tale of the plague and the fire. (1665.)
823.6014
—— De Foe, D. History of the plague in London. 1665. (*Works*, v. 5.) 823.2124
—— — *same.* 829.693
—— Rathbone, *Mrs.* M.. A. (M.) Cherry and Violet. 823.1093
Great fire in London, 1666. Ainsworth, W: H. Old Saint Paul's: a tale of the great plague and the fire. 823.24
JAMES II., 1685–1688.
—— Ainsworth, W: H. James II.; or, the revolution of 1688. 823.20

English Fiction. *Contin.*
England. *Contin.*
STUART PERIOD, 1603–1714. *Contin.*
JAMES II., 1685–1688. *Contin.*
—— Besant, W. For faith and freedom.
823.5531
—— Dryden, J: The hind and the panther. (*Works.*) p. 100, *in* 821.125
—— Kingston, W: H: G. Roger Willoughby; or, the times of Benbow. 808.1578
—— Maxwell, W: H. Grace Willoughby: a tale of the wars of King James. 823.5894
Monmouth rebellion. Griffin, G. Duke of Monmouth. 823.672
WILLIAM III. AND MARY (Mary died 1694), 1689–1702.
—— De Foe, D. The true-born Englishman: a satire. *in* 823.2124
—— James, G: P. R. The king's highway. 2 vols. (in 1.) 823.867
Darien scheme, 1698. Warburton, E. B. G: Darien; or, the merchant prince. 3 vols.
823.2048–50
ANNE, 1702–1714.
—— Ainsworth, W: H. John Law, the projector. 823.5602
—— — Saint James's; or, the court of Queen Anne. 823.28
—— — Mysteries of the court of Queen Anne. 823.5912
—— Holt, E. S.. Maidens' Lodge. 808.1529
—— Swift, J: A tale of a tub. (Satire on the churches of Rome and England.) (*Works.*) 820.97
War in Flanders.
—— Addison, J. The campaign; poem. (*Works*, v. 1.) p. 170, *in* 821.4
—— De Foe, D. Memoirs of Captain Carleton. p. 273, in 823.2123
—— Henty, G: A. Cornet of Horse: a tale of Marlborough's wars. 808.1574
—— Thackeray, W: M. History of Henry Esmond. 823.1575
—— — *Same.* 823.2242; 823.5008
MANNERS.
—— Ashton, J:, *ed.* A century of ballads. (Illustrative of the life, manners, etc., of the Eng. nation during the 17th cent.) 1887. ** 821.1285
—— Cibber, C. Careless husband; drama.
in * 822.8; *in* * 822.79
—— Gay, J: The beggar's opera. *in* * 822.11
—— — *Same.* *in* * 822.41; * 822.70
—— — *Same.* * 822.82; 822.681
—— Lillo, G: George Barnwell; trag.
in * 822.14
—— — *Same.* 822.739
—— Lytton, E: G: E. L. Bulwer- Devereux.
823.1025
—— — *Same.* 2 vols. ** 823.6257–8
—— — Not as bad as we seem. (*Dramatic works.*) p. 408, *in* 822.148
—— — *Same.* (*Dramatic works*, v. 1.)
p. 243, *in* 829.597
—— Marshall, *Mrs.* E. (M.) In Colston's days: a story of old Bristol. 823.5774
—— Pope, A. Rape of the lock; poem.
p. 67, *in* 821.315

English Fiction. *Contin.*
England. *Contin.*
STUART PERIOD, 1603-1714. *Contin.*
MANNERS. *Contin.*
—— Thackeray, W: M. Henry Esmond.
823.2242
—— — *Same.* 823.5008
—— — *Same.* (*Works,* v. 4.) 823.1575
Note.—See Adams, W: H: D. The merry monarch. (Charles II., 1660-1685.) 2 vols. 942.1279-80.
—Bancroft, G: History of the U. S. (1492-1748) vols. 1-3. 973.32-4.—Bayne, P: Chief actors in the Puritan revolution. 942.1385.—Bisset, R. Omitted chapters in the history of England. (1640-1653.) 2 vols. 942.1340-1.—Burton, J. II. History of the reign of Queen Anne. 3 vols. 1880. 942.473-5.—Carlyle, T: Oliver Cromwell's letters and speeches. 3 vols. 1885-6. * 923.1842-4.—Church, R: W: (Memoir of) Lord Bacon. 1884. 928.525.—Clavers the despot's champion: a Scot's biography. By A southern. 923.1982.—Cooper, *Miss* E.. Life of Thomas Wentworth, Earl of Strafford. 2 vols. 1866. 923.2009-10.—Cordery, B. M. Struggle against absolute monarchy. (1603-1688.) 942.288.—Cordery, B. M., *and* Phillpotts, J. S. King and commonwealth. (1558-1660.) 942.1323.—Coxe, W. Memoirs of the Duke of Marlborough. 3 vols. 1876. 923.108-10.—Creighton, L. Life of John Churchill, Duke of Marlborough. (1650-1721.) 1879. 923.2100.—Evelyn, J: Diary and correspondence. 4 vols. 1862. 826.13-16.—Forster, J: Arrest of the five members by Charles I. 942.1368;—Debates on the Grand Remonstrance. (1641.) 942.1367;—Life of Sir John Eliot. (1592-1632.) 2 vols. 1872. 923.1552-3;—Statesmen of the commonwealth. (1649-1660.) 923.81.—Fox, C: J. Reign of James II. (1685.) * 942.1375.—Fuller, T: Church history of Britain. (Earliest times to 1648.) 3 vols. 1837. 274.38-40.—Gardiner, S. R. First two Stuarts and the Puritan revolution. (1603-1660.) 1886. 942.1263;—History of England. (1603-1642.) 10 vols. 1884-7. 942.1330-9;—Personal government of Charles I. 2 vols. 942.1422-3.—Guizot, F. P. G. Cromwell and the commonwealth. 2 vols. 1854. 942.137-8;—English revolution of 1640. 1878. 942.43;—Memoirs of G: Monk, Duke of Albemarle. * 923.2014;—Richard Cromwell and the restoration of Charles II. (1658-1660.) 2 vols. 942.1349-50.—Hale, E. The fall of the Stuarts. (1678-1697.) 1876. 942.293.—Hallam, H: Constitutional history of England. 3 vols. 1876. 942.41-3.—Hamilton, A. Memoirs of Count Grammont. 1888. ** 923.1963.—Herbert, E:, *Lord* Cherbury. Autobiography. (1581-1648.) 923.2018.—Hume, D: History of England. (Tory.) (Earliest time to 1689.) 6 vols. 942.65-70.—Hutchinson, *Col.* Memoirs. (1616-1664.) 1880. 920.173.—Hyde, E:, *Earl of* Clarendon. Characters and episodes of the great rebellion selected from (his) history and autobiography. 1889. 942.1312;—History of the rebellion and civil wars in England. (1625-1660.) 6 vols. 1888. ** 942.1300-5.—James I. Prose works. (1599-1675.) ** 923.519-23.—Lingard, J: History of England. (Roman Catholic.) (B. C. 55-A. D. 1689.) 10 vols. 1874. 942.87-96.—Ludlow, E. Memoirs. (1640-1688.) (*and*) The case of King Charles I. ** 942.1377.—Macaulay, T: B., *Lord.* Francis Bacon. (*In his* Essays, v. 3.) p. 336, *in* 824.135;—Hallam's Constitutional history. (*In his* Essays, v. 1.) p. 433, *in* 824.134;—History of England. (Whig.) (1685-1702.) 5 vols. 1879. 942.102-6;—John Hampden. (*In his* Essays, v. 2.) p. 427, *in* 824.134;—Lord Nugent's memorials of Hampden. (*In his* Essays, v. 2.) p. 427, *in* 824.134;—Milton. (*In his* Essays, v. 1.) p. 202, *in* 824.134;—Sir James Mackintosh. (*In his* Essays, v. 3.) p. 251, *in* 824.135;—Sir William Temple. (*In his* Essays, v. 4.) p. 1, *in* 824.135.—Mackintosh, *Sir* J. History of the revolution in 1688. (1685-1694.) * 942.1374.—Masson, D. Charles II. (*In his* Life of Milton, v. 6.) 928.707;—Life of J: Milton: . . . political . . . history of his time. 6 vols. (and Index.) 7 vols. 1881-7. * 928.702-8.—May, T: History of the long parliament. (1640-41.) ** 942.1376.—Mitchell, D. G. English lands, letters, and kings. 1890. 820.177.—Morris, E. E. Age of Anne. 942.391.—Pattison, M. Life of Milton. 1880. 928.24.—Pepys, S: Memoirs and diary. 5 vols. 1828. 829.213-17.—Ranke, L. von. History of England. 6 vols. 1875. 942.466-71.—Raumer, F. L. G. v. Political history of England during the

English Fiction. *Contin.*
England. *Contin.*
STUART PERIOD, 1603-1714. *Contin.*
Note. Contin.
16th, 17th, and 18th centuries. 2 vols. 1837. * 942.1314-15.—Reign of Queen Anne. 36 pp. (*Edin. rev.,* v. 151. No. 310.) ** 52.5001.—Rogers, J. E. T. William Laud. (*In his* Hist. gleanings, 2d ser.) 923.966.—Smith, G. Pym and Cromwell. (*In his* Three Eng. statesmen.) pp. 1, 67, *in* 923.88.—Spedding, J. Life and times of Lord Bacon. 2 vols. 923.2028-9.—Stanhope, *Lord.* History of the reign of Queen Anne. (1701-13.) 942.1362.—Strickland, A. Lives of the queens of England. (1575-1714.) vols. 4-6. 920.201-3.—Swift, J. History of the last four years of Anne. (*Works,* v. 5.) 923.445.—Taine, H. A. History of English literature. 3 vols. 1876. 820.56-8.
See also Catalogues of this Library.
No. 2, 1880, pp. 72-74, 97.
No. 3, 1882, pp. 61-62, 83-84.
No. 4, 1884, pp. 94-95, 120-121.
No. 5, 1888, pp. 100-101, 187-189.

HANOVERIAN PERIOD, A. D. 1714-1891.
GEORGE I., A. D. 1714-1727.
—— De Foe, D. Life, adventures and piracies of Captain Singleton. (*Works,* v. 1.)
823.2122
—— — New voyage round the world. (Buccaneers.) (*Works,* v. 6.) *in* 823.2125
—— Grant, J. Lucy Arden. 823.637
—— Pyle, H. Rose of Paradise: . . . adventures (of) Captain John Mackra, in connection with the famous pirate, Edward England, in 1720 . . . 823.5288
Old Pretender's rebellion, 1715-1716.
—— James, G: P. R. Henry Smeaton: a Jacobite story of the reign of George I.
in 823.6247
—— Scott, *Sir* W. Rob Roy. 823.1408
—— — *Same.* *in* ** 823.6025
—— Swift, J. Travels into several remote nations of the world. (Satire on contemporary politics.) 823.2966
South Sea bubble, 1716-20. Ainsworth, W: H. John Law, the projector. 823.5602
GEORGE II., A. D. 1727-1760.
—— Ainsworth, W: H. The Lord Mayor of London. 823.5604
—— Fenn, G: M. Devon boys: a tale of the north shore. (French wars.) 808.1713
—— — In the king's name; or, the cruise of the " Kestrel." (Jacobite times.)
808.1714
—— Smollett, T. G: Roderick Random. (Bombardment of Carthagena, 1741.)
823.1473
—— Thackeray, W: M. The Virginians.
823.1581
Young Pretender's rebellion, 1745-1746. *See* Scotland.
—— Kotzebue, A. F. F. v. Eduard in Schottland; play. p. 55, *in* 832.74
—— Scott, *Sir* W. Waverley. 823.1413
—— — *Same.* *in* ** 823.6023
Methodists.
—— Charles, *Mrs.* E.. (R.) Diary of Kitty Trevylyan. 823.206
—— Dixon, *Mrs.* (—.) Walter: a tale of the times of Wesley. 808.1187
—— Foote, S: The minor; comedy.
in ** 822.2
—— — *Same.* *in* ** 822.110

English Fiction. *Contin.*
England. *Contin.*
HANOVERIAN PERIOD, A. D. 1714-1891.
Contin.
GEORGE II., A. D. 1727-1760. *Contin.*
Methodists. Contin.
—— Graves, *Rev.* R: Spiritual Quixote. 2
vols. (Barbauld, *Mrs.* A. L. (A.), *ed.*
The British novelists, vols. 32-3.)
** 823.2093-4
—— Smollett, T. G: Humphry Clinker.
823.1471
—— — *Same.* 2 vols. (Barbauld, *Mrs.* A.
L. (A.), *ed. The British novelists*, vols.
30-31.) ** 823.2091-2
Biographical. Reade, C: Peg Woffington.
823.1293
—— — *Same.* 823.5420
Manners.
—— Ainsworth, W: H. The flitch of bacon;
or, the custom of Dunmow: a tale of Eng-
lish home. 823.17
—— Composer's difficulty. (Handel and his
opera Messiah.) 7 pp. (*In* Robert . . .
and other stories.) p. 147, *in* 823.5811
—— Grant, J. Letty Hyde's lovers. (Brit-
ish service in 1742.) 823.636
—— Rathbone, *Mrs.* M., A. (M.) The old
Chelsea bun-house. ** 823.6715
Novelists.
—— Fielding, H: Adventures of Joseph An-
drews. (*In his* Novels, v. 1.) 823.6149
—— — *Same.* (Barbauld, *Mrs.* A. L. (A.),
ed. The British novelists, v. 18.)
** 823.2079
—— — History of Amelia. 823.6151
—— — History of Tom Jones, a foundling.
2 vols. 823.6149-50
—— — *Same.* 3 vols. (Barbauld, *Mrs.* A.
L. (A.), *ed. The Brit. novelists*, vols.
19-21.) ** 823.2080-2
—— Johnston, C: Chrysal; or, the adven-
tures of a guinea. 4 vols. (in 2).
* 823.7364-5
—— Lennox, *Mrs.* C.. (R.) Female Quixote;
or, the adventures of Arabella. 2 vols.
(Barbauld, *Mrs.* A. L. (A.), *ed. The Brit.*
novelists, vols. 24-5.) ** 823.2085-6
—— Richardson, S: Works. 12 vols.
** 823.6161-72
—— Smollett, T. G: Expedition of Humphry
Clinker. 823.1471
—— — *Same.* 2 vols. (Barbauld, *Mrs.* A.
L. (A.), *ed. The Brit. novelists*, vols. 30-1.)
** 823.2091-2
GEORGE III., A. D. 1760-1820.
—— Ainsworth, W: H. Lord Mayor of Lon-
don; or, city life in the last century.
823.5604
—— Collingwood, H. Under the meteor
flag. (French revolutionary war.) 808.1709
—— Marshall, *Mrs.* E. (M.) In four reigns:
recollections of Althea Allingham. 1785-
1842. 823.5770
—— Scott, *Sir* W. The surgeon's daughter.
823.1410
—— — *Same.* in 823.5329; in ** 823.6032
—— — The tapestried chamber. (*With his*
The talisman.) p. 270, *in* 823.1412

English Fiction. *Contin.*
England. *Contin.*
HANOVERIAN PERIOD, A. D. 1714-1891.
Contin.
GEORGE III., A. D. 1760-1820. *Contin.*
Gibraltar, 1779-83. Hamley, *Sir* E: B. Laz-
aro's legacy: a tale of the siege of Gibral-
tar. 64 pp. (*In* Tales from Blackwood, v.
2.) *in* ** 823.6648
Gordon riots, 1780.
—— Dickens, C: J: H. Barnaby Rudge.
823.384
—— — *Same.* 823.385; 823.5336; 823.5551
—— — *Same.* 2 vols. 823.5303-4
Lord Nelson. Chamier, F: Ben Brace;
the last of Nelson's Agamemnon.
823.197
Mutiny at the Nore, 1797. Marryat, *Capt.* F:
The king's own. 823.1100
—— — *Same.* 823.2916; ** 823.6662
Peninsular campaign, 1808.
—— Grant, J. King's Own Borderers.
823.633
—— — Romance of war; or, the Highland-
ers in Spain. 823.648
—— Maxwell, W: H. Stories of the Penin-
sular war. 823.1131
Luddite riots, 1813-1818. Henty, G: A.
Through the fray. 808.1484
—— — *Same.* 808.1612
Napoleonic wars. See also France.
—— Ballantyne, R. M. Battle and the
breeze. (*In his* Tales of adventure . . .)
in 808.1266
—— — *Same.* (*With his* Wrecked but not
ruined.) *in* 808.1265
—— Blackmore, R: D. Springhaven: a tale
of the great war. (Death of Lord Nelson.)
823.5151
—— — *Same.* 823.5514
—— Buchanan, R. W. Shadow of the
sword. 823.4166
—— Charles, *Mrs.* E.. (R.) Against the
stream: the story of a heroic age in Eng-
land. (Days of Clarkson and Wilberforce.)
823.202
Biographical.
—— Disraeli, B: Venetia. (*With his* Sybil.)
in 823.3230
—— — *Same.* 823.469
—— Ritchie, *Mrs.* A. I.. (T.) Miss Angel.
(Angelica Kaufman, Sir Joshua Reynolds,
etc.) 823.5986
MANNERS. (18th century.)
—— Brooke, H: Fool of quality; or, the
history of Henry, Earl of Moreland. 2
vols. 823.6532-3
—— Cobb, J. F. Watchers on the Loug-
ships: a tale of Cornwall in the last cen-
tury. 823.4532
—— Edgeworth, M. Belinda. (*In her* Tales
. . . , vols. 2-3.) ** 823.4647-8
—— — *Same.* 2 vols. (Barbauld, *Mrs.* A.
L. (A.), *ed. The Brit. novelists*, vols.
49-50.) ** 823.2110-11
—— Gaskell, *Mrs.* E.. C. Sylvia's lovers.
823.5867
Goldsmith, O. Vicar of Wakefield. 823.615
—— — *Same.* 823.4206; 823.5873; 823.6425

English Fiction. *Contin.*
England. *Contin.*
HANOVERIAN PERIOD, A. D. 1714-1891.
Contin.
MANNERS. (18th century.) *Contin.*
Goldsmith, O. *Contin.*
—— — *Same.* (Barbauld, *Mrs.* A. L. (A.),
ed. *The Brit. novelists*, v. 23.)
           p. 169, *in* ** 823.2084
—— — *Same.* (*In* Classic tales.)
           p. 111, *in* 823.4489
—— — *Same.* 91 pp. (*In* Lib. of famous
fiction.)   p. 447, *in* ** 823.6215
—— Grant, J. Strange story of the Duchess
of Kingston. 14 pp. (*With his* Ross-
shire Buffs.)   p. 188, *in* 823.649
—— Inchbald, *Mrs.* E.. (S.) Simple story.
(Barbauld, *Mrs.* A. L. (A.), ed. *The Brit.
novelists*, v. 28.)   ** 823.2089
—— Marshall, *Mrs.* E. (M.) On the banks
of the Ouse; or, life in Olney a hundred
years ago.   823.5411
—— Melville, G: J: Whyte- Cerise.
           823.7273
—— — *Same.* (*With his* Holmby House.)
           in ** 823.4667
—— Moore, J: Edward. 2 vols. 823.6462-3
—— Richardson, S: Clarissa (Harlowe); or,
the history of a young lady.   823.1316
—— — History of Clarissa Harlowe. 5
vols. (*Works*, vols. 4-8.)   823.6164-8
—— — *Same.* 8 vols. (Barbauld, *Mrs.* A.
L. (A.), ed. *The Brit. novelists*, vols.
1-8.)   ** 823.2062-9
—— — History of Sir Charles Grandison.
4 vols. (*Works*, vols. 9-12.)
           ** 823.6169-72
—— — *Same.* 7 vols. (Barbauld, *Mrs.* A.
L. (A.), ed. *The Brit. novelists*, vols.
9-15.)   ** 823.2070-6
—— — Pamela; or, virtue rewarded. 3 vols.
(*Works*, vols. 1-3.)   ** 823.6161-3
Bath life.
—— Ainsworth, W: H. Beau Nash.
           823.5790
—— Smollett, T. G: Humphry Clinker.
           823.1471
—— — *Same.* 2 vols. (Barbauld, *Mrs.* A.
L. (A.), ed. *The Brit. novelists*, vols. 30-
31.)   ** 823.2091-2
London life.
—— Arblay, *Mme.* F.. (B.) d'. Evelina. 2
vols. (in 1).   823.1911
—— — *Same.* 2 vols. (Barbauld, *Mrs.*
L. (A.), ed. *The Brit. novelists*, vols. 38-9.)
           ** 823.2099-2100
—— Dickens, C: J: H. Tale of two cities.
           823.5317
Middle and low life. Warren, S: Now and
then.   823.1685
Religious life. Holt, E. S.. Ashcliffe Hall.
           808.1520
Sea life.
—— Marryat, *Capt.* F: The dog fiend; or,
Snarleyow. (Smuggling.)   823.1096
—— — *Same.*   ** 823.6674
—— Russell, W: C. John Holdsworth, chief
mate.   *in* 823.5128

English Fiction. *Contin.*
England. *Contin.*
HANOVERIAN PERIOD, A. D. 1714-1891.
Contin.
MANNERS. (18th century.) *Contin.*
Sea life. *Contin.*
—— Smollet, T. G: Humphry Clinker.
           823.1471
—— — *Same.* 2 vols.   823.2091-2
—— — Peregrine Pickle.   823.1472
Note.—See also Sea stories.
Theatrical life.
—— Reade, C: Art: a dramatic tale. (*With
his* Christie Johnstone . . .)
          p. 231, *in* 823.1285
—— — Clouds and sunshine. (*With his*
Christie Johnstone . . .)
          p. 185, *in* 823.1285
MANNERS. (1st half of 19th century.)
—— Adams, H: C. School-days at Kings-
court: a tale of 1803.   808.1567
—— Austen, J.. Emma.   823.43
—— — Mansfield Park.   823.44
—— — Northanger Abbey.   823.2012
—— — *Same.* (*With her* Pride and preju-
dice.)   *in* 823.5341
—— — Pride and prejudice.   823.5341
—— — Persuasion. (*With her* Sense and
sensibility.)   *in* 823.47
—— — Sense and sensibility.   823.47
—— — *Same.*   823.5536
—— Cross, *Mrs.* M.. A. (E.) Adam Bede.
           823.996
—— Edgeworth, M. Belinda. (*In her* Tales
. . ., vols. 2-3.)   823.4647-8
—— — *Same.* 2 vols. (Barbauld, *Mrs.* A.
L. (A.), ed. *The British novelists*, vols.
49-50.)   ** 823.2110-11
—— — Manœuvring. (*In her* Tales of fash-
ionable life.)   *in* 823.506
—— — *Same.* (*In her* Tales . . ., v. 8.)
           * 823.4653
—— — Patronage. 2 vols. (*In her* Tales
. . ., vols. 11-12.)   * 823.4656-7
—— Scott, *Sir* W. St. Ronan's well.
           823.1411
—— — *Same.*   823.5326
—— — *Same.*   *in* ** 823.6030
—— Thackeray, W: M. Vanity fair.
           823.1580
London life. See Theodore Hook's novels.
Domestic life.
—— Ferrier, *Miss* S. E. Destiny; or, the
chief's daughter.   823.2051
—— — Inheritance.   823.2052
—— — Marriage.   823.1991
—— More, *Mrs.* H. Cœlebs in search of a
wife.   823.5749
Note.—See also Jane Austen's novels. (Begun 1811.)
Military life. See Napoleonic wars, *under*
France.
Political life.
—— Galt, J: The member: an autobiog-
raphy.   ** 823.6720
—— — The radical: an autobiography. (Na-
than Butt.)   ** 823.6721
—— Lytton, E: G: E. L. Bulwer-
2 vols.   823.1037-8
—— — *Same.*   823.5971-2

English Fiction. *Contin.*
England. *Contin.*
HANOVERIAN PERIOD, **A. D.** 1714-1891.
Contin.
MANNERS. (1st half of 19th century.) *Contin.*
Political life. Contin.
—— Ward, R. P.   De Vere; or, the man of
independence.   823.4054
—— ∸ Tremaine; or, the man of refinement.
                              ** 823.6733
Religious life. White, W. H. Revolution
in Tanner's lane.   823.5272
Rural life.
—— Irving, W. Bracebridge Hall; or, the
humourists: a medley.   823.1810
—— Lytton, E: G: E. L. Bulwer- Eugene
Aram.   823.1028
—— — *Same.*   823.6218
—— Mitford, M.. R. Our village. 2 vols.
                              823.2148-9
Note.—See also Jane Austen's novels for rural
gentry.
GEORGE IV., A. D. 1820-1830.
—— Croly, G. Marston; or, the soldier and
statesman. 2d ed. 3 vols.   * 823.5492-4
—— Marshall, *Mrs.* E. (M.) In four reigns.
1785-1842.   823.5770
WILLIAM IV., A. D. 1830-1837.
—— Cross, *Mrs.* M. A. (E.) Felix Holt, the
Radical.   823.999
—— Marshall, *Mrs.* E. (M.) In four reigns:
the recollections of Althea Allingham.
1785-1842.   823.5770
—— — Under the Mendips. (Bristol riots,
1831.)   823.5773
VICTORIA, A. D. 1837—.
Chartists.
—— Disraeli, B: Sybil; or, the two nations.
                              823.466
—— — *Same.*   823.3230
—— Kingsley, C: Alton Locke, tailor and
poet.   823.931
Crimean war, 1844-5.
—— Grant, J. Lady Wedderburn's wish.
                              823.634
—— — Laura Everingham.   823.635
—— — *Same.*   823.5682
—— — Lord Hermitage.   823.4797
—— — One of "The six hundred." 823.642
—— Henty, G: A. Jack Archer. 808.1532
—— Kingsley, H: Ravenshoe.   823.943
—— Melville, G: J: Whyte- The interpreter.
                              823.1853
—— — *Same.* (*With his* Digby Grand.)
                          in ** 823.4671
LIFE AND MANNERS.
London life.
—— Besant, W. Bell of St. Paul's.
                              823.6362
—— Charles, *Mrs.* E.. (R.) Winifred Ber-
tram.   823.212
—— Dickens, C: J: H. Martin Chuzzlewit.
4 vols.   823.420-3
—— — Nicholas Nickleby.   823.5553
—— — *Same.* 2 vols.
                    823.437-7½; 823.5298-9
—— — Oliver Twist.   823.5300
—— — *Same.* 823.5334; 823.5555; 823.6756
—— James, H:, *Jr.* A London life. 823.6536

English Fiction. *Contin.*
England. *Contin.*
HANOVERIAN PERIOD, **A. D.** 1714-1891.
Contin.
LIFE AND MANNERS. *Contin.*
London life. Contin.
—— Lovelace, F. The Moloch of fashion.
                          · 823.5491
—— Melville, G: J: Whyte- The Brookes of
Bridlemere.   823.1150
—— — *Same.* ** 823.4662; 823.7272
—— Savage, M. W. Bachelor of the Al-
bany.   ** 823.4674
—— Trollope, A. The three clerks.
                              823.1628
—— Whitty, E: M. Friends of Bohemia. 2
vols.   823.6155-6
Fashionable life.
—— Aïdé, H. Introduced to society.
                              823.5145
—— Aristocracy. (Anon.)   823.7237
—— Black, W: Prince Fortunatus. 823.7030
—— Burke, *Sir* J: B. Family romance; or,
episodes in the domestic annals of the aris-
tocracy.   823.152
—— Clemens, S: L. A Connecticut Yankee
in King Arthur's court.   823.6141
—— Collins, M. Marquis and merchant. 3
vols.   823.7369-71
—— Ellis, *Mrs.* S.. (S.) Pique: a tale of the
English aristocracy. (Anon.) 823.4633
—— Hook, T. E: Gurney married: a sequel
to Gilbert Gurney.   823.817
—— McCarthy, J., *and* Praed, *Mrs.* R. (M.-
P.) Campbell- The ladies' gallery.
                              823.7266
—— Yates, E. H. Broken to harness: a
story of English domestic life.   823.1749
Note.—See also novels by Disraeli, B:; Hook, T.
E:; Lytton, E: G: E. L. Bulwer-; Melville, G: J:
Whyte-; Trollope, *Mrs.* F.. E. (T.); Youge, C.. M..
Middle-class life. Yonge, C.. M.. The daisy
chain.   823.1764
Note.—See also novels by Jane Austen.
Low life. Warren, S: Ten thousand a year.
                              823.1689
Note.—See also novels by C: J: H. Dickens.
Politics.
—— Chesney, C: C. The battle of Dorking.
                              823.5649
—— Collins, W: W. The woman in white.
                              823.268
—— Dickens, C: J: H. Hard times. 2 vols.
(Social and political questions.)
                              823.411-12
—— — *Same.* *in* 823.5304; *in* 823.5336
—— Disraeli, B: Coningsby.   823.459
—— — *Same.* (*With his* Miriam Alroy.)
                          in 823.3002
—— — Endymion.   823.2313
—— — *Same.*   823.2314; 823.6157
—— — Vivian Grey.   823.470
—— Kingsley, C: Two years ago. 823.934
—— — Yeast: a problem.   823.936
—— Kingsley, H: Austin Elliot. 823.937
—— Lytton, E: G: E. L. Bulwer- The new
Timon. (Polit. satire.) p. 1, *in* 821.246
—— McCarthy, J., *and* Praed, *Mrs.* R. (M.-
P.) Campbell- "The Right Honourable."
                              823.5488

English Fiction. *Contin.*
England. *Contin.*
HANOVERIAN PERIOD, **A. D. 1714–1891.**
Contin.
LIFE AND MANNERS. *Contin.*
Politics. Contin.
—— Murray, E. C. G. Member for Paris.
823.6098
—— Trollope, A. Phineas Finn, the Irish
member. 823.1619
—— Ward, R. P. Tremaine. ** 823.6733
Parliamentary elections.
—— Lytton, E: G: E. L. Bulwer- My novel.
2 vols. 823.1037-8
—— — *Same.* 823.5971-2
—— Trollope, A. Ralph the heir. 823.1623
—— Warren, S: Ten thousand a year.
823.1689
Social and labor questions.
—— Besant, W. All sorts and conditions of
men. 823.3719
—— — Children of Gibeon. *in* 823.4985
—— — *Same.* 823.5020
—— — *Same.* 823.6962
—— Caird, *Mrs.* M. (A.) Wing of Azrael.
(Marriage and divorce.) 823.7199
—— Cross, *Mrs.* M.. A. (E.) Felix Holt.
823.999
—— Jenkins, E: Little Hodge. 823.900
—— Kingsley, C: Alton Locke. 823.931
—— Sime, W: King Capital. 823.4503
—— Trollope, *Mrs.* F.. (M.) Life . . . of
Michael Armstrong, the factory boy.
** 823.6222
Note.—See also novels by H. Martineau.
Socialism.
—— Gilbert, W: De profundis. 2d ed.
823.4087
—— Gresley, *Rev.* W: Charles Lever; or,
the man of the nineteenth century.
** 823.6772
—— James, H:, *Jr.* Princess Casamassima.
823.5744
—— Linton, *Mrs.* E. (L.) True history of
Joshua Davidson, communist. 823.4814
Manufacturing districts.
—— Hamerton, P. G. Wenderholme: a
story of Lancashire and Yorkshire.
823.693
—— Martineau, H. A Manchester strike.
(*In her* Illust. of polit. econ., v. 3.)
in ** 823.6708
—— Nicholls, *Mrs.* C.. (B.) Shirley.
823.128
Artist life. Collins, W: W. Hide-and-seek.
823.257
Note.—For Art novels, see p. 10.
Literary life. Murray, D: C. The weaker
vessel. 823.6424
Military life.
—— Grant, J. Frank Hilton. (In Arabia.)
823.627
—— — Oliver Ellis. (In West Indies.)
823.640
—— — The phantom regiment. (In Spain.)
823.644
—— Stannard, *Mrs.* H. E. V. (P.) Cavalry
life. 823.4990
Note.—See also novels by W: H. Maxwell.

English Fiction. *Contin.*
England. *Contin.*
HANOVERIAN PERIOD, **A. D. 1714–1891.**
Contin.
LIFE AND MANNERS. *Contin.*
Sea life.
—— Ballantyne, R. M. Shifting winds.
808.212
—— Black, W: White wings: a yachting ro-
mance. 823.2350
Chamier, F: Saucy Arethusa. 823.6347
—— Tom Bowling: a tale of the sea.
823.6348
—— Cupples, G: The green hand: adven-
tures of a naval lieutenant. 808.345
—— Kingston, W: H: G. From powder
monkey to admiral. 808.1033
—— — Paddy Finn; or, the adventures of a
midshipman. 808.1614
—— — Three lieutenants. 808.1616
—— — True Blue; or, the life . . . of a Brit-
ish seaman of the old school. 808.365
—— Russell, W: C. The Flying Dutchman.
(*With his* A sailor's sweetheart.)
in 823.2510
—— — Jack's courtship. 823.4947
—— — A sailor's sweetheart. 823.2510
—— — A sea queen. 823.4507
—— — Wreck of the "Grosvenor."
in 823.6702
—— Scott, M. The cruise of the Midge.
823.1389
—— — Tom Cringle's log. 823.1390
—— Stables, G. On special service. 808.1423
Note.—See also novels by Capt. F: Marryat.
Also Sea stories;—Whale fishery, in general al-
phabet.
Sporting life. Melville, G: J: Whyte- Sat-
anella. ** 823.4668
Note.—See also Hunting and sporting adventures,
in general alphabet.
University life.
—— Bradley, E: Adventures of Mr. Verdant
Green. 823.117
—— College theatricals. 38 pp. (*In Tales*
from Blackwood.) *in* ** 823.6648
—— Hughes, T: Tom Brown at Oxford.
823.837
—— — *Same.* (*With his* Tom Brown's
school-days.) *in* 823.5955
—— Kingsley, C: Alton Locke. 823.931
—— Kingsley, H: Ravenshoe. 823.943
—— Lockhart, J: G. Reginald Dalton.
823.4511
—— My college friends. Charles Russell,
the gentleman-commoner. (*In* Tales from
Blackwood, v. 4.) *in* ** 823.6650
—— — No. II. Horace Leicester. 45 pp.
(*In* Tales from Blackwood, v. 5.)
in ** 823.6652
—— — No. III. Mr. W. Wellington Hurst.
43 pp. (*In* Tales from Blackwood, v. 6.)
in ** 823.6652
—— Thackeray, W: M. Pendennis. 823.1576
—— — *Same.* 2 vols. 823.5006-7
School life.
—— Adams, H. C. Charlie Lucken at school
and college. 823.6333
—— — Schoolboy honour: a tale of Hal-
minster College. 808.1608
—— — Who was Philip? 808.1609

English Fiction. *Contin.*
England. *Contin.*
HANOVERIAN PERIOD, **A. D.** 1714–1891.
Contin.
LIFE AND MANNERS. *Contin.*
School life. *Contin.*
—— Dickens, C: J: H. Life and adventures
of Nicholas Nickleby. 2 vols. 823.5298–9
—— Grant, J. Dick Rodney. 823.624
—— Hughes, T: Tom Brown's school-days
at Rugby. 823.5167
—— *Same.* 823.835; 823.5955; *in* 823.6677
—— *Same.* *in* 823.6698
—— Kingston, W: H: G. Schoolboy days.
808.1543
—— Smedley, F. E. Frank Fairlegh; or,
scenes from the life of a private pupil.
823.1444
THEOLOGICAL MOVEMENTS.
—— Borrow, G: Lavrengo, the scholar, the
gipsy, the priest. 823.112
—— Disraeli, B: Tancred. (Defense of the
Jews.) 823.467
—— Holt, E. S.. Verena. 808.1521
—— McDonnell, W: Exeter Hall. 823.6158
—— Maitland, E: By and by. 823.1079
—— *Same.* 823.2354
—— — Higher law: a romance. 823.1080
—— — Pilgrim and the shrine. 823.1081
—— Mallock, W: H. A romance of the
nineteenth century. 823.5585
—— Ward, *Mrs.* M.. A. (A.) Robert Els-
mere. 823.5342
Note.—See also novels by Mrs. M. O. (W.) Oliphant.
High Church.
—— Chamberlain, N. H. The sphynx in
Aubrey parish. 823.7140
—— Yonge, C.. M.. Heir of Redclyffe.
823.1768
—— — Pillars of the house. 2 vols.
823.1772–3
Roman Catholic.
—— Disraeli, B: Lothair. (Catholicism in
England.) 823.464
—— — *Same.* 823.2751
REFORMS.
—— Dickens, C: J: H. Bleak House. (Delays
in Courts of chancery.) 823.390
—— — *Same.* 2 vols. 823.5313–14
—— — Little Dorrit. (Circumlocution office,
etc.) 823.419
—— — *Same.* 2 vols. 823.5315–16
—— Reade, C: Put yourself in his place.
(Legal trades unions.) 823.1294
—— — A woman-hater. (Difficulties, etc., in
pursuit of medical studies.) 823.1984
Note.—See also novels by H. Martineau.
Insane asylums.
—— Reade, C: Hard cash. 823.1290
—— Yates, E. H. Dr. Wainwright's patient.
823.5890
Poor and poor laws.
Besant, W. All sorts and conditions of men.
823.3719
—— Dickens, C: J: H. Adventures of Oliver
Twist. (Work-house abuses.) 823.5300
—— — *Same.* 823.5334; 823.5555
—— — *Same.* ** 823.6756
—— Farjeon, B: L. Toilers of Babylon.
823.6320

English Fiction. *Contin.*
- England. *Contin.*
HANOVERIAN PERIOD, **A. D.** 1714–1891.
Contin.
REFORMS. *Contin.*
Prison abuses.
—— Dickens, C: J: H. Posthumous papers of
the Pickwick club. 823.5173
—— — *Same.* 823.5556; 823.5677
—— — *Same.* 2 vols. 823.449–9¹; 823.5296–7
—— — *Same.* 4 vols. 823.445–8
—— James, G: P. R. The convict. 823.7307
—— Reade, C: It is never too late to mend.
823.1292
—— Smith, H. In prison and out.
823.1458
—— — *Same.* *in* 823.6687
Temperance. Jenkins, E: The devil's chain.
823.899

Life-saving service.
—— Ballantyne, R. M. Battles with the
sea. 808.1549
—— — The life-boat. 808.827
London fire brigade. Ballantyne, R. M.
Fire brigade. 808.208
Mail service. Ballantyne, R. M. Post
haste. 808.1271
Railroad system. Ballantyne, R. M. The
iron horse. 808.1261

COUNTRY LIFE.
—— Blackmore, R: D. Cradock Nowell.
823.5837
—— Cross, *Mrs.* M.. A. (E.) Adam Bede.
823.996
—— — Middlemarch: a study of provincial
life. *in* 823.6261
—— — *Same.* 2 vols. 823.1000–1001
—— Erskine, *Mrs.* T: Wyncote. 823.535
—— Gardiner, M. (P.) Country quarters.
823.599
—— Haggard, H: R. Colonel Quaritch, V.
C. 823.5529
—— Hamley, *Sir* E: B. Lady Lee's widow-
hood. 823.6072
—— Hardy, T: Far from the madding
crowd. 823.697
—— — *Same.* 823.5081; 823.5386
—— — Under the greenwood tree. 823.701
—— Howitt, W: Woodburn Grange. 3
vols. (in 1). 823.833
—— Melville, G: J: Whyte- Satanella: a
story of Punchestown. ** 823.4668
—— Mitford, M.. R. Our village.
823.2148–9
—— Sewell, E.. M. Margaret Percival.
823.4177
—— Stannard, *Mrs.* H. E. V. (P.) Army so-
ciety: life in a garrison town.
in 823.5040
—— Trollope, A. The Bertrams. 823.1604
—— — Eustace diamonds. 823.1608
—— — Orley Farm. 823.1618
—— — Sir Harry Hotspur of Humbleth-
waite. 823.1624
—— — *Same.* 823.5997
—— — Vicar of Bullhampton. 823.1629
—— — *Same.* 823.5999
—— — The warden. 823.1630

English Fiction. *Contin.*
England. *Contin.*
HANOVERIAN PERIOD, A. D. 1714-1891.
Contin.
COUNTRY LIFE. *Contin.*
—— Yonge, C.. M.. Beechcroft. 823.1760
In Berkshire. Kingsley, H: Silcote of Silcotes. 823.2033
In Cornwall.
—— Ballantyne, R. M. Deep down: a tale of the Cornish mines. 808.1264
—— — *Same.* in 823.6692
In Devonshire.
—— Blackmore, R: D. Christowell: a Dartmoor tale. 823.3916
—— Kingsley, H: Leighton Court. 823.942
—— Yonge, C.. M.. Two guardians. 823.1776
Note.—See also novels by C: Kingsley.
Isle of Man.
—— Barr, *Mrs.* A. E. (H.) Feet of clay. 823.7240
—— Caine, H. The deemster. 823.5448
In Lancashire. Hamerton, P. G. Wenderholme. 823.693
Scilly islands. Besant, W. Armorel of Lyonesse. 823.7163
In Sussex. Blackmore, R: D. Alice Lorraine. in 823.3916
—— — *Same.* 823.5836
In Wales.
—— Blackmore, R: D. Maid of Sker. 823.5831
—— Hardy, T: Wessex tales. 823.6190
In Yorkshire.
—— Blackmore, R: D. Mary Anerley. 823.2290
—— Dickens, C: J: H. Nicholas Nickleby. 823.5553
—— — *Same.* 2 vols. 823.437-7³
—— — *Same.* 823.5298-9
—— — *Same.* 4 vols. 823.433-6
—— Hamerton, P. G. Wenderholme. 823.693
—— Nicholls, *Mrs.* C.. (B.) Jane Eyre. 823.126
—— — *Same.* in 823.6261
—— — Shirley. 823.128
—— — Villette. 823.129
—— — *Same.* in 823.6261
—— Reid, T. W. Mauleverer's millions. in 823.5090
ANGLO-INDIAN LIFE. *See also* India.
—— Cunningham, H. S. Chronicles of Dustypore. 823.4375
Note.—See **Adolphus,** J. History of England. (1760-1804.) (Tory.) 7 vols. 942.441-7.—**Amos,** S. English constitution. (1830-1880.) 323.18;—Primer of the English constitution. 942.1342.—**Arblay,** *Mme.* F.. (B.) d'. Diary and letters. (1778-1840.) 2 vols. 1880. 928.363-4.—**Ashton,** J: Dawn of the 19th century in England. 2 vols. 1886. 942.1229-30.—**Bagehot,** W. English constitution. 1877. 342.5.—**Bancroft,** G: History of the United States. 10 vols. (1492-1782.) 973.32-41.—**Bloomfield,** G. (L.), *Baroness.* Reminiscences of court and diplomatic life. (1822-1871.) 923.2030.—**Browning,** O. Modern England. (1820-1874.) 1879. 942.403.—**Bryant,** W: C., *and* Gay, S. H. History of the United States. (Earliest times to 1865.) 4 vols. 1879. 973.11-13¾.—**Canning,** G:, *and others.* The poetry of the Anti-Jacobin. 1890. 821.1293.—**Cornwallis,** C:, *Marquis.* Correspondence. 3 vols. 1859. 816.49-51.—**David-**

English Fiction. *Contin.*
England. *Contin.*
HANOVERIAN PERIOD, A. D. 1714-1891.
Contin.
Note. Contin.
son, J. M. Eminent English liberals in and out of parliament. 923.798.—**Dilke,** *Sir* C: W. Problems of Greater Britain. 1890. (Relations of the English-speaking countries to the comparative politics of the countries under British government.) 327.62.—**Frothingham,** R: Rise of the republic of the United States. (1643-1790.) 1872. 324.10.—**Greville,** C: C. F. Memoirs: journal of the reigns of King George IV., King William IV., and Queen Victoria. 8 vols. v. 1: Journal of the reign of George IV. 1888. 923.1955.—**Hallam,** II. Constitutional history of England. (Accession of Henry VII. to death of George II., 1760.) 3 vols. 1876. 942.41-3.—**James,** W: Naval hist. of Gt. Brit. (1793-1827.) 6 vols. 1887. 304.1-2.—**Lecky,** W: L: H. History of England in the 18th century. 8 vols. 942. 71-2,2²-2².—**Ludlow,** J: M. The war of American independence. 1775-1783. 1876. 973.252.—**Macaulay,** T: B. *Mme.* F. B. d' Arblay. (*In his* Essays, v. 5.) p.248, *in* 824.136;—Barère. (1755-1841.) (*In his* Essays, v. 5.) p. 423, *in* 824.136;—Robert, Lord Clive. (*In his* Essays, v. 4.) p. 194, *in* 824.135;—Warren Hastings. (*In his* Essays, v. 5.) p. 1, *in* 824.136;—Samuel Johnson, Croker's ed. of Boswell's Life of. (*In his* Essays, v. 2.) p. 368, *in* 824.134;—William Pitt, Earl of Chatham. (*In his* Essays, v. 3.) p. 191, *in* 824.135;—Horace Walpole, Earl of Orford. (*In his* Essays, v. 3.) p. 143, *in* 824.135.—**McCarthy,** J. H. England under Gladstone. 1880-1884. 942.1325;—Epoch of reform. (1830-1850.) 942.868;—*Same.* 942. 1271;—History of our own times. (1837-1880.) 2 vols. 1880. 942.395-6.—**Markham,** *Admiral* J: A naval career during the old war. (1775-1826.) 923.2027.—**Martineau,** H. History of England. (1790-1854.) 4 vols. 1864. 942.112-15.—**Massey,** W: N. History of England. (1745-1801.) (Whig.) 4 vols. 1863.—**May,** T: Constitutional history. (1760-1860.) 2 vols. 1878. 942.171-2.—**Molesworth,** W: N. History of England. (1830-1874.) 3 vols. 1877. 942.265-7.—**Morris,** E. E. Early Hanoverians. (George I. and II.) (1713-1795.) 1886. 942.1266.—**Rogers,** J. E. T. Adam Smith. (1723-1790.) (*In his* Hist. gleanings, 1st ser.) p. 93, *in* 923.965;—John Horne Tooke. (1736-1812.) (*In his* Hist. gleanings, 2d ser.) p. 189, *in* 923.966;—Sir Robert Walpole, Earl of Orford. (1676-1745.) (*In his* Hist. gleanings, 1st ser.) p. 47, *in* 923.965;—John Wilkes. (1727-1797.) (*In his* Hist. gleanings, 2d ser.) p. 131, *in* 923.966.—**Rowley,** J. Settlement of the constitution. (1689-1784.) 1878. 942.308.—**Russell,** W: C. Horatio Nelson and the naval supremacy of England. 1890. 923.1926.—**Seeley,** J. R. Expansion of England. 1883. 942.922.—**Smiles,** S: Industrial biography. 1871. 926.19;—Life of George Stephenson. 925.38;—Life of James Watt. 926.39.—**Smith,** G. Foundation of the American colonies. (*In his* Lectures, 1859-61.) p. 185, *in* 907.2;—Pitt. 1784-1806. (*In his* Three Eng. statesmen.) 1878. 923.89.—**Smith,** S. Peter Plymley's letters. 816.63.—**Southey,** R. Life of Nelson. 1830. · 920.165;—Life of Wesley. 1876. 922.109.—**Stanhope,** P. H. (Lord Mahon.) History of England. (Tory.) 1713-1783. 7 vols. 1854. 942.330-6;—Notes of conversations with the Duke of Wellington. 1831-1851. 904.45.—**Stephen,** L. History of English thought in the 18th century. 2 vols. 1876. 192.21-2.—**Taine,** H. A. History of English literature. 3 vols. 820.56-8.—**Taucock,** O. W. England during the American and European wars. (1765-1820.) 1878. 942.326.—**Thackeray,** W: M. The four Georges. (Lectures.) (*Works,* v. x.) 823.1579.—**Waite,** R. Life of Wellington. 1879. 923.436.—**Walpole,** H. Memoirs. 2 vols. 923.2044-5;—Last journals of. Ed. by Dr. Doran. 2 vols. 923.2046-7.—**Walpole,** S. H. History of England. (1815-1861.) 5 vols. (Index in each vol.) 942.1351-5.—**Ward,** T: H. Reign of Victoria. (1837-1887.) 2 vols. 942. 1397-8.—**Wharton,** G., *and* P. Wits and beaux of society. 1873. 920.77.—**Wright,** T. Caricature history of the Georges. 942.198.

See also **Catalogues** of this Library.
No. 2, 1880, pp. 72-74; 97.
No. 3, 1882, pp. 61-62, 83-84.
No. 4, 1884, pp. 94-95, 120-121.
No. 5, 1888, pp. 100-101, 187-189.

English Fiction. *Contin.*
England. *Contin.*
LIFE AND MANNERS.

Note.—See **Adams**, W: H: D. The merry monarch; or, England under Charles II. (1630–1685.) 2 vols. 1885. 942.1279–80.—**Ashton**, J: The dawn of the 19th century in England. 2 vols. 1886. * 942.1229–30;—Men, maidens, and manners a hundred years ago. 1888. 942.1318;—Social life in the reign of Queen Anne. 2 vols. 1882. * 942.1190–1.—**Badeau**, A. Aristocracy in England. (1886.) 942. 1313.—**Balch**, E.. Glimpses of old English homes. Illus. 1890. * 942.1399.—**Besant**, W. Fifty years ago. 1888. 942.1278.—**Buckle**, H. T. History of civilization in England. 2 vols. 1878–9. 313. 35–6;—*Same.* 313.37–8;—*Same.* 3 vols. 313.55–7. —**Collier**, R. I.. English home life. 1886. 942. 1319.—**Colman**, H: European life and manners. 2 vols. 1849. 940.191–2.—**Gronow**, *Capt.* R. H. Reminiscences and recollections. 1810–1860. Illus. 2 vols. * 923.2025–6.—**Guild**, C. Britons and Muscovites. (Trav. and descrip., etc.) 1888. 914.467.—**Heath**, F. G: English peasantry. 1874. 942.1369. —**Holmes**, O. W. Our hundred days in Europe. 1888. 914.410.—**Hoppin**, J. M. Old England, its scenery, art, and people. 1878. 914.40.—**Howitt**, W: Visits to remarkable places. 1888. 914.440.— **Jesserand**, J. J. English wayfaring life in the middle ages. (14th cent.) 1889. 942.1284.—**Laugel**, A. A. England, political and social. 1874. 914.455.—**Lytton**, E: G: E. L. Bulwer- England and the English. 1874. 829.601.—**Mason**, E: T., *ed.* British letters illustrative of character and social life. 3 vols. 1888. 826.119–21.—**Miller**, H. First impressions of England and its people. 1873. 914. 54.—**Nadal**, E. S. Impressions of London social life. 1875. 914.39.—**Pascoe**, C: E. London of to-day. 1890. 914.454.—**Roberts**, G: Social history of the people of the southern counties of England. 1856. 942.1359.—**Shand**, A. I. Half a century; or, changes in men and manners. 2d ed. 1888. 942.1317.—**Smalley**, G: W. London letters. v. 2. 824.440.—**Thrupp**, J: The Anglo-Saxon home. (5th–11th cent.) 1862. 942.1358.—**Timbs**, J: Ancestral stories and traditions of great families illustrative of Eng. hist. 942.455;—Nooks and corners of English life, past and present. 1867. 942. 465.—**Wharton**, G., *and* P. Wits and beaux of society. 1873. 920.77.—**Wright**, T: Hist. of dom. manners during the middle ages. 1862. * 942.1396.

ENGLAND AS SEEN BY FOREIGNERS.

Blouet, P. [*Max O'Rell.*] John Bull and his island. 1887. 914.351;—*Same.* 942.958.—**Daryl**, P. Public life in England. (1884.) 942.1115.—**Emerson**, R. W. English traits. (1833–1847.) 1876. 914.53. —**Escott**, T: H. S. England: its people, polity and pursuits. 2 vols. 1879. 942.1364–5.—**Hawthorne**, N. Our old home. 1863. 915.55;—Passages from the English note-books. 1873. 914.37.—**Patten**, C. B. England as seen by an American banker. 914. 469.—**Taine**, H. Notes on England. 914.48.— **White**, R: G. England without and within. 1890. 914.456.—**Winter**, W: The trip to England. 1881. 914.465.

See also Poole's Index (to 1882). p. 408, *in* ** 50.1ᵃ;—*Same.* Jan. 1, 1882–Jan. 1, 1887. p. 141, *in* ** 50.1ᵇ.

IN GENERAL, AND FOR LONG PERIODS.

Note.—For bibliography, *see* **Adams**, C: K. Manual of historical literature. 1882. ** 907.4.—**Allen**, *Prof.* W: F. The reader's guide to English history. 1886. 907.8.—**Bright**, J. F. History of England. 4 vols. (Contains a list of authorities.) 942.398–400³. —**Gardiner**, S. R., *and* Mulliuger, J. B. Introduction to the study of English history. 1881. (pp. 200–202, by J. B. Mulliuger, on authorities.) 942.1424. —**Montgomery**, D. H. The leading facts of English history. 2d ed. 1889. (pp. 404–408. A short list of books on English history.) 942.1293.—**Sonnenschein**, W. S. The best books: classified bibliography. 1887. ** 17.238.

For comprehensive works, *see* **Allen**, J. Battles of the British navy. 2 vols. 1852. v. 1: 1190–1799. v. 2: 1800–1840. 942.338–9.—**Bright**, J. F. History of England. (A. D. 419–1880.) 4 vols. 942. 398–400–400¹.—**Green**, J: R: History of the English people. (A. D. 449–1885.) 4 vols. 942.225–7–7³.— **Hosmer**, J. K. Hist. of Anglo-Saxon freedom. (Polity of the Eng. speaking race.) 1890. 323.17.— **Hozier**, H. M. The invasions of England. 2 vols.

English Fiction. *Contin.*
England. *Contin.*
IN GENERAL, AND FOR LONG PERIODS. *Contin.*

Note. Contin.
(Norman conquest to A. D. 1805.) 1876. 942.1298–9. —**Hume**, D: History of England. (D. C. 55–A. D. 1689.) (Tory.) 6 vols. 942.65–70.—**Kennet**, W., *and* Hughes, J. Hist. of England (to 1701). 3 vols. ** 942.1418–20.—**Knight**, C: Popular history of England. (D. C. 56–A. D. 1848.) 942.79–86.—**Lingard**, J. History of England. (B. C. 55–A. D. 1689.) (Roman Catholic.) 10 vols. 942.87–96.—**Morris**, E: E., *ed.* Epochs of modern history, *viz.*: Beginning of the middle ages—England and Europe in the ninth century. By R. W. Church. 940.163;—Normans in Europe—Feudal system and England under Norman kings. By A. H. Johnson. 940.164;— Crusades. By G: W: Cox. 940.165;—Early Plantagenets—their relation to the history of Europe: foundation and growth of constitutional government. By W: Stubbs. 942.1267;—Edward III. By W. Warburton. 923.1836;—Houses of Lancaster and York—the conquest and loss of France. By J. Gairdner. 942.1268;—Era of the Protestant revolution. By F: Seebohm. 274.56;—Early Tudors. Henry VII., Henry VIII. By C. E. Moberley. 942. 1269;—Age of Elizabeth. By M. Creighton. 942. 1270;—Thirty years' war, 1618–1648. By S: R. Gardiner. 943.101;—Puritan revolution, and the first two Stuarts, 1603–1660. By S. R. Gardiner. 942.1263;— Fall of the Stuarts, and western Europe. By F: Hale. 942.1264;—Age of Anne. By E: E. Morris. 942.1265;—Early Hanoverians—Europe from the Peace of Utrecht to the Peace of Aix-la-Chapelle. By E: E. Morris. 942.1266;—Frederick the Great and the seven years' war. By F. W. Longman. 943.102;—French revolution and first empire. By W: O'C. Morris. App. by A. D. White. 944.628;— Epoch of reform, 1830–1850. By J. McCarthy. 942. 1271;—English restoration and Louis XIV. From Peace of Westphalia to Peace of Nimwegen. By O. Airy. 940.162.—**Ransome**, C. History of England. (B. C. 55–A. D. 1887.) 942.1308;—Rise of constitutional government in England. 1883. 323.16.— **Stone**, A. P. A history of England. (List of works for reference, pp. 226–233.) 1890. 942.1316. For British colonies, *see also* British North America.—United States: *Colonial period.*—West Indies.— **Bourne**, H. R. F. Story of our colonies. 1888. 942.1292.—**Froude**, J. A. Oceana; or, England and her colonies. 1888. 910.63.—**Lucas**, C. P. Hist. geography of the British colonies. v. 1. 1888. 942. 1384.

See also **Catalogues** of this Library.
No. 2, 1880, pp. 72–74, 97.
No. 3, 1882, pp. 61–62, 83–84.
No. 4, 1884, pp. 94–95, 120–121.
No. 5, 1888, pp. 100–101, 187–189.

See also Index to Consular reports. 1880–1885; 1886–1889. 2 vols. (U. S. Pub. Docs. *Dept. of State.*) *See also* Poole's Index (to 1882). pp. 408–15, *in* ** 50.1ᵃ;—*Same.* Jan. 1, 1882–Jan. 1, 1887. pp. 141–3, *in* ** 50.1ᵇ.

England's great protector. Herbert, H: W:
823.5687
English at the north pole. Verne, J. 823.6880
Same.   823.7126
English Bodley family. Scudder, H. E.
808.1853
English family Robinson. Reid, *Capt.* T: M.
808.431
English orphans, The. Holmes, *Mrs.* M.. J..
(H.)   823.793
English poetry, Stories from old. Richardson, *Mrs.* A. (S.)   808.1690
English squire, An. Coleridge, C. R.
in 823.5053
Ennery, Adolphe Philippe d'. *See* D'Ennery, A. P.
Ennui. Edgeworth, M.   823.505
Same.   p. 7, *in* ** 823.4652
Same.   p. 1, *in* 823.7427

English Fiction. *Contin.*

Eunice Lathrop, spinster. Noble, A. L.
823.7440

Europe. *See also* Crusades.—Reformation. *Also* names of particular countries, as France, Germany, Italy, Spain, etc.

—— Adams, W: T. Isles of the sea; or, Young America homeward bound. 808.494

—— Butterworth, H. Zigzag journeys in Europe. 808.1820

—— — Zigzag journeys in northern lands: the Rhine to the Arctic. 808.1814

—— — Zigzag journeys in the Orient: the Adriatic to the Baltic. 808.1818

—— Cox, *Sir* G: W:, *and* Jones, E. H. Popular romances of the middle ages. 940.54

—— Edgar, J: G: History for boys; or, annals of nations of modern Europe. 808.800

—— Forney, J: W. The new nobility: a story of Europe and America. 823.6089

—— Gould, S. Baring- Curious myths of the middle ages. 940.35

—— Hale, E: E., *and* Hale, S. A family flight through France, Germany, Norway and Switzerland. 808.1831

—— Saxon, *Mrs.* E. L., *ed.* Belt and spur: stories of the middle ages from the old chronicles. 808.1610

—— Scudder, H. E. Mr. Bodley abroad.
808.1851

—— Waddington, S:, *comp.* The sonnets of Europe. 1887. 821.1274

—— Wagner, *Dr.* W. Epics and romances of the middle ages. 823.6146

—— Whitney, *Mrs.* A. D. (T.) Sights and insights. 2 vols. 823.1699–1700

Note.—See Allison, A. History of Europe. (1789–1815.) 12 vols. * 940.36–47;—*Same.* 1815–1852. 8 vols. and index. 9 vols. * 940.182–90.—**Draper**, J: W: History of the intellectual development of Europe. 2 vols. 309.4–5.—**Dyer**, T: H: History of modern Europe. (1453–1857.) 4 vols. 940.9–12.—**Emerton**, *Prof.* E: Introduction to the study of the middle ages. (375–814.) 940.113.—**Freeman**, E: A. Four Oxford lectures, 1887. Fifty years of European history. Teutonic conquest in Gaul and Britain. 1888. 940.167;—The historical geography of Europe. 2 vols. Text and plates. 1882. 940. 129–30;—History of Europe. (Hist. primers.) 1881. 940.73.—**Geikie**, J. Pre-historic Europe. 1881. 81.6.—**Gibbon**, E: Decline and fall of the Roman empire. 6 vols. 937.8–13.—*Same.* 7 vols. 937.63–9.—**Hallam**, H: View of the state of Europe during the middle ages. 940.1;—*Same.* 3 vols. 940.2–4.—**Holmes**, O.W. Our hundred days in Europe. 1888. 914.410.—**Loe**, A. E. European days and ways. 1890. 914.466.—**Lilly**, W: S: Chapters in European hist. 2 vols. 1886. 940.193–4.—**Lord**, J. Character and society of the middle ages. (*In* Froissart, J. *Chronicles.*) 940.15.—**Murdock**, H. Reconstruction of Europe. Sketch of the diplomatic and military history of continental Europe; from the rise to the fall of the second French empire. 1889. (Bibliographical note, pp. 403–405.) 940.170.—**Myers**, P. V. N. Outlines of mediæval and modern history. 1889. 940.169.—**Traet**, J. van. Essays on the political history of the 15th–17th centuries. 1868. 940. 18.—**Russell**, W: History of modern Europe. With continuation, . . . to the present time by W: Jones. 3 vols. 1856. 940.18–20.—**Schlosser**, F. C. History of the 18th and 19th centuries, etc. 8 vols. * 940.151–8.—**Ungewitter**, F. H. Europe: its past and present condition. 1856. 940.168.—**Weir**, A. Hist. bases of modern Europe. (1760–1815.) 940.197.

See also **Catalogues** of this Library.

No. 2, 1880, p. 78. No. 4, 1884, p. 98.
No. 3, 1882, pp. 66–67. No. 5, 1888, p. 136.
See also **Poole's** Index (to 1882). pp. 429–31, *in* ** 50.1;—*Same.* Jan. 1, 1882–Jan. 1, 1887. p. 148, *in* ** 50.1².

English Fiction. *Contin.*

European slave life. 3 vols. (in 1). Hackländer, F. W. ** 823.6638

Europeans, The. James, H:, *Jr.* 823.884

Eustace diamonds. Trollope, A. 823.1608

Eustache de St. Pierre. 8 pp. Herbert, H: W: p. 107, *in* 823.4253

Eutaw. Simms, W: G. 823.1430

Eva St. Clair. James, G: P. R. 823.5892

Evan Harrington. Meredith, G: 823.1154

Évangéliste, L'. Daudet, A. 823.5566

Evans, Augusta J.. *See* Wilson, *Mrs.* A. J.. (E.)

Eve. Gould, S. Baring- 823.5403

Eve Effingham. Cooper, J. F. ** 823.6259

Evelina. 2 vols. (in 1). Arblay, *Mme.* F.. (B.) d'. 823.1911

Same. 2 vols. ** 823.2099–2100

Evelyn's folly. Brame, *Mrs.* C.. M. (L.) 823.5126

Evenings at Haddon Hall: a series of romantic tales of the olden time. 823.2151

Evenings at home. Aikin, J:, *and* Barbauld, *Mrs.* A.. L. (A.) 808.1664

Every-day business. Emery, M. S.
808.1586

Evil eye, The. Carleton, W: 823.171

Evil genius, The. Collins, W: W. 823.5647

Evil that men do. Fawcett, E. 823.6411

Evil that women do. Racowitza, H. von.
823.7025

Ewald, Herman F: The treasure of Kjœrsholm. 12 pp. — Olufsborg. 14 pp. (Vicary, J: F., *comp. A stork's nest.*)
in 823.5415

Ewing, *Gen.* Hugh Boyle. A castle in the air. 823.5497

Ewing, *Mrs.* Juliana Horatia (Gatty). A great emergency, and other tales. 823.536

—— Jackanapes, and other stories.
in 823.5090

—— Six to sixteen: a story for girls.
823.537

Executor, The. Hector, *Mrs.* A. (F.)
823.4621

Same. 823.4977

Exemplary novels of Miguel de Cervantes Saavedra. Tr. by W. K. Kelly. 823.6898

Exeter Hall. McDonnell, W: 823.6158

Exile of von Adelstein's soul. 78 pp. Underwood, F. H: 823.4174

Exiles, The. 46 pp. Balzac, H. de.
p. 229, *in* 823.7335

Exile's romance, An. Keyser, A. 823.7391

Expatriation. By the author of "Aristocracy." 823.7238

Expedition of Humphry Clinker. 2 vols. Smollett, T. G: ** 823.2091–2

Experiences of Richard Taylor, Esq. Johnstone, *Mrs.* C. I. * 823.6194

Experiment in marriage. Bellamy, C: J.
823.7167

Expiated. Prior, H. L. 823.5870

Expiation. French, A. 823.6950

Faber, Christian. Fickle fortune: a story of Place la Grève. 823.538

Fabiola. Wiseman, N: P. S. 823.4615

English Fiction. *Contin.*
Fables.

—— Æsop. A child's version of (his) fables ; with a supplement containing fables from La Fontaine and Krilof. (Ed. by) T. H. Stickney. 808.1470

—— —— Fables. Ed. by E: Garrett. 829.322

—— —— Fables, English and Hindoostance. * 894.3

—— —— Three hundred Æsop's fables. 829.379

—— Babrius. Mythiambics (Greek). 884.9

—— Bidpai, *or* Pilpay. Fables. Ed. by J. Jacobs. ** 899.29

—— Bleek, W. H. I. Reynard the fox in south Africa; or, Hottentot fables and tales. * 899.15

—— Bulfinch, T: Poetry of the age of fable. 821.53

—— Dryden, J: Fables. (*Poetical works.*) pp. 211-262, *in* 821.125

—— Dubois, J. A., *abbé.* Hindu fables. 6 pp. (*In his* Description . . . of India.) p. 502, *in* * 954.114

—— Eggleston, E: Modern fables. (*In his* Queer stories . . .) *in* 808.1418

—— Gay, J: Fables, with memoir. By A. Dobson. 821.907

—— Hood, T: The fox and the hen (poem). 4 pp. (*Works*, v. 2.) p. 263, *in* 828.52

—— —— The kangaroos (poem). 3 pp. (*Works*, v. 2.) p. 193, *in* 828.52

—— Iriarte, T. de. Fábulas literarias. (Spanish.) 861.3

—— Jefferies, R: Wood magic. 808.1595

—— La Fontaine, J. de. Fables (in French). 841.48

—— —— *Same.* (*Coll. des classiques français.*) p. 279, *in* 840.24

—— Lytton, E: R. Bulwer- Fables in song. 821.263

—— Phædrus. Fables. (*With* Terrence. *Comedies.*) p. 365, *in* 872.5

—— Saxe, J: G. Fables and legends of many countries (poems). 821.351

—— Tolstoi, *Count* L. N. Fables paraphrased from the Indian, and imitations. 33 pp. (*In his* The long exile, etc.) p. 211, *in* 808.1348

—— Wesselhoeft, *Mrs.* E.. F. (P.) The winds, the woods, and the wanderer: a fable for children. 808.1692

Fabre, Ferdinand. The abbé Tigrane, candidate for the papal chair. Tr. by Rev. L. W. Bacon. 823.4136

Face illumined. Roe, E: P. 823.1356

Facing death. Henty, G: A. 808.1482

Facino Cane. 22 pp. Balzac, H. de. p. 151, *in* 823.5428

Fainalls of Tipton. Johnson, V. W. 823.4784

Fair barbarian, A. Burnett, *Mrs.* F.. E. (H.) 823.4151

Fair but false. Brame, *Mrs.* C.. M. (L.) 823.5099

Fair emigrant, A. Mulholland, R. 823.7059

Fair god. Wallace, L. 823.1668

Fair Harvard. Washburn, W: T. 823.7115

Fair maid, A. Robinson, F: W: 823.7063

English Fiction. *Contin.*

Fair maid of Perth. Scott, *Sir* W. 823.1397

Same. *in* 823.5155; ** 823.6033

Fair mystery, A. Brame, *Mrs.* C.. M. (L.) *in* 823.5042

Fair play. Southworth, *Mrs.* E. D. E. (N.) 823.1486

Fair prospect, The. 12 pp. (Bushby, *Mrs.* —, *tr.* The Danes . . . , v. 3.) p. 1, *in* 823.6446

Fair Puritan, The. Herbert, H: W: 823.764

Fair Saxon. McCarthy, J. 823.1053

Fair women. Bridges, *Mrs. Col.*— 823.3157

Same. *in* 823.4990

Faire gospeller, Passages in the life of the. Rathbone, *Mrs.* M.. A. (M.) 823.4079

Fairer than a fairy. Grant, J. 823.626

Fairfax, Lina Redwood. Misfortunes of bro' Thomas Wheatley. 25 pp. (*In* Stories by Amer. authors, v. 6.) p. 68, *in* 823.4707

Fairfax. Cooke, J: E. 823.5509

Fairleigh, Frank, *pseud. See* Smedley, F. E:

Fairleigh Hall. Crake, A. D. 823.7098

Fairy book. Macé, J. 808.406

Fairy gold. Kirk, *Mrs.* E. W. (O.) 823.5900

Fairy guardians. Willoughby, F. 808.1693

Fairy legends and traditions of the south of Ireland. Croker, T: C. * 299.21

Fairy tales.

—— Abbott, J. Minigo; or, the fairy of Cairnstone Abbey. (*In his* Harper's story books, v. 11.) *in* 808.590

—— Andersen, H. C. Danish fairy legends and tales. 808.771

—— —— Fairy tales. (Complete ed.) 808.1928

—— —— The goloshes of fortune, and other stories. 808.600

—— —— The old church bell, and other stories. 808.605

—— —— Popular tales for children. 808.1729

—— —— The sand-hills of Jutland. 808.1730

—— —— Stories and tales. 808.377

—— —— Stories for the household. 808.1323

—— Arabian nights' entertainments. 808.398

—— Aulnoy, M. C. (J. de B.), *comtesse* d'. Fairy tales. 808.1927

—— Austin, *Mrs.* J.. (G.) Moonfolk: a true account of the home of the fairy tales. 808.396

—— Baumbach, R. Summer legends. 808.1660

—— Bunce, J. T. Fairy tales, their origin and meaning. 823.4509

—— Child's own book, and treasury of fairy stories. 808.1028

—— Cooley, *Mrs.* A. (K.) Ho ! for Elf-land. 808.1027

—— Craik, *Mrs.* D. M. (M.) Is it true? 808.114

—— Croker, T. C. Fairy legends and traditions of the south of Ireland. * 299.21

—— Dodgson, C: L. Alice's adventures in Wonderland. 808.688

—— —— Sylvie and Bruno. 808.1553

—— —— Through the looking-glass and what Alice found there. 808.687

English Fiction. *Contin.*
Fairy tales. *Contin.*
—— Drake, J. R. The culprit fay. 6 pp.
(Bryant, W: C. *New lib. of poetry*, v. 2.)
     p. 769, *in* * 821.44
—— Griffis, W: E. Japanese fairy world.
     808.1026
—— Grimm, J. L., *and* W. K: German
household stories.   808.793
—— —— German popular stories. With in-
trod. by J: Ruskin. Illus. by G: Cruik-
shank.   808.1592
—— —— German popular stories and fairy
tales.   808.1107
—— —— German popular tales.   808.411
—— —— *Same.*   808.1322
—— —— Household stories.   808.1315
—— Guiney, L. I. Brownies and bogles.
     808.1599
—— Hackländer, F. W. Enchanting and
enchanted.   808.1493
—— Hahn, J. G. v. Griechische und alban-
esische Märchen.   833.1050
—— Halliwell-Philipps, J. O. Illustrations
of the fairy mythology of Midsummer
night's dream. (*Shakes. Soc.*) ** 822.171
—— Harrison, *Mrs.* C. (C.) Bric-a-brac sto-
ries.   808.1685
—— —— Old-fashioned fairy book.   808.1365
—— Hauff, W. Longnose the dwarf, etc.
     808.1237
—— Hays, *Mrs.* H.. Adventures of Prince
Lazybones, and other stories. 808.1355
—— Hazlitt, W. C. Fairy tales, legends and
romances, illustrating Shakespeare and
other English writers.   * 822.309
—— Hebbel, F. Der Rubin: ein Märchen.
16 pp. (*Sämmt. Werke*, v. 9.)
     p. 189, *in* 839.69
—— Hood, T: The plea of the midsummer
fairies. 38 pp.—The two swans. 10 pp.
(poems.) (*Works*, v. 5.)
     pp. 213, 5, *in* 828.55
—— Household tales and fairy stories.
     808.1340
—— Hugessen, E. H. Knatchbull- Hig-
gledy-piggledy.   808.810
—— —— Moonshine. Fairy stories. 808.885
—— —— Puss-cat Mew, and other stories for
my children.   808.1679
—— —— Queer folk.   808.1049
—— —— Tales at tea-time.   808.886
—— —— Whispers from fairy-land.   808.763
—— Johnson, V. W. The Catskill fairies.
     808.636
—— Keary, E. Magic Valley; or, patient
Antoine.   808.1544
—— Kingsley, C: The heroes; or, Greek
fairy tales.   808.550
—— —— *Same.*   808.1006
—— Laboulaye, É. R. L. Fairy tales of all
nations.   808.672
—— —— Last fairy tales.   808.1312
—— Lang, A., *ed.* The blue fairy book.
     808.1687
—— —— The red fairy book.   808.1688
—— MacDonald, G: The princess and the
goblin.   808.1677
—— Macé, J. Home fairy tales.   808.406

English Fiction. *Contin.*
Fairy tales. *Contin.*
—— Mathews, C., *tr.* Indian fairy book.
     808.1330
—— Mitchell, S. W. Prince Little Boy, and
other tales out of Fairy-land. 808.1350
—— Pabke, M., *and* Pitman, *Mrs.* M. J. (D.)
Wonder-world stories from the Chinese,
French, German . . .   808.393
—— Paton, *Sir* J. N. Princess of Silverland,
and other tales.   808.1329
—— Rink, *Dr.* H: Tales and traditions of
the Eskimo.   299.16
—— Sanford, *Mrs.* M. M. (R.) Visit to El-
fay-gno-land.   808.768
—— Scudder, H. E. Dream children.
     808.1560
—— —— Seven little people and their friends.
     808.1559
—— Ségur, S. (R.), *comtesse* de. Fairy tales.
     808.1326
—— Smith, J. M. Tales of old Thulê.
     808.753
—— Stockton, F. R: The bee-man of Orn,
and other fanciful tales.   808.1349
—— —— The floating prince, and other fairy
tales.   808.1345
—— —— *Same.*   808.1902
—— —— Ting-a-ling.   808.1137
—— —— *Same.*   808.1410
—— Valentine, *Mrs.* —., *ed.* Eastern tales
by many story-tellers.   808.389
—— Wilde, O. O'F. F. W. The happy
prince, and other tales.   808.1643
—— Willoughby, F. Fairy guardians.
     808.1693
—— Wright, H. C. The princess Liliwin-
kins, and other stories.   808.1558
     See also Poole's Index (to 1882). p. 439, *in* **
     50.1;—*Same.* Jan. 1, 1882–Jan. 1, 1887. p. 151, *in* **
     50.1².
Fairy tales of all nations. Laboulaye, É. R.
L.   808.672
Faith and unfaith. Hungerford, *Mrs.* M.
     823.3989
Faith Gartney's girlhood. Whitney, *Mrs.* A.
D. (T.)   823.1693
Faithful Margaret. Ashmore, A.   823.42
Faithfull, Emily. A reed shaken with the
wind: a love story.   823.539
Falcon family, The. Savage, M. W.
     * 823.6144
Falconberg. Boyesen, H. H.   823.4217
Falkland. Lytton, E: G: E. L. Bulwer-
     823.1029
Same.   p. 145, *in* 823.5863
Same.   p. 149, *in* 823.5975
Fall of Asgard, The. Corbett, J.   823.5648
Fall of Damascus. Russell, C: W. 823.1375
Fall of England? Chesney, C: C. 823.4015
Fallen idol, A. Guthrie, F: A.   823.5676
Fallen pride. Southworth, *Mrs.* E. D. E.
(N.)   823.1487
False Christ, The. Charles, *Mrs.* E.. (R.)
     p. 65, *in* 823.5577
False or true. 19 pp. Opie, *Mrs.* A. (A.)
     p. 375, *in* 823.6136
Falsely accused: a criminal trial in Nürnberg.
1790. (*In* Tales from Blackwood, 2d ser.,
v. 3.)   *in* 823.7487

English Fiction. *Contin.*
Fame and sorrow, etc. Balzac, H. de.
    823.7177
Family affair, A. Fargus, F: J: 823.4912
   Same.   823.5069
Family doom, The. Southworth, *Mrs.* E. D.
E. (N.)   823.1488
Family feud, A. Harder, L.   823.6802
Family flight around home. Hale, E: E.,
and Hale, S.   808.1832
Family flight over Egypt and Syria. Hale,
E: E., *and* Hale, S.   808.1829
Family flight through France, Germany, Nor-
way and Switzerland. Hale, E: E., *and*
Hale, S.   808.1831
Family flight through Mexico. Hale, E: E.,
and Hale, S.   808.1830
Family fortunes. Mayo, *Mrs.* I. (F.)
    823.4465
Family romance. Burke, *Sir* J: B. 823.152
Family secrets. 3 vols. Ellis, *Mrs.* S.. (S.)
    823.527-9
Famous American Indians. *See* Eggleston,
E:, *and* Seelye, *Mrs.* L. (E.)
Famous boys and famous men. Illus.
    808.1666
   Contents:—Webster, D.—Drew, S:—Franklin, B:
—Burns, R.—Kane, E. K.—Clay, H:—Leyden, J:—
Montgomery, J.—Bowditch, N.—Havelock, H:—
Livingstone, D:—Evans, O.—Coleridge, S: T.—Fulton,
R.—Kitto, J:—Davy, H.—Lawrence, A.—Girard, S.
—Crompton, S:—Chalmers, T:—Laffitte, J.—Audu-
bon, J: J.—Jay, W:—Sherman, R.
Famous stories. De Quincey, T:, and others.
    823.1778
Famous victory, A. (Anon.)   823.4356
Fanchon the cricket. Dudevant, *Mme.* A. L.
A. (D.)   823.6847
Fane, Violet, *pseud. See* Singleton, *Mrs.* M..
(M. L.)
Fanshawe. Hawthorne, N.   823.727
Far above rubies. Riddell, *Mrs.* C.. E. L.
(C.)   823.1324
Far from the madding crowd. Hardy, T:
    823.697
   Same.   823.5081; 823.5386
Fardorougha, the miser. Carleton, W:
    823.172
Fargus, F: J: [*Hugh Conway.*] The Blatch-
ford bequest, and other stories. 823.5064
—— Bound by a spell.   *in* 823.5067
—— *Same.*   823.5068
—— Called back.   823.4913
—— *Same.*   *in* 823.5094
—— A cardinal sin: a novel.   823.4924
—— *Same.*   *in* 823.5125
—— Carriston's gift.   *in* 823.5012
—— Dark days.   823.4915
—— *Same.*   *in* 823.5106
—— *Same* (and other stories).   823.4817
—— The daughter of the stars, and other
tales.   *in* 823.5094
—— A family affair.   823.4912
—— *Same.*   823.5069
—— Living or dead.   *in* 823.4978
—— *Same.*   *in* 823.5056; 823.5066
—— Paul Vargas: a mystery; and other tales.
    in 823.4981
—— *Same.*   *in* 823.4982
—— Slings and arrows, and other stories.
    in 823.5046

English Fiction. *Contin.*
Farina, Salvatore. 1846—. Separation.
(Zimmern, H., *and* A. *Half-hours with
for. novelists.*)   *in* ** 823.6613
Farina. Meredith, G: *in* 823.5274
Farjeon, B: Leopold. Blade-o'-grass. (*Also*)
Golden grain. — Bread-and-cheese and
kisses.—The king of No-land.—(*And*) An
island Pearl.   823.6125
—— Bread-and-cheese and kisses. 76 pp.
(*With his* Blade-o'-grass.) *in* 823.6125
—— Bright star of life. (*With his* Nine of
hearts.)   *in* 823.6587
—— *Same.*   823.7122
—— Doctor Glennie's daughter: a story of
real life.   823.7373
—— The duchess of Rosemary lane.
    823.5865
—— Gautran; or, the House of White Shad-
ows. (*And*) Little Make-Believe. 823.6599
—— Golden grain. (A sequel to Blade-o'-
grass.)   823.5864
—— *Same.*   *in* 823.6125
—— The golden land; or, links from shore
to shore.   808.1711
—— Grif: a story of Australian life. 823.545
—— An island Pearl: a novel. 823.5859
—— *Same.*   *in* 823.6125
—— Jessie Trim.   823.6373
—— Joshua Marvel.   823.5860
—— The king of No-land.   823.5861
—— *Same.*   *in* 823.6125
—— Little Make-Believe. (*With his* Gau-
tran.)   *in* 823.6599
—— London's heart: a novel. 823.550
—— Love's victory: a novel. 823.5852
—— The murderer's confession. 9 pp. (*In*
Twenty novelettes . . .)
    p. 3, *in* 823.7183
—— The nine of hearts. (*With his* The
bright star of life.)   *in* 823.7122
—— *Same.* (*Also*) Bright star of life.—The
sacred nugget.—(*And*) A secret inheritance.
    823.6587
—— The sacred nugget. (*With his* Nine of
hearts.)   *in* 823.6587
—— A secret inheritance. (*With his* Nine of
hearts.)   *in* 823.6587
—— Shadows on the snow: a Christmas
story.   823.5866
—— Toilers of Babylon.   823.6320
Farm of Muiceron. Rheil, M. *in* 823.6285
Farmer, *Mrs.* Lydia Hoyt. A story book of
science.   808.1712
Farming for boys. Morris, E. 808.1547
Farquhar, G: Macauley, E. Tales of the
drama founded on . . . the comedies of
. . . Farquhar . . .   823.1051
Farquharson, Martha, *pseud. See* Finley, M.
Farrar, C: A. J. Down the west branch.
(Lake and forest ser., No. 3.) 808.1731
Farrers of Budge-Row, The. Martineau, H.
    in ** 823.6714
Farrier lass o' Piping Pebworth. 87 pp.
Chanler, *Mrs.* A. (R.) p. 81, *in* 823.5384
Fascinating woman, A. Adam, *Mme.* J. (L.)
    823.4527
Fashion and famine. Stephens, *Mrs.* A. S.
(W.)   823.1972

English Fiction. *Contin.*
Fashionable sufferer, A. Hoppin, A: 823.4616
Fast in the ice. Ballantyne, R. M. 808.673
  Same. *in* 808.1266 ; 808.1284
Fatal marriage, The. 59 pp. Maxwell, *Mrs.
  M.. E.. (B.)* 823.5108
  Same. 823.6604
Fatal marriage, The. Southworth, *Mrs. E.
  D. E. (N.)* 823.1489
Fatal repast, The. 20 pp. (*In* Tales from
  Blackwood, v. 10.) *in ** 823.6656
Fatal secret. Southworth, *Mrs. E. D. E.
  (N.)* 823.1490
Fatal whisper, The. Galt, J:
  p. 181, *in* 823.702
Fate, The. James, G: P. R. *in* 823.6247
Fate of Mansfield Humphreys. White, R:
  G. 823.4783
Fate of young Chubb. 5 pp. Clark, C: H.
  p. 75, *in* 823.5478
Fated to be free. Ingelow, J. 823.840
Father and daughter. Bremer, F. 823.2174
Father Connell. Banim, M. 823.57
Father of his country. Watson, H: C.
  808.726
Father Oswald: a genuine Catholic story.
  823.1178
Fathers and sons. Hook, T. E: 823.4286
Fathers and sons. Turgénef, I. S. 823.4211
Fatima. Jackman, A. S. 823.6561
Faust, Johann. Dr. Faustus. (Roscoe, T:
  The German novelists, v. 1.)
  p. 256, *in ** 823.6826
Faustine. Booth, *Mrs. E. M. J. (G.) von.*
  823.5779
Favourite Bible stories. Illus. 808.1582
Fawcett, Edgar. The adventures of a widow.
  823.4889
—— An ambitious woman. 823.6436
—— *Same.* 823.6560
—— The confessions of Claud. 823.5743
—— A daughter of silence. 823.7255
—— Divided lives: a novel. 823.5573
—— Douglas Duane. (*With* Sinfire. By J.
  Hawthorne.) *in* 823.5571
—— The evil that men do. 823.6411
—— A gentleman of leisure. 823.4238
—— The house at High Bridge. 2d ed.
  823.5741
—— How a husband forgave. 823.6451
—— A man's will. 823.5419
—— Miriam Balestier: a novel. 823.5572
—— Olivia Delaplaine. 823.5396
—— Tinkling cymbals. 823.5742
Fay, Theodore Sedgwick. (1807—.) Norman
  Leslie: a tale of the present times. 2 vols.
  ** 823.6759–60
  Note.—See **Griswold,** R. W. Prose writers of
  America. 1870. p. 449, *in * 829.110.
Fearful responsibility, and other stories.
  Howells, W: D. 823.1870
Feathers, furs, and fins; or, stories of animal
  life for children. 808.1910
Feats on the fiord. Martineau, H. 808.1198
Fedora. Bélot, A. 823.5727
Feet of clay. Barr, *Mrs. A. E. (H.)* 823.7240
Felbermann, Heinrich. Princess Dagomar
  of Poland. 29 pp. *in* 823.5084
—— *Same.* (*With* That terrible man. By
  W: E: Norris.) *in* 823.5089

English Fiction. *Contin.*
Felicitas. Dahn, F. 823.5728
Felina de Chambure. Dumas, A. D.
  823.5880
Felix Holt, the Radical. Cross, *Mrs. M.. A.
  (E.)* 823.999
Felmeres, The. Elliot, S. B. 823.525
Felon's reverie, The. 22 pp. (Bushby,
  Mrs. —, tr. The Danes . . , v. 1.)
  p. 177, *in* 823.6444
Female nihilist, A. Dragomonov, M.
  823.6188
Female Quixote. 2 vols. Lennox, *Mrs. C..
  (R.)* ** 823.2085–6
Fénelon, François de Salignac de la Mothe.
  Adventures of Telemachus. Tr. by J:
  Hawkesworth. 823.6211
—— Works, v. 1. 823.6916
  Contents:— Life of Fénelon. By A. de Lamar-
  tine.— Essay on the character and genius of
  Fénelon. By A. F. Villemain.—Critical opinions
  upon Fénelon and his works.—Telemachus.
Fenian alarm, A. 47 pp. (*In* Tales from
  Blackwood, 2d ser., v. 10.) *in* 823.7494
Fenn, G: Manville. The bag of diamonds.
  823.5591
—— Black blood: a peculiar case. (*With
  his* The parson o' Dumford.) *in* 823.2261
—— The chaplain's craze: being the mystery
  of Fiudon Friars. 823.5595
—— Commodore Junk. *in* 823.6698
—— The dark house: a knot unraveled.
  in 823.5046
—— Devon boys: a tale of the north shore.
  808.1713
—— Dick o' the fens: a tale of the great
  east swamp. 808.1444
—— The fanfare. 14 pp. (*In* Twenty nov-
  elettes . . .) p. 73, *in* 823.7183
—— Hollowdell Grange; or, holiday hours
  in a country home. 808.1498
—— In the king's name; or, the cruise of
  the "Kestrel." 808.1714
—— The master of ceremonies. 823.7374
—— Middy and ensign; or, the jungle sta-
  tion: a tale of the Malay peninsula.
  808.1222
—— *Same.* 823.5740
—— Morgan's horror: a romance of the
  "west countree." 823.5596
—— Mother Carey's chicken: her voyage to
  the unknown isle. 808.1438
—— Off to the wilds: being the adventures
  of two brothers in south Africa. 808.1183
—— *Same.* 808.1496
—— One maid's mischief: a novel. 823.5568
—— Parson o' Dumford: a story of Lincoln
  folk. *in* 823.5047
—— *Same.* *in* 823.5083
—— *Same.* (*Also*) Black blood: a peculiar
  case. 823.2261
—— Poverty corner. ("A little world.") A
  city story. 823.4906
—— *Same.* *in* 823.5047; *in* 823.5083
—— Quicksilver; or, the boy with no skid to
  his wheel. 808.1497
—— The Rosery folk. 823.4808
—— *Same.* *in* 823.4993
—— "Ship ahoy!" a yarn in thirty-six
  cable lengths. 823.5922

English Fiction. *Contin.*
Fenn, G: Manville. *Contin.*
—— The story of Antony Grace.　823.5569
—— Sweet Mace: a Sussex legend of the
iron times.　823.7117
—— The treasure hunters; or, the search for
the mountain mine.　823.5919
—— The vicar's people.　823.3926
Fenton's quest.　Maxwell, *Mrs.* M.. E. (B.)
823.2416
—— *Same.*　*in* 823.4991
Ferguson, *Sir* S: [*Michael Heffernan.*]
Father Tom and the pope. 67 pp. (John-
son, R., *ed.　Little classics,* v. 9.)
p. 131, *in* 829.132
—— *Same.* (*In* Tales from Blackwood, v. 3.)
** 823.6649
—— Hibernian nights' entertainments.
823.553
—— The wet wooing: a narrative of ninety-
eight. 65 pp. (*In* Tales from Blackwood,
v. 7.)　*in* ** 823.6653
Fernandez y Gonzalez, Manuel. Hermes-
enda; or, bishop, husband, & king.　Tr. by
J. R. and J. A. G.　823.7211
Ferne Fleming.　Warfield, *Mrs.* C. A. (W.)
823.1656
Ferrier, Susan Edmonstone. Destiny; or,
the chief's daughter.　823.2051
—— The inheritance.　823.2052
—— Marriage.　823.1991
Note.—Miss Clavering contributed a few pages
(the 'History of Mrs. Douglas').
Ferry on the Danube, The.　23 pp.　Gore,
Mrs. C. F.. G. (M.)　p. 227, *in* ** 823.6568
Festival of the Three Kings.　Gore,
Mrs. C. F. G. (M.)　p. 139, *in* ** 823.6569
Fetches, The.　Banim, J:　*in* 823.61
Feud of Oak Field creek.　Royce, J.
823.6506
Feuillet, Octave. (1812–1890.) [*Désiré Haz-
ard.*]　Camors.　823.7160
Issued also as Count de Camors.
—— Diary of a woman.　823.4234
Issued also as Woman's journal.
—— Julia de Trécœur.　(Zimmern, H.., *and*
A.　*Half-hours with for. novelists,* v. 2.)
in ** 823.6614
—— Led astray.　*in* 823.5064
—— Madame de Maurescamp: a story of Pa-
risian life.　Tr. by B. Page.　823.6965
—— Romance of a poor young man. 823.2495
—— *Same.*　823.4986; *in* 823.5021; 823.6864
—— *Same.*　Tr. by J. H: Hager.　823.6887
—— The story of Sibylle.　Tr. by M. H. T.
823.6287
Note.—For his life and writings, *see* **Brunetière,**
F. Octave Feuillet. 29 pp. (*Rev. d. d. Mondes,* 1891,
3e pér., v. 103.) p. 664, *in* ** 54.399¹⁹.—**Matthews,** J.
B. Octave Feuillet. 21 pp. (*In his* French drama-
tists of the 19th cent.) p. 203, *in* 842.39.—**Mauris,**
M. Octave Feuillet. 13 pp. (*In his* French men of
letters.) 1880. p. 187, *in* 928.179.—**Montégut,** E. La
nouvelle littérature française. M. O. Feuillet. 22
pp. (*Rev. d. d. Mondes,* 1858, 2e pér., v. 18.) p. 677,
in ** 54.223.

Féval, Paul Henri Corentin. The duke's
motto; or, the little Parisian. 96 pp.
** 823.6223
Few words on social philosophy, A. 33 pp.
(*In* Tales from Blackwood, v. 12.)
in ** 823.6658

English Fiction. *Contin.*
Fickle fortune.　Faber, C: J.　823.538
Field, *Mrs.* E. M.　Bryda: a story of the In-
dian mutiny.　823.7041
—— Ethne: being a truthful historie of the
great and final settlement of Ireland by
Oliver Cromwell, and certain other note-
worthy events, from the records of Ethne
O'Connor and of Roger Standfast, captain
in the Army of the Commons of England.
2d ed.　823.6400
Field, Horace. Glitter and gold.　823.554
Field, Margaret. The secret of Fontaine-la-
Croix.　823.7079
Field of ice, The.　Verne, J.　823.4343
Same.　*in* 823.7126
Fielding, H: (1707–54.) Adventures of Jos-
eph Andrews.　823.557
—— Amelia, History of.　823.555
—— *Same.* Illus. by G: Cruikshank.
823.7069
—— History of the adventures of Joseph An-
drews and his friend Mr. Abraham Adams.
With a short biog. by T: Roscoe.　Port. Il-
lus. by G: Cruikshank.　823.7070
—— *Same.* (Barbauld, *Mrs.* A. L. (A.), *ed.*
The British novelists, v. 18.)　** 823.2079
—— The history of Tom Jones, a foundling.
823 556
—— *Same.* Illus. by G: Cruikshank. 2 vols.
823.7071-2
—— *Same.* 3 vols. (Barbauld, *Mrs.* A. L.
(A.), *ed. The British novelists,* vols. 19–
21.)　** 823.2080-2
—— Joseph Andrews, Adventures of.
823.557
—— *Same.*　823.7070
—— *Same.* (Barbauld, *Mrs.* A. L. (A.), *ed.*
The British novelists, v. 18.)　** 823.2079
—— Novels. 5 vols.　823.6149-53
Contents.—v. 1. The adventures of Joseph Andrews.
vols. 2-3.–v. 1. The history of Tom Jones. (With Life and
works of the author.)
v. 4. The history of Amelia.
v. 5. The history of the life of the late Mr. Jona-
than Wild the Great; and, A journey from this
world to the next, etc.
—— Tom Jones, a foundling, History of.
823.556
—— *Same.* 2 vols.　823.7071-2
—— *Same.* 3 vols. (Barbauld, *Mrs.* A. L.
(A.), *ed. The British novelists,* vols. 19–
21.)　** 823.2080-2
Note.—For his life and writings, *see* **Dobson,** A.
Account of Fielding. 928.430.—**Forsyth,** W: (*In*
his Novels and novelists of the 18th cent., chapter
viii.) p. 255, *in* 820.35.—**Jeaffreson,** J: C. Henry
Fielding. 27 pp. (*In his* Novels, etc., v. 1.) p. 91,
in 820.186.—**Lowell,** J. R. Fielding. 24 pp. (*In*
his Democracy.) p. 65, *in* 829.670.—**Scott,** *Sir* W.
Henry Fielding. 40 pp. (*Misc. works,* v. 3.) p. 77,
in 920.366.—**Stephen,** L. Dictionary of national
biography, v. 18. *in* ** 920.330¹⁸.—**Thackeray,** W:
M. English humourists of the 18th century.
(*Works,* v. 10.) p. 524, *in* 823.1579.—**Whipple,** E. P.
Henry Fielding. 55 pp. (*In his* Essays and reviews, v. 2.) p. 303, *in* 829.274.
See also Allibone's Dict. of Eng. literature, v. 1.
pp. 591-5, *in* ** 803.6.
See also Poole's Index (to 1882). P. 451, *in* **
50.1;—*Same.* Jan. 1, 1882–Jan. 1, 1887. p. 155, *in* **
50.1³.

Fife, M. B. In Glenoran.　823.7191
Fight with fortune.　Collins, M.　823.246
Fighting Joe.　Adams, W: T.　808.511

English Fiction. *Contin.*
Fighting Phil: the life . . . of Philip Henry
Sheridan. Headley, P. C. 808.1600
Fighting the whales. Ballantyne, R. M.
808.674
Same. *in* 808.1266; *in* 808.1284
Figs and thistles. Tourgée, A. W. 823.1593
File No. 113. Gaboriau, É. 823.3014
Same. *in* 823.5115
Filleul, M. Pendower: a story of Cornwall
in the time of Henry the Eighth. 823.558
Final reckoning, A. Henty, G: A. 808.1476
Finger of fate. Reid, *Capt.* T: M. 823.5018
Finland. Crawford, J: M., *tr.* The Kale-
vala: the epic poem of Finland. 2 vols.
899.27-8
Finley, Martha. [*Martha Farquharson.*] Ca-
sella; or, the children of the valleys.
823.4109
—— Elsie's children: a sequel to "Elsie's
motherhood." 823.559
—— Elsie's motherhood: a sequel to "Elsie's
womanhood." 823.560
—— Elsie's widowhood: a sequel to "Elsie's
children." 823.4644
—— Grandmother Elsie: sequel to "Elsie's
widowhood." 823.4645
—— Mildred's married life, and a winter
with Elsie Dinsmore: sequel to "Mildred
and Elsie." 823.4747
—— Signing the contract, and what it cost.
823.561
—— The two Elsies: sequel to "Grandmother
Elsie." 823.4904
—— Wanted—a pedigree. 823.562
Fior d' Aliza. Lamartine, A. M. L: de P. de.
823.6873
Firdusi, Abu'l Kasim Mansur Ben Ahmed
Ben Fakhr Ed-Din. The epic of kings:
stories retold from Firdusi. Tr. by H..
Zimmern. 823.6143
Fire brigade. Ballantyne, R. M. 808.208
First and last crime. 25 pp. (*In* Tales from
Blackwood, v. 11.) *in* ** 823.6657
First and last kiss, The. 37 pp. (*In* Tales
from Blackwood, v. 10.) *in* ** 823.6656
First and true love. Dudevant, *Mme.* A. L.
A. (D.) 823.6296
First fam'lies of the Sierras. Miller, C. H.
823.1159
First love & last love. Grant, J. 823.628
First love is best. Dodge, M.. A. 823.694
First person singular. Murray, D: C.
823.4938
Same. *in* 823.5097
First violin, The. Fothergill, J. 823.586
Fisher, F.. C. *See* Tiernan, *Mrs.* F.. C.
(Fisher).
Fisherman's daughter, The. Conscience, H.
in 823.5706
Fishing girl. Björnson, B. 823.4224
Fishing stories. *See* Hunting and fishing.
Fitz-Boodle papers. Thackeray, W: M.
in 823.1572
Same. p. 161, *in* 823.6323
Five hundred dollars. Chaplin, H. W.
823.6937
Five hundred majority. Hume, J. F.
823.6097

English Fiction. *Contin.*
Five weeks in a balloon. Verne, J. 823.6924
Flag on the mill. Sleight, M.. B. 823.5406
Flagg, Edmund. De Molai: the last of the
military grand masters of the order of Tem-
plar Knights: a romance of history.
823.7043
Flamingo feather, The. Munroe, K.
808.1371
Flaminia, and other stories. Original, trans-
lated, and selected. 823.5815
Flammarion, Camille. Uranie. Tr. by M..
J. Serrano. 823.7257
Flatland. Abbott, E. A. 823.4902
Fleming, G:, *pseud.* *See* Fletcher, J. C.
Fleming, Geraldine. Only a girl's love.
823.4778
—— Slaves of the ring: a story of circus life.
823.7042
Fleming, *Mrs.* May Agnes (Early). Carried
by storm. 823.2034
—— A dark conspiracy. (*With her* Norine's
revenge.) *in* 823.578
—— For better for worse. (*With her* Nor-
ine's revenge.) *in* 823.578
—— Guy Earlscourt's wife. 823.579
—— The heir of Charlton. 823.574
—— Kate Danton; or, Captain Danton's
daughters. 823.575
—— A mad marriage. 823.576
—— Norine's revenge, and, Sir Noel's heir.
(*Also*) A dark conspiracy, (and) For bet-
ter for worse. 823.578
—— One night's mystery. 823.580
—— Silent and true; or, a little queen.
823.577
—— Sir Noel's heir. (*With her* Norine's re-
venge.) *in* 823.578
—— A terrible secret. 823.581
—— A wife's tragedy. 823.4205
—— A wonderful woman. 823.582
Fleming, Margaret. Brown, J:, *M. D.* Mar-
jorie Fleming. 32 pp. (Johnson, R.., *ed.*
Little classics, v. 10.) p. 108, *in* 829.133
Flemming, Harford, *pseud.* *See* McClellan,
Mrs. H. (H.)
Fletcher, Julia Constance. [*G: Fleming.*]
Head of Medusa. 823.2324
—— Kismet. 823.4301
Issued also as A Nile novel.
—— Mirage. By the author of Kismet.
823.1993
—— Vestigia. 823.4739
Fleurange. Craven, *Mme.* P. (de la F.)
823.6843
Flip. Harte, F. B. 823.4492
Flirtation Camp. Van Dyke, T. S. 823.7137
Flitch of bacon, The. Ainsworth, W: H.
823.17
Flitters, Tatters, and the counsellor. Mac-
Nabb, *Mrs.* M.. (L.) 823.4466
Floating beacon. 36 pp. (*In* Tales from
Blackwood, v. 1.) p. 59, *in* ** 823.6647
Floating city, A. Verne, J. 823.6243
Same. 823.7091
Floating light of the Goodwin Sands. Bal-
lantyne, R. M. 808.209
Floating prince, and other fairy tales. Stock-
ton, F. R: 808.1902

English Fiction. *Contin.*

Fortunes of the maid of Arc. Herbert, H:
W: p. 115, *in* 823.4253
Fortunes of the Scattergood family. Smith,
A. 823.1449
Forty-five guardsmen. Dumas, A. D. 823.5538
Same. 823.6515
Fosdick, C: A. [*Harry Castlemon.*] Rodney
the partisan. (War ser., v. 2.) 808.1704
Fothergill, Jessie. The first violin: a novel.
823.586
—— Healey. 823.4911
—— Made or marred. (*With her* One of
three.) *in* 823.1848
—— One of three, *and* Made or marred.
823.1848
—— Peril. 823.4903
—— Probation. 823.587
—— The Wellfields. 823.2336
Foul play. Reade, C:, *and* Boucicault, D.
823.1288
Found at Blazing Star. 84 pp. Harte, F. B.
p. 109, *in* 823.4492
Found dead. Payn, J. 823.6068
Found, yet lost. Roe, E: P. 823.5481
Four meetings. 42 pp. James, H:, *Jr.*
p. 321, *in* 823.4894
Four seasons, The. La Motte-Fouqué, F. H.
K: de. 823.5196
Four sisters, The. Bremer, F. 823.1919
Fox, *Mrs.* Emily. Gemini. 823.1998
Fox hunting. Stephens, C: A. 808.244
Fragoletta. Booth, *Mrs.* E. M. J. (G.) von.
823.3888
France. *See also* Paris.
—— Abbott, J. The little Louvre. [Picture
gallery.] (*Harper's story books*, v. 2.)
808.581
—— Adams, W: T. Palace and cottage; or,
Young America in France and Switzerland.
808.491
—— Champney, *Mrs.* E.. (W.) Three Vas-
sar girls abroad. Rambles . . . through
France . . . 808.1821
—— Hale, E: E., *and* Hale, S. A family
flight through . . . 808.1831
—— Longfellow, H: W. Poems of places.
2 vols. 821.217-18
—— Ritchie, L. Romance of history:
France. 823.1278
—— Thackeray, W: M. History of the next
French revolution. (From a forthcoming
history of Europe.) (*In his* Miscellanies.)
p. 470, *in* 823.6552
—— Yonge, C.. M.. Young folks' history of
France. 808.755
MEROVINGIAN DYNASTY, A. D. 428-752.
6TH CENTURY.
Clovis, A. D. 465-511. Bateman, J. C. Ierne
of Armorica: a tale of the time of Chlovis.
249.1
7TH CENTURY. Babo, J. M. Dagobert, king
of the Franks. p. 100, *in* ** 832.4
8TH CENTURY. Griffin, G. The invasion.
823.673
Note.—See Guizot, F. P. G. History of France
from earliest times to 1848. 6 vols. 944.4-9.—Hallam, H: Europe during the middle ages. 3 vols.
940.2-4.—Montalembert, C. F. de T., *comte* de.
Monks of the west. 2 vols. 271.4-5.—Thierry, J.
N. A. Lettres sur l'histoire de France. 1868. 940.71.

English Fiction. *Contin.*

France. *Contin.*

CARLOVINGIAN DYNASTY, A. D. 752-
987.
CHARLEMAGNE, A. D. 742-814. *See also*
Charlemagne, p. 37.
—— Ariosto, L. Orlando Furioso. 2 vols.
851.1-2
—— Baldwin, J. Story of Roland. 823.5624
—— Bulfinch, T: Legends of Charlemagne.
823.150
10TH CENTURY. Yonge, C.. M.. The little
duke. Richard the Fearless. 808.1576
Note.—See Guizot, F. P. G. History of civilization. (Lectures 19, 20, 24.) vols. 2, 3. 313.47-8; —
History of France from earliest times to 1848. 6
vols. 944.4-9.—Hallam, H: Europe during the
middle ages. 3 vols. 1872. 940.2-4.—James, G: P.
R. History of Charlemagne. 1832. 944.63.—Mul-
linger, J. B. Schools of Charles the Great.
1877. 370.245.—Palgrave, *Sir* F. History of Normandy and of England. (741-1101.) 4 vols. 942.
489-92.—Schmidt, E. A. Geschichte von Frank-
reich. (v. 1: 481-1328.) 944.773.
CAPETIAN DYNASTY, A. D. 987-1328.
CRUSADES, 1096-1291. *See* Crusades, p. 48.
12TH CENTURY.
—— Gobineau, J. A., *comte* de. Typhaines
Abbey. 823.7044
—— Hale, E: E. In his name: a story of the
Waldenses . . . 823.4037
—— Newton, W. W: Priest and man; or,
Abelard and Heloisa. 823.6527
PHILIP AUGUSTUS, A. D. 1180-1223.
—— James, G: P. R. Philip Augustus; or,
the brothers in arms. 2 vols. (in 1.)
823.874
—— Ponsard, F. Agnès de Méranie; trag.
(*Sem. littéraire*, t. 16.) p. 33, *in* 843.316
PHILIP THE FAIR, A. D. 1285-1340.
—— Conscience, H. The lion of Flanders.
823.6540
—— Flagg, E. De Molai: the last of the
military grand masters of the order of
Templar Knights. 823.7043
Note.—See Guizot, F. P. G. History of civiliza-
tion. 3 vols. 1852. 313.36-9.—Hallam, H: Eu-
rope during the middle ages. 3 vols. 1872. 940.
2-4.—Masson, G. The story of mediæval France.
(987-1514.) 1889. 944.749.—Michelet, J. History of
France. (B. C. 1200-A. D. 1483.) 2 vols. 944.28-9.
HOUSE OF VALOIS, A. D. 1327-1589.
PHILIP VI., A. D. 1328-1350.
—— Herbert, H: W. Eustache de St. Pierre;
or, the surrender of Calais. 1347. 8 pp.
(*In his* Chevaliers of France.)
p. 107, *in* 823.4253
—— Planché, J. R. William with the ring.
(Siege of Calais; poem.) 821.807
—— St. George for England: a tale of Cressy
and Poitiers. 808.1479
JOHN THE GOOD, A. D. 1350-1364.
—— Dulac, G: Before the dawn: a story of
Paris and the Jacquerie. 823.5402
—— James, G: P. R. The Jacquerie. 2 vols.
(in 1.) (Peasant's revolt, 1358.) 823.866
—— St. George for England: a tale of Cressy
and Poitiers. 808.1479
CHARLES V., A. D. 1364-1380.
Bertrand du Gueslin. Milnes, R: M. (*In his*
Poetical works.) p. 259, *in* 821.187
CHARLES VI., A. D. 1380-1422. Dumas, A.
D. Isabel of Bavaria. 823.3161

English Fiction. *Contin.*
France. *Contin.*
HOUSE OF VALOIS, A. D. 1327-1589. *Contin.*
CHARLES VII., A. D. 1422-1461.
—— James, G: P. R. Agnes Sorel (died 1450). 823.5058
—— *Same.* 823.5059
Joan of Arc.
—— Charles, *Mrs.* E,.. (R.) Joan the maid, deliverer of France and England. 823.209
—— Herbert, H: W: Fortunes of the maid of Arc. (1428.) (*In his* Chevaliers of France.) p. 115, *in* 823.4253
—— Robinson, J.. Maid of Orleans. 823.2025
—— Schiller, J. C. F. von. Maid of Orleans; drama. 832.36
—— Shakespeare, W: Henry VI. *in* ** 822.1026
Note.—For other editions, *see under* Shakespeare, *in* Catalogues of this Library.
No. 2, 1880, p. 207. No. 4, 1884, p. 265.
No. 3, 1882, p. 173. No. 5, 1888, pp. 317-18.
—— Southey, R. Joan of Arc (poem). (*Poetical works.*) *in* 821.1165
LOUIS XI., A. D. 1461-1483.
—— Hugo, V. M., *vicomte.* Notre-Dame; or, the bell-ringer of Paris. (Old Paris, 1482, etc.) 823.5611
—— —¬ Notre-Dame de Paris. (Another tr. of Notre-Dame.) 823.6291
—— *Same.* 823.6420; 823.7146
—— Phipps, E. King René's daughter; drama. *in* 822.696
—— Reade, C: Cloister and the hearth. 823.1286
Charles the Bold of Burgundy, 1433-1477.
—— James, G: P. R. Mary of Burgundy; or, the revolt of Ghent. 823.870
—— Scott, *Sir* W. Anne of Geierstein. (Battle of Nancy, 1474-7.) 823.1392
—— — *Same.* ** 823.6033
—— — Quentin Durward. 823.6030
—— — *Same.* *in* 823.5157; *in* ** 823.6030
15TH CENTURY. *Manners, etc.*
—— Smith, A. The armourer of Paris. 83 pp. (*With his* Fortunes of the Scattergood family.) p. 333, *in* 823.1449
FRANCIS I., A. D. 1515-1547.
—— Baillie, J. Basil. (Mantua, battle of Batavia); trag. 822.128
—— Dumas, A. D. Ascanio. 823.7161
HENRY II., A. D. 1547-1559.
—— Yonge, C.. M.. Chaplet of pearls; or, the white and black Ribaumont. 823.6004
—— — *Same.* 823.6096
Duke of Guise. (Assassinated 1558.) James, G: P. R. One in a thousand. 823.873
FRANCIS II. (married Mary, Queen of Scots), A. D. 1559-1560. *See* note on Scottish history.
CHARLES IX., A. D. 1560-1574. Dryden, J., *and* Lee, N. The duke of Guise; trag. *in* 822.139
St. Bartholomew's Day, 1572.
—— Du Bois-Melly, C: History of Nicolas Muss. 823.6570
—— Dumas, A. D. Marguerite de Valois. 823.5183
—— — *Same.* 823.6513

English Fiction. *Contin.*
France. *Contin.*
HOUSE OF VALOIS, A. D. 1327-1589. *Contin.*
CHARLES IX., A. D. 1560-1574. *Contin.*
St. Bartholomew's Day, 1572. *Contin.*
—— Herbert, H: W: Hamilton of Bothwelhaugh. 62 pp. (*In his* Chevaliers of France.) p. 247, *in* 823.4253
—— Holt, E. S.. Sister Rose. 823.7232
—— James, G: P. R. Man at arms; or, Henri de Cerons. 823.869
—— Marlowe, C. Massacre at Paris; drama. *in* 822.122
HENRY III., A. D. 1574-1589.
—— Ainsworth, W: H. Crichton. 823.16
—— Chapman, G: Bussy d'Ambois; trag. 822.886
—— Dumas, A. D. Chicot, the jester: sequel to "Marguerite de Valois." 823.4611
—— — *Same.* 823.6514
—— — La dame de Monsoreau. 3 vols. (in 2). 843.495-5²
—— — Forty-five guardsmen: sequel to "Chicot, the jester." 823.5538
—— — *Same.* 823.6515
—— James, G: P. R. Henry of Guise; or, the states of Blois. 823.863
—— Radcliffe, *Mrs.* A. (W.) Mysteries of Udolpho. 3 vols. ** 823.2106-8
16TH CENTURY. *Manners, etc.*
—— Dumas, A. D. Countess de Charny. 823.3099
—— — *Same.* 823.6521
—— — The two Dianas. 823.7347
—— Dutheil, E. Castle of Roussillon. 823.6871
—— Frith, H. Under Bayard's banner. 808.1606
—— James, G: P. R. Corse de Leon; or, the brigand. 823.853
—— Leonora d'Orco. 823.7233
—— Kip, L. Under the bells. 823.951
—— Lawrence, G: A. Brakespeare. 823.956
Note.—See **Baird**, *Prof.* H: M. History of rise of the Huguenots. 1515-1574. 2 vols. 1883. 944.21-2.—**Bray,** *Mrs.* A. E. (K.) Joan of Arc and the times of Charles VII. 1873. 923.1988.—**Comines,** P. de. Memoirs of (Louis XI., Charles VIII., and Charles the Bold). 2 vols. 1823. 944.457-8.—**Davila,** H. C. History of the civil wars of France. 2 vols. 1758. 944.188-9.—**Freeman,** E: A: Charles the Bold. (*In his* Essays, ser. 1.) p. 314, *in* 904.16.—**Froissart,** *Sir* J: Chronicles. 2 vols. 1874. 944.13-4.—**Gairdner,** J. Houses of Lancaster and York. 1875. 942.318.—**Guizot,** F. P. G. History of civilization. 3 vols. 1852. 313.46-9;—History of France. 6 vols. 1856. 944.4-9.—**Hallam,** H: Europe during the middle ages. 3 vols. 1872. 940.2-4.—**Jervis,** *Rev.* W: H. The Gallican church: a history of the church of France from the concordat of Bologna, A. D. 1516, to the revolution. 2 vols. 1872. 274.62-3.—**Lamartine,** A. M. L: de P. de. Jeanne d'Arc, with notes historical and philological and a vocabulary. 923.1952.—**Maimbourg,** L. History of the league, book 3. (Dryden; J: Works, v. 2.) p. 284, *in* 821.127A.—**Mérimée,** P. Chronique du règne de Charles IX. 1890. 944.692;—*Same.* Tr. by G: Saintsbury. 914.784.—**Monstrelet,** E. de. Chronicles. 2 vols. 1849. 944.112-3.—**Pardoe,** J. S. H. Court and reign of Francis I. (1521-1546.) 3 vols. 1887. 923.1993-5.—**Robinson,** *Mrs.* M. W. (F.) Henry III., King of France and Poland: his career and times. 3 vols. 1888. 923.1971-3.—**Schmidt,** E. A. Geschichte von Frankreich. (v. 2 1328-1559.) 944.774.—**Tuckey,** J. Joan of Arc, "the maid." 1886. 923.1954.—**White,**

English Fiction. *Contin.*
France. *Contin.*
HOUSE OF VALOIS, A. D. 1327-1589. *Contin.*

Note. Contin.
H: The massacre of St. Bartholomew. 1871. 944.
40.—**Willert**, P. F. Reign of Lewis XI. (1422-
1483.) 1876. 944.45.—**Wraxall**, N. W. History of
France. (1574-1610.) 6 vols. 1814. 944.664-9.

HOUSE OF BOURBON, A. D. 1589-1793.

HENRY IV., A. D. 1589-1610.
—— Dryden, J., *and* Lee, N. The Duke of
Guise; trag. *in* 822.139
—— Elliot, F.. Romance of old court-life
in France. 823.6050
—— James, G: P. R. Fate of the Duc de
Biron. (*In his* The desultory man, v. 1.)
p. 165, *in* 823.856
—— —— One in a thousand. 823.873
—— —— Rose d'Albret. 823.7234
—— Macaulay, T: B. Battle of Ivry; ballad.
p. 379, *in* 824.69
—— Voltaire, F. M. A. de. Henriade: epic.
(*Œuvres*, v. 10.) 841.11

Note.—See **Anquetil**, L: P. Intrigue du cabinet,
sous Henri IV., et Louis XIII., terminée par la
Fronde. 4 vols. 1780. * 944.934-7.—**Aumale**, H.
E. P. L: d'Orleans, *duc* d'. Histoire des princes de
Condé, pendant le 16e et 17e siècles. 6 vols. (v. 6, Atlas.) 1886-89. 944.699-704.—**Freer**, M. W. (*after-
ward* Mrs. Robinson). History of the reign of
Henry IV. 2 vols. 1860. 923.472-3.—**Guizot**, F. P.
G. History of civilization. 3 vols. 1856. 313.59-
61;—*Same.* 4 vols. 313.46-9;—History of France
from earliest times to 1848. 6 vols. 944.4-9.—**Jackson**, *Lady* C. C.. The first of the Bourbons. (1589-
1610.) 2 vols. 1890. 923.1904-5.—**Smiles**, S:
Huguenots in France after revocation of Edict of
Nantes. 1874. 944.37.—**Thierry**, J. N. A. Histoire du Tiers État. 1856. 940.73.—**White**, H. The
massacre of St. Bartholomew. 1871. 944.40.

LOUIS XIII., A. D. 1610-1643. (Regency of
Mary de Medici, 1610-1614.)
—— Anderdon, W: H: Antoine de Bonne-
val: Paris in the days of St. Vincent de
Paul. (1576-1660.) 823.39
—— Dumas, A. D. Three guardsmen; or,
the three mousquetaires. *in* 823.3229
—— —— *Same.* *in* 823.5088; 823.6930
—— —— Three musketeers. (Being the first
of the d'Artagnan romances.) 823.6509
—— Elliot, F.. Romance of old court-life
in France. 823.6050
—— Grant, J. Arthur Blane; or, the hun-
dred cuirassiers. 823.618

Richelieu, d. 1642.
—— James, G: P. R. De l'Orme. 823.7388
—— —— *Same.* 2 vols. ** 823.6248-9
—— Richelieu: a tale of France. 823.875
—— Lytton. Richelieu; play. 822.148
—— —— *Same.* 829.597
—— Marana, J: P. (?) The Turkish spy.
(In Paris, 1635-1682.) 8 vols. * 816.4-11
—— Vigny, A. V., *comte* de. Cinq-Mars; or,
a conspiracy under Louis XIII. 823.1873
—— —— *Same.* 2 vols. 823.6311-12

Manners, etc. Yonge, C.. M.. Stray pearls;
memoirs of Margaret de Ribaumont, vis-
countess of Bellaise. 823.6958

Note.—See **Anquetil**, L: P. L'intrigue du cabinet, sous Henri IV. et Louis XIII., terminée par
la Fronde. 2 vols. 1780. 4 vols. * 944.934-7.—
Bazin, A. de R. Histoire de France sous Louis
XIII. 1610-61. 4 vols. 1837. 944.730-3.

English Fiction. *Contin.*
France. *Contin.*
HOUSE OF BOURBON, A. D. 1589-1793.
Contin.

LOUIS XIV., A. D. 1643-1715.
—— Alcock, D. Geneviève; or, the children
of Port Royal: a story of old France.
823.7196
—— Bamford, M.. E. Marie's story.
808.1626
—— Bungener, L. L: F. Preacher and the
king; or, Bourdaloue in the court of Louis
XIV. 823.1875
—— Dumas, A. D. Bragelonne, the son of
Athos; or, ten years later: being a con-
clusion of "Twenty years after." 823.6302
—— —— The iron mask. ("The three guards-
men" ser., No. 4.) 823.5803
—— —— Louise La Vallière. ("The three
guardsmen" ser., No. 5.) 823.5802
—— —— Nanon. 823.7348
—— —— Twenty years after. (Sequel to "The
three musketeers.") 823.2748
—— —— *Same.* 823.6500; 823.6510
—— —— Vicomte de Bragelonne; or, ten
years later: completion of "The three mus-
keteers" and "Twenty years after." 2
vols. 823.6511-12
—— Fénelon, F. de S. de la M. Adventures
of Telemachus. (Satire on the reign of
Louis XIV.) 823.6211
—— Hugo, V. M., *vicomte*. Marion Delorme;
drame. (*Fr.*) *in* 840.47
—— —— *Same.* *in* 849.87
—— James, G: P. R. Lord Montagu's page.
3 vols. 823.6458-60
—— Smith, A. Marchioness of Brinvilliers,
the poisoner of the seventeenth century: a
romance of old Paris. 823.1450

The Fronde.
—— Anderdon, W: H: Antoine de Bonneval:
. . . Paris in the days of St. Vincent de
Paul. (1576-1660.) 823.39
—— Dumas, A. D. La guerre des femmes.
843.517
—— Herbert, H: W: The brothers: a tale of
the Fronde. 2 vols. ** 823.6241-2

Huguenots.
—— Dupuy, E. A. The Huguenot exiles.
823.489
—— G., H. Suzanne de l'Orme. 808.1659
—— James, G: P. R. The Huguenot.
823.865
—— —— *Same.* 2 vols. ** 823.6765-6
—— Keddie, H. The Huguenot family.
823.4098
—— Rathbone, *Mrs.* M.. A. (M.) Jacques
Bonneval; or, the days of the dragonnades.
823.4103
—— Raymond, G. How they kept the faith:
a tale of the Huguenots of Languedoc.
823.6367

Manners, etc.
—— Hoffmann, E. T. W. Cardillac, the jew-
eller. (*In his* Strange stories.)
p. 289, *in* 823.6807
—— Melville, G: J: Whyte- Sister Louise;
or, the story of a woman's repentance.
** 823 4665

English Fiction. *Contin.*
France. *Contin.*
HOUSE OF BOURBON, **A. D. 1589–1793.**
Contin.
Louis XIV., A. D. 1643–1715. *Contin.*
Manners, etc. Contin.
—— O'Reilly, A. J. Alvira, the heroine of
Vesuvius. (Canonization of St. Francis of
Jerome.) 823.1222
—— Zschokke, H. Alamontade. (*In* Tales
from the German.) p. 364, *in* 823.6276
Note.—See **Annale,** H. E. P. L. d'Orleans, *duc* d'.
Histoire des princes de Condé, pendant le 16e et 17e
siècles. 6 vols. (v. 6, Atlas.) 1886–9. 944.699-704.—
Dangeau, P. de C:, *marquis* de. Memoirs of the
court of France. 1684–1720. 2 vols. * 944.763-4.—
Ellis, G: J. W. A. True history of the state prisoner,
commonly called the Iron Mask. 1826. 944.767.—
Guizot, F: P. G. The French revolution. (Lecture
14. *In his* Hist. of civilization, v. 1.) 313.46.—**Hallam,** H: Europe during the middle ages. 3 vols.
1872. 940.2-4.—**Macaulay,** T: B. Louis XIV. of
France. 3 pp. (*In* Ferris, G. T. *Great leaders.*) p.
327, *in* 920.329.—**Martin,** H. History of France.
(1789–1881.) 3 vols. 944.10-11½.—**Pardoe,** J. Louis
the Fourteenth and the court of France. (1615–1715.)
3 vols. 944.751-3.—**Saint Simon,** L. de R., *duc* de.
Memoirs of the reign of Louis XIV., and the regency. 3 vols. 1876. 923.164-6.—**Schmidt,** E. A.
Geschichte von Frankreich. (vols. 3-4: 1559–1774.)
944.775-6.—**Smiles,** S: Huguenots in France after
the revocation of the Edict of Nantes. 1874. 944.37.
—**Tobin,** M. Man with the iron mask. 1870. 944.
157.—**Voltaire,** F. M. A. de. Siècle de Louis XIV.
1785. 3 vols. 20-22.) * 944.81-3.
—— **(Œuvres,** vols. 20-22.) * 944.81-3.

Louis XV., *including the regency,* A. D.
1715-1774.
—— Dumas, A. D. The conspirators; or, the
chevalier d'Harmental. 823.3164
—— — Joseph Balsamo. (*Same as* Memoirs
of a physician.) 823.5903
—— — Memoirs of a physician. 823.6518
—— — The regent's daughter. 823.2739
—— James, G: P. R. The ancient régime.
(1756–1770.) 3 vols. * 823.6403-5
Persecution of the Protestants. Buegener, L.
L: F. Priest and the Huguenot. 2 vols.
823.4064-5
Manners, etc.
—— Ainsworth, W: H. John Law. (Miss-
issippi bubble.) 823.5602
—— Melville, G: J: Whyte- Cerise.
823.1151
—— — *Same.* (*With his* Holmby House.)
in ** 823.4667
—— Shorthouse, J. H: Marquis Jeanne Hya-
cinthe de St. Palaye. 68 pp. (*With his* A
teacher of the violin.) p. 117, *in* 823.5438
Note.—See **Broglie,** C: J. V. A., *duc* de. The
king's secret. (Secret correspondence of Louis XV.
with his agents. (1752–1774.) 3 vols. 944.26-7.
—**Jackson,** *Lady* C. C. The old régime. 2 vols. (in
1). 944.418.—**Voltaire,** F. M. A. de. Siècle de
Louis XV. 1785. (Œuvres, v. 23.) * 944.84.

Louis XVI., A. D. 1774–1789.
—— Dumas, A. D. The queen's necklace.
(1734.) (Sequel to "Memoirs of a physi-
cian.") 823.3481
—— — *Same.* 823.6519
Manners, etc.
—— Dudevant, *Mme.* A. L. A. (D.) Anto-
nia. 823.6790
—— Kotzebue, A. F. F. v. Abbé de l'Epée;
drama. p. 253, *in* 832.75
—— Shorthouse, J: H: Countess Eve. (City
of Burgundy, 1785.) 823.5766

English Fiction. *Contin.*
France. *Contin.*
HOUSE OF BOURBON, **A. D. 1589–1793.**
Contin.
Louis XVI., A. D. 1774–1789. *Contin.*
Note.—See **Campan,** *Mrs.* J. L. Memoirs of the
court of Marie Antoinette. 2 vols. 1843. 923.
1752-3.—**Carlyle,** T: The diamond necklace. (*In
his* Essays, v. 3.) p. 1, *in* 824.401;—The French revolution. 2 vols. 944.23-4.—**Jackson,** *Lady* C. C.
French court and society. 2 pts. (in 1). 1881. 944.
426.—**Marmontel,** J. F. Memoirs. By W: D.
Howells. 2 vols. 1878. 928.230-1.—**Michelet,** J.
Historical view of the French revolution.
1848. 944.98.—**Sybel,** *Prof.* H. von. History of Europe during the French revolution. 4 vols. 1867-8.
944.151-4.—**Taine,** H. A. The ancient régime.
944.42.—**Vizetelly,** H. Story of the diamond
necklace. 944.424.

FRENCH REVOLUTION, A. D. 1789–1792.
—— Blyth, M. P. Antoinette: a tale of the
ancien régime. 2 vols. 823.7206-7
—— Breton maiden, A. By a French lady.
3 vols. 823.7208-10
—— Brougham, H: P: Albert Lunel; or, the
château of Languedoc. 3 vols. (in 1).
** 823.6685
—— Dickens, C: J: H. A tale of two cities.
823.414
—— — *Same.* 823.5317; *in* 823.5557
—— Dumas, A. D. The Countess de Charny:
sequel to "Taking the Bastile." 823.3099
—— — *Same.* 823.6521
—— Love and liberty. 823.6915
—— Six years later; or, taking of the
Bastile. 3d ser. of "The memoirs of a
physician." 823.6286
—— Taking the Bastile; or, six years
later: sequel to "The queen's necklace."
823.6520
—— Erckmann, É., *and* Chatrian, P. A. The
country in danger. (1792.) 823.6860
—— — *Same.* (*With their* The states gen-
eral.) *in* 823.7252
—— — Madame Thérèse; or, the volunteers
of '92. 823.6856
—— — States general. (1789.) 823.6859
—— — *Same.* 823.7252
—— Freeland, *Mrs.* C. J. In palace and
faubourg. 823.6368
—— Gayarré, A. Aubert Dubayet; or, the
two sister republics. (Seq. to "Fernando
de Lemos.") 823.4624
—— James, G: P. R. History of a French
artisan during the last revolution. 19 pp.
(*In his* The desultory man, v. 2.)
p. 189, *in* 823.856
—— Lytton, E: G: E. L. Bulwer- Zanoni.
823.5970
—— — *Same.* 823.5936
—— Martineau, H. French wine and poli-
tics. (*In her* Illust. of polit. econ., v. 4.)
in 823.6709
—— — Tales of the French revolution.
(*With her* Glen of the echoes.) 823.6602
—— Melville, G: J: Whyte- Rosine: a story
of the red revolution. *in* ** 823.4669
—— — *Same.* 823.7284
—— Mundt, T. Count Mirabeau. 823.6383
—— Paul, *Mrs.* M. A. (C.) Kintail place.
823.7200

English Fiction. *Contin.*
France. *Contin.*
FRENCH REVOLUTION, A. D. 1789–1792.
Contin.
—— Schwartz, *Mrs.* M. S. (B.) Birth and
education. 823.5808
Biographical.
—— Bölte, A. C.. E. M. Madame de Staël.
823.7093
—— Brachvogel, A. E. Beaumarchais.
823.6105
—— Croly, G: Marston; or, the soldier and
statesman. 2d ed. 3 vols. * 823.5492–4
—— Martineau, H. The prince. (*With her*
The peasant.) *in* 808.1199
Marie Antoinette. Mundt, *Mrs.* C. (M.)
Marie Antoinette and her son. 823.6329

Note.—See **Adams,** C: K. Democracy and monarchy in France. (1789–1870.) 1874. 320.9.—**Alison,**
Sir A. The reign of terror. 13 pp. (*In his* Essays,
polit., etc., v. 3.) p. 278, *in* 824.448.—**Bastille,** Tak-
ing of the. Tr. from the "Moniteur" newspaper
of July 20–23, 23 and 24, 1789. *See* Scottish rev., v.
14, July, 1889. * 52.6155¹¹.—**Bax,** E. D. Marat: a
biographical sketch. 1882. 923.2033.—**Beauchamp,**
A. Histoire de la guerre de la Vendée et des
Chouans. 3 vols. 1806. 944.696–8.—**Binghain,** D.
The Bastille. 2 vols. 1888. 944.647–8.—**Blind,** M.
Madame Roland. 1886. 928.664.—**Brougham,** H.
Baron. The French revolution. 43 pp. (*In his*
Statesmen, etc., v. 3.) p. 7, *in* 924.12.—**Buckle,**
H. T. Proximate causes of the French revolution.
95 pp. (*In his* Hist. of civilization.) 313.35.—**Burke,**
E. Reflections on the revolution in France. (1790.)
(*Works*, v. 2.) 944.61.—**Carlyle,** T: History of
the French revolution. 2 vols. 944.633–4.—**Daven-
port,** R. A. History of the Bastile. 944.770.—**Fau-
riel,** C. C: The last days of the consulate. 1885.
944.646.—**Imbert de Saint-Amand,** A. L. Marie
Antoinette and the end of the old régime. (1781–
1789.) 1890. 944.657.—**Jervis,** W: H. The Gallican church and the revolution: sequel to the "History of the church of France, etc." 1882. 274.64.—
Lamartine, A. M. L. de P. de. History of the
Girondists. 3 vols. 1878. 944.104–6.—**Lewes,** G: H:
Life of Robespierre. 1854. 923.1997.—**Lilly,** W: S: The
principles of '89. (*In his* Chapters in European
hist., v. 2.) p. 196, *in* 940.194.—**Michelet,** J. Histoire de la révolution française. 9 vols. 1877–78.
944.671–9.—**Paine,** T: Rights of man. (*In his* Political writings, v. 2.) *in* 324.2.—**Smyth,** *Prof.* W:
Lectures on the French revolution. 2 vols. 1860.
944.100–1.—**Stephens,** H. M. A history of the
French revolution. 3 vols. 1886. 944.652–4.—
Taine, H. A. The French revolution. (Unfavorable
to the revolutionists.) (v. 2 only.) 1878–80. 944.185.
—**Thiers,** A. History of the French revolution.
(1789–1801.) 4 vols. (in 2). 944.178–9.—**Vatel,** C.
Charlotte de Corday et les Girondins. 4 vols. 1864–
72. 944.705–8.—**Wachsmuth,** W. Geschichte
Frankreichs im Revolutionszeitalter. (vols. 1–3:
1774–1812.) 944.778–80.

FIRST REPUBLIC, A. D. 1792–1799.
NATIONAL CONVENTION, A. D. 1792–1795.
—— Dumas, A. D. Ingenue: an historical
romance. 823.3243
—— Erckmann, É., *and* Chatrian, P. A.
Madame Thérèse; or, the volunteers of '92.
823.4302
—— —— Year one of the republic—1793 : the.
story of a peasant. 823.6861
—— —— *Same.* 823.7253
—— Hugo, V. M., *vicomte.* Ninety-three.
823.6290
—— —— *Same.* 823.6419
—— Keddie, H. Citoyenne Jacqueline: a
woman's lot in the French revolution.
823.923
—— Roberts, M. On the edge of the storm.
823.1341

English Fiction. *Contin.*
France. *Contin.*
FIRST REPUBLIC, A. D. 1792–1799. *Contin.*
NATIONAL CONVENTION, A. D. 1792–1795.
Contin.
Reign of terror, A. D. 1793–1794.
—— Balzac, H. de. Episode under the Ter-
ror: scenes from political life. 24 pp. (*With
his* The Duchesse de Langeais.)
p. 191, *in* 823.5211
—— Dumas, A. D. Chevalier de Maison
Rouge: sequel to "The Countess de
Charny." 823.3108
—— —— *Same.* 823.6522
—— —— Ingenue. 823.3243
—— Henty, G: A. In the reign of terror:
adventures of a Westminster boy. 808.1435
—— Kip, L. The dead marquise. 823.4123
—— Roberts, M. Noblesse oblige. 823.1342
La Vendée, A. D. 1793–1796.
—— Hugo, V. M., *vicomte.* Ninety-three.
823.6290
—— Trollope, A. La Vendée. 823.2007
Wars.
—— Conscience, H. Veva. 823.5660
—— Erckmann, É., *and* Chatrian, P. A. La
guerre (drama). 822.1091

Note.—See **Alison,** *Sir* A. Miscellaneous essays.
1873. *in* 824.90.—**Carlyle,** T: (Essay on) Mirabeau.
(*In his* Essays, v. 3.) p. 77, *in* 824.401;—History of
the French revolution. 2 vols. 944.633–4.—**Farmer,**
L. II. Short history of the French revolution for
young people. 944.637.—**Gronlund,** L. Ça ira! or,
Danton in the French revolution. 944.699.—**Imbert de Saint-Amand,** A. L., *baron.* Citizeness
Bonaparte. (1796–1799.) 944.760.—**Lamartine,** A.
M. L. de P. de. History of the Girondists. 3 vols.
1878. 944.104–6.—**Macaulay,** T: B. Bertrand
Darère de Vieuzac. (*In his* Essays, v. 5.) p. 423, *in*
824.136;—Gabriel Honoré Riquetti, comte de Mirabeau. (*In his* Essays, v. 3.) p. 37, *in* 824.135.
—**McCarthy,** J. II. The French revolution. 2 vols.
1890. 944.658–9.—**Miguet,** F. A. M. History of the
French revolution. (1789–1814.) 1856. 944.99.—
Stephens, H. M. History of the French revolution. 3 vols. 1886. 944.652–4.—**Thiers,** A. History
of the great French revolution. (1789–1801.) 4 vols.
(in 2). 944.178–9.

NAPOLEONIC PERIOD, A. D. 1799–1814.
THE CONSULATE, A. D. 1799–1804. Erck-
mann, É., *and* Chatrian, P. A. Citizen
Bonaparte. (*With their* Year one of the
republic.) *in* 823.7253
THE EMPIRE, A. D. 1804–1814.
—— Dumas, A. D. The conscript. 823.6923
—— —— The twin captains. 823.5564
—— Erckmann, É., *and* Chatrian, P. A.
The conscript: a story of the French war
of 1813. 823.1850
—— Grant, J. Marquis of Lauriston. (*With
his* Constable of France.)
p. 232, *in* 823.623
—— Kavanagh, J. Madeleine: a tale of
Auvergne. 823.916
—— —— *Same.* 823.6592
—— Mundt, *Mme.* C. (M.) Empress Joseph-
ine. 823.6266
Peninsular war, A. D. 1808–1814. *See also
note* on Spanish history.
—— Grant, J. Adventures of an aide-de-
camp. 823.617
—— Lever, C: J. Charles O'Malley. 823.973
—— —— Tom Burke of "Ours." 823.994
—— —— *Same.* 2 vols. Illus. ** 823.6224–5

English Fiction. *Contin.*
France. *Contin.*
NAPOLEONIC PERIOD, A. D. 1799–1814. *Contin.*

THE EMPIRE, A. D. 1804–1814. *Contin.*
Peninsular war, A. D. 1808–1814. *Contin.*
—— Maxwell, W: H. The bivouac; or, stories of the peninsular war. 823.1127
—— — Stories of the peninsular war.
823.1131
War of 1813–14. *See also note* on German history.
—— Erckmann, É., *and* Chatrian, P. A. Blockade of Phalsburg: an episode of the end of the empire. 823.6854
—— — Invasion of France in 1814: comprising the night-march of the Russian army past Phalsburg. 823.6863
—— Roy, J. E. Adventures of a casket: an episode of the invasion of 1814. 823.6292
LOUIS XVIII., A. D. May 3, 1814–Mar. 20, 1815.
Hundred Days, Mar.–June, 1815.
—— Buchanan, R. W. Shadow of the sword.
823.4166
—— Dumas, A. D. The Count of Monte-Cristo. 823.6303
—— — *Same*. 823.6508
Waterloo, 1815.
—— Erckmann, É., *and* Chatrian, P. A. Waterloo: sequel to "The conscript of 1813." 823.5675
—— Henty, G: A. One of the 28th.
808.1668
—— Hugo, V. M., *vicomte*. Les misérables.
823.5645
—— — *Same*. 823.6289
—— Lever, C: J. Charles O'Malley. 823.973
—— Maxwell, W: H. Stories of Waterloo.
823.1133
—— Thackeray, W: M. Vanity fair: a novel without a hero. 823.5338
Poems on Napoleon. Lockhart, J: G. Napoleon. 2 pp. (*In* Tales from Blackwood, v. 1.) *in* ** 823.6647
See also Poems by Byron, V. M. Hugo, C. C. Colton, and others.
Note.—See Abbott, J: S. C. Confidential correspondence of the Emperor Napoleon and the Empress Josephine. 1858. 816.64.—**Berthier**, L: A. Mémoires. Campagne d'Egypte. 1827. 923.1989.—**Hamley,** *Lieut.-Gen. Sir* E: B. The operations of war examined and illustrated. (With 17 maps.) 1869. 355.73.—**Hillebrand,** K. Geschichte Frankreichs. (1830–1848.) 2 vols. 944.782-3.—**Jomini,** A. H., *baron* de. Atlas portatif pour l'intelligence des relations des dernières guerres, publiées sans plans. 2 vols. ** 914.768-9;—Same. 4 vols. With atlas. 5 vols. 1864. 923.1935-39.—**Labaume,** E. Circumstantial narrative of the campaign in Russia. 1815. 947.4.—**Lamartine,** A. M, L. de P. de. History of restoration of monarchy in France. 4 vols. 1865. 944.56-9.—**Lanfrey,** P. History of Napoleon. 4 vols. 1871–9. 923.1099-1102.—**Maitland,** F: L. Narrative of the surrender of Buonaparte and of his residence on board H. M. S. Bellerophon, May 24–Aug. 8, 1815. 1826. 944.670.—**Metternich,** C.W. N. L. *Fürst.* (*In his* Memoires.) (1773–1835.) 5 pts. (in 1.) 923.1049.—**Mitchell,** *Lieut.-Col.* J. Fall of Napoleon. 3 vols. 1845. 923.181-3.—**Napier,** *Lieut.-Gen. Sir* W: F. P. History of the war in the peninsula and in the south of France. (1807–1814.) 5 vols. 1862. 946.14-18.—**Napoleon** I., *Emperor of France*. Correspondence. (In French.) 32 vols. ** 944.572-603. (*See* account in Parton's Topics of the time. p. 316, *in* 829.187.)—Rémusat, C. E. J. G. de V., *Mme.* de. Memoirs.

English Fiction. *Contin.*
France. *Contin.*
NAPOLEONIC PERIOD, A. D. 1799–1814. *Contin.*

Note. Contin.
1802–8. 1880. 923.541.—**Reynier,** J. L. E., *comte.* Mémoires. Campagne d'Egypte. 2d part. 1827. 923.1990.—**Scott,** *Sir* W. Life of Napoleon. 9 vols. 1861. 923.439.—**Seeley,** J: R. A short history of Napoleon the First. 1888. 923.1940.—**Segur,** P. de. Hist. of the expedition to Russia, by Napoleon in 1812. 2 vols. 947.24-5.—**Thiers,** A. History of the consulate and the empire under Napoleon. 5 vols. 944.14-18.—**Wachsmuth,** W. Geschichte Frankreichs im Revolutionszeitalter. (v. 4; 1810–1830.) 944.781.—**Wilson,** *Sir* R. Private diary . . . during the campaign of 1812–14. 2 vols. 923.1199-1200.
Waterloo, June 18, 1815.—**Chesney,** C: C. Waterloo lectures: a study of campaign of 1815. 1869. 355.70.—**Gardner,** D. Quatre-Bras, Ligny, and Waterloo. 1882. 944.419.—**Gleig,** G: R. Story of the battle of Waterloo. 1861. 355.514.—**Siborne,** *Capt.* W. History of the war in France and Belgium in 1815. With atlas. 1848. 2 vols. * 944.729-729¹.
Elba and the Hundred Days.—**Campbell,** *Maj.-Gen. Sir* N. Napoleon at Fontainebleau and Elba. 1869. 923.1316.—**Maitland,** *Rear Admiral Sir* F: L. Narrative of the surrender of Buonaparte. 1826. 944.670.
Captivity, 1815–21.—**Forsyth,** W: History of the captivity of Napoleon at St. Helena. 3 vols. 1853. 920.212-14.—**O'Meara,** B. E. Napoleon in exile. 2 vols. (in 1). 1822. 923.433.

RESTORATION OF THE BOURBONS.
LOUIS XVIII., A. D. 1815–1824.
CHARLES X., A. D. 1824–1830.
SECOND REVOLUTION, 1830. Scribe, E. Bertrand et Raton; drama. (*Fr.*) *in* 842.99
LOUIS PHILIPPE, A. D. 1830–1848.
Revolution of 1848. Erckmann, É., *and* Chatrian, P. A. A man of the people. 2 vols. 823.7317-18
Note.—See Alison, *Sir* A. Fall of the throne of the barricades. 41 pp.; The French revolution of 1830. 42 pp. (*In his* Essays polit., etc., v. 1.) pp. 435, 253, *in* 824.448.—**Browning,** O. Modern France, 1814–79. 1880. 944.150.—**Guizot,** F. P. G. Last days of the reign of Louis Philippe. 1867. 944.663;—Memoirs to illustrate the history of my time. (1807–1840.) 4 vols. 944.738-41.—**Heine,** H. Französische Zustände. (*Sämmtl. Werke,* Bde. 8–11.) 3 vols. 1862. 839.63-5.—**Lamartine,** A. M. L. de P. de. History of the French revolution of 1848. 1870. 944.50;—Same. 944.95;—History of the restoration of monarchy in France. 4 vols. 1865. 944.56-9.—**Louis XVIII,** *King of France.* Correspondence of Prince Talleyrand and King Louis XVIII. during the congress in Vienna. 1881. 914.171.—**Turnbull,** D. The French revolution of 1830. 944.771.—**Williams,** H. N. Narr. of events which have taken place in France; with account of the present state of society and public opinion. (1815.) 944.757.

SECOND REPUBLIC, A. D. 1848. (Louis Napoleon, President.) Edmond Dantes. (Causes of the revolution.) 823.6120
SECOND EMPIRE, A. D. 1852–1870.
NAPOLEON III.
—— Murray, E. C. G. Member for Paris: a tale of the second empire. 823.6098
—— Sheppard, E. S. Rumor. 823.6043
Note.—See Hugo, V. M., *vicomte*. Hist. d'un crime. 2 vols. 944.648;—Same. Another tr. 944.649.
Society under Napoleon III.
—— Feuillet, O. Camors. 823.7160
—— Lytton, E: G: E. L. Bulwer- The Parisians. 2 vols. 823.1041-2
Franco-German war, 1870–1871.
—— Buchanan, R. Songs of the terrible year. (1870.) (*Works,* v. 2.)
p. 277, *in* 821.51

English Fiction. *Contin.*
France. *Contin.*
SECOND EMPIRE, A. D. 1852–1870. *Contin.*
NAPOLEON III. *Contin.*
Franco-German war, 1870–1871. *Contin.*
—— Collins, W: W. The new Magdalen.
823.262
—— Daudet, A. Robert Helmont: diary of
a recluse. 1870–1871. 823.6331
—— Erckmann, É., *and* Chatrian, P. A.
Brigadier Frederick. 823.6103
—— — The plébiscite. 823.6857
—— Gaboriau, E. Other people's money.
823.3014
—— — *Same.* 823.5057
—— Grant, J. Paquette. 27 pp. (*With his*
The queen's cadet.) p. 206, *in* 823.646
—— — Six years ago. 823.655
—— Kingsley, H: Valentin: a French boy's
story of Sedan. 823.946
—— Lucas, A. Léonie; or, light out of
darkness. 823.1020
—— Macquoid, *Mrs.* K.. S. Mère Suzanne.
823.7133
—— Smith, H. Max Kromer: a story of the
siege of Strasburg, 1870. 823.1461
The commune. Hugo, V. M., *vicomte.* L'an-
née terrible; poem. 840.54
Siege of Paris.
—— Champney, *Mrs.* E.. (W.) Three Vas-
sar girls in France. 808.1826
—— Du Boisgobey, F. The red band. 2 pts.
in 823.5130
—— King, E: Kentucky's love. 823.948
—— Lucas, A. Within iron walls. (*With*
her Léonie.) p. 190, *in* 823.1020
—— Lytton, E: G: E. L. Bulwer- The Pa-
risians. 2 vols. 823.1041-2
—— Peard, F.. M.. Mademoiselle. 823.7470
NATIONAL AND SOCIAL CHARACTER, *etc.*
—— Balzac, H. de. Bureaucracy; or, a civil
service reformer. 823.5460
—— Craven, *Mme.* P. (de la F.) Anne Sév-
erin. 823.6842
—— Curwen, H., *tr.* French love songs, and
other poems. 821.683
—— Hugo, V. M., *vicomte.* Les misérables.
823.6289
—— — *Same.* 823.6990
—— — *Same.* 5 vols. 823.6414-18
—— James, G: P. R. Domestic life in
France. 3 pp. (*In his* The desultory man,
v. 2.) p. 30, *in* 823.856
—— Sikes, *Mrs.* O. (L.) Château Frissac;
or, home scenes in France. 823.6116
—— Weyman, S. J. The house of the wolf.
(16th and 17th centuries.) 823.7299
    See also novels by E. F. V. About, H. de Balzac,
    Mme. A. L. A. (D.) Dudevant. [*G:* Sand.]
Middle and low life. See Novels by A. Belot;
É. Gaboriau.
Military life.
—— Balzac, H. de. A passion in the desert.
20 pp. (*With his* The Duchesse de Langeais.) (French in Egypt.)
p. 275, *in* 823.5211
—— Gaboriau, É. Military sketches. (*With*
his A thousand francs reward.)
in 823.6699

English Fiction. *Contin.*
France. *Contin.*
SECOND EMPIRE, A. D. 1852–1870. *Contin.*
NATIONAL AND SOCIAL CHARACTER, *etc.*
Contin.
Life in Paris.
—— Daudet, A. L'évangéliste. 823.5566
—— — The immortal; or, one of the "forty."
823.7012
—— — The nabob. 823.3189
—— — *Same.* 823.6884
—— — Sappho: Parisian manners.
* 823.5423
—— Diane Coryval. (Anon.) 823.4673
—— Droz, A. G. Around a spring.
823.4042
—— Hooper, *Mrs.* L. H. (J.) Under the tri-
color; or, the American colony in Paris.
823.1923
—— Hugo, V. M., *vicomte.* Les misérables.
823.6990
—— — *Same.* 823.6289
—— — *Same.* 5 vols. 823.6414-18
—— Irving, W. Sketches in Paris in 1825.
23 pp. (*With his* Wolfert's Roost . . .)
p. 215, *in* 823.1808
—— Kimball, R: B. Romance of student
life abroad. 823.5734
—— Laboulaye, É. R. L. Paris in America.
(Social and political criticisms.) 823.6870
—— Ohnet, G. A last love. 823.7180
—— Ruffini, G. D. Paragreens on a visit to
the Paris Universal Exhibition. 823.1374
—— Smith, A. Adventures of Mr. Ledbury
and his friend Jack Johnson. 823.1451
See also Novels by H. de Balzac.
Provincial life.
—— Balzac, H. de. César Birotteau.
823.5209
—— — The country doctor. 823.5149
—— — *Same.* 823.5570
—— — Eugénie Grandet. 823.3438
—— — *Same.* 823.4969
—— — Illustrious Gaudissart. 57 pp. (*With*
his The Duchesse de Langeais.)
p. 217, *in* 823.5211
—— — Sons of the soil. 823.6942
—— — The two brothers. 823.5213
—— Château Morville; or, life in Tour-
aine. 823.6877
—— Daudet, A. Stories of Provence.
823.4958
—— Dempster, *Mrs.* C.. L.. (H.) Ninette:
an idyll of Provence. 823.7080
—— — *Same.* 823.7291
—— Dudevant, *Mme.* A. L. A. (D.) Fan-
chon the cricket. 823.6847
—— — Monsieur Antoine. 823.6296
—— Field, M. The secret of Fontaine-la-
Croix. 823.7079
—— Jenkin, *Mrs.* C: A Psyche of to-day.
823.4240
—— Lamartine, A. M. L: de P. de. My
mother's manuscript . . . 823.6874
—— — Stone-mason of Saint Point.
823.6293
—— Pouvillon, É. Césette. 823.4484
—— Ritchie, *Mrs.* A. I.. (T.) Village on the
cliff. 823.1570

English Fiction. *Contin.*
France. *Contin.*
SECOND EMPIRE, **A. D. 1852–1870.** *Contin.*
NATIONAL AND SOCIAL CHARACTER, *etc.*
Contin.
Provincial life. *Contin.*
—— Sikes, *Mrs.* O. (L.) Château Frissac.
823.6116
—— Souvestre, E. Brittany and La Vendée.
823.6878
—— Teufel, *Mrs.* B. W. (H.) Guenn, a wave
on the Breton coast. 823.4672
Note.—See:
*Napoleon III.—***Bagehot**, W. Letters on the
French coup d'état of 1851. (*Works*, v. 2.) 1889.
p. 371, *in* 814.23.—**Browning**, O. Modern France,
1814–79. 944.150.—**Dernier des Napoléon.** 1872.
(Attributed to MM. de Beust, de Hubner, de
Kératry, and Lacroix.) 944.772.—**Falloux**, F. A. P.
de. Memoirs. (Royalist.) 2 vols. 1888. 923.
1924-5.—**Hugo**, V. M., *vicomte.* History of a crime.
944.425;—Things seen. (1838–1875.) 1887. 944.624.—
Jerrold, W. B. Life of Napoleon III. 4 vols. 1874–
1882. 923.1983–6.—**Lacroix**, P. Histoire politique
. . . de Napoléon III. 4 vols. 1853. ** 923.2038–41.
—**Lecomte**, F. Relation historique et critique de
la guerre franco-allemand. 1870–71. 4 tomes.
1872–74. 944.688–91.—**Lefèvre**, E. Documents of-
ficiels . . . Histoire de l'intervention française au
Mexique. 2 vols. 1869. 944.686–7.—**Maupas**, C. É. de.
Story of the coup d'état. 2 vols. 1884. 944.765–6.—
Napier, Sir C: J: History of the Baltic campaign
of 1854. 1857. 947.50.—**Napoléon III.**, *Emperor of
the French.* Works. 2 vols. 1852. 923.446–7.—
Wraxall, *Sir* F. C. L. Second empire as exhibited
in French literature. 1852–1863. 2 vols. 1865. 944.
785–6.
Crimean war, 1854–1856.—**Chambers**, W., *and* R.,
pubs. Pictorial history of the Russian war, 1854–56.
1856. 947.49.—**Kinglake**, A. W. Invasion of the
Crimea. 6 vols. 1863–88. 947.1–3, 3¹–3⁴.—**Napier**, C.
History of the Baltic campaign in 1854. 1857. 947.50.
—**Russell**, W: H. General Todleben's History of
the defence of Sebastopol, 1854–5; a review. 1865.
947.29.
Franco-German war, 1870–71.—**Borbstædt**, A.,
and Dwyer, F. The Franco-German war to
the catastrophe of Sedan and the fall of Strass-
burg. Maps and plans. 1873. 944.762.—**Busch**,
J. H. M. Bismarck in the Franco-German war.
1870–71. 2 vols. (in 1). 1884. 923.1979.—**Clarke**,
F. C. H. Franco-German war, 1870–71. (With
maps.) 2 vols. 1874–80. Text: ** 944.160–2, 165³;
Maps: ** 944.163–4.—**Daudet**, A. Recollections
of a literary man. 819.16.—**Deutsch-französische
Krieg**, 1870–71. Redigirt von der Kriegs-geschicht-
lichen Abth. des grossen Generalstabes. 5 vols.
1872–7. Text: ** 944.619–21; Maps: ** 944.622–3.—
Gladstone, W: E. Germany, France and
England. 1870. (*In his* Gleanings, etc.) p. 197, *in*
829.106.—**Lang**, H. Aus den Erinnerungen eines
Schlachten bummlers. 1870–71. 2 vols. 944.754–5.
—**Lecomte**, F. Relation historique et critique de
la guerre franco-allemand en 1870–71. 4 vols. 1872–
74. 944.668–91.—**Mommsen**, C. M. T., *and others.*
Letters on the war between Germany and France.
1871. 943.128.—**Rémusat**, P. de. Louis A. Thiers.
923.887.—**Russell**, W: H. My diary during the last
great war. 1874. 940.32.—**Washburne**, E. B.
Recollections of a minister to France, 1869–77. 2
vols. 944.625–6.
Sedan, 1870.—**Claretie**, J. Le champ de bataille
de Sedan. [1870.] 26 pp. (*Rev. d. d. Mondes*, v.
91, 2e pér. 1871.) p. 48, *in* ** 54.296.—**Fitz-George**,
G: W: A. Plan of the battle of Sedan. (1870.) 1871.
944.777.
See also **Poole's** Index (to 1882). p. 1175, *in* **
50.1;—*Same.* Jan. 1, 1882–Jan. 1, 1887. p. 394, *in*
** 50.1².
LIFE AND MANNERS.—**Blouet**, P. Jacques Bon-
homme. John Bull on the continent. From my
letter-box. 944.645.—**Carette**, *Mme.* Recollections
of the court of the Tuileries. 1889. 944.655;—Inner
life of the court of the Tuileries. (2d pt.) 944.655².
—**Coignet**, C. Francis the First and his times.
1889. 923.1885.—**Daudet**, A. Recollections of a literary man. p. 233, *in* 819.16.—**Gronow**, *Capt.* R.
H. Reminiscences and recollections. (1810–1860.)

English Fiction. *Contin.*
France. *Contin.*
SECOND EMPIRE, **A. D. 1852–1870.** *Contin.*
Note. *Contin.*
2 vols. * 923.2025–6.—**Jackson**, *Lady* C. C. The
French court and society. Reign of Louis XVI.
and first empire. 2 pts. (in 1). 944.426.—**Jarves**,
J. J. Parisian sights and French principles seen
through American spectacles. 914.275.—**Kingsley**,
C: Three lectures on the ancien régime. 1867.
944.661.—**Lacroix**, P. The eighteenth century, its
institutions, customs and costumes, 1700–1789. 1876.
* 944.93.—**Marshall**, F. French home life. 1874.
944.756.—**Taine**, H. A. Ancient régime. 944.42.—
Tocqueville, A. C: II. C. de. On the state of society in France before the revolution of 1789. 1856.
944.662.—**Uzanne**, O. The Frenchwoman of the
century; fashions,—manners,—usages. (19th cent.)
1887. ** 394.18.—**Vasili**, *Count* P. Society in Paris.
1890 944.761.
GENERAL HISTORIES.—**Allonville**, A. F., *comte*
d'. Mémoires secrets de 1770 à 1830. 6 vols. 1838–
45. 944.680–85.—**Bibliography.**—Brunet, J. C.
Table methodique: hist. de France. 75 pp. (*In
his* Manual, v. 6.) p. 1251, *in* ** 14.40.—**Masson**, G.
Early chroniclers of Europe: France. 944.460.—**Bon-
nemère**, J. E. Histoire des paysans, depuis la fin du
moyen age jusqu'à nos jours, 120°–1850. 2 vols.
1856. 944.693–5.—**Crowe**, E. E. History of France.
(A. D. 400–1814.) 3 vols. 944.139–41.—**Guizot**, F. P. G.
History of France from the earliest ages to the year
1848. 6 vols. 1872–81. 944.4–9.—**Kirkland**, *Miss*
E.. S. Short history of France for young people.
(B. C. 600–A. D. 1870.) 1890. 944.651.—**Kitchin**, G.
W. History of France down to the year 1453. 1877.
944.51.—**Martin**, H. Histoire de France . . . jus-
qu'en 1789. 17 vols. 1864–78. ** 942.432–48.—**Masson**,
G. Early chroniclers of Europe. France. (300–
1550.) 1879. 944.461.—**Michelet**, J. Histoire de
France. 9th ed. 19 vols. 1876–7. ** 944.710–28.

v. 1:	222 B. C.–	800 A. D.	944.710
v. 2:	814 A. D.–1180	"	944.711
v. 3:	1187	"–1304	" 944.711
v. 4:	1305	"–1364	" 944.712
v. 5:	1364	"–1409	" 944.713
v. 6:	1414	"–1438	" 944.714
v. 7:	1439	"–1465	" 944.715
v. 8:	1465	"–1483	" 944.716
v. 9:	1483	"–1515	" (La renaissance.) 944.718
v. 10:	1508	"–1547	" (La réforme.) 944.719
v. 11:	1547	"–1572	" 944.720
v. 12:	1548	"–1598	" 944.721
v. 13:	1598	"–1628	" 944.722
v. 14:	1629	"–1661	" 944.723
v. 15:	1661	"–1690	" 944.724
v. 16:	1689	"–1715	" 944.725
v. 17:	1715	"–1723	" 944.726
v. 18:	1724	"–1757	" 944.727
v. 19:	1758	"–1789	" 944.728

Petitot, C. B. *and* A., *and* Monmerqué, L. J. N.
Collection complète des mémoires relatifs à l'histoire de France, jusqu'au commencement du dix-
septième siècle. 1e ser. 1819–26. 52 vols. ** 944.277-
328;—*Same.* 2e ser. 1820–29. 78 vols. ** 944.329-
406½.—**Ranken**, A. History of France . . . from
the time of Clovis. (486–1793.) 9 vols. 1801–1822.
* 944.68–76.—**Stephen**, *Sir* J. Lectures on the history of France. 2 vols. 1852. 944.609–10.—**Thierry**,
J. N. A. Lettres sur l'histoire de France. 1868.
940–71.—**Voltaire**, F. M. A. de. Annales de l'empire depuis Charlemagne. (*Œuvres complètes*, v. 25.)
1785. 944.20.

See also **Catalogues** of this Library.
No. 2, 1890, pp. 86, 87. No. 4, 1884, pp. 108, 109.
No. 3, 1882, p. 74. No. 5, 1888, pp. 143, 144.

See also **Rowell**, J. C. Contents-index, pp. 177-
181. (*Lib. of Univ. of Cal.*) 1890. ** 19.134.

See also **Poole's** Index (to 1882). p. 472–82, *in* **
50.1;—*Same.* Jan. 1, 1882–Jan. 1, 1887. pp. 164–66,
in ** 50.1².

See also **Index** to Consular reports. 1880–1885;
1886–1889. 2 vols. (U. S. Pub. Docs. *Dept. of State.*)
** 350.5496¹·².

For a late work on the political affairs, etc., in
France, *see* **Hurlbert**, W: H: France and the republic (in 1889). (Bibliography **xxi**, xxii.) 1890.
944.750.

Frances. Collins, M., *and* Collins, *Mrs.* F..
(C.) 823.247

English Fiction. *Contin.*
Francillon, Robert E: A dog without a tail.
38 pp. (*In* Tales from Blackwood, 2d ser.,
v. 6.) *in* 823.7490
—— Grace Owen's engagement. (*In* Tales
from Blackwood, 2d ser., v. 2.) *in* 823.7486
—— Left-handed Elsa. (*In* Tales from
Blackwood, 2d ser., v. 12.) *in* 823.7496
—— A story of Eulenberg. (*In* Tales from
Blackwood, 2d ser., v. 8.) *in* 823.7492
—— Under Slieve-Ban: a yarn in seven
knots. 823.1897
—— Zelda's fortune. 823.5871
——, *and* Senior, W: The golden flood: a
cloud in seven colors. 823.4953
Franco, *Rev.* J: Joseph, *S. J.* Tigranes: a
tale of the days of Julian the Apostate.
823.6891
Frank Fairlegh. Smedley, F. E: 823.1444
Frank Forester's sporting scenes and characters. 2 vols. Herbert, H: W: 823.5754-5
Frank Hilton. Grant, J. 823.627
Frank Mildmay. Marryat, *Capt.* F: 823.1097
Same. ** 823.6659
Frank Sinclair's wife. Riddell, *Mrs.* C.. E.
L. (C.) 823.1325
Frank Warrington. Harris, *Mrs.* M. (C.)
823.703
Frankenstein. Shelley, *Mrs.* M.. W. (G.)
823.1421
Franklin, B:, 1706–1790. Abbott, J. Franklin the apprentice boy. (*Harper's story
books*, v. 4.) *in* 808.583
—— Abbott, J: S. C. (Life of) B: Franklin.
808.797
—— Hawthorne, N. Biographical stories.
14 pp. (*In his* Tales and sketches.) 1889.
p. 189, *in* 824.414
Note.—For accounts of Franklin's life and character, *see* Briggs, C. F. (*In* Homes of Amer. statesmen.) 1854. p. 65, *in* 917.36.—Brougham, H.,
Baron. Franklin. 5 pp. (*In his* Hist. sketches of
statesmen. v. 2.) p. 153, *in* 923.510.—Chasles, V. E.
P. Franklin. 34 pp. (*Rev. d. d. Mondes*, 1841. 4e
pér., v. 26.) p. 669, *in* ** 54.143.—Drake, S: A. Our
great benefactors. p 339, *in* ** 920.312.—Foster, J.
Franklin's correspondence. (*In his* Crit. essays, v.
2.) 1860. p. 411, *in* 824.117.—Griswold, R. W.
Prose writers of America. 1870. p. 57, *in* * 829.110.
—Howe, H: Memoirs of the most eminent Amer.
mechanics. 1858. p. 37, *in* 926.118.—Life of F. 20
pp. (Longacre & Herring. *Nat. portr. gallery*, v.
2.) p. 1, *in* ** 923.1598.—Parker, T. (*In his* Historic Americans.) 62 pp. p. 11, *in* 923.1109.—Sanderson, J: Signers of the Declaration, v. 2. p. 7, *in* **
920.94.—Sumner, C. B: Franklin and J: Sliddell at
Paris. 38 pp. (*Works*, v. 8.) p. 1, *in* 329.63.—
Tuckerman, H. T. B: Franklin, the American
philosopher. 20 pp. (*In his* Essays.) p. 456, *in*
824.224.
See also Poole's Index (to 1882). pp. 483-4, *in* **
50.1;—*Same.* 1st suppl. from Jan. 1, 1882–Jan. 1,
1887. p. 166, *in* ** 50.1².
See also Catalogues of this Library.
No. 2, 1880, p. 87.　　No. 3, 1882, p. 75.
Franklin, the apprentice boy. Abbott, J.
in 808.583
Franzos, Karl Emil. For the right. Tr. by
J. Sutter. 823.6551
—— The Jews of Barnow. Tr. by M. W.
MacDowall. 823.4474
Fraser, *Mrs.* —. The cousins. (*In* Standard tales, *etc.*, ed. by Mrs. C. I. Johnstone.)
in * 823.6194
—— *Same.* (Tieck, L. *The elves* . . .)
1864. p. 24, *in* 823.6328

English Fiction. *Contin.*
Fraser, Jessie. [*Tasma.*] In her earliest
youth. 823.6357
—— A Sydney sovereign, and other tales.
823.7201
—— Uncle Piper of Piper's Hill: an Australian novel. 823.6370
Fraser-Tytler, C. C. *See* Liddell, *Mrs.* C. C.
(F.-T.)
Frau Wilhelmine. Stinde, J. 823.5222
Freaks on the fell. Ballantyne, R. M.
808.213
Frederic, Harold. Brother Sebastian's friendship. 20 pp. (*In* Stories by Amer. authors, v. 6.) p. 145, *in* 823.4707
—— The Lawton girl. 823.6996
Frederick I. 1657–1713. *See also* Germany,
note.
—— Topelius, Z. Times of Frederick I.
(Surg. stories. 4th cyc.) 823.4701
Frederick II., *the Great, King of Prussia.*
1712–86.
—— Muudt, *Mrs.* C. (M.) Frederick the
Great and his court. 823.6280
—— —— Frederick the Great and his family.
823.5887
—— —— Old Fritz and the new era.
823.6270
Note.—*See* Abbott, J: S. C. Frederick, the Great.
263 pp. (*Harper's mag.*, v. 40, 1870: pp. 1, 161, 321,
490, 673, 834; v. 41, 1870: pp. 35, 200, 383, 518, 709, 869;
v. 42, 1871: pp. 41, 201, 364, 557, 680, 874. 3 vols. **
51.435-37.—Brougham, H., *Baron.* (*In his* Hist.
sketches of statesmen, v. 2.) p. 160, *in* 923.510.—
Carlyle, T: History of Frederick II. (*Works*,
vols. 9-14.) * 923.1845-50.—Dodge, T: A.
Frederick. (*In his* Great captains.) 1889. p. 140,
in 355.12.—Ferris, G. T. Great leaders. p. 357,
in 920.329.—Grimm, H. Voltaire and F.—F. and
Macaulay. (*In his* Literature.) *in* 804.9.—Lamb,
Lady C. (*In her* Warrior kings. . .) 35 pp. *in*
343, *in* 923.1413.—Macaulay, T: B., *Baron.* Frederick, the Great. 100 pp. (*In his* Essays . . . v. 5).
p. 148, *in* 824.136.—Sainte-Beuve, C. A. (*In his*
Monday-chats.) 40 pp. p. 248, *in* * 920.313.
See also Encyc. Britannica Index. p. 169, *in*
** 32.27p.
See also Catalogues of this Library.
No. 2, 1880, p. 87.　　No. 4, 1884, p. 109.
No. 3, 1882, p. 75.　　No. 5, 1888, p. 145.
See also Poole's Index (to 1882). p. 485, *in* ** 50.1;
—*Same.* Jan. 1, 1882–Jan. 1, 1887. p. 166, *in* ** 50.1².
Frederick the Great and his court. Mundt,
Mrs. C. (M.) 823.6280
Frederick the Great and his family. Muudt,
Mrs. C. (M.) 823.5887
Free Joe and other Georgian sketches. Harris, J. C. 823.5255
Free Lances, The. Reid, *Capt.* T: M.
823.6335
Free prisoners. Bruner, J.. W. 823.4384
Free, yet forging their own chains. Roe, M..
A. 823.1368
Freedom triumphant. Coffin, C: C. 808.1852
Freeland, *Mrs.* Carrie J. [*C. J. G.*] In
palace and faubourg: a story of the French
revolution. 823.6368
Freeman, *Mrs.* A. M. Somebody's Ned.
823.589
French, Alice. [*Octave Thanet.*] The bishop's vagabond. 42 pp. (*In* Stories by
Amer. authors, v. 7.) p. 5, *in* 823.4708
—— Expiation. 823.6950
—— Knitters in the sun. 823.5377
French, C.. Secret of the cliffs. *in* 823.5054

English Fiction. *Contin.*
French, Harry Willard. Castle Foam; or, the heir of Meerschaum: a Russian story.
823.590
—— The only one. 823.7450
—— Our boys in India: the wanderings of two young Americans in Hindustan, with their adventures on the sacred rivers and wild mountains, etc. Illus. 808.1872
French wines and politics. Martineau, H.
in ** 823.6709
Frere, M.. Old Deccan days; or, Hindoo fairy legends, current in southern India. With an introd. and notes by Sir H: B. E: Frere. 808.1035
Freres, The. Hector, *Mrs.* A. (F.) 823.4574
Same. 823.4976
Frescoes. La Ramée, L. de. 823.4730
Freshwater fisherman. Mitford, M.. R.
in * 823.6194
Fresneau, *Mme.* A. Theresa at San Domingo: a tale of the negro insurrection of 1791. Tr. by E. G. Magrath. 823.6938
Freytag, Gustav. Debit and credit. Tr. by L. C. C. 823.6277
—— The German professor, (Zimmern, H.., *and* A. *Half-hours with for. novelists,* v. 2.) *in* ** 823.6614
—— The lost manuscript. Tr. by Mrs. Malcolm. 823.6389
—— Our forefathers. Tr. by Mrs. Malcolm. 2 vols. 823.6797–8
1. Ingo. 823.6797
2. Ingraban. 823.6798
Fridolin's mystical marriage. Wilbrandt, A.
823.4759
Friedrich, *Mrs.* Bertha (Heyn). [*Georg Dannenberg.*] [*Golo Raimund.*] From hand to hand. Tr. by Mrs. A. L. Wister.
823.4548
Friend Barton's concern. 54 pp. Foote, *Mrs.* M.. (H.) p. 83, *in* 823.4705
Friend Fritz. Erckmann, É., *and* Chatrian, P. A. 823.1839
Friends: a duet. Ward, *Mrs.* E.. S. (P.)
823.5244
Friends of Bohemia. 2 vols. Whitty, E: M.
823.6155–6
Friends, though divided. Henty, G: A.
808.1575
Friendship. La Ramée, L. de. 823.1820
Friis, *Prof.* J. A. Lajla: a tale of Finmark. Tr. by I. Markhus. 823.6964
Frith, H: The hunting of the "Hydra;" or, the phantom prahu. 808.1495
—— Under Bayard's banner: a story of the days of chivalry. 808.1606
From canal boy to president. Alger, H., *Jr.*
808.1054
From dawn to daylight. Beecher, *Mrs.* E. W. (B.) 823.7375
From farm house to the White House. Thayer, W: M. 808.1727
From flag to flag. Ripley, E. McH.- 823.5439
From gloom to sunlight. Brame, *Mrs.* C.. M. (L.) *in* 823.5104
Same. 823.5133
From hand to hand. · Friedrich, *Mrs.* B. (H.)
823.4548

English Fiction. *Contin.*
From jest to earnest. Roe, E: P. · 823.1357
From my youth up. Terhune, *Mrs.* M.. V. (H.) 823.1553
From Olympus to Hades. Bridges, *Mrs. Col.*
in 823.3064
Same. *in* 823.5034
From post to finish. Smart, H. *in* 823.5116
From powder monkey to admiral. Kingston, W: H: G. 808.1033
From the earth to the moon. Verne, J.
823.2541
Same. 823.5485; 823.6305
Frontier schoolmaster. Thomas, C.
823.1842
Frontier series. 6 vols. 808.1653–6
General, The; or, twelve nights in the hunter's camp. By W: Barrows. 808.1653
Cabin on the prairie. By C: H. Pearson. 808.1654
Planting the wilderness; or, the pioneer boys. By J. D. McCabe, *Jr.* 808.1655
Young pioneers of the north-west. By C: H. Pearson. 808.1656
Frost, J: Old Hickory: young folks' life of Gen. Andrew Jackson, seventh president of the United States. 808.1715
Froude, James Anthony. Nemesis of faith.
823.4260
—— The two chiefs of Dunboy; or, an Irish romance of the last century. 823.5512
Frozen deep, and other tales. Collins, W: W.
823.256
Frozen dragon, A. Holder, C: F: 808.1904
Frozen hearts. Appleton, G. W. 823.7356
Fugitives, The. Ballantyne, R. M.
823.5636
Fuller, F.. Auretta. *See* Victor, *Mrs.* F.. A. (F.)
Fuller, Gardner A. Pennimans; or, the triumph of genius. 823.591
Fuller, J.. G. The Brownings: a tale of the great rebellion. (*Also*) Lucy Lee; or, all things for Christ. 808.1580
Fullerton, *Lady* Georgiana C.. (Leveson Gower.) Constance Sherwood: an autobiography of the 16th century. 823.6363
—— Ellen Middleton: a tale. 823.593
—— Lady-bird: a tale. 823.595
Fullom, Stephen Watson. The daughter of night: a story of the present time. 823.5926
Fur country, The. 2 pts. Verne, J.
823.6881–2
G., C. J. *See* Freeland, *Mrs.* Carrie J.
G., H. Suzanne de l'Orme: a story of France in Huguenot times. 808.1659
G. T. T. Hale, E: E. 823.682
Gaboriau, Émile. The amateur detective. (Zimmern, H.., *and* A. *Half-hours with for. novelists,* v. 2.) *in* ** 823.6614
—— Clique of gold. *in* 823.5022
—— *Same.* 823.6453
Issued also as The gilded clique.
—— The count's secret. 823.1890
—— *Same.* *in* 823.5127
—— The downward path. 823.5907
—— *Same.* 823.6174
—— File No. 113. *in* 823.5115
—— *Same.* (*Also*) Other people's money.
823.3014
—— The gilded clique. 823.2160

English Fiction. *Contin.*
Gaboriau, Émile. *Contin.*
—— In peril of his life. (*With his* Promise of marriage.)   *in* 823.2731
—— The little old man of Batignolles, and other stories. (*With his* Promise of marriage.)   *in* 823.2731
—— Marriage at a venture. Tr. by Vincenzo Calfa.   *in* 823.2463
—— *Same.*   *in* 823.5035
Issued also as Chance marriage.
—— Military sketches. (*With his* A thousand francs reward.)   *in* 823.6699
—— Monsieur Lecoq. 2 vols. (in 1).·   823.4259
—— *Same.*   823.6206
—— *Same.* Tr. by Mrs. L. E. Kendall. 2 pts.   *in* 823.5038
—— The mystery of Orcival.   823.2164
—— *Same.*   823.5034; 823.6079
—— Other people's money.   *in* 823.3014
—— *Same.*   *in* 823.5057
—— Promise of marriage.—In peril of his life. (*And*) The little old man of Batignolles, and other stories.   823.2731
—— A thousand francs reward. Tr. by M. J. Safford. (*Also*) Military sketches. Tr. by L. F. Kendall.   *in* 823.6699
—— The widow Lerouge.   *in* 823.5029
—— *Same.* (*Also*) Marriage at a venture. Tr. by V. Calfa.   823.2463
—— Within an inch of his life.   823.5070
—— *Same.*   823.6080
Gabriel Conroy. Harte, F. B.   823.712
Same.   823.6216
Gabrielle. McCarty, L.   823.7302
Gage, C: S. Mr. Bixby's Christmas visitor. 12 pp. (*In* Stories by Amer. authors, v. 9.)   p. 42, *in* 823.4710
Gagneur, *Mrs.* Louise (Mignerot). A nihilist princess.   823.1846
Gala-days. Dodge, M.. A.   823.1794
Galama. Liefde, J: B. de.   823.5847
Galatea. Cervantes Saavedra, M. de.   823.2121
Galdós, Benito Perez. *See* Perez Galdós, Benito.
Gally, J. W. Sand; and Big Jack Small. (Two stories.)   823.4162
Galt, J: The annals of the parish, and The Ayrshire legatees. With memoir of the author.   823.4191
—— The Ayrshire legatees. (*With his* The annals of a parish.)   *in* 823.4191
—— The book of life. (Picken, A., *ed.* *The club-book*, v. 2.)   *in* 823.702
—— The entail.   823.4193
—— The fatal whisper. (Picken, A., *ed.* *The club-book*, v. 2.)   p. 181, *in* 823.702
—— Haddad-Ben-Ahab the traveller. 9 pp. (Johnson, R., *ed.* *Little classics*, v. 9.)   p. 58, *in* 829.132
—— *Same.* (Picken, A., *ed.* *The club-book*, v. 2.)   p. 69, *in* 823.702
—— The member: an autobiography.   ** 823.6720
—— The painter: a Sicilian tale. (Picken, A., *ed.* *The club-book*, v. 2.)   *in* 823.702
—— Provost, and other tales.   823.4192

English Fiction. *Contin.*
Galt, J: *Contin.*
—— The radical: an autobiography.   ** 823.6721
—— The reform: being The member and The radical.   823.7376
—— Sir Andrew Wylie of that ilk.   823.4194
—— The unguarded hour. (Picken, A., *ed.* *The club-book*, v. 2.)   *in* 823.702
—— The wearyful woman. 10 pp. (*In* Tales from Blackwood, v. 3.)   *in* ** 823.6649
Gama, Vasco da. Towle, G: M. The voyages and adventures of Vasco da Gama.   808.740
Gambara. 86 pp. Balzac, H. de.   p. 173, *in* 823.5428
Gambler's wife, The. Grey, *Mrs.* E.. C.   *in* 823.5051
Same.   *in* 823.5058
Games and songs of American children. Newell, W: W., *comp.*   808.1876
Games and stories. *See* Higgins, E. M. Holidays at the grange.   808.1638
Garden of women. Keddie, H.   823.1783
Same.   823.4239
Gardiner, Marguerite (Power), *Countess of Blessington.* Country quarters: a love story.   823.559
Garfield, James Abram. (1831–81.) Alger, H., *Jr.* From canal boy to president.   808.1054
Note.—See Laveleye, É. de. Le président Garfield. 13 pp. (*Rev. d. d. Mondes*, v. 47. 3e pér. 1881.) p. 671, *in* ** 54.361.—Lowell, J. R. Garfield. 14 pp. (*In his* Democracy . . .) 1887. p. 43, *in* 829.670.—The poets' tributes to Garfield. *in* ** 923.1386.—U.S. Senate. Miscel. docs., v. 5. 1881–2. ** 350.2628.
See also Catalogues of this Library. No. 3, 1882, p. 78. No. 5, 1888, p. 175. No. 4, 1884, p. 113.
See also Poole's Index (to 1882). p. 500, *in* ** 50.1;—Same. Jan. 1, 1882–Jan. 1, 1887. p. 171, *in* ** 50.1².
Garland for girls, A. Alcott, L.. M.   808.1462
Garrett, E:, *pseud. See* Mayo, Mrs. I.. (Fyvie).
Garrett, E:, *and* Ruth, *pseud. See* Mayo, *Mrs.* I.. (Fyvie).
Garrison gossip. Stannard, *Mrs.* H. E. V. (P.)   823.4992
Garth. Hawthorne, J. C.   823.5868
Gascoyne, the sandal-wood trader. Ballantyne, R. M.   808.210
Gaskell, *Mrs.* E.. Cleghorn (Stevenson). Cranford.   823.600
—— *Same.*   823.5033
—— Moorland cottage.   823.603
—— Right at last, and other tales.   823.605
—— Sylvia's lovers: a novel.   823.5867
Gaspar, the gaucho. Reid, *Capt.* T: M.   808.1579
Gates ajar. Ward, *Mrs.* E.. S. (P.)   823.1255
Gates between, The. Ward, *Mrs.* E.. S. (P.)   823.5224
Gautier, Judith. *See* Mendès, *Mme.* Judith (Gautier).
Gautier, Théophile (1811–72). Captain Fracasse. Tr. by M. M. Ripley.   823.6883
—— The romance of a mummy. Tr. by A. McC. Wright.   823.4544

English Fiction. *Contin.*
Gautier, Théophile (1811–72). *Contin.*
— Spirite: a fantasy.   823.2316
— Same.   823.6454
Note.— For his life and writings *see* **Brunetière,**
F. T. Gautier. 11 pp. (*Rev. d. d. Mondes*, v. 84,
3e pér. 1887.) p. 693, *in* * 54.399.— **Mauris,** M.
French men of letters. 1880. p. 65, *in* 928.179.—
Sainte-Beuve, C. A. Gautier. (*In his* Premiers
lundis, v. 2.) 824.444; (*In* Gautier, T., *and others.*
Famous French authors.) p. 7, *in* 928.87.— **Swin-**
burne, A. C. Memorial verses on the death of G.
13 pp. (*Poems and ballads,* 2d s.) p. 84, *in* 821.397².
** *See also* Index to **Harper's** monthly. p. 271, *in*
** 51.475.
** *See also* Poole's Index (to 1882). p. 503, *in* **
50.1;—*Same.* Jan. 1, 1882-Jan. 1, 1887. p. 172, *in*
** 50.1³.
—, *and* Merimée,· Prosper. Tales before
supper. Tr. by M. Verelst, and delayed
with a proem by Edgar Saltus.   823.5737
Contents:—Introduction. (Sketch of T. Gautier.)
By E. Saltus.—Avatar. By T. Gautier.—Venus of
Ille. By P. Mérimée.
Gautran. Farjeon, B: L.   823.6599
Gaviota, La,—the sea-gull. Arrom, *Mme.*
C. (B. de F.)   823.6892
Gayarré, C: Étienne Arthur. Aubert Dub-
ayet: or, the two sister republics. (Sequel
to "Fernando de Lemos.")   823.4624
Gayworthys, The. Whitney, *Mrs.* A. D. (T.)
   823.1694
Geddie, J: Beyond the Himalayas: a story
of travel and adventure in the wilds of Thi-
bet.   808.1184
Geier-Wally. Hillern, *Mrs.* W. (B.) von.
   823.6806
Gemini. Fox, *Mrs.* E.   823.1998
General, The. Barrows, W: 808.1653
General Bounce. Melville, G: J: Whyte-
   ** 823.4664
Same.   823.7276
Geneva. *See also* Switzerland, *note.*
— Abbott, J. Rollo in Geneva.   808.926
Geneviève. Alcock, D.   823.7196
Genlis, Stéphanie-Félicité (Ducrest de Saint
Aubin), *comtesse* de. Adelaide and Theo-
dore; or, letters on education. 4th ed. 3
vols.   ** 823.4688–90
Gentle belle, A. Tiernan, *Mrs.* F.. C. (F.)
   823.5897
Gentle savage, The. King, E: 823.4547
Gentleman of leisure. Fawcett, E.   823.4238
Gentleman of the old school. James, G: P.
R.   823.859
Geoffrey Hampstead. Jarvis, T: S.   823.7449
Geoffrey the knight: a tale of chivalry of the
days of King Arthur. With engravings by
G. Doré.   * 823.5192
Geoffry Hamlyn, The recollections of. Kings-
ley, H: 823.944
Geographical novels. *See also* Sea stories.
— Andrews, J.. The seven little sisters
who live on the round ball that floats in
the air.   808.1428
— Stockton, F. R: Round-about rambles
in lands of fact and fancy.   808.1886
Note.—*See* novels by Adams, W: T. (*Young Amer-*
ica abroad.)–Ballantyne.—Butterworth.—Griswold.
—Kingston.–Knox, T. W.–Verne,–and others.
See also **Catalogues** of this Library.
   No. 2, 1880, p. 91.   No. 4, 1884, p. 114.
   No. 3, 1882, p. 79.   No. 5, 1888, p. 177.

English Fiction. *Contin.*
George Caulfield's journey. Maxwell, *Mrs.*
M.. E.. (B.)   *in* 823.4991
George Christy. Halsey, H.   823.5054
George Geith of Fen Court. Riddell, *Mrs.*
C.. E. L. (C.)   823.1326
George Julian. Cockton, H: 823.240
George Silverman's explanation. 29 pp.
Dickens, C: J: H.   p. 449, *in* 808.686
Same.   p. 449, *in* 942.1259
Georgia scenes, characters, incidents, etc.
Longstreet, A: B.   823.1012
Georgina's reasons. James, H:, *Jr.*
   p. 159, *in* 823.4894
Georgy Sandon. Ogle, A.   823.1225
Gerald Estcourt. Lean, *Mrs.* F. (M.)
   823.219
Gerald Ffrench's friends. Jessop, G: H.
   823.6574
Geraldine Hawthorne. Butt, B.. M.
   823.4570
Gerard, Dorothea. Orthodox.   823.7078
Gérard's marriage. Theuriet, A.   823.2315
Gerda. Schwartz, *Mrs.* M. S. (B.)
   823.1944
German emigrants. Göthe, J. W. von.
   p. 357, *in* 823.2183
German household stories. 2d ser. Grimm,
J. L., *and* W. K: 808.1538
German novelists. 4 vols. Roscoe, T:, *tr.*
   ** 823.6826–9
German popular stories. Grimm, J. L., *and*
Grimm, W. K: 808.1592
German popular tales. Grimm, J. L., *and*
W. K: 808.1322
German tales. Auerbach, B.   823.7013
Germany. *See also* notes under Austria.—
France. *Also* Reformation.
— Adams, W: T.. Down the Rhine; or,
Young America in Germany.   808.489
— Hale, E: E., *and* Hale, S. A family
flight through . . . Germany.   808.1831
— Longfellow, H: W. Poems of places.
2 vols.   821.215-16
— Wagner, W. Book of ballads on Ger-
man history (in German; arranged and
annotated. (A. D. 410-1871.)   831.122
— Wratislaw, A. H., *tr.* Upper and lower
Lusatian stories. (*In his* Sixty folk-tales,
etc.) 1890.   p. 92, *in* 823.6946
— Yonge, C.. M.. Young folks' history
of Germany.   943.5
HERMANN, or ARMINIUS, *destroys the Ro-*
mans under Varus, A. D. 9.
— —; drama. Kleist, H. B. W. von. 830.2
— —; drama. Klopstock, F. G.   832.11
Note.—*See* Ancient Germans. (*In* Univ. hist.,
anc. pt., v. 17.) p. 1, *in* ** 909.47.—**Caesar's** Commentaries. 937.53; 937.61.—**Freytag,** G. Aus der
Römerzeit. 101 pp. (*In his* Bilder aus der deutschen
Vergangenheit, v. 1.) p. 27, *in* 943.11.—**Gibbon,** E.
History, *etc.*, v. 1. Chap. 9. p. 249, *in* 937.8.—**Mot-**
ley, J: L. Hist. introd. (*In his* The rise of the
Dutch republic, v. 1.) p. 1, *in* 949.10.—**Stubbs,** W:
Caesar and Tacitus. 28 pp. (*In his* Constitutional
hist. of England, v. 1.) p. 13, *in* 942.451.—**Tacitus.**
Germany. (*Works.*) 2 vols. 937.71-2.
4TH CENTURY, A. D. Freytag, G. Ingo.
(A. D. 357.)   823.6797
5TH CENTURY, A. D. Dahn, F. Felicitas.
(Early Christianity.)   823.5728

English Fiction. *Contin.*
Germany. *Contin.*
8TH CENTURY, A. D. Freytag, G. Iugraban.
823.6798
Genoveva, or *Geneviève of Brabant.*
—— Hebbel, F. Genoveva. (*Sämmtl.*
Werke, v. 3.) ' p. 1, *in* 832.91
—— Moncrieff, R. H. Geneviève of Brab-
ant. 76 pp. (*In his* Stories of old renown.)
p. 223, *in* 808.1686
CHARLEMAGNE, A. D. 742–814. *See also*
Charlemagne, p. 37.
—— Bulfinch, T: Legends of Charlemagne.
823.150
9TH CENTURY, A. D. Bates, A. Albrecht.
(The Black Forest.) 823.6951
10TH CENTURY, A. D. Scheffel, J. von.
Ekkehard. 833.364
11TH CENTURY, A. D.
Henry IV., 1056–1106. Bresciani, *Rev.* A.
Mathilda of Canossa, and Yoland of Gron-
ingen. (Submission to Pope at Canossa,
1076.) 823.1904
CRUSADES, 1096–1291. *See* Crusades, p. 48.
12TH CENTURY, A. D. Meredith, G: Farina.
(Cologne.) (*With his* The shaving of Shagpat.) *in* 823.5274
13TH CENTURY, A. D.
Otho IV., 1208–1215.
—— James, G: P. R. Castle of Ehrenstein.
in 823.6247
—— —— Philip Augustus. 823.874
Frederick II., 1215–1250. Immermann, K.
L. Kaiser Friedrich der Zweite.
p. 151, *in* 832.28
Rudolph von Hapsburg, 1273–1291.
—— —; drama. Kotzebue, A. F. F. von.
(*Theater,* v. 34.) *in* 832.82
—— —; poem. Schiller, J. C. F. von. 831.54
14TH CENTURY. Crucifix of Baden. 823.5817
15TH CENTURY, A. D.
—— Ebers, G. M. Gred of Nuremberg.
823.7039
—— —— Margery: a tale of old Nuremberg.
2 vols. (Another tr. of Gred.) 823.6571–2
—— Reade, C: The cloister and the hearth.
823.1286
—— Spindler, C. Der Jude. 2 vols.
833.425–6
—— Wolff, J. Salt master of Lüneburg.
823.7185
Hussites. Kotzebue, A. F. F. von. Die Hus-
siten von Naumburg. (1432.) Play.
p. 259, *in* 832.73
Maximilian, 1459–1519. (*Emperor,* 1493.)
James, G: P. R. Mary of Burgundy.
823.870
Vehmgerichte.
—— Scott, *Sir* W. Anne of Geierstein. 2
vols. (in 1). 823.1392
—— —— *Same.* ** 823.6033
Manners. Yonge, C. M.. The dove in the
eagle's nest. (Domestic feudal manners.)
823.1765
Note.—See Dunham, S. A. History of Europe
during the middle ages. 4 vols. 1833-4. 940.177-
80.—Hallam, H. View of the state of Europe during the middle ages. 3 vols. 1872. 940.2-4.—Modern part of an universal history. vols. 25-7. 3
vols. 1782. ** 909.73-5.

English Fiction. *Contin.*
Germany. *Contin.*
15TH CENTURY, A. D. *Contin.*
Note. *Contin.*
See also **Catalogues** of this Library.
No. 2, 1830, p. 78. No. 4, 1834, p. 115.
No. 3, 1882, pp. 80, 81. No. 5, 1888, p. 184.
16TH CENTURY, A. D.
—— Göthe, J. W. von. Götz von Berlich-
ingen; drama. 830.20
—— —— *Same.* 822.34
—— Hausrath, A. Klytia: a story of Heid-
elberg castle. *in* 823.4973
—— Hoffmann, E. T. W. The cooper of
Nuremberg. (*In his* Strange stories.)
p. 13, *in* 823.6807
—— Kleist, H. von. Michael Kohlhaas. (*In*
Tales from the German.)
p. 165, *in* 823.6276
—— Labadye, A. de. The baron of Hertz: a
tale of the Anabaptists. 823.6868
—— Morier, J., *ed.* The banished: a Swab-
ian historical tale. (Würtemberg.)
* 823.6182
—— Roberts, M. In the olden time. (Peas-
ant war.) 823.5792
Reformation, 1517, etc.
—— Charles, *Mrs.* E.. (R.) Chronicles of
the Schönberg-Cotta family. 823.204
—— Kingston, W: H: G. Count Ulrich.
823.5782
Luther. Meredith, O. Thomas Müntzer to
Martin Luther. (*In his* Chronicles and
characters, v. 2.) *in* 821.1345
Rudolph II., 1576–1612. Spindler, C. Der
Bastard. 2 vols. 833.437–8
Manners.
—— Aleman, M. Guzman d'Alfarache.
863.17
—— Arnim, L. A. von. Isabella von
Aegypten. (Gipsy life.) 833.664
Note.—See Gindely, A. Rudolf II. und seine
Zeit. (1600-1612.) 2 vols. 1868. 943.124-5.—
Ranke, L. von. History of the Reformation in
Germany. 2d ed. 3 vols. 1845-7. 274.59-61.—
Robertson, W. Charles V. 4 vols. 923.121-4.
17TH CENTURY, A. D.
—— Arnim, L. A. von. Die Capitulation
von Oggersheim, 1621; drama. *in* 832.112
—— —— Vertreibung der Spanier aus Wesel
im Jahre 1629. *in* 832.111
—— Marryat, *Capt.* F: The phantom ship.
823.1111
—— —— *Same.* ** 823.6670
Thirty years' war, 1618–1648.
—— Byron, G: G. N., *Baron.* Werner; trag.
p. 133, *in* 821.73
—— —— *Same.* *in* 822.730
—— De Foe, D. Memoirs of a cavalier.
(Tilly & Gustavus Adolphus.) (*In his*
Novels, v. 2.) 823.2123
—— Duellist, The: a tale of the "Thirty
years' war." 28 pp. (*In* Tales from Black-
wood, v. 10.) *in* ** 823.6656
—— James, G: P. R. Heidelberg. 823.862
—— Lee, *Miss* H. The German's tale. (*In*
her Canterbury tales, v. 2.) 823.967
—— Liefde, J. B. de. The maid of Stral-
sund. 823.2181
—— Topelius, Z. Times of Gustav Adolf.
823.4476

English Fiction. *Contin.*
Germany. *Contin.*
17TH CENTURY, A. D. *Contin.*
Thirty years' war, 1618-1648. *Contin.*
—— Velde, E. K. van der. Axel. (*In* Tales from the German.) p. 119, *in* 823.6276
Wallenstein.
—— Schiller, J. C. F. von. Piccolomini.
p. 179, *in* 832.35
—— — *Same.* Tr. by Coleridge.
p. 479, *in* 829.480
—— — Death of Wallenstein. 832.35
—— — *Same.* Tr. by Coleridge.
p. 609, *in* 829.480
Witchcraft. Meinhold, J. W. Mary Schweidler, the amber witch. 823.4246
Note.—See **Fletcher, C. R. L.** Gustavus Adolphus and the struggle of Protestantism for existence. 1890. 923.2050.—**Gardiner, S. R.** Letters illust. the relations between England and Germany at commencement of the 30 years' war. 2 ser. 1: 1618-1619; 2: 1629-30. 2 vols. ** 942.1060; 1068;—Thirty years' war, 1618-1648. 1887. 943.101.—**Gindely,** *Prof.* A. History of the Thirty years' war. 2 vols. 1884. 943.89-90.—**Malleson,** *Col.* G. B. The battlefields of Germany, outbreak of Thirty years' war to Blenheim. 1884. 943.95.—**Schiller,** J. C. F. von. History of the Thirty years' war. 1873. 949.3.—**Smith,** W: Lectures on modern history. 2 vols. 1854. 901.9-10.—**Trench,** *Abp.* R. C. Gustavus Adolphus in Germany. 1886. 943.92.

18TH CENTURY, A. D.
—— Auerbach, B. Poet and merchant: a picture of life from the times of Moses Mendelssohn. 823.6793
—— Dr. Goethe's courtship: a tale of domestic life. 823.4249
—— Friedmann Bach. 19 pp. (*In* Robert . . . , and other stories.)
p. 153, *in* 823.5811
—— Müller, O: Charlotte Ackerman: a theatrical romance. 823.6812
—— Richter, J. P. F. Invisible lodge.
823.4613
—— Shorthouse, J. H: Little school-master Mark: a spiritual romance. *in* 823.4993
—— Smart, H. Courtship in 1720.
823.4331
—— Zschokke, H. Die Prinzessin von Wolfenbüttel. (German.)
p. 3, *in* 833.1038
Frederick, the Great, 1740-1786. *See* Frederick II., the Great, p. 96.
Maria Theresa, 1717-1780. *See under* Austria, *Maria Theresa*, p. 13.
Seven years' war, 1756-1763.
—— Lessing, G. E. Minna von Barnhelm; com. 832.34
—— Mundt, *Mrs.* C. (M.) Frederick the Great and his court. 823.6280
—— — Frederick the Great and his family.
823.5887
—— Paalzow, *Mrs.* H. (W.) von. Citizen of Prague. 823.6073
—— Zschokke, H. Bückwirkungen. (German.) p. 223, *in* 833.1041
Note.—See **Broglie,** C: J. V. A., *duc* de. Frederick the Great and Maria Theresa. 1740-42. 2 vols. 1883. 943.111-12. — **Carlyle,** T: Frederick the Great. (*Works,* vols. 9-14.) 6 vols. 1886-7. 923. 1845-50.—**Frederic** II., *of Prussia.* History of the seven years' war. (vols. 3-4 *of his* Œuvres post., 1788.) 2 vols. 943.28-9.

English Fiction. *Contin.*
Germany. *Contin.*
18TH AND 19TH CENTURIES, A. D.
War with France, 1793-1815. *See* France, *note,* p. 92.
—— Göthe, J. W. von. Hermann and Dorothea (life in small town with French immigrants); poem. 821.1021
—— Mundt, *Mrs.* C. (M.) Louisa of Prussia and her times. 823.6268
—— — Napoleon and Blücher. 823.6269
—— — Napoleon and the Queen of Prussia.
823.5801
Note.—See **Seeley,** *Prof.* J. R. Life and times of Stein. (1780-1831.) 2 vols. (Germany and Prussia in Napoleonic times.) 923.134-5.
Revolution of 1848.
—— Auerbach, B. Waldfried. (Political movements, 1848-72.) 823.6794
—— Freytag, G. Debit and credit.
823.6277
—— — Soll und Haben. 2 Bde. 823.126-7
—— Spielhagen, F. Through night to light.
823.6822
Note.—See **Maurice,** C. E. Revolutionary movement of 1848-9 in Italy . . . Germany. 1887. 943.313.
Franco-German war. See France, *Franco-German war,* pp, 93, 94.
—— Erckmann, E., *and* Chatrian, P. A. Brigadier Frederick. 823.6103
LIFE AND MANNERS.
—— Auerbach, B. Master Bieland and his workmen. 823.4590
—— — *Same.* 823.6629
—— — The villa on the Rhine. 2 vols.
823.4333-4
—— Behrens, B. Lora, the major's daughter.
823.6321
—— Bürstenbinder, E.. At a high price.
823.4991
—— — *Same.* 823.6704
—— — Banned and blessed. 823.4614
—— Crawford, F. M. Greifenstein.
823.5455
—— Edwards, M. B. Betham- Doctor Jacob.
823.4099
—— — *Same.* 823.5055; *in* 823.5068
—— Hackländer, F. W. European slave life. 3 vols. (in 1). (Illustrations of all classes of European society.) ** 823.6638
—— — Forbidden fruit. 823.7094
—— Heyse, J. L. P. The romance of the canoness. 823.5618
—— Hillern, *Mrs.* W. (B.) von. By his own might. 823.7095
—— — Only a girl; or, a physician for the soul. 823.5617
—— John, E. At the councillor's. 823.2775
—— — The bailiff's maid. 823.4060
—— — Countess Gisela. 823.2654
—— — Gold Elsie. 823.6601
—— — In the counselor's house. (*Same as* At the councillor's.) *in* 823.6693
—— — In the Schillingscourt. 823.2023
—— — *Same.* 823.2444
—— — The little moorland princess.
823.3052
—— — The old mam'selle's secret. 823.5781
—— — The second wife. 823.2455

English Fiction. *Contin.*
Germany. *Contin.*
LIFE AND MANNERS. *Contin.*
— Powers, S. Papers from Germany.
(*With his* Muskingum legends.)
p. 47, *in* 823.4145
— Reichenbach, M. von. The Eichhofs.
823.4345
— Schobert, H. Picked up in the streets.
823.5271
— Spielhagen, F. The Hohensteins.
823.4281
— Streckfuss, A. F. K. Too rich.
823.6824
— Tautphœus, J. (M.) *Freiherrin* von.
Cyrilla. 823.6439
— — The initials. 823.1796
— — Quits. 823.1798
— Teufel, *Mrs.* B. W. (H.) The open door.
823.6209
— Trollope, *Mrs.* F.. E. (T.) Sacristan's
household. 823.6001
— Waller, M. E. The rose-bush of Hildes-
heim: a cathedral story. * 823.6140
— Williams, A. B. The giant dwarf.
808.1639
Life among the aristocracy.
— Brink, *Mrs.* M. (di S.) ten. Not in their
set; or, in different circles of society.
823.7111
— Dingelstedt, F. *Freiherr* von. The
Amazon. 823.6825
— Glümer, C. von. A noble name.
823.4549
— Harder, L. A family feud. 823.6802
— Menger, R. Countess Loreley.
823.7055
Life at watering places.
— About, E. F. V. Rouge et noir: a tale
of Baden-Baden. 823.6282
— Turgénef, I. S. Smoke. 823.4214
Musical life.
— Beethoven. 18 pp. (*In* Cruc. of Baden.)
p. 135, *in* 823.5817
— Cornish, *Mrs.* —. Alcestis. 823.806
— Dudevant, *Mme.* A. L. A. (D.) Con-
suelo. 823.6214
— — *Same.* 823.6885
— Sheppard, E.. S. Charles Auchester.
(Seraphael is Mendelssohn; Miss Benette
is Jenny Lind.) 823.5960
— — *Same.* 3 vols. ** 823.6233-5
— — Counterparts; or, the cross of love.
823.6127
Peasant life. Göthe, J. W. von. Hermann
and Dorothea; poem. 821.1021
See also Novels by B. Auerbach.
University life.
— Powers, S. German student fraterni-
ties. 20 pp. (*With his* Muskingum le-
gends.) p. 103, *in* 823.4145
— Student rambles in Prussia. 34 pp.
(*With his* Muskingum legends.)
p. 103, *in* 823.4145
School life. Owen, *Mrs.* J. A. A winter
school in the upper Eifel. (*With her* After
shipwreck.) p. 167, *in* 823.6945
Literary life. Mundt, *Mrs.* C. (M.) Goethe
and Schiller. 823.6267

English Fiction. *Contin.*
Germany. *Contin.*
LIFE AND MANNERS. *Contin.*
Mining life. Bürstenbinder, E.. Good luck !
823.6264
Travelling apprentices. Göthe, J. W. von.
Wilhelm Meister's apprenticeship and trav-
els. 2 vols. 823.6799–6800
Bavaria.
— Peard, F.. M.. Castle and town.
823.5641
— Tautphœus, J. (M.) *Freiherrin* von.
At odds. 823.1797
Breslau. See Tales by G. Freytag.
Black Forest. Auerbach, B. Black Forest
village stories. 823.5730
Mecklenburg. Reuter, F. An old story of
my farming days. 2 pts. (in 1).
in 823.5030
Posen. See Tales by G. Freytag.
Prussia.
— Lindau, P. Lace: a Berlin romance.
823.7264
— Stinde, J. The Buchholz family.
Sketches of Berlin life. 2 vols.
823.5220-1
— — Frau Wilhelmine. Concluding pt.
of The Buchholz family. 823.5222
See also Tales by G. Freytag (Polish); and F.
Spielhagen.
Note.—See Child, T. Impressions of Berlin. 16
pp. (*Harper's mag.*, v. 81, Aug. 1890.) p. 340, *in* ⁕
51.A16⁺.
See also Rowell, J. C. Contents-index. (*Lib. of
Univ. of Cal.*) p. 51, *in* ⁑ 19.134.
The Rhine.
— Cooper, J. F. The Heidenmauer: a le-
gend of the Rhine. 823.295
— Häring, G. W. H. Hans Preller: a
legend. 26 pp. (*In* Tales from Blackwood.
3d ser., v. 2.) p. 90, *in* 823.7498
— Legend of the Rhine. (*In* Stray leaves
. . .) p. 146, *in* 823.5810
— Lytton, E: G: E. L. Bulwer. The pil-
grims of the Rhine. (*With his* Leila.)
in 823.1035
— — *Same.* *in* 823.5957
— Saintine, J. X. B. The myths of the
Rhine. 293.9
— Thackeray, W: M. Legend of the
Rhine. 45 pp. (*Works*, v. 8.)
p. 421, *in* 823.1577
— — *Same.* p. 205, *in* 823.5010
— — *Same.* p. 394, *in* 823.6552
Saxony. See Tales by G. Freytag.
South Germany. Hillern, *Mrs.* W. (B.) von.
A graveyard flower. 823.4733
Swabia. See Tales by B. Auerbach.
— Hauff, W. The cold heart. (*In* Tales
from the German.) p. 51, *in* 823.6276
Note.—See Freytag, G. Bilder aus der deutschen Vergangenheit. 4 vols. (In 5). (Mittelalter-
1848.) 1876. 943.11–15;—Pictures of German life in
the xviii. and xix. centuries. 2 vols. (in 1). 1863.
943.148.—Gould, S. Baring- Germany, past and
present. 1882. 943.82.—Howitt, W: Rural and domestic life in Germany. (1840–2.) 1842. 943.118.—Mayhew, H: German life and manners as seen in Saxony. 1865. 943.147.—Smalley, G: W. Prince Bismarck.—Count Herbert Bismarck.—The German
emperor. 1895. (*In his* Londou letters . . . v. 1.)
1891. p. 1, *in* 824.439.—Whitman, S. Imperial Germany: a critical study of fact and character. 1889.
914.447.

English Fiction. *Contin.*
Germany. *Contin.*

IN GENERAL, AND FOR LONG PERIODS.
Note.—See **Bibliography.** Dahlmann, F. C.
Quellenkunde der deutschen Geschichte. 1875. **
15.274.—Janssen, J. Geschichte des deutschen
Volkes. (1462–1618.) Bücherverzeichniss, v. 4. pp.
xviii–xxxi.) 6 vols. 943.134–9.—**Bryce**, J. The holy
Roman empire. 1877. 943.55.—**Bülau**, F. Geschichte Deutschlands von 1806–1830. (Fortsetzung
von Pfister's.) 943.145.—**Frederick**, crown prince
and emperor: a biographical sketch . . . By R. Rodd.
923.1932.—**Kohlrausch**, H. F. T. History of Germany. 1876. 943.31.—**Lewis**, C. T. History of
Germany from the earliest times. 1874. 943.127.—
Lowe, C: Prince Bismarck: an historical biography. 2 vols. (1886.) 923.1980–81.—**Menzel**, W.
History of Germany from the earliest period to the
present time. 1879. 2 vols. 943.22–3;—*Same.* 3 vols.
943.83–5.—**Pfister**, J. C. v. Geschichte der Teut-
schen (B. C. 320–A. D. 1807.) 5 vols. 943.140–4.—**Tulloch**, W. W. Story of the life of the emperor
William of Germany. 1888. 923.1999.—**Turner**, S:
E. Sketch of the Germanic constitution from early
times to dissolution of the empire. (B. C. 113–A.
D. 1806.) 1888. 323.13.—**Tuttle**, H. History of
Prussia. 3 vols. 1884. 943.91, 91¹, 91². v. 1: 1134–1740;
v. 2: 1740–1745; v. 3: 1745–1756.—**Wyatt**, W. J. History of Prussia from the earliest times to the present
day. 2 vols. 1871. (v. 1: A. D. 700–1390; v. 2: A. D.
1390–1525.) 943.116–17.—**Zimmermann**, W. History
of Germany from the earliest period to the present day. 4 vols. 1878. 943.1–3½.
See also Austria, *note*, p. 14.
See also **Catalogues** of this Library.
   No. 2, 1880, p. 93.   No. 4, 1884, p. 115.
   No. 3, 1882, pp. 79–80.   No. 5, 1888, p. 184.
See also Poole's Index (to 1882). pp. 512–518, *in* **
50.1;—*Same.* Jan. 1, 1882–Jan. 1, 1887. pp. 175–177.
in ** 50.1³.
See also Index to Consular reports, 1880–1885;
1886–1889. 2 vols. (U. S. Pub. Docs. *Dept. of State.*)
** 350.5496¹⁻².

Germany in storm and stress. Old Fritz and
the new era. Mundt, *Mrs.* C. (M.)
               823.6270

Gerund de Campazas. Isla, *Father* J. F.
History of the famous preacher Friar Ge-
rund de Campazas: otherwise Gerund
Zotes. 2 vols.   ** 823.6153–4

Gesta Romanorum. Swan, *Rev.* C:, *tr.*
               823.2132

Ghost, The. O'Connor, W: D.   823.4131

Ghost stories. *See also* Spiritualism in story.
—Strange tales. — The supernatural in
story.—Theosophy in story.
—— Aunt Ann's ghost story. 35 pp. (*In*
Tales from Blackwood. 2d ser., v. 9.)
            in 823.7493
—— Collins, W: W. The ghost's touch. 43
pp.   *in* 823.6686
—— Crowe, *Mrs.* C. (S.) The night side of
nature; or, ghosts and ghost-seers. 823.5925
—— *Same.*   133.19
—— Grant, J. A string of ghost stories. 23
pp. (*With his* The queen's cadet.)
         p. 307, *in* 823.646
—— Henty, G: A. A pipe of mystery. (*In
his* Tales of daring and danger.)
       p. 71, *in* 808.1669
—— Johnson, R. Little classics. v. 8: Mys-
tery.   829.131
Contents:—
Crowe, *Mrs.* C. (S.) The advocate's wedding-day.
Cunningham, A. The haunted ships.
Dickens, C: J. II. The signal-man.
Edwards, A. B. The four-fifteen express.
Hawthorne, N. The birthmark.
Lowell, R. T. S. A raft that no man made.
O'Connor, F. The invisible princess.
O'Connor, W: D. The ghost.

English Fiction. *Contin.*
Ghost stories. *Contin.*

—— Kennedy, P. Witchcraft, sorcery,
ghosts and fetches. 56 pp. (*In his* Legendary fictions . . .) p. 147, *in* 823.2115
—— Lytton, E: G: E. L. Bulwer- The
haunted and the haunters: or, the house
and the brain. (*With his* Pausanias the
Spartan.)   p. 379, *in* 823.1045
—— MacCallum, *Mrs.* M. C. (S.) The ghost
of Morcar's tower. 25 pp. (*In* Tales from
Blackwood. 3d ser., v. 3.)
         p. 390, *in* 823.7499
—— MacDonald, G: The portent: a story of
the inner vision of the Highlanders, commonly called the second sight. 823.1066
—— *Same.*   *in* 823.4995; *in* 823.5141
—— Mayo, *Mrs.* I.. (F.) A ghost story.
(*With her* The dead sin.) p. 69, *in* 823.1138
—— Modern ghosts; selected and tr. from
the works of Guy de Maupassant, and
others.   823.7349
—— Oliphant, F. R. The grateful ghosts.
81 pp. (*In* Tales from Blackwood. 3d ser.,
v. 6.)   p. 233, *in* 823.7502
—— Ralston, W. R. S. Ghost stories. (*In
his* Russian folk-tales.) p. 238, *in* 823.1282
—— Schiller, F. v. The apparitionist.. (Ros-
coe, T: *German novelists*, v. 3.)
        p. 120, *in* ** 823.6828
—— Tieck, L. The Klausenburg. (*In* Tales
from the German.) p. 231, *in* 823.6276
Note.—In addition to the works mentioned under
"Spiritualism " in this Catalogue, *see* Brand, J:
Popular antiquities of Gt. Britain, v. 3. 942.384.
—**Calmet**, A. The phantom world. 1850. 133.20.—
Chambers, R. Book of days. 2 vols. ** 32.6–7.—
Ingersoll, R. E. The ghosts. 70 pp. *in* 204.37.—
Owen, R. D. Footfalls on the boundary of another
world. 1875. 133.53.—**Signs before death.** 1875.
133.86.
See also "**Apparitions**" in Catalogues of this
Library. No. 2, 1880, p. 11. No. 3, 1882, p. 8.

Ghost-hunter and his family. Banim, J:, *and*
M.   823.58

Ghost's touch, The. 43 pp. Collins, W: W.
         in 823.6686

Giannetto. Majendie, *Lady* M. 823.1090

Giant dwarf, The. Williams, A. B. 808.1639

Giant raft. (Pt. 1.) Verne, J. 823.4350
  Same. (Pt. 2.)   823.4491
  Same. (2 pts.)   823.6310

Giants. Smithson, I., *and* Barnes, G: F.
About giants and other wonder people.
         808.1598

Giant's robe. Guthrie, F: A. 823.4754

Gibbon, C: The golden shaft. 823.3873
—— One of his inventions. *in* 823.4993

Giberne, Agnes. The rector's home: a story.
         823.607

Gibraltar gallery, The. Abbott, J. 808.587

Gideon, Trial of. Hawthorne, J. C:
         823.5683

Gideon Fleyce. Lucy, H: W. 823.4573

Gift, Theo., *pseud. See* Boulger, *Mrs.* Dora
Henrietta (Havers).

Gil Blas, Adventures of. Le Sage, A. R.
         823.2137
  Same.   823.4287

Gilbert, W: De profundis: a tale of the social deposits. 2d ed.   823.4087

English Fiction. *Contin.*
Goldsmith, Oliver. (1728–74.) *Contin.*
—— *Same.* (*In* Classic tales.) 1885.
p. 111, *in* 823.4489
—— *Same.* 91 pp. (*In* Lib. of famous fiction, etc.) p. 447, *in* ** 823.6215
—— *Same.* (*Also*) The traveller (poem). (*and*) The deserted village (poem). With a life of Goldsmith, by W: Black. 823.6425
—— *Same.* (*Also*) Paul and Virginia. By J. H. B. de Saint-Pierre. 823.4206

—— Macauley, E. Tales of the drama founded on . . . the comedies of . . . Goldsmith . . . 823.1051
Note.—For his life and writings, *see* Cucheval-Clarigny. Oliver Goldsmith: sa vie et ses écrits. 37 pp. (*Rev. d. d.''Mondes*, 1857, 2e pér., v. 12.) p. 855, *in* ** 54.217.—Do Quincey, T: (*In his* Sketches. 40 pp. *Works*, v. 4.) p. 288, *in* 829.682.—Drake, S: A. Our great benefactors. 1884. p. 53, *in* * 920.312.—Giles, H. Lectures and essays, v. 1. p. 288, *in* 824.35.—Howitt, W: Homes . . . of British poets, v. 1. p. 195, *in* 914.10.—Jeaffreson, J. C. Novels and novelists, v. 1. p. 223, *in* 820.186.—Lytton, E: G: E. L. Bulwer- (*In his* Miscellaneous prose works, v. 1.) p. 49, *in* 824.9.—Scott, Sir W. (*In his* Miscellaneous works, v. 3.) p. 231, *in* 920.366.—Thackeray, W: M. *In his* English humourists. 820.180.—Timbs, J. *In his* Anecdote lives of wits and humorists. 1872. p. 251, *in* 828.129.
See also Catalogues of this Library.
No. 2, 1880, p. 95. No. 5, 1888, p. 186.
No. 3, 1882, p. 81.
See also Poole's Index (to 1882). p. 534, *in* ** 50.1:—*Same.* Jan. 1, 1882-Jan. 1, 1887. p. 182, *in* ** 50.1².

Gold-worshippers. Robinson, J.. 823.1343
Goloshes of fortune, and other stories. Andersen, H. C. 808.600
Gooch, *Mrs.* Fani (Pusey). Miss Mordeck's father. 823.7002
Good for nothing. Melville, G: J: Whyte- *in* ** 823.4670
Same. 823.7277
Good hater, A. Boyle, F: 823.5109
"Good hour," The. Auerbach, B. 823.5626
"Good luck!" Bürstenbinder, E.. 823.6264
Good stories. Reade, C: 823.5520
Good stories of man and other animals. Reade, C: *in* 823.5520
Good women, The. 22 pp. Göthe, J. W. von. p. 461, *in* 823.2183
Good-bye sweetheart. Broughton, R. 823.133
Same. *in* 823.2745
Goodman, E: J. Too curious. 823.5360
Gooroo Simple, Strange . . . adventures of the venerable . . . ** 823.1855
Gordian knot, The. Brooks, C: S. 823.6179
Gordon, *Mrs.* —. Sir Gervase Grey. 3 vols. (in 2). 823.7314-15
Gordon, W: J: The captain-general; being the story of the attempt of the Dutch to colonize New Holland. Map. 823.7045
Gordonhaven: scenes and sketches of fisher life in the north. By an old fisherman. With an introd. by W. Alexander. 823.7202
Gore, *Mrs.* Catherine Grace F.. (Moody). Hungarian tales. 3 vols. ** 823.6567-9

English Fiction. *Contin.*
Gore, *Mrs.* Catherine Grace F.. (Moody). *Contin.*
—— The maid of honour. (*In* Standard tales, etc., ed. by Mrs. C. I. Johnstone.) *in* * 823.6194
—— *Same.* 16 pp. (Tieck, L. *The elves* . . .) 1864. p. 53, *in* 823.6328
—— Percy; or, fortune's frolics. 823.6263
Gorilla hunters. Ballantyne, R. M. 808.211
Goss, Warren Lee. Jed: a boy's adventures in the army of '61–'65: a story of battle and prison, of peril and escape. 808.1561
Göthe, Johann Wolfgang von. (1749–1842.) Elective affinities. 823.6801
—— Novels and tales. 823.2183
Contents: Elective affinities;—The sorrows of Werther;—German emigrants;—The good women; and a nouvelette.
—— Sorrows of Werter. Tr. by W. Render. ** 823.6646
—— Wilhelm Meister's apprenticeship. Tr. by R. D. Boylan. 823.2133
—— *Same.* Tr. by T: Carlyle. 2 vols. 823.6799-6800

—— Lazarus, E. Alide: an episode of Goethe's life. 823.964
Note.—For his life and works, *see* Arnold, M. A French critic on Goethe. 30 pp. (*In his* Mixed essays.) p. 206, *in* 824.407.—Calvert, G: H. Göthe. 36 pp. (*In his* Coleridge, Shelley . . .) p. 259, *in* 928.182.—Carlyle, T: Goethe. 45 pp. (*Crit. and misc. essays*, v. 1.) p. 610, *in* * 824.399;—Goethe's works. 21 pp. (*Crit. and misc. essays*, v. 2.) p. 323, *in* * 824.400.—Emerson, R. W. Göthe; or, the writer. 29 pp. (*In his* Representative men.) p. 257, *in* 920.73.—Hale, E: E. Lights of two centuries. p. 411, *in* 920.314.—Hedge, F: H. Prose writers of Germany. p. 263, *in* 839.2.—Helmholtz, H. L. F. On Göthe's scientific researches. 27 pp. (*In his* Popular lectures.) p. 33, *in* 504.2.—Hutton, H. R. Goethe and his influence. (*In his* Essays.) p. 1, *in* 824.143.—Littré, E. Œuvres d'histoire naturelle de Gœthe. 14 pp. (*Rev. d. d. Mondes*, 1838, 4e pér., v. 14.) p. 94, *in* ** 54. 131.—Mendelssohn-Bartholdy, K: Goethe and Mendelssohn (1821-31.) 2d ed. 1874. 927.104.—Ossoli, S.. M. (F.), *Marchesa* d'. Life without and life within. 1875. p. 23, *in* 829.307.—Scherer, E. Goethe. 56 pp. (*Études* . . . v. 6.) p. 295, *in* 844.37;—Le Faust de Gœthe. 13 pp. (*Études* . . . v. 2.) p. 81, *in* 844.33.
See also Catalogues of this Library.
No. 2, 1880, p. 94. No. 4, 1884, p. 117.
No. 3, 1882, p. 81. No. 5, 1888, p. 186.
See also Poole's Index (to 1882). pp. 530-531, *in* ** 50.1:—*Same.* Jan. 1, 1882-Jan. 1, 1887. p. 181, *in* ** 50.1².

Gœthe and Schiller. Mundt, *Mrs.* C. (M.) 823.6267
Gotthelf, Jeremiah, *pseud. See* Bitzius, A.
Gottschalck, C. F. Popular traditions and tales of the Germans. 89 pp. (Roscoe, T: *The German novelists*, v. 2.) p. 90, *in* ** 823.6827
Gould, Sabine Baring- Alexander Nesbitt, ex-schoolmaster. 44 pp. (*In* Tales from Blackwood. 3d ser., v. 1.) p. 254, *in* 823.7497
—— Arminell. 823.6577
—— Court Royal: a story of cross currents. *in* 823.4978
—— *Same.* *in* 823.4984; *in* 823.5056
—— Eve. 823.5403
—— Grettir the outlaw. (*In* Tales from Blackwood. 3d ser., v. 1.) 808.1661
—— Last words of Joseph Barrable. 48 pp. p. 275, *in* 823.7499

English Fiction. *Contin.*
Gould, Sabine Baring- *Contin.*
—— Little Tu' penny.								823.5579
—— The Pennycomequicks.						823.6966
Gould, Jeanie T. *See* Lincoln, *Mrs.* J. T. (G.)
Gowden Gibbie. Cunningham, A.
												in 823.702
Gower, *Lord* Francis Leveson. *See* Egerton, F. L. G.
Gowrie. James, G: P. R.						823.861
Grace and Isabel. McIntosh, M. J.. 823.4845
Grace Lee. Kavanagh, J.						823.914
Grace Seymour. 2 vols.		** 823.6253-4
Grace Willoughby. Maxwell, W: H.
												823.5894
Graham, Barbara. Arden Court. *in* 823.5012
Graham, Ennis, *pseud.* *See* Molesworth, *Mrs.* M.. L.. (S.)
Graham, J: W. Neæra: a tale of ancient Rome.										823.6904
Grande Florine, La. Belot, A.		823.2774
Grandfather, The. Pickering, E.		823.6071
Grandfather's chair. Hawthorne, N.
												in 808.548
Same.										*in* 808.1890
Grandissimes, The. Cable, G: W.	823.2442
Grandmother Elsie. Finley, M.		823.4645
Grant, James. Adventures of an aide-de-camp.										823.617
—— The adventures of Rob Roy.		823.647
—— Arthur Blane; or, the hundred cuirassiers.									823.618
—— The "Black Watch;" or, Forty-Second Highlanders.						823.619
—— Bothwell; or, the days of Mary, queen of Scots.							823.620
—— The Cameronians.					823.4799
—— The captain of the guard.		823.621
—— The cavaliers of fortune; or, British heroes in foreign wars.		823.622
—— Colville of ' the Guards.'		823.5681
—— *Same.*								823.6525
—— The constable of France, and other military historiettes.			823.623
	Contents:—The constable of France.—The chevalier d' Artagnam, captain-lieutenant of the mousquetaires du roi.—The traitor and his victim.—Story of private Thomas Keith, who became aga of the Mamelukes and governor of Medina.—A memoir of General Wolfe.—Sir Andrew Wood of Largo, captain of the "Yellow Frigate" and admiral of James III.—The marquis of Lauriston, grand veneur of France.—The Scots Fusilier Guards.
—— The dead tryst. (*And*) A haunted life.
												823.4794
—— Derval Hampton: a story of the sea.
												823.5680
—— *Same.*								*in* 823.6524
—— Dick Rodney; or, the adventures of an Eton boy.						823.624
—— Did she love him? a novel.		823.625
—— The Duke of Albany's Own Highlanders.
												823.4796
—— *Same.*								823.5679
—— Dulcie Carlyon.						823.6526
—— Fairer than a fairy.				823.626
—— First love & last love: a tale of the Indian mutiny.				823.628
—— Frank Hilton; or, "the Queen's Own."
												823.627
—— The girl he married.				823.629

English Fiction. *Contin.*
Grant, James. *Contin.*
—— Harry Ogilvie; or, the Black Dragoons.
												823.630
—— A haunted life. (*With his* The dead tryst.)							*in* 823.4794
—— Jack Chaloner; or, the fighting Forty-Third.						823.4801
—— Jack Manly: his adventures by sea and land.							823.631
—— Jane Seton; or, the king's advocate: a Scottish historical romance.	823.632
—— The King's Own Borderers: a military ,romance.						823.633
—— Lady Wedderburn's wish: a tale of the Crimean war.					823.634
—— Laura Everingham; or, the Highlanders of Glen Ora.					823.635
—— *Same.*								823.5682
—— Letty Hyde's lovers; or, the Household Brigade.						823.636
—— The Lord Hermitage.				823.4797
—— Lucy Arden; or, Hollywood Hall.
												823.637
—— Mary of Lorraine.					823.638
—— Miss Cheyne of Essilmont.		823.4798
—— Morley Ashton: a story of the sea.
												823.639
—— Oliver Ellis; or, the Fusiliers.	823.640
—— One of "The six hundred:" a novel.
												823.642
—— Only an ensign: a tale of the retreat from Cabul.					823.643
—— The phantom regiment; or, stories of "Ours."						823.644
—— Philip Rollo; or, the Scottish musketeers.
												823.645
—— Playing with fire: a story of the Soudan war.						823.6523
—— The queen's cadet, and other tales.
												823.646
—— The romance of war; or, the Highlanders in Spain.					823.648
	Issued also as Guerrilla chief.
—— The Ross-shire Buffs (and other stories).
												823.649
—— The Royal Highlanders; or, the Black Watch in Egypt.				823.5678
—— *Same.*				823.6530; *in* 823.6699
—— The Royal Regiment, and other novelettes.							823.650
—— The Scots Brigade, and other tales.
												823.4795
—— The Scottish cavalier; or, the First Royal Scots.					823.651
—— The Scottish soldiers of fortune: their adventures and achievements in the armies of Europe.					823.5932
—— Second to none: a military romance.
												823.652
—— The secret dispatch; or, the adventures of Captain Balgonie.		823.653
—— Shall I win her? the story of a wanderer.
												823.654
—— Six years ago.						823.655
—— Vere of "Ours," the Eighth or King's.
												823.4800
—— Violet Jermyn; or, tender and true.
												823.4802

English Fiction. *Contin.*
Grant, James. *Contin.*
—— The white cockade; or, faith and forti-
tude. 823.657
—— The Yellow Frigate; or, the three sisters.
823.658
Grant, Maria M. Artiste. 823.659
—— Once and forever; or, bright morning.
823.641
Issued also as Bright morning.—So dear a dream.
—— Sun-maid. 823.661
Grant, Robert. Jack Hall; or, the school
days of an American boy. 808.1716
—— Jack in the bush; or, a summer on a
salmon river. 808.1636
——, *and others.* The king's men. 823.4786
Grant, Ulysses Simpson (*originally* Hiram
Ulysses). 1822–85.
—— Adams, W: T. Our standard-bearer; or,
the life of G. 808.1555
—— Denison, C: W. The tanner boy.
808.224
Note.—See Arnold, M. General Grant: an esti-
mate. 66 pp. 923.1812.—Badeau, A. Grant in
peace. From Appomattox to Mount McGregor.
923.1830.—Boutwell, G: S. Gen. Grant. 82 pp.
(*In his* The lawyer, the statesman, and the soldier.)
p. 150, *in* 920.315.—Chesney, C: C. Military life of
General Grant. (*In his* Essays.) p. 1, *in* 923.395.—
Childs, G: W: Grant. (*In his* Recollections.) p.
70, *in* 923.1998.—Headley, J. T. Grant and Sherman:
their campaigns and generals. 1861–1865. 923.1852.—
List of his swords, presents, etc. (*In* Bost. Herald,
Jan. 26, 1885.) ** 51.2532.—McClellan, C. The per-
sonal memoir and military hist. of U. S. Grant ver-
sus the record of the army of the Potomac. 1887.
973.701.—Personal memoirs. 2 vols. 1885. 923.
1761–62.
See also United States. *Civil war, note.*
See also Catalogues of this Library.
No. 2, 1880, p. 96. No. 4, 1884, p. 120.
No. 3, 1882, p. 82. No. 5, 1888, p. 187.
See also Poole's Index (to 1882). p. 540, *in* **
50.1;—*Same.* Jan. 1, 1882–Jan. 1, 1887. p. 184, *in* **
50.1⁵.
Granville de Vigne. La Ramée, L. de.
823.1821
Grapes and thorns. Tincker, M.. A.
823.6307
Grateful negro, The. Edgeworth, Mrs.
p. 113, *in* ** 823.4651
Grattan, T: Colley. Heiress of Bruges: a tale.
823.78
Graves, *Rev.* R: The spiritual Quixote; or,
the summer's ramble of Mr. Geoffry Wild-
goose. A comic romance. Prefixed, the
life of the author. 2 vols. (Barbauld, Mrs.
A. L. (A.), *ed. The British novelists*, vols.
32–33.) ** 823.2093-4
Graveyard flower, A. Hillern, Mrs. W. (B.)
von. 823.4733
Gray, Arnold. Periwinkle: an autobiography.
823.5035
Graysons, The. Eggleston, E: 823.5516
Graziani, Giovanni Magherini- Fioraccio.
Tr. by M.. A. Craig. 32 pp. (*In* Mod.
ghosts.) p. 157, *in* 823.7349
Graziella. Lamartine, A. M. L: de P. de.
823.2353
Great Amherst mystery, The. Hubbell, W.
823.6199
Great bank robbery, The. Hawthorne, J. C.
823.5446
Great Britain. *See* England.
Great Elm, The. Abbott, J. 808.588

English Fiction. *Contin.*
Great emergency, and other tales. Ewing,
Mrs. J. H. (G.) 823.536
Great earthquake at Lisbon. 38 pp. (*In*
Tales from Blackwood. 2d ser., v. 12.)
in 823.7496
Great expectations. Dickens, C: J: H.
823.409
Same. 823.4968; 823.5318; 823.5332
Same. 823.6935
Great Hesper, The. Barrett, F. *in* 823.4998
Great Hoggarty diamond, History of Sam-
uel Titmarsh and the. Thackeray, W: M.
823.1577
Same. *in* 823.2537
Great match, The. Smith, Mrs. M.. P. (W.)
823.5615
Great treason, A. Marks, Mrs. M.. A. M.
(H.) *in* 823.5037
Greatest heiress in England. Oliphant, Mrs.
M. O. (W.) 823.2272
Same. 823.4943; 823.5016
Great-organ prelude, A. 21 pp. Underwood,
F. H: p. 146, *in* 823.4174
Gred of Nuremberg. Ebers, G. M.
823.7039
Greece. Adams, W: T. Cross and crescent;
or, Young America in Turkey and Greece.
808.496
—— Bonner, J: A child's history of Greece.
2 vols. 808.621-2
v. 1: B. C. 500–D. C. 456.
v. 2: B. C. 447–A. D. 1843.
—— Butterworth, H. Zigzag journeys in
classic lands; or, Tommy Toby's trip to
Mount Parnassus. 808.1816
—— Church, *Rev.* A. J: Three Greek chil-
dren: a story of home in old time.
808.1705
—— Cox, G: W:¹ Tales of ancient Greece.
808.837
—— Longfellow, H: W. Poems of places.
821.225
—— White, J: S., *ed.* The boys' and girls'
Herodotus: being parts of the history of
Herodotus. 808.1880
—— Yonge, C.. M.. Young folks' history of
Greece. 808.748

Greece, Ancient.
MYTHICAL.
—— Bulfinch, T. Age of fable. 292.10
—— Church, A. J:, *tr.* Stories from the
Greek tragedians. 808.1378
—— — *Same.* 823.4155
—— Cox, G: W: Tales from Greek mythol-
ogy. 292.43
—— Hahn, J. G. von. Griechische und al-
banesische Märchen. 833.1050
—— Hawthorne, N. Tanglewood tales.
808.1890
—— The wonder-book. 808.548
—— — *Same.* 808.1890
—— Kingsley, C: The heroes. 808.550
—— — *Same.* 808.1006
—— Larned, A. Old tales retold from Gre-
cian mythology. 808.1551
—— Lytton, E: R. Bulwer- Tales from He-
rodotus. (*In his* Chronicles and characters,
v. 1.) 821.1344

English Fiction. *Contin.*
Greece, Ancient. *Contin.*

Note. Contin.
D. 1864.) 7 vols. 1877. 938.60–6.—**Grote**, G: History of Greece. (to B. C. 300.) 12 vols. 938.1–12.—**Harrison**, J. A. The story of Greece. (*Story of the nations.*) 1890. 938.109.—**Herodotus.** History. (to B. C. 478.) With notes by G. Rawlinson. 4 vols. 930.36–9.—**Lloyd**, W: W. The age of Pericles: history of the politics and arts of Greece. (B. C. 480–431.) 2 vols. 1875. 938.92–3.—**Mahaffy**, J: P. Greek life and thought from the age of Alexander to the Roman conquest. (B. C. 323–146.) 1887. 938.104;— The story of Alexander's empire. 938.110.—**Plutarchus.** Greek history. (B. C. 490–323.) 938.111.— **Universal** hist. (anc.) vols. 6–8. * 930.6–8.— **Wheeler**, J. T. Analysis and summary of Thucydides. 1855. 889.5.
LIFE AND MANNERS.—**Becker**, W. A. Charicles; or, illustrations of the private life of the ancient Greeks; with notes and excursuses. 1889. 938.107.—**Mahaffy**, J. P. Social life in Greece from Homer to Menander. 1875. 391.5.—**Sewell**, W. Domestic virtues and manners of the Greeks . . . compared with . . . the most refined states of Europe. (*Oxf. prize essays*, v. 4.) p. 185, *in* 824.314.
MYTHOLOGY.—**Anthon**, C. Classical dictionary. 1888. 930.26.—**Gladstone**, W: E. Juventus mundi: the gods and men of the heroic age. 1869. 883.39.—**Preller**, L. Griechische Mythologie: römische Mythol. 2 vols. 1872. 292.36–7.—**Ruskin**, J: The queen of the air. 1878. 824.141.—**Smith**, W: Dictionary of Greek and Roman biography and mythology. 3 vols. 1880. v. 1: A-D; v. 2: E-N; v. 3: O-Z. ** 920.242–4.

Greece, Modern.
—— About, E. F. V. King of the mountains.   823.6976
—— Bikelas, D. Loukis Laras. Reminiscences of a Chiote merchant during the Greek war of independence. 823.4198
—— *Same.*   823.6115
—— Byron, G: G. N. Bride of Abydos.   p. 67, *in* 821.61
—— — Childe Harold's pilgrimage.   p. 38, *in* 821.1042
—— — The corsair.   p. 127, *in* 821.61
—— — Giaour.   p. 1, *in* 821.61
—— — Siege of Corinth.   p. 273, *in* 821.61
—— Hemans, *Mrs.* F. D. Modern Greece; poem.   p. 169, *in* 821.154
—— Hope, T: Anastasius; or, memoirs of a Greek: written at the close of the eighteenth century. 3 vols. 823.2057–9

Note.—See Finlay, *Dr.* G: History of the Greek revolution to A. D. 1864. (*In his* History of Greece, vols. 5 and 6.) 938.65–6.—**Freeman**, *Prof.* E: A. Byzantine empire. (*Hist. essays*, v. 3.) p. 231, *in* 904.21; —First impressions of Athens. (*Hist. essays*, v. 3.) p. 278, *in* 904.21;—Mediæval and modern Greece. (*Hist. essays*, v. 3.) p. 303, *in* 904.21.—**Hertzberg**, G. F. Geschichte Griechenlands. (395–1878.) 4 vols. (Heeren, A. H. L., *and others*. Gesch. der europ. Staaten.) 1876–9. 949.88–91.—**Hobhouse**, J. C. Journey through Albania . . . during 1809–1810. 1813. ** 914.340.—**Maximilian**, *Emperor*. On the wing. 1868. 914.21.— **Metternich**, C. W. N. L, *Fürst* von. Memoirs. 1815–29. *in* 923.1049.—**Stephens**, J. L. Incidents of travel in Greece, Turkey, Russia, and Poland. 1859. 914.254.—**Taylor**, B. Travels in Greece and Russia, 1859. 914.18.—**Timayenis**, T. T. A history of Greece from earliest times to the present. 2 vols. 1881. 938.58–9.—**Webster**, D. The revolution in Greece. 20 pp. (*In his* Great speeches.) p. 57, *in* 825.54.

Greek hero stories. Niebuhr, B. G. 808.1541
Same.   823.6813
Greek romances. Smith, *Rev.* R., *tr.*   823.2134
Greek tragedians, Stories from. Church, A. J: 823.4155
Green, A.. K.., *now* Rohlfs, *Mrs.* A.. K.. (G.)

English Fiction. *Contin.*
Green, Annie Douglas. *See* Robinson, *Mrs.* A. D. (G.)
Green, Evelyn Everett. Dorothy's vocation.   823.7377
—— The stronger will.   823.7378
Green, Will Semple. Sacrifice; or, the living dead.   823.6244
Green gate, The. Wichert, E.   823.6819
Green hand, The. Cupples, G: 808.345
Green mountain boys, The. 2 vols. (in 1). Thompson, D. P.   823.1587
Same.   ** 823.5992
Green pastures and Piccadilly. Black, W: 823.81
Green ray, The. Verne, J.   823.7420
Greene, Homer. The blind brother: a story of the Pennsylvania coal mines. (*Also*) Dick, the door-boy.   808.1357
Greene, *Mrs.* S.. Pratt (McLean). Cape Cod folks.   823.1849
—— Towhead: the story of a girl. 823.4473
Greenough, *Mrs.* R: S. *See* Greenough, *Mrs.* S.. D. (L.)
Greenough, *Mrs.* S.. Dana (Loring). Arabesques: Monaré.—Apollyona.—Domitia. —Ombra.   823.665
—— In extremis: a novelette.   823.666
Greenway, Grandfather, *pseud. See* Cannon, C: J.
Greenwood, James. The adventures of Reuben Davidger; seventeen years and four months captive among the Dyaks of Borneo.   823.6018
—— A night in a workhouse. 29 pp. (Johnson, R., *ed. Little classics*, v. 1.)   p. 56, *in* 829.124
Greey, E: The bear-worshippers of Yezo and the island of Karafuto (Saghalin); or, the adventures of the Jewett family and their friend Oto Nambo. Illus. 808.1892
—— The golden lotus and other legends of Japan.   808.1128
—— Young Americans in Japan. Illus.   808.1873
Greg, Percy. Guy Neville's ghost. 38 pp. (*In* Tales from Blackwood. 2d ser., v. 9.)   *in* 823.7493
Greifenstein. Crawford, F. M. 823.5455
Gresley, *Rev.* W: Charles Lever; or, the man of the nineteenth century. 2d ed.   ** 823.6772
Grettir the outlaw. Gould, S. Baring-   808.1661
Gréville, H:, *pseud. See* Durand, *Mrs.* A. M. C. (H.)
Grey, *Mrs.* E.. Caroline. The gambler's wife. (Anon.)   *in* 823.5051
—— *Same.*   *in* 823.5058
—— The trials of life. 2 vols. ** 823.6255–6
Grey, H: A key to the Waverley novels, in chronological sequence, with index of the principal characters. Rev. ed.   ** 823.6776
Grey, *Mrs.* Maria Georgina (Shirreff). Passion and principle.   823.6208
Note.—Written in conjunction with her sister, Miss Emily Shirreff.
Grey, Maxwell, *pseud. See* Uttiet, M. G.

English Fiction. *Contin.*
Grey Dolphin. 37 pp. Barham, R: H.
　　　　　　　　　　　　in 823.5478
Greyslaer. 3 vols. Hoffman, C: F.
　　　　　　　　　　　　823.5874–6
Grif. Farjeon, B: L.　　　823.545
Griffin, Gerald. The collegians: a tale of
Carryowen.　　　　　　　823.671
—— Duke of Monmouth.　　823.672
—— The invasion.　　　　　823.673
—— Mr. Tibbot O'Leary, the curious. 42 pp.
(Johnson, R., *ed. Little classics,* v. 5.)
　　　　　　　　p. 145, *in* 829.128
—— The rivals, and, Tracy's ambition.
　　　　　　　　　　　　823.676
—— The swans of Lir. 26 pp. (Johnson,
R., *ed. Little classics,* v. 1.)
　　　　　　　　p. 30, *in* 829.124
—— Tales of the Munster festivals. 823.667
—— *Same.* (2d ser.)　　　823.668
—— Talis qualis; or, tales of the jury-room.
　　　　　　　　　　　　823.677
—— Tracy's ambition.　　*in* 823.676
—— *Same.*　　　　　　　　823.4960
——; Lover, S:; Carleton,W:; *and* Lever, C:
James. Half hours with Irish authors. Se-
lections from . . .　　　　823.1073
Griffis, W: Elliot. Japanese fairy world.
Stories from the wonder-lore of Japan.
Illus.　　　　　　　　　808.1026
Griffith, Cecil. Victory Deane. *in* 823.4982
Same.　　　　　　　　*in* 823.5068
Griffith, Robert. Boys' useful pastimes.
Comprising chapters on the use and care of
tools . . . instructions by means of which
boys can make . . . a large number of toys,
household ornaments . . .　　808.1645
Griffith Gaunt. Reade, C:　823.1289
Same.　　　　　　　　*in* 823.6263
Griffiths, Arthur. Lola: a tale of Gibraltar.
　　　　　　　　　　　　823.678
Grimm, Jakob Ludwig, *and* Wilhelm, K:
German household stories. 2d ser.
　　　　　　　　　　　　808.1538
—— German popular stories. (Tr. and) ed.
by E. Taylor. With introd. by J: Ruskin.
Illus. by G: Cruikshank. 2d ser. 808.1592
—— German popular tales.　　808.1322
—— Popular traditions. 52 pp. (Roscoe, T:
The German novelists, v. 2.)
　　　　　　　　p. 235, *in* ** 823.6827
Grinnell, G: Bird. Pawnee hero stories and
folk-tales, with notes on the origin, cus-
toms, and character of the Pawnee people.
　　　　　　　　　　　　808.1717
Grogan, *Mrs.* Millicent. [*Erick Mackenzie*].
The Roua pass; or, Englishmen in the
Highlands. 3 vols.　　　823.7308–10
Gross, F. Not dead: a Christmas story.
　　　　　　　　　　　in 823.5084
Same.　　　　　　　　*in* 823.5089
Grumbler, The. Pickering, E.　823.6070
Guardian, The. 3 vols. Carlén, *Mrs.* E. (S.)
　　　　　　　　　　　　823.7229–31
Guardian angel, The. Holmes, O. W.
　　　　　　　　　　　　823.805
Guenn. Teufel, *Mrs.* B. W. (H.)　823.4672
Guénot, C:, *abbé.* The vengeance of a Jew.
　　　　　　　　　　　　823.616

English Fiction. *Contin.*
Guerndale. Stimson, F: J.　　823.5358
Guerrazzi, Francesco Domenico. Beatrice
Cenci: a historical novel of the sixteenth
century. Tr. by L. Monti. 2 vols. (in 1).
　　　　　　　　　　　　823.7379
—— Manfred; or, the battle of Benevento.
Tr. by L. Monti. .　　　823.6890
Gueullette, T: Simon. Mogul tales, Tartarian
tales, (*and*) Chinese tales. (Weber, H:
Tales of the east, v. 3.)　*in* ** 823.6232
Guild court. MacDonald, G:　823.3382
Same.　　　　　　　　　823.5373
Guilt and innocence. Schwartz, *Mrs.* M. S.
(B.)　　　　　　　　　　823.6046
Guilty river, The. Collins, W: W. 823.5646
Guiney, Louise Imogen. Brownies and bo-
gles.　　　　　　　　　808.1599
Gulliver, Lemuel, *pseud. See* Swift, Jonathan.
Gulliver's travels. Swift, J.　823.2966
Same.　　　　　p. 279, *in* 823.4489
Same.　　　　　p. 539, *in* 823.6215
Gunnar. Boyesen, H. H.　　823.1990
Gunter, Archibald Clavering. Mr. Barnes of
New York.　　　　　　　823.6019
—— Mr. Potter of Texas.　　823.5408
—— That Frenchman!　　　823.5505
Gurney married. Hook, T. E:　823.817
Guthrie, F: Anstey. [*F. Anstey.*] The black
poodle, and other tales.　　823.5597
—— A fallen idol.　　　　　823.5676
—— The giant's robe.　　　823.4754
—— The tinted Venus: a farcical romance.
　　　　　　　　　　　　823.4872
—— A toy tragedy. 20 pp.　*in* 823.4981
—— *Same.*　　　　　　*in* 823.4999
—— *Same.* (*With* As it fell upon a day. By
Mrs. M. Hungerford.)　*in* 823.4982
—— Vice versâ; or, a lesson to fathers.
　　　　　　　　　　　　823.4472
Guy Deverell. Le Fanu, J. S.　823.6177
Guy Earlscourt's wife. Fleming, *Mrs.* M. A.
(E.)　　　　　　　　　　823.579
Guy Fawkes. Ainsworth, W: H.　823.18
Guy Livingstone. Lawrence, G: A. 823.959
Guy Mannering. Scott, *Sir* W.　823.1399
Same.　　823.5327; *in* ** 823.6023
Guy Rivers. Simms, W: G.　823.1432
Guy Waterman. 3 vols. Saunders, J:
　　　　　　　　　823.5153,3⁹,3³
Guy's marriage. Durand, *Mme.* A. M. C.
(H.)　　　　　　　　　　823.4610
Gwendoline's harvest. Payn, J.　823.6066
Gymnastics. Stables, G.; Hicks, C. S., *and
others.* The boys' own book of indoor
games and recreations.　　808.1096
　　Note.—See **Betz,** C. System of physical culture,
v. 1: Free gymnastics. 1888. 613.257.—**Checkley,**
E. A natural method of physical training. Illus.
1890. 613.270.—**Combe,** G: Education: its principles and practice.; ed. by Jolly. 1879. D 2.3.—
Higginson, T: W. Gymnastics. 46 pp.; The murder of the innocents. 28 pp. (*In his* Out-door
papers.) pp. 131, 77, *in* 824.434.—**Hunt,** L. B. Handbook of light gymnastics. 87 pp. 1882. 613.102.—
Klemm, C. Muscle-beating. 56 pp. 1889. 613.269.
—**Maclaren,** A. A military system of gymnastic
exercises. 1877. 613.64;—A system of physical education. 1869. 613.46.—**Procter,** R: A. Strength
and happiness. 613.254.—**Ravenstein,** E. G., *and*
Hulley, J: A handbook of gymnastics and athletics.
613.91.

English Fiction. *Contin.*
Gypsy life.
—— Borrow, G: Lavengro. (Spanish gypsies.) 823.112
—— —— The Romany Rye. (Spanish gypsies.) 823.4586
—— Cross, *Mrs.* M.. A. (E.) The Spanish gypsy; poem. 821.905
—— Leland, C: H., *and others.* English-gipsy songs. 821.718
—— Melville, G: J: Whyte- Katerfelto. 823.1152
—— —— *Same.* 823.4661
—— Mitford, M.. R. Our village. (Contains scenes of gypsy life.) 2 vols. · 823.2148-9

Note.—See **Bibliography.** Boston Pub. Lib. *Bulletin.* Jan. 1881. v. 4. p. 281, *in* ** 17.135;—Encyclop. Brit. v. 10. p. 551, *in* ** 32.280.—**Groome,** F. H. In gipsy tents. 1880. 949.62.—**Leland,** C: G. English gipsies and their language. 1873. 949. 46.—**Simson,** W. History of the gipsies. 1878. 949.38.

H— family, The. Bremer, F.
p. 285, *in* 823.2120
Habberton, J: The Barton experiment. 823.4090
—— The Bowsham puzzle. 823.5694
—— Brueton's bayou. (*Also*) Miss Defarge. By Mrs. F.. E. (H.) Burnett. 823.5634
—— Country luck. 823.5695
—— The crew of the "Sam Weller." 823.7401
—— Helen's babies. 823.4533
—— The Jericho road: a story of western life. 823.679
—— Little Guzzy, and other stories. 823.7134
—— Mrs. Mayburn's twins: with her trials in the morning, noon, afternoon and evening of just one day. 823.4562
Issued also as Just one day.
—— Scripture club of Valley Rest ; or, sketches of everybody's neighbours. 823.4091
Hackländer, Friedrich Wilhelm. Behind blue glasses. Tr. by M.. A. Robinson. 823.5563
—— Enchanting and enchanted. Tr. by Mrs. A. L. Wister. 808.1493
—— European slave life. Tr. by E. Woltmann. 3 vols. (in 1). ** 823.6638
—— Forbidden fruit. Tr. by R. Kaufman. 823.7094
—— The volunteer. (Zimmern, H.., *and* A. *Half-hours with foreign novelists.*)
in 823.6613
Haco the dreamer. Sime, W: *in* 823.5108
Haddad-Ben-Ahab. Galt, J:
p. 69, *in* 823.702
Hagg, W: J. Woman the stronger. 823.1804
Haggard, H: Rider. Allan Quatermain. 823.5072
—— *Same.* 823.7154
—— Allan's wife, and other tales. 823.6987
—— Beatrice. 823.6988
—— Colonel Quaritch, V. C.: a tale of country life. 823.5529
—— Dawn. *in* 823.5072
—— *Same.* 823.7155

English Fiction. *Contin.*
Haggard, H: Rider. *Contin.*
—— Jess. 823.5074
—— *Same.* 823.5075; 823.7156
—— *Same.* (*Also*) King Solomon's mines. 823.6591
—— King Solomon's mines. *in* 823.5071
—— *Same.* *in* 823.6591; *in* 823.6606
—— *Same.* 823.7157
—— Maiwa's revenge: a novel. 823.5530
—— Mr. Meeson's will: a novel. 823.5528
—— My fellow laborer. (*With his* A tale of three lions.) *in* 823.6606
—— She: a history of adventure. 823.5071
—— *Same.* 823.7158
—— A tale of three lions. (*Also*) King Solomon's mines.—My fellow laborer. (*And*) The wreck of the "Copeland." 823.6606
—— Witch's head. *in* 823.5071
—— *Same.* 823.7159
—— The wreck of the "Copeland." (*With his* A tale of three lions.) *in* 823.6606
——, *and* Lang, Andrew. The world's desire. 823.7380
Hajji Baba, Adventures of. Morier, J. 823.4280
—— *Same.* * 823.6183
Hajji Baba in England. Morier, J. * 823.6184
Hale, E: Everett. [*J. T: Darragh.*] [*Col. F: Ingham.*] Back to back: a story of to-day. *in* 823.5562
—— The children of the public. 44 pp. (Johnson, R., *ed. Little classics,* v. 12.)
p. 134, *in* 829.135
—— Christmas eve and Christmas day. 823.680
—— Crusoe in New York, and other tales. 823.4330
—— The fortunes of Rachel. 823.5691
—— G. T. T.; or, the wonderful adventures of a pullman. 823.682
—— His level best, and other stories. 823.681
—— How they lived in Hampton: a study of practical Christianity applied in the manufacture of woollens. 823.5693
—— In His name: a story of the Waldenses, seven hundred years ago. 823.4037
—— The Ingham papers: some memorials of the life of Capt. Frederic Ingham, U. S. N. 823.4309
—— The man without a country. 36 pp. (Johnson, R., *ed. Little classics,* v. 1.)
p. 101, *in* 829.124
—— Mr. Tangier's vacations. 823.5254
—— Mrs. Merriam's scholars: a story of the "original ten." 823.2342
—— My friend the boss: a story of to-day. 823.5692
—— Our Christmas in a palace: a traveller's story. 823.4741
—— Our new crusade: a temperance tale. 823.683
Issued also as Good time coming.
—— Philip Nolan's friends: a story of the change of western empire. . 823.684
—— The skeleton in the closet. 14 pp. (Johnson, R., *ed. Little classics,* v. 5.)
p. 112, *in* 829.128

English Fiction. *Contin.*
Hale, E: Everett. *Contin.*
—— Stories of adventure, told by adventurers.   808.1367
Contents:—Marco Polo.—Sir John Mandeville and the crusades.—Bertrandon in Palestine.—Geoffrey of Vinsauf.—Hernando Cortes's letters.—Fra Marco and Coronado.—The Jesuit relations.—Northern discoveries.—Humboldt's travels.—A young man's voyage.—The northwest.—Siberia and Kamtschatka.

—— Stories of discovery, told by discoverers.   808.1369
Contents:—Introd.—DaGama and the east.—Magalhaens and the Pacific.—Sir Francis Drake.—The Atlantic coast.—Voyages in the Pacific.—The northwest passage.—Source of the Nile.—Mouth of the Niger.—West of the Mississippi.—The Antarctic continent.

—— Stories of invention, told by inventors and their friends.   808.1426
Contents:—Archimedes.—Friar Bacon.—Benvenuto Cellini.—Bernard Palissy.—Benjamin Franklin.—Theorists of the 18th century.—James Watt.—Robert Fulton.—George Stephenson, and the locomotive.—Eli Whitney.—James Nasmyth.—Sir H: Bessemer.—The last meeting.

—— Stories of the sea, told by sailors.   808.1368
Contents:—Columbus's return from his first voyage.—The Chancellor voyage.—Spanish Armada.—Battle of Lepanto.—Sir Richard Grenville.—Alexander Selkirk.—The buccaneers.—Paul Jones and Richard Pearson.—Nelson and Trafalgar.—The English navy.—Pitcairn's island.—Naval battles.—Shipwrecks.

—— Stories of war, told by soldiers.   808.1370
Contents:—Introd.—Life at Little Crastis.—First Bull Run.—Fort Henry and Fort Donelson.—Gen. McClellan and the peninsula.—West Virginia.—Antietam.—Pittsburgh Landing.—Vicksburg.—Gettysburg.—Chickamauga and Chattanooga.—Grant's advance on Richmond.—The wilderness.—Sheridan's ride.—Sherman's great march.—Nashville.—Siege of Richmond.—The last week.—The end.

—— *Same.*   823.5164
—— Ten times one is ten: the possible reformation.   823.685
—— *Same.*   823.4540
—— Ups and downs: an every-day novel.   823.686
——, *and* Hale, Susan. A family flight around home.   808.1832
—— A family flight over Egypt and Syria.   808.1829
—— A family flight through France, Germany, Norway and Switzerland.   808.1831
—— A family flight through Mexico.   808.1830
Hale, Gertrude E.. Little flower-people.   808.1465
Hale, Lucretia Peabody, *and* Bynner, Edwin Lassetter. An uncloseted skeleton.   823.6960
Hale, Susan, *joint author. See* Hale, E: E.
Halévy, Ludovic. L' abbé Constantin. Tr. by E. H. Hazen.   823.3845
Same. Tr. by K. Sullivan.   823.4563
Same.   *in* 823.6690
Half brothers, The. Dumas, A. D.   823.7085
Half hours with Irish authors.   823.1073
Half-hours with foreign novelists.   2 vols. Zimmern, H., *and* Zimmern, A.
** 823.6613-14
Half-hours with great story tellers.   823.5478
Contents:—Barham, R: H.   Grey Dolphin.—Browne, C: F. [*Artemus Ward.*] Moses, the sassy.—

English Fiction. *Contin.*
Half-hours with great story tellers. *Contin.*
Contents. Contin.
Mr. Columbus Coriander's gorilla.—Clark, C: H. [*Max Adeler.*] The fate of young Chubb.—Dickens, C: J: H.   Boots at the Holly-tree inn.—Oxenford, J: The enthusiast in anatomy.—Macdonald, G: "The light princess."—Lover, S: Legend of the little weaver.

Half-way: an Anglo-French romance.
in 823.5065
Haliburton, T: Chandler. [*Sam Slick.*] The attaché; or, Sam Slick in England.
823.687
—— The clockmaker: sayings and doings of Samuel Slick of Slickville. Illus. by F. O. C. Darley.   823.688
—— The letter-bag of the Great Western.
823.689
—— The season-ticket.   823.690
Hall, *Mrs.* A.. Maria (Fielding). The last in the lease.   20 pp.   (*With* Fortunes of the Colville family. By F. E: Smedley.)
p. 252, *in* 823.1443
—— Sketches of Irish character.   823.691
Hall, *Capt.* C: W.   Adrift in the ice-fields.
808.1321
—— Drifting round the world: a boy's adventures by land and sea.   808.1869
Hall, James. Legends of the west: sketches illustrative of the . . . habits of the pioneers of the West.   823.6316
Hall, *Mrs.* S. C.   *See* Hall, *Mrs.* A.. M. (F.)
Hall in the grove, The.   Alden, *Mrs.* I.. (McD.)   808.1512
Hall of Hellingsley.   3 vols.   Brydges, *Sir* S: E.   823.146-8
Hall porter, The.   31 pp.   Lover, S:
in 823.6692
Halpine, C: Graham. [*Miles O'Reilly.*] Life and adventures, songs, services, and speeches of private Miles O'Reilly.
823.7083
Halsey, Calista.   Two of us.   823.692
Halstead, Ada L.   The death trust.
823.6502
Halstead, Leonora B. [*Barbara Elbon.*] Bethesda.   823.4726
Halves.   Payn, J.   823.6067
Hamerling, Robert. Aspasia: a romance of art and love in ancient Hellas.   Tr. by M.. J. Safford.   2 vols.   823.4312-13
Hamerton, Philip Gilbert. [*Adolphus Segrave.*]   Her picture.   823.7047
—— Marmorne.   823.2001
—— Wenderholme: a story of Lancashire and Yorkshire.   823.693
Hamilton, Alice King.   Mildred's cadet.   An idyl of West Point.   823.1860
—— One of the Duanes.   823.4887
Hamilton, *Mrs.* Celia V. (Dakin). Crown from the spear.   823.6099
Hamilton, Gail, *pseud.*. *See* Dodge, M.. A.
Hamilton of Bothwelhaugh.   62 pp.   Herbert, H: W.   p. 247, *in* 823.4253
Hamley, C: The light on the hearth. (*In* Tales from Blackwood.   2d ser., v. 5.)
in 823.7489
—— Wassail. (*In* Tales from Blackwood.   2d ser., v. 6.)   *in* 823.7490

English Fiction. *Contin.*
Hamley, *Lieut.-Gen. Sir* E: Bruce. Lady
Lee's widowhood. (From Blackwood's
mag.)   823.6072
—— Lazaro's legacy: a tale of the siege of
Gibraltar. 64 pp. (*In* Tales from Black-
wood, v. 2.)   ** *in* 823.6648
—— Legend of Gibraltar. 67 pp. (*In* Tales
from Blackwood, v. 1.)   *in* ** 823.6647
Hamlin, *Mrs.* Marie Caroline Watson. Le-
gends of le Détroit. Illus.   823.4756
Hammer, The. Church, A. J:, *and* Seeley, R.
   823.6940
Hammer and anvil. Benedict, F. L. 823.69
Hammer and anvil. Spielhagen, F. 823.6821
Hammersmith: his Harvard days. Severance,
M: S.   823.1415
Hammond, *Mrs.* —. [*L.. Capsadell.*] A wait-
ing heart.   823.4810
Hammond, W: Alexander. Lal.   823.4781
—— *Same.*   823.7017
—— Mr. Oldmixon.   823.4857
Hampden, J: (1597-1643.)
—— Butterworth, H. (*In his* Zigzag journeys
in the British Isles.)   808.1807[11]
Note.—For his life, *see* **Disraeli,** I: Elliot,
Hampden and Pym. 1832. 920.368.—**Forster,** J:
Statesmen of the Commonwealth of England. 1846.
p. 241, *in* 923.81.—**Grenville,** G. N. T. Memorials
of Hampden. 1874. 920.193.—**Hallam,** H: Con-
stitutional history of England. 1876. p. 249, *in* 942.
123.—**Macaulay,** T: B. Essays, v. 2. p. 427, *in*
824.134.
Hampdens, The. Martineau, H.   823.7400
Hancock, Sallie J. Etna Vandemir: a romance of Kentucky, and "the great up-
rising."   823.1877
Hand and glove. Edwards, A. B. *in* 823.2522
Same.   823.4385
Hand and ring. Rohlfs, *Mrs.* A.. K.. (G.)
   823.4696
Hand of Ethelberta. Hardy, T: 823.698
Händel, Georg Friedrich. (1684-1759.)
—— Barnard, C: Handel and Haydn. (*The
tone masters,* v. 2.)   808.1619
—— The composer's difficulty. (Handel and
his opera Messiah.) 7 pp. [*In* Robert
. . . and other stories.]
   p. 147, *in* 823.5811
Handy Andy. Lover, S: 823.1014
Hannah. Craik, *Mrs.* D. M. (M.)   823.328
Hannah Thurston. Taylor, B.   823.1544
Hans Brinker. Dodge, *Mrs.* M.. E.. (M.)
   808.1417
Hans of Iceland. Hugo, V. M.   823.6159
Hanson, C: H: Old Greek stories simply
told. The siege of Troy and The wander-
ings of Ulysses.   808.1492
—— *Same.*   808.1573
—— The wanderings of Æneas, and the
founding of Rome.   808.1494
Happiness of being rich, The. Conscience,
H.   823.5704
Happy boy, The. Björnson, B. *in* 823.4218
Happy Dodd. Cooke, *Mrs.* R. (T.) 823.5635
Happy man, The. 70 pp. Lover, S:
   in 823.6692
Happy prince, and other tales. Wilde, O.
O'F. F. W.   808.1643
Happy-Thought Hall. Burnand, F. C.
   823.153

English Fiction. *Contin.*
Harben, Will N. White Marie: a story of
Georgian plantation life.   823.7258
Hard cash. Reade, C: 823.1290
Hard times. Dickens, C: J: H.   *in* 823.414
Same.   823.4750; *in* 823.5304; *in* 823.5336
Same. 2 vols.   823.411-12
Harder, Ludwig. A family feud. Tr. by
Mrs. A. L. Wister.   823.6802
Harding, Victor Eugenio, *and* Braga, Teofilo.
Twelve Portuguese legends. 12 pp. Tr.
by Mrs. F.. C. Henderson. (Henderson,
Mrs. F.. C. *Dunderviksborg* . . .) 1881.
   p. 305, *in* 823.6534
Hardman, F: Major Moss: a campaigning
reminiscence. 56 pp. (*In* Tales from
Blackwood, v. 11.)   *in* ** 823.6657
—— My English acquaintance. 69 pp. (*In*
Tales from Blackwood, v. 7.)
   in ** 823.6653
—— My friend the Dutchman. 63 pp. (*In*
Tales from Blackwood, v. 6.)
   in ** 823.6652
—— The smuggler's leap: a passage in the
Pyrenees. 19 pp. (*In* Tales from Black-
wood, v. 10.)   *in* ** 823.6656
Hardy, Arthur Sherburne. But yet a woman.
   823.4496
—— *Same.*   823.4618
—— Passe Rose.   823.5452
Hardy, T: Desperate remedies.   823.696
—— Far from the madding crowd. 823.697
—— *Same.*   823.5081; *in* 823.5386
—— The hand of Ethelberta: a comedy in
chapters.   823.698
—— A Laodicean; or, the castle of the De
Stancy's: a tale of to-day.   823.3596
—— Mayor of Casterbridge.   *in* 823.4984
—— *Same.*   823.5105
—— A mere interlude. 30 pp. (*With* Mrs.
Smith of Longmains. By R. Broughton.)
   in 823.5046
—— A pair of blue eyes.   823.699
—— *Same.*   *in* 823.4991
—— The return of the native.   823.700
—— Romantic adventures of a milkmaid.
   in 823.4999
—— Trumpet-major.   823.4041
—— *Same.*   *in* 823.5135; *in* 823.5136
—— Two on a tower.   823.3747
—— Under the greenwood tree: a rural
painting of the Dutch school.   823.701
—— Wessex tales: strange, lively, and com-
monplace.   823.6190
—— The woodlanders.   *in* 823.5136
—— *Same.*   *in* 823.5186
Hardy Norseman, A. Bayly, A. E. 823.6565
Harkut, Frank, *ed.* The conspirator: a ro-
mance of real life, by Count Paul P—. 2
vols.   823.7327-8
Harland, H: [*Sidney Luska.*] As it was
written: a Jewish musician's story.
   823.4914
—— The yoke of the Thorah.   823.5198
Harland, Marion, *pseud. See* Terhune, *Mrs.*
M.. V. (H.)
Harley, *Dr.* —. The young Crusoe; or, the
adventures of a shipwrecked boy: a story
for boys.   808.375

English Fiction. *Contin.*

Harold. Lytton, E: G: E. L. Bulwer-
823.6000
Harper establishment, The. Abbott, J.
808.583
Harper's story books. 12 vols. Abbott, J.
808.580-91
Harpe's Head. Hall, J. *in* 823.5634
Harrington, G: F., *pseud. See* Baker, *Rev.* W: M.
Harrington. Edgeworth, M. ** 823.4658
Same. 823.7438
Harris, Joel Chandler. [*Uncle Remus.*] Daddy Jake, the runaway, and short stories told after dark. * 808.1808
—— Free Joe, and other Georgian sketches.
823.5255
Harris, *Mrs.* Miriam (Coles). Frank Warrington. 823.703
—— Louie's last term at St. Mary's. 823.704
—— A perfect Adonis. 823.705
—— Phœbe. 823.4753
—— Richard Vandermarck: a novel.
823.706
—— Rutledge. 823.707
—— St. Philip's. 823.708
—— The Sutherlands. 823.709
Harrison, *Mrs.* Burton. *See* Harrison, *Mrs.* C. (C.)
Harrison, *Mrs.* Constance (Cary). Bar Harbor days. 823.5256
—— Bric-a-brac stories. Illus. by W. Crane.
808.1685
—— The old-fashioned fairy book. 808.1365
Harrison, Jennie. Whose fault? 823.7381
Harrison, *Mrs.* Rose G. (Kingsley). [*Lucas Malet.*] Colonel Enderby's wife.
823.4830
—— *Same.* *in* 823.4973
—— A counsel of perfection. 823.5404
—— Mrs. Lorimer: a study in black and white. 823.7268
Harrison, Lewis. A strange infatuation.
823.7077
Harry Bolton's curacy. 48 pp. (*In* Tales from Blackwood, v. 9.) *in* ** 823.6655
Harry Coverdale's courtship and marriage. Smedley, F. E: 823.1445
Harry Harson. Irving, J: T. 823.4026
Harry Heathcote of Gangoil. Trollope, A.
823.5889
Harry Lorrequer. Lever, C: J. 823.981
—— *Same.* ** 823.6221
Harry Marline, The adventures of. Porter, D: D. 823.6142
Harry Muir. Oliphant, *Mrs.* M. O. (W.)
in 823.5108
Harry Ogilvie. Grant, J. 823.630
Harry Racket Scapegrace, Fortunes . . . of. Smedley, F. E: 823.6387
Harry Richmond, Adventures of. Meredith, G: 823.5275
Harsha, *Judge* —. Ploughed under: the story of an Indian chief, told by himself; with an introduction by Inshta Theamba (Bright Eyes). 823.4158
Hart, *Col.* Joseph C. Miriam Coffin; or, the whale-fishermen. 2 vols. (in 1). 823.6110
Same. 823.6210

English Fiction. *Contin.*

Harte, Bret. *See* Harte, F. B.
Harte, Francis Bret. The argonauts of North Liberty. 823.5286
—— By shore and sedge. 823.4876
Contents: — An apostle of the tules. — Sarah Walker. — A ship of '49.
—— Condensed novels. 823.711
—— The crusade of the Excelsior.
823.5284
—— Devil's Ford. (*With his* A millionaire of Rough-and-Ready.) *in* 823.5152
—— A drift from Redwood camp. (*With his* A Phyllis of the Sierras.) *in* 823.5281
—— Drift from two shores. 823.5285
—— Flip, and, Found at Blazing Star.
823.4492
—— Found at Blazing Star. (*With his* Flip.)
in 823.4492
—— Gabriel Conroy. 823.712
—— *Same.* 823.6216
—— The heritage of Dedlow Marsh and other tales. 823.6911
Contents:—The heritage of Dedlow Marsh.—A knight-errant of the foot-hills.—A secret of Telegraph hill.—Captain Jim's friend.
—— In the Carquinez woods. 823.4623
—— The Luck of Roaring camp. 14 pp. (Johnson, R., *ed. Little classics*, v. 4.)
p. 46, *in* 829.127
—— *Same*, and other sketches. 823.713
—— *Same*, and other stories, including earlier papers, Spanish and American legends, Tales of the Argonauts, etc.
823.4322
—— Maruja. 823.5282
—— A millionaire of Rough-and-Ready, and Devil's Ford. 823.5152
—— Mrs. Skaggs's husbands, and other sketches. 823.717
—— On the frontier. 823.4792
—— The outcasts of Poker Flat. 16 pp. (Johnson, R., *ed. Little classics*, v. 1.)
p. 85, *in* 829.124
—— A Phyllis of the Sierras, and, A drift from Redwood camp. 823.5281
—— A Sappho of Green Springs. (*Lipp. mag.*, May, 1890.) 823.6394
—— Snow-bound at Eagle's. 823.5280
—— The story of a mine. 823.2041
—— Tales of the Argonauts, and other sketches. 823.714
—— Thankful Blossom: a romance of the Jerseys. 1779. 823.2042
—— The twins of Table Mountain, and other stories. 823.715
—— A waif of the plains. 823.6999
—— A ward of the Golden Gate. 823.7382
Hartley, *Mrs.* May (Laffan), *now* MacNabb, *Mrs.* M. (L.)
Hartner, Eva. Severa. Tr. by Mrs. A. L. Wister. 823.4271
Hartwell farm, The. Comins, L. B.
823.2359
Harveys, The. Kingsley, H: 823.939
Hasselt, André-Henri-Constant van. [*Alfred d'Aveline.*] Menshikoff; or, the peasant prince. 823.7172
Hathercourt. Molesworth, *Mrs.* M. L.. (S.)
823.1164

English Fiction. *Contin.*

Hatton, Joseph. Not in society, and other
tales. 823.718
—— Queen of Bohemia. 823.719
—— The Tallants of Barton: a tale of for-
tune and finance. 823.720
Hauff, Wilhelm. Arabian days' entertain-
ments. Tr. by H. P. Curtis. 823.4327
—— Longnose the dwarf (and other fairy
tales). 808.1237
Issued also as Little Mook, and other fairy tales.
Haunted and the haunters. Lytton, E: G: E.
L. Bulwer- p. 379, *in* 823.1045
Haunted Enghenio, The. 17 pp. (*In* Tales
from Blackwood. 2d ser., v. 11.)
in 823.7495
Haunted homestead, and other novelettes.
Southworth, *Mrs.* E. D. E. (N.) 823.1493
Haunted life, A. Brame, *Mrs.* C.. M. (L.)
in 823.5019
Haunted life, A. Grant, J. *in* 823.4794
Hauntings. Paget, V. 823.7021
Hausrath, Adolf. [*G: Taylor.*] Klytia: a
story of Heidelberg Castle. Tr. by S. F.
Corkran. *in* 823.4973
Hawaiian islands.
—— Jarves, J. J. Kiana: a tradition of Ha-
waii. 823.1903
—— Kalakaua, D:, *King.* Legends and
myths of Hawaii. 1888. 291.87
—— Newell, C: M. Kalani of Oahu: an his-
torical romance of Hawaii. 823.6132
Note.—See Coan, T. Life in Hawaii: an autobio-
graphic sketch . . . (1835-1881.) 1882. 922.335.
—Cumming, *Miss* C. F. Gordon- Fire-fountains:
kingdom of Hawaii, volcanoes, etc. 2 vols. 1883.
919.119-20.—Grant, *Mrs.* M. F. Scenes in Hawaii;
or, life in the Sandwich islands. 1888. 919.122.
See also "Sandwich islands" *in* Catalogues of this
Library.
No. 2, 1880, p. 201. No. 4, 1884, p. 257.
No. 3, 1882, p. 168. No. 5, 1888, p. 195. (Hawaiian
islands.)
See also Poole's Index (to 1882). pp. 574-7, 1149-
50, *in* ** 50.1;—*Same.* Jan. 1, 1882-Jan. 1, 1887. pp.
198, 385, *in* ** 50.1².
See also Index to Consular reports. 1880-1885;
1886-1889. 2 vols. (U. S. Pub. Docs. *Dept. of State.*)
** 350.5496¹⁻².
See also Index to Appleton's Amer. cyclopædia.
1867-1887. p. 59, *in* ** 31.36¹¹.
Hawkesworth, J: Almoran and Hamet: an
oriental tale. (Barbauld, *Mrs.* A. L. (A.),
ed. The British novelists, v. 26.)
p. 135, *in* 823.2087
Haworth's. Burnett, *Mrs.* F. H. 823.158
Hawthorne, Julian Crowinshield. An Ameri-
can penman; from the diary of Inspector
Byrnes. 823.5444
—— Another's crime; from the diary of
Inspector Byrnes. 823.5752
—— Archibald Malmaison. 823.5684
—— Beatrix Randolph. 823.4744
—— Bressant: a novel. 823.722
—— Calbot's rival. (*With his* Constance.)
in 823.5507
—— Constance, and Calbot's rival: tales.
823.5507
—— Countess Almara's murder. (*With his*
The trial of Gideon.) *in* 823.5683
—— A dream and a forgetting. 823.5443
—— Dust. 823.4742
—— Fortune's fool. 823.4699
—— Garth: a novel. 823.5868

English Fiction. *Contin.*

Hawthorne, Julian Crowinshield. *Contin.*
—— The great bank robbery; from the diary
of Inspector Byrnes. 823.5446
—— Idolatry: a romance. 823.724
—— John Parmelee's curse. 823.6787
—— Kildhurm's oak. (*Also*) A strange
friend. 823.7383
—— Mrs. Gainsborough's diamonds.
823.5685
—— The professor's sister. 823.5689
—— Sebastian Strome. 823.6390
—— Section 558; or, the fatal letter; from
the diary of Inspector Byrnes. 823.5269
—— Sinfire. (*Also*) Douglas Duane. By
Edgar Fawcett. 823.5571
—— A strange friend. (*With his* Kildhurm's
oak.) p. 138, *in* 823.7383
—— A tragic mystery; from the diary of
Inspector Byrnes. 823.5400
—— The trial of Gideon, and, Countess Al-
mara's murder. 823.5683
Hawthorne, Nathaniel. (1804-1864.) The
birthmark. 24 pp. (Johnson, R., *ed.*
Little classics, v. 8.) p. 207, *in* 829.131
—— The Blithedale romance. (*With his*
The scarlet letter.) *in* 823.733
—— David Swan: a fantasy. 8 pp. (John-
son, R., *ed. Little classics,* v. 4.)
p. 99, *in* 829.127
—— Dr. Grimshawe's secret. Ed. with pre-
face and notes by Julian Hawthorne.
823.4551
—— The Dolliver romance, and other pieces.
in 823.727
—— *Same.* 823.4083
—— Ethan Brand. 23 pp. (Johnson, R., *ed.*
Little classics, v. 1.) p. 7, *in* 829.124
—— Fanshawe, The Dolliver romance, and
other pieces. 2 vols. (in 1). 823.727
—— Grandfather's chair. (*With his* A won-
der-book.) *in* 808.548
—— The house of seven gables. 823.728
—— *Same,* and The snow image, and other
twice-told tales. 823.5878
—— The marble faun; or, the romance of
Monte Beni. 2 vols. 823.4362-3
—— *Same.* 823.6553-4
Issued also as Transformation; or, the romance of
Monte Beni.
—— Mosses from an old manse. 2 vols.
(in 1). 823.730
—— Our old home, and Septimius Felton.
2 vols. (in 1). 823.731
—— Peter Goldthwaite's treasure. 21 pp.
(*In* Famous stories. By De Quincey and
others.) p. 64, *in* 823.1778
—— The scarlet letter. 823.7509
—— *Same,* and The Blithedale romance.
823.733
—— Septimius Felton; or, the elixir of life.
in 823.731
—— *Same.* 823.5166
—— The snow image, and other twice-told
tales. 823.734
—— *Same.* *in* 823.5878
—— Tanglewood tales for girls and boys: be-
ing a second wonder-book. 808.549
—— *Same.* *in* 808.1890

English Fiction. *Contin.*
Hawthorne, Nathaniel. *Contin.*
—— The threefold destiny. 11 pp. (John-
son, R., *ed. Little classics,* v. 12.)
p. 204, *in* 829.135
—— Twice-told tales. 2 vols. (in 1).
823.5561
—— *Same.* (*Works,* v. 1.) 823.6195
—— *Same.* 2 vols. 823.735-6
—— A wonder-book, and Grandfather's
chair. 2 vols. (in 1). 808.548
—— *Same,* Tanglewood tales, and Grandfather's chair. 808.1890
Note.—For his life and writings, *see* **Fields,** J. T.
Hawthorne. 28 pp. (*In his* Yesterdays with authors.) 1876. p. 39, *in* 928.76.—**Forgues,** P. E. D.
Poëtes et romanciers américains. N. Hawthorne.
29 pp. (*Rev. d. d. Mondes,* 1852, n. pér., v. 14.) p.
337, *in* ** 54.187.—**Harris,** A. B. N. Hawthorne. 20
pp. (*In her* Amer. authors for young folks.) 1887.
p. 87, *in* 820.157.—**Hawthorne,** J. Nathaniel Hawthorne and his wife. 2 vols. 1889. 928.714-15.—
Hodgkins, L. M. Hawthorne. 5 pp. (*In her* A
guide to the study of 19th cent. authors.) p. 15, *in*
820.155.—**Hutton,** R: H. Nathaniel Hawthorne.
59 pp. (*In his* Essays in llt. crit.) p. 98, *in* 824.143.
—**James,** H:, *Jr.* Hawthorne. (*Eng. men of letters
ser.*) 1880. 928.419.—**Lathrop,** G: P. Biog. sketch
of Hawthorne. 70 pp. p. 439, *in* 824.414.—**Longfellow,** H: W. (Review of) Twice-told tales. 7 pp.
(*Prose Works,* v. 1.) p. 360, *in* 820.103.—**Montégut,**
E. Un romancier pessimiste en Amérique. 36 pp.
(*Rev. d. d. Mondes,* 1860, 2e pér., v. 28.) p. 668, *in*
** 54.233.—**Nichol,** J: Nathaniel Hawthorne. 31
pp. (*In his* Amer. lit. 1620–1880.) p. 322, *in* 820.160.
—**Poe,** E. A. Hawthorne. 13 pp. (*Works,* v. 3.)
p. 188, *in* 829.503.—**Stedman,** E. C. Hawthorne
and other poems. 1877. 821.632.—**Stephen,** L. N.
Hawthorne. 34 pp. (*In his* Hours in a library, v.
1.) p. 204, *in* 824.86.—**Whipple,** E. P. N. Hawthorne. 25 pp. (*In his* Character and characteristic
men.) p. 218, *in* 824.195.
See also **Poole's** Index (to 1882). pp. 575–76, *in* **
50.1;—*Same.* Jan. 1, 1882–Jan. 1, 1887. p. 198, *in* **
50.1².

Hay, Elzey, *pseud. See* Andrews, F.
Hay, J: (?) The bread-winners: a social
study. (Anon.) 823.4692
Hay, M.. Cecil. The Arundel motto.
823.5080
—— *Same.* (*Also*) Back to the old home.
91 pp. 823.2790
—— Back to the old home. *in* 823.2790
—— *Same.* *in* 823.4986; *in* 823.5021
—— Brenda Yorke. (*With her* For her dear
sake.) *in* 823.2472
—— *Same,* and Upon the waters.
in 823.4998
—— A dark inheritance. 99 pp. *in* 823.6694
—— Dorothy's venture. *in* 823.5063
—— *Same.* (*Also*) Victor and vanquished.
823.3146
—— For her dear sake. *in* 823.5057
—— *Same.* (*Also*) Brenda Yorke. 98 pp.
823.2472
—— Hidden perils. (*Also*) Old Myddelton's
money. 823.3093
—— Lester's secret. *in* 823.4973
—— Missing. 823.4361
—— My first offer and other stories. (*With
her* The squire's legacy.) *in* 823.3394
—— Nora's love test. 823.2978
—— Old Myddelton's money. *in* 823.3093
—— *Same.* 823.5077
—— The squire's legacy. *in* 823.5128
—— *Same.* (*Also*) My first offer, and other
stories. 823.3394

English Fiction. *Contin.*
Hay, M.. Cecil. *Contin.*
—— Upon the waters. (*With her* Brenda
Yorke.) *in* 823.4998
—— Victor and vanquished. *in* 823.4998
—— *Same.* 823.5079
—— A wicked girl. 823.5078
Hayden, *Mrs.* Sumner. Little Goldie: a
story of woman's love. *in* 823.5101
Haydn, Franz Joseph. (1732–1809.)
—— Barnard, C. Handel and Haydn. (*The
tone masters,* v. 2.) *in* 808.1619
—— Haydn's first lesson in music and love.
(*In* Robert . . . and other stories.)
p. 196, *in* 823.5811
—— Haydn's struggle and triumph. (*In*
Robert . . . and other stories.)
p. 196, *in* 823.5811
Hayes, A: Allen. The Denver express. 37
pp. (*In* Stories by Amer. authors, v. 6.)
p. 131, *in* 823.4707
Hayes, H:, *pseud. See* Kirk, *Mrs.* E. W.
(O.)
Hayes, I: Israel. Cast away in the cold: an
old man's story of a young man's adven-
tures, as related by Captain John Hardy,
mariner. 808.367
Hays, *Mrs.* H.. Adventures of Prince Lazy-
bones, and other stories. 808.1355
Hays, *Mrs.* W. J. *See* Hays, *Mrs.* H..
Hazard, Désiré, *pseud. See* Feuillet, O.
Hazard of new fortunes. 2 vols. Howells,
W: D. 823.7018-19
Hazel Kirke. Walsh, M. 823.4843
Same. *in* 823.5115
He. 69 pp. Lang, A., *and* Latimer, D.
823.5076
He fell in love with his wife. Roe, E: P.
823.5540
He knew he was right. Trollope, A. 823.1611
He that will not when he may. Oliphant,
Mrs. M. O. (W.) 823.2701
He would be a gentleman. Lover, S:
823.1784
Head of Medusa. Fletcher, J. C. 823.2324
Head of the family. Craik, *Mrs.* D. M. (M.)
823.329
Headley, Phineas Camp. Fighting Phil: the
life and military career of Philip Henry
Sheridan, general of the army of the United
States. (*Young folks' heroes of the rebel-
lion.*) 808.1600
Headsman, The. Cooper, J. F. 823.294
Same. *in* 823.7458
Headsman, The: a tale of doom. 83 pp. (*In*
Tales from Blackwood, v. 3.)
in ** 823.6649
Healy, M.. *See* Bigot, *Mrs.* M.. (H.)
Healy. Fothergill, J. 823.4911
Heaps of money. Norris, W: E: 823.4464
Hearn, Lafcadio. Chita: a memory of Last
Island. 823.7141
—— Stray leaves from strange literature:
stories, reconstructed from the Anvari-So-
heïlí, Baitál Pachísí, Mahabbarata, Panch-
atantra, Gulistan, Talmud, Kalewala, etc.
823.4791
—— Youma: the story of a West-Indian
slave. 823.6354

English Fiction. *Contin.*
Heart. 81 pp. Tupper, M. F.
           p. 105, *in* 823.6090
Heart of it, The. Stoddard, W: O. 823.2035
Heart of Mid-Lothian. Scott, *Sir* W.
           823.1400
Same.   p. 287, *in* ** 823.6025
Heart of steel. Tiernan, *Mrs.* F.. C. (F.)
           823.4475
Heartbreak cameo. 22 pp. Champney, *Mrs.*
E.. (W.)   p. 94, *in* 823.4707
Hearts and hands. Tiernan, *Mrs.* F.. C. (F.)
           823.5896
Hearts and homes. 3 vols. Ellis, *Mrs.* S..
(S.)   823.530–2
Hearts: queen, knave and deuce. Murray,
D: C.   823.3712
Same.   823.4949 ; *in* 823.5024
Heartsease. Yonge, C.. M..   823.1767
Heat. Abbott, J.   808.716
Hector, *Mrs.* Annie (French). [*Mrs. Alex-*
ander.] The admiral's ward.   823.4569
—— *Same.*   *in* 823.5034
—— At bay.   823.4839
—— *Same.*   823.4981; 823.4982
—— The Australian aunt. 50 pp. (*With*
her Forging the fetters.)   *in* 823.6694
—— Beaton's bargain.   823.4978
—— *Same.*   *in* 823.4984; *in* 823.4996
—— *Same.*   *in* 823.5056; *in* 823.5422
—— By woman's wit.   *in* 823.5017
—— The executor.   823.4621
—— *Same.*   *in* 823.4977
—— Forging the fetters, and other stories.
           823.6623
—— *Same,* and The Australian aunt. 50 pp.
           in 823.6694
—— The Freres.   823.4574
—— *Same.*   823.4976
—— Her dearest foe.   823.741
—— *Same.*   *in* 823.5107
—— The heritage of Langdale.   823.742
—— *Same.*   823.4980
—— Look before you leap.   823.4469
—— *Same.*   *in* 823.5125
—— Maid, wife, or widow?   823.743
—— *Same.*   *in* 823.5128
—— Mrs. Vereker's courier maid.
           in 823.5089
—— Ralph Wilton's weird: a novel.
           823.746
—— *Same.*   *in* 823.5015
—— A second life.   823.4909
—— *Same.*   823.4979
—— To Paris for pleasure. 16 pp. (*In*
Twenty novelettes . . .)
           p. 225, *in* 823.7183
—— Valerie's fate.   *in* 823.5119
—— Which shall it be?   823.747
—— *Same.*   *in* 823.5098
—— The wooing o't.   823.748
—— *Same.*   *in* 823.5070
Hector O'Halloran, The fortunes of. Max-
well, W: H.   823.1129
Hector Servadac. Verne, J.   823.6111
Hedged in. Ward, *Mrs.* E.. S. (P.) 823.1256
Hedri. Reeves, *Mrs.* H.. B. (M.)   823.7054
Heffernan, Michael, *pseud. See* Ferguson,
Sir S:

English Fiction. *Contin.*
Heiberg, Thomasine Christine. [*Carl Bern-*
hard.] Aunt Francisca. 98 pp. (Bushby,
Mrs. —, *tr.* The Danes . . . v. 2.)
           p. 49, *in* 823.6445
—— The bankrupt. 32 pp. (Bushby, *Mrs.*
—, *tr.* The Danes . . . v. 3.)
           p. 197, *in* 823.6446
—— Cousin Carl. (Bushby, *Mrs.* —, *tr.*
The Danes . . . v. 1.)   p. 1, *in* 823.6444
—— Damon and Pythias. 42 pp. (Bushby,
Mrs. —, *tr.* The Danes . . . v. 2.)
           p. 221, *in* 823.6445
Heidelberg. James, G: P. R.   823.862
Heidenmauer, The. Cooper, J. F.   823.295
Same.   823.7458
Heimburg, W., *pseud. See* Behrens, B.
Heir of Charlton. Fleming, *Mrs.* M. A. (E.)
           823.574
Heir of Linne. Buchanan, R. W.
           in 823.6594
Heir of Redclyffe. Yonge, C.. M.. 823.1768
Heir of the ages. Payn, J.   823.7060
Heiress, The. Stephens, *Mrs.* A. S. (W.)
           823.1967
Heiress of Bruges. Grattan, T: C.   823.78
Heiress of Kilorgan. Sadlier, *Mrs.* M.. A.
(M.)   823.1379
Heiress of Sweetwater. Randolph, J. T.
           823.1283
Heldmann, Bernard. The mutiny on board
the Leander: a story of the sea. 808.1637
Helen and Arthur. Hentz, *Mrs.* C. L. (W.)
           823.756
Helen Gardner's wedding-day. Terhune,
Mrs. M.. V. (H.)   823.1554
Helen of Glenross. 4 vols. (in 2). Martin,
H.   ** 823.6763–4
Helen's babies. Habberton, J: 823.4533
Heliodorus. The Ethiopics; or, adventures
of Theagenes and Chariclea. (*In* Greek
romances . . . Tr. by Rev. R. Smith.)
           p. 1, *in* 823.2134
Helm, Clementine. Child and woman. Tr.
by J. Z. Cocke.   823.6805
Helme, *Mrs.* E.. St. Clair of the isles; or,
the outlaws of Barra: a Scottish tradition.
           823.6437
Heloise. Robinson, *Mrs.* T. H. L. (von J.)
           823.1542
Helps, *Sir* Arthur. Casimir Maremma.
           823.749
—— *Same.*   823.5459
—— Ivan de Biron; or, the Russian court in
the middle of last century.   823.750
—— Realmah.   823.4612
Hemlock swamp, The. Whittlesey, E. L.
           823.4764
Henderson, *Mrs.* F.. C. Dunderviksborg and
other tales: forming an epitome of modern
European literature.   823.6534
Contents:—
Alarcon, P. A. de. Black eyes. Tr. from Spanish.
Celestin, F. Roza; play. Tr. from Slavonian.
Dequet, A. Theodore, conte de la vie littéraire.
    Tr. from French.
Eckstein, E. Cards for four. Tr. from German.
Harding, V. E., *and* Braga, T. Twelve Portuguese
    legends.
Henderson, *Mrs.* F.. C. Priscilla Baker, the freed-
    woman.
Karpinsky, F. Taxes; com. Tr. from Polish.

English Fiction. *Contin.*

Henderson, *Mrs.* F.. C. Dunderviksborg and other tales: forming an epitome of modern European literature. *Contin.*

Contents. Contin.

Kisfaludy, K. Three at once; farce. Tr. from Hungarian.

Krypow, *Dr.* —. Leka; or, remiuiscences of a physician. Tr. from Serbian.

Milan, N. Amanda; farce. Tr. from Croatian.

Palarik, J. Friendship at the harvest-feast; farce. Tr. from Slovack.

Pfleger, G. Revenge. Tr. from the Bohemian.

Pushkin, A. G. The snow-storm. Tr. from Russian.

Rask, C. E. The storm-bride. Tr. from Danish.

Straparola *de Cararaggio*, G. F. Salardo. Tr.from Italian.

Stroobant, E. Rue des Pierres, No. 60. A Flemish play with a French name. Tr. from Flemish.

Van Doossclaeve, T. S. No happiness without virtue; drama. Tr. from the Dutch.

Zedritz, K: E. The double wedding at Dunderviksborg. Tr. from Swedish.

2d ed., *containing two additional stories, is issued as* An epitome of modern European literature.

Henderson, I: Agatha Page: a parable.   823.5750

—— The prelate.   823.6618

Henrietta Temple. Disraeli, B: 823.461

Same.   *in* 823.3002

Henry VIII. Mundt, *Mrs.* C. (M.) Henry the Eighth and his court.   823.5886

See also England. *Tudor period.*

Henry, Edgar, *ed.* "89: edited from the original manuscript.   823.5441

Henry Esmond. Thackeray, W: M. 823.1575

Same.   823.2242; 823.5008

Henry Masterton. James, G: P. R.   823.864

Henry of Guise. James, G: P. R.   823.863

Henry Powers (banker). Kimball, R: B.   823.4097

Henry St. John, Gentleman. Cooke, J: E.   823.2017

Henry Smeaton. James, G: P. R. *in* 823.6247

Henry the Eighth, and his court. Mundt, *Mrs.* C. (M.)   823.5886

Henty, G: Alfred. Bonnie Prince Charlie: a tale of Fontenoy and Culloden.   808.1443

—— The boy knight, who won his spurs fighting with King Richard of England: a tale of the Crusades.   808.1491

—— The bravest of the brave; or, with Peterborough in Spain.   808.1473

—— By pike and dyke: a tale of the rise of the Dutch republic.   808.1588

—— By sheer pluck: a tale of the Ashanti war.   808.1486

—— Captain Bayley's heir: a tale of the gold fields of California.   808.1475

—— The cat of Bubastes: a tale of ancient Egypt.   808.1605

—— The Cornet of Horse: a tale of Marlborough's wars.   808.1574

——The curse of Carne's Hold: a tale of adventure.   823.7048

—— The dragon and the raven; or, the days of King Alfred.   808.1480

—— Facing death; or, the hero of the Vaughan pit: a tale of the coal mines.   808.1482

—— A final reckoning: a tale of bush life in Australia.   808.1476

—— For name and fame; or, through Afghan passes.   808.1472

English Fiction. *Contin.*

Henty, G: Alfred. *Contin.*

—— For the temple: a tale of the fall of Jerusalem.   808.1439

—— Friends, though divided: a tale of the civil war.   808.1575

—— In freedom's cause: a story of Wallace and Bruce.   808.1478

—— In the reign of terror: the adventures of a Westminster boy.   808.1435

—— In times of peril: a tale of India.   808.1481

—— Jack Archer: a tale of the Crimea.   808.1532

—— The lion of St. Mark: a tale of Venice.   808.1458

—— One of the 28th: a tale of Waterloo.   808.1668

—— Orange and green: a tale of the Boyne and Limerick.   808.1457

—— Out on the pampas; or, the young settlers.   808.1611

—— St. George for England: a tale of Cressy and Poitiers.   808.1479

—— A shark's fin. 9 pp. (*In* Twenty novelettes . . .)   p. 173, *in* 823.7183

—— Tales of daring and danger.   808.1669

—— Through the fray: a tale of the Luddite riots.   808.1484

—— *Same.*   808.1612

—— True to the old flag: a tale of the American war of independence.   808.1434

—— Under Drake's flag: a tale of the Spanish main.   808.1487

—— With Clive in India; or, the beginnings of an empire.   808.1474

—— With Lee in Virginia: a story of the American civil war.   808.1670

—— With Wolfe in Canada; or, the winning of a continent.   808.1477

—— The young buglers: a tale of the Peninsular war.   808.1471

—— The young Carthaginian: a story of the times of Hannibal.   808.1436

——, *joint author. See* Forbes, A.

Hentz, *Mrs.* Caroline Lee (Whiting). Aunt Patty's scrap-bag.   823.751

—— The banished son, and other stories of the heart.   823.752

—— Courtship and marriage; or, the joys and sorrows of American life.   823.753

—— Eoline; or, Magnolia vale; or, the heiress of Glenmore.   823.754

—— Ernest Linwood; or, the inner life of the author.   823.755

—— Helen and Arthur; or, Miss Thusa's spinning-wheel.   823.756

—— Linda; or, the young pilot of the Belle Creole.   823.757

—— The lost daughter, and other stories of the heart.   823.758

—— Love after marriage, and other stories of the heart.   823.759

Issued also as Victim of excitement.

—— Marcus Warland; or, the Long Moss Spring.   823.760

—— The planter's northern bride; or, scenes in Mrs. Hentz's childhood.   823.761

—— Rena; or, the snowbird.   823.762

English Fiction. *Contin.*

Hentz, *Mrs.* Caroline (Lee) Whiting. *Contin.*
—— Robert Graham. A sequel to "Linda."
823.763
Her dearest foe. Hector, *Mrs.* A. (F.)
823.741
Same. *in* 823.5107
Her friend. Benedict, F. L. 823.65
Her gentle deeds. Keddie, H. *in* 823.4999
Her great ambition. Earle, A. R. 823.7339
Her great idea, and other stories. Walford, *Mrs.* L. B. (C.) 823.5499
Her Johnnie. Whyte, V. *in* 823.5133
Her lord and master. Lean, *Mrs.* F. (M.)
823.5841
Her majesty the queen. Cooke, J: E.
823.275
Her martyrdom. Brame, *Mrs.* C.. M. (L.)
823.4919
Same. *in* 823.5103
Her mother's sin. Brame, *Mrs.* C.. M. (L.)
in 823.5022
Her own doing. 89 pp. Norris, W: E:
in 823.5015
Her own sister. Williamson, *Mrs.* E. S.. (C.)
in 823.4983
Her picture. Hamerton, P. G. 823.7047
Her sailor love. Macquoid, *Mrs.* K.. S.
823.4564
Her second love. Brame, *Mrs.* C.. M. (L.)
823.5127
Herbert, H: W: [*Frank Forester.*] The brothers: a tale of the Fronde. 2 vols.
** 823.6241-2
—— The chevaliers of France from the crusades to the marechals of Louis XIV.
823.4253
Contents:—Sir Hugues de Coucy: a chivalric legend of the Low countries.—Eustache de St. Pierre; or, the surrender of Paris.—The fortunes of the maid of Arc a superstitious legend of the English wars in France.—Hamilton of Bothwelhaugh; or, the massacre of St. Bartholomew: a dark scene in Paris.—Ahsahgunushk Numamahtahseng; or, the Reed-shaken-by-the-wind.
—— The fair Puritan: an historical romance of the days of witchcraft. 823.764
—— Frank Forester's sporting scenes and characters. With a life of the author . . . 2 vols. 823.5754-5
—— Oliver Cromwell; or, England's great protector. 823.765
—— *Same.* 823.2352; 823.5687
—— The Roman traitor; or, the days of Cicero, Cato and Cataline [*sic.*]: a true tale of the republic. 2 vols. (in 1). 823.5620
Herbert Massey in eastern Africa, Adventures of. Cameron, V. H: L. 808.1433
Hereward the Wake. Kingsley, C: 823.932
Same. 823.6422
Heriot's choice. Carey, R. N. 823.7362
Heritage of Dedlow Marsh. 86 pp. Harte, F. B. 823.6911
Heritage of Langdale, The. Hector, *Mrs.* A. (F.) 823.742
Same. 823.4980
Hermann Agha. Palgrave, W: G. 823.1229
Hermesenda. Fernandez y Gonzalez, M.
823.7211
Hero, A. Craik, *Mrs.* D. M. (M.) 823.330
Same. 823.5508

English Fiction. *Contin.*

Herodotus. Church, A. J: Stories of the east from Herodotus. 808.1546
Contents:—The story of King Croesus.—Croesus wishing to make war against the Persians, consulteth the oracles.—King Croesus is defeated and the city of Sardis is taken.—Croesus is saved from death. Of Lydia, the Lydians, and of certain Greeks that dwelt in Asia.—Birth and bringing up of Cyrus.—Cyrus overthroweth Astyvages, and taketh the kingdom to himself.—The city of Babylon. Cyrus taketh it.—Cyrus maketh war against the Massagetæ and dieth.—Of the manners of the Egyptians.—Of certain kings of Egypt.—Of certain other kings of Egypt.—The Persians conquer Egypt.—Cambyses maketh war . . , is stricken with madness, and so dieth.—The false Smerdis is slain.—The kingdom of Darius.—Babylon rebelleth against the king and is taken.—King Darius maketh war upon the Scythians.—Of the Scythians and other nations.
—— — Story of the Persian war from Herodotus. 823.5671
—— White, J: S. The boys' and girls' Herodotus: being parts of the history of Herodotus. Ed . . . with an introd. Illus.
808.1880
Heroes. Kingsley, C: 808.550
Same. 808.1006
Heroes of the desert. Rathbone, *Mrs.* M.. A. (M.) 823.5583
Heroes of the olden times. 3 vols. *See* Baldwin, J.
Heroic tales of ancient Greece. Niebuhr, B. G. * 808.1682
Hero-worship and its dangers. Lever, C: J. p. 360, *in* 829.699
Herr Paulus. Besant, W. 823.5885
Herr Regenbogen's concert. 36 pp. Underwood, F. H: p. 110, *in* 823.4174
Heseltine, W: The last of the Plantagenets: an historical narrative, illustrating some of the public events, and domestic and ecclesiastical manners of the fifteenth and sixteenth centuries. 3d ed. (Anon.)
823.1813
Hesperus. 2 vols. Richter, J. P. F.
823.6814-15
Hester. Oliphant, *Mrs.* M. O. (W.)
823.7132
Hester Howard's temptation. Warfield, *Mrs.* C. A. (W.) 823.1657
Hester Morley's promise. Smith, H.
823.1457
Hester Stanley of St. Marks. Spofford, *Mrs.* H. E.. (P.) 823.5756
Hetty. Kingsley, H: 823.6374
Same, and other stories. Kingsley, H:
823.940
Hetty's strange history. Jackson, *Mrs.* H.. M. (F.) 823.1992
Hetzel, Pierre Jules. [*P. J. Stahl.*] Maroussia, a maid of Ukraine. Tr. by C. W. Cyr.
808.1725
Heyse, Johann Ludwig Paul. 1830 —. Children of the world. 3 vols. (in 1).
** 823.6633
—— *Same.* 3 vols. 823.6455-7
—— The huntsman. (Zimmern, H.., *and* A. *Half-hours with foreign novelists*, v. 2.)
in ** 823.6614
—— In Paradise. 2 vols. 823.2327-8

English Fiction. *Contin.*
Heyse, Johann Ludwig Paul. *Contin.*
—— Laurella. (*With his* The maiden of Treppi.) 823.6803
Issued also as The fury (L'Arrabiata).
—— The maiden of Treppi; or, love's victory. Tr. by A. W. H. (*Also*) Laurella. 823.6803
—— The romance of the canoness: a life-history. Tr. by J. M. Percival. 823.5618
—— Tales from the German. 823.2332
Contents:—Count Ernest's home.—The dead lake. —The fury (L'Arrabiata).—Judith Stern.
Heyse, Paul. *See* Heyse, J. L. P.
Hibernian nights' entertainments. Ferguson, *Sir* S: 823.553
Hidden hand. Southworth, *Mrs.* E. D. E. (N.) 823.5176
Hidden masterpiece, The. Balzac, H. de. p. 297, *in* 823.5211
Hidden path, The. Terhune, *Mrs.* M.. V. (H.) 823.1555
Hidden perils. Hay, M.. C. 823.3093
Hidden power. Tibbles, T. H. 823.1844
Hidden sin, The. Brown, F.. 823.5027
Hidden terror, A. Albert, M.. 823.4983
Hide-and-seek. Collins, W: W. 823.257
Higgins, Emily Mayer. Holidays at the grange; or, a week's delight. Games and stories for parlor and fireside. 808.1638
Higginson, *Mrs.* S. J. Java, the pearl of the east. Map. 808.1601
Higginson, T: Wentworth. A book of American explorers. (*Young folks ser.*) 808.298
Contents:—The legends of the Northmen. (985-1008.)—Columbus and his companions. (1492-1503.)—Cabot and Verrazzano. (1497-1524.)—The strange voyage of Cabeza de Vaca. (1528-1533.)—The French in Canada. (1534-1536.)—Adventures of De Soto. (1538-1542.)—The French in Florida. (1534-1536.)—Sir Humphrey Gilbert. (1583.)—The lost colonies of Virginia. (1584-1590.)—Unsuccessful New England settlements. (1602-1607.)—Captain John Smith. (1606-1631.)—Champlin on the war-path. (1609.)—Henry Hudson: the New Netherlands. (1609-1626.)—The Pilgrims at Plymouth. (1620-1621.)—The Massachusetts Bay Colony. (1629-1631.)
—— Malbone: an Oldport romance. 823.766
—— The monarch of dreams. 823.7256
Higgledy-piggledy. Hugessen, E: H. Knatchbull- 808.810
High Mills. Cooper, *Mrs.* K.. (S.) 823.6087
High priest's daughter. 52 pp. Holt, E. S.. p. 43, *in* 808.1517
Higher law. Maitland, E: 823.1080
Higher than the church. Hillern, *Mrs.* W. (B.) von. 823.5722
Highland widow, The. 96 pp. Scott, *Sir* W. p. 273, *in* 823.1394
Same. *in* 823.4803; *in* 823.5328
Hilary's folly. Brame, *Mrs.* C.. M. (L.) *in* 823.5019
Same. 823.5472
Hilda. Brame, *Mrs.* C.. M. (L.) *in* 823.5094
Hilda and I. Benjamin, E. B. 823.2018
Hill, J: Waters of Marah. 823.5073
Hill & the valley. Martineau, H. *in* ** 823.6706

English Fiction. *Contin.*
Hillern, *Mrs.* Wilhelmine (Birch) von. By his own might. 823.7095
—— Ernestine. Tr. by S. Baring-Gould. 2 vols. 823.4017-18
Issued also as Only a girl.
—— Geier-Wally: a tale of the Tyrol. 823.6806
Issued also as Elsa and her vulture.—The vulture maiden.
—— A graveyard flower. Tr. by C. Bell. 823.4733
—— Higher than the church: an art legend of ancient times. Tr. by M.. J. Safford. 823.5722
—— Only a girl; or, a physician for the soul: a romance. Tr. by Mrs. A. L. Wister. 823.5548
Issued also as Ernestine.
—— *Same.* 823.5617
Hills of Shatemuc. Warner, S. 823.1677
Hillyars and the Burtons. Kingsley, H: 823.941
Hillyer, Shaler. The Marable family. 823.768
Hilt to hilt. Cooke, J: E. 823.5525
Hindoo tales. Jacob, P. W., *tr.* 823.4365
His inheritance. Knox, *Mrs.* A. (T.) 823.1601
His level best. 22 pp. Hale, E: E. 823.681
His little mother. Craik, *Mrs.* D. M. (M.) 823.3294
His opportunity. Pearson, H: C. 823.7135
His sombre rivals. Roe, E: P. 823.4609
His young wife. Smith, J. P. 823.1466
Historic girls. Brooks, E. S. 808.1925
History. Strickland, A. Stories from history. 808.294
History, Ancient.
—— Abbott, J. Story of ancient history, from the earliest periods to the fall of the Roman empire. (*In his* Harper's story books, v. 5.) 808.584
—— True stories from ancient history: chronologically arranged. By a mother. 808.296
See also novels by A. J: Church.—G. M. Ebers, and others.
Note.—*See* Allen, W: F., *and* Myers, P. V. N. Ancient history. 1888. 930.214.—Adams, *Prof.* C: K. Bibliography. 18 pp. (*In his* Manual of historical literature, 3d ed.) 1889. p. 75, *in* * 907.4*.—Duneker, M. W. Hist. of antiquity. 1872-1882. 6 vols. * 930.145-50.—Heeren, A. H. L. Ancient history. 1833. 930.67.—Herodotus. From the text of Schweighæuser. 2 vols. 1858. 930.215-16.—Niebuhr, B. G. Lectures on ancient history. 3 vols. 1852. 930.202-4.—Rawlinson, G: Five great monarchies. 3 vols. 1873. 930.33-5.—Manual of ancient history. 1875. 930.21.—Rollin, C. Ancient history. 8 vols. 1821. 930.59-66.—Sayce, A. H: The ancient empires of the east. 1889. 930.228.—Smith, P. History of the world: ancient history. 3 vols. 1873. 930.30-2.—Zerffi, *Dr.* G. G. Studies on the science of general history. v. 1: Anc. history. 1887. 930.227.
History, Modern.
—— Eggleston, G: C. Strange stories from history for young people. 808.1432
—— Historical tales. (Middle ages and modern.) (*In* Entertaining knowledge, by popular authors.) *in* 829.659

English Fiction. *Contin.*
History, Modern. *Contin.*
—— Museum of history; or, narratives of adventures, etc.   * 909.93
—— True stories from modern history: chronologically arranged, from the death of Charlemagne to the battle of Waterloo. By the author of "True stories from ancient history."   808.295

Note.—See **Adams,** H. B. Study of history in American colleges and universities. (U. S. Bureau of Educ. *Circulars, etc.,* No. 2.) 1887. 3701.22.—**Arnold,** T: Introductory lectures on modern history. 1878. 904.2.—**Bibliography.** Adams, C: K. General works on modern hist. (*In his* Manual of hist. lit.) 1889. p. 203, *in* * 907.4³.—Smyth, W: Lectures on modern history from the irruption of the northern nations to the close of the American revolution. 2 vols. 1848. (List of books. v. 1: pp. xi-xx.) 940.175-6.—**Gervinus,** G. G. Geschichte des 19. Jahrhunderts. 8 vols. (in 6) 1855-66. 940.94-101.—**Michelet,** J. Modern history. (1453-1789.) 940.202.—**Monceriell,** A. R. H. Famous historical scenes from three centuries. (1492-1799.) 1875. 904.133.—**Myers,** P. V. N. Outlines of mediæval and modern history. (A. D. 476-A. D. 1880.) 1888. 940.169.—**Schlosser,** F. C. History of the 18th and 19th cent. 8 vols. 1843-52. 940.151-8.—**Smyth,** W: Lectures on modern history. (476-1791.) 904.1;—*Same.* 2 vols. (With list of books referred to each lecture. v. 1: pp. vii-xvi.) 901.9-10.—**Taylor,** W. C. Student's manual of modern history. 1866. 904.4.—**Zerffi,** Dr. G. G. Studies on the science of general history. v. 2: Mediæval. v. 3: Mod. 940.199-200.

See also **Catalogues** of this Library.
No. 2, 1880, pp. 108-109.   No. 4, 1884, p. 133.
No. 3, 1882, pp. 92-93.   No. 5, 1888, pp. 203-204.

History for boys. Edgar, J: G: 808.800
Same.   808.803
History of a week. Walford, *Mrs.* L. B. (C.)   823.4935
History of Abdalla, the son of Hanif. (Weber, H: *Tales of the east,* v. 3.)
     p. 593, *in* ** 823.6232
History of Amelia. Fielding, H: 823.555
Same.   823.6151
History of Clarissa Harlowe. 5 vols. Richardson, S: ** 823.6164-8
History of Henry Esmond. Thackeray, W: M.   823.1575
Same.   823.5008
History of . . . Joseph Andrews and his friend Mr. Abraham Adams. Fielding, H: ** 823.2079
History of King Arthur. 3 vols. Malory, *Sir* T:, *comp.*   * 823.6615-17
History of Lady Julia Mandeville. Brooke, *Mrs.* F.. (M.)   ** 823.2088
History of Mr. John Decastro and his brother Bat. 4 vols. Mathers, J., *and* A solid gentleman (*pseud.*)   ** 823.6609-12
History of New England. Cady, *Mrs.* H. N.   808.1901
History of Nicolas Muss. Du Bois-Melly, C: 823.6570
History of Nourjahad. 34 pp. (Weber, H:, *comp.* Tales of the east, v. 2.)
     p. 691, *in* ** 823.6231
History of Pendennis. Thackeray, W: M.   823.1576
Same. 2 vols.   823.5006-7
History of Pompey the Little. Coventry, F.   ** 823.2084
History of Rasselas. Johnson, S: 823.903
Same.   ** 823.2087

English Fiction. *Contin.*
History of Samuel Titmarsh and the great Hoggarty diamond. Thackeray, W: M.   823.1577
Same.   823.6324; 823.6552
History of Sir Charles Grandison. 4 vols. Richardson, S: ** 823.6169-72
Same. 7 vols.   ** 823.2070-6
History of the adventures of Joseph Andrews, and his friend Mr. Abraham Adams. Fielding, H: 823.7070
History of the famous preacher Friar Gerund de Campazas. 2 vols. Isla, *Father* J. F.   ** 823.6153-4
History of the ingenious gentleman Don Quixote of La Mancha. 4 vols. Cervantes Saavedra, M. de.   823.6899-902
History of the life of the late Mr. Jonathan Wild the Great. Fielding, H: 823.6152
History of Tom Jones. Fielding, H: 823.556
Same. 2 vols.   823.6149-50; 823.7071-2
Same. 3 vols.   ** 823.2080-2
Hitherto. Whitney, *Mrs.* A. D. (T.)   823.1695
Ho ! for Elf-land ! Cooley, *Mrs.* A. (K.)   808.1027
Hoey, *Mrs.* Cashel. *See* Hoey, *Mrs.* F.. S.. (J.)
Hoey, *Mrs.* F.. S.. (Johnston). A golden sorrow.   *in* 823.6262
—— The lover's creed.   823.4824
Hoffman, C: Fenno. Greyslaer: a romance of the Mohawk. 3 vols.   823.5874-6
—— The man in the reservoir. 10 pp. (Johnson, R., *ed. Little classics,* v. 4.)
     p. 189, *in* 829.127
Hoffman, M.. J. Agnes Hilton; or, practical views of catholicity: a tale of trials and triumphs.   823.769
—— The orphan sisters; or, the problem solved.   823.773
Hoffmann, Ernst Theodor (Amadeus *properly*) Wilhelm. Strange stories.   823.6807
—— Weird tales. Tr. with a biog. memoir by J. T. Bealby. 2 vols.   823.4884-5
Hofland, *Mrs.* Barbara (Wreaks). Reflection: a tale.   823.4597
Hogbin, *Rev.* Alfred C. Elsa: a romance.   823.780
Hogg, James. [*The Ettrick shepherd.*] The bogle o' the brae: a queer courting story. (Picken, A., *ed. The club-book,* v. 2.)
     in 823.702
—— The Laidlaws and the Scotts: a border tradition. (Picken, A., *ed. The club-book,* v. 2.)   *in* 823.702
—— Singular letter from southern Africa. 13 pp. (*In* Tales from Blackwood, v. 5.)
     in ** 823.6651
—— Tales and sketches. Including the Brownie of Bodsbeck, etc. And several pieces not before printed. Illus. 5 vols.   823.774-8
Hohensteins, The. Spielhagen, F. 823.4281
Holberg, Ludwig, *Baron* von. [*Nicholas Klimius.*] A journey to the world underground. By Nicholas Klimius. Tr. from the Latin.   ** 823.6778
—— *Same:* being the subterraneous travels of Niels Klim. (*Another tr.*)   823.7384

English Fiction. *Contin.*
Holder, C: F: A frozen dragon, and other
 tales: a story-book of natural history for
 boys and girls.   808.1904
Holding, Carlisle B. Reuben: a prince in
 disguise.   823.7259
Holiday romance. 38 pp. Dickens, C: J:
 H.   p. 411, *in* 808.686
 Same.   p. 409, *in* 942.1259
Holidays at the grange. Higgins, E. M.
                                    808.1638
Holland, Josiah Gilbert. Arthur Bonnicastle:
 an American novel.   823.785
—— The Bay-path: a tale of New England
 colonial life.   823.784
—— Miss Gilbert's career: an American
 story.   823.781
—— *Same.*   823.5257
—— Nicholas Minturn: a study in a story.
                                    823.782
—— Sevenoaks: a story of to-day.   823.783
Holland. *See also* Netherlands.
—— Abbott, J. Rollo in Holland.   808.918
—— Longfellow, H: W. Poems of places.
                        p. 231, *in* 821.220
—— Scudder, H. E. Bodley grandchildren
 and their journey in Holland.   808.1852
Holley, Marietta. Miss Richards' boy, and
 other stories.   823.6119
Hollister, Gideon Hiram. Kinley Hollow.
                                    823.4575
Hollowdell Grange. Fenn, G: M.   808.1498
Holmby House. Melville, G: J: Whyte-
                                 ** 823.4667
 Same.   823.7278
Holmes, *Mrs.* E.. (Emra). Scenes in our
 parish. 1st and 2d series.   ** 823.6745
Holmes, *Mrs.* M.. J.. (Hawes). Bessie's for-
 tune.   823.4848
—— The Cameron pride; or, purified by suf-
 fering: a novel.   823.786
—— Château d'Or. (*Also*) Norah, and, Kitty
 Craig.   823.4846
—— Christmas stories.   823.4850
—— Cousin Maude, and Rosamond.   823.787
—— Daisy Thornton, and Jessie Graham.
                                    823.788
—— Darkness and daylight.   823.789
—— Dora Deane; or, the East India uncle;
 and Maggie Miller; or, old Hagar's secret.
                                    823.790
—— Edith Lyle: a novel.   823.791
—— Edna Browning; or, the Leighton home-
 stead: a novel.   823.792
—— The English orphans; or, a home in the
 new world.   823.793
—— Ethelyn's mistake; or, the home in the
 west: a novel.   823.794
—— Forrest House.   823.795
—— The homestead on the hillside, and
 other tales.   823.796
—— Hugh Worthington.   823.797
—— Jessie Graham. (*With her* Daisy Thorn-
 ton.)   *in* 823.788
—— Kitty Craig. (*With her* Château d'Or.)
                               in 823.4846
—— 'Lena-Rivers.   823.798
—— Madeline.   823.4849

English Fiction. *Contin.*
Holmes, *Mrs.* M.. J.. (Hawes). *Contin.*
—— Maggie Miller; or, old Hagar's secret.
 (*With her* Dora Deane.)   *in* 823.790
—— Marian Grey; or, the heiress of Red-
 stone Hall.   823.1924
—— Meadow Brook.   823.799
—— Mildred: a novel.   823.800
—— Millbank; or, Roger Irving's ward.
                                    823.1922
—— Norah. (*With her* Château d'Or.)
                               in 823.4846
—— Queenie Hetherton: a novel.   823.4847
—— The rector of St. Mark's. (*With her*
 West Lawn.)   *in* 823.803
—— Rosamond. (*With her* Cousin Maude.)
                               in 823.787
—— Rose Mather: a tale.   823.801
—— Tempest and sunshine; or, life in Ken-
 tucky.   823.802
—— West Lawn, and, The rector of St.
 Mark's.   823.803
Holmes, Oliver Wendell (1809—.) Elsie
 Venner: a romance of destiny.   823.804
—— The guardian angel.   823.805
—— Iris. 76 pp. (Johnson, R., *ed. Little
 classics,* v. 7.)   p. 7, *in* 829.130
—— A mortal antipathy.   823.4864
 Note.— For his life and writings, *see* **Bolton,**
 Mrs. S.. K. Oliver Wendell Holmes. 22 pp. (*In
 her* Famous Amer. authors.) 1887. p. 133, *in* 820.
 99.—**Brown,** E. E. Life of H. 1884. 928.547.—
 Kennedy, W: S. Oliver Wendell Holmes. 1883.
 928.444.—**Stedman,** E. C. Oliver Wendell Holmes.
 31 pp. (*In his* Poets of Amer.) 1890. p. 273, *in*
 820.188.
   See also **Poole's** Index (to 1882). p. 598, *in* **
 50.1¹;—*Same.* Jan. 1, 1882–Jan. 1, 1887. p. 205, *in* **
 50.1².
Holst, Hans P: Lisette's castles in the air.
 24 pp. (Bushby, *Mrs.* —, *tr. The Danes
 . . v. 3.)   p. 65, *in* 823.6446
Holt, Emily S.. All for the best; or, Bernard
 Gilpin's motto.   808.1516
—— Ashcliffe Hall: a tale of the last century.
                                    808.1520
—— At ye Grene Griffin; or, Mrs. Treadwell's
 cook: a tale of the fifteenth century.
                                    823.7102
—— Clare Avery: a story of the Spanish Armada.   808.1523
—— Earl Hubert's daughter; or, the polish-
 ing of the pearl: a tale of the thirteenth
 century.   808.1525
—— For the Master's sake: a story of the
 days of Queen Mary.   808.1514
—— Imogen: a story of the mission of Augustine.   823.5725
—— In all time of our tribulation: the story
 of Piers Gavestone.   823.5616
—— In convent walls: the story of the Des-
 pensers. (Following "In all time of our
 tribulation.")   823.5608
—— Isoult Barry of Wynscote: her diurnal
 book: a tale of Tudor times.   808.1519
—— Joyce Morrell's harvest; or, the annals of
 Selwick Hall: a story of the reign of Elizabeth.   823.7103
—— The King's daughters; or, how two girls
 kept the faith.   808.1526
—— Lady Sybil's choice: a tale of the crusades.   823.808

English Fiction. *Contin.*
Horse-shoe Robinson. Kennedy, J: P.
823.927
Hostages to fortune. Maxwell, *Mrs.* M.. E..
(B.)　　　　　　　　　　*in* 823.2407
Same. in 823.5049; *in* 823.5050; 823.6075
Hot plowshares. Tourgée, A. W.　823.4538
Houp-la. 79 pp. Stannard, *Mrs.* H. E. V.
(P.)　　　　　　　　　　*in* 823.5046
House at High Bridge, The. Fawcett, E.
823.5741
House behind the poplars. Beckwith, *Mrs.*
J. R.　　　　　　　　　　823.63
House by the medlar-tree. Verga, G.
823.7186
House by the works, The. Mayo, *Mrs.* I..
(F.)　　　　　　　　　　823.1925
House divided against itself, A. Oliphant,
Mrs. M. O. (W.)　　　　　823.4945
Same.　　　　　　　　*in* 823.5040
House of a merchant prince. Bishop, W: H:
823.4480
House of Ross, The. Riddle, A. G.　823.7144
House of the seven gables. Hawthorne, N.
823.728
Same.　　　　　　　　　823.5878
House of the wolf. Weyman, S. J.　823.7299
House of Walderne. Crake, A. D.　823.5658
House of Yorke. Tincker, M.. A.　823.5993
House on the beach, The. Meredith, G:
823.5563
House on the marsh, The. James, *Mrs.* F.
A. (P.)　　　　　　　　*in* 823.5094
House on the moor. Oliphant, *Mrs.* M. O.
(W.)　　　　　　　　　　823.1198
Same.　　　　　　　　*in* 823.5044
Household of Bouverie. Warfield, *Mrs.* C.
A. (W.)　　　　　　　　823.1658
Household tales and fairy stories.　808.1340
House-party, A. La Ramée, L. de.
823.5747
How a husband forgave. Fawcett, E.
823.6451
How could he help it? Roe, A. S.　823.1362
How he won her. Southworth, *Mrs.* E. D.
E. (N.)　　　　　　　　　823.1982
Same.　　　　　823.4061; 823.5174
How old Wiggins wore ship. 12 pp. Coffin,
R. F.　　　　　　　　p. 139, *in* 823.4710
How private Geo. W. Peck put down the re-
bellion. Peck, G: W.　　　　823.7409
How she did it. Cruger, M..　　823.5498
How they kept the faith. Raymond, G.
823.6367
How they lived in Hampton. Hale, E: E.
823.5693
Howard, Blanche Willis, *now* Teufel, *Mrs.*
B. W. (H.)
Howe, Edgar Watson. A man story.
823.5470
—— A moonlight boy.　　　　823.5277
—— The mystery of the locks.　823.4875
—— The story of a country town.　823.4868
Howe, Maud, *now* Elliott, *Mrs.* M. (H.)
Howells, W: Dean. Annie Kilburn: a novel.
823.5541
—— April hopes.　　　　　　823.5522
—— A boy's town: described for "Harper's
Young people."　　　　　　808.1718

English Fiction. *Contin.*
Howells, W: Dean. *Contin.*
—— A chauce acquaintance.　　823.828
—— A day's pleasure, and other sketches.
823.5765
—— Dr. Breen's practice.　　　823.4279
—— Fearful responsibility, and other stories.
823.1870
—— A foregone conclusion.　　823.829
—— A hazard of new fortunes. 2 vols.
823.7018-19
—— Indian summer.　　　　　823.5619
—— The lady of the Aroostook.　823.2004
—— The minister's charge; or, the appren-
ticeship of Lemuel Barker.　823.5778
—— A modern instance.　　　823.4545
—— The rise of Silas Lapham.　823.4867
—— A romance of real life. 17 pp. (John-
sou, R., *ed. Little classics,* v. 4.)
p. 26, *in* 829.127
—— The shadow of a dream.　823.7166
—— Suburban sketches.　　　823.830
—— The undiscovered country.　823.4306
—— Their wedding journey. With an addi-
tional chapter on Niagara revisited twelve
years after.　　　　　　　823.831
—— A woman's reason.　　　823.4625
—— Macoun, M. Character and comment
selected from the novels of W. D. Howells.
823.6991
Howitt, W: A boy's adventures in the wilds
of Australia; or, Herbert's note-book.
808.193
—— Johnny Darbyshire, a primitive Quaker.
38 pp. (Johnson, R., *ed. Little classics,*
v. 9.)　　　　　　p. 168, *in* 829.132
—— *Same.* 10 pp. (Tieck, L. *The elves
. . .*)　　　　　　p. 136, *in* 823.6328
—— *Same.* (*In* Standard tales, etc., ed. by
Mrs. C. I. Johnstone.)　　*in* * 823.6194
—— Woodburn Grange: a story of English
country life. 3 vols. (in 1).　823.833
——, *and* Howitt, *Mrs.* M.. (Botham). Sto-
ries of English and foreign life.　823.2135
Howleglass, the merry jester. (Roscoe, T:
The German novelists, v. 1.)
p. 141, *in* ** 823.6826
Hubback, *Mrs.* M. Love and duty.　823.834
Hubbell, *Mrs.* Martha (Stone). [*A pastor's
wife.*] The shady side; or, life in a country
parsonage.　　　　　　　823.4639
Hubbell, Walter. The great Amherst mystery: a true narrative of the supernatural.
823.6199
Hudson, W. C. [*Barclay North.*] Vivier of
Vivier, Longman & Company, bankers.
823.7260
Hudson's bay.
—— Kingston, W: H: G. Snow-shoes and
canoes.　　　　　　　　808.1590
Note.—See **Ballantyne,** R. M. Hudson bay; or,
every-day life in the wilds of North America. 1888.
9176.64 —**Bancroft,** H. H. Hist. of Oregon. (1834-
1888.) 2 vols. * 970.93-4.—**Barrows,** W: Oregon:
the struggle for possession. * 977.156.—**Gray,** W.
H. Hist. of Oregon. (1792-1849.) 977.38.—**Robinson,** H. M. The great fur land. 1879. 9171.15.—
Simpson, T. Narrative of the discoveries on the
north coast of America, effected by the officers of
the Hudson's Bay Company. (1836-1839.) 1840. 917.
56.—**Winsor,** J. Hudson's Bay. (*In his* Narr. and
crit. hist. of America, vols. 3, 4, 8.) * 970.127², ', ⁸.

English Fiction. *Contin.*
Humor, satire, etc. *Contin.*
—— Locke, D: R. Ekkoes from Kentucky.
828.200
—— — Morals of Abou Ben Adhem.
828.201
—— — "Swingin' round the cirkle."
828.202
—— Lowell, J. R. Humor and satire (poems). (*In his* Heartsease and rue.)
p. 149, *in* 821.1185
—— Maistre, X. de. A journey round my room. 824.274
—— Mayhew, H:, *and* A: S. The image of his father. 823.5479
—— Nye, E. W. Remarks. 828.217
—— —, *and* Riley, J. W. Fun, wit, and poetry. 828.219
—— Peele, G: Merry conceited jests. 32 pp. (*Works*, v. 2.) p. 373, *in* ** 822.1086
—— Taylor, C. J. In the "400" and out. (Comic designs from "Puck.") ** 828.214
—— Timbs, J. Anecdote lives of wits and humorists. 2 vols. 1872. 828.129-30
—— Welch, P. H: Said in fun. Illus.
828.216
—— Welcker, A. Snob papers. 823.4888
See also **Catalogues** of this Library.
No. 2, 1880, p. 113.   No. 4, 1884, p. 138.
No. 3, 1882, p. 96.   No. 5, 1888, p. 207.
See also **Poole's Index** (to 1882). p. 614, *in* **
50.1;—*Same.* Jan. 1, 1882-Jan. 1, 1887. p. 211, *in* **
50.1².
See also **Stedman**, E. C., *and* Hutchinson, E.
M. Library of American literature. (*General index*,
v. 11.) p. 626, *in* ** 820.131¹.
Humphrey, F.. A. Adventures of early discoverers. 808.1905
Humphry Clinker. Smollett, T. G. 823.1471
Same. 2 vols. ** 823.2091-2
Hungarian tales. 3 vols. Gore, *Mrs.* C. G. F.. (M.) ** 823.6567-9
Hungary. *See* Austria.
Hungerford, James. The old plantation, and what I gathered there in an autumn month.
823.839
Hungerford, *Mrs.* Margaret. [*The Duchess.*]
"Airy fairy Lilian:" a novel. 823.740
—— "As it fell upon a day." 19 pp.
in 823.4981
—— *Same.* *in* 823.4982
—— Beauty's daughters. 823.2504
—— A born coquette. 823.7089
—— Faith and unfaith. 823.3989
—— Lady Branksmere: a novel. 823.4917
—— Loys, Lord Berresford, and other tales.
823.5788
—— Mrs. Geoffrey. 823.3440
—— *Same.* 823.4189
—— Molly Bawn. 823.744
—— Phyllis. 823.745
—— Portia; or, "by passions rocked."
823.5787
Hunt, *Mrs.* Alfred W. *See* Hunt, *Mrs.* M. (R.)
Hunt, *Mrs.* H.. Maria (Fiske). *See* Jackson, *Mrs.* H.. M. (F.)
Hunt, James H: Leigh. Romances of real life. 2 vols. 823.5461-2

English Fiction. *Contin.*
Hunt, James H: Leigh. *Contin.*
—— Stories from the Italian poets. With critical notices of the lives and genius of the authors. 2 vols. 823.7081-2
Contents:—v. 1. Dante, Alighieri. v. 2. **Tasso,** B.
— Ariosto, L. G.—Pulci, L.
Hunt, Leigh. *See* Hunt, J. H: L.
Hunt, *Mrs.* Margaret (Raine). Barrington's fate. 823.4510
Issued also as Self-condemned.
—— The leaden casket. 823.4165
—— That other person. 1st hf. *in* 823.5187
Hunted down. Dickens, C: J: H. *in* 823.5323
Hunter, Hay, *and* White, Walter. Crime of Christmas-day: a tale of the Latin quarter.
in 823.5084
—— My ducats and my daughter. 823.4855
—— *Same.* *in* 823.5047; *in* 823.5083
Hunting adventures on land and sea. 2 pts. Knox, T: W. 808.1846-7
Hunting, fishing and sporting adventures.
—— Adams, W: H: D. The forest, the jungle, and the prairie; or, scenes with the trapper . . . in many lands. 808.131
—— — Scenes with the hunter and trapper in many lands. 808.129
—— Barrows, W: The general; or, twelve nights in the hunter's camp. 808.1653
—— Campbell, W. The old forest ranger; or, wild sports of India. 915.29
—— Grant, R. Jack in the bush; or, a summer on a salmon river. 808.1636
—— Knox, T: W. Hunting adventures on land and sea. 2 pts. 808.1846-7
—— Reid, *Capt.* T: M. Bruin: the grand bear hunt. 808.426
—— — The young voyageurs; or, the boy hunters in the north. 808.1681
—— Souvestre, E. The chamois-hunter.
823.5941
—— Stephens, C: A. Fox-hunting, as recorded by Raed. 808.244
—— — The young moose-hunters: a backwoods story. 808.1889
—— Van Dyke, T: S. Flirtation camp; or, the rifle, rod and gun in California.
823.7137
—— — Rifle, rod and gun in California. (*Same as* Flirtation camp.) 823.4157
Note.—See **Baker,** *Sir* S: W. The rifle and
the hound in Ceylon. 1877. 915.26.—**Barnum,**
P. T. The wild beasts, birds and reptiles of the
world: the story of their capture. 1889. 590.117.—
Barras, J. India and tiger-hunting. 2 vols. 915.
359-60.—**Bumstead,** J: On the wing. 187c. 799.22.
—**Burdett,** C: Life of Kit Carson. 923.415.—**Cumming,** R. G. A hunter's life in south Africa. (1855.)
916.65.—**Elliott,** W: Carolina sports, by land and
water. 1846. 799.74.—**Gillmore,** P. Gun, rod, and
saddle. 799.125.—**Greenwood,** J. Wild sports of
the world. 1870. 910.140. — **Hammond,** S. H.
Hunting adventures in the northern wilds. (1863.)
799.79;— Wild northern scenes. (1863.) 799.80.—
Herbert, H: W: Frank Forester's field sports
of the U. S. and Brit. provinces of N. Amer. 2
vols. 1873. * 799.87-8.— **Holub,** *Dr.* E. Seven
years in south Africa (1872-79). 2 vols. 1881. 916.
112-13.—**Inglis,** J. Tent life in tigerland: being
sporting reminiscences of a pioneer planter in an
Indian frontier district. Plates. 1888. * 915.364.—
Krider's sporting anecdotes. 1853. 799.102.—
Leffingwell, W: B., *ed.* Shooting on upland
marsh and stream. Illus. 1890. * 799.124.—**Lewis,**
E. J. The Amer. sportsman . . . hints for sports-
men . . . 1879. * 799.92.—**Mayer,** A. M. Sport with

English Fiction. *Contin.*
India. *Contin.*
Hindus.
—— Burton, R: F., *ed.* Vikram and the
vampire; or, tales of Hindu devilry.
823.4154
—— Taylor, M. Confessions of a Thug.
823.4276
—— — *Same.* 3 vols. * 823.4629-31
Jungle life.
—— Cumming, *Lt.-Col.* W. G. Wild men
and wild beasts. 823.6581
—— Fenn, G: M. Middy and ensign: a tale
of the Malay Peninsula. 823.5740
BENGAL.
—— Chatterjee, B. C. The poison-tree.
823.4936
—— Day, L. B. Folk-tales of Bengal.
808.1691
SOUTHERN INDIA. Frere, M.. Old Deccan
days; or, Hindoo fairy legends. 808.1035

Note.—See Elliot, *Sir* H.-M. **Bibliographical
index** to the historians of Muhammedan India. 4
vols. v. 1. 1859. (No more has been published.)
* 951.110.—**Castaneda,** H. L. de. Discovery and
conquest of India by the Portuguese. (Kerr, R.
Gen. hist . . . of voy. . ., v. 2.) p. 292, *in* ** 913.
113.—**Correa,** G. Three voyages of Vasco da
Gama and his viceroyalty. (*Hakluyt Soc.,* 1869.)
** 954.34.—**Discoveries** . . . of the Portuguese in
India. 1505-39. (Kerr, R. *Gen. hist. . . of voy.*
. . ., v. 6.) p. 69, *in* ** 913.117.—**Frederick,** C.
Voyages and travels in India. 1503-81. (Kerr, R.
Gen. hist. . . . of voy. . v. 7.) p. 142, *in* ** 913.
118.—**Heeren,** A. H. L. Hist. researches into the
politics, intercourse, and trade of the prin. nations
of antiquity. v. 3: Asiatic nations: Indians. 1883.
* 950.4.—**History of the Indians.** (*Univ. history*
(anc.), chap. 88, v. 18.) ** 909.48.—**Hooker,** W. J.
Himalayan journals: notes of a naturalist in Bengal . . . 2 vols. 1855. 915.87-8.—**Hunter,** W. W.
Orissa. v. 2. 1872. 915.216.—**Major,** R. H., *ed.*
India in the 15th century. ** 954.35.—**Réclus,**
J. J. E. The earth and its inhabitants. Asia.
v. 3: India and Indo-China. Ed. by A. H. Keane.
Maps. Illus. 1884. 915.377.—**Robertson,** W: Hist.
disquisition concerning the knowledge the ancients
had of India. 1804. 954.14.—**Roe,** *Sir* T: Voyage
to India. 1614-15. (*Pinkerton's voy.,* v. 8.) p. 1, *in*
** 913.16.—**Rousselet,** L: India and its native
princes. 1878. * 915.127.—**Sleeman,** *Sir* W. H.
Journey through . . Oude. 1849-50. 2 vols. 1858.
915.251-2.—**Taylor,** R. Visit to India . . . 1875.
915.41.—Travels of two Mohammedans through
India . . . in the 9th cent. (*Pinkerton's voy.,* v. 7.)
p. 179, *in* ** 913.13.—**Vartheina,** L. di. Voyages
and travels in . . . India . . . A.D. 1503-8. ** 915.
132.—**Vincent,** F., *Jr.* The land of the white elephant. 1874. 915.21;—Through and through the
tropics. 1874. 910.126.—**Wheeler,** J. T. History
of India from the earliest ages. 4 vols. 1867-76;
954.115-18.—Short history of India, Afghanistan,
Nipal and Burma. 1880. 954.93.

British India.—**Auber,** P. Rise and progress of
the British power in India. 2 vols. 1837. 954.23-4.
—Macaulay, T: B. Lord Robert Clive. (*In his* Essays, v. 4.) p. 194, *in* 824.135.—Malcolm, *Sir* J. Life
of Clive. 3 vols. 923.2022-24.—Burke, E. Reports
of administration of justice in India. Charge against
Warren Hastings. 2 vols. (*Works,* vols. 4-5.) 1880.
825.113-114.—**Hastings,** W., The history of the trial
of. Feb. 7, 1786-Apr. 23, 1795. 1796. 340.163.—Gleig,
Rev. G. R. Memoirs of the life of **Hastings** (1733-
1818). 3 vols. 1841. 923.513-15.—**Hunter,** *Sir* W:
W. The Marquess of Dalhousie. (*Rulers of India*
ser.) 1890. 954.102.—**Marshman,** J: C. History
of India from the earliest period to 1858. 3 vols.
1871. 954.103-5.—**Martin,** R. M. British colonial
library, vols. 4 and 5: West Indies. 2 vols. 1844.
979.1-2.—**Mill,** J. British history of India. (1527-
1833.) 10 vols. (in 9.) 1858. * 954.65-73.

French in India.—**Malleson,** *Maj.* G. B. History
of the French in India. (1674-1761.) 1868. 954.86.

English Fiction. *Contin.*
India. *Contin.*
Note. *Contin.*
Indian mutiny, 1857-8.—**Holmes,** T. R. E. History of the Indian mutiny. 2d ed. 1885. 954.106.—
Kaye, *Sir* J: W: History of the Sepoy war in
India. 3 vols. 1870-76. * 954.78-80.—**Malleson,**
Col. G. W. History of the Indian mutiny, 1857-1858;
commencing from the close of the second volume
of Sir J: Kaye's History of the Sepoy war. 2 vols.
1878-79. 954.81-2.
Religion.—**Clarke,** J. F. Ten great religions.
1878. 208.2.—**Fergusson,** J. Tree and serpent
worship. (Plates only.) 294.33.—**Hodgson,** B. H. Oriental religions. v. 2: India. 1873. 299.2.—**Wilson,**
H. H. Essays . . . on the religion of the Hindus.
2 vols. (*Works,* vols. 1-2.) 1862. 894.15-16.
Manners and customs.—**Cust,** R: N. Pictures of
Indian life, sketched with the pen from 1852-1881.
Maps. 915.372.—**Dubois,** J. A., *abbé.* Description
of the character, manners and customs of the people of India. 1817. * 954.114.—**Oman,** J: C. Indian
life (Hindu and Muhammedan), religious and social. 1889. 915.349.
For description and recent history, *see* Arnold,
Sir E. India revisited. 1886. 915.346.—**Duff,** J. G.
History of Mahrattas. (1323-1822.) Maps. 3 vols.
1826. 954.107-9.—**Feudge,** *Mrs.* F. (R.) (Description and recent history of) India. (1880.) 954.57.—
Hodgson, B. H. Misc. essays relating to Indian
subjects. 2 vols. 1880. 494.29-30.—**Holcomb,** *Mrs.*
H. H. Bits about India. (1888.) 915.357.—**Karaka,**
D. F. Hist. of the Parsis, including their manners,
customs, religion, and present position. Illus. 2
vols. 1884. * 295.12-13.—**Robinson,** P. Under the
sun. 1882. 504.63.

See also **Catalogues** of this Library.
No. 2, 1880, pp. 116, 117. No. 4, 1884, p. 142.
No. 3, 1882, p. 98. No. 5, 1888, pp. 211, 212.
See also **Poole's Index** (to 1882). pp. 628-35, *in* **
50.1;—*Same.* Jan. 1, 1882-Jan. 1, 1887. pp. 217-19, *in*
** 50.1².
See also **Index to Consular reports.** 1880-1885;
1886-1889. 2 vols. (U. S. Pub. Docs. *Dept. of State.*)
** 350.5496¹-².

India. Southworth, *Mrs.* E. D. E. (N.)
823.1494
Indian fairy book. Mathews, C. 808.1330
Indian summer. Howells, W: D. 823.5619
Indian tales. *See* Kipling, R.
Indiana. Dudevant, *Mme.* A. L. A. (D.)
823.6848
Indians.
—— Ballantyne, R. M. Away in the wilderness. 808.631
—— — *Same.* (*With his* Lost in the forest.)
in 808.1279
—— — *Same.* (*In his* Tales of adventure.)
in 808.1268
—— Bird, R. M. Nick of the woods.
823.79
—— Campbell, T: Gertrude of Wyoming;
poem. p. 77, *in* 821.78
—— Clark, *Mrs.* C.. (M.) Baby Rue.
823.1872
—— Cooper, J. F. Leather stocking tales,
viz.:
1: The deerslayer. 823.293
2: Last of the Mohicans. 823.320
3: The pathfinder. 823.304
4: The pioneers. 823.306
5: The prairie. 823.307
—— — Stories of the prairie and other adventures of the border. 808.1127
—— — The wept of Wish-Ton-Wish.
823.316
—— — Wyandotté. 823.318
—— Cozzens, S: W. Young silver seekers.
808.1630
—— — Young trail hunters; or, the wild
riders of the plains. 808.1628

English Fiction. *Contin.*
Indians. *Contin.*

—— Eggleston, E:, *and* Seelye, *Mrs.* L. (E.) Brant and Red Jacket. Including an account of the early wars of the six nations and the border warfare of the revolution.
808.767

—— —— Tecumseh and the Shawnee prophet.
808.1589

—— Grinnell, G: B. Pawnee hero stories and folk-tales, with notes. 808.1717

—— Halleck, F.-G. Wyoming; poem. (*Poet. writings.*) p. 30, *in* 821.1323

—— Herbert, H: W. Ahsahgunushk Numamahtahseng; or, the Reed-Shaken-by-the-Wind. 91 pp. (*In his* Chev. of France.)
823.4253

—— King, *Capt.* C: Marion's faith.
823.4967

—— Kingston, W: H: G. Adventures of Dick Onslow among the redskins.
808.1554

—— Longfellow, H: W. The song of Hiawatha. p. 1, *in* 821.239

—— — *Same.* p. 141, *in* 821.888

—— McKnight, C: Captain Jack, the scout; or, the Indian wars about old Fort Duquesne. 823.4335

—— — *Same.* 823.7139

—— Matthews, C. Enchanted moccasins and other legends of the American Indians.
808.1856

—— — Indian fairy book from original legends. 808.1330

—— Moorehead, W. K. Wanneta, the Sioux.
823.6470

—— Murray, C: A. The prairie-bird.
823.1179

—— Poston, C: D. Apache-land. 821.318

—— Schoolcraft, H. R. The myth of Hiawatha. 291.32

—— Simms, W. G. Yemassee. 823.1441

—— Smith, E. H. Ma-ka-tai-me-she-kiakiak; or, Black Hawk and scenes in the west; poem. 1848. ** 1000.122

—— Southey, R. Songs of the American Indians. p. 259, *in* 821.1165

—— Stoddard, W: O. Red Beauty: a story of the Pawnee trail. 808.1485

—— — Talking leaves. 808.1359

—— — Two Arrows: a story of red and white.
808.1429

—— Tibbles, T. H. Hidden power: a secret history of the Indian ring. 823.1844

—— Webber, C: W. Old Hicks the guide; or, adventures in the Camauche country in search of a gold mine. 823.1691

—— Wraxall, F: C: L. Golden-hair.
823.1745

See also Tales by G. Aimard.

Bibliography.—The Indian question. Bost. Pub. Lib. *Bulletin* No. 49. v. 4. p. 68, *in* ** 17.135.—Brooks, F. S. Best one hundred books on the American Indian. 7 pp. (*In his* The story of the Amer. Indian.) 1887. p. 301, *in* 970.129.—Field, T: W. An essay towards an Indian bibliography: being a catalogue of (his) library. 1873. ** 16.14.

Origin.—Bradford, A. W. American antiquities and researches into the origin and history of the red race. 1841. 970.14.—Journal of American folk-lore. vols. 1-3. 1888-1890. 3 vols. 291.81-81².

English Fiction. *Contin.*
Indians. *Contin.*

Religion.—Brinton, D. G. American hero-myths. 1882. 291.39.—McClintock, J:, *and* Strong, J. Cyclop. v. 4. p. 558, *in* 203.9.

Manners and customs.—Catlin, G. Illustrations of the manners, customs, etc., of North American Indians. 2 vols. 1857. 970.12-13;—*Same.* 970.52-3.—Schoolcraft, H. R. The Indian in his wigwam. 1848. 9170.42.

For recent descriptions, *see* Brooks, E. S. The story of the American Indian. 1887. (Best one hundred books on the American Indian. pp. 301-308.) 970.129;—*Same.* 970.134.—Burdett, C. Life of Kit Carson, the great western hunter and guide. 1865. 923.415.—Custer, *Mrs.* E.. (B.) Following the guidon. 1890. 9173.488.—Custer, *Gen.* G: A. Wild life on the plains. 1866. 9173.484.—Drake, S: G. The aboriginal races of North America. 1859. 970.22.—Dunn, J. P., *Jr.* Massacres of the mountains: hist. of the Indian wars of the far west. Illus. 1886. 970.133.—Jackson, *Mrs.* H.. M. (F.) A century of dishonor: U. S. gov't dealings with Indians. 973.597.—Schoolcraft, H. R. Indian tribes of the United States. 6 vols. 1853-6. * 970.1-6;—Notes on the Iroquois. 1847. 970.50.—Smith, *Col.* J. An account of . . . captivity with the Indians. 1870. 9170.45.—Thomas, C. The Cherokees in pre-Columbian times. (*Fact and theory papers.*) 1890. 970.132.

See also Catalogues of this Library.
No. 2, 1880, p. 117 (and p. 235, U. S. Pub. Docs. *Indian frauds*).
No. 3, 1882, p. 98 (and p. 193, U. S. Pub. Docs. *Indians*).
No. 4, 1884, pp. 142-143.
No. 5, 1888, pp. 212-213 (and p. 365, U. S. Pub. Docs. *Indian affairs*.)

See also Poole's Index (to 1882). pp. 635-638, *in* ** 50.1;—*Same.* Jan. 1, 1882-Jan. 1, 1887. p. 219, *in* ** 50.1².

See also Catalogue of government publications of the U. S. 1774-1881. pp. 1302-4, *in* ** 15.202.

See also New England, *note.*

Inez. Wilson, *Mrs.* A. J.. (E.) 823.4009
Infanta at Presburg. Gore, *Mrs.* C. G. F.. (M.) p. 169, *in* ** 823.6569
Infelice. Wilson, *Mrs.* A. J.. (E.) 823.1707
Infernal marriage, The. Disraeli, B:
in 823.458

Ingelow, Jean. Don John. 823.3426
—— Fated to be free. 823.840
—— John Jerome: his thoughts and ways. A book without beginning. 823.5613
—— Off the Skelligs. 823.841
—— Sarah de Berenger. 823.5791
—— — *Same.* 3 vols. 823.7385-7
—— Studies for stories. 823.842

Ingemann, Bernhard Severin. The aged rabbi. 54 pp.—All Souls' Day. 58 pp.—The death ship. 6 pp. (Poem.) (Bushby, *Mrs.* —, *tr.* The Danes . . . v. 3.)
in 823.6446

—— The doomed house. 30 pp.—The secret witness. 8 pp. (Bushby, *Mrs.* —, *tr.* The Danes . . . v. 1.) *in* 823.6444

Ingenious gentleman, Don Quixote of La Mancha. 4 vols. Cervantes Saavedra, M. de. 823.5235-38

Ingenue. Dumas, A. D. 823.3243

Ingersoll, Ernest. The silver caves: a mining story. 808.1719

Ingham, *Col.* F:, *pseud. See* Hale, E: Everett.

Ingham papers. Hale, E: E. 823.4309

Ingledew House. Brame, *Mrs.* C.. M. (L.)
in 823.5132

Ingo. Freytag, G. 823.6797

English Fiction. *Contin.*

Ingraban. Freytag, G. 823.6798

Ingraham, *Rev.* Joseph Holt. The pillar of fire; or, Israel in bondage. 249.13
—— The prince of the house of David; or three years in the holy city. Being a ser. of letters . . . relating . . . all the scenes and wonderful incidents in the life of Jesus of Nazareth from his baptism in Jordan to his crucifixion on Calvary. 823.2167
—— The throne of David: . . . to the rebellion of prince Absalom. 823.7441

Inheritance, The. Ferrier, S. E. 823.2052

Initials. Tautphœus, J. (M.) *Freiherrin* von. 823.1796

Inland voyage. Stevenson, R. L:
in 823.5015

Inner house, The. Besant, W. 823.6603

Innocent. 2 parts (in 1). Oliphant, *Mrs.* M. O. (W.) 823.5028
Same. 823.6365

Inside. Baker, *Rev.* W: M. 823.5927

Inside the bar. Melville, G: J: Whyte-
in ** 823.4668
Same. *in* 823.7282

Inspired lobbyist, An. 35 pp. De Forest, J: W:
p. 137, *in* 823.4705

Interpreter, The. Melville, G: J: Whyte-
823.1853
Same. *in* 823.4671

Into unknown seas. Ker, D: 808.1360

Introduced to society. Aidé, H. *in* 823.5145
Same. *in* 823.5187

Invaders, The, and other stories. Tolstoï, *Count* L. N. 823.5242

Invasion, The. ·Griffin, G. 823.673

Invasion of France in 1814. Erckmann, E., *and* Chatrian, P. A. 823.6863

Inventions.
—— Hale, E: E. Stories of invention: told by inventors and their friends. 808.1426
—— Timbs, J: Stories of inventors and discoverers in science and the useful arts. 1860. D 3.118
Note.—See Coryton, J. Accidental inventions. (*Macmillan's mag.,* v. 4.) p. 75, *in* ** 52.1764.—Knight, E. II. Crude and curious inventions. (*Atlantic monthly,* v. 39, pp. 517, 645; v. 40, pp. 22, 689; v. 41, pp. 19, 426.) ** 51.913-15.—Timbs, J: Wonderful inventions. 1870. 609.1.—Tissandier, G., *and* Frith, H: Marvels of invention and scientific puzzles. (*Sci. rec. ser.*) 608.150.—Towle, G: M. Heroes and martyrs of invention. 1890. 609.14. *See also* Catalogues of this Library. No. 2, 1880, p. 118. No. 4, 1884, p. 145. No. 3, 1882, p. 100. No. 5, 1888, p. 214. *See also* Poole's Index (to 1882). p. 651, *in* ** 50.1¹—*Same.* Jan. 1, 1882–Jan. 1, 1887. p. 224, *in* ** 50.1¹.

Invisible empire, The. Tourgée, A. W. 823.2189
Same. *in* 823.4176

Invisible lodge. Richter, J. P. F. 823.4613

Involuntary experimentalist, The. 17 pp. (*In* Tales from Blackwood, v. 12.)
** *in* 823.6658

Involuntary voyage, An. Biart, L. 823.6837

Ipomydon, Lyfe of. Weber, H: W:
p. 279, *in* * 821.1240

Ireland.
—— Adams, W: T. Shamrock and thistle; or, Young America in Ireland and Scotland. 808.492

English Fiction. *Contin.*

Ireland. *Contin.*

—— Butterworth, H. Zigzag journeys in the British Isles. 808.1813
—— Croker, T. C. Fairy legends and traditions of the south of Ireland. 299.21
—— — Killarney legends. 299.22
—— Curtin, J. Myths and folk-lore of Ireland. 291.83
—— — *Same.* 291.86
—— Emerald gems: . . . Irish fireside tales, historic, domestic, and legendary. 823.1190
—— Half-hours with Irish authors. Selections from Griffin, Lover, Carleton and Lever. 823.1073
—— Irish fireside stories, tales and legends. 823.6145
—— Kennedy, P. Legendary fictions of the Irish Celts. 823.2115
—— Knox, T: W. The boy travellers in Great Britain and Ireland. 808.1930
—— Longfellow, H: W. Poems of places. 821.211
—— Lover, S: Legends and stories of Ireland. 823.1016
—— — *Same.* 823.5154
—— McAnally, D: R., *Jr.* Irish wonders: the ghosts . . . and other marvels of the emerald isle: popular tales as told by the people. 808.1908
—— Martineau, H. Ireland. (*In her* Illus. of polit. econ., v. 3.) *in* ** 823.6708
—— Towle, G: M. Young people's history of Ireland. 941.133
—— Wilde, *Lady* J.. F. S. (E.) Ancient legends, mystic charms, and superstitions of Ireland. 291.90

5TH CENTURY, A. D. Shirley, J. Saint Patrick for Ireland; drama.
p. 363, *in* * 822.1111

8TH CENTURY, A. D.
—— Griffin, G. The invasion. 823.673
—— Smyth, P. G. King and viking; or, the ravens of Lochlan: a tale of the Danish invasion of Ireland. (795.) 823.7305

12TH CENTURY, A. D.
—— Adams, J. Q. Dermot MacMorrogh; or, the conquest of Ireland (poem). 821.1377
—— O'Byrne, M. L: The court of Rath Croghan. 823.7304

16TH CENTURY, A. D.
—— O'Grady, S. Red Hugh's captivity. 823.7222
—— Sadlier, *Mrs.* M.. A. (M.) MacCarthy More; or, the fortunes of an Irish chief in the reign of Queen Elizabeth. 823.1380

17TH CENTURY, A. D.
—— Banim, J: Boyne-water. 823.54
—— — The denounced; or, the last baron of Crana. (Battle of Aughrim, 1691.) 823.56
—— Caddell, C. M.. Nellie Netterville. 823.163
—— Field, *Mrs.* E. M., *ed.* Ethne: a truthful historie of the great and final settlement of Ireland by Oliver Cromwell . . . 823.6400
—— Henty, G: A. Orange and green: a tale of the Boyne and Limerick. 808.1457

English Fiction. *Contin.*
Ireland. *Contin.*
17TH CENTURY, A. D. *Contin.*
—— Sadlier, *Mrs.* M.. A. (M.) Confederate chieftains. 823.1377
—— — Heiress of Kilorgan: or, evenings with the old Geraldines. 823.1379
—— Smyth, P. G. The wild rose of Lough Gill: a tale of the Irish war. 823.7306
18TH CENTURY, A. D.
—— Edgeworth, M. Castle Rackrent. (*In her* Tales . . . v. 1.) p. 1, *in* ** 823.4646
—— Froude, J. A. Two chiefs of Dunboy. 823.5512
—— Lever, C: J. The Martins of Cro' Martin. 823.987
—— — *Same.* 2 vols. 823.5708–9
—— — The O'Donoghue. 823.989
—— Lover, S: Rory O'More. 823.1017
Insurrection of 1798–1799.
—— Argyle, A.. Olive Lacey. 823.41
—— Banim, M. The croppy. 823.55
—— Conyngham, D: P. The O'Mahony: chief of the Comeraghs. 823.273
—— Damant, M.. Peggy Thornhill. 823.7171
—— Neville, R. Lloyd Pennant. 823.1187
19TH CENTURY, A. D.
—— Savage, M. W. The Falcon family; or young Ireland. 823.6144
—— Trollope, A. Kellys and the O'Kellys. 823.1612
—— — The Macdermots of Ballycloran. 823.1615
—— — Phineas Finn, the Irish member. 823.1619
See also Trench, W. S. Realities of Irish life. 941.44
Legislative union, 1801. Lever, C: J. Knight of Gwynne. 2 vols. 823.5712–13
Famine, 1847.
—— Carleton, W: The black prophet. 823.168
—— Keary, A. Castle Daly: the story of an Irish home . . . 823.922
—— Trollope, A. Castle Richmond. 823.1606
Catholics and Protestants. Sadlier, *Mrs.* M.. A. (M.) New lights; or, life in Galway. 823.1382
Church imposts. Carleton, W: The tithe-proctor. 823.175
Fenians.
—— McCarthy, J. Maurice Tyrone; or, the fair Saxon. 823.1053
—— — *Same.* 823.5748
Landlords and agents.
—— Carleton, W: Poor scholar. (*In his* Traits and stories . . . v. 2.) *in* 823.5820
—— — *Same.* (*In his* Traits and stories . . . v. 4.) ** 823.6644
—— — Tubber Derg. (*In his* Traits and stories . . . v. 2.) *in* 823.5820
—— — *Same.* (*In his* Traits and stories . . . v. 4.) ** 823.6644
—— — Valentine M'Clutchy. 823.179
Land system.
—— Carleton, W: The emigrants of Ahadarra. 823.170
—— Trollope, A. The land leaguers. 823.6590

English Fiction. *Contin.*
Ireland. *Contin.*
19TH CENTURY, A. D. *Contin.*
Penal laws.
—— Carleton, W: Willy Reilly. 823.180
—— Griffin, G. Tracy's ambition.
in 823.676
—— — *Same.* 823.4960
·IRISH CHARACTER. ·
—— Ballyblunder: an Irish story. 823.6431
—— Banim, M. Mayor of Wind-gap. 823.59
—— Boyce, J: Mary Lee; or, the Yankee in Ireland. 823.113
—— — Shandy M'Guire: a story of the north of Ireland. 823.114
—— Carleton, W: The black baronet. 823.167
—— — The evil eye. 823.171
—— — Fardorougha, the miser. 823.172
—— — Jane Sinclair; or, the fawn of Springvale. 823.173
—— — *Same.* 823.5517
—— — Poor scholar, and other tales of Irish life. 823.174
—— — Tubber Derg, and other tales. 823.178
—— — Willy Reilly, and his dear Coleen bawn. 823.180
—— Griffin, G. Tales of the Munster festivals. 823.667
—— — Talis qualis; or, tales of the jury-room. 823.677
—— Hall, *Mrs.* A.. M. (F.) Sketches of Irish character. 823.691
—— Lever, C: J. Charles O'Malley. 823.973
—— — Harry Lorrequer. 823.981
—— — Tom Burke of "Ours." 823.994
—— Lover, S: Handy Andy. 823.1014
—— — He would be a gentleman. 823.1784
—— Lunn, *Mrs.* J. C. Shamrock and rose. 3 vols. 823.7218–20
—— Maunsell, W. P. Poisoned chalice. 823.7221
—— Morgan, *Lady* S. (O.) Florence Macarthy. 823.1174
—— — Wild Irish girl. 3 vols. * 823.2361–3
—— O'Brien, W: When we were boys. 823.7023
—— Reade, C: The wandering heir. p. 211, *in* 823.1983
—— Smart, H. The master of Rathkelly. 823.5589
—— Wilde, W. R. Irish popular superstitions. *in* ** 1000.106
See also Novels by J: and M. Banim; *Mrs.* A.. M. (F.) Hall; C: J. Lever; S: Lover.
Life among the aristocracy.
—— Edgeworth, M. Ormond. (*In her* Tales . . . vols. 13–14.) p. 285, *in* ** 823.4658–9
Peasant life.
—— Carleton, W: Traits and stories of the Irish peasantry. 823.7363
—— — *Same.* 2 vols. 823.5819–20
—— — *Same.* 5 vols. ** 823.6641–5
—— Mick Tracy, the Irish scripture reader: or; the martyred convert and the priest. By the author of "Tim Doolan." 823.7190

English Fiction. *Contin.*
Ireland. *Contin.*
IRISH CHARACTER. *Contin.*
Peasant life. Contin.
—— Mulholland, C. Kathleen Mavourneen.
823.7178
—— Roy, G. For her sake.   ·   823.6369
See also Novels by J: and M. Banim.
Claddagh. Sadlier, *Mrs.* M.. A. (M.) Maureen Dhu, the admiral's daughter.
823.1381
Leinster. See Tales by J: and M. Banim.
Munster.
—— Griffin, G. The collegians: a tale of Carryowen.   823.671
Note.—Rural middle class life in Munster, Ireland; the source of Boucicault's play "Colleen Bawn."
—— —— Sketches illustrative of life and manners in the south of Ireland. (*With his* Munster festivals.)   p. 374, *in* 823.667
—— —— Tales of the Munster festivals. 2 ser.
823.667-8
Ulster.
—— Carleton, W: Traits and stories of the Irish peasantry. 2 vols.   823.5819-20
—— —— *Same.* 5 vols.   ** 823.6641-5
See also Novels of W: Carleton.
In poetry.
—— Ballads and songs (of Ireland), with music.   821.128
—— Duncathail, —, *comp.* Ballads, popular poetry, and household songs of Ireland. 1882.   821.1349
—— Graves, A. P. Irish songs and ballads. 1880.   * 821.1338
—— —— Songs of Irish wit and humour. 1884.
821.1047
—— Hardiman, J., *ed.* Irish minstrelsy; or, bardic remains of Ireland. 2 vols. 1831.
* 821.1335-6
—— Hayes, E. Ballads of Ireland. 2 vols.
821.149-50
—— Longfellow, H: W. Poems of places: Ireland.   821.211
Note.—See Annals of the kingdom of Ireland, by the Four Masters, from the earliest period to 1616, ed. by J. O'Donovan. 7 vols. 1856. * 9411.75-81.—**Ball,** J: T. Historical review of the legislative systems operative in Ireland. (1172-1800.) 1888. 328. 730.—**Barnard,** F. P., *tr.* Strongbow's conquest of Ireland. (1166-86.) 1888. (Authorities, pp. 202-9.) 9411.65.—**Bellings,** R. History of the Irish confederation and the war in Ireland. 1641-1648. 6 vols. 1882-1890. vols. 1-2: 9411.3-4; vols. 3-6: 9411. 46-46*.—**Bibliography,** Madden, R. R. The history of the Irish periodical literature, from the end of the 17th to the middle of the 19th century. 2 vols. 1867. 820.41-2.—**Power,** J. Irish literary periodicals. 1730-1865. (*Notes and queries,* 3d ser., v. 9, Mar., 1866.) p. 173, *in* ** 52.652.—**Calendar** of the state papers relating to Ireland, of the reign of James I. 1603-1625. 5 vols. (*Gt. Brit. Rolls. chron.*) 1872-80. ** 9411.82-6.—**Carlyle,** T: Oliver Cromwell letters and speeches. (Campaign in Ireland, 1649.) (*Works,* vols. 6 and 7.) 923.1842-3.—**Cusack,** M. F. Compendium of Irish history. 941.21.—Illustrated history of Ireland. 1868. 941.46.—**Daunt,** W: J. O'N. Eighty-five years of Irish history. 1880-1884. (*With*) suppl. chapter . . to 1887. 1888. 9411.55.—**Froude,** J. A. The English in Ireland in the 18th century. 3 vols. 1881. 941.64-6.—**Gilbert,** J: T. History of the Irish confederation and the war in Ireland. v. 7: 1646-49. 1891. 9411.46*.—**Hassencamp,** *Dr.* R. The history of Ireland. (1660-1760.) 1888. 9411.74.—**Hay,** E. History of the Irish insurrection of 1798. 1846. 9411.61.—**Lawless,** E. The story of Ireland. 1889. 9411.67.—**McGee,** T: d'A. Popular history. 2 vols. 1880. 941.18-19.—

English Fiction. *Contin.*
Ireland. *Contin.*
Note. Contin.
Montalembert, C: F. de T., *comte* de. Monks of the west. 2 vols. (Era of St. Patrick and the early Christian history.) 271.4-5.—**Moore,** T. History of Ireland. 4 vols. 1835-46. 9411.92-5.—**O'Connell,** D., Correspondence of. (1792-1847.) 816.53-4;—Memoir on Ireland, native and Saxon. 1172-1660. 1843. (Styled by Daunt "an indictment of England.") 9411.68.—**O'Rourke,** J: The history of the great Irish famine of 1847. 1875. 9411.96.—**Taylor,** W. C. History of Ireland. (Anglo-Norman invasion to the union in 1801.) 2 vols. 1839. 941.53-4.
For the Catholic emancipation, *see* Burke, E. Works. 6 vols. 825.110-15.
On the relations of England and Ireland, *see also* Arnold, M. Irish essays and others. 1882. (Written partly before and partly after the passage of the present land act.) 824.319.—**Atkins,** T. de C. The case of Ireland stated. 1881. 9411.87.—**Blackwood,** F. T.H., *Earl of Dufferin.* Irish emigration and the tenure of land in Ireland. 1867. (Favors emigration and discourages small farming.) 9411.88.—**Daunt,** W: J. O'N. Eighty-five years of Irish history. 1800-1884. 9411.55.—**Higgins,** C: Home rule; or, the Irish land question. 9411.54.—**Hurlburt,** W: H: Ireland under coercion: the diary of an American. 1888. 9411.56.—**Ingram,** T. D. The Irish parliament of James II. 90 pp. (*In his* Two chapters of Irish history.) 1888. p. 1, *in* 9411.58;—Alleged violation of the treaty of Limerick. 47 pp. (*In his* Two chapters of Irish history.) p. 93, *in* 9411.58.—Irish seditions, from 1792-1880. 9411.90.—**Jervish,** H. J. W. Ireland under the British rule. 1868. 9411.89.—**McCarthy,** J: Ireland's cause in England's parliament. 1888. 9411.60.—**Maguire,** J. G. Ireland and the pope: a brief history of papal intrigues against Irish liberty, from Adrian IV. to Leo XIII. 1888. 9411.57.—**Martin,** R. M. Ireland before and after the union with Great Britain. (English side.) 1843. 9411.66.—**O'Connor,** T: P., *and* McWade, P. Gladstone-Parnell, and the great Irish struggle. (1886.) 9411.59.—**Russell,** *Sir* C: The Parnell commission: the opening speech for the defence. 3d ed. 1889. 340.161.—**Rutherford,** J: The secret history of the Fenian conspiracy. 2 vols. 1877. 9411.69-70.—**Staples,** R. Agitation in Ireland, from a landlord's point of view. 1881. 9411.91.—**Sullivan,** A. M. New Ireland. 1878. 941.16.—**Thornton,** W: T. A plea for peasant proprietors. 1874. 9411.73.—**Tuke,** J. H. Irish distress and its remedies. The land question. A visit to Donegal and Connaught in the spring of 1880. 1880. 9411.71.
For manners and customs in general, *see* **Hall,** *Mrs.* A.. M. Sketches of Irish character. 823.691.—**O'Curry,** E. On the manners and customs of the ancient Irish. 3 vols. * 9411.62-4.—**Smith,** G. Irish history and Irish character. 1862. 9411.72.—**Thébaud,** A: J. Irish race in the past and present. 1873. 941.14.

See also Catalogues of this Library.
 No. 2, 1880, p. 119. No. 4, 1884, pp. 145-46.
 No. 3, 1882, p. 100. No. 5, 1888, p. 215.

See also Poole's Index (to 1882). pp. 652-663, *in* ** 50.1;—*Same.* Jan. 1, 1882-Jan. 1, 1887. pp. 224-229, *in* ** 50.1².

See also Index to Consular reports. 1880-1885 ; 1886-1889. 2 vols. (U. S. Pub. Docs. *Dept. of State.*) ** 350.5496¹⁻³.

Ireland's dream. 2 vols. Lyon, E. D.
823.6401-2

Irene Magillicuddy. Oliphant, L. 823.4059

Irene, the missioary. De Forest, J: W:
823.1789

Irish character, Sketches of. Hall, *Mrs.* A.. M. (F.)   823.691

Irish Charles Dickens, The. *See* MacNabb, *Mrs.* May (Laffan).

Irish fireside stories: tales and legends.
823.6145

Irish wonders. McAnally, D: R., *Jr.*
808.1908

Iron horse, The. Ballantyne, R. M.
808.1261

English Fiction. *Contin.*
Italy. *Contin.*
18TH CENTURY, A. D. *Contin.*
Politics. Foscolo, N. U. Jacque Ortis.
843.514
Brigandage.
—— De Mille, J. The American baron.
823.5844
—— Oliphant, L. The brigand's bride: a tale of southern Italy. 35 pp. (*In* Tales from Blackwood. 3d ser., v. 1.) *in* 823.7497
Manners.
—— Goldoni, C. (1707-93.) Collezioni completa delle commedie. 30 vols. 1827-29.
** 812.4-33
—— Moore, *Dr.* J: Zeluco. Various views of human nature, taken from life and manners, foreign and domestic. 2 vols. (Barbauld, *Mrs.* A. L. (A.) *The Brit. novelists,* vols. 34-5.) ** 823.2095-6
19TH CENTURY.
—— Bresciani, A. Ubaldo and Irene. 2 vols. 823.6888-9
—— Browning, *Mrs.* E.. (B.) Napoleon III. in Italy; poem. p. 309, *in* 821.33
—— Cooper, J. F. Wing-and-Wing; or, le Feu-Follet. 823.317
—— — *Same.* 823.6173
—— Jenkin, *Mrs.* C: "Who breaks—pays."
823.897
—— Wallace, *Mrs.* E. D. Strife: a romance of Germany and Italy. 823.2358
Revolution, 1848. Browning, *Mrs.* E.. (B.) Casa Guido windows, Tuscany, 1848-51; poem. p. 243, *in* 821.35
Battle of Solferino, 1859. Walmsley, H. M. Chasseur d'Afrique. 823.1670
Garibaldi, 1807-1882.
—— Browning, *Mrs.* E.. (B.)
p. 164, *in* 821.35
—— Whittier, J: G. p. 350, *in* 821.431
Note.—See Botta, C. G. G. Storia d' Italia. 1534-1789. 10 vols. 1837. 945.102-11.—**Brosch,** M. Geschichte des Kirchenstaates. (1500-1870.) 2 vols. 1880-82. 945.112-13.—**Colletta,** *Gen.* P. History of Naples. (1734-1825.) 2 vols. 945.15-15A.—**Gallenga,** A. The pope and the king. 2 vols. .1879. 945.36-7.—**Hunt,** W: History of Italy. 476-1870. (Hist. course for schools.) 1883. 945.87.—**Leo,** H. Geschichte von Italien. (568-1830.) 5 vols. (fn 4.) 1829-32. 945.83-6.—**Maurice,** C. E. Revolutionary movement of 1848-9 in Italy . . . 1887. 943.313.—**Mazade,** C: de. Life of Cavour. (1810-1861.) 923.2015.—O'Clery, K. History of the Italian revolution: 1st period (1796-1849). 1875. 945.91.—**Probyn,** J: W. Italy from fall of Napoleon I. (1815) to death of Victor Emanuel (1878). 1884. 945.73.—**Spalding,** W: Italy and the Italian islands from the earliest ages. (B. C. 510-A. D. 1840.) 3 vols. 945.28-30.—**Wrightson,** R. H. History of modern Italy. (1789-1850.) 1865. 954.116.
See also Catalogues of this Library.
No. 2, 1880, p. 120. No. 4, 1884, p. 147.
No. 3, 1882, p. 101. No. 5, 1888, p. 216.
See also Index to Consular reports. 1880-1885; 1886-1889. 2 vols. (U. S. Pub. Docs. *Dept. of State.*) ** 350.5496¹·³.
See also Poole's Index (to 1882). pp. 669-73, *in* ** 50.1;—*Same.* Jan. 1, 1882-Jan. 1, 1887. pp. 231-2, *in* ** 50.1¹.

ITALIAN LIFE, CHARACTER, ETC.
—— Amicis, E. de. Cuore: an Italian schoolboy's journal. 808.1657
—— Andersen, H. C. The improvisatore.
823.4223

English Fiction. *Contin.*
Italy. *Contin.*
ITALIAN LIFE, CHARACTER, ETC. *Contin.*
—— Björnson, B. Captain Mansana.
823.4477
—— Byron, G: G. N., *Lord.* Childe Harold's pilgrimage; poem. (4th canto.)
p. 220, *in* 821.69
—— Collins, W: W. Woman in white.
823.268
—— Comyn, L. N. Elena. (Country life.)
823.272
—— Craven, *Mme.* P. Fleurange. 823.6843
—— Dickens, C: J: H. Little Dorrit. (Partly in Italy.) 823.419
—— — *Same.* 2 vols. 823.5315-16
—— Elliot, F.. The Italians. (In Luca.)
823.526
—— Hawthorne, N. The marble faun; or, the romance of Monte Beni. 2 vols.
823.4362-3
—— — *Same.* 823.6553-4
—— Howells, W: D. A foregone conclusion.
823.829
—— La Ramée, L. de. Signa. (Village life.) 823.1827
—— — Village commune. 823.4028
—— Lytton, E: G: E. L. Bulwer- My novel. 2 vols. 823.1037-8
—— Macquoid, *Mrs.* K.. (S.) Checco: a tale of Perugia. (*With her* The little vagabond.) *in* 808.1622
—— Marks, *Mrs.* M.. A. M. (H.) Story of carnival. 823.4572
—— Maturin, E: Bianca: a tale of Erin and Italy. 823.1123
—— Meredith, G: Vittoria. 823.5586
—— Richter, J. P. F. Titan. 2 vols.
823.6810-11
—— Rogers, S: Italy; poem. 821.343
—— Ruffini, G. Lavinia. 3 vols. (in 1.)
823.7128
—— Staël-Holstein, A. L. G. (N.), *baronne.* Corinne; or, Italy. 823.4258
—— — *Same.* *in* 823.6261; 823.6297
—— Stowe, *Mrs.* H. E.. (B.) Agnes of Sorrento. 823.2038
—— Thomson, J. Liberty; poem. (pts. 1 and 3.) 821.410
—— Tincker, M.. A. Signor Monaldini's niece. 823.2000
—— Trollope, T: A. Diamond cut diamond: a story of Tuscan life. *in* 823.5073
—— Verga, G. The house of the medlartree. (Southern fishing life.) 823.7186
Artist life.
—— Serrao, T. Brushes and chisels.
823.7514
—— Vosmaer, C. The amazon. 823.4804
Musical life.
—— Dudevant, *Mme.* A. L. A. (D.) Consuelo. 823.6214
—— — *Same.* 823.6703; 823.6885
Brigandage.
—— Dudevant, *Mme.* A. L. A. (D.) Le Piccinino (in Sicily, etc.). 843.470
—— Irving, W. Italian banditti. (*In his* Tales of a traveller.) p. 313, *in* 823.844

English Fiction. *Contin.*
Italy. *Contin.*
ITALIAN LIFE, CHARACTER, ETC. *Contin.*
In poetry.
—— Longfellow, H: W. Poems of places.
  3 vols. 821.222-4
—— Miller, C. H. Songs of Italy. 821.268
—— *Same.* (*In his* Poems.) *in* 821.1314
Florence.
—— La Ramée, L. de. In a winter city.
  823.1823
—— Waller, M. E. Giotto's sheep: a cathe-
dral story. 808.1907
Padua. Antonio di Carrara. A Paduan tale.
  79 pp. (*In* Tales from Blackwood, v. 10.)
  in ** 823.6656
Rome.
—— Ainsworth, W: H. A night's adventure
in Rome. (1830.) (*With his* Auriol.)
  in 823.27
—— Crawford, F. M. Marzio's crucifix.
  823.5231
—— — Sant' Ilario. (Sequel to Saracinesca.)
  823.6548
—— — Saracinesca. 823.4970
—— Henderson, I: The prelate. (Old Catholicism, opposed to celibacy.) 823.6618
—— Stahr, *Mrs.* F. (L.) Stella. 823.5055
—— Tincker, M.. A. By the Tiber.
  823.4152
Sicily. Lytton, E: R. Bulwer- The Oread's
son; poem. (*In his* Lost tales of Miletus.)
  p. 105, *in* 821.1313
Venice. Saxon, *Mrs.* E. L. City in the sea:
stories of the deeds of the old Venetians
from the chronicles. 823.7173
Note.—For society and manners, *see* Amicis, E.
de. Military life in Italy. (19th cent.) 1882. 945.
59.—Blunt, J. J. Vestiges of ancient manners and
customs discoverable in modern Italy. 1823. 945.77.
—Carr, *Mrs.* C. North Italian folks. Sketches of
town and country life. 1878. 945.90.— Doran, J.
"Mann" and manners at the court of Florence,
1740-1786. 2 vols. 1876. 945.46-7.—Hazlitt, C. History of the Venetian republic. 4 vols. 1860. 945.
16-19.—Howells, W: D. Venetian life. 1876. 914.
102.—Jarves, J. J. Italian sights and papal princi-
ples, seen through American spectacles. 914.290.—
Moore, J. E. View of society and manners in
Italy. 2 vols. 1781. 945.88-9.—Symonds, J: A.
Sketches and studies in southern Europe. 2 vols.
1880. 940.195-6.
Ivan de Biron. Helps, *Sir* A. 823.750
Iván Ilyitch, and other stories. Tolstoi, *L.*
N. 823.5243
Ivanhoe. Scott, *Sir* W. 823.1401
—— *Same.* 823.5160; p. 345, *in* ** 823.6026
Ixion in heaven. Disraeli, B: 823.458
Jack. Daudet, A. *in* 823.2827
—— *Same.* 823.6566; 823.6845
Jack Archer. Henty, G: A. 808.1532
Jack Chaloner. Grant, J. 823.4801
Jack Hall. Grant, R. 808.1716
Jack Hinton. Lever, C: J. 823.983
Jack Horner. Tiernan, *Mrs.* M.. S. (N.)
  823.6944
Jack in the bush. Grant, R. 808.1636
Jack Manly. Grant, J. 823.631
Jack of all trades. 57 pp. Reade, C:
  in 823.6697
Jack Sheppard. Ainsworth, W: H. 823.19
Jack the fisherman. Ward, *Mrs.* E.. S. (P.)
  823.6196

English Fiction. *Contin.*
Jack, the shepherd (*pseud.*) Dicky Dawkins;
or, the bookmaker of the outer ring. 16
pp. (*In* Tales from Blackwood. 3d ser., v.
6.) p. 35, *in* 823.7502
Jack Tier. Cooper, J. F. 823.298
—— *Same.* 823.7468
Jackanapes. 26 pp. Ewing, *Mrs.* J. H. (G.)
  in 823.5090
Jackman, Abi S. Fatima: a dream of passion.
  823.6561
Jack's courtship. Russell, W: C. 823.4947
—— *Same.* *in* 823.5092
Jackson, *Gen.* Andrew. (1767-1845.)
—— Frost, J: Old Hickory. 808.1715
—— Life of A. Jackson: embracing anec-
dotes illustrative of his character. (*Young
Amer's. lib. of famous generals.*) 808.744
  Note.—See Baldwin, J. G. Andrew Jackson and
Henry Clay. (*In his* Party leaders.) 1868. p. 277,
in 923.328;—*Same.* 923.329.—Dusenbery, B. M.
Monument to the memory of J . . . preceded by a
sketch of his life. 1848. 923.316.—Godwin, P.
Jackson. (*In* Homes of Amer. statesmen.) 1854.
p. 341, *in* * 917.36.—Young, A. W. Jackson. (*In his*
Amer. statesmen.) 1858. p. 476, *in* * 973.259.
  See also Catalogues of this Library.
No. 2, 1880, p. 120. No. 4, 1884, p. 147.
No. 3, 1882, p. 101. No. 5, 1888, p. 216.
  See also Poole's Index (to 1882). pp. 674-5, *in*
** 50.1;—*Same.* (Jan. 1, 1882-Jan. 1, 1887.) p. 232, *in*
** 50.1³.
Jackson, *Mrs.* H.. Maria (Fiske). [*H. H.*]
[*Saxe Holm.*] Between whiles. 823.5264
—— Hetty's strange history. 823.1992
—— Mercy Philbrick's choice. 823.4304
—— Ramona. 823.4865
—— Saxe Holm's stories. 1st and 2d ser.
2 vols. 823.891-2
—— Zeph. A posthumous story. 823.5266
Jacob, P. W., *tr.* Hindoo tales; or, the ad-
ventures of ten princes. 823.4365
Jacob Faithful. Marryat, *Capt.* F:
  823.1098
—— *Same.* ** 823.6660
Jacobi, *Mrs.* M. (Putnam). Martyr to sci-
ence. 46 pp. (*In* Stories by Amer. authors,
v. 2.) p. 24, *in* 823.4703
Jacobins in Hungary. 2 vols. Pulszky, F. A.
  823.5732-3
Jacquerie, The. James, G: P. R. 823.866
Jacques Bonneval. Rathbone, *Mrs.* M.. A.
(M.) 823.4103
Jak, *pseud.* *See* Williams, A. B.
James, *Mrs.* Florence Alice (Price). [*Flor-
ence Warden.*]
—— At the world's mercy. *in* 823.4993
—— Deldee; or, the iron hand. *in* 823.4995
—— *Same.* *in* 823.5202
—— Doris's fortune. *in* 823.5015
—— The house on the marsh. *in* 823.5094
—— A prince of darkness. *in* 823.5103
—— A vagrant wife. 823.4988
James, G: Payne Rainsford.
—— Agincourt. ** 823.6716
—— Agnes Sorel. 823.5058
—— *Same.* 823.5059
—— Aims and obstacles. (*With his* Beau-
champ.) *in* 823.6247
—— The ancient régime: a tale. 3 vols.
  * 823.6403-5

English Fiction. *Contin.*
James, G: Payne Rainsford. *Contin.*
—— Arabella Stuart. A romance from English history. 3 vols.   * 823.6406–8
—— Attila. (*Also*) My aunt Pontypool.
     823.848
—— Same.   823.7020
—— Beauchamp; or, the error. (*Also*) The castle of Ehrenstein.—Pequinillo: a tale.— Aims and obstacles. — The fate: a tale of stirring times.—Henry Smeaton: a Jacobite story of the reign of George the First.— Margaret Graham, or, the reverses of fortune. (*And*) The last of the fairies: a Christmas tale.   823.6247
—— Bertrand de la Croix; or, the siege of Rhodes. (Picken A., *ed. The club-book.*)
     in 823.702
—— The bride of Landeck.   *in* 823.5562
—— Castelneau; or, the ancient régime.
     ** 823.6705
—— The castle of Ehrenstein . . . (*With his* Beauchamp.)   *in* 823.6247
—— The cavalier.   823.7107
—— Charles Tyrrell; or, the bitter blood. 2 vols. (in 1).   823.850
—— The convict.   823.7307
—— Corse de Leon; or, the brigand. 2 vols. (in 1).   823.853
—— Delaware; or, the ruined family.
     823.2157
'Issued also as "Thirty years since."
—— De l'Orme.   823.7388
—— Same. 2 vols.   ** 823.6248–9
—— The desultory man.   823.856
—— Eva St. Clair, and other collected tales. 3 vols. (in 1).   823.5892
—— The fate. (*With his* Beauchamp.)
     in 823.6247
—— Forest days: a romance of old times.
     823.6377
—— The gentleman of the old school. 2 vols. (in 1).   823.859
—— Gowrie; or, the king's plot.   823.861
—— Heidelberg.   823.862
—— Henry Masterton; or, the adventures of a young cavalier. 2 vols. (in 1).   823.864
—— Henry of Guise; or, the states of Blois.
     823.863
—— Henry Smeaton: a Jacobite story of the reign of George the First. (*With his* Beauchamp.)   *in* 823.6247
—— The Huguenot: a tale of the French Protestants. 2 vols. (in 1).   823.865
—— Same. 2 vols.   ** 823.6765–6
—— The jacquerie. 2 vols. (in 1).   823.866
—— John Marston Hall; or, Little Ball o' Fire.   823.4323
—— The king's highway. 2 vols. (in 1).
     823.867
—— The last of the fairies: a Christmas tale. (*With his* Beauchamp.)   *in* 823.6247
—— Leonora d'Orco.   823.7233
—— Life . . . of John Marston Hall. 2 vols. (in 1).   823.868
—— Lord Montagu's page. 3 vols.
     823.6458–60
—— The man at arms; or, Henri de Cerons.
     823.869

English Fiction. *Contin.*
James, G: Payne Rainsford. *Contin.*
—— The man in black.   823.5898
—— Margaret Graham.   823.4920
—— Same.   *in* 823.6247
—— Mary of Burgundy; or, the revolt of Ghent.   823.870
—— Morley Ernstein; or, the tenants of the heart.   823.872
—— My aunt Pontypool. (*With his* Attila.)
     in 823.848
—— Same.   823.7020
—— The Old Dominion.   823.5427
—— One in a thousand; or, the days of Henry Quatre.   823.873
—— Pequinillo: a tale. (*With his* Beauchamp.)   *in* 823.6247
—— Philip Augustus; or, the brothers in arms. 2 vols. (in 1).   823.874
—— Richelieu: a tale of France.   823.875
—— Rose d'Albret.   823.7234
—— Russell: a tale of the reign of Charles II.   823.877
—— The step-mother.   823.879
—— The string of pearls.   823.880
—— Ticonderoga; or, the black eagle.
     823.6385
—— A whim and its consequences.   823.881
—— The woodman.   823.882
James, H:, *Jr.* The American.   823.883
—— The Aspern papers. (*Also*) Louisa Pallant; (*and*) The modern warning.
     823.5780
—— The author of Beltraffio. (*Also*) Pandora.—Georgina's reasons.—The path of duty; (*and*) Four meetings.   823.4894
—— Confidence.   823.1928
—— The Europeans.   823.884
—— Four meetings. (*With his* The author of Beltraffio.)   *in* 823.4894
—— Georgina's reasons. (*With his* The author of Beltraffio.)   *in* 823.4894
—— The liar. (*With his* A London life.)
     in 823.6536
—— A light man. 47 pp. (*In* Stories by Amer. authors, v. 5.)   p. 5, *in* 823.4706
—— A London life. (*Also*) The Patagonia. —The liar; (*and*) Mrs. Temperly.
     823.6536
—— Louisa Pallant. (*With his* The Aspern papers.)   *in* 823.5780
—— Mrs. Temperly. (*With his* A London life.)   823.6536
—— The modern warning. (*With his* The Aspern papers.)   *in* 823.5780
—— Pandora. (*With his* The author of Beltraffio.)   *in* 823.4894
—— A passionate pilgrim, and other tales.
     823.885
—— The Patagonia. (*With his* A London life.)   *in* 823.6536
—— The path of duty. (*With his* The author of Beltraffio.)   *in* 823.4894
—— The Pension Beaurepas. (*With his* The siege of London.)   *in* 823.4524
—— The point of view. (*With his* The siege of London.)   *in* 823.4524
—— Portrait of a lady.   823.5251
—— Princess Casamassima.   823.5744

English Fiction. *Contin.*
James, H:, *Jr. Contin.*
—— The Reverberator. 823.5412
—— Roderick Hudson. 823.886
—— The siege of London. (*Also*) The Pension Beaurepas; (*and*) The point of view.
823.4524
—— The tragic muse. 2 vols. 823.7332-3
—— Washington square. 823.2346
—— Watch and ward. 823.887
—— *Same.* 823.5405
James, T: P. Mystery of Edwin Drood. Pt. 2. (*Prefixed*, Pt. 1, by C: Dickens.)
823.6122
James Braithwaite, the supercargo. Kingston, W: H: G. 808.1139
James Gordon's wife. (Anon.) *in* 823.5049
Same. *in* 823.5050
James Montjoy. Roe, A. S. 823.2022
James the Second. Ainsworth, W: H.
823.20
Jan Vedder's wife. Barr, *Mrs.* A. E. (H.)
823.5703
Jane Eyre. Nicholls, *Mrs.* C.. (B.) 823.126
Same. *in* 823.6261
Jane Seton. Grant, J. 823.632
Jane Sinclair. Carleton, W: 823.173
Same, and other tales. 823.5517
Jane Talbot. Brown, C: B. 823.140
Same. * 823.6204
Janet's repentance. Cross, *Mrs.* M.. A. (E.)
in 823.6687
Janson, Kristofer Nagel. Spell-bound fiddler: a Norse romance. Tr. by A. Forestier. Introd. by R. B. Anderson. 823.2020
Janvier, T: Allibone. [*Ivory Black.*] The Aztec treasure-house: a romance of contemporaneous antiquity. 823.7165
—— Pancha: a story of Monterey. 39 pp. (*In* Stories by Amer. authors, v. 10.)
p. 5, *in* 823.4711
Japan.
—— Ayrton, C. Child-life in Japan and Japanese child stories. 808.1871
—— Dickins, F. V., *tr.* Old bamboo-hewer's story: the earliest of the Japanese romances; written in the tenth century. * 823.6430
—— Greey, E: The golden lotus and other legends of Japan. 808.1128
—— — Young Americans in Japan.
808.1873
—— Griffis, W: E. Japanese fairy world.
808.1026
—— Knox, T: W. The boy travellers in the far east. Pt. 1. 808.1835
—— Longfellow, H: W. Poems of places.
p. 233, *in* 821.229
—— Maclay, A. C. Mito Yashiki: a tale of old Japan. 823.6963
—— Mitford, A. B. Tales of old Japan.
823.4245
—— — *Same.* 2 vols. 891.8-9
—— Wingfield, L. Curse of Koshiu: a chronicle of old Japan. 823.7192
17TH CENTURY. Mendès, *Mme.* J. (G.) The usurper. (1615.) 823.4785
18TH CENTURY. Tamenaga Shunsui. The loyal Ronins. 823.6083

English Fiction. *Contin.*
Japan. *Contin.*
19TH CENTURY. Shigemi, S. A Japanese boy. (A boy's life.) 808.1742
Note.—See **Bibliography.** Guissani, C. List of works, essays, etc., relating to Japan. (Asiatic Soc. of Japan. Trans. 1886. v. xiv. 87-118.) ** 952. 15[14].—**Bishop,** *Mrs.* I.. L. (B.) Unbeaten tracks in Japan. 1880. 915.332.—**Hulsh,** M. B. Japan and its art. Illus. 1889. 952.15.—**Pearson,** G: C. Flights inside and outside Paradise. 1886. 915.373.—**Rein,** J: J. The industries of Japan. 1889. 915.351;—Japan: travels and researches. 1884. 915.333.—**Stern,** S. A. Jottings of travel in China and Japan. 1888. 915. 374.—**Taylor,** B., *comp.* Japan of our day. 1887. 915.355.
See also Décennale du "Tour du monde." 1860-1870. ** 913.138[1].
For general histories, *see* **Adams,** F. O. History of Japan from the earliest period. 2 vols. 1874. 952.13-14.—**Bramsen.** W: Japanese chronological tables. (645-1873.) 952.17.
For manners and customs, *see* **Morse,** E. S. Japanese homes and their surroundings. 1886. 915. 382.—**Silver,** J. M. W. Sketches of Japanese manners and customs. 1867. 952.16.
See also **Catalogues** of this Library.
No. 2, 1880, p. 121. No. 4, 1884, p. 148.
No. 3, 1882, p. 102. No. 5, 1888, p. 217.
See also Index to **Consular reports.** 1880-1885; 1886-1889. 2 vols. (U. S. Pub. Docs. *Dept. of State.*) ** 350.5496[1·3].
See also Ency. **Brit. Index.** p. 474, *in* ** 32.295.— Index to **Harper's** monthly. p. 337, *in* ** 51.475.
See also **Poole's** Index (to 1882). pp. 677-79, *in* ** 50.1;—*Same.* Jan. 1, 1882-Jan. 1, 1887. pp. 233-34, *in* ** 50.1[2].
See also Catalogue of the gov't pubs. of the U. S. 1774-1881. ** 15.202.
Japanese boy, A. Shigemi, S. 808.1742
Japanese fairy world. Griffis, W: E.
808.1026
Japheth in search of a father. Marryat, *Capt.* F: 823.1099
Same. ** 823.6661; ** 823.6742
Jarl's daughter. Burnett, *Mrs.* F.. E. (H.)
823.5633
Jarves, James Jackson. Kiana: a tradition of Hawaii. 823.1903
Jarvis, T: Stinson. Geoffrey Hampstead.
823.7449
Jasper. Abbott, J. *in* 808.590
Jaufry the knight and the fair Brunissende. Mary-Lafon, J. B. 823.6104
Java.
—— Higginson, *Mrs.* S. J. Java, the pearl of the east. 808.1601
—— Knox, T: W. The boy travellers in the far East. Pt. 2. 808.1836
—— Nordhoff, C: Java. (*In his* Stories of the island world.) p. 87, *in* 808.165
Java, the pearl of the east. Higginson, *Mrs.* S. J. 808.1601
Jay, Harriett. *See* Buchanan, *Mrs.* H. (J.)
Jeaffreson, J: Cordy. Not dead yet.
823.5951
Jealous husband. Maillard, *Mrs.* A. M.
823.6117
Jealousy. Dudevant, *Mme.* A. L. A. (D.)
823.6849
Jean Têterol's idea. Cherbuliez, V.
823.2331
Jeanie's quiet life. Stephenson, *Mrs.* E. (T.)
823.5990
Jed. Goss, W. L. 808.1561
Jefferies, R: Wood magic: a fable. 808.1595

English Fiction. *Contin.*

Jefferson, T: (1743–1826.) Cooke, J: E. The youth of Jefferson; or, a chronicle of college scrapes at Williamsburg . . . A. D. 1764.   823.7421

Note.—See Abbott, J: S. C. Lives of the presidents. p. 97, *in* 923.259.—Baldwin, J. G. Thomas Jefferson and Alexander Hamilton. (*In his* Party leaders.) 1868. p. 17, *in* 923.328;—*Same.* 923.329. —Godwin, P. Jefferson. (*In* Homes of Amer. statesmen.) 1854. p. 79, *in* * 917.36.—Lincoln, R. W. Jefferson. (*In his* Lives of the presidents.) 1839. p. 97, *in* ** 923.1110.—Parker, T. Jefferson. (*In his* Hist. Amer.) 1878. p. 260, *in* 923.1109.— Sainte-Beuve, C. A. Jefferson. (*In his* Premiers lundis, v. 2.) p. 126, *in* 824.444.

See also in the lives of Washington, Adams, Hamilton, etc., and in Bancroft's Hist. of the United States.

See also Catalogues of this Library.
No. 2, 1880, p. 122.   No. 4, 1884, p. 149.
No. 3, 1882, p. 102.   No. 5, 1888, p. 217.

See also Poole's Index (to 1882). pp. 680–1, *in* ** 50.1;—*Same.* Jan. 1, 1882–Jan. 1, 1887. p. 234, *in* ** 50.1².

Jenifer. Cudlip, *Mrs.* A. H. (T.)   823.4999

Jenkin, *Mrs.* C. *See* Jenkin, *Mrs.* H. C. (J.)

Jenkin, *Mrs.* Henrietta Camilla (Jackson). Jupiter's daughters.   823.895

—— A Psyche of to-day.   823.4240

—— Skirmishing.   823.896

—— "Who breaks—pays." ("*Chi rompe-paga.*")   823.897

—— Within an ace.   823.898

Jenkins, E: The devil's chain.   823.899

—— Little Hodge.   823.900

—— A paladin of finance: contemporary manners.   823.4559

—— A week of passion; or, the dilemma of Mr. George Barton the younger.   823.5061

Jenner, G. A philanthropist: a tale of the vigilance committee at San Francisco. 40 pp. (*In* Tales from Blackwood. 3d ser., v. 6.)   p. 193, *in* 823.7502

Jennings, Hargrave, *ed.* One of the thirty (pieces of silver for which Jesus Christ was sold): a strange history.   823.4589

Jennings, L: J. The millionaire.
    in 823.5091

Jephson, Philippa Prittie. An April day.
    in 823.4993

Jerdan, W: The sleepless woman. (Picken, A., *ed. The club-book*, v. 1.)
    p. 198, *in* 823.702

Jericho road, The. Habberton, J: 823.679

Jerome, Jerome K., *pseud. See (in Appendix)* Arrowsmith, J. W.

Jerrold, Douglas W: Mrs. Caudle's curtain lectures.   823.2598

—— Works, v. 2.   823.4828
Contents:—Story of a feather, and Cakes and ale.

Jerry. Elliott, S.. B.   823.7533

Jerusalem. *See also* Crusades.—Jews.—Syria.

—— Eddy, D. C. Walter in Jerusalem.
    808.1647

Jess. Haggard, H: R.   823.5074

Same.   823.5075; 823.6591; 823.7156

Jessamine. Terhune, *Mrs.* M.. V. (H.)
    823.1557

Jessie Cameron. Butler, *Lady* R.   823.7319

Jessie Graham. Holmes, *Mrs.* M.. J.. (H.)
    in 823.788

English Fiction. *Contin.*

Jessie Trim. Farjeon, B: L.   823.6373

Jessop, G: H. Gerald Ffrench's friends.
    823.6574

—— Judge Lynch: a romance of the California vineyards.   823.6528

Jesus Christ in Flanders. 28 pp. Balzac, H. de.   p. 201, *in* 823.7335

Jet. Edwardes, *Mrs.* A.   823.2905

Jewel in the lotos. Tincker, M.. A.
    823.4743

Jewett, S.. Orne. Country by-ways.
    823.1864

—— A country doctor.   823.5263

—— Deephaven.   823.4071

—— The King of Folly island, and other people.   823.5261

—— A marsh island.   823.4862

—— The mate of the Daylight, and friends ashore.   823.4807

—— Old friends and new.   823.5385

—— Strangers and wayfarers.   823.7389

—— Tales of New England.   823.7175

—— A white heron, and other stories.
    823.5262

Jews, The.

—— Brooke, E. S. Son of Issachar: a romance of the days of Messias.   823.7164

—— Cædmon. Exodus and Daniel. 1888.
    821.1306

—— Church, A. J:, *and* Seeley, R. The hammer: a story of the Maccabean times.
    823.6940

—— Cooley, *Mrs.* A. (K.) Asaph.
    823.7478

—— Cooley, W: F. Emmanuel: the story of the Messiah.   823.6575

—— Cutler, *Mrs.* M.. C. Philip: a story of the first century.   823.7248

—— Delitzsch, F. José and Benjamin: a tale of Jerusalem in the time of the Herods.
    823.7124

—— Escrich, E. P. Martyr of Golgotha: a picture of oriental tradition. 2 vols.
    823.7152–3

—— Ingraham, J. H. The pillar of fire; or, Israel in bondage.   249.13

—— — Prince of the house of David. (Jerusalem under Herod.)   823.2167

—— — The throne of David . . . to the rebellion of prince Absalom. (Grandeur of Hebraic hist.)   823.7441

—— Klopstock, F. G. Der Messias; poem.
    831.40

—— Longfellow, H: W. The divine tragedy. (Death of Christ.)   851.7

—— Milton, J: Paradise regained; poem.
    821.487

—— Osborne, S: D. Spell of Ashtaroth.
    823.5215

—— Pascheles, W. Sammlung jüdischer Volksagen, etc. 1883.   296.62

—— Story, W: W. A Roman lawyer in Jerusalem; poem.   *in* 819.53

—— Wallace, L. Ben-Hur: a tale of the Christ.   823.4860

—— Ware, W: Julian; or, scenes in Judea. 2 vols.   823.1650–1

English Fiction. *Contin.*
Jews, The. *Contin.*
Wandering Jew.
—— Conway, M. D. (Legend of) the Wandering Jew.   291.33
—— Croly, G: Salathiel.   823.5558
—— —— *Same.* Enl. ed. 3 vols.   823.345-7
—— Gould, S. Baring- Curious myths of the middle ages.   p. 1, *in* 940.35
—— McHenry, *Mrs.* J. The Wandering Jew (poem).   821.561
—— Reddall, H: F: Fact, fancy and fable.
pp. 517-22, *in* ** 803.34
—— Sue, E. The Wandering Jew.   823.5014
—— —— *Same.*   823.5799
Jerusalem taken, 70 A. D.
—— Crowne, J. Destruction of Jerusalem; trag. (*Dram. works*, v. 2.)
p. 215, *in* 822.533
—— Henty, G: A. For the temple.
808.1439
—— Melville, G: J: Whyte- The gladiators.
823.4670
—— Milman, H. H. Fall of Jerusalem; drama.   p. 1, *in* 821.1327
Jews and Christians.
—— Aguilar, G. The edict: a tale of 1492. (*In her* Home scenes.)   p. 118, *in* 823.8
—— —— The vale of cedars. (Expulsion from Spain, 15th cent.)   823.10
—— Berry, E: P. Leah of Jerusalem: a story of the times of Paul.   823.6396
—— Cooper, J. F. Mercedes of Castile. (Persecution of Jews.)   823.300
—— Cross, *Mrs.* M.. A. (E.) Daniel Deronda. 2 vols. (A supposed Christian discovers himself to be a Jew.)   823.997-8
—— Harland, H: The yoke of the Thorah.
823.5198
—— Scott, *Sir* W. Ivanhoe.   823.1401
—— —— *Same.*   823.5160; *in* ** 823.6026
—— Spindler, C. Der Jude. (Worms, 1414.) 2 vols.   833.425-6
Jewish character.
—— Aguilar, G. Home scenes.   823.8
—— Auerbach, B. Poet and merchant: a picture of life from the times of Moses Mendelssohn.   823.6793
—— —— Spinoza.   823.4576
—— Church, A. J:, *and* Seeley, R. The hammer: a story of the Maccabean times.
823.6940
—— Cumberland, R: The Jew; drama.
** 822.27
—— —— *Same.*   ** 822.88; * 822.744
—— Disraeli, B: Alroy.   823.458
—— —— Coningsby.   823.459
—— —— *Same.*   *in* 823.3002
—— —— Tancred.   823.467
—— Erckmann, É., *and* Chatrian, P. A. The Polish Jew.   823.6858
—— Guenot, C. Vengeance of a Jew.
823.616
—— Harland, H: As it was written: a Jewish musician's story.   823.4914
—— Lessing, G. E. Nathan the wise; drama. (Protest against uncharitable views of the Jewish character.)   ** 832.42
—— Marlowe, C. The Jew of Malta. 822.122

English Fiction. *Contin.*
Jews, The. *Contin.*
—— Shakespeare, W: Merchant of Venice; drama.   822.270
—— —— *Same.*   822.290; 822.651; 822.807
See also Novels by K. E. Franzos.
For parody, *see* Edgeworth, M. Harrington. (*In her* Tales, etc.)   ** 823.4658.

Note.—See **Bibliography.** Fuerst, J. Bibliotheca Judaica. 3 vols. (in 2). 1863. ** 16.64-5.—Jacobs, J. The Jewish question. 1875-1884: a bibliographic hand-list. 96 pp. 1885. * 16.225.—Lippe, C. D. Bibliographisches Lexicon der gesammten jüdischen Literatur der Gegenwart. 1881. 893.5.
For ancient history, *see* Allen, J. H. Hebrew men and times from the patriarchs to the Messiah. 922.94.—Ewald, *Prof.* G. H. A. The antiquities of Israel. 1876. * 933.22;—History of Israel (viz.: vols. 1-5: to estab. of Roman supremacy; v. 6: Christ and his times; v. 7: Apostolic age.) 7 vols. (1867-71.) 1883. 933.17-21².—Hosmer, J. K. The story of the Jews; ancient, mediæval and modern. (*Story of the nations*.) 933.67.—Jewish and Christian history. 3 vols. 1882. 220.181-3.—Josephus, F. Works. 1857. 933.1;—*Same.* 933.23;—Kuenen, *Dr.* A. Prophets and prophecy in Israel. 1877. 224.12;—Religion of Israel to fall of the Jewish state. 3 vols. 1881-3. 933.57-9.—Lenormant, F., *and* Chevallier, E. The Israelites. (*In their* Man. of anc. hist., v. 1.) 1871. p. 79, *in* 930.23.—Leo of Modena The hist. of the present Jews. 1707. ** 1000.79.—Morrison, W. D. The Jews under Roman rule. 1890. (List of authorities, pp. xvii-xviii.) 933.65.—Renan, E. History of the people of Israel till the time of King David. 1888. 933.55.—Schürer, E. A history of the Jewish people in the time of Jesus Christ. 3 vols. 1855-6. 933.62-4.
For history in general, *see* Cassel, D: Manual of Jewish history and literature. 1883. 933.66.—Hosmer, J. K. The story of the Jews; ancient, mediæval and modern. (*Story of the nations*.) 1889. 933.67.—Jewish and Christian history. 3 vols. 1882. 220.181-3.—Macaulay, T: B. Civil disabilities of the Jews. (*In his* Essays, v. 2.) p. 307, *in* 824.134.—Milman, *Dr.* H: H. History of the Jews. (to 1860.) 3 vols. 1883. 933.4-6.—Palmer, *Prof.* E. H. History of the Jewish nation to the present day. 1883. 933.70.—Philipson, D: The Jew in English fiction. 1889. 296.193.—Simon, *Mrs.* B. A. The ten tribes of Israel historically identified with the aborigines of the western hemisphere. 1836. 933.71.—Wolf, S. Influence of the Jews on the progress of the world: a lecture. 46 pp. 1888. 933.61.
For religion, *see* Clarke, J. F. Ten great religions. 1878. 208.2.—Gould, S. Baring- Origin and development of religious belief. 1870. 209.27.
For manners and customs, *see* Edersheim, *Dr.* Sketches of Jewish social life. 933.23.—Fenton, J. Early Hebrew life. 1880. 933.68.
See also **Catalogues** of this Library.
No. 2, 1880, p. 123.   No. 4, 1884, p. 150.
No. 3, 1882, pp. 102, 103.   No. 5, 1888, p. 218.
See also **Poole's Index** (to 1882). pp. 689-91, *in* ** 50.1;—*Same.* Jan. 1, 1882-Jan. 1, 1887. pp. 236-7, *in* ** 50.1².
See also **M'Clintock,** *and* **Strong.** Cyclopædia, v. 4. p. 905, *in* ** 203.9.
See also Catalogue of gov't pubs. of the **United States.** "Israelites, Treatment of, in Europe." p. 1306, *in* ** 15.202.
Also, Index to **Consular reports.** 1886-1889. U. S. Pub. Docs. *Dept. of State*.) p. 83, *in* ** 350.5496².

PALESTINE.
Note.—See **Bibliography.** McClintock, *and* Strong. Cyclopædia of Biblical . . . literature, v. 7. (With authorities, pp. 580-82.) p. 551, *in* ** 203.11².—Sewall, W. H. Travels in Palestine, 1788-1884. (N. & Q. 1881-1884.) See Index. p. 98, *in* ** 52.5316.—Stapfer, E. Palestine in the time of Christ. 1886. (Bibliography, pp. 502-508.) 956.36.—Conder, C. R. Palestine. (*The world's great explorers . . .*) 915.358.—Geikie, C. The Holy Land and the Bible. 2 vols. 1888. 915.361-2.—Thomson, W: M. The land and the Book; or, Biblical illustrations drawn from the manners and customs, the scenes and scenery, of the Holy Land, southern Palestine and Jerusalem. (1880.) * 915.110².

English Fiction. *Contin.*
Jews, The. *Contin.*
PALESTINE. *Contin.*
  Note. Contin.
  See also Catalogues of this Library.
  No. 2, 1880, p. 174. No. 4, 1884, p. 214.
  No. 3, 1882, p. 141. No. 5, 1888, p. 275.
  See also Poole's Index (to 1882). pp. 960–1, *in*
** 50.1;—*Same.* Jan. 1, 1882–Jan. 1, 1887. p. 327, *in*
** 50.1².
Jews, The, of Barnow. Franzos, K. E.
                                823.4474
Jill and Jack. Dillwyn, E. A. 823.6909
Jim Skaggs of Skaggsville. Legif, L.
                                823.4357
Joan. Broughton, R.   *in* 823.3062
Joan of Arc. (1411?–1431.)
—— Calvert, G: H: The maid of Orleans: an
  historical tragedy. 1874.   822.1101
—— Schiller, J. C. F. von. Maid of Orleans;
  drama.   p. 328, *in* 832.36
—— Shakespeare, W: Henry VI.
                               ** 822.859
—— — *Same.*   ** 822.1008; 822.1026
—— — *Same.* 2 vols.   ** 822.876–7
—— Southey, R. (*Poetical works.*)
                                821.1165
  Note.—See Adams, W: H: D. The maid of Or-
  leans: and the great war of the English in France.
  1889. 923.1977.—Barthélemy de Beauregard, E.
  J. Histoire de Jeanne d'Arc. 2 vols. 1847. (Catalogue raisonné des ouvrages qui ont paru sur Jeanne
  d'Arc, pp. 457–9.) 923.2056–7.—Bibliography. Boston Pub. Lib., *Bulletin* No. 34. p. 363, *in* ** 17.134.
  —Bray, *Mrs.* A.. E. (K.) Joan of Arc and the
  times of Charles the Seventh, King of France.
  1874. 923.1988.—Delepierre, O. Jeanne d'Arc.
  (1430.) 11 pp. (*In his* Hist. difficulties . . .) 1868.
  p. 105, *in* 904.27.—De Quincey, T: Joan of Arc.
  43 pp. (*In his* Misc. essays.) p. 81, *in* 829.84.—
  Lamartine, A. M. L: de P. de. Joan of Arc.
  69 pp. (*In his* Memoirs of celebrated characters.) p. 49, *in* 920.371.—Parr, H. Life and death
  of Jeanne d'Arc. 2 vols. 1866. 923.2053–4.—Stanhope, P. H. Joan of Arc. (*In his* Hist. essays.) p.
  1, *in* 904.24.
  See also Poole's Index (to 1882). p. 692, *in* ** 50.1;
  —*Same.* Jan. 1, 1882–Jan. 1, 1887. p. 237, *in* 50.1².
  See also Ency. Brit. Index. p. 479, *in* ** 32.295.
  See also under France, Charles VII., p. 89.
Joan the maid. Charles, *Mrs.* E.. (R.)
                                823.209
Joan Wentworth. Macquoid, *Mrs.* K.. S.
                                823.5628
Joe Bently naval cadet. Clark, H. H.
                                823.7035
Johannes Olaf. Wille, E.. de. 823.4088
John, Eugenie. [*E. Marlitt.*] At the coun-
  cillor's; or, a nameless history. Tr. by
  Mrs. A. L. Wister.   823.2775
  Issued also as In the counselor's house.
—— The bailiff's maid: a romance. Tr. by
  Mrs. A. L. Wister.   823.4060
—— Countess Gisela. Tr. by Mrs. A. L.
  Wister.   823.2654
—— Gold Elsie. Tr. by Mrs. A. L. Wister.
                                823.6601
—— In the counselor's house. *in* 823.6693
—— In the Schillingscourt. Tr. by Mrs. A.
  L. Wister.   823.2023
—— *Same.*   823.2444
—— The little moorland princess. Tr. by
  Mrs. A. L. Wister.   823.3052
—— Old mam'selle's secret. Tr. by Mrs. A.
  L. Wister.   823.5781
—— The second wife. Tr. by Mrs. A. L.
  Wister.   823.2455

English Fiction. *Contin.*
John, Eugenie. [*E. Marlitt.*] *Contin.*
—— The twelve 'apostles. (Zimmern, H..,
  and A. *Half-hours with for. nov.*, v. 2.)
                          in ** 823.6614
John. Oliphant, *Mrs.* M. O. (W.) 823.1200
  Same.   *in* 823.5109
John Andross. Davis, *Mrs.* R.. B. (H.)
                                823.361
John Bodewin's testimony. Foote, *Mrs.* M..
  (H.)   823.4896
John Brent. Winthrop, T.   823.1725
John Charáxes. Boylston, P: 823.7032
John Deane. Kingston, W: H: G. 808.1577
John Dorrien. Kavanagh, J.   823.915
John Eax. Tourgée, A. W.   823.4303
John Godfrey's fortunes. Taylor, B.
                                823.1545
John Halifax, Gentleman. Craik, *Mrs.* D.
  M. (M.)   823.331
John Halsey, the anti-monopolist. Collins,
  R. U.   823.4827
  Note.—Based on John H. Burke's "bonanza suits."
John Holdsworth, chief mate. Russell, W: C.
                          in 823.5128
John Inglesant. Shorthouse, 'J. H:
                                823.4531
John Jerome. Ingelow, J.   823.5613
John Law. Ainsworth, W: H.   823.5602
John Marchmont's legacy. Maxwell, *Mrs.*
  M.. E.. (B.)   *in* 823.2400
  Same.   *in* 823.5045
John Marston Hall. James, G: P. R.
                                823.868
  Same.   823.4323
John Milton and his times. Ring, M.
                                823.5964
John Nicholson, The misadventures of.
  Stevenson, R. L: 823.5776
John Parmelee's curse. Hawthorne, J. C.
                                823.6787
John Rintoul; or, the fragment of a wreck.
  (*In* Tales from Blackwood, v. 11.)
                          in ** 823.6657
John Thompson, and other stories. Parr,
  Mrs. L.. (T.)   823.1233
John True. Abbott, J.   808.585
John Ward, preacher. Deland, *Mrs.* M. W.
  (C.)   823.5278
John Winter. Mayo, *Mrs.* I.. (F.) 823.5753
John Worthington's name. Benedict, F. L.
                                823.5833
Johnny Darbyshire, a primitive Quaker.
  Howitt, W: *in* * 823.6194
Johnson, *Col.* —. The white fawn: a North
  American story. (*In* Standard tales, etc.,
  ed. by Mrs. C. I. Johnston.) *in* * 823.5194
—— *Same.* 10 pp. (Tieck, L. *The elves*
  . . .) 1864.   p. 127, *in* 823.6328
Johnson, Edwin Rossiter. *See* Johnson, R.
Johnson, *Mrs.* H.. (Kendrick). Raleigh West-
  gate; or, Epimenides in Maine: a romance.
                                823.5502
Johnson, Rossiter, *ed.* Little classics. 18 vols.
                                829.124–141
  Contents:—Vol. I. Exile: Ethan Brand, by N.
  Hawthorne; The swans of Lir, by G. Griffin; A night
  in a workhouse, by J. Greenwood; The outcasts of
  Poker Flat, by F. B. Harte; The man without a
  country, by E: E. Hale; Flight of a Tartar tribe, by
  T: De Quincey.   829.124

English Fiction. *Contin.*
Johnson, Rossiter, *ed.* Little classics. *Contin.*
Contents. Contin.

Vol. II. **Intellect:** The house and the brain, by E:
G: E. L. Bulwer-Lytton; D'outre mort, by Mrs. H.
E..(P.) Spofford; The fall of the house of Usher, by E.
A. Poe; Chops, the dwarf, by C: J: H. Dickens; Wake-
field, by N. Hawthorne; Murder considered as one
of the fine arts, by T: De Quincey; The captain's
story, by Mrs. R.. H. Davis.   829.125
Vol. III. **Tragedy:** The murders in the Rue
Morgue, by E. A. Poe; The Lawson tragedy, by J:
W: De Forest; The iron shroud, by W: Mudford;
The bell-tower, by H. Melville; The Kathayan slave,
by Mrs. E. (C.) Judson; The story of La Roche, by
H: Mackenzie; The vision of sudden death, by T:
De Quincey.   829.126
Vol. IV. **Life:** Rab and his friends, by J: Brown,
M. D.; A romance of real life, by W: D. Howells;
The Luck of Roaring camp, by F. B. Harte; Jerry
Jarvis's wig, by R: H. Barham; Beauty and the
beast, by N. P. Willis; David Swan, by N. Haw-
thorne; Dreamthorp, by A. Smith; A bachelor's
revery, by D. G. Mitchell; The grammar of life, by
B: F. Taylor; My châteaux, by G:W: Curtis; Dream-
children, by C: Lamb; The man in the reservoir, by
C: F. Hoffman; Westminster abbey, by J. Addison;
The puritans, by T: B. Macaulay; Gettysburg, by A.
Lincoln.   829.127
Vol. V. **Laughter:** A Christmas carol, by C: J:
H. Dickens; The haunted crust, by Mrs. K.. (S.)
Cooper; A dissertation upon roast pig, by C: Lamb;
The total depravity of inanimate things, by Mrs.
E. A. Walker; The skeleton in the closet, by E: E.
Hale; Sandy Wood's sepulchre, by H. Miller; A visit
to the asylum for aged and decayed punsters, by O.
W. Holmes; Mr. Tibbot O'Leary, the curious, by G.
Griffin; Neal Malone, by W: Carleton.   829.128
Vol. VI. **Love:** Love and skates, by T. Win-
throp; The maid of Malines, by E: G: E. L. Bulwer-
Lytton; The story of Ruth, from the Bible; The rise
of Iskander, by B: Disraeli.   829.129
Vol. VII. **Romance:** Iris, by O. W. Holmes; The
Rosicrucian, by Mrs. D. M. (M.) Craik; The South
Breaker, by Mrs. H. E..(P.) Spofford; The snow-
storm, by J: Wilson; The king of the peak, by A.
Cunningham.   829.130
Vol. VIII. **Mystery:** The ghost, by W: D. O'Con-
nor; The four-fifteen express, by A. B. Edwards;
The signal-man, by C: J: H. Dickens; The haunted
ships, by A. Cunningham; A raft that no man made,
by R. T. S. Lowell; The invisible princess, by F.
O'Connor; The advocate's wedding-day, by Mrs. C.
(S.) Crowe; The birthmark, by N. Hawthorne.
                829.131
Vol. IX. **Comedy:** Barny O'Reirdon, the naviga-
tor, by S: Lover; Haddad-Ben-Ahab, the traveller,
by J: Galt; Bluebeard's ghost, by W: M. Thackeray;
The picnic party, by H. Smith; Father Tom and
the pope, by S: Ferguson; Johnny Darbyshire, by
W: Howitt; The gridiron, by S: Lover; The box
tunnel, by C: Reade.   829.132
Vol. X. **Childhood:** A dog of Flanders, by L. de
La Ramée; The king of the golden river, by J: Rus-
kin; The lady of Shalott, by Mrs. E. S. (P.) Ward;
Majorie Fleming, by J: Brown, M. D.; Little Jakey,
by Mrs. S.. H.. (A.) De Kroyft; The lost child, by H:
Kingsley; Goody gracious! and the forget-me-not,
by J: Neal; A faded leaf of history, by Mrs. R..(H.)
Davis; A child's dream of a star, by C: J: H. Dickens.
                829.133
Vol. XI. **Heroism:** Little Briggs and I, by F. H.
Ludlow; Ray, by Mrs. H. E..(P.) Spofford; Three No-
vember days, by B: F. Taylor; The forty-seven
Rônins, by A. B. Mitford; A chance child, by Mrs.
I.. (F.) Mayo; A leaf in the storm, by L. de La Ra-
mée.   829.134
Vol. XII. **Fortune:** The gold-bug, by E. A. Poe;
The fairy-finder, by S: Lover; Murad, the unlucky,
by M. Edgeworth; The children of the public, by
E: E. Hale; The rival dreamers, by J: Banim; The
threefold destiny, by N. Hawthorne.   829.135
Vol. XIII. **Poems narrative:** The deserted vil-
lage, by O. Goldsmith; The ancient mariner, by S:
T. Coleridge; The prisoner of Chillon, by Lord Byron;
Bingen on the Rhine, by C. Norton; O'Connor's child,
by T. Campbell; The culprit fay, by J. R. Drake;
The sensitive plant, by P. B. Shelley; The eve of St.
Agnes, by J: Keats; Paradise and the peri, by T:
Moore; The raven, by E. A. Poe; The skeleton in
armor, by H: W. Longfellow; The haunted house,
by T: Hood; The writing on the image, by W:

English Fiction. *Contin.*
Johnson, Rossiter, *ed.* Little classics. *Contin.*
Contents. Contin.

Morris; Tam O'Shanter, by R. Burns; The forging
of the anchor, by S: Furguson; Morte d'Arthur, by
A. Tennyson; Horatius, by T: B. Macaulay. 829.136
Vol. XIV. **Poems lyrical. XV. Minor poems.**
XVI. **Authors.** Biographical sketches of the
authors represented in the series. With a general
index.   829.137-9
Vol. XVII. **Nature:** A-hunting of the deer, by
C: D. Warner; Dogs, by P. G. Hamerton; In the
hemlocks, by J: Burroughs; A winter walk, by H.
D: Thoreau; Buds and birds voices, by N. Haw-
thorne; The fens, by C: Kingsley; Ascent of the
Matterhorn, by E: Whymper; Ascent of Mt. Tyn-
dall, by C. King; The firmament, by J: Ruskin.
                829.140
Vol. XVIII. **Humanity:** Chumming with a sav-
age, by C: W. Stoddard; Doctor Marigold, by C: J: H.
Dickens; A brace of boys, by F. H. Ludlow; George
the Third, by W:M. Thackeray; Jullet, by Mrs. A. B.
(M.) Jameson; Is life worth living? by W: H. Mal-
lock.   829.141
Johnson, S: History of Rasselas, prince of
Abyssinia.   823.903
—— *Same.*   823.4964
—— *Same.* (Barbauld, *Mrs.* A. L. (A.), *ed.*
The British novelists, v. 26.) ** 823.2087
—— *Same.* (*In* Classic tales.)
                p. 5, *in* 823.4489
Johnson, Virginia Wales. The Catskill fairies.
                808.636
—— The Fainalls of Tipton.   823.4784
—— A foreign marriage; or, buying a title.
                823.6040
—— The image of San Donato. 35 pp. (*In*
Stories by Amer. authors, v. 7.)
                p. 145, *in* 823.4708
Johnston, C: Chrysal; or, the adventures of
a guinea. By an adept. 4 vols. (in 2).
                823.7364-5
Same. 4 vols.   ** 823.4518-21
Johnston, R: Malcolm. Mr. Absalom Bil-
lingslea, and other Georgian folk.
                823.5267
—— Ogeechee cross-firings.   823.6558
—— Widow Guthrie.   823.7390
Johnstone, *Mrs.* Christian Isobel. Experi-
ences of Richard Taylor, Esq. (*viz.:*
Young Mrs. Roberts' three Christmas din-
ners;—Mary Anne's hair: a London love
story;—Governor Fox;—Little Fanny
Bethel;—Frankland the barrister.) (*In*
her Standard tales, etc.)   * 823.6194
—— Mrs. Mark Luke; or, West country ex-
clusives. (*In her* Standard tales, etc.)
                in * 823.6194
—— The Sabbath night's supper. 12 pp.
(Tieck, L. The elves . . .) 1864.
                p. 12, *in* 823.6328
——, *ed.* Standard tales by standard authors.
                * 823.6194
Contents:—Crowe, Mrs. C. (S.) Story of Martha
Guinnis and her son.—Fraser, Mrs. —. The cous-
ins.—Gore, Mrs. C. G. F.. (M.) Maid of honour.—
Howitt, W: Johnny Darbyshire, a primitive Quak-
er.—Johnson, Col. —. White fawn.—Johnstone,
Mrs. C. I. Experiences of Richard Taylor, Esq.;—
Mrs. Mark Luke;—Sabbath night's supper.—Lau-
der, Sir T: D. Story of Farquharson of Inverey.—
Mitford, M.. R. Freshwater fisherman.—Nicander,
K: A. The renounced treasure. Tr. by W: Howitt.
—Quillinan, E: Rangers of Connaught.—Tieck, L.
The elves.—Tytler, M. Fraser- The deformed.
Jókai, Mór. (*Germ.* Maurus.) A modern
Midas. Tr. by Mrs. L. C. Bullard and E.
Herzog.   823.4927

English Fiction. *Contin.*
Jókai, Mór. (*Germ.* Maurus.) *Contin.*
—— The plague. (Zimmern, H.., *and* A. Half-hours with for. nov., v. 1.)
in 823.6613
Jolly good times. Smith, *Mrs.* M.. P. (W.)
808.1004
Jonathan. Liddell, *Mrs.* C. C. (F.-T.)
823.1644
Jones, C: H: Davault's mills. 823.904
Jones, Ethel, *pseud.* *See* Wharton, T:
Jones, J: B. The rival belles; or, life in Washington. 823.905
Issued also as Spanglers and tinglers.
—— Wild western scenes: a narrative of adventures in the western wilderness wherein the exploits of Daniel Boone . . . are particularly described. 823.906
Jones, *Rear-Admiral* J: Paul. Abbott, J: S. C. Life and adventures of J. 808.546
Joost Avelingh. Maartens, M. 823.7448
José and Benjamin. Delitzsch, F. 823.7124
Joseph and his friend. Taylor, B. 823.1546
Joseph Andrews, Adventures of. Fielding, H: 823.557
Same. in ** 823.2079; 823.6149; 823.7070
Joseph Balsamo. Dumas, A. D. 823.5903
Joseph in the snow. Auerbach, B. 823.4347
Joseph II., and his court. Mundt, *Mrs.* C. (M.) 823.6301
Joseph's coat. Murray, D: C. 823.4319
Joshua. Ebers, G. M. 823.6998
Joshua Haggard's daughter. Maxwell, *Mrs.* M.. E.. (B.) 823.2412
Same. in 823.5130; 823.6078
Joshua Marvel. Farjeon, B: L. 823.5860
Journey from this world to the next. Fielding, H: p. 189, in 823.6152
Journey to the centre of the earth, A. Verne, J. 823.6160
Journey to the world underground, A. Holberg, L., *Baron* v. ** 823.6778
Same. 823.7384
Joy after sorrow. Riddell, *Mrs.* C.. E. L. (C.) 823.1328
Joyce. Oliphant, *Mrs.* M. O. (W.) 823.5914
Joyce Morrell's harvest. Holt, E. S.. 823.7103
Judd, Sylvester. Margaret: a tale of the real and the ideal. 823.907
—— Richard Edney and the governor's family. 823.2340
Judge Justin. Abbott, J. 808.590
Judge Lynch. Jessop, G: H. 823.6528
Judith. Terhune, *Mrs.* M.. V. (H.) 823.4698
Judith Shakespeare. Black, W: 823.5535
Judson, *Mrs.* Emily (Chubbuck). [*Fanny Forester.*] Alderbrook: a collection of Fanny Forester's village sketches, poems, etc. 2 vols. (in 1). 823.908
—— The Kathayan slave. 16 pp. (Johnson, R., *ed.* *Little classics,* v. 3.)
p. 149, in 829.126
Julia and her Romeo. 62 pp. Murray, D: C. in 823.5131
Julia de Roubigné. Mackenzie, H: p. 115, in ** 823.2090

English Fiction. *Contin.*
Julian. 2 vols. Ware, W: 823.1650–1
Julius Courtney. Cobban, J. M. 823.7246
Juncker, F. *See* Schmieden, *Mrs.* E. (J.)
June. Bridges, *Mrs.* Col. —. in 823.4986
Same. in 823.5021
Jupiter's daughters. Jenkin, *Mrs.* H. C. (J.)
823.895
Just as I am. Maxwell, *Mrs.* M.. E.. (B.) in 823.2417
Same. in 823.5112
Just sixteen. Woolsey, S.. C. 808.1534
Justin Harley. Cooke, J: E. 823.276
Kalani of Oahu. Newell, C: M. 823.6132
Kaloolah. Mayo, W.: S. 823.1144
Kangaroo hunters, The. Bowman, A. 808.892
Karma. Sinnett, A. P. 823.4937
Kate Beaumont. De Forest, J: W: 823.5855
Kate Clarendon. Bennett, E. 823.72
Kate Coventry. Melville, G: J: Whyte- ** 823.4669
Same. 823.7279
Kate Danton. Fleming, *Mrs.* M. A. (E.) 823.575
Katerfelto. Melville, G: J: Whyte- 823.1152
Same. ** 823.4661; 823.7280
Katharine Walton. Simms, W: G. 823.1433
Katherine Regina. Besant, W. 823.6603
Kathleen. Burnett, *Mrs.* F.. E. (H.) 823.5631
Kathleen mavourneen. Mulholland, C. 823.7178
Katia. Tolstoï, *Count* L. N. 823.5240
Katy of Catoctin. Townsend, G: A. 823.7446
Kauffmann, Maria Angelica (Mrs. A. K. Zucchi.) 1741–1807.
—— Ritchie, *Mrs.* A. I.. (T.) Miss Angel. 823.5986
Note.—*See* Nouvelle biographie générale. p. 479, in ** 920.270.
See also Poole's Index (to 1882). p. 703, in ** 50.1; —*Same.* Jan. 1, 1882–Jan. 1, 1887. p. 241, in ** 50.1².
Kavanagh, Julia. Adèle: a tale. 823.909
—— Beatrice. 3 vols. (in 1). 823.910
—— Bessie. 823.5924
—— Daisy Burns: a tale. 823.912
—— Grace Lee. 823.914
—— John Dorrien. 823.915
—— Madeleine: a tale of Auvergne, founded on fact. 823.916
—— *Same.* 823.6592
—— Nathalie: a tale. 823.917
—— Queen Mab. 3 vols. (in 1). 823.918
—— Rachel Gray: a tale founded on fact. 823.919
—— Seven years, and other tales. 3 vols. (in 1). 823.920
—— Silvia. 823.5920
—— Sybil's second love. 3 vols. (in 1). 823.921
—— Two lilies. 823.5745
Kavanagh. Longfellow, H: W. 823.1010
Keary, Annie. Castle Daly: the story of an Irish home thirty years ago. 823.922
—— A York and a Lancaster rose. 808.1489

English Fiction. *Contin.*
Keary, Eliza. The Magic Valley; or, patient Antoine. 808.1544
Keddie, Henrietta. [*S.. Tytler.*] Citoyenne Jacqueline; a woman's lot in the French revolution. 823.923
—— Days of yore. 2 vols. 823.924-5
—— Duchess Frances. 2 vols. 823.7226-7
—— A garden of women. 823.1783
—— *Same.* 823.4239
—— Girl neighbours; or, the old fashion and the new. 823.5474
—— Her gentle deeds. *in* 823.4999
—— The Huguenot family. 823.4098
—— Papers for thoughtful girls, with sketches of some girls' lives. 808.325
—— Phemie Millar. 3 vols. (in 2). 823.7312-13
Keeler, Ralph. Gloverson and his silent partners. 823.926
Keeling, Elsa d'Esterre- Three sisters; or, sketches of a highly original family. *in* 823.5060
Keena Karmody. Kerr, E. 823.7189
Keenan, H: Francis. The money-makers: a social parable. 823.4856
Keepsake stories. Scott, *Sir* W. *in* 823.7473
Keller, Gottfried. 1819—. Clothes make men. (*Also*) The funeral. (Zimmern, H.., *and* A. Half-hours with for. nov., v. 2.) *in* ** 823.6614
Kellys and the O'Kellys. Trollope, A. 823.1612
Kelp-gatherers, The. Trowbridge, J: T. 808.1728
Kendall, May. 'Such is life.' 823.7262
Kenelm Chillingly. Lytton, E: G: E. L. Bulwer- 823.1032
Kenilworth. Scott, *Sir* W. 2 vols. (in 1). 823.1402
Same. 823.5155; ** 823.6028
Kennedy, J: Pendleton. [*Solomon Secondthoughts, schoolmaster.*] Horse-shoe Robinson: a tale of the Tory ascendency. 823.927
—— Quodlibet: containing some annals thereof, with an authentic account of the origin . . . of the borough, and the sayings and doings of sundry of the townspeople: interspersed with sketches of the most remarkable. . . . characters of that place. By Solomon Secondthoughts, schoolmaster. 3d ed. 823.930
—— Rob of the bowl: a legend of St. Inigoe's. 823.928
—— *Same.* 2 vols. ** 823.6630-1
—— Swallow Barn; or, a sojourn in the Old Dominion. 823.929
Kennedy, Patrick. Legendary fictions of the Irish Celts. 823.2115
Kent, W. C: The vision of Cagliostro: a tale of the five senses. 42 pp. (*In* Tales from Blackwood, v. 10.) *in* ** 823.6656
Kentuckian in New York. Neal, J: 2 vols. ** 823.6239-40
Kentucky colonel, A. Read, O. P. 823.6465

English Fiction. *Contin.*
Kentucky's love. King, E: 823.948
Ker, D: Into unknown seas; or, the cruise of two sailor-boys. 808.1360
—— The lost city; or, the boy explorers in central Asia. 808.1361
Kerr, Eliza. Keena Karmody. (*Also*) Mervyn's meed. 823.7189
Key to the Waverley novels. Grey, H: ** 823.6776
Keyser, Arthur. An exile's romance; or, realities of Australian life. 823.7391
Kiana. Jarves, J. J. 823.1903
Kibboo Ganey. Gilman, J: B. 808.1537
Kidd, *Captain* W: Abbott, J: S. C. Captain William Kidd, and others of the pirates . . . who ravaged the seas . . . two hundred years ago. (*Amer. pioneers* . . .) 808.540
Kidnapped. Stevenson, R. L: *in* 823.5051
Same. *in* 823.5067; 823.7442
Kielland, Alexander L. Siesta. Tr. from the German version of M. von Borch by C: F. McClumpha. 20 pp. (*In* Mod. ghosts.) p. 59, *in* 823.7349
Kildhurm's oak. Hawthorne, J. C. 823.7383
Kilmeny. Black, W: 823.83
Kimball, R: Burleigh. Henry Powers (banker): how he achieved a fortune, and married. 823.4097
—— Romance of student life abroad. 823.5734
King, *Capt.* C: Between the lines. 823.6544
—— The colonel's daughter; or, winning his spurs. 823.7392
—— Marion's faith; a sequel to "The colonel's daughter." 823.4967
—— Starlight ranch and other stories of army life on the frontier. 823.7176
King, Clarence. Democracy: an American novel. 823.4577
King, E: The gentle savage. 823.4547
—— Kentucky's love; or, roughing it around Paris. 823.948
King, K.. Ethel Mildmay's follies. 823.5090
King, R: Ashe. [*Basil.*] A coquette's conquest. *in* 823.5062
—— A drawn game. 823.4833
—— *Same.* *in* 823.5062
—— Passion's slave. 823.7050
—— "The wearing of the green." 823.4825
—— *Same.* *in* 823.5109
King and not a king, A. Rice, M. S. 808.1724
King and viking. Smyth, P. G. 823.7305
King Arthur. Craik, *Mrs.* D. M. (M.) *in* 823.4978
Same. *in* 823.4984; 823.5056; 823.5389
King Arthur, History of. 3 vols. Malory, *Sir* T:, *comp.* * 823.6615-17
King Capital. Sime, W: 823.4503
King of Folly island, and other people. Jewett, S.. O. 823.5261
King of No-land. Farjeon, B: L. 823.5861
Same. *in* 823.6125
King of the conjurors. Borlase, J. S. 823.111

English Fiction. *Contin.*
King of the mountains. ' About, E. F. V.
823.6976
King Solomon's mines. Haggard, H: R.
in 823.5071
Same. *in* 823.6591; *in* 823.6606; 823.7157
King Solomon's wives. Lang, A., *and* Latimer, D. (?) 823.5019
King Veric. 12 pp. Tupper, M. F.
p. 239, *in* 823.1443
Kingdom of coins. Gilman, J: B. 808.1805
King's daughters, The. Holt, E. S..
808.1526
King's highway, The. James, G: P. R.
823.867
King's men, The. Grant, R., *and others.*
823.4786
King's Own, The. Marryat, *Capt.* F:
823.1100
Same. 823.2916; ** 823.6662
King's Own Borderers, The. Grant, J.
823.633
King's servants, The. Smith, H. 823.1459
King's treasure house, The. Walloth, W.
823.6986
Kingsbury, Alice. *See* Cooley, *Mrs.* A. (K.)
Kingsford, J.., *pseud. See* Barnard, C:
Kingsley, C: (1819–1875.) Alton Locke, tailor and poet: an autobiography. With a prefatory memoir by T: Hughes. 823.931
—— At last: a Christmas in the West Indies.
823.5746
—— Hereward the Wake, "Last of the English." 823.932
—— *Same.* 823.6422
—— Heroes; or, Greek fairy tales for my children. 808.550
Contents:—Perseus.—The Argonauts.—Theseus.
—— *Same.* 808.1006
—— Hypatia; or, new foes with an old face.
823.933
—— Madam How and Lady Why; or, first lessons in earth lore for children. 808.933
—— Two years ago. 823.934
—— The water-babies: a fairy tale for a land-baby. *in* 823.5094
—— Westward ho! or, the voyages and adventures of Sir Amyas Leigh . . . in the reign of . . . Queen Elizabeth. 823.935
—— Yeast: a problem. 823.936
Note.—For his life and writings, *see* **Bayne,** P.
Kingsley. 42 pp. (*In his* Essays in biog. and crit.)
p. 9, 824.186.—**Greg,** W. R. Kingsley and Carlyle.
31 pp. (*In his* Lit. and social judgments.) p. 115,
in 824.153.—**Harris,** A.B. Little biographies. (1887.)
p. 93, *in* 928.692.—**Kingsley,** C: His letters and
memories of his life. 1890. 928.709.—**Miller,** F:
M. Kingsley. 21 pp. (*In his* Biog. essays.) p. 258.
in 928.621.
See also **Poole's** Index (to 1882). pp. 708–9, *in* **
50.1;—*Same.* Jan. 1, 1882–Jan. 1, 1887. p. 243, *in* **
50.1².
Kingsley, H: Austin Elliot. 823.937
—— Geoffry Hamlyn, Recollections of.
823.944
—— The Harveys. 823.939
—— Hetty. 823.6374
—— *Same,* and other stories. 823.940
—— Hillyars and the Burtons: a story of two families. 823.941
—— Hornby mills, and other stories.
823.2040

English Fiction. *Contin.*
Kingsley, H: *Contin.*
—— Leighton Court: a country house story.
823.942
—— The lost child. 8 pp. (Johnson, R., *ed.
Little classics,* v. 10.) p. 174, *in* 829.133
—— Old Margaret. 823.2032
—— Ravenshoe. 823.943
—— The recollections of Geoffry Hamlyn.
823.944
—— Silcote of Silcotes. 823.2033
—— Stretton. 823.945
—— *Same.* 823.5935
—— Valentin : a French boy's story of Sedan. 823.946
Kingsley, Maurice. The Puerto de Medina.
37 pp. (*In* Tales from Blackwood. 3d ser.,
v. 2.) p. 117, *in* 823.7498
Kingston, W: H: Giles. Adventures of Dick Onslow among the redskins. 808.1554
—— Count Ulrich: a tale of the reformation in Germany. 823.5782
—— The cruise of the "Dainty;", or, rovings in the Pacific. 808.890
—— From powder monkey to admiral: a story of naval adventure. 808.1033
—— Hurricane Hurry; or, the adventures of a naval officer afloat and ashore. 808.1613
—— In the eastern seas. 808.350
—— In the Rocky mountains. 808.362
—— James Braithwaite, the supercargo.
808.1139
—— John Deane: historic adventures by land and sea. 808.1577
—— Mark Seaworth: a tale of the Indian ocean. 808.874
—— The missing ship; or, notes from the log of the "Ouzel" galley. 808.358
Issued also as Ouzel galley; or, notes from an old sea log.
—— My first voyage to the southern seas.
808.351
—— Old Jack: a tale for boys. 808.355
—— On the banks of the Amazon. 808.364
—— Paddy Finn; or, the adventures of a midshipman. 808.1614
—— Peter Trawl; or, the adventures of a whaler. 808.1014
—— Roger Willoughby; or, the times of Benbow: a tale of the sea and land. 808.1578
—— Round the world. 808.346
—— Saved from the sea; or, the loss of the "Viper" and the adventures of her crew in the great Sahara. 808.349
—— Schoolboy days; or, Ernest Bracebridge.
808.1543
—— The seven champions of Christendom; compiled from the most ancient chronicles . . . 808.617
—— Snow-shoes and canoes; or, the early days of a fur-trader in the Hudson's Bay territory. 808.1590
—— The south sea whaler; . . . loss of the "Champion" and the adventures of her crew. 808.352
—— Stories of the sagacity of animals. The horse and other animals. 808.1445
—— Three hundred years ago; or, the martyr of Brentwood. 808.1615

English Fiction. *Contin.*
Knox, T: Wallace. *Contin.*
—— The boy travellers in the Russian empire. 808.1844
—— The boy travellers on the Congo. 808.1843
—— Hunting adventures on land and sea. 2 pts. 808.1846-7
Pt. 1: The young Nimrods in North America.
Pt. 2: The young Nimrods around the world.
—— Voyage of the "Vivian" to the north pole and beyond. Adventures . . . in the open polar sea. 808.1845
Kompert, Leopold. The silent woman. Tr. by C: F. McClumpha. 36 pp. (*In* Mod. ghosts.) p. 189, *in* 823.7349
Kongo river. *See also* Africa, *note.*
Kophetua the Thirteenth. Corbett, J. 823.6910
Korea. Allen, H. N., *tr.* Korean tales: being a collection of stories translated from the Korean folk-lore. 823.6535
Note.—*See* Griffis, W. E. Corea, the hermit nation. (Bibliography, pp. xi-xvii.) * 951.28.—
Carles, W. R. Life in Corea. 1888. 915.343.—
Griffis, W: E. Corea, without and within. 1885.
915.322.—Lowell, P. Chosön: the land of the morning calm. 1888. 915.342.—Oppert, E. A forbidden land: voyages to the Corea. 1880. 915.45.—
Treaties with Great Britain, 1883; Japan, 1876; United States, 1883. (*See* Chronicle & directory for China . . . , for 1886.) *in* ** 910t.75ᴴᵈ.
See also "Corea" *in* Index to Consular reports. 1880-1885; 1886-1889. 2 vols. (U. S. Pub. Docs. *Dept. of State.*) ** 350.5496ⁱ⁻³.
See also "Corea" *in* Poole's Index (to 1882). pp. 301-2, *in* ** 50.1;—*Same.* Jan. 1, 1882-Jan. 1, 1887. p. 103, *in* ** 50.1³.
Korean tales. Allen, H. N., *tr.* 823.6535
Kouns, Nathan Chapman. Arius the Libyan: a romance of the primitive church. 823.7239
Kraszewski, Joseph Ignatius. 1812—. The foundling. (Zimmern, H.., *and* A. *Half-hours with for. novelists,* v. 2.) *in* ** 823.6614
Krypow, *Dr.* —. Leka; or, reminiscences of a physician. 16 pp. Tr. by Mrs. F.. C. Henderson. (Henderson, *Mrs.* F.. C. *Dunderviksborg* . . .) 1881. p. 355, *in* 823.6534
Kyng Alisaunder. 2 pts. Weber, H: W: p. 1, *in* * 821.1239
Labadye, Albert de. The baron of Hertz: a tale of the Anabaptists. 823.6868
Laboulaye, Édouard René Lefèbvre.
—— Abdallah; or, the four-leaved shamrock. Tr. by M.. L. Booth. 823.4100
—— Fairy tales of all nations. Tr. by M.. L. Booth. 808.672
—— Last fairy tales. Tr. by M.. L. Booth. 808.1312
—— Paris in America. Tr. by M.. L. Booth. 823.6870
Labour stands on golden feet. Zschokke, J. H. D. 823.6833
Lace. Lindau, P. 823.7264
Laconia. Scribner, J. P. 823.1782
Ladies' gallery, The. McCarthy, J., *and* Praed, *Mrs.* R. (M.-P.) C. 823.7266
Ladies Lindores, The. Oliphant, *Mrs.* M. O. (W.) 823.6593
Ladies of Lone Leventhorpe. Linskill, M.. p. 141, *in* 823.6562

English Fiction. *Contin.*
Lad's love, A. Bates, A. 823.5576
Lady Audley's secret. Maxwell, *Mrs.* M.. E.. (B.) *in* 823.2405
Same. 823.5104
Lady Branksmere. Hungerford, *Mrs.* M. 823.4917
Lady Car. Oliphant, *Mrs.* M. O. (W.) 823.6309
Lady Damer's secret. Brame, *Mrs.* C.. M. (L.) 823.237
Same. *in* 823.5117
Lady Ernestine. Warfield, *Mrs.* C.. A. 823.1659
Lady Gay's pride. Miller, *Mrs.* A. McV. 823.5043
Lady Gwendoline's dream. Brame, *Mrs.* C.. M. (L.) *in* 823.5064
Lady Judith. McCarthy, J. 823.6378
Lady Julia Mandeville, History of. Brooke, *Mrs.* F.. (M.) ** 823.2088
Lady Lee's widowhood. Hamley, *Sir* E: B. 823.6072
Lady Marabout's troubles. La Ramée, L. de. *in* 823.1817
Lady Muriel's secret. Middlemass, J. *in* 823.5093
Lady of the Aroostook. Howells, W: D. 823.2004
Lady of the ice. De Mille, J. 823.5829
Lady of the isle. Southworth, *Mrs.* E. D. E. (N.) 823.1496
Lady, or the tiger? and other stories. Stockton, F. R: 823.4735
Lady Silverdale's sweetheart. 30 pp. Black, W: *in* 823.2885
Lady Sybil's choice. Holt, E. S.. 823.808
Lady Wedderburn's wish. Grant, J. 823.634
Lady Willoughby. Rathbone, *Mrs.* M.. A. (M.) 823.7394
Lady-bird. Fullerton, Lady G. C.. (L. G.) 823.595
Lady's mile, The. Maxwell, *Mrs.* M.. E.. (B.) *in* 823.2399
Same. *in* 823.5096
Lafayette, Marie Jean Paul Roch Yves Gilbert de Motier, *marquis* de. Life of L., with anecdotes illustrative of his character. (*Young Amer. lib* . . .) 808.727
Same. 808.745
Laffan, May. *See* MacNabb, *Mrs.* M. (L.)
Lafon, Mary- *See* Mary-Lafon, J. B.
Laidlaws and the Scotts, The. Hogg, J. *in* 823.702
Lajla. Friis, *Prof.* J. A. 823.6964
Lake breezes. Adams, W: T. 808.503
Lakeville. Bigot, *Mrs.* M.. (H.) 823.5872
Lal. Hammond, W: A. 823.4781
Same. 823.7017
Lamartine, Alphonse Marie L: de Prat de. (1791-1869.) Fior d'Aliza. Tr. by G: Perry. 823.6873
—— Graziella: a story of Italian love. Tr. by J. B. Runnion. 823.2353
—— My mother's manuscript: being a true picture of the private life of a French family during . . . the nineteenth century. With annotations, etc. Tr. by M.. L.. Helper. 823.6874

English Fiction. *Contin.*

Lamartine, Alphonse Marie L: de Prat de. (1791–1869.) *Contin.*

—— Raphael; or, pages of the book of life at twenty. 823.6875

—— The stone-mason of Saint Point: a village tale. 823.6293

Note.—For his life and writings, *see* **Alison,** *Sir* A. Lamartine. (*In his* Misc. essays.) p. 163, *in* 824.90.—**Gautier,** T., *and others.* Famous French authors. 1879. p. 145, *in* 928.87.—**Lacretelle,** H. de. Lamartine and his friends. 1880. 923.509.—**Lamartine,** A. M. L: de P. de. Twenty-five years of my life. *in* 928.644.—**Mazade,** C. de. Lamartine. 57 pp. (*Rév. d. d. Mondes,* 1870, 2 per. v. 88, p. 563; v. 89, p. 585; v. 90, p. 38.) ** 54.293-5. *See also* **Catalogues** of this Library. No. 2, 1880, p. 130. No. 3, 1882, p. 106. *See also* **Poole's** Index (to 1882). p. 719, *in* ** 50.1;—*Same.* Jan. 1, 1882–Jan. 1, 1887. p. 246, *in* ** 50.1².

Lamb, C: (1775–1834.) The adventures of Ulysses. *in* 823.5562

—— Dream children: a revery. 5 pp. (Johnson, R., *ed. Little classics,* v. 4.) p. 183, *in* 829.127

—— Mrs. Leicester's school; or, the history of several young ladies related by themselves. (*In his* Mrs. Leicester's school, and other writings in prose and verse.) 824.415

Note.—For his life and writings, *see* **Ainger,** C. (Account of) Lamb. 928.369.—**De Quincey,** T: C: Lamb. 53 pp. (*Works,* v. 2.) p. 293, *in* 824.426.—**Drake,** S: A. Our great benefactors. 6 pp. 1884. p. 81, *in* * 920.312.—**Forcade,** E. C: Lamb, sa vie intime et littéraire. 24 pp. (*Rév. d. d. Mondes,* 1849, n. pér., v. 1.) p. 177, *in* ** 54.174.—**Harris,** A. B. Little biographies. 14 pp. (1887.) p. 33, *in* 928.692.—**Hunt,** T. W. The prose style of L. 23 pp. (*In his* Rep. Eng. prose, etc.) 1887. p. 363, *in* 820. 120.—**Lytton,** E: G: E. L. B-, *Baron.* C: Lamb and some of his companions. 40 pp. (*In his* Quarterly essays.) p. 86, *in* 829.602.—**Martin,** B: E. In the footprints of Charles Lamb. With a bibliog. by E. D. North. 1890. * 928.725.—**Patmore,** P: G: C: Lamb. 100 pp. (*In his* My friends, etc., v. 1.) p. 1, *in* * 923.1745.—**Swinburne,** A. C: Charles Lamb. 44 pp. (*In his* Miscellanies.) 1886. p. 157, *in* 824.405. *See also* **Catalogues** of this Library. No. 2, 1880, p. 130. No. 4, 1884, p. 157. No. 3, 1882, p. 106. *See also* **Poole's** Index (to 1882). p. 719, *in* ** 50.1; —*Same.* Jan. 1, 1882–Jan. 1, 1887. pp. 247–8, *in* ** 50.1².

——, *and* Lamb, M.. Tales from Shakespeare. 808.783

—— *Same.* 823.953

Lamb, M.. Mrs. Leicester's school; or, the history of several young ladies related by themselves. (Lamb, C: *Mrs. Leicester's school, etc.*) *in* 824.415

——, *joint author. See* Lamb, C:

Lament of Dives. Besant, W. 823.7029

La Motte-Fouqué, Friedrich Heinrich K: *Freiherr* de. The four seasons. 823.5196 *Contents:*—Undine.—The two captains.—Sintram. —Aslauga's knight.

—— The magic ring: a knightly romance. 823.5480

—— Minstrel love: a romance. 823.6865

—— Popular traditions. (Roscoe, T:, *tr. The German novelists,* v. 2.) p. 306, *in* ** 823.6827

—— Sintram and his companions. 823.3892

—— Thiodolf the Icelander. 823.6866

English Fiction. *Contin.*

La Motte-Fouqué, Friedrich Heinrich K: *Freiherr* de. *Contin.*

—— Undine; or, the water-spirit. 52 pp. (*In* Lib. of famous fiction, etc.) p. 900, *in* ** 823.6215

—— *Same,* and other tales. Tr. by F. E. Bunnett. 823.4762 *Contents*—Undine.—Two captains.—Aslauga's knight.—Sintram and his companions.

Lamplighter, The. Cummins, M. S. 823.356

Lancashire witches, The. Ainsworth, W: H. 823.21

Lancaster, Albert Edmund. "All's dross but love": a strange record of two reincarnated souls. 64 pp. 823.5490

Lancaster's choice. Miller, *Mrs.* A. McV. 823.5036

Lancelot Ward, M. P. Temple, G: *in* 823.4987

Land at last. Yates, E. H. 823.1753

Land leaguers, The. Trollope, A. 823.6590

Land of gold, The. Spurr, G: G. 823.4336

"**Land** of the sky," The." Tiernan, *Mrs.* F.. C. (F.) 823.6044

Lander, Meta, *pseud. See* Lawrence, *Mrs.* M. (W.)

Lander, S.. West. Spectacles for young eyes. 8 vols. 823.97–104

Berlin.	808.98.	Pekin.	808.101
Boston.	808.97.	Rome.	808.102
Moscow.	808.99.	St. Petersburg	808.103
New York.	808.100.	Zürich.	808.104

Landers, J. King Bemba's point: a west African story. 47 pp. (*In* Tales from Blackwood. 3d ser., v. 1.) p. 288, *in* 823.7497

—— The story of James Barker: a tale of the Congo coast. 68 pp. (*In* Tales from Blackwood. 3d ser., v. 5.) p. 141, *in* 823.7501

Landolin. Auerbach, B. 823.6791

Landor, Owen. Three sisters of the Briars. 27 pp. (*With* A Polish Jew. By E. Erckmann and P. A. Chatrian.) *in* 823.5089

Lane, E. W., *tr.* The thousand and one nights; or, the Arabian nights' entertainments. 2 vols. 823.4057–8

Lang, Andrew, *ed.* The blue fairy book. 3d ed. 808.1687

—— The mark of Cain. *in* 823.5026

—— The red fairy book. 808.1688

——, *joint author. See* Haggard, H: R.

——, *and* Latimer, Darsie. [*Hyder Ragged.*] He. 69 pp. 823.5076

—— "It." (Anon.) *in* 823.5472

—— King Solomon's wives. 823.5019

Lang, *Mrs.* Andrew. Dissolving views. 823.5049

—— *Same.* 823.5050

Langbein, August Friedrich Ernst. Popular tales. (Roscoe, T:, *tr. The German novelists,* v. 4.) p. 133, *in* ** 823.6829

Lanier, Sidney. Tiger-lilies. 823.7110

——, *ed.* The boy's Mabinogion. *Same as* Knightly legends of Wales.

—— Knightly legends of Wales; or, the boy's Mabinogion; being the earliest Welsh tales of King Arthur in the famous Red book of Hergest. 808.1899

English Fiction. *Contin.*

Laodicean, A. Hardy, T: 823.3596

Lapsed but not lost. Charles, *Mrs.* E.. (R.) 823.2158

Lapstone. Abbott, J. *in* 808.599

La Ramée, Louise de. ["*Ouida.*"] Ariadne: the story of a dream. 823.1814

—— Beatrice Boville, and other stories. 3d ser. 823.1815

—— Bébée; or, two little wooden shoes. 823.1816

—— Cecil Castlemaine's gage; Lady Marabout's troubles, and other stories. 823.1817

—— Chandos. 823.1818

—— A dog of Flanders. 48 pp. (Johnson, R., *ed. Little classics*, v. 10.) p. 7, *in* 829.133

—— Don Gesualdo. (*With her* A house-party.) *in* 823.5747

—— Folle-farine. 823.1819

—— Frescoes, etc. Dramatic sketches. 823.4730

—— Friendship: a story of society. 823.1820

—— Granville de Vigne; or, held in bondage: a tale of the day. 823.1821

—— A house-party,—Don Gesualdo,—and A rainy June. 823.5747

—— Idalia. 823.1822

—— In a winter city: a story of the day. 823.1823

—— In Maremma: a story. 823.5482

—— Lady Marabout's troubles. (*With her* Cecil Castlemaine's gage.) 823.1817

—— A leaf in the storm. 41 pp. (Johnson, R., *ed. Little classics*, v. 11.) p. 202, *in* 829.134

—— Moths. 823.2172

—— Othmar. 823.4956

—— Pascarel: only a story. 823.1824

—— Princess Napraxine: a novel. 823.5483

—— *Same.* 823.5627

—— A Provence rose. 27 pp. (*With* Daughters of Eve. By P. Meritt.) *in* 823.7056

—— Puck: his vicissitudes . . . Related by himself. 823.1825

—— A rainy June. 32 pp. *in* 823.4994

—— *Same.* *in* 823.5747

—— Randolph Gordon, and other stories. 2d ser. 823.1826

—— Signa. 823.1827

—— Strathmore; or, wrought by his own hand: a life romance. 823.1828

—— Syrlin; or, position. 823.7024

—— Tricotrin: the story of a waif and stray. 823.1829

—— Under two flags. 823.1830

—— A village commune. 823.4028

—— Wanda, Countess von Szalras: a novel. 823.5484

Note.—For reviews of Ouida's novels, *see* Murray, V. E. H. Ouida's novels. 15 pp. (*Contemp. rev.*, v. 22. 1873.) p. 921, *in* ** 52.5372.—(Ouida.) Novels. Rev. of. 26 pp. (*Westm. rev.*, n. s., v. 49. 1876.) p. 360, *in* ** 52.2040.—Shepard, W: *In his* Pen pictures of modern authors. p. 331, *in* 820.163.

Larned, Augusta. Old tales retold from Grecian mythology, in talks around the fire. 808.1551

English Fiction. *Contin.*

La Rochere, *Mme.* Eugénie de, *pseud. See* Dutheil, E.

La Salle, Robert Cavelier de. Abbott, J: S. C. Adventures of La Salle. 808.1050

Last abbot of Glastonbury. Crake, A. D. 823.7097

Last chronicle of Barset. Trollope, A. *in* 823.6262

Last days at Apswich. (Anon.) *in* 823.4997

Last days of Pompeii. Lytton, E: G: E. L. Bulwer- 823.6308

Same. 2 vols. ** 823.6734-5

Last fairy tales. Laboulaye, E. R. L. 808.1312

Last in the lease. 20 pp. Hall, *Mrs.* A.. M. (F.) p. 252, *in* 823.1443

Last love, A. Ohnet, G. 823.7180

Last meeting, The. Matthews, J. B. 823.5367

Last of the barons. Lytton, E: G: E. L. Bulwer- 823.5933

Same. 823.5977

Last of the fairies. James, G: P. R. *in* 823.6247

Last of the Macallisters. Barr, *Mrs.* A. E. (H.) 823.5513

Last of the Mohicans. Cooper, J. F. 823.320

Same. *in* 823.7457

Last of the Mortimers. Oliphant, *Mrs.* M. O. (W.) 823.1203

Same. 823.5939

Last of the Plantagenets. Heseltine, W: 823.1813

Late for the train. 53 pp. (*In* Tales from Blackwood. 2d ser., v. 2.) *in* 823.7486

Late Miss Hollingford. Mulholland, R. *in* 823.5074

Late Mrs. Null, The. Stockton, F. R: 823.5217

Late remorse, A. Benedict, F. E. 823.5699

Lathrop, G: Parsons. Afterglow. 823.1996

—— An echo of passion. 823.5364

—— In the distance. 823.5365

—— Newport. 823.4700

—— Somebody else. 823.4108

—— Two purse-companions. 38 pp. (*In* Stories by Amer. authors, v. 3.) p. 62, *in* 823.4704

——, *and* Rideing, W: H: The letter of credit. 823.7213

Latimer, *Mrs.* M.. E.. (Wormeley). —— My wife and my wife's sister. 823.4348

—— Salvage. 823.2339

Latimer family, The. Arthur, T. S. 823.5911

Latreaumont. Sue, M. J. 823.5893

Latter-day saint, A. Wharton, T: 823.4635

Lauder, *Sir* T: Dick. Story of Farquharson of Inverey. (*In* Standard tales, etc., ed by Mrs. C. I. Johnstone.) *in* * 823.6194

—— *Same.* (Tieck, L. The elves . . .) 1864. p. 146, *in* 823.6328

Laura Everingham. Grant, J. 823.635

Same. 823.5682

Laurel bush, The. Craik, *Mrs.* D. M. (M.) 823.332

English Fiction. *Contin.*
Literature. *See also* Books and reading, p. 23.

Axon, W: E: A. Stray chapters in literature, folk-lore and archæology. 1888. 829.678.—**Beloe**, W: Anecdotes of literature and scarce books. 6 vols. 1808-14. ** 828.207-12.—**D'Israeli**, I. Curiosities of literature. 4 vols. 1877. 820.26-9.—**Griswold**, W: M. Directory of writers for the literary press particularly in the U. S. 3d ed. 1890. ** 9101. 83².—**Hargreaves**, J: G: Literary workers; or, pilgrims to the temple of honour. 1889. 801.4.—**Hazlitt**, W: C. Studies in jocular literature. 1890. 818.3.—**Hennequin**, A. The art of play writing. 1890. 812.76.—**Moulton**, C. W., *ed.* Queries with answers in literature, etc. 1st ser., 2d ed. 1888. 374.18.—**Posnett**, H. M. Comparative literature. (*Inter. sci. ser.*, v. 54.) 1886. 800.8.—**Schaff**, P. Literature and poetry. 1890. 800.6.—**Whipple**, E. P. Outlooks on society, literature and politics. 1888. 304.21.

See also **Catalogues** of this Library.
No. 2, 1880, pp. 135, 136.   No. 4, 1884, p. 166.
No. 3, 1882, p. 111, 112.   No. 5, 1888, p. 234.

Dictionaries.
Alden's cyclopedia of universal literature. vols. 1-15. (A.-N.) ** 803.15-29. **Beeton's** dictionary of literature, fine arts and amusements. ** 803.32. —**Brewer**, E. C. Dictionary of phrase and fable. * 803.1:—**Reader's** handbook of allusions, references, plots and stories. 1880. ** 803.2.—**Encyclopædia Britannica**. 24 vols. and index. ** 32.271-95;— Supplement. 4 vols. ** 32.296-99.—**Reddall**, H: F:, *comp.* Fact, fancy and fable. 1889. ** 803.34.— **Wheeler**, W: A. Explanatory and pronouncing dictionary of noted names of fiction. 19th ed. 1889. ** 803.31;—Who wrote it? 1881. * 803.9;—*and* C: G. Familiar allusions. 1882. * 803.12.

History and criticism.
Books that have helped me. (*Forum*, v. 3, 1886-87.) p. 29. 10 pp. Hale, E: E.; p. 142. 10 pp. Harris, *Prof.* W: T.; p. 263. 10 pp. Bascom, J:; p. 339. 6 pp. Lang, A.; p. 458. 8 pp. Peabody, *Prof.* A. P.; p. 578. 9 pp. Eggleston, E: *in* * 51.4701².—**Botta**, *Mrs.* A.. C.. (L.) Handbook of universal literature (to 1885). 1890. 809.103.—**Brandes**, G. Eminent authors of the nineteenth century. 1886. 809.67.— **Dowden**, E: Studies in literature. 1789-1877. 4th ed. 800.4.—**Dunlop**, J: History of fiction. 1876. 809.2.—**Gayley**, C: M., *and* Scott, F. N. Literature. (*In their* Guide to the lit. of æsthetics.) 1890. pp. 108-14, *in* ** 16.227.—**Grimm**, H. Literature. 1886. 804.9.—**Hallam**, H: Introd. to the literature of Europe in the 15th, 16th and 17th centuries. 2 vols. 1871. 809.3-4.—**Hardy**, T: The profitable reading of fiction. 14 pp. (*Forum*, v. 5, 1888.) p. 57, *in* * 51.4701².—**Hedge**, *Prof.* F: H. The hundred authors. (*Forum*, v. 2, 1886-7.) p. 293, *in* * 51.4701.— **Henley**, W. E. Views and reviews: essays in appreciation. 1890. 824.451.—**Klein**, J. L. Geschichte des Dramas. 13 vols. (in 15). u. Register Bd. 16 vols. 1865-76. * 832.95-110.—**Knight**, W: Idealism and experience in literature, etc. 49 pp. (*In his* Essays in philosophy.) 1890. 104.21.—**Lang**, A. Letters on literature. 3d ed. 1889. 804.11.—**Lewin**, W. The abuse of fiction. 14 pp. (*Forum*, v. 7, 1889.) p. 659, *in* * 51.4701.—Literature. (*Forum*, v. 4.) p. 29. 9 pp. Jessopp, *Dr.* A.; p. 207. 6 pp. Gilder, J. L.; p. 314. 9 pp. Matthews, B.; p. 388. 9 pp. Hill, *Dr.* T:; p. 536. 9 pp. Conway, M. D.; p. 604. 8 pp. Pitman, R. C. * 51.4701³.—**Lowell**, J. R. Writings. 10 vols. 1890. 824.455-64.—**Marmontel**, J. F. Élémens de littérature. 4 vols. (*Œuvres*, vols. 12-15.) 849.44-7.—**Morley**, J: Critical miscellanies. 3 vols. 1888. 814.19-21.—**Oliphant**, *Mrs.* M. O. (W.) Success in fiction. (*Forum*, v. 7, 1889. p. 314, *in* * 51.4701².—**Oncü**, S. M. (F.) Marchioness. Art, literature and drama. 1889. 829.97. —Perry, T: S. From Opitz to Lessing: a study of pseudo-classicism in literature. 1885. 809.102.— **Prescott**, W: H. Biographical and critical miscellanies. (Repr. from North Amer. rev.) 824.437.— **Prölss**, R. Geschichte des neueren Dramas. 3 vols. (in 6). 1881-3. 812.68-73.—**Sainte-Beuve**, C: A. Essays on men and women. 1890. 824.452.— **Salt**, H. S. Literary sketches. 824.454.—**Scherr**, J. Allgemeine Geschichte der Literatur. 809.5.— **Schlegel**, A. W. Lectures on dramatic art and literature. 2d ed. 1886. 812.67.—**Schlegel**, K. W. F. v. Lectures on the history of literature: ancient and modern. 1885. 809.100.—**Smith**, G: B. Poets and novelists. 1876. 829.237.—**Sully**, J. The fu-

English Fiction. *Contin.*
Literature. *Contin.*
History and criticism. *Contin.*
ture of fiction. 14 pp. (*Forum*, v. 9, 1890.) p. 644, *in* * 51.4701².—**Taylor**, I: History of the transmission of ancient books to modern times. 1827. 809. 101.

See also **Catalogues** of this Library.
No. 2, 1880, pp. 135-6.   No. 4, 1884, p. 166.
No. 3, 1882, pp. 111-12.   No. 5, 1888, p. 234.
Also "Periodicals" in **Catalogues** of this Library.
No. 2, 1880, pp. 178-9.   No. 4, 1884, pp. 218-22.
No. 3, 1882, pp. 144-7.   No. 5, 1888, pp. 279-85.
Also **Poole's** Index (to 1882). pp. 753-5; *in* ** 50.1:—*Same*, to Jan. 1, 1887. pp. 260-1, *in* ** 50.1².

AMERICAN LITERATURE. *Bibliography.*
Adams, O. F. A brief handbook of Amer. authors. 1884. ** 820.100.—**Allibone**, S: A. Dictionary of Eng. literature and . . . Amer. authors. 3 vols. ** 803.6-8.—**Brewer**, E. C. Authors and their works, with dates. 1884. ** 15.272.—**Hickcox**, J: H. United States government publications. A monthly catalogue. vols. 1-12. 1885-6. 2 vols. ** 17.247-8.—**Smith**, G. J. A synopsis of Eng. and Amer. lit. 1890. 820.200.—**Trübner**, W. Bibliographical guide to Amer. literature. * 16.12.— **Whitney**, J. L. A modern Proteus; or, a list of books published under more than one title. 1884. * 14.17.

See also "Bibliography" in **Catalogues** of this Library.
No. 2, 1880, p. 23.   No. 4, 1884, pp. 26-7.
No. 3, 1882, p. 20.   No. 5, 1888, pp. 33-5.
Also **Poole's** Index (to 1882). *in* ** 50.1;—*Same*, to Jan. 1, 1887. *in* ** 50.1².

—— *Periodicals.*
Annual Amer. catalogue. 1886. ** 15.261;— *Same*. 1887. ** 15.263;—*Same*. 1888. ** 15.263²;— *Same*. 1889. ** 15.263³;—*Same*. 1890. ** 15.264.— **Author**, The. v. 1, Jan.-Dec. 15, 1889. * 51B.2.— **Book buyer**. vols. 4-5, Feb. 1887-Jan. 1889. ** 11.358¹·².—**Book chat**. vols. 3-4, 1888-9. * 51. 5105¹·²·—**Critic**. vols. 1-4, Jan. 1884-Dec. 1885. 4 vols. * 51.1421-2²;—*Same*. vols. 8-11, 1887-9. 4 vols. * 51.1427¹·²;—*Same*. v. 13, 1890. * 51.1426². —**Dial**, The. vols. 1-10, 1880-90. * 51.476¹·¹⁰.—**Literary news**. vols. 7-9, 1886-8. (N. S.) * 51.207¹·².— **Literary world**. vols. 18-20, 1887-9. * 805.666-8.— **Literary world**. (Duyckinck.) vols. 1-13, 1847-53; 13 vols. ** 51.3301-13.—**Publishers'** trade list annual. 1888-90. 3 vols. ** 11.357¹·².—**Publishers' weekly**. vols. 31-37, 1887-1890. 7 vols. ** 11. 871·¹⁰.—**Student's journal**. vols. 16, 18, 1887; 1889. * 653.65¹·³.—**Writer**. vols. 1-3, 1887-9. * 51.5103¹·³.

—— *Collections and selections.*
Bates, C.. F., *comp.* Cambridge book of poetry and song. 1882. * 821.1246.—**Crandall**, C: H: Representative sonnets by Amer. poets. 1890. 821.1340. —**Duyckinck**, E., *and* G: Cyclopædia of Amer. literature. Ed. by M. L. Simons. 2 vols. ** 803.10-11. —**Eggleston**, G: C., *ed.* Amer. war ballads and lyrics. 2 vols. 1889. * 821.1271-2.—**Higginson**, T: W., *and* Bigelow, E. H., *comps.* Amer. sonnets. 1890. 821.1342.—**Keene**, J:, *ed.* The poets of America. ** 821.1187.—**Lambert**, W. H. *In his* Memory gems. 1884. 829.664.—**Martin**, *Prof.* B: N. Choice specimens of Amer. literature and literary reader. 1879. 829.387.—**Mason**, E: T., *ed.* Humorous masterpieces of Amer. lit. 3 vols. 1888. 828.225-7.— **Smith**, H., *ed.* A century of Amer. literature, Benjamin Franklin to James Russell Lowell. (1889.) 820.156.—**Stedman**, E. C., *and* Hutchinson, E. M. Library of Amer. literature from the earliest settlement to the present time. 11 vols. 1890. 820. 122-31².—**Willmoth**, R. A. Poets of the 19th century. 1884. 821.1324.

See also "Extracts" in **Catalogues** of this Library.
No. 2, 1880, pp. 79-80.   No. 4, 1884, p. 100.
No. 3, 1882, pp. 68-9.   No. 5, 1888, p. 137.

—— *Dictionaries.*
Allibone, S. A. Dictionary of Eng. literature and . . . Amer. authors. 3 vols. ** 803.6-8.—**Cushing**, W: Anonyms: a dictionary of revealed authorship. 1889. ** 14.52:—Initials and pseudonyms. 2 vols. 1885-8. ** 14.18-18².—**Griswold**, W: M. A directory of writers for the literary press particularly in the U. S. 3d ed. 1890. ** 9101.83².—**Ward**, A.. L., *ed.* Dictionary of quotations from Eng. and Amer. poets. 1883. ** 821.1235.—**Wilson**, J. G.,

English Fiction. *Contin.*
Literature. *Contin.*
AMERICAN LITERATURE. *Contin.*
—— *Dictionaries. Contin.*
and Fiske, J:, *eds.* Appleton's cyclopædia of Amer. biography. 6 vols. ** 920.320-5.
—— *History, criticism and manuals.*
Adams, O. F. A brief handbook of Amer. authors. 1884. * 820.100.—American fiction. 34 pp. (*Edin. rev.*, v. 173, Jan. 1891.) p. 31, *in* * 52.5012°.—
Bancroft, H. H. The early Amer. chroniclers. 45 pp. 1883. 904.37.—Beers, H: A. An outline sketch of Amer. literature. 1888. 820.101.—Blaisdell, A. F. First steps with Amer. and Brit. authors. 1888. 820.154.—Bolton, *Mrs.* S.. (K.) Famous Amer. authors. 1887. 820.99;—*Same.* 820.176.—
Gilder, J. L., *and* J. B., *eds.* Authors at home. Personal and biographical sketches of well-known Amer. writers. (1888.) 820.159.—Hand-book of Amer. literature, historical, biographical and critical. (1640-1854.) 820.132.—Harris, A. B. Amer. authors for young folks. (1887.) 820.157.—Hart, J: S. A manual of Amer. literature. (1872.) 820.106.
—Herringshaw, T: W. Local and national poets of Amer., with biographical sketches. 1890. 820. 183.—Higginson, T: W. Short studies of Amer. authors. 60 pp. 1880. 820.102.—Hodgkins, L. M. Guide to the study of nineteenth century authors. 1889. 820.155.—Morris, C:, *ed.* Half-hours with the best Amer. authors. 4 vols. 1887. 820.108-11. —Nichol, J: American literature as historical sketch. 1620-1880. 1882. 820.160.—Richardson, C. F., Primer of Amer. literature. 820.80;—Amer. literature, 1607-1885. 2 vols. 820.206-7.—Royse, N. K. A manual of Amer. literature. Rev. ed. (1882.) 820.193.—Stedman, E. C. Poets of America. 1890. 820.188.—Tyler, M. C. History of Amer. literature. (1706-1765.) 2 vols. 1878. 820.59-60.—Welsh, A. H. Digest of Eng. and Amer. literature. 1890. 820.192. —Whipple, E. P. Amer. literature. 1887. 820.179. —White, G. Sketch of the philosophy of Amer. literature. 1891. 820.202.
See also "Literature" in Catalogues of this Library.
No. 2, 1880, pp. 135-6. No. 4, 1884, p. 166.
No. 3, 1882, pp. 111-12. No. 5, 1888, p. 234.
—— *Poetry. See also before under* American literature, *History, etc.*
The Library has poems of Trumbull, J: 1750-1831.—Freneau, P. 1752-1832.—Allston, W. 1779-1843.—Pierpont, J: 1785-1866.—Dana, R: H: 1787-1879.— Halleck, F.-G. 1790-1867.—Sprague, C: 1791-1875.—Bryant, W: C. 1794-1878.—Drake, J. R. 1795-1820.—Percival, J. G. 1795-1856.—Brainerd, J: G. C. 1796-1828.—Alcott, A. B. 1798-1887.—Sands, R. C. 1799-1832.—Morris, G: P. 1802-1864.—Pinkney, E: C. 1802-1828.—Emerson, R. W. 1803-1882.—Hoffman, C: F. 1806-1884.—Willis, N. P. 1806-1867.—Longfellow, H: W. 1807-1882.—Whittier, J: G. 1807- .—Gallagher, W: D. 1808- .—Poe, E. A. 1809-1849.—Holmes, O. W. 1809- .—Street, A. B. 1811-1881.—Linton, W. J. 1812- .—Cranch, C. P. 1813- .—Sargent, E. 1813-1880.—Saxe, J: G. 1816-1887.—Story, W: W. 1819- .—Lowell, J. R. 1819- .—Whitman, W. 1819- .—Holland, J. G. 1819-1881.—Taylor, B: F. 1819-1887.—Parsons, T: W. 1819- .—Howe, *Mrs.* J. W. 1819- .—Welby, A. B. 1821- .—Read, T: B. 1822-1872. —Boker, G: H. 1823- .—Preston, M. J. 1825- . —Taylor, B. 1825-1878.—Dorr, Julia C. R. 1825- . —Stoddard, R: H: 1825- .—Larcom, Lucy. 1826-1888.—Powers, H. N. 1826-1890.—Trowbridge, J: T. 1827- .—Timrod, H: 1829-1867.—Hayne, P. H. 1830-1886.—Jackson, H.. M. F. 1831-1885.— Stedman, E. C. 1833- .—Realf, R: 1834-1878.— Moulton, Louise E. 1835- .—Tilton, T. 1835- . —Platt, J: J. 1836- .—Thaxter, C. 1836- .—Aldrich, T: B. 1836- .—Hay, J: 1838- .—Dodge, M.. M. 1838- .—Harte, F. B. 1839- .—Sill, E: R. 1841-1887.—Miller, Joaquin. 1841- .—Lanier, S. 1842-1881.—Stoddard, C: W. 1843- .—Gilder, R: W. 1844- .—Coolbrith, I. C. (?).—Fawcett, E. 1847- .—Woolsey, S.. C. (?).—Beers, H: A. 1847- . —DeKay, C: 1848- .—Cheney, J: V. 1848- .—Lazarus, E. 1849-1888.—Bates, A. 1850- .—Thomas, E. M. 1854- .—Peck, S: M. 1854- .—Bunner, H: C. 1855- .—Sherman, F. D. 1860- .—Scollard, C. 1860- .
See also "Poetry" in Catalogues of this Library.
No. 2, 1880, p. 183. No. 4, 1884, p. 231.
No. 3, 1882, pp. 151-2. No. 5, 1888, pp. 289-90.

English Fiction. *Contin.*
Literature. *Contin.*
AMERICAN LITERATURE. *Contin.*
—— *Poetry. Contin.*
Also Poole's Index (to 1882). pp. 31-2, *in* ** 50.1; —*Same*, to Jan. 1, 1887. p. 11, *in* ** 50.1³.
—— *Prose.*
For· prose writers, *see* Catalogues of this Library.
No. 2, 1880. No. 4, 1884. No. 6, 1891.
No. 3, 1882. No. 5, 1888.
ANGLO-SAXON LITERATURE.
Earle, J: Anglo-Saxon lit. 820.208.
See also English literature, p. 158.
ARABIC LITERATURE.
Burckhardt, J. L. Arabic proverbs. 1830. 916.142.—Clouston, W. A. Arabian poetry for English readers. 1881. * 821.933.
See also Poole's Index (to 1882). p. 50, *in* ** 50.1; —*Same*, to Jan. 1, 1887. p. 18, *in* ** 50.1³.
ARMENIAN LITERATURE. Dulaurier, E. Les chants populaires de l'Arménie. 32 pp. (*Revue d. d. Mondes*, 1852, n. pér., v. 14.) p. 224, *in* ** 54.187.
ASSYRIAN LITERATURE.
Birch, S., *ed. In his* Records of the past. 6 vols. 930.50-5.—Schrader, *Dr.* E. Die Höllenfahrt der Istar. Nebst Proben assyrischer Lyrik. 1874. 493.33. *See also* Poole's Index (to 1882). p. 69, *in* ** 50.1; —*Same*, to Jan. 1, 1887. p. 25, *in* ** 50.1³.
BABYLONIAN LITERATURE.
Birch, S. *In his* Records of the past. 6 vols. 1878-81. 930.50.—Sayce, A. H. Babylonian literature: lectures. 899.25;—*In his* Records of the past. v. 1. 930.256.
See also Poole's Index (to 1882). p. 84, *in* ** 50.1.
BASQUE LITERATURE. *See* Poole's Index (to 1882). p. 101, *in* ** 50.1;—*Same*, to Jan. 1, 1887. p. 36, *in* ** 50.1³.
BOHEMIAN LITERATURE.
Bowring, *Sir* J. Cheskian anthology. 831.11.— Literature of Bohemia. 25 pp. (*Westm. rev.*, n. s., v. 23, 1865.) p. 23, *in* ** 52.2014.—Ward, A. W. Bohemian literature in the 14th century. 8 pp. (*Macmillan's mag.*, v. 38, 1878.) p. 40, *in* ** 52. 1798.
See also Poole's Index (to 1882). p. 145, *in* ** 50.1.
CELTIC LITERATURE, *History, criticism, etc.*
Arnold, M. On the study of Celtic literature. 1883. 896.13.—Morley, H. Old Celtic literature. (*In his* Eng. writers, v. 1.) 820.170.
See also Poole's Index (to 1882). p. 210, *in* ** 50.1;—*Same*, to Jan. 1, 1887. *in* ** 50.1³.
CHINESE LITERATURE.
Davis, J. E. On the poetry of the Chinese. 1834. * 891.16.—Lau Tsze. Speculations. Tr. by Chalmers. 891.15.—Legge, J. Chinese classics. 3 vols. v. 1: Confucius; v. 2: Mencius; v. 3: She King. (Müller, F. M. *Sacred books of the east.*) 299.11-13. —Loomis, A. W., *ed.* Confucius and the Chinese classics. 1867. 299.24;—*Same.* 1882. 891.18.—Martin, W. A. P. The Chinese: their education, philosophy and letters. 891.10.—Sealy, T: H: Chinese legends. 828.81.—Stent, G. C. Jade chaplet: songs from the Chinese. * 821.765.—White, C. A. Classic literature . . with some account of the . . . Chinese. . . . 1889. p. 401, *in* 810.54.
See also Poole's Index (to 1882). p. 236, *in* ** 50.1;—*Same*, to Jan. 1, 1887. p. 80, *in* ** 50.1³.
CLASSICAL LITERATURE, *Bibliography.* Moss, J. W: Manual of classical bibliography. 2 vols. 1837. ** 16.1-2.
—— *History, criticism, etc.*
Morris, C: Manual of classical literature. 3d ed. 1888. 880.29.—Ramage, C. T. Bible echoes in ancient classics. 1878. 215.77.—Taylor, I: History of the transmission of ancient books to modern times. 1879. 809.32.—White, C. A. Classic literature, principally Sanskrit, Greek and Roman, etc. 1889. 810.54.
See also Greek literature.—Latin literature.
DANISH LITERATURE.
Griffin, G. W. Glance at Danish literature. 34 pp. (*In his* My Danish days.) 1875. p. 259, *in* 948. 11.—Thorpe, B., *ed.* Yule-tide stories. 823.4231.— Vicary, J: F. A stork's nest. 823.5415.
See also Andersen, H. C., p. 7.
See also Denmark, p. 52.
Also, Poole's Index (to 1882). p. 331, *in* ** 50.1.
DUTCH LITERATURE.
Bowring, J:, *and* Van Dyk, H. S. Batavian anthology; or, specimens of Dutch poets. 1824. 899.8.

English Fiction. *Contin.*
Literature. *Contin.*

—**Knuttel**, *Dr.* W. P. C. Nederlandsche bibliographie van Kergeschiedenis. 1889. ** 15.273.—**Marmier**, X. Poésie populaire de la Hollande. 16 pp. (*Rev. d. d. Mondes*, 1836, 4e pér., v. 6.) p. 488, *in* ** 54.123.
See also **Poole's** Index (to 1882). p. 373, *in* ** 50.1.

EGYPTIAN LITERATURE.

Birch, A. H. *In his* Records of the past. 6 vols. 930.50-55.— **Bunsen**, C. C. J. Book of the dead. (*In his* Egypt's place, v. 5.) *in* 962.7.—**Mahaffy**, J. P. Survey of old Egyptian literature. *in* 930.140.—**Sayce**, A. H. *In his* Records of the past. New ser., v. 1. 930.236.
See also **Poole's** Index (to 1882). p. 397, *in* ** 50.1.

ENGLISH LITERATURE.

See also **Books** and reading, pp. 23-4.
6th century. **Gildas** (*the Wise*), Works of. pp. 293-380, *in* 942.139.
7th century.
Bede *or* **Bæda Venerabilis**. 673-735. Be domes dæge, de judicii; an old English version of the Latin poem ascribed to Bede. Ed. (with other short poems) by J. R. Lumby. (*Early Eng. Text. Soc.*, No. 65.) ** 806.1¹⁴.—**Beowulf**; poem. Tr. by T. Arnold. ** 899.17;—*Same*. Tr. by J. M. Garnett. 821.938;—*Same*. Tr. by Thorpe. 429.11;—*Same*. With ... transliteration and notes by J. Zupitza. (*Early Eng. Text. Soc.*, No. 77.) ** 806.1¹¹. *Note.*—"The text of Beowulf took, about the close of the 7th or the beginning of the 8th century, substantially the shape in which it has come down to us." *Ten Brink*.—**Caedmon**. —680. Exodus and Daniel. By T. W. Hunt. (*Lib. of Ang.-Sax. poetry*, v. 2.) 821.1306.
8th century. **Cynewulf**. Crist; Elene; Juliana. Ed. by Grein. *in* 899.36-7.
9th century.
Alfred, *King of the West-Saxons, The Great.* Orosius. Ed. by H: Sweet. Pt. 1: Old Eng. text and Lat. orig. (*Early Eng. Text. Soc.*, No. 79.) ** 806.7¹⁹;—Works. 2 vols. (*Early Eng. Text Soc.*, Nos. 45, 50.) ** 806.1¹⁸.—**Anglo-Saxon** chronicle. (55 A. D. to 1154 A. D.) 2 vols. v. 1: Ang.-Sax; v. 2: Tr. by Thorpe. ** 942.539-40.—**Nennius**. *Abbot of Bangor.* History of the Britons. Rev. and aug. from the tr. of Rev. W. Gunn by J. A. Giles. (*With Six old chron.*) 1841. p. 381, *in* ** 942.139.
10th century.
Ælfric. *Abbott, called* Grammaticus. —1006. Lives of the saints; sermons on saints' days formerly observed by the Eng. Church. Ed. by W. W. Skeat. pts. 1-3. (*Early Eng. Text Soc.*, Nos. 76, 82, 94.) 806.1¹⁴·³·⁴.—**Dunstan**, *St. Abp. of Canterbury*, 925-988. Stubbs, W: Memorial of Saint Dunstan. 1874. (*Gt. Brit. Rolls. chron.*) * 942.642.
12th century.
Florence, *of Worcester.* d. 1118? Chronicle of. Tr. with notes and illus. by T: Forrester. 1854. 942.341.— **Geoffrey**, *of Monmouth.* Circa 1110-54. British history. Tr. by A. Thompson. Ed. with notes by J. A. Giles. (*With Six old chron.*) 1848. 942.139.—**Henry**, *of Huntington.* History of the English, from A. C. 55 to A. D. 1154, in eight books. (*Lat.*) Ed. by T: Arnold. 1879. (*Gt. Brit. Rolls. chron.*) * 942.653.—**Lancelot of the Laik.** (*Early Eng. Text. Soc.*, No. 6.) ** 806.1¹.—**Map**, *or* **Mapes**, Walter. 1143?-1210? De nugis curialium distinctiones V. Ed. by T: Wright. 1850. (*Camden Soc.*, No. 50.) ** 942-1020;—Latin poems; coll. and ed. by T: Wright. 1850. (*Camden Soc.*, No. 17.) ** 942.986.—**Seint Graal** (or Grail), Legend of the. (1167?) (*Early Eng. Text. Soc.*, No. 44.) ** 806.1¹⁸. *Note.*—Sometimes called. The romance of Joseph of Arimathea; written, according to H: Morley, at least twenty years later than Geoffrey of Monmouth's chronicle.—**William** *of Malmesbury.* (d. after 1142.) De gestis pontificum Anglorum libri V. (*Lat.*) Ed. by N. E. S. A. Hamilton. 1870. (*Gt. Brit. Rolls. chron.*) * 942.617.
13th century.
Bacon, Roger. Circa 1214-92. Opera quædam hactenus inedita. Ed. by J. S. Brewer. 1859. (*Gt. Brit. Rolls. chron.*) * 942.523A.—**Grosseteste**, Robert. *Bp. of Lincoln.* Circa 1175-1253. Epistolæ. (*Lat.*) Ed. by H: R: Luard. 1861. (*Gt. Brit. Rolls. chron.*) * 942.543;—Weymouth, R. F. Bishop Grosseteste's "Castle off Ioue." 94 pp. (Philol. Soc.

English Fiction. *Contin.*
Literature. *Contin.*
ENGLISH LITERATURE. *Contin.*

13th century. Contin.
Lon., *Trans.*, 1862-3.) ** 405.60.—**Havelok, the Dane.** The lay of. 1280. Re-ed. by W. W. Skeat. (*Early Eng. Text Soc.*, ex. ser., No. 4.) ** 806.2⁴;—*Same.* (*In* Spec. of early Eng., pt. 1.) p. 222, *in* 420.19.—**King Horn**; poem. (*Early Eng. Text Soc.*, No. 14.) ** 806.1⁴;—*Same.* (*In* Spec. of early Eng., pt. 1.) p. 237, *in* 420.19.—**Matthew Paris.** (-1259.) Chronica majora. Ed. by H: R: Luard. 5 vols. 1872-80. (*Gt. Brit. Rolls. chron.*) * 942.626-30; Historia Anglorum, sive, ut vulgo, dicitur, Historia minor. Item, ejusdem abbreviatio chronicorum Angliæ. Ed. by Sir F. Madden. 3 vols. 1866-69. (*Gt. Brit. Rolls. chron.*) * 942.601-3.
14th century.
Chaucer, Geoffrey. Canterbury tales, annotated and accented, with illus. of Eng. life in Chaucer's time. By J: Saunders. 1889. 821.1248;— Minor works. Ed. by W. W. Skeat. 1888. 821.1296;—Poetical works. Ed. by R. Bell. 4 vols. 821.477-80;—Prologue and Knight's tale, designed to serve as an introd. to the study of Eng. lit. By S. H. Carpenter. 1872. 420.4;—Treatise on the astrolabe. Ed. by W. W. Skeat. (*Early Eng. Text Soc.*, ex. ser., No. 16.) ** 806.2¹⁶;—Boethius, A: M. T. S. De consolatione philosophiæ. Tr. by Chaucer. Ed. by R: Morris. 1868. (*Early Eng. Text Soc.*, ex. ser., No. 5.) ** 806.2⁴. *See also* Catalogue of this Library, No. 2, 1880, p. 44.—**Gower**, J: about 1330-1448. Confessio amantis (about 1393). Ed. by Dr. R. Pauly. 3 vols. 1857. * 821.842-2A-2B.—**Higden**, Ranulph, or Ralph, *of Chester.* -1363. Polychronicon: together with the Eng. tr. of J: Trevisa and of an unknown writer of the 15th century. Ed. by C. Babington and J. R. Lumby. 7 vols. 1865-82. (*Gt. Brit. Rolls. chron.*) * 942.590-6. — **Langland**, W: about 1332-about 1400. Pierce the ploughman's crede (about 1394). Ed. by W. W. Skeat. (*Early Eng. Text Soc.*, No. 30.) ** 806.1¹;—Richard the redeles. 1399. (*Early Eng. Text Soc.*, No. 54.) ** 806.1¹⁴;—The vision and creed of Piers ploughman. Ed. by T: Wright. 2 vols. 1856. 821.501-2;—The vision of William concerning Piers the plowman, together with vita de Dowel, Dobet, et Dobest. Ed. by W. W. Skeat. 4 pts. (in 5). (*Early Eng. Text Soc.*, Nos. 28, 38, 54, 67, 81.) ** 806.1¹·⁴·⁶·⁸·¹¹.—**Langtoft**, P: Chronicle, in French verse, from the earliest period to the death of King Edward I. Ed. by T: Wright. (With Eng. tr.) 2 vols. 1866-68. (*Gt. Brit. Rolls. chron.*) * 942.606-7.—**Wiclif**, J: about 1324-84. An apology for Lollard doctrines, attributed to Wicliffe, with notes by J. H. Todd. 1842. (*Camden Soc.*, No. 20.) * 942.990;—English works of Wyclif hitherto unpublished. Ed. by F. D. Matthew. (*Early Eng. Text Soc.*, No. 74.) ** 806.1¹⁴;—Fasciculi zizaniorum magistri J. Wyclif cum tritico, ascribed to T: Netter of Walden. Ed. by W. W. Shirley. 1858. (*Gt. Brit. Rolls. chron.*) * 942.506.
15th century.
Caxton, W: Blades, W: Biography and typography of Caxton. Illus. 1877. * 926.23;—*Same.* 2d ed. 1882. * 23.3;—Knight, C: William Caxton, the first English printer. Illus. 1877. 928.294.—**Fortescue**, *Sir* J: De laudibus legum Angliæ. With notes by A. Amos. 1874. * 343.123;—Governance of England. Rev. with notes by C: Plummer. 1885. 340.155.—**James I.**, *of Scotland.* Poetical remains. Ed. by Rev. C: Rogers. 1873. p. 297, *in* ** 906.6.—**Lydgate**, J: (about 1375-1460.) The childe of Bristow; poem. Ed. by C. Hopper. 1859. (*Camden Soc.*, No. 73.) *in* ** 942.1023.—**Malory**, *Sir* T: Circa 1430-96. La mort d'Arthure. History of King Arthur and of the Knights of the Round Table. Ed. from the text of the ed. of 1634, with an introd. and notes by T: Wright. 3 vols. 1866. ** 823.6773-5.—**Pecock**, Reginald. 1390?-1461. The repressor of over much blaming of the clergy. Ed. by C. Babington. 2 vols. 1860. (*Gt. Brit. Rolls. chron.*) * 942.527-8.—**Skelton**, J: 1460-1529. Of the death of the noble prince, Kynge Edwarde the Forthe. 1483.—Upon the doulourous dethe and muche lamentable chaunce of the most honorable Erle of Northumberlande. 1489. (*Poet. works.*) 821.367.
16th century.
Ascham, Roger. 1515-1568. Toxophilus. (Arber, E: Eng. reprints.) ** 829.20;—Whole works. Rev. with life of author by Rev. Dr. Giles. 4 vols. 1864. 370.22-5.—**Bacon**, Francis. *Baron Verulam, Viscount St. Albans.* (1561-1626.) Works. 15 vols.

English Fiction. *Contin.*
Literature. *Contin.*
ENGLISH LITERATURE. *Contin.*
16th century. *Contin.*
(16th and 17th centuries.) 01.1–15.—**Cranmer, T:**
Abp. of Canterbury. Miscellaneous writings and
letters. Ed. by Rev. J: E. Cox. 1846. (*Parker Soc.*)
02.19;—Writings and disputations relative to the
sacrament of the Lord's Supper. Ed. by Rev. J: E.
Cox. 1844. (*Parker Soc.*) 02.18.—**Erasmus, Des-**
iderius. Colloquies. Tr. by N. Bailey. Ed. with
notes by Rev. E. Johnson. 2 vols. 1878. * 829.568–9.
—**Fisher, J:** *Bp. of Rochester.* 1459–1535. English
works collected by J: R. B. Mayor. Pt. 1. (*Early
Eng. Text Soc.*, ex., ser. No. 27.) ** 806.2²¹.—**Hooker,**
R: 1553–1600. Laws of ecclesiastical polity. (Books
I–IV, 1594; V, 1597.) (*Works*, vols. 1–2.) 283.41–2.—
Howard, H: *Earl of Surrey.* Songs and sonnets.
(Arber, E: *Eng. reprints.*) 829.410.—**Jewel,** J: *Bp. of
Salisbury.* 1522–1571. Works, ed. by Rev. J: Ayre.
4 vols. 1845–50. (*Parker Soc.*) 02.23–26.—**Jonson,**
Ben. 1573–1637. Every man in his humour
(acted 1596–1598);—Every man out of his humour
(acted 1599). (*Works.*) *in* 822.121.—**Latimer,**
Hugh. 1491–1555. Sermon on the ploughers. 1549.
(Arber, E: *Eng. reprints.*) *in* ** 829.13;—Seven ser-
mons before Edward VI. (Arber, E: *Eng. re-
prints.*) *in* ** 829.18.—**Lyly,** J: 1553–1606. Eu-
phues: the anatomy of wit. 1579;—Euphues and his
England. 1580. (Arber, E: *Eng. reprints.*) * 829.
15.—**Lyndesay,** *Sir* D: about 1490–1555. Works, ed.
by F. Hall and J. A. H. Murray. (*Early Eng. Text
Soc.*, Nos. 11, 19, 35, 37, 47.) ** 806.1.—**Marlowe,**
Christopher. 1564–1593. Works, with notes by
Rev. A. Dyce. 822.122.—**More,** *Sir* T: 1480–1535.
Utopia. Tr. by R. Robinson. (Arber, E: *Eng. reprints.*) *in* * 829.18.—**Shakespeare,** W: 1564–1616.
See Catalogues of this Library: No. 2, 1880, pp. 207–8;
No. 3, 1882, p. 173; No. 4, 1884, p. 265; No. 5, 1888, pp.
317–19.—**Sidney,** *Sir* Philip. 1554–1586. An apology
for poetrie. (Arber, E: *Eng. reprints.*) * 829.16;—
Complete poems. Ed. with notes by A. B. Grosart.
3 vols. 821.364–6.—**Skelton,** J: 1460–1529. Merie
tales. 1566–7. (Hazlitt, W. C. *Old Eng. jest books.*)
** 828.33;—Poetical works. Ed. by A. Dyce. 821.367.
—**Southwell,** Robert. 1560?–1595. Complete poems.
Ed. with notes by A. B. Grosart. (*Fuller
worthies' lib.*) ** 821.1076.—**Spenser,** Edmund.
1552–1599. Amoretti (1595). Colin Clouts come home
againe (1595). (Hitchcock, A. E. *Spencer's poem,
etc.*) 821.575;—Works, with life by Rev. II: J:
Todd. 821.382.—**Tyndale,** W: 1485–1536. Answer
to Sir T. More's Dialogue; Supper of the Lord; W:
Tracy's Testament expounded. Ed. by H: Walter.
1850. (*Parker Soc.*) 02.40;—Doctrinal treatises on
introductions to the Scriptures. Ed. by H: Walter.
1848. (*Parker Soc.*) 02.39;—Expositions and notes
. . . on Scripture with practice of prelates. Ed. by
H: Walter. 1849. (*Parker Soc.*) 02.38;—Translation
of the Bible. *in* ** 225.45.—**Udall,** N: English
verses and ditties at the coronation procession of
Queen Anne Boleyn. 9 pp. (Arber, E: *An Eng.
garner,* v. 2.) *in* * 819.4;—Ralph Roister Doister. (Hazlitt, W. C. *Old Eng. plays,* v. 3.) p. 53, *in*
* 822.294;—Same. (*Dodsley's old plays,* v. 3.) p. 1, *in*
** 822.181;—Roister Doister. (Arber, E: *Eng. reprints.*) *in* * 829.12.—**Wyatt,** *Sir.* T:, *the elder.*
Songs and sonnets. (Arber, E: *Eng. reprints.*)
* 829.410.

17th century.
Addison, Joseph. 1672–1719. Account of the
greatest English poets. 1694. Latin poems in the
Musæ Anglicanæ. 1699. (*Works,* v. 1.) 819.33.—
Bacon, Francis. *Baron Verulam. Viscount St.
Albans.* 1561–1626. Works. 15 vols. 01.1–15.—**Beaumont,** Francis, *and* Fletcher, J: Works. 2 vols.
822.118–19.—**Bunyan,** J: 1628–1688. Divine emblems,
with pref. by A. Smith. 821.612;—The pilgrim's
progress. (1628–1684.) ** 249.27.—**Butler,** S: 1612–
1680. Poetical works. 2 vols. (in 1). 821.56.—**Congreve,** W: 1670–1729. Dramatic works. *in* 822.
126.—**Cowley,** Abraham. 1618–1667. Essays, with
life and notes by Dr. Hurd and others. 824.160.—
Denham, *Sir* J: 1615–1668. Cooper's Hill; poem.
(1642.) 821.1008.—**Dryden,** J: 1631–1700. Drama-
tick works. 6 vols. * 42.5–15.—Poetical works,
with memoir. 5 vols. (in 2). 821.126–7.—**Hobbes,** T:
1588–1679. English works. Ed. by Sir W: Molesworth. 11 vols. * 42.5–15.—**Hooker,** R: 1553–1600.
Laws of ecclesiastical polity. Books, vi–viii. 1618.
(*Works,* v. 2.) 283.42.—**Jonson,** Ben. Works, with

English Fiction. *Contin.*
Literature. *Contin.*
ENGLISH LITERATURE. *Contin.*
17th century. *Contin.*
biog. memoir, by W: Gifford. 822.121.—**Locke,** J:
1632–1704. Works. 8th ed. 4 vols. * 42.1–4.—**Milton,**
J: 1608–1674. Complete poetical works, with life and
notes by Rev. G: Gilfillan. 821.270–1;—Prose works,
with notes by J. A. St. John. 5 vols. 820.68–72.—
Prynne, W: 1600–1669. A short . . . prescription
to recover our kingdom, church and nation from
their present . . . confusion. 1659. (*Harl. misc.*) p.
89, *in* ** 942.853.—**Shirley,** J. Dramatic works and
poems. 6 vols. 1833. 822.1108–13.—**Spenser,** Edmund. 1552–1599. View of the state of Ireland.
1633. 941.6.—**Taylor,** Jeremy. *Bp. of Down and
Connor.* 1613–1667. Holy living and dying. 1650–
1651. 241.4;—Works. 3 vols. 200.45–7.

18th century.
The Library has works of **Addison,** Joseph. 1672–
1719.—**Alison,** A. 1757–1839.—**Beckford,** W: 1760–
1844.—**Bentham,** J. 1748–1832.—**Berkeley,** G: *Bp.
of Cloyne.* 1684–1753.—**Blackstone,** *Sir* W: 1723–
1780.—**Boswell,** J. 1740–1795.—**Burke,** Edmund.
1729–1797.—**Burney,** F.. 1752–1840.—**Burns,** Robert.
1759–1796.—**Butler,** Joseph. *Bp. of Durham.* 1692–
1752.—**Chesterfield,** *Lord.* 1699–1751.—**Churchill,**
C: 1731–1764.—**Cibber,** Colley. 1671–1757.—**Coleridge,** S: Taylor. 1772–1834.—**Cooper,** Anthony.
Lord Shaftesbury. 1671–1713.—**Cowper,** W: 1731–
1800.—**Defoe,** Daniel. 1661–1731.—**Disraeli,** I:
1766–1848.—**Dryden,** J: 1631–1700.—**Ferguson,** A.
1724–1816.—**Fielding,** H: 1707–1754.—**Gibbon,** E:
1737–1794.—**Godwin,** W: 1756–1836.—**Goldsmith,**
Oliver. 1728–1774.—**Hartley,** D:, *M. D.* 1705–1757.—
Hervey, J. 1714–1758.—**Hume,** D: 1711–1776.—
Hutcheson, Francis. 1694–1747.—**Johnson,** *Dr.*
S: 1709–1784.—"**Junius.**"—**Lamb,** C: 1775–1834.—
Locke, J: 1632–1704.—**Lowth,** R. 1710–1787.—**Lyt-
tleton,** G: *Lord.* 1709–1773.—**Malone,** E. 1741–1821.—
Mason, W: 1725–1797.—**More,** H. 1745–1833.—
Paley, W: 1745–1805.—**Pope,** Alexander. 1688–
1744.—**Priestley,** *Dr.* Joseph. 1733–1804.—**Rad-
cliffe,** *Mrs.* A. 1764–1823.—**Reid,** *Dr.* T: 1710–1796.
—**Richardson,** S: 1689–1761.—**St. John,** H: *Lord
Bolingbroke.* 1678–1751.—**Scott,** *Sir* Walter. 1771–
1832.—**Sheridan,** R: Brinsley Butler. 1751–1816.
—**Smith,** Adam. 1723–1790.—**Smollett,** Tobias G:
1721–1771.—**Spectator, The.** *See* Addison, J. Works.
vols. 2, 4. 819.34, 36.—**Steele,** *Sir* R: 1671–1729.—
Sterne, Laurence. 1713–1768.—**Stewart,** Dugald.
1753–1828.—**Swift,** Jonathan. 1667–1745.—**Tindal,** M.
1657–1733.—**Warton,** J. 1722–1800.—**Warton,** T:
1728–1790.—**Wesley,** J: 1703–1791; *and* C: 1708–1788.—
White, G. 1720–1793.—**Wordsworth,** W: 1770–
1850.—**Young,** E: 1684–1765; and others.
Note.—See Catalogues of this Library.
No. 2, 1880.   No. 4, 1884.   No. 6, 1891.
No. 3, 1882.   No. 5, 1888.
19th century.
The Library has works of **Arnold,** Matthew.
1822–1888.—**Arnold,** T: 1795–1842.—**Austen,** J.. 1775–
1817.—**Bagehot,** W: 1826–1877.—**Bentham,** J.
1748–1832.—**Besant,** W: 1838- .—**Black,** W: 1841- .
—**Blackmore,** R: D. 1825- .—**Bowles,** W: L. 1762–
1850.—**Brontë,** C. 1816–1855.—**Brontë,** E. 1818–1848.
—**Broughan,** H: *Lord.* 1778–1868.—**Browning,**
Mrs. E.. (Barrett). 1806–1861.—**Browning,** Robert.
1812–1890.—**Buchanan,** R. 1841- .—**Buckle,** H:
T: 1822–1862.—**Burns,** Robert. 1759–1796.—**Byron,** *Sir*
Gordon Noel. G: Lord. 1788–1824.—**Carlyle,** T:
1795–1881.—**Clough,** A. H. 1819–1861.—**Cobbett,** W:
1762–1835.—**Coleridge,** S: Taylor. 1772–1834.—**Col-
lins,** W: 1824–1889.—**Darwin,** C: R. 1809–1882.
—**Dickens,** C: J: Huffam. 1812–1870.—**Disraeli,**
B:, *Lord Beaconsfield.* 1804–1881.—**Dowden,** E:
1843- .—**Edgeworth,** M. 1767–1849.—**Eliot,** G:
1819–1880.—**Fitzgerald,** E: 1809–1883.—**Freeman,**
E: A: 1823- .—**Froude,** J. A. 1818- .—**Gardiner,**
S: R. 1829- .—**Gladstone,** W: Ewart. 1809.—
Godwin, W: 1756–1836.—**Green,** J: R: 1837–1883.—
Grote, G: 1794–1871.—**Hallam,** H: 1777–1859.—
Hardy, T: 1840- .—**Helps,** *Sir* A. 1817–1875.—
Hemans, *Mrs.* F. D. 1794–1835.—**Hunt,** J. H: L.
1784–1859.—**Huxley,** T: H: 1825- .—**James,** G: P.
R. 1801–1860.—**Jeffrey,** F. 1773–1850.—**Keats,** J:
1795–1821.—**Kinglake,** A. W. 1811- .—**Kings-
ley,** C: 1791–1875.—**Lamb,** C: 1775–1834, *and* M..—
Landor, W. S. 1775–1864.—**Lang,** A. 1844- .
—**Lecky,** W: E: H. 1838- .—**Lever,** C: J. 1809-
1872.—**Lewes,** G: H: 1817–1878.—**Lockhart,** J: G.

English Fiction. *Contin.*
Literature. *Contin.*
ENGLISH LITERATURE. *Contin.*
19th century. Contin.

1794-1854.—**Lytton,** E: G: **E. L. Bulwer-** 1805-1873.—**Macaulay,** T: B., *Lord.* 1800-1859.—**MacDonald,** G: 1824- —**Malthus,** T: R. 1766-1876.—**Martineau,** H. 1802-1876.—**Masson,** D: 1822- —**Maurice,** J: F. D. 1805-1872.—**Meredith,** G: 1828- —**Mill,** J: S. 1806-1873.—**Miller,** H. 1802-1856.—**Milnes,** M. *Lord Houghton.* 1809-1885.—**Mitford,** M.. R. 1786-1866;—**Mitford,** W: 1744-1827.—**Moore,** T: 1779-1852.—**More,** H. 1745-1833.—**Morley,** J: 1838- .—**Müller,** F. Max. 1823- —**Napier,** *Sir* W: 1785-1860.—**Newman,** J: H:, *Cardinal.* 1801-1890.—**Oliphant,** *Mrs.* 1820- .—**Ople,** *Mrs.* 1769-1853.—**Paley,** W: 1745-1805.—**Palgrave,** *Sir* F. 1788-1861.—**Pater,** W. H. 1839- .—**Patmore,** C. 1823- .—**Peacock,** T: L. 1785-1866.—**Procter,** B. W. 1787-1874.—**Pusey,** E: B. 1800-1882.—**Reade,** C: 1814-1884. — **Robertson,** F: W. 1816-1853. — **Rossetti,** Dante Gabriel. 1828-1882.—**Ruskin,** J: 1819- .—**Scott,** *Sir* Walter. 1771-1832. — **Shelley,** Percy Bysshe. 1792-1822.—**Smith,** G. 1823- .—**Smith,** S. 1771-1845.—**Southey,** R. 1774-1843.—**Spencer,** Herbert. 1820- .—**Stephen,** L. 1832- .—**Stevenson,** R. L: 1845- .—**Stewart,** Dugald. 1753-1828. —**Stubbs,** W: 1825- .—**Swinburne,** A. C: 1837- .—**Symonds,** J: A. 1840- .—**Tennyson,** Alfred, *Lord.* 1809- .—**Thackeray,** W: Makepeace. 1811-1863.—**Tooke,** J: H. 1736-1812.—**Trench,** R: C. 1807-1886.—**Trollope,** A. 1815-1882.—**Tyndall,** J: 1820- .—**Wallace,** A. R. 1822- —**Whately,** R: 1787-1863.—**Whewell,** W: 1794-1866.—**White,** G. 1759-1833.—**Wilson,** J: *(Christopher North.)* 1785-1854.—**Wordsworth,** W: 1770-1850.—**Yonge,** C.. M.. 1823; and others.

Note.—See **Catalogues** of this Library.
No. 2, 1880.   No. 4, 1884.   No. 6, 1891.
No. 3, 1882.   No. 5, 1888.

—— *Bibliography.*

Adams, O. F. Brief handbook of Eng. authors. 4th ed. 1887. 820.205.—**Allibone,** S. A. Critical dictionary of Eng. literature. 3 vols. 1886. ** 803.6-8.—**Bent,** W: London catalogue of books. 1800-1822. ** 15.264.—**Brewer,** E. C. Authors and their works, with dates. 1884. ** 15.272.—**Collier,** J. P. Bibliographical and critical account of the rarest books in the English language. 4 vols. 1866. ** 20.4-7.—**Grey,** H. A bird's eye view of Eng. literature. (A. D. 610-A. D. 1882.) 820.191.—**Harris,** A. B. Little biographies. Eng. authors. (1887.) 928.692.—**Hazlitt,** W. C. Hand-book to the popular, poetical and dramatic literature of Gt. Britain. 1867. ** 15.20.—**Hodgson,** T: The London catalogue of books published in Gt. Britain. 1816-1851. ** 15.12.—**Jones,** L. E. The best reading. 2d ser. 1882. ** 17.2²;—*Same.* 3d ser. For the five years ending Dec. 1, 1886. * 17.2³.—**Low,** S. The Eng. catalogue of books. Jan. 1835-Jan. 1863. ** 15.13;—*Same.* Jan. 1863-Jan. 1872. ** 15.14;—*Same.* Jan. 1872-Dec. 1880. ** 15.14²;—Index to the Brit. catalogue of books published during 1837 to 1857 inclusive. ** 15.15;—*Same.* (Eng. catalogue.) v. 2: 1856-Jan. 1876. ** 15.16;—*Same.* v. 3: Jan. 1874-Dec. 1880. ** 15.17;—*and others.* The Eng. catalogue. 1881-1885. 5 vols. ** 15.61¹⁻⁵;—*Same.* 1888-90. 3 vols. ** 15.61⁶⁻¹⁰.—**Lowndes,** W. T. Bibliographer's manual of Eng. literature. 5 vols. (in 10) and app. 1877-8. ** 15.1-11.—**Maclean,** G: E., *ed.* A chart of Eng. lit. with references. 1891. 820.204.—**Porter,** N. Books and reading. 1882. D2.19.—**Ryland,** F: Authors and their works. (*In his* Chronolog. outlines of Eng. lit.) 1890. p. 241, *in* 820.195.—**Smith,** G. J. A synopsis of Eng. and Amer. lit. 1890. 820.200.—**Sonnenschein,** W: S. The best books. 1891. ** 17.238².—**Sotheran,** H: A catalogue of superior second-hand books in literature, science and the fine arts. 1888. ** 18.270.—**Van Rhyn,** G. A. F. What and how to read. 1875. * 17.1.—**Watt,** R. Bibliotheca Britannica. 4 vols. 1824. ** 15.13-16.—**Whitaker,** J. A reference catalogue of current literature. 1875. ** 11. 102;—*Same.* 1877. ** 11.29;—*Same.* 1880. ** 11.30; —*Same.* 1888. ** 11.30²;—*Same.* 1889. ** 11.30³.

See also "**Bibliography**" in **Catalogues** of this Library.
No. 2, 1880, p. 23.   No. 4, 1884, pp. 26-29.
No. 3, 1882, pp. 20-1.   No. 5, 1888, pp. 33-4.
Also **Poole's Index** (to 1882.) ** 50.1;—*Same,* to Jan. 1, 1887. ** 50.1².
Also **Books** and reading, pp. 23, 24.

English Fiction. *Contin.*
Literature. *Contin.*
ENGLISH LITERATURE. *Contin.*

—— *Bibliography. Periodicals.*

Athenæum. Jan. 1869-June 1890. 31 vols. ** 52.261-2675².—**Bibliographer.** vols. 1-6. Dec. 1881-Nov.1884. ** 10.13¹⁻⁶.—**Bookseller.** Jan. 1887-Dec. 1889. 5 vols. ** 11.231¹⁻⁴.—**Classical review.** vols. 2. Feb. 1888-Dec. 1889. 2 vols. * 805. 4¹⁻².—**Library.** v. 1. 1889. * 19.133.—**Library chronicle.** vols. 1, 5. 1884, 1888. 2 vols. * 19.67; 67².—**New monthly magazine and literary journal.** vols. 1-68. 1821-1843. 68 vols. ** 52.549-617.—**Publishers' circular.** vols. 50-52. 1887-1889. 3 vols. 11.292¹⁻³.

—— *Collections.*

Arber, E: English garner. 7 vols. 1877-83. * 810.3-9. *Note.—*For contents, *see* Catalogue of this Lib., No. 5, 1888, pp. 21-2.—**Baker,** G: M. The favorite speaker . . . selections published in the Reading club. Nos. 17-20. 1889. 825.202.—**Carpenter,** J. E. Popular readings in prose and verse. 5 vols. 825.22-6.—**Early English Text Society.** Publications, Nos. 1-51; 56-94. 56 vols. ** 806.1-1¹;¹ᵃᵉ⁻⁹ᵏ.— *Same.* Ex. ser., Nos. 1-58. 1867-90. 58 vols. ** 806.2-2ᵃ⁸.—**Forbes,** W. K. Five minute recitations. 1887. 825.189.—**Fuller worthies' library.** Ed. by Rev. A. B. Grosart. 1868-78. 39 vols. ** 821.1048-86. *Note.—*For contents, *see* Catalogue of this Lib. No. 5, 1888, p. 174.—**Fulton,** R. I., *and* **Trueblood,** T. C., *comps.* Choice readings from standard and popular authors. 1885. 825.191.—**Garnett,** J. M., *comp.* Selections in Eng. prose (1580-1880). 820.203. —**Garrett,** P., *comp.* Speaker's garland and literary bouquet. Nos. 1-28. (4 vols. in 1.) 7 vols. 1885-8. 825.192-8.—**Harlow,** W. B. An introd. to early Eng. lit. (to 1552). 820.201.—**Hazlitt,** W. C. Shakespeare's library: a coll. of the plays, romances, novels, poems and histories employed by Shakespeare in the composition of his works. 1875. 6 vols. 822. 236-41.—**Hudson,** H: N. Classical English reader. 1888. 825.203.—**Morris,** R: Specimens of early English. v. 1: A. D. 1150-A. D. 1300. 1882. 420. 19. — **New Shakspere Society.** Publications. *Note.—*For contents, *see* Catalogue of this Lib. No. 5, 1888, p. 266.—**Riddle,** G: Readings. 1888. 829.676.—**Saintsbury,** G: Specimens of Eng. prose style from Malory to Macaulay. 1886. 820.121.—**Sargent,** E. Intermediate standard speaker. (*Ser. of speakers,* No. 2.) 1858. 825.188.—**Skeat,** W. W. Specimens of Eng. literature. (A. D. 1394-A. D. 1579.) 821.678.

See also "**Extracts and selections**" in **Catalogues** of this Library.
No. 2, 1880, pp. 79-80.   No. 4, 1884, p. 100.
No. 3, 1882, pp. 68-69.   No. 5, 1888, p. 137.
See also **Fables,** p. 81.—**Fairy tales,** p. 81.

—— *Dictionaries.*

Adams, W: H: D. Dictionary of Eng. literature. ** 803.30.—**Allibone,** S: A. Dictionary of Eng. and Amer. literature. 3 vols. ** 803.6-8.—**Brewer,** E. C. Dictionary of phrase and fable. 803.1;—Reader's hand-book. 1880. 803.2. — **Chambers,** W., *and* Chambers, R., *pubs.* Cyclopædia of Eng. literature. 2 vols. ** 820.15-16.—**Halkett,** S., *and* Laing, J: Dictionary of the anonymous and pseudonymous literature of Great Britain. 4 vols. 1888. v. 1: A-E; v. 2: F-N; v. 3: O-Tis; v. 4: Tit-Z. ** 14.11-13¹.—**Reddall,** H: F: Fact, fancy and fable. 1889. ** 803.34.—**Wheeler,** W. A., *and* Wheeler, C. G. Familiar allusions. 1882. * 803.12.

—— *History, criticism, manuals.*

Adams, W: H: D. The merry monarch; or, England under Charles II. Its art, literature and society. 2 vols. 1885. 942.1279-80.—**Angus,** J. The handbook of Eng. literature. 820.168.—**Arnold,** M. A guide to Eng. literature. 20 pp. (*In his* Mixed essays.) 1883. p. 134, *in* 824.407.—**Arnold,** T: Manual of Eng. literature, historical and critical. 1885. 820.165.—**Backus,** T. J., *and* Brown, H. D. The great English writers from Chaucer to George Eliot. 1889. 820.167. —**Bagehot,** W. Literary studies. (*Works,* vols. 1, 2.) 1889. 814.22-3.—**Blaisdell,** A. F: First steps with Amer. and Brit. authors. 1888. 820.154.—**Brink,** B. ten. Early Eng. literature (to Wiclif, 1384). Tr. by H. M. Kennedy. 1889. 820. 153.—**Brooke,** *Rev.* S. (Primer of) Eng. literature. 1890. 820.4.—**Buckland,** A.. Story of Eng. literature. (A. D. 264-19th cent.) 1882. 809.55.—**Burt,** B. C. References for students in Eng. literature. 42 pp. 1887. 820.181.—**Chambers,** R. History of the Eng. language and literature. 1835. 820.96.—

English Fiction. *Contin.*
Literature. *Contin.*
ENGLISH LITERATURE. *Contin.*
—— *History, criticism, manuals. Contin.*
Collier, W: F. A hist. of Eng. literature in a series
of biog. sketches. New ed. 1888. 820.196.—Courthope, W: J: The liberal movement in Eng. literature. (Essays.) 820.190.—Craik, G: L. Compendi-
ous history of Eng. literature and language from
the Norman conquest. 2 vols. 1875. 820.21-2.—Day,
H: N. Introd. to the study of Eng. literature. (1868.)
820.107.—Demaus, R. Class-book of Eng. prose.
1350-1866. 1871. 820.182.—Dowden, E: Transcripts
and studies. 1888. 824.421.—Gosse, E. W: History
of eighteenth century literature. (1660-1780.) 1889.
820.133.—Hodgkins, L. M. Guide to the study of
nineteenth century authors. 1889. 820.155.—Hunt,
T. W. Representative Eng. prose and prose writers. 2d ed. 1887. 820.120.—Hutton, L. Literary landmarks of London. 820.178.—Hutton, R:
H. Essays on some of the modern guides to English thought in matters of faith. 1888. 824.474.—
Jusserand, J. J. The Eng. novel in the time of
Shakespeare. 1890. 813.1.—L'Estrange, Rev. A.
G. K. Hist of Eng. humour. 2 vols. 1878. 828.169-70.
—M'Cormick, W: S. Three lectures on Eng. literature. 1889. 820.166.—Minto, W: Characteristics of Eng. poets from Chaucer to Shirley. 1889.
820.169.—Mitchell, D. G. Eng. lands, letters and
kings. From Celt to Tudor. 1889. 820.164:—Same.
From Elizabeth to Anne. 1890. 820.177.—Morgan,
A. Shakespeare in fact and in criticism. 1888.
824.453.—Morley, Prof. H: Eng. literature in the
reign of Victoria. 1882. 820.85;—Same. An
attempt towards a history of Eng. literature. vols.
1-4. 1887-9. 820.170-73;—A first sketch of Eng. literature. 820.46;—Same. 13th ed. 1887. 820.189;—
Manual of Eng. literature (670 A. D. to date). 1879.
809.11.—Nicoll, H: J. Landmarks of Eng. literature. 1883. 809.59.—Oliphant, Mrs. M. O. (W.)
Literary history of England. (End of 18th and beginning of 19th cent.) 2 vols. 1882. 820.88-9.—
Perry, T: S. Eng. literature in the eighteenth
century. 1883. 809.56.—Ryland, F: Chronological outlines of Eng. literature. 1890. 820.195.—
Saintsbury, G: W. A history of Elizabethan literature. (1560-1660.) 1887. 820.134.—Salt, H. S.
Literary sketches. 1888. 824.454.—Senior, N. W.
In his Essays on fiction. 1864. 824.354.—Shepard,
W:, ed. In his Pen pictures of earlier Victorian authors. 1884. 820.158.—Taine, H. History of Eng.
literature. 3 vols. 820.56-8.—Thackeray, W: M.
Eng. humourists of the eighteenth century: lectures. 1853. 820.180;—Same. (Works, v. 10.) in
823.1579.—Timbs, J: Anecdote lives of wits and
humorists. 2 vols. 1872. 828.129-30.—Tucker-
man, B. A history of Eng. prose fiction from Sir
Thomas Malory to George Eliot. 1882. 820.198.—
Washburn, E. W. Studies in early Eng. literature. (600-1660.) 1884. 820.135.—Welsh, A. H. A
digest of Eng. and Amer. literature. 1890. 820.192.
—Wright, J: C. Outline of Eng. literature. 1889.
820.194.
See also Roberts, W: The earlier history of
Eng. bookselling. 1889. 686.8.
Also " Literature" in Catalogues of this Library.
No. 2, 1880, pp. 135-6.   No. 4, 1884, p. 166.
No. 3, 1882, pp. 111-12.   No. 5, 1888 (Eng. lit.), p. 132.
Also Poole's Index (to 1882). pp. 415-19, in **
50.1;—Same, to 1887. pp. 143-5, in ** 50.1².
—— Drama.
16th century. See also before under English literature,
16th cent., p. 158.
The Library has works of Chettle, H: (2d hf. of
16th cent.)—Churchyard, T: 1520-1604.—Gascoigne, G: about 1536-1577.—Greene, R. 1560-
1592.—Greville, Sir Fulke. 1554-1628.—Heywood,
J: 1506(?)-1565.—Kyd, T: (end of 16th cent.)—
Lindsay, Sir D: 1490(?)-1555.—Lodge, T: 1558-
1625.—Lyly, J: 1553-1603.—Marlowe, C. 1564-1593.
—Munday, A. 1554-1633.—Nash, T: (2d hf. of 16th
cent.)—Peele, G: 1558(?)-1598(?).—Skelton, J: about
1460-1529.—Udall, N. 1504(?)-1556; and others.
17th century. See also before under English literature,
17th cent., p. 159.
Beaumont, 1586(?)-1616, and Fletcher. 1579-
1625.—Behn, A. 1640-1689.—Congreve, W: 1559(?)-
1634.—Crowne, J: (2d
hf. of 17th cent.)—Davenant, Sir W: 1606-1668.
—Dekker, T: 1570(?)-1637(?).—Dryden, J: 1631-1700.

English Fiction. *Contin.*
Literature. *Contin.*
ENGLISH LITERATURE. *Contin.*
—— *Drama. Contin.*
17th century. Contin.
—Farquhar, G: 1678-1707.—Ford, J: 1586-1666.
—Heywood, T: 1581(?)-1640(?).—Jonson, B. 1573-
1637.—Lee, N. 1655-1692.—Marston, J: 1575(?)-1633.
—Massinger, P. 1584-1640.—Mayne, J: 1604-1672.
—Middleton, T: 1570-1627.—Otway, T: 1651-1685.
—Randolph, T: 1606(?)-1634(?).—Rowley, W: (1st
hf. of 17th cent.)—Shadwell, T: 1640-1692.—
Shakespeare, W: 1564-1616.—Shirley, J. 1596-
1666.—Southern, T: 1660-1746.—Vanbrugh, Sir
J: 1666(?)-1726.—Villiers, G: Duke of Buckingham.
1627-1688.—Webster, J: 16th and 17th cent.—
Wycherley, W: 1640-1725; and others.
18th century. See also before under English literature,
18th cent., p. 159.
The Library has works of Addison, J. 1672-1719.
—Centlivre, S. 1680(?)-1722.—Cibber, C. 1671-
1757.—Colman, G: 1732-1794.—Cowley, H. 1743-
1809.— Cumberland, R: 1732-1811.—Dibdin, C:
1745-1814.—Foote, S: 1719-1777.—Garrick, D: 1716-
1779.—Gay, J: 1688-1732.—Goldsmith, O. 1728-
1774.—Home, J: 1722-1808.—Hughes, J: 1677-1720.
—Inchbald, E.. 1753-1821.—Johnson, S: 1709-
1784.—Lillo, G: 1693-1739.—Moore, E: 1712-1757.—
Rowe, N. 1673-1718.—Sheridan, R: B. B. 1751-
1816; and others.
Modern period. See also before under English literature, 19th cent., p. 159.
The Library has works of Baillie, J. 1762-1851.—
Boucicault, D. 1822-1890.—Brougham, J: 1810-
1880.—Browning, R. 1812-1889.—Buckstone, J: B.
1802-1889.—Byron, Lord. 1788-1824—Dibdin, T:
1771-1841.—Gilbert, W. S. 1836-——Jerrold, D. W:
1803-1857.—Knowles, J. S. 1784-1862.—Landor, W.
S. 1775-1864.—Lytton, Lord. 1805-1873.—Milman,
H: H. 1791-1868.—Mitford, M.. R. 1786-1855.—
Planché, J. R. 1796-1880.—Poole, J: 1786-1872.—
Robertson, T: W. 1829-1871.—Swinburne, A. C:
1837-——Talfourd, Sir T: N. 1795-1854.—Taylor,
Tom. 1817-1880; and others.
Note.—For Drama and Drama, Collections, see also
Catalogues of this Library.
No. 2, 1880, p. 65.   No. 4, 1884, pp. 84-5.
No. 3, 1882, pp. 54-5.   No. 5, 1888, p. 78.
—— Drama. History and criticism.
Archer, W: Eng. dramatists of to-day. 1882.
822.1083.—Coleridge, S: T. Lectures upon Shake-
speare and some other dramatists. 1854. (Comp.
works, v. 4.) 822.291.—Collier, J: P. History of
Eng. dramatic poetry. 3 vols. 1831. 822.152-4.—
Donnelly, I. The great cryptogram: Francis
Bacon's cipher in the so-called Shakespeare plays.
1888. * 822.1082.—Dryden, J: An essay of dramatic
poesy. Ed. by T: Arnold. 1889. 812.75.—Fitzgerald, P. Romance of the Eng. stage. 1875. 822.
1097.—Gayley, C: M., and Scott, F. N. Literature. 34
pp. (In their A guide to the lit. of æsthetics.) 1890. p.
73, in ** 16.227.—Golden, W: E. A brief history of
the Eng. drama. 1890. 822.1102.—Grey, H: Plots of
some of the most famous of old English plays. 1888.
822.1120.—Halliwell-Phillipps, J. O. Dictionary of
old Eng. plays. 822.451.—Hazlitt, W. C. Handbook
to the popular, poetical and dramatic literature of
Gt. Britain. 1867. * 15.20.—Klein, J. L. Geschichte
des englischen Drama's. 832.108-9. Linton, W. J.,
and Stoddard, R: H: Dramatic scenes and characters. 1887. 822.1019.—Lowe, R. W. Bibliographical account of Eng. theatrical literature, from the
earliest times to the present day. 1888. ** 16.230.
—Prölss, R. Das neuere Drama der Engländer.
(In his Geschichte des neueren Dramas. v. 2, pt. 2.)
1882. 812.71.—Russell, W: C. Representative actors
. . . from the 16th to the present century. 927.289.
—Ward, A. W. History of Eng. dramatic literature. 2 vols. 1875. 822.1095-6.
See also before under English literature, History, criticism, and manuals, p. 160.
—— Fiction. History and criticism.
Forsyth, W. Novels and novelists of the 18th
cent. 1871. 820.86.—Gayley, C: M., and Scott, F.
N. Literature. 34 pp. (In their A guide to the lit.
of æsthetics.) 1890. p. 73, in ** 16.227.—Jeaffreson, J. C. Novels and novelists from Elizabeth to
Victoria. 2 vols. 1858. 820.186-7.—Jusserand, J.
J. The Eng. novel in the time of Shakespeare.
Illus. 1890. 813.1.—Lanier, S. The Eng. novel
and the principle of its development. 1883. 820.86.

English Fiction. *Contin.*
Literature. *Contin.*
ENGLISH LITERATURE. *Contin.*
—— *Fiction. History and criticism. Contin.*
—Stephen, L. Hours in a library. 3 vols. 1874–79. 824.86; 824.320; 824.320².—Tuckerman, B. History of Eng. prose fiction from Sir T: Malory to G: Eliot. 1882. 809.54.
See also before under English literature, *History, criticism, and manuals.* p. 160.

ENGLISH LANGUAGE. *History.*
Earle, J: Philology of the Eng. tongue. 1879. 420.12.—Guest, E. A history of Eng. rhythms. Ed. by W. W. Skeat. 1882. 426.5.—Hadley, J. Brief history of the Eng. language. (Webster, N. *Dictionary.* 1890. pp. xxix–xliv.) 423.27².—Marsh, G: P. Origin and history of the Eng. language. 1862. 420.1.—Meiklejohn, J. M. D. The Eng. language: its grammar, history and literature. 1888. 425.60.—Morris, R: Historical outlines of Eng. accidence. 1880. 425.35.—Sievers, E. An old Eng. grammar. Tr. and ed. by A. S. Cook. 1885. 425.59.—Welsh, A. H. Development of Eng. literature and language. 2 vols. 1882. 809.52–3.
See also papers by various authors in **Early Eng. Text. Soc.** Publications, Nos. 1–94, in 56 vols. 1864–90. ** 806.1–1¹¹; ** 806.1¹⁶.²⁴;—*Same.* Ex. ser., Nos. 1–58. 58 vols. 1867–90. ** 806.2–2⁵⁸.
Also, **Philological Society.** Publications. 9 vols. ** 405.51–5; ** 405.58–61;—Transactions. 1842–1876. 22 vols. ** 405.1–22.
See also **Catalogues** of this Library.
  No. 2, 1880, pp. 74–5.   No. 4, 1884, pp. 95–6.
  No. 3, 1882, p. 63.   No. 5, 1888, pp. 131–2.

ENGLISH POETRY. *Collections and selections.*
Aitkin, M. C., *comp.* Scottish song. (*Gold. treas. ser.*) 1874. 821.1220.—Ashton, J:, *ed.* A century of ballads (illustrative of the life, manners and habits of the Eng. nation during the 17th cent.) Illus. 1887. ** 821.1285;—Modern street ballads. 1888. 821.1270.—Bates, C., F., *comp.* Cambridge book of poetry and song. * 821.1246.—Bullen, A. H., *ed.* England's Helicon. A coll. of lyrical and pastoral poems: pub. in 1600. 1887. 821.1237;—Lyrics from the song-books of the Elizabethan age. 1889. 821.1238.—Dowden, E:, *ed.* Lyrical ballads. Repr. from 1st ed. of 1798. 1890. 821.1358.—Ellis, G: Specimens of early Eng. poets. 3 vols. 1803. * 821.873–5.—Fuller worthies' library. Ed. by Rev. A. B. Grosart. 39 vols. * 821.1048–86. (For contents, *see* Catalogue of this Lib. No. 5, 1888, p. 174.)—Garrett, P., *comp.* Speaker's garland and literary bouquet; combining 100 choice selections. Nos. 1–28. 4 vols. (in 1) 7 vols. 1885–8. 825.192–8.—Hazlitt, W: C., *ed.* Remains of the early popular poetry of England. 4 vols. 1864. 821.1110–13.—Historical poems of the 16th cent. (*In* Camden Soc., No. 61.) ** 942.1031.—Hullah, J: F., *ed.* The song book. (*Gold. treas. ser.*) 1884. 821.1226.—Hunt, J. H: L. Imagination and fancy. 1883. 821.1234.—Koelle, I,. L. C., *comp.* Music in song. From Chaucer to Tennyson. 1883. 821.1242.—Lear, H. L. S., *comp.* Five minutes' daily readings of poetry. 4th ed. 1882. 821.1280.—Linton, W. J., and Stoddard, R: H: English verse. Ballads and romances. 1887. 821.1232;—*Same.* Chaucer to Burns. 1887. 821.1231;—*Same.* Translations. 1883. 821.1229.—Mackay, C:, *comp.* 1001 gems of Eng. poetry. (1867.) * 821.1039.—Melville, G: J: Whyte- Songs and verse. 821.1311.—Morris, M., *ed.* Poet's walk: an introd. to Eng. poetry. 3d ed. 821.1276.—Oxenford, J:, *comp.* Old English ditties sel. from W: Chappell's "Popular music of the olden time" . . . , the symphonies . . . by G: A. Macfarren. 2 vols. * 784.37–8.—Palgrave, F. T., *ed.* Children's treasury of Eng. song. (*Gold. treas. ser.*) 1887. 821. 1222;—Golden treasury of the best songs and lyrical poems in the Eng. language. (*Gold. treas. ser.*) 1888. 821.1223;—The treasury of sacred song. 1890. 821.1309.—Peele, G: Miscellaneous poems. 16 pp. (1627.) (*Works,* v. 2.) p. 357, *in* ** 822.1086.—Rump poems. (Royalist.) 1639–61. 2 vols. * 821.991–2.—Skeat, W. W. Specimens of Eng. literature. 1879. 821.678.—Swinburne, A. C: Poems and ballads, 2d ser. 1878. 821.397¹.—Tennyson, A. Ballads and other poems. (*Works,* v. 6.) 1888. 821.1212.—Thackeray, W: M. Ballads. (*Works,* v. 11.) *in* 823.1573.—Willmott, R. A. Poets of the 19th cent. 1884. 821.1324.—Wright, T: *ed. and tr.* Political songs of England. John to Edward II. (*Camden Soc.,* No. 6.) 1839. ** 942.976.

English Fiction. *Contin.*
Literature. *Contin.*
ENGLISH POETRY. *Collections and selections. Contin.*
See also "Poetry " in **Catalogues** of this Library.
  No. 2, 1880, p. 183.   No. 4, 1884, p. 231.
  No. 3, 1882, pp. 151–2.   No. 5, 1888, pp. 289–90.
See also before under English literature.
—— *Dictionaries.*
Allibone, S. A. Poetical quotations from Chaucer to Tennyson. ** 821.10.—Bysshe, E: The art of English poetry. 1725. ** 829.592.—Dictionary of quotations from the British poets. 3 vols. 1824. ** 821.1201–3.—Ward, A.. L., *ed.* Dictionary of quotations from Eng. and Amer. poets. Based upon Bohn's ed. (1883.) ** 821.1235.
—— *History and criticism.*
Brooke, *Mrs.* S.. (W.) English poetry and poets. (1890.) 820.184.—Coleridge, S: T. Notes and lectures upon Shakespeare, and some old poets and dramatists. (*Comp. works,* v. 4.) 822.291.—Collier, J. P. Poetical Decameron; or, ten conversations on Eng. poets and poetry. 2 vols. 1820. ** 821.100–101.—Dawson, W. J. The makers of modern English. 1890. 820.197.—De Vere, A. T: Essays chiefly on poetry. 2 vols. 1887. 821.1191–2.—Ellis, G: Historical sketch of the rise and progress of the Eng. poetry and language. 2 vols. 1801. (*In his* Spec. of the early Eng. poets, vols. 1–2.) 821.873–4.—Gayley, C: M., *and* Scott, F. N. Literature. 34 pp. (*In their* Guide to the lit. of æsthetics.) 1890. p. 73, *in* ** 16.227.—Genung, J: F. Tennyson's In memoriam: its purpose and its structure. 3d ed. 1888. 811.17.—Hazlitt, W. Lectures on the Eng. poets and Eng. comic writers. 1880. 824.113.—Minto, W. Characteristics of Eng. poets. 1874. 820.169.—Pater, W. Appreciations, with an essay on style. 1889. 811.22.—Simonds, W: E: Sir Thomas Wyatt and his poems. 1889. 824.417.—Stedman, E. C. The Victorian poets. 1876. 821. 383.—Swinburne, A. C: A century of Eng. poetry. 25 pp. (*In his* Miscellanies.) 1886. p. 25, *in* 824.405;—Short notes on Eng. poets. 24 pp. (*In his* Miscellanies.) 1886. p. 1, *in* 824.405.—Ward, T. H., *ed.* Eng. poets. Selections, with crit. introd. 4 vols. 1881. 821.705–8.—Warton, T: Hist. of Eng. poetry from 11th to 17th cent. 821.420;—*Same.* 12th to 16th cent. Ed. by W. C. Hazlitt. 4 vols. 1871. 811.9–12.
See also **Catalogues** of this Library.
  No. 2, 1880, p. 183.   No. 4, 1884, p. 231.
  No. 3, 1882, p. 151.   No. 5, 1888, p. 290.
See also before under English literature, *History, criticism, manuals,* p. 160.

—— SINGLE AUTHORS.
Early period. The Library has works of Cockayne, O.—Grosseteste, R., *Bp. of* Lincoln.
Chaucer to Shakespeare. See also before under English literature, 14th–16th centuries. p. 158.
  The Library has works of Chaucer, G. 1340 (or, 1328)–1400.—Dunbar, W: 1460(?)–1530(?).—Gascoigne, G: 1536–1577.—Googe, B. 1540–1594.—Henry, *the minstrel.* (Blind Harry.) 15th cent.—James I., *King of Scotland.* 1391–1437.—Lydgate, J: d. about 1460.—Roy, W: 16th cent.—Skelton, J: circa 1460–1529.—Spenser, E. 1552–1599; and others.
Elizabethan to 1625. See also before under English literature, 16th–17th centuries, pp. 158, 159.
  The Library has works of Barnfield, R: 1574–1627.—Breton, N. 1554(?)–1624.—Brooke, C. 17th cent.—Curew, T: 1598–1639(?).—Churchyard, T: 1520(?)–1604.—Constable, H: 1562–1613.—Daniel, S: 1562–1619.—Davies, *Sir* J: 1569–1626.—Donne, J: 1573–1631.—Dyer, *Sir* E. circa 1540–1607.—Fletcher, G. circa 1588–1623.—Fletcher, J: 1579–1625.—Fraunce, A. 16th cent.—Gifford, H. 16th cent.—Greville, F., *Lord Brooke.* 1554–1628.—Harbert, W: 17th cent.—Herbert, G: 1593–1633.—Heywood, T: 1581(?)–1640(?).—Jonson, Ben. 1573 -1637.—Lever, C. 17th cent.—Lodge, T: 1558(?)- 1625.—Markham, G. 1570–1655.—Marston, J: 1575 (?)–1633.—Parker, M. 17th cent.—Peele, G: 1558(?)- 1598(?).—Randolph, T: 1606(?)–1634(?).—Sackville, T:, *Earl of Dorset.* 1536–1608.—Sandys, G: 1577- 1644.—Shakespeare, W: 1564–1616.—Sidney, *Sir* P. 1554–1586.—Southwell, R. 1560(?)–1595.—Taylor, J: *The water-poet.* 1580–1654.—Thynne, F. 16th cent.—Watson, T: circa 1560–1592.—Wotton, *Sir* H: 1568–1639; and others.
17th century (from 1625). See also before under English literature, 17th cent., p. 159.

English Fiction. *Contin.*
Literature. *Contin.*
ENGLISH POETRY. *Contin.*
—— SINGLE AUTHORS. *Contin.*
17th century (from 1625). *Contin.*
The Library has works of Baxter, R: 1615-1691.
—Beaumont, J. 1615-1699.—Bunyan, J: 1628-1688.—Butler, S: 1612-1680.—Carey, P. 17th cent.
—Cary, L., 2 *Viscount Falkland.* 1610(?)-1643.—Congreve, W: 1670-1729.—Cowley, A. 1618-1667.—Crashaw, R. 1613(?)-1650(?).—Davenant, *Sir* W: 1606-1668.—Denham, *Sir* J: 1615-1668.—Dryden, J: 1631-1700.—Fletcher, P. 1582-1650.—Glapthorne, H: 17th cent.—Habington, W: 1605-1654.—Harvey, C. 1597-1603.—Herrick, R. 1591-1674.—Marvell, A. 1621-1678.—Milton, J: 1608-1674.—More, H: 1614-1687.—Norris, J: 1657-1711.—Otway, T: 1651-1685.—Prior, M. 1664-1721.—Quarles, F. 1592-1644.—Suckling, *Sir* J: 1609-1641.—Taylor, Jeremy. 1613-1667.—Vaughan, H. 1622(?)-1695.—Villiers, G:, *Duke of Buckingham.* 1627-1688.—Waller, E. 1605-1687.—Walton, I. 1593-1683.—Washbourne, T: 17th cent.—Wilmot, J:, *Earl of Rochester.* 1647-1680.—Wither, G: 1588-1667; and others.

18th century. See also *before under* English literature, 18th cent., p. 159.
The Library has works of Addison, J. 1672-1719.—Akenside, M: 1721-1770.—Barbauld, *Mrs.* A. L. 1743-1825.—Beattie, J. 1735-1803.—Brooke, H: 1706-1783.—Burns, R. 1759-1796.—Chatterton, T: 1752-1770.—Churchill, C: 1731-1764.—Collins, W: 1721-1756.—Colman, G., *Jr.* 1762-1836.—Congreve, W: 1670-1729.—Cowper, W: 1731-1800.—Crabbe, G: 1754-1832.—Darwin, E: 1731-1802.—Defoe, D. 1661-1731.—Dyer, J: 1700(?)-1758.—Falconer, W: 1732-1769.—Farquhar, G: 1678-1707.—Garrick, D: 1716-1779.—Gay, J: 1688-1732.—Glover, R: 1712-1785.—Goldsmith, O. 1728-1774.—Gray, T: 1716-1771.—Hughes, J: 1677-1720.—Johnson, S: 1709-1784.—Langhorne, J: 1735-1779.—McPherson, J. 1738-1796.—Moore, E: 1712-1757.—Parnell, T: 1679-1717.—Pope, A. 1688-1744.—Prior, M. 1664-1721.—Ramsay, A. 1685-1758.—Rogers, *Rev.* S: 1763-1855.—Rowe, N. 1673-1718.—Shenstone, W: 1714-1763.—Somerville, W: 1692-1742.—Swift, J. 1667-1745.—Thomson, J: 1700-1748.—Tickell, T: 1686-1740.—Warton, T: 1728-1790.—Watts, I: 1674-1748.—Wesley, C: 1708-1788. *and* J: 1703-1791.—Whitehead, W: 1715-1785.—Wolcott, J: 1738-1819.—Young, E: 1681-1765; and others.

Modern period. See also *before under* English literature, 19th ceut., p. 159.
The Library has works of Arnold, *Sir* E. 1831- .—Arnold, M. 1822-1888.—Austin, A. 1835- .—Aytoun, W: E. 1813-1865.—Bailey, P. J. 1816- .—Baillie, J. 1762-1851.—Barnes, W: 1800-1886.—Beddoes, T: L. 1803-1849.—Blake, W: 1757-1827.—Bloomfield, R. 1766-1823.—Bowles, W: L. 1762-1850.—Browning, *Mrs.* E. B. 1809-1861.—Browning, R. 1812-1889.—Buchanan, R. 1841- .—Byron, G: G. N., *Lord.* 1788-1824.—Calverley, C: S. 1831-1884.—Campbell, T: 1777-1844.—Chambers, R. 1802-1871.—Clough, A. H. 1819-1861.—Coleridge, H. 1796-1849.—Coleridge, S: T. 1772-1834.—Combe, W: 1741-1823.—Craik, *Mrs.* D. M. (M.) 1826-1887.—Croker, J: W. 1780-1857.—Cross, *Mrs.* M.. A. (E.) 1819-1880.—Cunningham, A. 1785-1842.—DeVere, A. T. 1814- .—Dobell, S. T. 1824-1874.—Dobson, H: A. 1840- .—Elliott, E. 1781-1849.—Fitzgerald, E: 1809-1883.—Frere, J: H. 1769-1846.—Heber, R. 1783-1826.—Hemans, *Mrs.* F. D. 1794-1835.—Hogg, J. 1772-1835.—Hood, T: 1798-1845.—Hunt, J. H. L. 1784-1859.—Ingelow, J. 1830- .—Ireland, W: H: 1777-1835.—Keats, J: 1795-1821.—Keble, J: 1792-1866.—Kingsley, C: 1819-1875.—Lamb, C: 1775-1834, and M..—Landor, W: S. 1775-1864.—Locker, F: 1821- .—Lytton, E: G: E. L. Bulwer- 1 *Baron.* 1806-1873.—Lytton, E: R. Bulwer- 2 *Baron.* 1831- .—MacDonald, G: 1824- .—Mahony, F. S. 1804-1866.—Marston, J: W. 1820- .—Milman, H: H. 1791-1868.—Montgomery, J. 1771-1854.—Moore, T: 1779-1852.—More, H. 1745-1833.—Morris, L. 1835- .—Morris, W: 1834- .—Motherwell, W: 1797-1835.—Newman, J: H: *Cardinal.* 1801-1890.—Percy, T: 1728-1811.—Pollok, R. 1799-1827.—Praed, W: M. 1802-1839.—Procter, A. A. 1825-1864.—Procter, B. W. 1787-1874.—Rogers, S: 1763-1855.—Rossetti, C. G. 1830- .—Rossetti, D. G. 1828-1882.—Scott, *Sir* W. 1771-1832.—Shelley, P. B. 1792-1822.—Southey, R. 1774-1843.—Swinburne, A: C:

English Fiction. *Contin.*
Literature. *Contin.*
ENGLISH POETRY. *Contin.*
—— SINGLE AUTHORS. *Contin.*
Modern period. *Contin.*
1837- .—Symonds, J: A. 1840- .—Tannahill, R. 1774-1810.—Taylor, *Sir* H: 1805-1886.—Taylor, T. 1817-1880.— Tennyson, A. *Lord.* 1809- .—Thomson, J. 1834-1882.—Tupper, M. F. 1810-1889.—White, H: K. 1785-1806.—Wilson, J: 1785-1854.—Wordsworth, W: 1770-1850; and others.

FINNISH LITERATURE.
Geoffroy, A. La Finlande et la Kalevala. 21 pp. (*Rev. d. d. Mondes*, 1810, 2 pér., v. 91.) p. 300, *in* ** 54. 296.—Kalevala, Selections from the. Tr. by J: A. Porter. 1873. 821.317.—Marmier, X. De la poésie finlandaise. 24 pp. (*Rev. d. d. Mondes*, 1842, 4 s., v. 32.) p. 68, *in* ** 54.149.
See also Poole's Index (to 1882). p. 454, *in* ** 50. 1;—*Same,* to Jan. 1, 1887, p. 156, *in* ** 50. 1³.

FRENCH LITERATURE, *Bibliography.*
Blanc, J. Bibliographie italico-française universelle. 1475-1885. 2 vols. ** 15.270-1.—Lorenz, O. Catalogue général de la librairie française pendant 1840-65, et 1866-75. 8 vols. 1807-80. ** 15.31-8.—Nisard, M. E. C. Histoire des livres populaires. 2 vols. 1854. 840.27-8.—Quérard, J. M. La littérature française contemporaine. 1827-1849. 6 vols. * 15.64-9.

—— *Collections and selections.*
Carey, *Mrs.* M., *tr.* Fairy legends of the French provinces. 1887. 291.76.—Curwen, H., *tr.* French love songs and other poems. 1871. 821.683.—Fontaine, C. Les poètes français du XIXe siecle. 1889. 842.157.—Legrand d'Aussy, P. J. B. Fabliaux. Tr. by G. L. Way. 3 vols. 1815. 841.2.—Masson, G. French classics with English notes. 7 vols. (In French.) vols. 1-3: Plays by Corneille, Molière and Racine; v. 4: Letters of Mme. de Sévigné; v. 5: Tales by mod. writers; v. 6: Plays by Regnard, Brueys, and Palaprat; v. 7: Louis XIV., and his contemporaries. 849.14-20;—La lyre française (with Eng. notes). 842.151. —Saintsbury, G:, *ed.* French lyrics. 1883. 841.32;—Specimens of French literature: Villon to Hugo. 840.26.

—— *History, criticism, etc.*
Arnold, M. *In his* Essays in criticism. 824.3.—Besant, W. The French humourists from the 12th to the 19th century. 1877. 928.147.—Buckle, H: T: State of historical literature in France, from the end of the 16th to the end of the 18th century. (*In his* Hist. of civ. in Eng., v. 1.) 1878. p. 553, *in* 313.37.—Houssaye, A. *In his* Behind the scenes of the Comédie Française, and other recollections. 1889. 842.152.—Hutson, C: W. A history of French literature. 1889. 840.69.—James, H:, *Jr.* French poets and novelists. 1884. 840.68.—Laun, H. van. History of French literature. 3 vols. 1877. 840. 2-4.—Matthews, J. B. French dramatists of the 19th century. 1881. 842.39.—Nisard, J. M. N. D. Histoire de la littérature française. 4 vols. 1889. 840.70-3.—Nisard, M. E. C. Histoire des livres populaires, ou, de la littérature du colportage. 2 vols. 1854. 840.27-8.—Parès, A. P. Ancient French romances. 50 pp. (*With* Longfellow, H: W. *Kavanagh.*) p. 190, *in* 823.1010.—Saintsbury, G: Primer of French literature. 1880. 840.14;—Short history of French literature. 1882. 840.23.—Scherer, E. *In his* Études sur la littérature contemporaine. 9 vols. 1885-9. 844.32-40.—Stael-Holstein, *Mme.* de. *In her* The influence of literature upon society. v. 2. ** 810.21.
For collected works of French authors, *see* Catalogues *of this Library.*
No. 4, 1884, pp. 325-32. No. 5, 1888, pp. 145-73.

FRENCH POETRY, *History, criticism, etc.*
Besant, W. Studies in early French poetry. 1877. 841.20.—Dowden, E: On some French writers of verse. 1830-1877. 35 pp. (*In his* Studies in lit., etc.) p. 392, *in* 800.4.—James, H:, *Jr.* French poets and novelists. 1884. 840.68.
See also Poole's Index (to 1882). p. 488-90, *in* ** 50.1;—*Same,* to Jan. 1, 1887. pp. 167-8, *in* ** 50.1³.

GERMAN LITERATURE, *Bibliography.*
Allgemeine Bibliographie für Deutschland. 1884-90. 7 vols. * 15.273¹⁻¹.—Heinsius, W. Allgemeines Bücher-Lexikon, 1700-1879. 14 vols. 1812-81. ** 11.195-208.—Janssen, J. Kunst u. Volksliteratur bis 1618. (*In his* Gesch. des deutschen Volkes, v. 6.) 1888. 943.139.—Kayser, C. G. Vollständiges Bücher-Lexikon, 1750-1886; u. Sachregis-

English Fiction. *Contin.*
Literature. *Contin.*
GERMAN LITERATURE, *Bibliography. Contin.*
ter. (1838.) 25 vols. ** 11.88–98¹². —Maltzahn, W. *Freiherr* von. Deutscher Bücherschatz des 16., 17., 18. bis um die Mitte des 19. Jahrhunderts. 1882. * 15.62.—Vierteljahrs-Catalog aller neuen Erscheinungen im Felde der Literatur in Deutschland. 1880–1890. 11 vols. ** 15.30⁰⁸⁻⁴⁸.

—— *Collections and selections.*
Baskerville, A. Poetry of Germany. 1879. 831.72.—Beauties of German literature. (*Chandos classics.*) 830.51.—Buchheim, C. A., *ed.* Deutsche Lyrik. (*Gold. treas. ser.*) 1886. 831.123.—Härtel, A. Deutsches Liederlexikon. * 784.2.—Hedge, F. H. Prose-writers of Germany. 1870. 839.2.—Heine, H. Wit, wisdom and pathos; with pieces from the "Book of songs." 1888. 830.61.—Müller, F: M. The German classics from the 4th to the 19th century. 2 vols. 839.59–60.—Pletsch, O., *and* Füllhaas, J., *and others.* Deutscher Humor in Poesie. 1872. 831.36.—Schwab, G., *ed.* Fünf Bücher deutscher Lieder und Gedichte. 1857. 831.35.—Storm, T. Hausbuch aus deutschen Dichtern seit Claudius. 1872. 831.108.

—— *History, criticism, etc.*
Dippold, G: T. Great epics of mediæval Germany. 1882. 830.47. —Gervinus, G. G. Geschichte der deutschen Dichtung. 5 vols. 1874. 839.7–11.—Göthe, J. W. von. Deutsche Literatur. (*Werke,* v. 26.) *In* 830.30.—Hebbel, F. Charakteristiken.—Kritiken. (*Sämml. Werke,* vols. 11, 12.) pp. 3, 163, *in* 839.71–2.—Heine, H. The romantic school in German literature. Tr. by S. L. Fleischman. 1882. 830.48.—Hettner, H. Deutsche Literatur im 18. Jahrhundert. 4 vols. 1879. 809.23–6.—Hosmer, J. K. Short history of German literature. 1879. 830.1.—Janssen, J. Geschichte des deutschen Volkes. v. 6: Kunst u. Volksliteratur (bis 1618). 1–12. Aufl. 1888. 943.139.—Koenig, R. Deutsche Literaturgeschichte. 1879. 830.52.—Moschzisker, F. A. A guide to German literature. 2 vols. 1850. * 830.53–4.—Müller, F: M. German literature. 50 pp. (*In his* Chips from a German workshop, v. 3.) p. 1, *in* 824.296.—Parker, T. German literature. 24 pp. (*In his* Crit. writings.) p. 161, *in* 829.185.—Staël-Holstein, *Mme. de. In her* Germany, v. 1. *in* 914.61;—*In her* Influence of literature upon society, v. 2. *in* ** 810.21.—Taylor, B. Studies in German literature. 1879. 830.37.—Taylor, W., *of Norwich.* Historic survey of German poetry. 3 vols. 1828. 831.7–9.—Teuffel, W. S. Studien und Charakteristiken zur . . . deutschen Literaturgeschichte. 1871. 809.6.—Weir, A. National literature and art in Germany. 42 pp. (*In his* Hist. basis of modern Europe.) 1886. p. 506, *in* 940.197.
See also Catalogue of this Library. No. 5, 1888. p. 18₄.
Also Poole's Index (to 1882) pp. 513–14, *in* ** 50.1;—*Same*, to Jan. 1, 1887. pp. 175–6, *in* ** 50.1³.

GREEK LITERATURE, *Bibliography.*
Engelmann, W. Bibliotheca scriptorum classicorum 1700–1878. 1. Abth., scriptores Græci. 1880. ** 16.70.—Fabricius, J. A. Biblioth. Græca sive notitia scriptorum veterum Græcorum. 14 vols. 1718–28. ** 880.14–27.—Moss, J. W. Manual of classical bibliography. 2 vols. 1837. ** 16.1–2.

—— *Collections and selections.*
Brunck, R. F. P. Gnomici poetæ Græci. (*Gr.*) 1784. 884.10.—Church, A. J: Stories from the Greek tragedians. 1879. 808.1378;—*Same.* 882.18.—Elton, C: A. Specimens of the Greek and Roman classic poets. 3 vols. 1854. 811.3–5.—Marlager, P. Pictures of Hellas. Five tales of ancient Greece. Tr. by M.. J. Safford. 1888. 823.5279.—Meleager *of Gadara.* Fifty poems. (*Gr. and Eng.*) Tr. by W. Headlam. 1890. 821.1343.—Pollard, A. W., *ed.* Odes from the Greek dramatists. (*Gr.*) & tr. 1890. 881.18.

—— *Dictionaries.*
Anthon, C: Classical dictionary. 1888. 930.26. —Lempriere, J. Bibliotheca classica. 15th ed. 1875. ** 930.28.—Smith, W. Dictionary of Greek and Roman biography and mythology. 3 vols. 1880. ** 930.242–4.

—— *History, criticism, etc.*
Anthon, C: Manual of Greek literature. 1859. 889.7.—Browne, R. W. History of classical literature: Greek literature. 809.47.—Dunbar, G. Of the literature of the Greeks. (Potter, J: *Archæol. Græca,* v. 2.) 1813. p. 56, *in* ** 938.97.—Geddes, W: D. The

English Fiction. *Contin.*
Literature. *Contin.*
GREEK LITERATURE. *Contin.*
—— *History, criticism, etc. Contin.*
problem of the Homeric poems. 1878. 880.42.—Grote, G: *In his* History of Greece, vols. 1, 2, 4, 8. 938.1, 2, 4, 8.—Haigh, A. E. The Attic theatre. 1889. 882. 22.—Jebb, R. C. Greek literature. 1878. 880.5.—Jevons, F. B. History of Greek literature . . . to the death of Demosthenes. 1886. 880.28.—Klein, J. L. Geschichte des griechischen . . . Drama's. 2 vols. (*In his* Gesch. des Drama's, vols. 1–2.) * 832. 95–6.—Lawton, W: C. On the origin and spirit of Attic tragedy. 20 pp. p. 1, *in* 882.21.—Lounge, A. History of Greek and Roman classical literature. 1873. 880.6.—Mahaffy, *Rev.* J: P. A history of classical Greek literature. 2 vols. 889.8–9.—Moulton, R: G: The ancient classical drama. 1890. 872.11.—Snider, D. J. Homer's Iliad: a commentary. 880. 41.—Symonds, J: A. Studies of the Greek poets. 2 vols. 1880. 881.1–2.—Teuffel, W. S. Studien und Charakteristiken zur griechischen . . . Literaturgeschichte. 1871. 809.6.
See also Poole's Index (to 1882) pp. 554–6, *in* ** 50.1;—*Same*, to Jan. 1, 1887. pp. 190–1, *in* ** 50.1³.

HEBREW LITERATURE, *Bibliography.*
Fürst, J. Bibliotheca Judaica. 2 vols. 1863. ** 16.64–5.—Lippe, C. D. Bibliog. Lexikon der gesammten jüdischen Literatur der Gegenwart. 1881. 893 5.—Neubauer, A. Catalogue of the Hebrew manuscripts in the Bodleian Library. 1886. ** 16. 207. —Steinschneider, M. Bibliog. Handbuch über die Literatur für heb. Sprachkunde. 1859. * 16.109.

—— *Collections and selections.*
Hurwitz, H. Hebrew tales; tr. from the ancient Hebrew sages. Prefixed, essay on the uninspired literature of the Hebrews. 1847. 893.4.—Lazarus, E. Jewish poems; translations. (*Poems,* v. 2.) 1889. 821.129⁴.—Pascheles, W., *comp.* Sippurim: Sammlung jüdischer Volkssagen. 1883. 296.62.

—— *History, criticism, etc.*
Coles, A. New rendering of the Hebrew psalms into Eng. verse. 1888. 223.24.—Heilprin, M. Historical poetry of the Hebrews. 2 vols. 1879. 899. 20–1.—Lowth, R. Lectures on the sacred poetry of the Hebrews. Tr. by G. Gregory. 1847. 893.6.—Rothschild, C., *and* A. de. History and literature of the Israelites. 2 vols. 1870. 933.42–3.—Taylor, I: Spirit of Hebrew poetry. 1873. 811.2.—Zuns, L. *In his* Gesammelte Schriften. 2 vols. (in 1). 1875–6. 296.70.
See also Catalogue of this Library. No. 5, 1888. pp. 196–200.
Also Poole's Index (to 1882) pp. 581–2, *in* ** 50.1;—*Same*, to Jan. 1, 1887. p. 199, *in* ** 50.1³.

HUNGARIAN LITERATURE.
Bowring, *Sir* J. Poetry of the Magyars. 831.10. —Czink, J. Historical sketches of Hungarian literature. (*In his* Complete . . . gram. of Hung. lang.) 1883. * 499.23.
See also Poole's Index (to 1882). p. 615, *in* ** 50.1.

ICELANDIC LITERATURE. *See also* Scandinavian literature.
Anderson, R. A. The younger Edda. 1880. 293.4.—Die Edda, die ältere und jüngere. Übers. von K. Simrock. 1876. 293.2.—Sæmund, *the learned.* The (elder) Edda. 1866. 899.19.—Snorro Sturluson. Heimskringla; or, the sagas of the Norse Kings. Tr. by S: Laing. 2d ed. 4 vols. 1889. * 948.29–32.—Vigfusson, G., *and* Powell, F. Y. Corpus poeticum boreale. 2 vols. 1883. 898. 134–5.

—— *History, criticism, etc.*
Metcalfe, F. The Englishman and the Scandinavian; or, a comparison of Anglo-Saxon and old Norse literature. 1880. 809.37.
See also Iceland, p. 127.
See also Poole's Index (to 1882). p. 622, *in* ** 50.1;—*Same*, to Jan. 1, 1887. p. 214, *in* ** 50.1³.

IRISH LITERATURE, *History, criticism, etc.*
Madden, R: R. History of Irish periodical literature from the end of the 17th to the middle of the 19th cent. 2 vols. 1867. 820.41–2.—Mills, A. Literature and literary men of Gt. Brit. and Ireland. 2 vols. 1858. 820.77–8.—Murray, J: O'K. Prose and poetry of Ireland. 1878. 829.178.
See also Ireland, p. 132.
See also Poole's Index (to 1882). p. 662, *in* ** 50.1;—*Same*, to Jan. 1, 1887. p. 228, *in* ** 50.1³.

English Fiction. *Contin.*
Literature. *Contin.*

ITALIAN LITERATURE.
Hallam, A. H: Influence of Italian works of imagination on the same class of compositions in England. 46 pp. (*In his* Remains in verse and prose.) 1863. p. 180, *in* 829.111.—Howells, W: D. Modern Italian poets: essays and versions. 1887. 854.3.
—— *Bibliography.*
Blanc, J. Bibliographie italico-française universelle. 1475-1885. 2 vols. ** 15.270-1.
—— *Collections and selections.*
Parnaso italiano ovvero raccolta de' poeti classici italiani. 56 vols. 1784-91. ** 851.24-79.—Rossetti, D. G. Dante and his circle. 1876. 851.8.
—— *History, criticism, and manuals.*
Klein, J. L. Geschichte des italienischen Drama's. 4 vols. (*In his* Gesch. des Drama's, vols. 4-7.) * 832.98-102.—Prescott, W: H. Poetry and romance of the Italians. (*In his* Biog. . . . misc.) *in* 920.150.—Simpson, L. F. Literature of Italy to the death of Boccacio. 1859. 850.1.—Sismondi, J. C. L. S. de. Literature of southern Europe. 2 vols. 1877. 809.19-20.—Symonds, J: A. An introduction to the study of Dante. 2d ed. 1890. 850.31;—Renaissance in Italy. vols. 4-5: Italian literature. 2 vols. 1881. 850.29-30.—Tiraboschi, G. Storia della letteratura italiana. 16 vols. 1822-6. 850.3-18.
JAPANESE LITERATURE, *History, criticism, etc*
Bousquet, G. Japon littéraire. 34 pp. (*Rev.d. d. Mondes.* 1878. 3 pér., v. 29.) p. 747, *in* ** 54.343.—Chamberlain, B. H. The classical poetry of the Japanese. (*Trübner's Orient. ser.*) 1880. 899.30.—White, C. A. Classic literature . . . with some account of the . . . Japanese, etc. 1889. p. 421, *in* 810.54.
See also Poole's Index (to 1882). p. 679, *in* ** 50.1;—*Same*, to Jan. 1, 1887. p. 234, *in* ** 50.1².
LATIN LITERATURE. *Bibliography.*
Bibliotheca scriptorum classicorum. ** 16.54.—Fabricius, J: A. Bibliotheca Lat. mediæ et infimæ ætatis. 5 vols. 1634-46. ** 16.111-15.—Mayor, J: E. B. Bibliog. clue to Latin literature. 1875. 870.11.—Moss, J. W. Manual of classical bibliog. 2 vols. 1837. ** 16.1-2.
—— *Dictionaries.*
Anthon, C. Classical dictionary. 1888. ** 930.26.—Lempriere, J. Bibliotheca classica. 1875. ** 930.28.—Rich, A. Dictionary of Greek and Roman antiquities. 1874. ** 930.29.—Smith, W: Dictionary of Greek and Roman antiquities. 1878. ** 930.27;—Dictionary of Greek and Roman biography and mythology. 3 vols. 1880. ** 920.242-4.
—— *History, criticism, etc.*
Crutwell, C: T: History of Roman literature. 1877. 870.2.—Klein, J. L. Geschichte des griechischen und römischen Drama's. 2 vols. (*In his* Gesch. des Drama's, vols. 1-2.) * 832.95-6.—Louage, A. History of Greek and Roman classical literature. 1873. 880.6.—Merivale, C: *In his* History of the Romans. vols. 2, 6. 937-79, 81.—Moulton, R: G. The ancient classical drama. 1890. 872.11.—Quackenbos, J: D. Illustrated history of ancient literature, oriental and classical. 1879. 899.9.—Schmitz, L. History of Latin literature. 1877. 870.3.—Sellar, W: Y. The Roman poets of the republic. 3d ed. 870.18.—Simcox, G: A. Latin literature from Ennius to Boethius. 2 vols. 1883. 809.57-8.—Studien u. Charakteristiken zur . . . römischen . . . Literaturgeschichte. 1871. 809.6.—Teuffel, W. S. Geschichte der römischen Literatur. 1875. 870.4.—Thompson, H:, ed. History of Roman literature. (*Encycl. metrop.*) 1852. 879.2.
See also Poole's Index (to 1882). p. 727, *in* ** 50.1;—*Same*, to Jan. 1, 1887. p. 250, *in* ** 50.1².
NORSE LITERATURE. *See* Icelandic literature.—Scandinavian literature.
ORIENTAL LITERATURE.
Fürst, J. *In his* Bibliotheca Judaica. 3 vols. 1863. ** 16.63-5.—Zenker, J. T. Bibliotheca orientalis. 2 vols. (in 1). 1846-61. ** 16.66.
See also Arabic, Hebrew, Persian, Sanskrit, etc., literature.
PERSIAN LITERATURE.
White, C. A. Classic literature . . . with some account of the Persian, etc. p. 371, *in* 810.54.
See also Poole's Index (to 1882). p. 992, *in* ** 50.1; —*Same*, to Jan. 1, 1887. p. 336, *in* ** 50.1².

English Fiction. *Contin.*
Literature. *Contin.*

POLISH LITERATURE, *History, criticism, etc.*
Bowring, J: Specimens of Polish poets, with notes on the literature of Poland. 1827. 899.3.—Klaczko, J. La poésie polonaise au 19e siècle. 60 pp. (*Rev. d. d. Mondes.* 1862. 2 pér., v. 37.) p. 5, *in* ** 54.242.
See also Poole's Index (to 1882). p. 1025, *in* ** 50.1;—*Same*, to Jan. 1, 1887. p. 347, *in* ** 50.1².
PORTUGUESE LITERATURE, *History, criticism, etc.*
Bouterweck, F: History of Spanish and Portuguese literature. 2 vols. 1823. 860.2-3.—Sismondi, J. C. L. S. de. Literature of the south of Europe. 2 vols. 1877. 809.19-20.
See also Poole's Index (to 1882). p. 1037, *in* ** 50.1.
PROVENÇAL LITERATURE, *History, criticism, etc.*
Fauriel, C. C. History of Provençal poetry. Tr. by G. J. Adler. 1860. 841.26.—Hueffer, F. The troubadours: history of Provençal life and literature in the middle ages. 1878. 840.15.—Preston, H. W. Troubadours and trouvères: new and old. 1876. 841.15.—Sismondi, J. C. L. S. de. *In his* Literature of the south of Europe. v. 1. *in* 809.19.
See also Poole's Index (to 1882). p. 1059, *in* ** 50.1.
ROMAN LITERATURE. *See* Latin literature.
RUSSIAN LITERATURE, *History, criticism, etc.*
Bazau, Mrs. E. P. Russia: its people and its literature. 1890. 890.7.—Delaveau, H. La littérature et la vie militaire en Russie. 36 pp. (*Rev. d. d. Mondes.* 1856. 2 pér., v. 4.) p. 775, *in* ** 54.209.—Dupuy, E. Great masters of Russian literature in the 19th century. Tr. by N. H. Dole. 1886. 890.4.—Jauffret, A. De la littérature russe. 17 pp. (*Rev. d. d. Mondes.* 1831. v. 2.) p. 99, *in* ** 54.103.—Saint Julien, C: de. La littérature en Russie. 34 pp. (*Rev. d. d. Mondes.* 1851. n. pér., v. 12.) p. 67, *in* ** 54.185.—Turner, C: E: Studies in Russian literature. 1882. 897.11.—Vogüé, E. M. de. The Russian novelists. (Cop. 1887.) 690.6.
See also Poole's Index (to 1882). p. 1138, *in* ** 50.1;—*Same*, to Jan. 1, 1887. p. 381, *in* ** 50.1².
See also Gogol, N. V.; Pushkin, A. S.; Tolstoï, L. N.; Turgenief, I. S., in gen. alphabet.
SANSKRIT LITERATURE, *History, criticism, etc.*
Burnouf, E. La littérature sanscrite. 14 pp. (*Rev. d. d. Mondes.* 1833. 2 pér., v. 1.) p. 246, *in* ** 54.110.—Kaegi, A. The Rigveda: the oldest literature of the Indians; with add. to the notes by R. Arrowsmith. 1886. 899.31.—Muir, J. Original Sanskrit texts on the origin and history of the people of India. 5 vols. 1872. * 954.51-5.—Poor, L. E. Sanskrit and kindred literature. 1880. 894.8;—*Same*. 1890. 899.32.—Reed, E. A. Hindu literature. 1891. 899.33.—Weber, A. Akademische Vorlesungen über indische Literaturgeschichte. 2. Aufl. 1876. 894.27.—White, C. A. Classic literature, principally Sanskrit, Greek, and Roman, etc. 1889. p. 5, *in* 810.54.—Williams, Sir M. Indian epic poetry; lectures: analysis of the Rámáyana, and of the Mahá-bhárata. 1863. 894.28.—Wilson, H. H. Essays on Sanskrit literature. (*Works*, vols. 3-5.) 1864. 894.17-19.
See also Poole's Index (to 1882). p. 1151, *in* ** 50.1;—*Same*, to Jan. 1, 1887. p, 386. *in* ** 50.1².
SCANDINAVIAN LITERATURE, *History, criticism, etc.*
Gosse, E. Northern studies. 1890. 898.136.—Horn, F: W. History of Scandin. literature. Tr. by Anderson; bibliog. by Solberg. 1884. 898.130.—Howitt, W:, *and* M.. Literature and romance of northern Europe. 2 vols. 1852. 804.13-14.—Schweitzer, P. Geschichte der altskandinavischen Litteratur . . bis zur Reformation. 1885. 898.133.
See also before *under* Icelandic literature.
Also "Scandinavia" in the general alphabet.
Also Poole's Index (to 1882). p. 1155, *in* ** 50.1; —*Same*, to Jan. 1, 1887. p. 387, *in* ** 50.1².
SERVIAN LITERATURE.
Bowring, J: Servian popular poetry. 1827. 899.2;—*Same*. 899.7.—Cazaux, J. de. La poésie légendaire chez les Serbes. 3 pp. (*Rev. d. d. Mondes.* 1868. 2e pér., v. 76.) p. 503, *in* ** 54.281.—Majatovies, Mme. E., L., *tr.* Serbian folk-lore. Ed. with introd. by Rev. W. Denton. 1874. 897.10.
See also Poole's Index (to 1882). p. 1180, *in* ** 50.1.
SPANISH LITERATURE, *History, criticism, etc.*
Berard, A. E. A manual of Spanish art and literature. 1866. 860.10.—Bibliography of Spau-

English Fiction. *Contin.*
Literature. *Contin.*

SPANISH LITERATURE. *History, criticism, etc. Contin.*
ish books. (*In* Misc. Hisp.-Amer., vols. 2, 3, 4.) 1829.
in 980.7, 8, 9.—**Bouterwek,** F: History of Spanish
literature. 1847. 860.1;—History of Spanish and
Portuguese literature. 2 vols. 1823. 860.2-3. —
Klein, J. L. Geschichte des spanischen Drama's.
4 vols. (in 5). (*In his* Gesch. des Drama's, vols. 8-
11.) * 832.103-107.—**Sismondi,** J. C. L. S. de. Literature of the south of Europe. v. 2. 1877. p. 86, *in*
809.20.—**Ticknor,** G: History of Spanish literature.
3 vols. 1872. 860.4-6. *Note.*—Reviewed by W: H.
Prescott. *In his* Miscellanies.
—— *Collections and selections.*
Bowring, J: Ancient poetry and romances of
Spain: selected and translated. * 861.2.—**Lock-
hart,** J. G., *tr.* Spanish ballads. 821.854.—**Southey,**
R., *tr.* Chronicle of the Cid. *in* 821.854.
See also Poole's Index (to 1882). p. 1231, *in* **
50.1;—*Same,* to Jan. 1, 1887. p. 413, *in* ** 50.1².
SWEDISH LITERATURE. **Howitt,** W:, *and* **Howitt,** *Mrs.*
M.. (B.) Literature and romance of northern Eu-
rope. v. 2. 804.14.
See also Sweden in the gen. alphabet.
See also Poole's Index to (1882). p. 1274, *in* **
50.1;—*Same,* to Jan. 1, 1887. p. 428, *in* ** 50.1².
TURKISH LITERATURE. *See* Poole's Index (to 1882).
p. 1333, *in* ** 50.1;—*Same,* to Jan. 1, 1887. p. 448, *in*
50.1².
Little barefoot. Auerbach, B.   823.3053
Little classics. vols. 1-18. Johnson, R., *ed.*
  829.124-141
Little dinner at Timmins's. 23 pp. Thack-
eray, W: M.   *in* 823.1572
Little Dorrit. Dickens, C: J: H.   823.419
Same. 2 vols.   823.5315-16
Little duke, The. Yonge, C.. M..   808.1576
Little flower-people. Hale, G. E..   808.1465
Little folks' history of England. Knox, *Mrs.*
I. (C.)   808.616
Little folks in feathers and fur and others in
neither. Miller, *Mrs.* H. (M.)   808.1888
Little Golden; or, the pride of the family.
By the author of "The fatal mistake."
  823.4770
Little Goldie. Hayden, *Mrs.* S.
  in 823.5101
Little good-for-nothing, The. Daudet, A.
  823.6846
Little Guzzy and other stories. Habberton,
J: 823.7134
Little Hodge. Jenkins, E: 823.900
Little journey in the world, A. Warner, C:
D.   823.6579
Little Loo. Russell, W: C.   823.4776
Same.   *in* 823.4977
Little Louvre, The. Abbott, J.   808.581
Little Make-Believe. Farjeon, B: L.
  in 823.6599
Little moorland princess. John, E.
  823.3052
Little neighbors at Elmridge. Church, *Mrs.*
E. (R.)   808.1633
Little Nell. Dickens, C: J: H.   808.1571
Little old man of Batignolles, The. Gabor-
iau, E.   *in* 823.2731
Little ones annual. Stories and poems for
little people.   808.1923
Little Paul. Abbott, J.   *in* 808.591
Little Pierre, the pedlar of Alsace; or, the re-
ward of filial piety. Tr. by J. M. C.
  823.6839
Little pilgrim, A. Oliphant, *Mrs.* M. O. (W.)
  in 823.5038
Same.   *in* 823.6695

English Fiction. *Contin.*
Little savage. Marryat, *Capt.* F: 823.1101
Little schoolmaster Mark. Shorthouse, J.
H: 823.4881
Same.   *in* 823.4993; 823.5413
Little sister. Yardley, *Mrs.* J..   823.4535
Little Tu'penny. Gould, S. Baring-
  823.5579
Little vagabond, The. Macquoid, *Mrs.* K..
S.   808.1622
Little Venice, and other stories. Litchfield,
G. D.   823.7395
Living link, The. De Mille, J.   823.5852
Same.   823.6214
Living or dead. Fargus, F: J: *in* 823.4978
Same.   *in* 823.5056; *in* 823.5066
Living too fast. Adams, W: T.   823.1831
Same.   823.5339
Livingstone, David, Story of. Rathbone,
Mrs. M.. A. (M.)   823.5583
Livius Patavinus, Titus. Church, A. J:
Stories from Livy. Illus.   808.1545
Contents:—The story of Romulus and of Numa.
—The story of Alba.—The story of the elder Tar-
quin.—The story of Servius.—The story of Brutus.—
The story of Lars Porsenna.—The story of Corio-
lanus.—The story of the Fabii.—The story of Cin-
cinnatus.—The story of the Decemvirs and of Vir-
ginia.—The story of Veii.—The story of Camillus.—
The story of Rome and the Gauls.—The story of
Manlius of the twisted chain.—Stories of certain
great Romans.—The story of the passes of Caudium.
Livy. *See* Livius Patavinus, Titus.
Liza. Turgenef, I. S.   823.4212
Lloyd, D: Demarest. Poor Ogla-Moga. 35
pp. (*In* Stories by Amer. authors, v. 3.)
  p. 99, *in* 823.4704
Lloyd Pennant. Neville, R.   823.1187
Lobeira, Vasco de. Amadis of Gaul. Tr.
from the Spanish version of Garciordoñez
de Montalvo. By. R. Southey. 3 vols.
  ** 823.6893-5
Lobeyra, V. de. *See* Lobeira, V. de.
Locke, D: Ross. [*Petroleum V. Nasby.*]
—— A paper city.   823.1008
Locke, *Mrs.* M.. In far Dakota.   823.7217
Locke Amsden. Thompson, D. P.
  823.4171
Lockhart, J: Gibson. Reginald Dalton.
(Anon.)   823.4511
—— Valerius: a Roman story. (Anon.)
  823.4513
—— *Same.* 2 vols.   ** 823.6718-19
Lockhart, Laurence W: Maxwell.
—— A night with the Volunteers of Strath-
kinahan. 59 pp. (*In* Tales from Black-
wood.)   *in* 823.7485
—— Unlucky Tom Griffin, his love and his
luck. 82 pp. (*In* Tales from Blackwood,
2d ser., v. 4.)   *in* 823.7488
Lockwood, Ingersoll. Travels and adventures
of little Baron Trump and his wonderful
dog Bulger. Illus. by G: W. Edwards.
  808.1895
Lodge, *Mrs.* —. Under a ban.   823.4767
Same.   *in* 823.5023
Logan, Olive, *now* Sikes, *Mrs.* O. (L.)
Lola: a tale of Gibraltar. Griffiths, A.
  823.678
Lombard street mystery. Robertson, M.
  823.5457

English Fiction. *Contin.*
Ludovic and Gertrude. Conscience, H.
823.5659
Lukin, James. Amongst machines: a description of various mechanical appliances used in the manufacture of wood, metal and other substances; a book for boys. 808.630
—— The boy engineers; what they did and how they did it. 808.1662
Lumsden, K.. M. How I fell among thieves. 26 pp. (*In* Tales from Blackwood. 3d ser., v. 3.) 823.7499
—— A vendetta. 12 pp. (*In* Tales from Blackwood. 3d ser., v. 1.)
p. 325, *in* 823.7497
Lunn, *Mrs.* J. Calbraith. Shamrock and rose. 3 vols. 823.7218-20
Luska, Sidney, *pseud. See* Harland, H:
Lutaniste of St. Jacobi's. Drew, C.
823.1847
Luttrell of Arran. Lever, C: J. 823.986
Lyall, Edna, *pseud. See* Bayly, A. E.
Lyndon, *pseud. See* Bright, *Mrs.* M. A.
Lynx-hunting. Stephens, C: A. 808.245
Lyon, *Capt.* E. D. Ireland's dream: a romance of the future. 2 vols. 823.6401-2
Lyon, Sidney. For a mess of pottage.
823.7052
Lyster, Annette. My treasure. 45 pp. (*In* Tales from Blackwood. 3d ser., v. 2.)
p. 199, *in* 823.7498
Lytton, E: G: Earle Lytton Bulwer-, 1 *Baron Lytton.* [*Pisistratus Caxton.*] (1805-73.)
—— Alice; or, the mysteries: a sequel to "Ernest Maltravers." 823.5931
—— Calderon the courtier. (*With his* Leila.) *in* 823.1035
—— *Same.* 823.5957
—— The Caxtons: a family picture. 823.1023
—— *Same.* 823.6217
—— The coming race; or, the new Utopia.
823.1024
—— *Same.* (*Also*) Falkland,—Zicci,—*and,* Pausanias the Spartan. 823.5863
—— *Same.* 823.5975
—— Devereux. 823.1025
—— *Same.* 2 vols. **823.6257-8
—— The disowned. 823.1026
—— *Same.* 823.6337
—— Ernest Maltravers; or, the Eleusinia.
823.1027
—— *Same.* 823.5976
This story is continued in "Alice."
—— *Same.* 2 vols. **823.6757-8
—— Eugene Aram. 823.1028
—— *Same.* 823.6218
—— Falkland. (*With his* The coming race.)
in 823.5863
—— *Same.* 823.5975
—— *Same,* and Zicci. 823.1029
—— Godolphin. 823.5956
—— Harold; the last of the Saxon kings.
823.6000
—— The haunted and the haunters; or, the house and the brain. (*With his* Pausanias the Spartan.) *in* 823.1045
Issued also as The house and the brain.
—— *Same.* 63 pp. (*In* Tales from Blackwood, v. 10.) *in* **823.6656

English Fiction. *Contin.*
Lytton, E: G: Earle Lytton Bulwer-, 1 *Baron Lytton.* [*Pisistratus Caxton.*] (1805-73.)
Contin.
—— The house and the brain. 53 pp. (Johnson, R., *ed. Little classics,* v. 1.)
p. 7, *in* 829.125
—— Kenelm Chillingly: his adventures and opinions. (Port.) 823.1032
—— The last days of Pompeii. 823.6308
—— *Same.* 2 vols. **823.6734-5
—— The last of the barons. 823.5933
—— *Same.* 823.5977
—— Leila; or, the siege of Granada; (*Also*) Calderon the courtier; *and* The pilgrims of the Rhine. 823.1035
—— *Same.* 823.5957
—— Lucretia; or, the children of night.
823.1036
—— *Same.* 823.5934
—— The maid of Malines. 38 pp. (Johnson, R., *ed. Little classics,* v. 6.)
p. 90, *in* 829.129
—— "My novel." By Pisistratus Caxton. 2 vols. 823.1037-8
—— *Same.* 823.5971-2
—— Night and morning. 823.1040
—— *Same.* 823.6219
—— The Parisians. 2 vols. 823.1401-2
—— Paul Clifford. 823.1044
—— Pausanias the Spartan: an unfinished historical romance. 2d ed. 823.5729
—— *Same.* *in* 823.5863; *in* 823.5975
—— *Same.* (*Also*) The haunted and the haunters; or, the house and the brain.
823.1045
—— Pelham; or, adventures of a gentleman.
823.1046
—— Pilgrims of the Rhine. (*With his* Leila.) *in* 823.1035
—— *Same.* 823.5957
—— Rienzi: the last of the Roman tribunes.
823.1039
—— *Same.* **823.6762
—— A strange story. 823.1043
—— What will he do with it? By Pisistratus Caxton. 2 vols. (in 1). 823.6679
—— *Same.* 2 vols. 823.1047-8
—— *Same.* 823.5973-4
—— Zanoni. 823.5936
—— *Same.* 823.5970
—— Zicci. *in* 823.1029
—— *Same.* *in* 823.5863; *in* 823.5975

Note.— For his life and writings, *see* Bayne, P. The modern novel . . . Bulwer. (*In his* Essays in biog., etc., 1st ser.) 1880. p. 363, *in* 824.185.—Brimley, G: "My novel." 24 pp. (*In his* Essays.) 1861. p. 327, *in* 824.6.—Horne, R. H. Lytton. (*In his* New spirit of the age.) 1844. p. 297, *in* 928.77.—Jeaffreson, J: C. Sir E: L. Bulwer-Lytton. 24 pp. (*In his* Novels, etc., v. 1.) p. 198, *in* 820.187.—Lytton, E: R. Bulwer- Memoir of Lyttou. (Lytton, E: G: E. L. Bulwer- Speeches, v. 1.) p. vii, *in* 928.384.— Mathews, W. Bulwer. (*In his* Men, places and things.) p. 53, *in* 824.397.—Roscoe, W. C. Sir E. B. Lytton, novelist, philosopher and poet. 39 pp. (*In his* Poems and essays, v. 2.) p. 354, *in* 821.1383. —Shepard, W: Edward Bulwer, Lord Lytton. 37 pp. (*In his* Pen pictures of earlier Victorian authors.) 1884. p. 50, *in* 820.158.—Smiles, S: Brief biographies. 1877. p. 117, *in* 923.841.
See also Catalogues of this Library.
No. 3, 1882, p. 114. No. 4, 1884, p. 170.

English Fiction. *Contin.*
MacDonald, G: (1824—.) *Contin.*
—— What's mine's mine. *in* 823.5082
—— Wilfrid Cumbermede: an autobiograph-
ical story. 823.5370
Note.—For his life and writings, *see* Harris, A.
B. Little biographies. (1887.) p. 122, *in* 928.692.
See also Poole's Index (to 1882). p. 782, *in* **
50.1¹—*Same.* Jan. 1, 1882–Jan. 1, 1887. p. 270, *in* **
50.1¹.
Macdonald, J: Narrative of prince Charlie's
escape. 28 pp. (*In* Tales from Blackwood.
2d ser., v. 10.) *in* 823.7494
McDonnell, W: Exeter Hall: a theological
romance. 823.6158
MacDowall, Cameron. A queen among
queens: a tale of the desert. 823.7188
McDowell, *Mrs.* K.. Sherwood (Bonner).
—— Dialect tales. 823.6121
—— Suwanee river tales. 823.4891
Macé, Jean. Fairy book. Home fairy tales.
Tr. by M.. L. Booth. 808.406
MacFarlane, C: Romance of history: Italy.
823.1072
MacGahan, *Mrs.* Barbara (Elagina). Xenia
Repnina: a story of the Russia of to-day.
With introd. by V. Verestchagin. 823.7267
McGlasson, Eva Wilder. Diana's livery.
823.7397
McIntosh, Maria J.. Grace and Isabel; or, to
seem and to be. 823.4845
—— Two pictures; or, what we think of our-
selves, and what the world thinks of us.
823.4078
McKay, James Thompson. Stella Grayland.
42 pp. (*In* Stories by Amer. authors, v. 7.)
p. 103, *in* 823.4708
Mackay, W: The devil's ward. 13 pp.
in 823.5084
Same. *in* 823.5089
McKenna, *Mrs.* C.. M. Stanley-
—— The secret of a birth. 823.4811
—— The fortunes, good and bad, of a sewing-
girl. *in* 823.4988
Mackenzie, Erick, *pseud. See* Grogan, *Mrs.*
M.
Mackenzie, H: The man of feeling, *and*,
Julia de Roubigné. (Barbauld, *Mrs.* A. L.
(A.), *ed. The British novelists*, v. 29.)
** 823.2090
—— The story of La Roche. 18 pp. (John-
son, R., *ed. Little classics*, v. 3.)
p. 165, *in* 829.126
Mackenzie, Robert Shelton. Tressilian and
his friends. 823.1074
McKnight, C: Captain Jack, the scout; or, the
Indian wars about old Fort Duquesne.
823.1075
Issued also as Captain Jack.—Old Fort Duquesne.
Same. 823.4335; 823.7139
McLandburgh, Florence. Automaton ear, and
other sketches. 823.1076
Maclaren, *Miss* —. "Thrust out;" an old
legend. 823.1185
Maclay, Arthur Collins. Mito Yashiki: a
tale of old Japan. 823.6963
McLean, Sally Pratt. *See* Greene, *Mrs.* S..
P. (McL.)
Macleod, Norman. The starling.
in 823.4999

English Fiction. *Contin.*
Macleod of Dare. Black, W: 823.1914
MacNabb, *Mrs.* May (Laffan). [*Irish C:*
Dickens.]
—— Christy Carew. 823.3119
—— Flitters, Tatters, and the counsellor, and
other sketches. 823.4466
—— Ismay's children. 823.5686
—— A singer's story. 823.4954
—— *Same.* *in* 823.5042
Macnish, Robert. The metempsychosis. 38
pp. (*In* Famous stories. By DeQuincey,
and others.) p. 201, *in* 823.1778
—— *Same.* 59 pp. (*In* Tales from Black-
wood, v. 2.) *in* ** 823.6648
Macquoid, *Mrs.* K.. S.
—— A charming widow. 823.7398
—— At an old château. 823.6461
—— Checco: a tale of Perugia. (*With her*
The little vagabond.) *in* 823.1622
—— Her sailor love. 823.4564
—— Joan Wentworth: a novel. 823.5628
—— The little vagabond: a story. (*And*)
Checco: a tale of Perugia. 808.1622
—— Louisa. 823.4835
—— Lucy. 13 pp. (*In* Twenty novelettes,
etc.) p. 159, *in* 823.7183
—— Mère Suzanne, and other stories.
823.7133
—— The mill of St. Herbot: a Breton story.
823.5563
—— Patty. 823.1077
—— Rookstone. 823.5979
—— Too soon: a study of a girl's heart.
823.5918
Mad betrothal, A. Libbey, L. J. 823.7263
Mad love, A. By the author of "Lover and
lord." *in* 823.4981
Same. *in* 823.4982
Mad marriage, A. Fleming, *Mrs.* M.-A. (E.)
823.576
Mad world and its inhabitants. Chambers,
J. 823.196
Madagascar.
—— Ballantyne, R. M. The fugitives; or,
the tyrant queen of Madagascar. 823.5636
—— Nordhoff, C: Madagascar. (*In his*
Stories of the island world). 808.165
Note.—*See* Catalogues of this Library.
No. 2, 1880, p. 143. No. 5, 1888, p. 240.
No. 4, 1884, p. 172.
See also Index to Consular reports. 1880–1885;
1886–1889. 2 vols. (U. S. Pub. Docs. *Dept. of State.*)
** 350.5496¹.
See also Poole's Index (to 1882). p. 785, *in* **
50.1;—*Same.* Jan. 1, 1882–Jan. 1, 1887, p. 271, *in* **
50.1¹.
Madam. Oliphant, *Mrs.* M. O. (W.)
in 823.4989
Madam How and Lady Why. Kingsley, C:
808.933
Madame Agnes. Dubois, C: 823.6285
Madame de Chamblay. Dumas, A. D.
823.5879
Madame de Fleury. Edgeworth, M.
in 823.506
Same. p. 55, *in* 823.7431
Madame de Maurescamp. Feuillet, O.
823.6965
Madame de Presnel. Poynter, E. F.. 823.4907
Same. *in* 823.5055; *in* 823.5068

English Fiction. *Contin.*
Madame de Staël. Bölte, A. C.. E. M.
823.7093
Madame Delphine. Cable, G: W. 823.1895
Madame Firmiani. 57 pp. Balzac, H. de.
823.4256
Madame Gosselin. Ulbach, L: 823.2320
Madame Jane Junk and Joe. Bornemann,
Mrs. M.. 823.5813
Madame Thérèse. Erckmann, É., *and* Chatrian, P. A. 823.4302
Same. 823.6856
Madcap Violet. Black, W: 823.84
Made or marred. Fothergill, J. *in* 823.1848
Madeleine. Kavanagh, J. 823.916
Same. 823.6592
Madeleine. Sandeau, L. S. J. 823.6832
Madeleine Graham. Robinson, J..
823.1344
Madeline. Holmes, *Mrs.* M.. J.. (H.)
823.4849
Madeline. Opie, *Mrs.* A. (A.)
p. 9, *in* 823.6134
Mademoiselle. Peard, F.. M.. 823.7470
Mademoiselle Bismarck. Rochefort, H.
823.4187
Madman and the pirate. Ballantyne, R. M.
808.1277
Madolin Rivers. Libbey, L. J. *in* 823.5095
Madolin's lover. Brame, *Mrs.* C.. M. (L.)
in 823.5134
Madonna. 19 pp. Spicer, H:
p. 182, *in* 823.1778
Madonna Mary. Oliphant, *Mrs.* M. O. (W.)
823.5944
Madonna of the tubs, The. Ward, *Mrs.* E..
S. (P.) 823.6212
Magdalen Férat. Zola, É. 823.5401
Magdalen Hepburn. Oliphant, *Mrs.* M. O.
(W.) *in* 823.5084
Magellan, Fernando. Towle, G: M. Magellan; or, the first voyage round the world.
808.738
Maggie Miller. Holmes, *Mrs.* M.. J.. (H.)
in 823.790
Magic ring, The. La Motte-Fouqué, F. H.
K:, *Freiherr* de. 823.5480
Magic skin, The. Balzac, H. de. 823.5212
Magic Valley. Keary, E. 808.1544
Magicians, Stories of the. Church, *Rev.* A.
J: 823.5663
Maginn, W: Bob Burke's duel with ensign
Brady. 39 pp. (*In* Tales from Blackwood,
v. 3.) *in* ** 823.6649
—— Story without a tail. 23 pp. (*In* Tales
from Blackwood, v. 2.) *in* ** 823.6648
Magnetic man, and other stories. Van Zile,
E: S. 823.7298
Magnhild. Björnson, B. 823.4478
Magruder, Julia. Across the chasm. (Anon.)
823.5607
Maid Ellice. Boulger, *Mrs.* D. H. (H.)
823.721
Maid of Athens. McCarthy, J. 823.5039
Maid of honour. Gore, *Mrs.* C. F. G. (M.)
in * 823.6194
Maid of Killeena, and other stories. Black,
W: 823.5839
Maid of Orleans. Robinson, J.. 823.2025

English Fiction. *Contin.*
Maid of Sker. Blackmore, R: D. 823.5831
Same. 823.5906
Maid of Stralsund, The. Liefde, J. B. de.
823.2181
Maid, wife or widow? Hector, *Mrs.* A. (F.)
823.743
Same. *in* 823.5128
Maiden & married life of Mary Powell.
Rathbone, *Mrs.* M.. A. (M.) 823.4763
Maiden of Treppi. Heyse, J. L. P.
823.6803
Maiden widow. Southworth, *Mrs.* E. D. E.
(N.) 823.1980
Maidens' Lodge. Holt, E. S.. 808.1529
Mail-cart robbery. Wood, *Mrs.* E. (P.)
in 823.4994
Maillard, *Mrs.* Annette Marie. Jealous husband. A story of the heart. 823.6117
Maine. *See* New England.
Mainstone's housekeeper. Meteyard, E.
823.1155
**Mairet, Jeanne, *pseud.* *See* Bigot, *Mrs.* M..
(H.)
Maitland, E: [*Herbert Ainslie.*]
—— By and by: an historical romance of the
future. 823.1079
—— *Same.* 823.2354
—— Higher law: a romance. 823.1080
—— Pilgrim and the shrine. 823.1081
Maitland, James A.
—— The diary of an old doctor. 823.1082
—— The lawyer's story; or, the orphan's
wrongs. 823.1083
—— The old patroon; or, the great Van
Broek property. 823.1084
—— Sartaroe: a tale of Norway. 823.1085
—— The three cousins. 823.1086
—— The wanderer. 823.1087
—— The watchman. 823.1088
Maiwa's revenge. Haggard, H: R. 823.5530
Majendie, *Lady* Margaret E.. Dita. 823.1089
—— *Same.* 823.5037
—— A French speculation. 45 pp. (*In*
Tales from Blackwood. 3d ser., v. 2.)
p. 1, *in* 823.7498
—— Giannetto. 823.1090
—— Past forgiveness. 823.6984
—— A railway journey. 29 pp. (*In* Tales
from Blackwood. 2d ser., v. 6.)
in 823.7490
Major and minor. 2 vols. Norris, W: E:
823.5574-5
Making of a man. Baker, *Rev.* W: M.
823.4900
Malbone. Higginson, T: W. 823.766
Malcolm. MacDonald, G: 823.1064
Same. 823.5962; 823.5981
**Malet, Lucas, *pseud.* *See* Harrison, *Mrs.* R.
G. (K.)
Mallock, W: Hurrell. New Paul and Virginia; or, positivism on an island.
823.1091
—— The new republic; or, culture, faith and
philosophy in an English country house.
823.1092
—— The old order changes. 823.5584
—— A romance of the nineteenth century.
823.5585

English Fiction. *Contin.*

Malory, *Sir* T: The boy's King Arthur: being (a) history of King Arthur and his knights of the Round Table. Ed. for boys with an introd. by Sidney Lanier. Illus. 808.1870

—— La mort d'Arthure. The history of King Arthur and of the knights of the Round Table. Ed. by T: Wright. 2d ed. 3 vols. * 823.6615-17

—— *Same.* ** 823.6773-5

Malot, Hector Henri. No relations. Tr. by Mrs. M.. (L.) MacNabb. 823.3556

Mamelon. Tourgée, A. W. *in* 823.4303

Mam'zelle Eugénie. Durand, *Mme.* A. M. C. (H.) 823.4934

Man and wife. Collins, W: W. 823.259

Man as he is not. Bage, R. ** 823.2109

Man at arms. James, G: P. R. 823.869

Man in black, The. James, G: P. R. 823.5898

Man in the bell. 10 pp. (*In* Tales from Blackwood, v. 6.) *in* ** 823.6652

Man of feeling. Mackenzie, H: ** 823.2090

Man of his word, A. 50 pp. Norris, W: E: *in* 823.5036

Man of honor, A. 73 pp. Stannard, *Mrs.* H. E. V. (P.) *in* 823.5046

Man of the family, The. Williams, A. B. *in* 808.1640

Man of the people. 2 vols. Erckmann, E., *and* Chatrian, P. A. 823.7317-8

Man of the world. North, W: 823.1191

Man story, A. Howe, E. W. 823.5470

Man who laughs. 2 vols. (in 1). Hugo, V. M. 823.6288

Same. 823.6412

Man with five wives, The. Dumas, A. D. 823.5882

Man with the broken ear, The. About, E. F. V. 823.3436

Same. 823.6804

Manch. Bryan, *Mrs.* M.. E. 823.143

Manchester strike, A. Martineau, H. *in* ** 823.6708

Manfred. Guerrazzi, F. D. 823 6890

Manmat'ha. 24 pp. DeKay, C: *p.* 88, *in* 823.4711

Manning, Anne. *See* Rathbone, *Mrs.* M.. A. (M.)

Manning, E: Six months on a slaver. 823.6959

Man-of-war life. Nordhoff, C: 808.167

Same. 808.1898

Manœuvring. Edgeworth, M. 823.506

Same. *in* ** 823.4653; *p.* 1, *in* 823.7428

Man's will, A. Fawcett, E. 823.5419

Mansfield Park. Austen, J.. 823.44

Manuel, Juan, *prince,* Count Lucanor; or, the fifty pleasant stories of Patronio. Tr. by J. York. Illus. 823.7513

Manzoni, Alessandro. The betrothed. (*I promessi sposi.*) 823.5048
Issued also as "The betrothed lovers."—"Lucia, the betrothed."

—— *Same.* (Another tr.) 823.7399

—— I promessi sposi. The betrothed. 823.2138

English Fiction. *Contin.*

Marable family, The. Hillyer, S. 823.768

Marannos, The. Carey, J. H., *tr.* 823.6123

Marbeck, John, The story of. Marshall, *Mrs.* E. (M.) 823.5578

Marble faun, The. 2 vols. Hawthorne, N. 823.4362-3

Same. 823.6553-4

Marchioness of Brinvilliers. Smith, A. 823.1450

Marco Paul series. *See* Abbott, J.

Marcus Warland. Hentz, *Mrs.* C. L. (W.) 823.760

Margaret. Bright, *Mrs.* M. A. 823.1248

Same. 823.2047

Margaret. Judd, S. 823.907

Margaret Graham. James, G: P. R. 823.4920

Same. *in* 823.6247

Margaret Kent, Story of. Kirk, *Mrs.* E. W. (O.) 823.5527

Margaret Maitland of Sunnyside, Passages in the life of. Oliphant, *Mrs.* M. O. (W.) 823.4821

Margaret Moncrieffe. Burdett, C: 823.2061

Margaret Percival. Sewell, E.. M. 823.4177

Margaret Roper. Stewart, A. M. 823.1894

Margarethe. Schmieden, *Mrs.* E. (J.) 823.6808

Margery. 2 vols. Ebers, G. M. 823.6571-2

Margery Daw. (Anon.) *in* 823.4990

Margery's son. Holt, E. S.. 823.809

Margret Howth. Davis, *Mrs.* R.. B. (H.) 823.4257

Marguerite de Valois. Dumas, A. D. 823.5183

Same. 823.6513

Maria. Isaacs, J. 823.6641

Maria Theresa, and her fireman. Mundt, *Mrs.* C. (M.) *p.* 243, *in* 823.5888

Mariager, Peder. Pictures of Hellas. Five tales of ancient Greece. Tr. by M.. J. Safford. 823.5279

Marian Grey. Holmes, *Mrs.* M.. J.. (H.) 823.1924

Marianela. Perez Galdós, B. 823.4495

Marie. Pushkin, A. S. 823.4225

Marie Antoinette and her son. Mundt, *Mrs.* C. (M.) 823.6329

Marie's story. Bamford, M.. E. 808.1626

Marion, *Brig.-Gen.* Francis. Life of. 808.742

Marion Berkley. Comins, L. B. 823.270

Marion Graham. Lawrence, *Mrs.* M. (W.) 823.7323

Marion Scatterthwaite. Symington, C.. 823.4036

Marion's faith. King, *Capt.* C: 823.4967

Maritime novels. *See* Sea stories.

Marius the epicurean. 2d ed. 2 vols. Pater, W. H. 823.6197-8

Marjorie. 2 pts. Brame, *Mrs.* C.. M. (L.) *in* 823.5140

Same. 823.5186; 823.5195

Marjorie Daw and other people. Aldrich, T: B. 823.6926

Marjorie Daw and other stories. Aldrich, T: B. 823.36

English Fiction. *Contin.*

Marjorie's quest. Lincoln, *Mrs.* J. T. (G.)
     823.4084
Mark of Cain, The. Lang, A. *in* 823.5026
Mark Seaworth. Kingston, W: H: G.
     808.874
Marked "In haste." Macchetta, *Mrs.* B. R.
(T.)   823.4728
Market Harborough. Melville, G: J: Whyte-
     in ** 823.4668
Same.   823.7282
Markham, R: Aboard the Mavis (. . . how
five boys and five girls cruise . . . about
the east end of Long Island and how . . .
they learn something of the early history
of their country.)   808.1866
—— Colonial days. Being stories and bal-
lads for young patriots as recounted by
five boys and five girls in "Around the Yule
log," "Aboard the Mavis," "On the edge
of winter."   808.1865
Markof, the Russian violinist. Durand, *Mme.*
A. M. C. (H.)   823.6920
Marks, *Mrs.* M.. A. M. (Hoppus).
—— A great treason: a story of the war of in-
dependence.   *in* 823.5037
—— Masters of the world. 3 vols.
     823.7203-5
—— A story of carnival.   823.4572
Marlitt, E., *pseud. See* John, E.
Marmorne. Hamerton, P. G.   823.2001
Marooned. Russell, W: C.   823.6319
Maroussia. Hetzel, P. J.   808.1725
Marquis and merchant. Collins, M.
     823.6380
Same. 3 vols.   823.7369-71
Marquis Jeanne Hyacinthe de St. Palaye.
68 pp. Shorthouse, J. H:
     p. 117, *in* 823.5438
Marquis of Carabas. Spofford, *Mrs.* H. E..
(P.)   823.4463
Marquis of Lossie. MacDonald, G:
     823.1951
Marriage. Ferrier, S. E.   823.1991
Marriage at a venture. Gaborian, É.
     in 823.2463
Same.   *in* 823.5035
Marriage of convenience. Buchanan, *Mrs.*
H. (J.)   823.5060
Marriage of Moira Fergus. 68 pp. Black,
W: *in* 823.2885
Married belle, The. Smith, J: P.   823.1467
Married by proxy. Dupree, F.   823.7251
Married in haste. Maxwell, *Mrs.* M.. E..
(B.)   *in* 823.5117
Married in haste. Stephens, *Mrs.* A. S. (W.)
     823.1960
Marryat, Florence, *now* Lean, *Mrs.* F. (M.)
Marryat, *Capt.* F: The children of the New
Forest.   823.1095
—— The dog fiend; or, Snarleyyow. 823.1096
—— *Same.*   ** 823.6674
—— Frank Mildmay; or, the naval officer.
     823.1097
—— *Same.*   ** 823.6659
—— Jacob Faithful.   823.1098
—— *Same.*   ** 823.6660
—— Japhet in search of a father.   823.1099
—— *Same.*   ** 823.6661; 823.6742

English Fiction. *Contin.*

Marryat, *Capt.* F: *Contin.*
—— The king's own.   823.1100
—— *Same.*   823.2916; ** 823.6662
—— The little savage.   823.1101
—— Masterman Ready; or, the wreck of the
Pacific.   808.1499
—— Midshipman Easy. *See* Mr. Midship-
man Easy.
—— The mission; or, scenes in Africa: writ-
ten for young people.   808.775
—— *Same.*   808.1500
—— Mr. Midshipman Easy.   823.1105
—— *Same.*   ** 823.6663
—— Monsieur Violet, Travels . . . of, in Cal-
ifornia, Sonora, and western Texas.
     .   823.1104
—— *Same.*   ** 823.6664
—— Newton Forster; or, the merchant ser-
vice.   823.1106
—— *Same.*   ** 823.6665
—— Olla podrida.   823.1107
—— *Same.*   ** 823.6666
—— The pacha of many tales.   823.1108
—— *Same.*   ** 823.6667
—— Percival Keene.   823.1109
—— *Same.*   ** 823.6668
—— Peter Simple.   823.1110
—— *Same.*   ** 823.6669
—— The phantom ship.   823.1111
—— *Same.*   ** 823.6670
—— The pirate, and The three cutters.
     823.1112
—— *Same.*   ** 823.6671
—— The poacher.   823.1113
—— *Same.*   ** 823.6672
—— Poor Jack.   823.1114
—— Privateersman; adventures by sea and
land, in civil and savage life, one hundred
years ago.   823.1115
—— Rattlin, the reefer.   823.1116
—— *Same.*   ** 823.6673
—— The settlers in Canada: written for
young people.   808.776
—— *Same.*   823.1118
—— Stories of the sea.   ** 823.6730
—— The three cutters. (*With his* The pi-
rate.)   *in* 823.1112
—— *Same.*   *in* ** 823.6671
—— Travels and adventures of Monsieur
Violet in California, Sonora, and western
Texas.   823.1104
—— *Same.*   ** 823.6664
—— Valerie: an autobiography.   823.1119
—— *Same.*   ** 823.6675
Marse Chan. 36 pp. Page, T: N.
     p. 5, *in* 823.4710
Marsh, *Mrs.* Anne (Caldwell). Tales of the
woods and fields.   ** 823.6732
Marsh, C: L. Opening the oyster: a story of
adventure.   823.6322
Marsh island, A. Jewett, S.. O.   823.4862
Marshall, *Mrs.* Emma (Martin).
—— Alma; or, the story of a little music mis-
tress.   823.7138
—— Dayspring; a story of the time of Wil-
liam Tyndale, reformer, scholar, and mar-
tyr.   823.5775

English Fiction. *Contin.*
Marshall, *Mrs.* **Emma (Martin).** *Contin.*
—— In Colston's days: a story of old Bristol.
823.5774
—— In four reigns: the recollections of Al-
thea Allingham, 1785–1842.   823.5770
—— In the ,east country with Sir Thomas
Browne.   823.5771
—— John Marbeck, The story of.   823.5578
—— Memories of troublous times: being the
history of Dame Alicia Chamberlayne of
Ravensholme, Gloucestershire.   823.5772
—— Now-a-days; or, King's daughters.
823.1120
—— On the banks of the Ouse; or, life in
Olney a hundred years ago.   823.5411
—— The story of John Marbeck: a Windsor
organist of three hundred years ago; his
work and his reward.   823.5578
—— Under Salisbury spire in the days of
George Herbert. The recollections of Mag-
dalene Wydville.   823.7269
—— Under the mendips.   823.5773
Marston, Owen. Beauty's marriage. 823.7301
—— A dark marriage morn.   823.4771
—— Lover and husband.   823.7300
Marston. 3 vols. Croly, G: * 823.5492–4
Martha, the gypsy. 20 pp. Hook, T. E:
in 823.5182
Martin, H: Helen of Glenross. 4 vols.
(in 2).   ** 823.6763–4
Martin, *Mrs.* Herbert. *See* Martin, *Mrs.* M..
E.
Martin, *Mrs.* M.. E. "For a dream's sake."
in 823.5041
Martin Chuzzlewit, Life and adventures of.
2 vols. (in 1). Dickens, C: J: H.   823.424
Same.   823.5848
Same. 2 vols.   823.5305–6
Same. 4 vols.   823.420–3
Martin Paz. Verne, J.   p. 265, *in* 823.5162
Same.   p. 219, *in* 823.5204; 823.5380
Martin Rattler. Ballantyne, R. M. 808.263
Martin the foundling. Sue, M. J.   823.6299
Martin the skipper. Cobb, J. F.   808.1627
Martineau, Harriet. Deerbrook.   823.7352
—— *Same.* 2 vols.   ** 823.6740–1
—— Feats on the fiord.   808.1198
—— Glen of the echoes; or, Dan Mahony
and Dora Sullivan: a tale of Ireland.
(*Also*) Sowers not reapers; or, Chatham
and Mary Kay. (*And*) Tales of the
French revolution.   823.6602
—— The Hampdens.   823.7400
—— Illustrations of political economy.   9
vols. *viz.:*   ** 823.6706–14
v. 1. Brooke and Brooke farm.—Hill and the valley.
—Life in the wilds.   ** 823.6706
v. 2. Demerara. —Ella of Garveloch. ** 823.6707
woe in Garveloch.
v. 3. Cousin Marshall.—Ireland.—A Manchester
strike.   ** 823.6708
v. 4. For each and for all.—French wines and politics.—Homes abroad.   ** 823.6709
v. 5. Berkeley, the banker.—Charmed sea.
** 823.6710
v. 6. The loom and the lugger.—Messrs. Vanderput and Snoek.   ** 823.6711
v. 7. Cinnamon and pearls.—Sowers not reapers.—
Tale of the Tyne.   ** 823.6712
v. 8. Briery creek.—Three ages.   ** 823.6713
v. 9. The Farrers of Budge-Row.—Moral of many
fables.   ** 823.6714

English Fiction. *Contin.*
Martineau, Harriet. *Contin.*
—— Illustrations of political economy. *Con-
tin.*
—— — No. 1: Life in the wilds.   ** 823.6748
—— — No. 4: Demerara.   ** 823.6749
—— — No. 6: Weal and woe in Garveloch.
** 823.6750
—— — No. 13: The charmed sea.
** 823.6751
—— — No. 15: Berkeley the banker.   Pt. 2.
** 823.6752
—— — No. 16: Messrs. Vanderput and
Snoek.   ** 823.6753
—— The peasant and The prince.   808.1199
—— The prince. (*With her* The peasant.)
in 808.1199
—— Sowers not reapers; or, Chatham and
Mary Kay. (*With her* Glen of the echoes.)
in 823.6602
—— Tales of the French revolution. (*With
her* Glen of the echoes.)   *in* 823.6602
Martingale, Hawser, *pseud. See* Sleeper, J:
S.
Martins of Cro' Martin. Lever, C: J.
823.987
Same. 2 vols.   823.5708–9
Martyr of Golgotha. 2 vols. Escrich, E. P.
823.7152–3
Martyr to science. 46 pp. Jacobi, *Mrs.* M..
(P.)   p. 24, *in* 823.4703
Martyrdom of Madeline, The. Buchanan, R.
W.   *in* 823.6600
Martyrs of Spain. Charles, *Mrs.* E.. (R.)
823.6598
Maruja. Harte, F. B.   823.5282
Marvel, Ik, *pseud. See* Mitchell, D. G.
Mary Anerley. Blackmore, R: D.   823.2290
Mary Derwent. Stephens, *Mrs.* A. S. (W.)
823.1959
Mary Gresley. Trollope, A.   823.1616
Mary Lee. Boyce, J: 823.113
Mary Marston. MacDonald, G: 823.4168
Same.   823.6102
Mary of Burgundy. James, G: P. R.
823.870
Mary of Lorraine. Grant, J.   823.638
Mary Ogilvie. Picken, A.   823.7235
Mary Powell, Maiden & married life of.
Rathbone, *Mrs.* M.. A. (M.)   823.4763
Mary Schweidler, the amber witch. Mein-
hold, J. W.   823.4246
Mary-Lafon, Jean Bernard. Jaufry the
knight and the fair Brunissende. Tr. by
A. Elwes.   823.6104
Marzio's crucifix. Crawford, F. M.
823.5231
"—mas has come." 29 pp. Kip, L.
p. 152, *in* 823.4710
Mason, T: Adam Dickson; or, sae sweet, sae
bonnilie.   823.7187
Massachusetts. *See* New England.
Massachusetts bay. *See* New England.
Massinger, Philip. Macauley, E. Tales of
the drama founded on the tragedies of
. . . Massinger, etc.   823.1051
Master Bieland and his workmen. Auerbach,
B.   823.4590
Same.   823.6629

English Fiction. *Contin.*

Master Humphrey's clock. Dickens, C: J:
H. 823.425
Same. *in* 823.426; *in* 823.5331
Same. *in* 823.5554
Master of Ballantrae. Stevenson, R. L:
823.6934
Master of ceremonies. Fenn, G: M.
823.7374
Master of Greylands. Wood, *Mrs.* E. (P.)
823.6007
Master of Rathkelly, The. Smart, H.
823.5589
Master of the forges. Ohnet, G.
in 823.5043
Master of the magicians. Ward, *Mrs.* E.. S.
(P.), *and* Ward, H. D. 823.7342
Master of the mine. Buchanan, R. W.
in 823.5138
Master Vorhagen's wife. Lowell, R. T. S.
p. 234, *in* 823.1019
Masterman Ready. Marryat, *Capt.* F:
808.1499
Masters of the world. 3 vols. Marks, *Mrs.*
M.. A. M. (H.) 823.7203-5
Matapan affair, The. Du Boisgobey, F.
823.6595
Matchmaker, The. Sheppard, E.. S..
823.1420
Mate of the Daylight. 33 pp. Jewett, S.. O.
823.4807
Mate to mate. Sharkey, T. K. 823.1416
Mathers, H.., *now* Reeves, *Mrs.* H.. B. (M.)
Mathers, J:, *and* A solid gentleman, (*pseud.*)
The history of Mr. John Decastro, and his
brother Bat, commonly called Old Crab. 4
vols. ** 823.6609-12
Mathews, Cornelius, *comp.* The enchanted
moccasins, and other legends of the Ameri-
can Indians. 808.1856
Issued also as The Indian fairy book.
—— The Indian fairy book. 808.1330
Mathews, Julia A. Bessie Harrington's ven-
ture. 823.1122
Mathias Sandorf. 3 pts. (in 1 v.) Verne, J.
in 823.5028
Mathilda of Canossa, and Yoland of Gron-
ingen. Bresciani, *Rev.* A. 823.1904
Matilda. 2 vols. Cottin, *Mme.* S. (R.)
823.5652-3
Matrimony. Norris, W: E: 823.1893
Matt. 93 pp. Buchanan, R. W. 823.5141
Same. 823.5188
Matter of millions, A. Rohlfs, *Mrs.* A. K..
(G.) 823.7512
Matthews, Brander. *See* Matthews, J. B.
Matthews, James Brander.
—— The last meeting: a story. 823.5367
—— A secret of the sea, &c. 823.5366
—— Venetian glass. 26 pp. (*In* Stories by
Amer. authors, v. 3.) p. 172, *in* 823.4704
——, *and* Bunner, H: Cuyler. The docu-
ments in the case. 50 pp. (*In* Stories by
Amer. authors, v. 1.) p. 33, *in* 823.4702
Maturin, E: Bianca: a tale of Erin and Italy.
823.1123
Maturin, *Rev.* Robert C: Melmoth, the wan-
derer. 4 vols. ** 823.6681-4

English Fiction. *Contin.*

Mauleverer's millions. Reid, T. W.
in 823.5090
Maunsell, W. Pryce. The poisoned chalice.
823.7221
Maupassant, Guy de. *See* Maupassant, H.
R. A. G. de.
Maupassant, Henri René Albert Guy.
—— The Horla. Tr. by J. Sturges. 58 pp.
(*In* Mod. ghosts.) p. 1, *in* 823.7349
—— The odd number: thirteen tales. Tr. by
Jonathan Sturges. With introd. by H:
James. 823.6933
—— On the river. Tr. by Jonathan Sturges.
16 pp. (*In* Mod. ghosts.)
p. 113, *in* 823.7349
—— Pierre and Jean. Tr. by Hugh Craig.
823.6936
Mauprat. Dudevant, *Mme.* A. L. A. (D.)
823.6850
Maureen Dhu. Sadlier, *Mrs.* M.. A. (M.)
823.1381
Maurice Dering. Lawrence, G: A. 823.961
Maurice Tiernay, the soldier of fortune.
Lever, C: J. 823.988
Maurice Tyrone. McCarthy, J. 823.1053
Same. 823.5748
Mauritius; or, Isle of France.
—— St. Pierre, J. H: B. de. Paul and Vir-
ginia. 823.217
—— *Same.* 823.4206
Note.—See Backhouse, J. Narrative of a visit
to Mauritius and South Africa. 1844. 916.55.—Mar-
tin, R. M. History of southern Africa: Mauritius,
etc. 1843. 968.1.
Max Kromer. Smith, H. 823.1461
Maxwell, *Lady* Caroline E.. S.. (Sheridan)
Sterling- Lost and saved. 823.7405
—— Old Sir Douglas. 823.1192
—— *Same.* ** 823.6636
—— The wife and Woman's reward. 2 vols.
(Anon.) ** 823.6746-7
—— Woman's reward. (*With her* The wife,
etc., vols. 1-2.) 823.6746-7
Maxwell, Cecil. A story of three sisters.
823.1132
Maxwell, *Mrs.* M.. E.. (Braddon).
—— Asphodel. 823.1589
—— *Same.* *in* 823.5045
—— *Same.* (*Also*) Rupert Godwin.
823.2415
—— Aurora Floyd: a love story. *in* 823.5066
—— *Same.* 823.5904
—— Barbara; or, splendid misery.
in 823.5036
—— *Same.* (*Also*) John Marchmont's leg-
acy. 823.2400
—— Birds of prey. *in* 823.4987
—— *Same.* (*Also*) Charlotte's inheritance.
823.2403
—— Charlotte's inheritance. *in* 823.2403
—— *Same.* *in* 823.5048
—— Cloven foot. *in* 823.2416
—— *Same.* *in* 823.5114
—— Cut by the county; or, Grace Darnel.
in 823.5108
—— The day will come. 823.7198
—— Dead men's shoes. 823.5125
—— *Same.* (*Also*) Hostages to fortune.
823.2407

English Fiction. *Contin.*
Maxwell, *Mrs.* M.. E.. (Braddon). *Contin.*
—— Dead-sea fruit.   823.6076
—— *Same.* (*Also*) The golden calf.
     823.2413
—— Diavola; or, nobody's daughter. 2 pts.
     in 823.5119
Issued also as Run to earth.
—— The doctor's wife.   *in* 823.4977
—— *Same.* (*Also*) Only a clod.   823.2408
—— Dudley Carleon; or, the brother's secret; and George Caulfield's journey.
     in 823.4991
—— The fatal marriage, and The shadow in the corner.   823.5108
—— *Same.* (*And*) Put to the test.
     823.6604
—— Fenton's quest.   *in* 823.4991
—— *Same.* (*Also*) The cloven foot.
     823.2416
—— George Caulfield's journey. (*With her* Dudley Carleon.)   *in* 823.4991
—— The golden calf. (*With her* Dead-sea fruit.)   *in* 823.2413
—— Hostages to fortune.   *in* 823.2407
—— *Same.*   *in* 823.5049; *in* 823.5050
—— *Same.*   823.6075
—— An Ishmaelite.   *in* 823.5051
—— *Same.*   *in* 823.5058
—— John Marchmont's legacy. *in* 823.2400
—— *Same.*   *in* 823.5045
—— Joshua Haggard's daughter.
     in 823.5130
—— *Same.*   823.6078
—— *Same.* (*Also*) Taken at the flood.
     823.2412
—— Just as I am; or, a living lie.
     in 823.2417
—— *Same.*   *in* 823.5112
—— Lady Audley's secret.   *in* 823.2405
—— *Same.*   823.5104
—— Lady's mile.   *in* 823.2399
—— *Same.*   *in* 823.5096
—— The lawyer's secret. (*Also*) The mystery at Fernwood. (*With* Saints and sinners. By V. Cherbuliez.)   *in* 823.6384
—— The Lovels of Arden.   823.6081
—— Married in haste.   823.5117
—— The mistletoe bough. Christmas, 1885.
     in 823.5012
—— *Same,* 1886.   *in* 823.5059
—— *Same.*   *in* 823.5067
—— Mohawks.   823.5107
—— Mount Royal.   *in* 823.4979
—— *Same.* (*Also*) Just as I am.   823.2417
—— The mystery at Fernwood. 20 pp. (*With her* The lawyer's secret.)
     in 823.6384
—— The octoroon. (Anon.)   823.5029
—— *Same.*   *in* 823.6689
—— One thing needful; or, the penalty of fate.   823.5131
—— Only a clod.   *in* 823.2408
—— *Same.*   *in* 823.5061
—— Only a woman.   *in* 823.5126
—— *Same.*   *in* 823.6695
—— An open verdict.   823.6077
—— Phantom fortune.   *in* 823.5116

English Fiction. *Contin.*
Maxwell, *Mrs.* M.. E.. (Braddon). *Contin.*
—— Publicans and sinners; or, Lucius Davoren. Pt. 1.   *in* 823.5135
—— *Same.* Pt. 2.   *in* 823.5186
—— *Same.* 2 pts. 2 vols. (in 1).   823.2401
Issued also as Lucius Davoren.
—— *Same.*   823.5140
—— Put to the test.   823.5106
—— *Same.*   *in* 823.6604
—— Rupert Godwin.   *in* 823.2415
—— *Same.*   *in* 823.5114
—— The shadow in the corner. (*With her* The fatal marriage.)   823.5108
—— *Same.*   *in* 823.6604
—— Sir Jasper's tenant.   823.4955
—— *Same.* (*Also*) Lady's mile.   823.2399
—— A strange world.   *in* 823.2409
—— *Same.*   823.2639
—— Strangers and pilgrims.   823.3067
—— *Same.*   823.5018; 823.6208
—— *Same.* (*Also*) A strange world.
     823.2409
—— Taken at the flood.   *in* 823.2412
—— *Same.*   823.5112
—— To the bitter end.   823.5103
—— *Same.*   *in* 823.6208
—— *Same.* (*Also*) Lady Audley's secret.
     823.2405
—— Under the red flag.   823.4769
—— *Same.*   *in* 823.5029
—— Vixen.   *in* 823.5124
—— *Same.* (*Also*) Weavers and weft.
     823.2404
—— Weavers and weft; or, "Love that hath us in his net."   *in* 823.2404
—— *Same.*   *in* 823.5017
—— Wyllard's weird.   *in* 823.5096
Maxwell, W: Hamilton. Adventures of Captain Blake; or, my life.   823.1124
—— The bivouac; or, stories of the Peninsular war. 3 vols. (in 1).   823.1127
—— Captain Blake, Adventures of.
     823.1124
—— Flood and field; or, the recollections of a soldier of fortune.   823.1128
—— The fortunes of Hector O'Halloran.
     823.1129
—— Grace Willoughby; a tale of the wars of King James.   823.5894
—— Hector O'Halloran, The fortunes of.
     823.1129
—— Luck is everything; or, the adventures of Brian O'Linn.   823.1125
—— Sports . . . in the Highlands and islands of Scotland: a sequel to the " Wild sports of the west."   823.1130
—— Stories of the Peninsular war.
     823.1131
—— Stories of Waterloo.   823.1133
Maxwell. Hook, T. E: 823.820
May, Sophie, *pseud. See* Clarke, R.. S.
May. Oliphant, *Mrs.* M. O. (W.) 823.5945
May Blossom. Lee, M.   823.5054
May Flower, and miscellaneous writings. Stowe, *Mrs.* H. E.. (B.)   823.2037
May Lane. M., C. M. (*With* The well of the desert. By E. S.. Holt.)
     p. 185, *in* 823.5768

English Fiction. *Contin.*
May Martin, and other tales of the Green mountains. Thompson, D. P.　823.1851
Mayhew, A: Septimus, *joint author. See* Mayhew, H:
Mayhew, H:, *and* Mayhew, A: Septimus. The image of his father; or, one boy is more trouble than a dozen girls: being a tale of a "young monkey."　823.5479
Mayo, *Mrs.* I.. (Fyvie). [*E: and Ruth Garrett.*]
—— At any cost.　　　*in* 823.4995
—— *Same.*　　　　　*in* 823.5202
—— By still waters.　　　823.1135
—— A chance child. 37 pp. (Johnson, R., *ed. Little classics*, v. II.)
　　　　　　　p. 165, *in* 829.134
—— Crooked places: a story of struggles and hopes.　　　　　　823.1136
—— The crust and the cake.　823.1137
—— The dead sin, and other stories.
　　　　　　　　　823.1138
—— Doing and dreaming. (*Also*) A real lady.　　　　　　　823.1139
—— Family fortunes: a domestic story.
　　　　　　　　　823.4465
—— Gold and dross.　　　823.1140
—— The house by the works.　823.1925
—— John Winter: a story of harvests.
　　　　　　　　　823.5753
—— The mystery of Allan Grale.
　　　　　　　in 823.5138
—— The occupations of a retired life.
　　　　　　　　　823.1141
—— Premiums paid to experience: incidents in my business life.　　　823.1142
—— The quiet Miss Godolphin; and A chance child.　　　　　　823.4050
—— A real lady. (*With her* Doing and dreaming.)　　　　*in* 823.1139
—— White as snow.　　　823.5723
Mayo, W: Starbuck. The Berber; or, the mountaineer of the Atlas: a tale of Morocco.　　　　　　823.1143
Issued also as Mountaineer of the Atlas.
—— Kaloolah; or, journeyings to the Diébel Kumri: an autobiography of Jonathan Romer.　　　　　　823.1144
—— Never again.　　　823.1145
Mayor of Casterbridge. Hardy, T:
　　　　　　　in 823.4984
Same.　　　　　*in* 823.5105
Mayor of Wind-gap. Banim, M.　823.59
Meadow Brook. Holmes, *Mrs.* M.. J.. (H.)
　　　　　　　　　823.799
Mecklenburg, *Mrs.* Alfhilda (Svenson). [*Ivar Ring.*] Furugaard. 16 pp.—The snowball. 24 pp. (Vicary, J: F., *comp. A stork's nest.*)　　　*in* 823.5415
Mediterranean. Campbell, *Sir* G. Dark stories from the sunny south; or, legends of the Mediterranean.　　823.7242
Meinhold, Johann Wilhelm. Mary Schweidler, the amber witch. The most interesting trial for witchcraft ever known. Printed from an imperfect manuscript by her father, Abraham Schweidler, the pastor of Coserow, in the island of Usedom. Tr. by Lady L. D. Gordon.　　823.4246

English Fiction. *Contin.*
Melbourne house. Warner, S.　823.1678
Meldrum, D: S. Rathillet. 57 pp. (*In* Tales from Blackwood. 3d ser., v. 6.)
　　　　　　　p. 350, *in* 823.7502
Mellichampe. Simms, W: G.　823.1434
Melmoth, the wanderer. 4 vols. Maturin, *Rev.* R. C:　　　** 823.6681-4
Melville, G: J: Whyte-
—— Black but comely; or, the adventures of Jane Lee.　　　** *in* 823.4665
—— *Same.*　　　　　823.7270
—— "Bones and I;" or, the skeleton at home.　　　** *in* 823.4660
—— *Same.*　　　　　823.7271
—— The Brookes of Bridlemere.　823.1150
—— *Same.*　　　　　823.7272
—— *Same.* (*Also*) Sarchedon: a legend of the great queen.　　** 823.4662
—— Cerise: a tale of the last century.
　　　　　　　　　823.1151
—— *Same.*　　*in* ** 823.4667; 823.7273
—— Contraband; or, a losing hazard.
　　　　　　　　　823.7274
—— *Same.* (*Also*) Roy's wife.
　　　　　　　** 823.4666
—— Digby Grand; an autobiography.
　　　　　　　　　823.7275
—— *Same.* (*Also*) The interpreter: a tale of the war.　　** 823.4671
—— General Bounce; or, the lady and the locusts.　　　　　823.7276
—— *Same.* (*Also*) Tilbury Nogo; or, passages in the life of an unsuccessful man.
　　　　　　　** 823.4664
—— The gladiators: a tale of Rome and Judæa.　　　　　823.7402
—— *Same.* (*Also*) Good for nothing; or, all down hill.　　** 823.4670
—— Good for nothing; or, all down hill.
　　　　　　　in ** 823.4670
—— *Same.*　　　　　823.7277
—— Holmby house: a tale of old Northamptonshire.　　　　823.7278
—— *Same.* (*Also*) Cerise: a tale of the last century.　　** 823.4667
—— Inside the bar; or, sketches at Soakington.　　　　*in* ** 823.4668
—— *Same.*　　　*in* 823.7282
—— The interpreter: a tale of the war.
　　　　　　　　　823.1853
—— *Same.*　　*in* ** 823.4671
—— Kate Coventry: an autobiography.
　　　　　　　　　823.7279
—— *Same.* (*Also*) Rosine: a story of the red revolution.　　** 823.4669
—— Katerfelto: a story of Exmoor.
　　　　　　　　　823.1152
—— *Same.*　　　　　823.7280
—— *Same.* (*Also*) M. or N. "Similia similibus curantur."　　** 823.4661
—— M. or N. "Similia similibus curantur."
　　　　　　　in ** 823.4661
—— *Same.*　　　　　823.7281
—— Market Harborough; or, how Mr. Sawyer went to the shires. (*With his* Satanella.)　　　*in* ** 823.4668
—— *Same.* (*Also*) Inside the bar; or, sketches at Soakington.　　823.7282

English Fiction. *Contin.*
Melville, G: J: Whyte- *Contin.*
—— The queen's Maries: a romance of Holyrood. 823.7283
—— *Same.* (*Also*) The white rose.
** 823.4663
—— Rosine. *in* ** 823.4669
—— *Same.* 823.7284
—— Roy's wife. *in* ** 823.4666
—— *Same.* 823.7285
—— Sarchedon: a legend of the great queen.
in ** 823.4662
—— *Same.* 823.7286
—— Satanella: a story of Punchestown.
823.7287
—— *Same.* (*Also*) Market Harborough; or, how Mr. Sawyer went to the shires. (*And*) Inside the bar; or, sketches at Soakington.
** 823.4668
—— Scotland and the moors. 40 pp. (*With his* Tilbury Nogo.) p. 323, *in* 823.7289
—— Sister Louise; or, the story of a woman's repentance. 823.7288
—— *Same.* (*Also*) Black but comely; or, the adventures of Jane Lee. ** 823.4665
—— Tilbury Nogo; or, passages in the life of an unsuccessful man. (*With his* General Bounce.) *in* ** 823.4664
—— *Same.* (*Also*) Scotland and the moors.
823.7289
—— Uncle John. 823.7290
—— *Same.* (*Also*) "Bones and I;" or, the skeleton at home. ** 823.4660
—— The white rose. 823.1153
—— *Same.* *in* ** 823.4663
Melville, Herman. The bell-tower. 20 pp. (Johnson, R., *ed.* *Little classics*, v. 3.)
p. 128, *in* 829.126
—— Moby-Dick; or, the whale. 823.1146
—— Pierre: or, the ambiguities. 823.1147
—— The refugee. 823.1148
—— White-Jacket; or, the world in a man-of-war. 823.1149
Member, The. Galt, J: ** 823.6720
Member for Paris. Murray, E. C. G.
823.6098
Memoirs and resolutions of Adam Graeme of Mossgray. Oliphant, *Mrs.* M. O. (W.)
in 823.5089
Memoirs of a cavalier. De Foe, D.
in 823.2123
Memoirs of a millionaire. Ames, L. T.
823.6556
Memoirs of a physician. Dumas, A. D.
823.6518
Memoirs of Barry Lyndon. Thackeray, W: M. *in* 823.1575
Same. p. 3, *in* 823.6552
Memoirs of Captain Carleton. De Foe, D.
in 823.2123
Memoirs of Henry VIII. Herbert, H: W:
823.5726
Memoirs of Mr. C. J. Yellowplush. Thackeray, W: M. *in* 823.1577
Same. 823.6323
Memorable murder, A. 35 pp. Thaxter, *Mrs.* C. (L.) p. 135, *in* 823.4704
Memories. Müller, F. M. 823.4020

English Fiction. *Contin.*
Memories of troublous times. Marshall, *Mrs.* E. (M.) 823.5772
Men, women, and ghosts. Ward, *Mrs.* E.. S. (P.) 823.1257
Ménard, Théophile, *pseud.* *See* Roy, J. J. E.
Mendelssohn, Moses. (1729–1786.)
—— Auerbach, B. Poet and merchant: a picture of life from the times of Moses Mendelssohn. 823.6793
Note.—See Hedge, F. H. Life of M., with examples of his writings. 20 pp. (*In his* Prose writers of Germany.) p. 99, *in* 839.2.—Samuels, M. Memoirs of M., incl. the correspondence on the Christian religion with Lavater. 1827. 921.35.
Mendelssohn-Bartholdy, Jakob Ludwig Felix. (1809–1847.)
—— Barnard, C: Mozart and Mendelssohn. (*The tone masters*, v. 1.) 808.1619
See also Grove, *Sir* G: Dictionary of music and musicians, v. 2. p. 253, *in* ** 780.20.—Moscheles, I. Recent music and musicians. 1873. 780.6.
Mendès, *Mme.* Judith (Gautier). The usurper: an episode in Japanese history. Tr. by A. L. Alger. 823.4785
Menger, Rudolf. Countess Loreley. Tr. by Miss Dandridge. 823.7055
Men's wives. Thackeray, W: M. *in* 823.1572
Same. *in* 823.6324
Menshikoff. Hasselt, A. H. C. van.
823.7172
Mercedes of Castile. Cooper, J. F. 823.300
Same. *in* 823.7454
Merchant of Antwerp. Conscience, H.
823.2445
Merchant of Berlin, The. Mundt, *Mrs.* C. (M.) 823.5888
Merchant vessel, The. Nordhoff, C:
808.166
Merchant's clerk. Warren, S: 823.4994
Mercy Philbrick's choice. Jackson, *Mrs.* H.. M. (F.) 823.4304
Mere adventurer. Andrews, F. 823.5842
Mere interlude, A. 30 pp. Hardy, T: (*With* Mrs. Smith of Longmains. By R. Broughton.) *in* 823.5046
Mère Suzanne and other stories. Macquoid, *Mrs.* K.. S. 823.7133
Meredith, G: Adventures of Harry Richmond. 823.5275
—— Beauchamp's career. 823.5276
—— Diana of the crossways. *in* 823.5060
—— The egoist. 823.2264
—— *Same.* 823.6620
—— *Same.* 3 vols. 823.4369–71
—— Evan Harrington; or, he would be a gentleman. 823.1154
—— Farina. (*With his* The shaving of Shagpat.) *in* 823.5274
—— The house on the beach: a realistic tale.
823.5563
—— The ordeal of Richard Feverel: a history of father and son. * 823.6619
—— Rhoda Fleming. 823.5381
—— Sandra Belloni, originally Emilia in England. 823.5382
—— The shaving of Shagpat: an Arabian entertainment; and, Farina. 823.5274
—— The tragic comedians: a study in a well-known story. 2 vols. * 823.4682–3
—— Vittoria. 823.5586

English Fiction. *Contin.*
Merimée, Prosper. Carmen: the power of love. 65 pp. (*With* A thousand francs reward. By E. Gaboriau.)   *in* 823.6699
Meritt, Paul. Daughters of Eve. Founded on the drama of "New Babylon." *Also* A Provence rose. By L. de La Ramée.
       823.7056
Merkland. Oliphant, *Mrs.* M. O. (W.)
       823.7406
Merry men, and other tales and fables. Stevenson, R. L.   823.5017
Merton. Hook, T. E: 823.821
Mervyn Clitheroe. Ainsworth, W: H.
       823.22
Mervyn's meed. Kerr, E.   *in* 823.7189
Mesopotamia. *See also* Babylon.
—— Longfellow, H: W. Poems of places.
       p. 109, 821.228
Message from the sea, A. Dickens, C: J: H.
       823.5557
Messrs. Vanderput & Snoek. Martineau, H.
       in ** 823.6711
Same.   ** 823.6753
Meta Holdenis. Cherbuliez, V.   823.2318
Same.   823.2378
Metamorphoses. Apuleius, L.   823.2116
Metamorphoses: a tale. (*In* Tales from Blackwood. 2d ser., v. 4.)   *in* 823.7488
Metempsychosis, The. 38 pp. Macuish, R.
       p. 201, *in* 823.1778
Meteyard, Eliza. [*Silverpen.*] Mainstone's housekeeper.   823.1155
Metzerott, shoemaker. Woods, K.. P.
       823.6995
Mexico.
—— Francis, F. Mosquito: a tale of the Mexican frontier.   823.7517
—— Hale, E: E., *and* Hale, *Miss* S. A family flight through Mexico.   808.1830
—— Knox, T: W. Boy travellers in Mexico, The. Adventures . . . in a journey to northern and central Mexico, Campeachey, and Yucatan, with a description . . . of Central America and of the Nicaragua canal.   808.1841
—— Miller, C. H. Songs of the Mexican seas.   821.1315
—— Ober, F: A. Young folks' history of Mexico.   978.75
Conquest period.
—— Dryden, J. Indian emperor; trag.
       ** 822.135
—— —— Indian queen; trag.   ** 822.135
Montezuma.
—— Eggleston, E:, *and* Seelye, *Mrs.* L. (E.) Montezuma, and the conquest of Mexico.
       808.826
—— Ober, F: A. Montezuma's gold mines.
       823.5539
—— Voltaire, F. M. A. de. Alzire; trag.
       p. 418, *in* 842.16
Aztec civilization. Wallace, L. The fair god; or, the last of the 'Tzins; a tale of the conquest of Mexico.   823.1668
19TH CENTURY, A. D.
—— Bishop, W: H: The yellow snake.
       823.6391

English Fiction. *Contin.*
Mexico. *Contin.*
19TH CENTURY, A. D. *Contin.*
—— Janvier, T: A. The Aztec treasure-house.   823.7165
—— Kingsley, M. The Puerto de Medina. 37 pp. (*In* Tales from Blackwood. 3d ser., v. 2.)   p. 117, *in* 823.7498
—— Maitland, E: Higher law.   823.1080
—— Ober, F: A. The silver city: a story of adventure in Mexico.   808.1878
—— Reid, *Capt.* T: M. The Free Lances: a romance of the Mexican valley. 823.6335
—— —— The scalp hunters; or, adventures among the trappers.   808.437
—— Ripley, E. McH. From flag to flag: a woman's adventures and experiences . . . in Mexico.   823.5439
—— Stoddard, W: O. The red mustang: a story of the Mexican border.   808.1587
Note.—For ancient Aztec civilization, *see* Prescott, W: H. History of the conquest of Mexico. v. 1. chaps. i-vi. 978.11.
For Spanish conquest under Cortes, *see* Cortes, H. Despatches addressed to the Emperor Charles V. 1843. 978.39.—**Helps**, A. The Spanish conquest in America. vols. 2, 3. 1857. 970.38-9.
For general histories, etc., *see* **Bancroft**, H. H. History of Mexico. 5 vols. (*Works*, vols. 9-13.) *970. 73-77. *Contents:*—v. 1: 1516-1521, * 970.73; v. 2: 1521-1600, * 970.74; v. 3: 1600-1803, * 970.75; v. 4: 1804-1824, * 970.76; v. 5: 1824-1861, * 970.77;—History of the north Mexican states. (*Works*, vols. 15-.) *Contents:*—v. 1: 1531-1800, 970.79.—**Frost**, J. History of Mexico and its wars (to 1882). 1877. 978.77.—**Hale**, S. The story of Mexico. (*Story of the nations*.) 1891. 978.76.—**Janvier**, T: A. The Mexican guide. 1890. * 9102.2.—**Noll**, A. H. Short hist. of Mexico. (1325-1888.) 1890. 978.78.—**Ober**, F: A. Young folks' history of Mexico. 1883. 978.65.—**Tylor**, E: B. Anahuac; or, Mexico and the Mexicans, ancient and modern. (Re-is. of 1861.) 978.54.—**Winsor**, J. Mexico and Central America. (*In his* Narr. and crit. hist. of Amer., v. 1, pp. 133-208.) * 970.127[1].
For war with the United States, *see* **Jay**, W: Review of the causes and consequences of the Mexican war. 2d ed. 1849. 973.708.—**Jenkins**, J: S. History of the war between the United States and Mexico. 1859. 973.88.—**Mayer**, B. History of the war between Mexico and the United States. 1848. 978.79.—**Ripley**, *Maj.* R. S. War with Mexico. 2 vols. 1849. 978.82-3.
See also United States, *note*: *War with Mexico.*
For empire of Maximilian, *see* **Elton**, *Capt.* J. F. With the French in Mexico. 978.18.—**Schrœder**, S. Fall of Maximilian's empire. 1887. 978.80.
For manners and customs, *see* **Gooch**, *Mrs.* F. C. Face to face with the Mexicans. 1887. * 9178.62.
For description of modern Mexico, *see* **Aubertin**. A flight to Mexico. 1882. 9178.65.—**Brockleburst**, T: U. Mexico to-day. 1883. * 917.57.—**Castro**, L. The republic of Mexico in 1882. 9178.64.—**Crawford**, C. H. The land of the Montezumas. 1889. 9178.63.—**Haven**, G. Our next-door neighbor. 1875. 9178.44.—**Janvier**, T: A. The Mexican guide. 1890. * 9102.2.
See also **Anderson**, A. D. Mexico from the material stand-point. 1884. (American and English authorities. pp. 137-156, etc.) 978.81.
See also Catalogues of this Library.
No. 2, 1880, p. 153.   No. 4, 1884, p. 185.
No. 3, 1882, p. 122.   No. 5, 1888, p. 253.
See also Poole's Index (to 1882). pp. 832-4, *in* ** 50.1;—*Same.* Jan. 1, 1882-Jan. 1, 1887. pp. 286-7, *in* ** 50.1[1].
See also Index to Consular reports. 1880-1889. 2 vols. (U. S. Pub. Docs. *Dept. of State.*) *in* ** 350.5496[1-2].

Mexico, Gulf of. Hearn, L. Chita: a memory of Last Island.   823.7141
Meyer, Konrad Ferdinand. The tempting of Pescara. Tr. by Mrs. Clara Bell. 823.7351

English Fiction. *Contin.*
Meyers, Robert C. Miss Margery's roses.
823.1156
Michael Armstrong, Life and adventures of.
Trollope, *Mrs. F..* (M.)   ** 823.6222
Michael Rudolph. Dupuy, E. A.   823.4284
Michael Strogoff. Verne, J.   823.6112
Michel Lorio's cross. 45 pp. Smith, H.
p. 249, *in* 823.1460
Mick Tracy, the Irish scripture reader. By
the author of "Tim Doolan."   823.7190
Middle ages. *See also* Charlemagne.—Le-
gends.—For Wandering Jew, *see note under*
Jews.
—— Cox, *Sir* G: W:, *and* Jones, E. H.
Popular romances of the middle ages.
823.7193
For contents, *see* Cox, *Sir* G: W:, *and* Jones, E. H.
—— Saxon, *Mrs.* E. L. Belt and spur: sto-
ries of the knights of the middle ages from
the old chronicles.   808.1610
Middlemarch. Cross, *Mrs.* M.. A. (E.)
in 823.6261
Same. 2 vols.   823.1000-1
Middlemass, Jean. Lady Muriel's secret.
in 823.5093
—— Silvermead.   *in* 823.4987
Middlemore, *Mrs.* S. G. C. Round a posada
fire: Spanish legends. Illus.   823.4745
Middy and ensign. Fenn, G: M.   808.1222
Same.   823.5740
Midnight sun. Bremer, F.   *in* 823.5023
Same.   823.6109
Midshipman Easy. Marryat, *Capt.* F:
823.1105
Mignon. Bridges, *Mrs. Col.* —.   823.584
Mignon. Stannard, *Mrs.* H. E. V. (P.)
in 823.4994
Mignon's secret. 82 pp. Stannard, *Mrs.* H.
E. V. (P.)   *in* 823.5015
Mildred. Holmes, *Mrs.* M.. J.. (H.)
823.800
Mildred's cadet. Hamilton, A. K.   823.1860
Mildred's married life, and a winter with Elsie
Dinsmore. Finley, M.   823.4747
Miles O'Reilly, Life and adventures of. Hal-
pine, C. G.   823.7083
Miles Wallingford. Cooper, J. F.   823.301
Same.   *in* 823.7456
Military adventure in the Pyrenees. By a
peninsular medallist. 98 pp. (*In* Tales
from Blackwood. 2d ser., v. 3.)
in 823.7487
Military sketches. Gaboriau, É.
in 823.6699
Military sketches and stories. Forbes, A.,
and others.   823.6281
Military stories and sketches.
—— Forbes, A., *and others.* Military sketches
and stories.   823.6281
—— Grant, J. Cavaliers of fortune; or, Brit-
ish heroes in foreign wars.   823.622
—— — Constable of France.   823.623
—— — Legend of the old 55th; or, the regiment of Flanders. 30 pp. (*With his* Ross-
shire Buffs.)   p. 267, *in* 823.649
—— — Scottish soldiers of fortune: their ad-
ventures and achievements in the armies of
Europe.   823.5932

English Fiction. *Contin.*
Military stories and sketches. *Contin.*
—— King, *Capt.* C: Starlight ranch, and
other stories of army life on the frontier.
823.7176
Note.—For American military and naval biography, *see* Dudley, D. Officers of our Union army
and navy. v. 1. 923.684.—Hamersley, T: H. S.
Complete army and navy register of the United
States of America. 1776-1887. 1888. ** 973.616.—
Johnson, R. U., *and* Buel, C. C., *eds.* Battles and
leaders of the civil war. 4 vols. * 973.630-33.—
Peterson, C: J. Military heroes of the war of 1812
and Mexico. 1858. 923.396.—Shea, J. G. The fallen brave. 1861. 923.393.—Snow, W. P. Southern
generals, who they are and what they have done.
1865. 920.396.—Wilson, T: Biography of the principal American military and naval heroes. 2 vols.
1817. 920.396-7.
For British military biography, *see* Cust, *Sir* E:
Lives of the warriors of the 17th century. 6 vols.
1865-9. 920.390-95.—Kaye, *Sir* J. W. Lives of Indian officers. 3 vols. 1880. 920.387-89.—Mitchell,
Maj.-Gen. J. Biographies of eminent soldiers of
the last four centuries. 1865. 920.386.
For military life in general, *see* Zogbaum, R. F.
Horse, foot and dragoons: sketches of army life at
home and abroad. 1888. 355.512.
See also notes under England.—France.—United
States.
Mill and the tavern, The. Arthur, T. S.
823.5758
Mill mystery, The. Rohlfs, *Mrs.* A.. K.. (G.)
823.7148
Mill of St. Herbot, The. Macquoid, *Mrs.* K..
S.   823.5563
Mill on the Floss. Cross, *Mrs.* M.. A. (E.)
823.1002
Millbank. Holmes, *Mrs.* M.. J.. (H.)
823.1922
Miller, *Mrs.* Alex. McVeigh. A dreadful
temptation.   823.7057
—— Lady Gay's pride; or, the miser's treas-
ure.   823.5043
—— Lancaster's choice.   823.5036
—— Laurel Vane; or, the girl's conspiracy.
in 823.5043
—— An old man's darling.   823.7058
—— Sworn to silence.   *in* 823.5044
Miller, *Mrs.* Annie (Jenness). 'Twixt love
and law: a novel.   823.5506
Miller, Cincinnatus Hiner. [*Joaquin Miller.*]
—— Danites in the Sierras.   823.4204
—— The destruction of Gotham.   823.5388
—— *Same.*   823.5769
—— First fam'lies of the Sierras. 823.1159
—— The one fair woman.   823.7403
Miller, *Mrs.* Harriet (Mann). [*Olive Thorne
Miller.*] Little folks in feathers and fur,
and others in neither.   808.1888
Miller, Hugh. Sandy Wood's sepulchre. 8
pp. (Johnson, R., *ed. Little classics, v. 5.*)
p. 127, *in* 829.128
—— Scenes and legends of the north of
Scotland; or, the traditional history of
Cromarty.   823.1157
—— Tales and sketches. Ed., with a preface,
by Mrs. Miller.   823.1158
Contents:—Recollections of Ferguson.—Recollec-
tions of Burns.—The salmon-fisher of Udoll.—Let-
ters on the herring fishery.—The Iykewake.—Bill
Whyte.—The young surgeon.—A true story of the
life of a Scotch merchant of the 18th century.
Miller, Joaquin, *pseud. See* Miller, Cincin-
natus Hiner.
Miller, Olive Thorne, *pseud. See* Miller, *Mrs.*
Harriet (Mann).

English Fiction. *Contin.*

Missing bride, The. Southworth, *Mrs.* E. D.
E. (N.) 823.1500
Missing ship, The. Kingston, W: H: G.
808.358
Mission, The. Marryat, *Capt.* F: 808.775
Same. 808.1500
Mist of error. Dickens, M.. A. 823.7228
Mr. Absalom Billingslea, and other Georgian
folk. Johnston, R: M. 823.5267
Mr. and Mrs. Morton. Williams, *Dr.* H.,
and Williams, *Mrs.* H. 823.4550
Mr. Barnes of New York. Gunter, A. C.
823.6019
Mr. Bixby's Christmas visitor. 12 pp. Gage,
C: S. p. 42, *in* 823.4710
Mr. Bodley abroad. Scudder, H. E.
808.1851
Mr. Butler's ward. Robinson, F. M.
in 823.4987
Mr. Columbus Coriander's gorilla. 22 pp.
(*In* Half-hours with great story tellers.)
p. 53, *in* 823.5478
Mr. Ghim's dream. 823.1898
Mr. Isaacs. Crawford, F. M. 823.4471
Mr. Jonathan Wild the great, The history of
the life of the late. Fielding, H:
823.6152
Mr. Ledbury and his friend Jack Johnson,
Adventures of. Smith, A. 823.1451
Mr. Meeson's will. Haggard, H: R.
823.5528
Mr. Midshipman Easy. Marryat, *Capt.* F:
823.1105
Same. ** 823.6663
Mr. Oldmixon. Hammond, W: A. 823.4857
Mr. Peter Crewitt. Denison, *Mrs.* M.. (A.)
823.377
Mr. Phillips' goneness. Bailey, J. M.
823.52
Mr. Potter of Texas. Gunter, A. C.
823.5408
Mr. Scarborough's family. Trollope, A.
823.6596
Mr. Schermerhorn's marriage and widowhood.
Lowell, R. T. S. p. 99, *in* 823.1019
Mr. Smith. Walford, *Mrs.* L. B. (C.)
823.1665
Same. 823.6700
Mr. Tangier's vacations. Hale, E: E.
823.5254
Mistletoe bough, The. Christmas, 1885.
Maxwell, *Mrs.* M.. E.. (B.), *ed.*
in 823.5012
Same. 1886. *in* 823.5059; *in* 823.5067
Mistress and maid. Craik, *Mrs.* D. M. (M.)
823.335
Same. *in* 823.6263
Mrs. Armington's ward. Wright, D. T.
823.4092
Mrs. Arthur. Oliphant, *Mrs.* M. O. (W.)
823.5946
Mistress Beatrice Cope. Le Clerc, M. E.
823.6504
Mrs. Beauchamp Brown. Austin, *Mrs.* J..
(G.) 823.6625
Mrs. Beauchamp's vengeance. 50 pp. (*In*
Tales from Blackwood. 2d ser., v. 11.)
in 823.7495

English Fiction. *Contin.*

Mrs. Carr's companion. Wightman, M. G.
823.4993
Mrs. Caudle's curtain lectures. Jerrold, D.
W. 823.2598
Mrs. Dymond. Ritchie, *Mrs.* A.. I.. (T.)
in 823.5138
Mrs. Forrester's secret. Godfrey, *Mrs.* G.
W. *in* 823.5064
Mrs. Gainsborough's diamonds. Hawthorne,
J. C. 823.5685
Mrs. Geoffrey. Hungerford, *Mrs.* M.
823.3440
Same. 823.4189
Mistress Judith. Liddell, *Mrs.* C.. C. (F.-T.)
823.1645
Mrs. Keith's crime. Clifford, *Mrs.* L. (L.)
823.5045
Mrs. Knollys. 21 pp. Stimson, F: J.
p. 70, *in* 823.4703
Mrs. Leicester's school. Lamb, C: 824.415
Mrs. Lorimer. Harrison, *Mrs.* R. G. (K.)
823.7268
Mrs. Mark Luke. Johnstone, *Mrs.* C. I.
in * 823.6194
Mrs. Mayburn's twins. Habberton, J:
823.4562
Mrs. Merriam's scholars. Hale, E: E.
823.2342
Mistress of Beech Knoll. Burnham, *Mrs.*
C. L. (R.) 823.6993
Mistress of the house. Chamberlain, P. B.
823.195
Mrs. Skaggs's husband, and other sketches.
·Harte, F. B. 823.717
Mrs. Smith of Longmains. 34 pp. Brough-
ton, R. *in* 823.5046
Mrs. Temperly. 59 pp. James, H:, *Jr.*
p. 317, *in* 823.6536
Mrs. Vereker's courier maid. Hector, *Mrs.*
A. (F.) *in* 823.5089
Same. *in* 823.6623
Misunderstood. Montgomery, F. 823.1165
Mitchell, Donald Grant. [*Ik Marvel.*]
—— A bachelor's revery. 26 pp. (Johnson,
R., *ed. Little classics,* v. 4.)
p. 126, *in* 829.127
—— Doctor Johns: being a narrative of cer-
tain events in the life of an orthodox min-
ister in Connecticut. 823.1161-2
—— Dream life: a fable of the seasons.
823.5290
—— Reveries of a bachelor; or, a book of the
heart. 823.5289
—— Seven stories, with basement and attic.
823.5291
Mitchell, E: Page. The ablest man in the
world. 28 pp. (*In* Stories by Amer. auth-
ors, v. 10.) p. 45, *in* 823.4711
—— The Tachypomp: a mathematical dem-
onstration. 24 pp. (*In* Stories by Amer.
authors, v. 5.) p. 142, *in* 823.4706
Mitchell, Silas Weir. In war-time. 823.5399
—— Prince Little Boy, and other tales out of
Fairy-land. 808.1350
—— Roland Blake. 823.5245
Mitford, A. Bertram. The forty-seven Rōnins.
25 pp. (Johnson, R., *ed. Little classics,* v.
11.) p. 141, *in* 829.134

English Fiction. *Contin.*
Moon.
—— Verne, J. From the earth to the moon direct in 97 hours 20 minutes. 823.5485
—— —— *Same.* (*Added*) A trip round it.
823.6305
—— —— Round the moon: a sequel to "From the earth to the moon." 823.5487
—— —— *Same.* 823.2855
Note.—For general works, *see* Naismith, J., *and* Carpenter, J. The moon considered as a planet, a world. and a satellite. 26 pl. 1885. 523.34.—**Nelson,** E. The moon. 1876. * 523.42.—**Proctor,** R: A. The moon: motions, aspects, scenery, etc. Illus. 1878. * 523.10.
See also Poole's Index (to 1882). pp. 865 and 866, *in* ** 50.1;—*Same.* Jan. 1, 1882–Jan. 1, 1887. p. 296, *in* ** 50.1².
For humorous works, *see* **Harley.** *Rev.* T. Moon lore. 1885. 291.69.—**Locke,** R. A. The moon hoax. 1852. 829.581;—*Same.* Ed. by W. N. Griggs. 1852. 525.6.
Moondyne. O'Reilly, J: B. 823.1223
Moonfolk. Austin, *Mrs.* J.. (G.) 808.396
Moonlight boy, A. Howe, E. W. 823.5277
Moonshine. 20 pp. Marryat, *Capt.* F: p. 213, *in* ** 823.6730
Moonstone, The. Collins, W: W. 823.260
Moore, E: Macauley, *Miss* E. Tales of the drama founded on the tragedies of . . . Moore, etc. 823.1051
Moore, *Dr.* J: Edward. Various views of human nature, taken from life and manners, chiefly in England. 2 vols.
823.6462-3
—— *Same.* 4 vols. ** 823.6768-71
—— Zeluco. Various views of human nature, taken from life and manners, foreign and domestic. 2 vols. (Barbauld, *Mrs.* A. L. (A.), *ed.* The British novelists, vols. 34-35.)
** 823.2095-6
Moore, Nina. Pilgrims and Puritans: the story of the planting of Plymouth and Boston. 808.1720
Moore, T: Epicurean: a romance. 187.2
Moorehead, Warren K. Wanneta, the Sioux. Illus. from life. 823.6470
Moorland cottage. Gaskell, *Mrs.* E.. C. (S.)
823.603
Moral tales. *See* Edgeworth, M.
Mordaunt, C: *Earl of Peterborough.*
—— Henty, G: A. The bravest of the brave; or, with Peterborough in Spain. 808.1473
Note.—*See* Russell, W: Eccentric personages. 1865. 920.369.—**Warburton,** G. Memoir of C. Mordaunt, Earl of Peterborough and Monmouth. 2 vols. 1853. 923.2076-77.
More, Hannah. Cœlebs in search of a wife.
823.5749
—— *Same.* (*Also*) Essays on various subjects. (*And*) Moriana. 823.6069
—— The repository tales. 823.1168
—— Shepherd of Salisbury plain and other tales. 823.1172
More bitter than death. Brame, *Mrs.* C.. M. (L.) *in* 823.5132
More happy thoughts, &c., &c. Burnand, F. C. 823.154
Morford, H: Sprees and splashes; or, droll recollections of town and country: a book for railroad rides and odd half-hours.
823.1173

English Fiction. *Contin.*
Morgan, *Lady* Sydney (Owenson).
—— Florence Macarthy: a national tale.
823.1174
—— The wild Irish girl: a national tale. 3 vols. * 823.2361-3
Morgan's horror. Fenn, G: M. 823.5596
Morier, James. Abel Allnutt. * 823.6180
—— Adventures of Hajji Baba, in Turkey, Persia and Russia. ¯ 823.4280
—— The adventures of Hajji Baba, of Ispahan. * 823.6183
Issued also as Adventures of Hajji Baba, in Turkey, Persia and Russia.
—— The adventures of Hajji Baba, of Ispahan, in England. * 823.6184
—— Ayesha, the maid of Kars. * 823.6181
—— The banished: a Swabian historical tale.
* 823.6182
—— The Mirza. * 823.6185
—— Zohrab the hostage. * 823.6186
Morley, *Countess of.* *See* Parker, F.. Talbot, *Countess of Morley.*
Morley Ashton. Grant, J. 823.639
Morley Ernstein. James, G: P. R. 823.872
Morris, Edmund. Farming for boys: what they have done, and what others may do, in the cultivation of farm and garden; how to begin, how to proceed, and what to aim at. 808.1547
Morris, W: News from nowhere; or, the epoch of rest. Being some chapters from a (*sic*) Utopian romance. 823.7404
—— A tale of the house of the Wolfings, and all the kindreds of the mark written in prose and in verse. 829.697
Mort d'Arthure, La. 3 vols. Malory, *Sir* T:
* 823.6615-17
Same. ** 823.6773-5
Mortal antipathy, A. Holmes, O. W.
823.4864
Mortomley's estate. Riddell, *Mrs.* C.. E. L. (C.) 823.1331
Moscow.
See also note under Russia.
—— Lander, S.. W. Moscow. 808.99
Mose Evans. Baker, W: M. 823.50
Moses, the sassy. 7 pp. Browne, C: F. p. 46, *in* 823.5478
Mosquito. Francis, F. 823.7517
Mosses from an old manse. 2 vols. (in 1). Hawthorne, N. 823.730
Moss-side. Terhune, *Mrs.* M.. V. (H.)
823.1559
Mother Carey's chicken. Fenn, G: M.
808.1438
Mother Molly. Peard, F.. M. 823.4040
Mother-in-law, The. Southworth, *Mrs.* E. D. E. (N.) 823.1501
Mother's recompense, The. Aguilar, G.
823.9
Moths. La Ramée, L. de. 823.2172
Moulton, *Mrs.* Ellen Louise (Chandler).
—— My third book. 823.2307
—— Some women's hearts. 823.1176
Mount of Sorrow. 24 pp. Spofford, *Mrs.* H. E.. (P.) p. 141, *in* 823.4703
Mount Royal. Maxwell, *Mrs.* M.. E.. (B.)
823.2417
Same. 823.4979

English Fiction. *Contin.*
Mountain, Story of a. Lawrence, *Uncle.*
808.1894
Mountain-White heroine, A. Gilmore, J. R.
823.6364
Mowatt, *Mrs.* A.. C. *See* Ritchie, *Mrs.* A..
C. (O.)
Mozart, Johann Chrysostom Wolfgang Amadeus. (1756–1791.)
—— Barnard, C: Mozart and Mendelssohn.
(*The tone masters*, v. 1.) 808.1619
—— Rau, H. Mozart: a biographical romance. 823.7350
Mudfog papers. Dickens, C: J: H. 823.4046
Mudford, W: First and last. 14 pp. (*In*
Tales from Blackwood, v. 4.)
in ** 823.6650
—— The iron shroud. 20 pp. (Johnson, R.,
ed. *Little classics*, v.3.) p. 108, *in* 829.126
—— *Same.* 22 pp. (*In* Tales from Blackwood, v. 1.) *in* ** 823.6647
Mügge, Theodor. Afraja; or, life and love
in Norway. Tr. by E: J. Morris. 823.6809
Mühlbach, L.., *pseud. See* Mundt, *Mrs.*
Clara (Müller).
Muir, Alan. "Golden girls: " a picture-gallery. *in* 823.5037
—— Tumbledown Farm. *in* 823.5064
Mulholland, Clara. Kathleen mavourneen.
823.7178
Mulholland, Rosa. A fair emigrant. 823.7059
—— Late Miss Hollingford. *in* 823.5074
Müller, Christine, *pseud. See* Walrée, *Mrs.*
E. C. W. (Gobie) van.
Müller, Friedrich Max. Memories: a story of
German love. Tr. by G: P. Upton.
823.4020
Müller, O: Charlotte Ackerman: a theatrical
romance, founded upon interesting facts in
the life of a young artist of the last century. Tr. by Mrs. C. Coleman and her
daughters. 823.6812
Mummy, The. London, *Mrs.* J.. (W.)
823.1013
Mumu. Turgenef, I. S. 823.4740
Mundt, *Mrs.* Clara (Müller). [*L. Mühlbach.*]
—— Andreas Hofer. 823.6265
—— Bernthal; or, the son's revenge. 823.5915
—— The daughter of an empress. Tr. by N.
Greene. 823.5800
—— The Empress Josephine: an historical
sketch of the days of Napoleon. Tr. by
Rev. W. Binet. 823.6266
—— Frederick the Great and his court. Tr.
by Mrs. C. Coleman and her daughters.
823.6280
—— Frederick the Great and his family. Tr.
by Mrs. C. Coleman and her daughters.
823.5887
—— Goethe and Schiller. Tr. by C. Coleman.
823.6267
—— Henry the Eighth and his court.
823.5886
—— Joseph II. and his court. 823.6301
—— Louisa of Prussia and her times. (Napoleon in Germany.) Tr. by F. Jordan.
823.6268
—— Marie Antoinette and her son. Tr. by
W. L. Gage. 823.6329

English Fiction. *Contin.*
Mundt, *Mrs.* Clara (Müller). [*L. Mühlbach.*]
Contin.
—— The merchant of Berlin.* Tr. by A.
Coffin. (*Also*) Maria Theresa and her fireman. 823.5888
   * *Issued also as* Frederick the Great and his merchant.
—— Napoleon and Blücher. (Napoleon in
Germany.) Tr. by F. Jordan. 823.6269
—— Napoleon and the Queen of Prussia. Tr.
by F. Jordan. 823.5801
—— Old Fritz and the new era. (Germany
in storm and stress.) Tr. by P: Langley.
823.6270
—— Prince Eugene and his times. Tr. by A.
de V. Chaudron. 823.6271
—— Two life-paths: a romance. Tr. by N.
Greene. 823.5899
Mundt, Theodore. Count Mirabeau. Tr. by
T. J. Radford. 823.6383
Munroe, Kirk. Derrick Sterling: a story of
the mines. 808.1440
—— The flamingo feather. 808.1371
—— The golden days of '49: a tale of California diggings. 823.6318
—— Wakulla: a story of adventure in Florida. 808.1372
Murdoch, *Rev.* D: Royalist's daughter and
the rebels; or, the Dutch Dominie of the
Catskills: a tale of the revolution.
823.1177
Murfree, M.. Noailles. [*C: Egbert Craddock.*] The despot of Broomsedge cove.
823.5469
—— Down the ravine. 808.1343
—— In the Tennessee mountains. 823.5232
—— The prophet of the Great Smoky mountains. 823.4880
—— Where the battle was fought. 823.4893
Murger, H: (1822–1861.) Francine's muff. 11
pp. (*Also*) The passage of the Red sea.
9 pp. (Zimmern, H.., *and* A. *Half-hours
with foreign novelists.*) *in* ** 823.6613
Murphy, Arthur. Macauley, *Miss* E. Tales
of the drama founded on the tragedies of
. . . Murphy, etc. 823.1051
Murphy's master. Payn, J. 823.6062
Murray, *Hon.* C: A: The prairie-bird.
823.1179
Murray, D: Christie. Aunt Rachel: a rustic
sentimental comedy. *in* 823.5105
—— Bull-dog and butterfly; and, Julia and
her Romeo: a chronicle of Castle Barfield.
in 823.5131
—— By the gate of the sea. 823.5038
—— Cynic fortune: a tale of a man with a
conscience. *in* 823.5131
—— First person singular. 823.4938
—— *Same.* *in* 823.5097
—— Hearts: queen, knave, and deuce.
823.4949
—— *Same.* *in* 823.5024
—— *Same.* (*Also*) Valentine Strange: a
story of the primrose way. 823.3712
—— Joseph's coat. 823.4319
—— Julia and her Romeo: a chronicle of
Castle Barfield. (*With his* Bull-dog and
butterfly.) *in* 823.5131

English Fiction. *Contin.*
Murray, D: Christie. *Contin.*
—— A life's atonement. 823.4940
—— *Same.* *in* 823.5024; 823.6597
—— Rainbow gold. 823.4948
—— *Same.* *in* 823.5081
—— Valentine Strange: a story of the primrose way. *in* 823.3712
—— *Same.* *in* 823.5065
—— "The way of the world." *in* 823.5023
—— The weaker vessel. 823.6424
Murray, Eustace Clare Grenville. [*Trois-Etoiles.*] The member for Paris: a tale of the second empire. 823.6098
Murray, W: H: Harrison. Adirondack tales. v. 1. 823.6326
Musæus, Johann K: August.
—— Dumb love, Libussa, *and* Melechsala. (Carlyle, T:, *tr. Tales by Musæus, etc.*, v. 1.) 823.6830
—— The dumb lover. (Roscoe, T: *The German novelists*, v. 3.) ** 823.6828
Museum; The; or, curiosities explained. Abbott, J. *in* 808.585
Music and musicians. Lillie, *Mrs.* L. C. (W.) Story of music and musicians for young readers. 808.1459
Musical novels. *See also* Biographical stories, p. 20.
—— Andersen, H. C. The improvisatore. 823.4223
—— — Only a fiddler. 823.4219
—— — The soprano. 823.6632
—— Barnard, C: The tone masters. 3 vols. (v. 1: Mozart and Mendelssohn; v. 2: Handel and Haydn; v. 3: Bach and Beethoven.) 808.1619-21
—— Bartol, M. Honor May. 823.7558
—— Brewster, A. H. M. Compensation. 823.7559
—— Cornish, *Mrs.* —. Alcestis. (Gluck and Faustina Hässe.) 823.806
—— Dudevant, *Mme.* A. L. A. (D.) Consuelo. 823.6214
—— — *Same.* 823.6703; 823.6885
—— — Countess of Rudolstadt. (Sequel to "Consuelo.") 823.6921
—— — *Same.* 823.7090
—— — Lucrezia Floriani (in French). (Prince Karol is Chopin, and Count Salvator Albani is Liszt.) 843.461
—— — Malgrétout (in French). 843.467
—— Marshall, *Mrs.* E. (M.) Alma; or, the story of a little music mistress. 823.7138
—— Musical moments: short selections . . . for music lovers. 821.1333
—— Polko, E. Musical sketches. 823.6452
—— Rau, H. Mozart: a biographical romance. 823.7350
—— Shedlock, E. L. A trip to music-land: a fairy tale. 808.1933
—— Sheppard, E.. S. Charles Auchester. 823.5960
—— — *Same.* 3 vols. ** 823.6233-5
—— — Counterparts. (Shelley and Byron.) 823.6127
—— — Rumor. (Beethoven.) 823.6043
—— Stephenson, *Mrs.* E. (T.) St. Olave's. 823.7554

English Fiction. *Contin.*
Musical novels. *Contin.*
—— Trollope, *Mrs.* F. E. (T.) Mabel's progress. 823.6130
Note.—For **Bibliography**, *see* Dörffel, A. Musikalische Literatur. 1861. (*Also*) Erster Nachtrag. 1890. 2 vols. (in 1). 1861-1890. ** 16.228.—Works on music. (*Lit. news*, v. 8, 1887.) pp. 84-5, *in* ** 15.207².
General history.—Burgh, A. Anecdotes of music, historical and biographical. 3 vols. 1814. * 780.89-91.—Engel, K. Musical myths and facts. 2 vols. 1876. 780.87-8.—Niecks, F: Frederick Chopin as a man and musician. 2 vols. 1888.' 927.291-2.—Pougin, A. Verdi: great anecdote history of his life and works. (Catalog. of his comp., pp. 295-300.) 1887. 927.290.—Ritter, F. L: History of music, in the form of lectures. 2 vols. (Cop. 1870-74.) 780.84-5;—Music in America (1620-1880). 1890. 780.83.—Stafford, W. C. History of music. 1830. 780.86.—Upton, G: P. The standard operas: their plots, etc. 1887. 782.4.
See also **Catalogues** of this Library.
No. 2, 1880, p. 162. No. 4, 1884, p. 196.
No. 3, 1882, p. 129. No. 5, 1888, pp. 260-1.
For biographies of musicians, *see* Hueffer, F., *ed.* The great musicians, *viz.:* **Bach.** By R. L. Poole. 927.250.—**Beethoven.** By H. A. Rudall. 927.287.—**English church composers.** By W: A. Barrett. 927.251.—**Handel.** By Mrs. J. Marshall. 927.252.—**Haydn.** By P. D. Townsend. 927.253.—**Mendelssohn.** By W: S. Rockstro. 927.254.—**Mozart.** By Dr. F. Gehring. 927.255.—**Purcell.** By W. H. Cumming. 927.256.—**Rossini.** By H: S. Edwards. 927.257.—**Schubert.** By H. F. Frost. 927.258.—**Schumann.** By J.A. F. Maitland. 927.259. — **Wagner.** By F. Hueffer. 927.260.—**Weber.** By Sir J. Benedict. 927.261.
See also **Poole's** Index (to 1882). pp. 882-84, *in* ** 50.1;—*Same.* Jan. 1, 1882-Jan. 1, 1887. pp. 302-3, *in* ** 50.1².
For biographical dictionaries, *see* **Champlin**, J: D., *Jr., and* Apthorp, W: F., *eds.* Cyclopedia of music and musicians. v. 1: A-D; v. 2: E-M; v. 3: N-Z. 1888-90. ** 780.72-72².—**Grove**, *Sir* G. Dictionary of music and musicians. (A. D. 1450-1889.) 4 vols. ** 780.19-202. v. 1: A-Imp.; v. 2: Impr.-Plain; v. 3: Planché-Sumer; v. 4: Sumer (*contin.*)-Z.

Musical sketches. Polko, *Mrs.* E. (V.) 823.6452

Muskingum legends. Powers, S. 823.4145

Mutinies. *See also* Sea stories.
—— Heldmann, B. Mutiny on board the Leander. 808.1637
—— Marryat, *Capt.* F: The king's own. (Mutiny at the Nore, May 27, 1797.) 823.1100
—— Russell, W: C. Wreck of the Grosvenor. *in* 823.6702
Note.—*See* **Belcher**, *Lady* D. Mutineers of the Bounty, and their descendants in Pitcairn and Norfolk islands. 1871. 9190.18.—**Mackenzie**, A. S. Defence; Somers' mutiny case. 1843. *in* ** 41.1.—**Pitcairn's island** and mutiny of the ship "Bounty." 9109.39.
See also **Index** to **Harper's** monthly. p. 459, *in* ** 51.475.
See also **Poole's** Index (to 1882.) p. 886, *in* ** 50.1.

Mutiny on board the Leander. Heldmann, B. 808.1637
My after-dinner adventures with Peter Schlemihl. 43 pp. (*In* Tales from Blackwood. 2d ser., v. 9.) *in* 823.7493
My Apingi kingdom. Du Chaillu, P. B. 808.691
My aunt Margaret's mirror. Scott, *Sir* W. p. 385, *in* ** 823.6034
My aunt Pontypool. James, G: P. R. *in* 823.848
—— *Same.* *in* 823.7020

English Fiction. *Contin.*
My brother's keeper. Warner, A.. B.
823.1673
My brother's wife. Edwards, A. B.
in 823.2522
My college friends.—Charles Russell, the
gentleman-commoner. (*In* Tales from
Blackwood, v. 4.) *in* ** 823.6650
— No. II. Horace Leicester. 45 pp. (*In*
Tales from Blackwood, v. 6.)
in ** 823.6652
— No. III. Mr. W. Wellington Hurst. 43
pp. (*In* Tales from Blackwood, v. 6.)
in ** 823.6652
My daughter Elinor. Benedict, F. L.
823.5834
My days and nights on the battle-field. Cof-
fin, C: C. 973.643
My desire. Warner, S. 823.1679
My ducats and my daughter. Hunter, H.,
and White, W. 823.4855
Same. *in* 823.5047; *in* 823.5083
My enemy's daughter. McCarthy, J.
823.6355
My fellow laborer. 77 pp. Haggard, H: R.
in 823.6606
My first love and My last love. Riddell, *Mrs.*
C.. E. L. (C.) 823.1332
My first offer. 19 pp. Hay, M.. C.
in 823.3394
My first voyage to southern seas. Kingston,
W: H: G. 808.351
My friend Jim. Norris, W: E: *in* 823.4985
Same. *in* 823.5020
My friend the boss. Hale, E: E. 823.5692
My good friend. Belot, A. 823.7005
My health. Burnand, F. C. 823.155
My hero. Bridges, *Mrs.* —. *in* 823.3157
My husband and I.. Tolstoï, *Count* L. N.
in 823.6702
My investment in the far west. 50 pp. (*In*
Tales from Blackwood. 2d ser., v. 12.)
in 823.7496
My Kalulu, prince, king, and slave. Stanley,
H: M. 808.1420
My lady coquette. Booth, *Mrs.* E. M. J. (G.)
von. *in* 823.6691
My Lady Pokahontas. Cooke, J: E.
823.5690
My lady's money. Collins, W: W.
in 823.3563
My last love. Riddell, *Mrs.* C.. E. L. (C.)
in 823.1332
My little girl. Besant, W., *and* Rice, J.
823.6213
My little lady. Poynter, E. F.. 823.6977
My little love. Terhune, *Mrs.* M.. V. (H.)
823.1560
My lord and my lady. Bridges, *Mrs. Col.* —.
823.3945
My mother and I. Craik, *Mrs.* D. M. (M.)
823.336
My mother's manuscript. Lamartine, A. M.
L: de P. de. 823.6874
"My novel." Lytton, E: G: E. L. Bulwer-
2 vols. 823.1037-8
Same. 823.5971-2
My poor wife. By the author of "Addie's
husband." *in* 823.5062

English Fiction. *Contin.*
My shipmate Louise. Russell, W: C.
823.6466
My sister Jeannie. Dudevant, *Mme.* A. L.
A. (D.) 823.6852
My sister Kate. 29 pp. Brame, *Mrs.* C.. M.
(L.) *in* 823.4994
My southern friends. Gilmore, J. R.
823.611
My third book. Moulton, *Mrs.* E. L. (C.)
823.2307
My time and what I've done with it. Bur-
nand, F. C. 823.156
My trivial life and misfortune. 2 pts. Barter,
K.. 823.4504-5
My uncle the curate. Savage, M. W.
823.5916
My uncle's garret window. 46 pp. Lewis, M.
G. p. 1, *in* 823.4275
My wife and I. Stowe, *Mrs.* H. E.. (B.)
823.1525
My wife and my wife's sister. Latimer, *Mrs.*
E.. (W.) 823.4348
My wife's niece. By the author of "Dr.
Edith Romney." 823.4842
Same. 823.5046
My wonder-story. Benedict, A. K. 808.1900
My young Alcides. Yonge, C.. M..
823.1770
Mysteries of Paris. Sue, M. J. 823.6187
Same. 823.6586
Mysteries of Redgrave Court. 34 pp. Smed-
ley, F. E: p. 115, *in* 823.1443
Mysteries of the court of Queen Anne. Ains-
worth, W: H. 823.5912
Mysteries of the unseen. Campbell, *Sir* G.
823.7243
Mysteries of Udolpho. Radcliffe, *Mrs.* A.
(W.) 823.1280
Same. 3 vols. ** 823.2106-8
Mysterious hunters. Carleton, L. C.
in 823.5141
Same. *in* 823.5188
Mysterious island, The. 3 pts. (in 1). Verne,
J. 823.5784
Same. 823.6306
Mystery, The. Wood, *Mrs.* E. (P.)
823.2921
Same. 823.6229
Mystery at Fernwood. Maxwell, *Mrs.* M..
E.. (B.) *in* 823.6384
Mystery of Allan Grale. Mayo, *Mrs.* I.. (F.)
in 823.5138
Mystery of an omnibus. Du Boisgobey, F.
in 823.6702
Mystery of Colde Fell, The. Brame, *Mrs.*
C.. M. (L.) 823.4992
Mystery of Dark Hollow. Southworth, *Mrs.*
E. D. E. (N.) 823.1502
Mystery of Edwin Drood. Dickens, C: J: H.
in 823.384
Same. 823.432; 823.5323
Same. *in* 823.5331; 823.6122
Mystery of Metropolisville. Eggleston, E:
823.523
Mystery of Mrs. Blencarrow. Oliphant, *Mrs.*
M. O. (W.) 823.7418
Mystery of Orcival. Gaboriau, É. 823.2164
Same. 823.5034; 823.6079

English Fiction. *Contin.*
Mystery of the holly-tree. Brame, *Mrs.* C..
M. (L.) *in* 823.5133
Mystery of the locks. Howe, E. W.
823.4875
Mystery of the "Ocean Star," The. Russell,
W: C. 823.5588
Mythology.
—— Hawthorne, N. Tanglewood tales.
in 808.1890
—— A wonder-book. 808.548
Note.—For ancient mythologies, *see* **Thomas,** J.
Universal dictionary of biography and mythology.
** 920.227.
For myths of American aborigines, *see* **Brinton,**
D. G. American hero myths. 1882. * 291.39;—
Myths of the new world. 2d ed. 1876. 291.19.—
Réville, A. The native religions of Mexico and
Peru. (*Hibbert lectures,* 1884.) 1884. 299.33.
For Egyptian mythology, *see* **Renouf,** P. le P.
Origin and growth of religion of ancient Egypt.
(*Hibbert lectures,* 1879.) 1880. 299.23.—**Tiele,** *Dr.*
C. P. History of Egyptian religion. 1882. 299.25.
For English myths, *see* **Child,** *Prof.* F. J., *ed.*
The English and Scottish popular ballads. 8 vols.
(in 4). 1878-85. 821.89-92.
For German mythology, *see* **Grimm,** J. Teutonic
mythology. 4 vols. 1882-8. 293.28-31.
For Greek and Roman mythology, *see* **Glad-
stone,** W: E. Juventus mundi. 1869. 883.39.—
Roscher, W. H. Lexikon der griech. u. röm.
Mythologie. 292.44.—**Smith,** W. Dictionary of
Greek and Roman biography and mythology. 3
vols. v. 1: A-D; v. 2: E-N; v. 3: O-Z. ** 920.242-4.
See also **Catalogues** of this Library.
No. 2, 1880, pp. 162-3. No. 4, 1884, p. 197.
No. 3, 1882, pp. 129-30. No. 5, 1888, p. 261.
See also **Ency. Brit.** Index (Amer. repr.) p.
620, *in* ** 32.295.
See also **Poole's Index** (to 1882). pp. 890-891, *in* **
50.1.—*Same.* Jan. 1, 1882-Jan. 1, 1887. pp. 304-305, *in*
** 50.1¹.
See also **Greece.**
See also **Fairy tales.—Folk-lore.**
Nabob. Daudet, A. 823.3189
Same. 823.6884
Nameless nobleman, A. Austin, *Mrs.* J..
(G.) 823.5786
Nancy. Broughton, R. 823.134
Same. 823.3062
Nanon. Dumas, A. D. 823.7348
Nantucket scraps. Austin, *Mrs.* J.. (G.)
823.5674
Naples. *See also note under* **Italy.**
—— Abbott, J. Rollo in Naples. 808.921
Napoleon I., *Emperor of the French.* (1769-
1821.)
—— Mundt, *Mme.* C. (M.) Napoleon and
the Queen of Prussia. 823.5801
Note.—For bibliography, *see* **Bibliography** ap-
pended to the article Napoléon Ier, in the Nouvelle
biographie générale, v. 37. *in* ** 920.275.
For biography, *see* **Abbott,** J: S. C. History of
Napoleon Bonaparte. (Popular.) 2 vols. 1883. 923.
1923-3¹.—**Jomini,** A. H. Life of Napoleon. 4 vols.
and atlas. 1864. * 923.1935-39.—**Junot,** L. P.,
duchesse d'Abrantes. Memoirs of N., his court
and family. 2 vols. 1855. 920.215-16.—**Lanfrey,**
P. History of Napoleon I. 4 vols. 1871-79. 923.
1099-1102.—**Metternich,** C. W. N. L. *Fürst* v. *In
his* Memoirs. vols. 1 and 2. 923.1049.—**Napoleon**
III. Napoleonic ideas. 1859. 320.39.—**Rémusat,** C.
E. J. G. de V., *Mme.* de. Memoirs. 1802-08. 1880.
923.541.—**Seeley,** J: R. Short history of Napoleon
I. 1888. 923.1940.
See also **Catalogues** of this Library.
No. 2, 1880, p. 163. No. 4, 1884, pp. 197-8.
No. 3, 1882, p. 130. No. 5, 1888, p. 262.
See also **Poole's Index** (to 1882). pp. 893-5, *in* **
50.1.—*Same.* Jan. 1, 1882-Jan. 1, 1887. pp. 305-6, *in*
** 50.1¹.
Napoleon and Blücher. Mundt, *Mrs.* C. (M.)
823.6269

English Fiction. *Contin.*
Napoleon and the Queen of Prussia. Mundt,
Mrs. C. (M.) 823.5801
Napoleon in Germany. Louisa of Prussia.
Mundt, *Mrs.* C. (M.) 823.6268
—— Napoleon and Blücher. Mundt, *Mrs.*
C. (M.) 823.6269
Nares, E: Thinks-I-to-myself: a serio-ludicro,
tragico-comico tale written by Thinks-I-to-
myself, Who? 2 vols. (in 1). 823.1180
Narka, the Nihilist. O'Meara, K. 823.5214
Narrative of certain uncommon things that
did formerly happen to me, Herbert
Willis, B. D. 61 pp. (*In* Tales from
Blackwood, v. 7.) *in* ** 823.6653
Nash, Willard G. A century of gossip; or,
the real and the seeming. 823.1181
Nathalie. Kavanagh, J. 823.917
Natolian story-teller. 69 pp. (*In* Tales from
Blackwood, v. 11.) *in* ** 823.6657
Natural history. *See also* **Animals.**
—— Abbott, J. Water and land. 808.715
—— Aikin, J:, *and* Barbauld, *Mrs.* A.. L. (A.)
Evenings at home; or, the juvenile budget
opened. 808.1664
—— Church, *Mrs.* E. (R.) Little neighbors
at Elmridge. 808.1633
—— Daubeny, C. G. B. Fugitive poems con-
nected with nat. hist., etc. 821.793
—— Feathers, fur, and fins; or, stories of an-
imal life for children. 808.1910
—— Gosse, P. H. Romance of natural his-
tory. 500.35
—— Hale, G. E.. Little flower-people.
808.1465
—— Holder, C: F: A frozen dragon.
808.1904
—— Hooper, M.. Ways and tricks of animals. 808.470
—— Kingsley, C: Madam How and Lady
Why; or, first lessons in earth lore for chil-
dren. 808.933
—— Kirby, M.., *and* E.. The sea and its
wonders. 808.1875
—— The world by the fireside; or, pic-
tures and scenes from far-off lands.
808.1891
—— Miller, *Mrs.* H. (M.) Little folks in
feathers and fur, and others in neither.
808.1888
—— Stockton, F. R: Round-about rambles
in lands of fact and fancy. 808.1886
—— Tales out of school. 808.1887
—— Tolstoï, *Count* L. N. Tales from zoölogy.—Stories from botany. 29 pp. (*In his*
The long exile, etc.) p. 187, *in* 808.1348
—— Wagner, H. Entdeckungsreisen in der
Wohnstube. 808.1879
—— Wood, J: G: Rutledge's picture book
of fishes, insects, etc. 808.1885
Note.—For a late work giving titles of important
publications, *see* **Kingsley,** J. S. The riverside
natural history. 6 vols. (1888.) * 590.108-13. v.
1: Lower invertebrates. * 590.108; v. 2: Crustacea
and insects. * 590.109; v. 3: Lower vertebrates. *
590.110; v. 4: Birds. * 590.111; v. 5: Mammals. * 590.
112; v. 6: Man. * 590.113.
For periodical literature, *see* **Catalogue** of this
Library. No. 5, 1888, p. 263.
See also **Catalogues** of this Library.
No. 2, 1880, pp. 163-4. No. 4, 1884, pp. 198-9.
No. 3, 1882, pp. 130-1. No. 5, 1888, p. 263.

English Fiction. *Contin.*
Natural philosophy.
—— Abbott, J. Rollo's experiments.
           808.913
—— — Rollo's philosophy—Air.   808.907
—— — Rollo's philosophy—Fire.   808.905
—— — Rollo's philosophy—Sky.   808.910
—— — Rollo's philosophy—Water.   808.915
—— — Science for the young.—Force.
           808.1105
—— — Science for the young.—Heat.
           808.716
—— — Science for the young.—Light.
           808.798
—— Aikin, J:, *and* Barbauld, *Mrs.* A.. L.
(A.) Evenings at home; or, the juvenile
budget opened.   808.1664
—— Lawrence, *Uncle.* In search of a son.
           808.1893
—— Paris, J: A. Philosophy in sport made
science in earnest. (Anon.)   808.991
—— Pepper, J: H: Scientific amusements for
young people.   808.69
—— Tolstoï, *Count* L. N. Stories from
physics. 11 pp. (*In his* The long exile.)
      p. 176, *in* 808.1348
Note.— See **Bibliographies.** Burker, G. F.
Physical bibliography. 1883–1884, in 2 vols.; 1885, 4
vols. (Smithson. Inst. *Ann. rep.*, 1883–1885.) **
500.22⁶–22⁸.—**Clarke,** F. W. Text-books relating
to chemistry and physics. (U. S. Bureau of Educ.
Circulars of information, No. 6, 1880.) pp. 157–66,
in * 370.189.—**Daniell,** A. A text-book of the principles of physics. 2d ed. 1885. (Representative
list for further reading, pp. 668–671.) * 530.102.—
Faraday, M. The various forces of nature and
their relation. 1874. 530.19.—**Guillemin,** A. The
forces of nature: popular introduction to physical
phenomena. 1873. 530.2.—**Helmholtz,** *Prof.* H.
Popular lectures on scientific subjects. 2 vols. 1881.
504.2.—**Proctor,** R: A. Light science for leisure
hours. 1871. 504–6.—**Tait,** *Prof.* P. G. Lectures on
some recent advances in physical science. 1885.
D4.29.—**Thomson,** *Sir* W., *and* Tait, *Prof.* P. G.
Treatise on natural philosophy. 2 vols. 1879. 530.61–
61³.—**Tyndall,** *Prof.* J: Natural philosophy in easy
lessons. 530.77.—**Wead,** C: K. Aims and methods
of the teaching of physics. 1884. (U. S. Dept. of Int.
Bureau of Educ. Circulars, No. 7, 1884.) *in* * 370.244.
See also **Catalogues** of this Library.
   No. 2, 1880, p. 164.   No. 4, 1884, p. 199.
   No. 3, 1882, p. 131.   No. 5, 1888, p. 263.
Nature and art. Inchbald, *Mrs.* E.. (S.)
      p. 213, *in* ** 823.2088
Nature's serial story. Roe, E: P.   823.5524
Nautical novels. *See* Sea stories.
Neal, J: (1793–1876.) The down-easters, &c.,
&c., &c. 2 vols.   ** 823.6237–8
—— Goody Gracious! and the forget-me-not.
18 pp. (Johnson, R., *ed. Little classics,*
v. 10.)   p. 183, *in* 829.133
—— The Kentuckian in New York; or, the
adventures of three southerns. 2 vols.
      ** 823.6239–40
*Note.—*For Neal's writings, *see* **Griswold,** R. W.
Prose writers of America. 1870. p. 313, *in* *829.110.
See also **Allibone's** Dict. of Eng. lit., v. 2. p.
1404, *in* ** 803.7.
Near to happiness. Potter, F. H., *tr.*
      823.5504
Near to nature's heart. Roe, E: P.   823.1359
Neæra. Graham, J: W.   823.6904
Nearer and dearer. Bradley, *Rev.* E:
      823.4134
Necromancer, The. Reynolds, G: W. M.
      823.6339

English Fiction. *Contin.*
Needell, *Mrs.* J. H. Lucia, Hugh, and an-
other.   823.4853
Same.   823.5075
Neele, H: Romance of history, England.
      823.1182
Neighbours, The. Bremer, F.   823.2117
Same.   823.2175
Neighbours on the green. Oliphant, *Mrs.*
M. O. (W.)   823.6905
Nellie Harland. Vance, E. E.   823.5175
Nellie Netterville. Caddell, C. M..   823.163
Nellie's memories. Carey, R. N.   823.2594
Nelly Kinnard's kingdom. Douglas, A. M.
      823.482
Nelly's dark days. Smith, H.   823.1462
Nemesis. Terhune, *Mrs.* M.. V. (H.)
      823.1561
Nemesis of faith. Froude, J. A.   823.4260
Nenuphar: a fancy. 48 pp. (*In* Tales from
Blackwood. 2d ser., v. 12.)   *in* 823.7496
Nero. 2 vols. Eckstein, E.   823.7150–1
Netherlands.
—— Adams, W: T. Dikes and ditches.
      808.488
—— Young, A. Young folks' history of the
Netherlands.   949.83
12TH CENTURY, A. D.
—— Herbert, H: W: Sir Hugues de Coucy:
a chivalric legend of the Low Countries.
(1200.) (*In his* The chevaliers of France.)
      p. 7, *in* 823.4253
14TH CENTURY, A. D.
—— Conscience, H. Count Hugo of Craen-
hove. (Antwerp, 1360.)   823.5705
—— Taylor, *Sir* H: Philip van Artevelde.
(Insurrection in Ghent, 1379–1382); drama.
      822.485
15TH CENTURY, A. D.
—— James, G: P. R. Mary of Burgundy; or,
the revolt of Ghent. (1477.)   823.870
—— Kingsley, H: Old Margaret. (Ghent,
1400, etc.)   823.2032
—— Lytton, E: R. Bulwer- Jacqueline. (*In
his* New poems.)   p. 394, *in* 821.569
16TH CENTURY, A. D.
—— Charles, *Mrs.* E.. (R.) The liberation
of Holland. (*With her* Martyrs of Spain.)
      p. 143, *in* 823.6598
—— Conscience, H. The amulet. (Ant-
werp life, etc.)   p. 157, *in* 823.5707
—— — Ludovic and Gertrude. (Antwerp,
1566.)   823.5659
—— Ebers, G. The burgomaster's wife.
(Siege of Leyden, 1574.)   823 4311
—— Liefde, J: B. de. Galama.   823.5847
—— Lytton, E: R. Bulwer- Adolphus, Duke
of Guelders. (*In his* New poems.)
      p. 441, *in* 821.569
Egmont, executed 1568. Drama. Göthe, J.
W. von.   p. 117, *in* 830.20
William, Prince of Orange. 1533–1584.
—— Henty, G: A. By pike and dyke.
      808.1588
17TH CENTURY, A. D.
—— Dumas, A. D. The black tulip. (Hague,
1672.)   823.6450
—— Kotzebue, A. von. Hugo Grotius; play.
      in 832.73

English Fiction. *Contin.*
New England. *Contin.*
MAINE.
—— Farrar, C: A. J. Down the west branch; or, camps and tramps around Katahdin.
808.1731
—— Harrison, *Mrs.* C. (C.) Bar Harbor days. 823.5256
—— Stephens, C: A. Camping out. 808.241
—— — Lynx-hunting. 808.245
—— Stowe, *Mrs.* H. E.. (B.) Pearl of Orr's Island. 823.1528
—— Trowbridge, J: T. The kelp-gatherers.
808.1728
—— Wells, H: P. City boys in the woods.
808.1802
—— Whittier, J: G. The bridal of Penna-cook; poem. p. 15, *in* 821.431
—— — Mogg Megone; poem.
p. 1, *in* 821.431
—— — Norembega; poem.
p. 347, *in* 821.431
MASSACHUSETTS BAY.
—— Andrews, G: H. The scarlet letter; drama, based on Hawthorne. 822.511
—— Austin, *Mrs.* J.. (G.) A nameless no-bleman. (Dr. Francis Lebaron.) 823.5786
—— Bliss, W: R. Colonial times on Buzzard's bay. 2d ed. 823.6537
—— Castleton, D. R. Salem: a tale of the 17th century. (Witchcraft.) 823.183
—— Dawes, R. Nix's mate. (Revolution of 1689 in Boston.) 2 vols. (in 1). ** 823.6236
—— Hawthorne, N. The scarlet letter. (Gov. Bellingham's time.) 823.733
—— — "Twice-told tales." 823.5561
—— *Same.* 2 vols. 823.735-6
—— Herbert, H: W: The fair Puritan: an historical romance of the days of witch-craft. 823.764
—— Holland, J. G. Bay path. (Agawam, Springfield, in 1638.) 823.784
—— Longfellow, H: W. Giles Corey of the Salem farms; trag. (Witchcraft.)
p. 397, *in* 822.1072
—— — John Endicott; trag. (Persecution of the Quakers.) p. 313, *in* 822.1072
—— The Puritan and the Quaker. 289.28
—— White, E. O. Miss Brooks. 823.7184
—— Whittier, J: G. "The witch of Wen-ham." (*Atlantic monthly,* v. 39.)
p. 129, *in* ** 51.913
—— Wilkins, M.. E. The adventures of Ann. (Colonial times.) 808.1932
Regicides.
—— Cooper, J. F. The wept of Wish-Ton-Wish. 823.316
—— Southey, R. Oliver Newman: a New England tale; poem. p. 263, *in* 821.378
NEW HAMPSHIRE.
—— King, T: S. The White hills: their legends, landscapes, and poetry. 9174.123
—— Scribner, J. P. Laconia; or, legends of the White mountains and Merry Meeting bay. 823.1782
—— Whitney, *Mrs.* A. D. (T.) A summer in Leslie Goldthwaite's life. 823.1701
Note.—See McClintock, J: N. Hist. of N. H., 1623-1888. 1889. 974.148.

English Fiction. *Contin.*
New England. *Contin.*
PLYMOUTH COLONY.
—— Austin, *Mrs.* J.. (G.) Dr. Le Baron and his daughters. 823.7360
—— — Standish of Standish. 823.6543
—— Longfellow, H: W. Courtship of Miles Standish; poem. 821.888
—— Moore, N. Pilgrims and Puritans.
808.1720
KING PHILIP'S WAR. Cooper, J. F. The wept of Wish-Ton-Wish. 823.316
RHODE ISLAND.
—— Cooper, J. F. The red rover. (Slave trade at Newport in the last century.)
823.309
—— Stowe, *Mrs.* H. E.. (B.) The minister's wooing. 823.1524
VERMONT.
—— Song of the Vermonters. 1779. (*Duyck-incks's Cyclop. of Amer. lit.,* v. 1.)
p. 477, *in* * 803.10
—— Thompson, D. P. The Green moun-tain boys. 823.1587
—— — *Same.* 823.5992
—— Locke Amsden. 823.4171
—— — May Martin, and other tales of the Green mountains. 823.1581
—— — The rangers. 823.4170
Note.—See Dana, H: S. Hist. of Woodstock, Vt. 1760-1887. 974.146.
LIFE AND MANNERS.
—— Austin, *Mrs.* J.. (G.) Nantucket scraps.
823.5674
—— Beecher, H: W. Norwood. 823.64
—— Bellamy, E: Six to one. 823.7162
—— Brown, T. Red-shanty boys; or, pictures of New-England school life thirty years ago. 808.1617
—— Burnham, *Mrs.* C. L. (R.) Young maids and old. 823.5458
—— Chaplin, H. W. Five hundred dollars.
823.6937
—— Coffin, C: C. Caleb Krinkle. 823.244
—— Cooke, *Mrs.* R. (T.) Somebody's neigh-bors. 823.4169
—— Cummins, M. S. The lamplighter.
823.356
—— — Mabel Vaughan. 823.357
—— Damon, S. M. Old New-England days.
823.5379
—— Emery, S.. A. Three generations.
823.5858
—— Greene, *Mrs.* S.. P. (McL.) Cape Cod folks. 823.1849
—— Hale, E: E. Mr. Tangier's vacations.
823.5254
—— Haliburton, T: C. The clockmaker: sayings and doings of Samuel Slick of Slickville. 823.688
—— — *Same.* 828.30
—— Hart, *Col.* J. C. Miriam Coffin. 823.6110
—— — *Same.* 823.6210
—— Hawthorne, N. Blithedale romance. (*With his* The scarlet letter.) *in* 823.733
—— — House of the seven gables. 823.728
—— — *Same.* 823.5878
—— — Tales and sketches. 824.414
—— — Twice-told tales. 823.5561

English Fiction. *Contin.*
New England. *Contin.*
LIFE AND MANNERS. *Contin.*
—— Holland, J. G. Arthur Bonnicastle.
823.785
—— — Bay-path. 823.784
—— Holmes, O. W. Elsie Venner: a ro-
mance of destiny. 823.804
—— — The guardian angel. 823.805
—— Howells, W: D. Annie Kilburn.
823.5541
—— — Doctor Breen's practice. 823.4279
—— — Suburban sketches. 823.830
—— Jewett, S.. O. Country by-ways.
823.1864
—— — A country doctor. 823.5263
—— — Deephaven. 823.4071
—— — Strangers and wayfarers. 823.7389
—— — Tales of New England. 823.7175
—— — A white heron. 823.5262
—— Judd, S. Margaret: a tale of the real
and the ideal, etc. 823.907
—— — Richard Edney and the governor's
family. 823.2340
—— Kirk, *Mrs.* E. W. (O.) Walford. (N.
E. manufacturing town.) 823.7393
—— Lee, M.. C. A Quaker girl of Nan-
tucket. 823.6961
—— Longfellow, H: W. Kavanagh. (*Prose
Works,* v. 3.) 823.1010
—— Lowell, R. T. S. Antony Brade. (Col-
lege life.) 823.1018
—— Nash, W. G. Century of gossip.
823.1181
—— Neal, J. The down-easters. 2 vols.
** 823.6237-8
—— Prentiss, *Mrs.* E.. (P.) Pemaquid: a
story of the old times in New England.
823.1274
—— Robinson, *Mrs.* A. D. (G.) Peter and
Polly; or, home life in New England a
hundred years ago. 823.4072
—— Rollins, *Mrs.* E. C. (H.) Old-time
child-life. 808.1530
—— Round, W: M. F. Achsah: a New Eng-
land life-study. 823.1371
—— Smith, J. E. Oakridge. 823.1463
—— Smith, *Mrs.* M. P. (W.) Jolly good
times; or, child-life on a farm. 808.1004
—— Stowe, *Mrs.* H. E.. (B.) The minister's
wooing. 823.1524
—— — Oldtown folks. 823.1527
—— — Pink and white tyranny. 823.1529
—— — Poganuc people: their loves and
lives. 823.1530
—— — Sam Lawson's Oldtown fireside sto-
ries. 823.1936
—— Thompson, D. P. Locke Amsden; or,
the schoolmaster. 823.4171
—— Ward, *Mrs.* E.. S. (P.) Jack the fisher-
man. 823.6196
—— — The madonna of the tubs. 823.6212
—— — The silent partner. 823.1259
—— Warner, S. The wide, wide world.
823.1683
—— Whittier, J: G. Ballads of New Eng-
land. 821.433
—— — Snow-bound; poem.
p. 286, *in* 821.431

English Fiction. *Contin.*
New England. *Contin.*
LIFE AND MANNERS. *Contin.*
—— Wilkins, M.. E. A humble romance,
and other stories. 823.7336
——.— New England nun, and other stories.
823.7557
—— Winthrop, T. Edwin Brothertoft. (18th
century.) 823.1724
—— Wraxall, F: C: L. Golden-hair. (17th
century.) 823.1745
See also novels by T: B. Aldrich.—Mrs. A. D. (T.)
Whitney.
Note.—For a bibliographical work with critical
essay, *see* Deane, C: New England. (Winsor, J.,
ed. Narr. and crit. hist. of Amer., v. 3.) pp. 295-
384, *in* ** 970.127².
For general histories, *see* Hubbard, W: Indian
wars in New England. 2 vols. 1865. 9174.11.—
Palfrey, J. G. History of New England. 5 vols.
1859-90. 974.1-1⁵. vols. 1-3: History of New England during the Stuart dynasty; v. 4: History of New
England from the revolution of the 17th century;
v. 5: History of New England from the revolution of
the 17th century to the revolution of the 18th.—Savage, J. Genealogical dictionary of first settlers in
New England. 4 vols. (with index). 5 vols. 1860-62.
** 929.61-4-64².—Weeden, W: B. Economic and
social history of New England. 1620-1789. 2 vols.
1890. 974.149-50.—Winthrop, J: History of New
England. (1630-49.) Ed. by J. Savage. 1825. 2
vols. 1853. * 9174.98-9.
See also Catalogues of this Library.
No. 2, 1880, p. 166. No. 4, 1884, p. 202.
No. 3, 1882, pp. 133-4. No. 5, 1888, p. 265.
See also Poole's Index (to 1882). pp. 909-910, *in*
** 50.1;—*Same.* Jan. 1, 1882-Jan. 1, 1887. p. 310, *in*
** 50.1².
For illustrations of the revolutionary period, *see*
United States, *note.*
For manners and customs, *see* Felt, J. B. Cus-
toms of New England. 1853. 9174.198.—Lunt, G:,
ed. Old New England traits. 1873. 974.31.
New England nun, and other stories. Wil-
kins, M.. E. 823.7557
New England story-book. Whitney, *Mrs.*
A. D. (T.), *and others.* 808.1864
New France. *See* British North America, p.
28.
New Guinea. *See* Pacific Ocean.
New Hampshire. *See* New England.
New Holland. *See* Australia, p. 12.
Newman, J: H:, *Cardinal.* (1801-1890.)
—— Callista: a sketch of the third century.
823.1188
Note.—For an account of Cardinal Newman, *see*
Hutton, R: H. Cardinal Newman. 922.343.—
Shepard, W: Pen pictures of modern authors.
1886. p. 68, *in* 820.163.
See also Motzley, *Rev.* T. Reminiscences. v. 1.
922.256.
See also Catalogues of this Library.
No. 2, 1880, p. 166. No. 3, 1882, p. 134.
See also Poole's Index (to 1882). p. 912, *in* **
50.1;—*Same.* Jan. 1, 1882-Jan. 1, 1887. p. 311, *in* **
50.1².
Newport. Lathrop, G: P. 823.4700
News from nowhere. Morris, W: 823.7404
Newton, *Sir* I: (1642-1727.)
—— Hawthorne, N. Biographical stories. 9
pp. (*In his* Tales and sketches.) 1889.
p. 157, *in* 824.414
Newton, *Rev.* R: Bible animals and the
lessons taught by them. 808.1722
Newton, W: Wilberforce. Priest and man;
or, Abelard and Heloisa: an historical ro-
mance. 823.6527
Newton Forster. Marryat, *Capt.* F:
823.1106
Same. ** 823.6665

English Fiction. *Contin.*
New York.
—— Lander, S.. W. New York. (*Spec. for young eyes.*) 808.100
New Zealand.
—— Nordhoff, C: New Zealand. (*In his* Stories of the island world.)
p. 238, *in* 808.165
—— Verne, J. Voyage round the world. N. Zealand. 823.5545
Next door. Burnham, *Mrs.* C. L. (R.)
823.6953
Niagara revisited (twelve years after their wedding journey). Howells, W: D.
in 823.831
Nicander, K: August. The renounced treasure. 10 pp. (Tieck, L. *The elves.*)
p. 43, *in* 823.6328
Nicholas Minturn. Holland, J. G. 823.782
Nicholas Nickleby. Dickens, C: J: H.
823.5553
Same. 2 vols. 823.437–7½; 823.5298–9
Same. 4 vols. 823.433–6
Nicholls, *Mrs.* C.. (Brontë). [*Currer Bell.*] (1816–1855.)
—— Jane Eyre. 823.126
—— *Same.* 823.6261
—— The professor. 823.127
—— Shirley. 823.128
—— Villette. 823.129
—— *Same.* *in* 823.6261
Note.—For an account of Mrs. Nicholls's life and writings, *see* **Gaskell**, *Mrs.* E.. C. (S.) Life of Charlotte Brontë. 1874. 928.59.—**Harris**, A. B. Little biographies. (1887.) p. 175, *in* 928.692.—**Jeaffreson**, J: C. Charlotte (Brontë) Nicholls. 21 pp. (*In his* Novels, etc., v. 2.) p. 282, *in* 820.187.—**Martineau**, H. Charlotte Brontë. 7 pp. (*In her* Biog. sketches.) p. 360, *in* 928.33.—**Montégut**, E. Miss Brontë, sa vie et ses œuvres. 89 pp. (*Rev. d. d. Mondes*, 1857, 2e pér., v. 10.) pp. 139, 423, *in* 54.215.—**Swinburne**, A. C: Note on Charlotte Brontë. 1877. 928.60.
See also Poole's Index (to 1882). pp. 166–167, *in* 50.1;—*Same.* Jan. 1, 1882–Jan. 1, 1887. p. 57, *in* 50.1².
Nichols, G: Ward. The sanctuary: a story of the civil war. 823.1189
Nicholson, J. Shields. A dreamer of dreams: a modern romance. 823.5501
Nicholson, *Rev.* Joseph J. The Blemmertons; or, dottings by the wayside. 823.4267
Nick of the woods. Bird, R. M. 823.79
Nick Whiffles, the trapper guide. Robinson, *Dr.* J. H. 823.1353
Nicolas Muss, History of. Du Bois-Melly, C:
823.6570
Niebuhr, Barthold Georg. Greek hero-stories. Tr. by B: Hoppin. 823.6813
Contents:—The voyage of the Argonauts.—Stories of Hercules.—The Herakleidae and Orestes.
Issued also as Heroic tales of ancient Greece.
—— *Same.* 808.1541
—— Heroic tales of ancient Greece. Tr. and ed., with notes, etc., by F. Summerly.
* 808.1682
Night and morning. Lytton, E: G: E. L. Bulwer- 823.1040
Same. 823.6219
Night side of nature, The. Crowe, *Mrs.* C. (S.) 823.5925
Night-wanderer of an Afghaun fort. 52 pp. (*In* Tales from Blackwood. 2d ser., v. 5.)
in 823.7489

English Fiction. *Contin.*
Nihilist princess, A. Gagneur, L. M.
823.1846
Nimport. Bynner, E. L. 823.4034
Nina's atonement, and other stories. Tiernan, *Mrs.* F.. C. (F.) 823.5805
Nine days' wonder. Aïdé, H. 823.5828
Nine of hearts. Farjeon, B: L. 823.6587
Same. *in* 823.7122
Ninette. Dempster, *Mrs.* C.. L.. (H.)
823.7080
Same. 823.7291
Ninety-three. Hugo, V. M. 823.6290
Same. 823.6419
Nisbet, James. The siege of Damascus: a historical romance. 3 vols. ** 823.6947–9
Nix's mate. 2 vols. (in 1). Dawes, R.
** 823.6236
No alternative. Cudlip, *Mrs.* A. H. (T.)
823.1583
No laggards we. Raymond, R. 823.1843
No medium. Cudlip, *Mrs.* A. H. (T.)
823.5012
No name. Collins, W: W. 823.263
No new thing. Norris, W: E: 823.4571
No quarter! Reid, *Capt.* T: M. 823.6336
No relations. Malot, H. H. 823.3556
No saint. Sergeant, A. *in* 823.5078
No thoroughfare. Dickens, C: J: H., *and* Collins, W: W. *in* 823.6689
Noble, Annette Lucille.
—— Eunice Lathrop, spinster. 823.7440
—— In a country town. 823.7325
Noble, Lucretia Gray.
—— A reverend idol. (Anon.) 823.4546
Noble deeds of our fathers. Watson, H: C.
808.386
Noble life, A. Craik, *Mrs.* D. M. (M.)
823.4285
Noble lord, A. Southworth, *Mrs.* E. D. E. (N.) 823.1503
Noble name, A. Glümer, C. von. 823.4549
Noble wife, A. Saunders, J: *in* 823.5073
Noble woman, A. Stephens, *Mrs.* A. S. (W.)
823.1963
Noblesse oblige. Roberts, M. 823.1342
Same. 823.5789
Nobody's fortune. Yates, E. H. 823.1754
Nobody's husband. Cozzens, S: W. 823.321
Norah. Holmes, *Mrs.* M.. J.. (H.)
p. 223, *in* 823.4846
Nora's love test. Hay, M.. C. 823.2978
Nora's return. Cheney, *Mrs.* E. D. (L.)
823.7322
Nordhoff, C: Man-of-war life: a boy's experience in the United States navy, during a voyage around the world in a ship of the line. 808.167
—— *Same.* 808.1898
—— The merchant vessel: a sailor boy's voyages to see the world. 808.166
—— Stories of the island world. 808.165
—— Whaling and fishing. 808.165
Norine's revenge. Fleming, *Mrs.* M. A. (E.)
823.578
Norman Leslie. 2 vols. Fay, T: M,
** 823.6759–60
Norman Sinclair. 3 vols. Aytoun, W: E.
823.6137–9

English Fiction. *Contin.*
Norris, W: E: Adrian Vidal. *in* 823.5047
—— *Same.* *in* 823.5083
—— A bachelor's blunder. *in* 823.5120
—— The baffled conspirators. 823.7341
—— Chris. 823.5594
—— The Duffer. 12 pp. (*In* Twenty nove-
lettes, etc.) p. 27, *in* 823.7183
—— Heaps of money. 823.4464
—— Her own doing. 89 pp. *in* 823.5015
—— Major and minor. 2 vols. 823.5574-5
—— A man of his word. 50 pp.
in 823.5036
—— Matrimony. 823.1893
—— Misadventure. 823.7292
—— My friend Jim. *in* 823.4985
—— *Same.* *in* 823.5020
—— No new thing. 823.4571
—— The rogue. 823.5582
—— That terrible man. 44 pp. 823.5084
—— *Same.* *in* 823.5089
—— Thirlby Hall. *in* 823.5091
Norseman's pilgrimage, A. Boyesen, H. H.
823.5670
Norston's Rest. Stephens, *Mrs.* A. S. (W.)
823.1958
North, Barclay. The diamond button: whose
was it? A tale from the diary of a lawyer
and the note-book of a reporter. 823.6956
North, W: The man of the world. 823.1191
Issued also as Slave of the lamp.
North Pole. *See* Arctic regions, p. 9.
North America. *See also* Alaska.—America.
—Arctic regions.—British North America.
—Hudson's Bay.—Mexico.—New England.
—Nova Scotia.—Sonora.—United States.
—— Knox, T: W. Hunting adventures on
land and sea. 2 pts. 808.1846-7
Northanger Abbey. Austen, J.. 823.2012
Same. *in* 823.5341
Northern lands. Adams, W: T. 808.495
Norton, *Hon. Mrs.* Caroline E.. S.. (Sheri-
dan). *See* Maxwell, *Lady* C. E.. S.. (S.)
Stirling-
Norway. *See also* Scandinavia.
—— Adams, W: T. Up the Baltic; or, Young
America in Norway, Sweden, and Den-
mark. 808.498
—— Hale, E: E., *and* Hale, S. A family
flight through . . . Norway, etc. 808.1831
—— Scudder, H. E. The Viking Bodleys.
808.1854
EARLY LEGENDARY.
—— Ballantyne, R. M. Erling the Bold.
808.1273
—— Dasent, G: W., *tr.* The story of Gisli
the outlaw. * 823.6448
—— Snorri Sturleson. Heimskringla; or, the
sagas of the Norse kings. 4 vols.
** 948.29-32
12TH CENTURY. Björnson, B. Sigurd Slembe.
Tr. by W: M. Payne. 822.1087
LIFE AND MANNERS.
—— Ballantyne, R. M. Chasing the sun.
808.637
—— — *Same.* (*In his* Tales of adventure,
etc.) *in* 808.1269
—— — *Same.* (*With his* Up in the clouds.)
808.1281

English Fiction. *Contin.*
Norway. *Contin.*
LIFE AND MANNERS. *Contin.*
—— Ballantyne, R. M. *Contin.*
—— — Papers from Norway. (*With his*
Freaks on the fells.) p. 357, *in* 808.213
—— Björnson, B. Arne: a sketch of Nor-
wegian country life. 823.4218
—— — *Same.* 823.4364
—— — The bridal march. 823.4467
—— — Fishing girl. 823.4224
—— — The happy boy: a tale of Norwegian
peasant life. (*With his* Arne.)
in 823.4218
—— — Synnöve Solbakken. 823.4236
—— Boyesen, H. H. Gunnar: a tale of
Norse life. 823.1990
—— Friis, *Prof.* J. A. Lajla: a tale of Fin-
mark. 823.6964
—— Hugo, V. M., *vicomte.* Hans of Ice-
land; or, the demon of the north. 823.6159
—— Lie, J. L. I. Barque Future; or, life in
the far north. 823.4230
—— Maitland, J. A. Sartaroe: a tale of Nor-
way. 823.1085
—— Martineau, H. Feats on the fiord.
808.1198
—— — *Same.* 808.1621
—— Mecklenburg, *Mrs.* A. (S.) Furugaard.
The snow-ball. (Vicary, J: F., *comp. A*
stork's nest.) *in* 823.5415
—— Mügge, T. Afraja; or, life and love in
Norway. 823.6809
In poetry.
—— Longfellow, H: W. Poems of places.
p. 177, *in* 821.214
—— Taylor, B. Lars: a pastoral of Norway.
821.402
—— — *Same.* 821.1351
Note.—See **Bibliography. Botten-Hansen,** P.
La Norvège littéraire. 19e siècle. 1868. ** 15.82.
—**Boyesen,** *Prof.* H. H. The story of Norway.
1889. 948.34.—**Carlyle,** T: The early kings of
Norway. 1875. 923.220.—**Sidgwick,** C. The story
of Norway. (Popular.) 1885. 948.48.
See also **Catalogues** of this Library.
No. 2, 1880, p. 168. No. 4, 1884, p. 207.
No. 3, 1882, p. 137. No. 5, 1888, p. 270.
See also **Index to Consular reports.** 1880-1885;
1886-1889. 2 vols. (U. S. Pub. Docs. *Dept. of State.*)
** 350.5496¹·².
See also **Poole's Index** (to 1882). pp. 929-30, *in*
** 50.1;—*Same.* Jan. 1, 1882-Jan. 1, 1887. pp. 316-17,
in ** 50.1².
Norwood. Beecher, H: W. 823.64
Not dead. Gross, F. 5 pp. *in* 823.5084
Same. *in* 823.5089
Not dead yet. Jeaffreson, J: C. 823.5951
Not for him. Holt, E. S.. 808.1527
Not in society, and other tales. Hatton, J.
823.718
Not in their set. Brink, *Mrs.* M. (di S.) ten.
823.7111
Not to be won. Bell, *Mrs.* L.. 823.4779
Not wisely but too well. Broughton, R.
823.135
Same. *in* 823.2338
Notary's daughter, The. Donnet, *Mme.* L.
823.6912
Notary's nose, The. About, E. F. V.
823.6836
Notre-Dame. Hugo, V.-M. 823.5611
Same. 823,6291; 823.6420; 823.7146

English Fiction. *Contin.*
Nourjahad, History of. Sheridan, *Mrs.* F..
(C.) p. 691, *in* ** 823.6231
Nouvelette, A. Göthe, J. W. von.
p. 483, *in* 823.2183
Nova Scotia.
—— Butterworth, H. Zigzag journeys in
Acadia and New France. 808.1811
—— De Mille, J. The lily and the cross: a
tale of Acadia. 823.373
—— Hall, C: W. Twice taken. (Reduction
of Louisburg, 1763.) 823.7523
—— Lougfellow, H: W. Evangeline; poem.
(Dispossession of the French in Nova Scotia
by the British, 1755.) *in* 821.237
—— — *Same.* *in* 821.888
—— Reeves, M. C. L., *and* Read, E. Pilot
Fortune. 823.7444
Note.—See **Drake, S**: A. The taking of Louis-
burg. 1745. 1891. 972.32.—**Nova Scotia Histori-**
cal Society. Report and collections for the years
1878-1888. 6 vols. ** 972.33-33°.—Smith, C. C.
Acadia. (Winsor, J., *ed. Narr. and crit. hist. of*
Amer., v. 4.) pp. 135-162. *in* * 970.127⁴.
See also **Catalogues** of this Library.
No. 2, 1880, p. 169. No. 5, 1888, p. 270.
No. 3, 1882, pp. 137.
See also **Poole's** Index (to 1882). p. 931, *in* **
50.1;—*Same.* Jan. 1, 1882-Jan. 1, 1887. p. 317, *in*
** 50.1².
Novels.
Robertson, M. A Lombard street mystery.
Stimson, F: J. The residuary legatee. 823.5457

Brame, *Mrs.* C.. M. (L.) Hilary's folly.
Lang, A., *and* Latimer, D. "It." 823.5472

Hale, E: E. Back to back.
James, G: P. R. Bride of Landeck.
Lamb, C: Adventures of Ulysses. 823.5562

Hackländer, F. W. Behind blue glasses.
Macquoid, K.. S. Mill of St. Herbot.
Meredith, G: House on the beach. 823.5563

Grey, *Mrs.* M. G. (S.) Passion and principle.
Maxwell, M.. E.. (B.) Strangers and pilgrims.
—— To the bitter end.
Oliphant, *Mrs.* M. O. (W.) For love and life.
—— Minister's wife. 823.6208

Cudlip, *Mrs.* A. H. (T.) Denis Donne.
De Mille, J. The living link.
Dudevant, *Mme.* A. L. A. (D.) Consuelo.
Lever, C: J. That boy of Norcott's.
Riddell, *Mrs.* C.. E. L. (C.) A life's assize. 823.6214

Cross, *Mrs.* M.. A. (E.) Middlemarch.
Nicholls, *Mrs.* C.. (B.) Jane Eyre.
—— Villette.
Ritchie, *Mrs.* A. I.. (T.) Old Kensington.
Staël-Holstein, A. L. G. (N.), *baronne* de. Corinne.
823.6261

Hoey, *Mrs.* F.. S.. (J.) A golden sorrow.
Trollope, A. The last chronicle of Barset.
—— Doctor Thorne.
—— The Belton estate. 823.6262

Craik, *Mrs.* D. M. (M.) Mistress and maid.
Cudlip, *Mrs.* A. H. (T.) A passion in tatters.
Godwin, W: Adventures of Caleb Williams.
Gore, *Mrs.* C. G. E. (M.) Percy.
Reade, C: Griffith Gaunt. 823.6263

Hughes, T: Tom Brown's school-days at Rugby.
Reade, C: The Knightsbridge mystery. 29 pp.
—— The picture 31 pp.
—— Tit for tat. 30 pp.
—— Singleheart and Doubleface. 823.6677

Stowe, *Mrs.* H. (B.) Betty's bright idea and other
stories. (*viz.:* Let every man mind his own business.—Bolton and his friends.)
Zschokke, J. H. D. The broken pitcher. 823.6678

English Fiction. *Contin.*
Novels. *Contin.*
Collins, W: W. The ghost's touch; and,
Percy and the prophet.
Parr, *Mrs.* L.. (T.) Robin.
Reade, C: The picture. 823.6686

Novels and tales. Göthe, J. W. von.
823.2183
Now and then. Warren, S: 823.1685
Now-a-days. Marshall, *Mrs.* E. (M.)
823.1120
Nugents of Carriconna. Hopkins, T.
823.7354
Numa Roumestan. Daudet, A. 823.4289
Same. 823.5664
Nun's curse, The. Riddell, *Mrs.* C.. E. L.
(C.) 823.5368
Nuttie's father. Yonge, C.. M.. 823.5761
O. T. Andersen, H. C. 823.6788
"O thou, my Austria!" Kirschner, L.
823.7415
Oak openings. Cooper, J. F. 823.303
Same. 823.7461
Oakridge. Smith, J. E. 823.1463
Ober, F: Albion. The Knockabout Club in
north Africa. 808.1924
—— Montezuma's gold mines. 823.5539
—— The silver city: a story of adventure in
Mexico. (*Also*) Cicique Jack. 808.1878
—— Young folks' history of Mexico.
978.75
O'Brien, Fitz James. The spider's eye. 24
pp. (*In* Stories by Amer. authors, v. 3.)
p. 1, *in* 823.4704
O'Brien, W: When we were boys. 823.7023
O'Byrne, M. L. The court of Rath Croghan;
or, dead but not forgotten. 823.7304
Occidental sketches. Truman, B. C.
823.5185
Occupations of a retired life. Mayo, *Mrs.* I..
(F.) 823.1141
"Ocean Star," The mystery of the. Russell,
W: C. 823.5588
O'Connor, Francis. The invisible princess.
21 pp. (Johnson, R., *ed. Little classics.*
v. 8.) p. 169, *in* 829.131
O'Connor, W: Douglas. The ghost. 823.4131
—— *Same.* 64 pp. (Johnson, R., *ed. Lit-*
tle classics, v. 8.) p. 7, *in* 829.131
Octoroon, The. Maxwell, *Mrs.* M.. E.. (B.)
823.5029
Same. *in* 823.6689
Octouian Imperator. 85 pp. Weber, H:
W: p. 155, *in* 821.1241
Odd couple, An. Oliphant, *Mrs.* M. O. (W.)
823.1211
Odd number, The. Maupassant, H. R. A. G.
de. 823.6933
Odd, or even? Whitney, *Mrs.* A. D. (T.)
823.2024
Odd volume, The. Illustrated by Seymour
and Cruikshank. 823.350
Odd-fellows' offering for 1848. Ridgely, J. L.,
and Donaldson, P., *eds.* ** 823.6220
O'Donoghue, *Mrs.* Nannie (Lambert) Power.
Unfairly won. *in* 823.4975
—— *Same.* 823.7179
O'Donoghue, The. Lever, C: J. 823.989
O'Dowd, Cornelius, *pseud. See* Lever, C: J.

English Fiction. *Contin.*

Oliver and the Jew Fagin. Dickens, C: J: H.
in 808.1570
Oliver Cromwell. Herbert, H: W: 823.765
Same.   823.2352; 823.5687
Oliver Ellis. Grant, J.   823.640
Oliver Twist. Dickens, C: J: H.   823.5300
Same.   823.5334; 823.5555; 823.6352
Same.   ** 823.6756; 823.6935
Oliver's bride. 50 pp. Oliphant, *Mrs.* M. O.
(W.)   *in* 823.5046
Olivia Delaplaine. Fawcett, E.   823.5396
Olla podrida. Marryat, *Capt.* F: 823.1107
Same.   ** 823.6666
Olney, Ellen W. *See* Kirk, *Mrs.* E. W. (O.)
O'Mahony, The, chief of the Comeraghs.
Conyngham, D: P.   823.273
Ombra. Oliphant, *Mrs.* M. O. (W.)
823.5024
Same.   823.6147
O'Meara, Kathleen. [*Grace Ramsay.*]
—— Narka, the Nihilist.   823.5214
Omen, The. Galt, J: *in* 823.4192
Omnia vanitas. Bridges, *Mrs. Col.* —.
in 823.4986
Same.   *in* 823.5021
On both sides. Baylor, F.. C.   823.4899
On both sides of the sea. Charles, *Mrs.* E..
(R.)   823.210
On guard. Cudlip, *Mrs.* A. H. (T.)
in 823.6246
On her wedding morn. Brame, *Mrs.* C.. M.
(L.)   *in* 823.5133
On special service. Stables, G.   808.1423
On the Amazon. Stephens, C: A.   808.242
On the banks of the Amazon. Kingston,
W: H: G.   808.364
On the banks of the Ouse. Marshall, *Mrs.*
E. (M.)   823.5411
On the blockade. Adams, W: T.   808.1701
On the edge of the storm. Roberts, M.
823.1341
On the eve. Turgenef, I. S.   823.4213
On the frontier. Harte, F. B.   823.4792
On the heights. 2 vols. Auerbach, B.
823.5642-3
On the verge. Shirley, P.   823.1424
On the Wallaby track. 20 pp. (*In* Tales
from Blackwood. 3d ser., v. 6.)
p. 331, *in* 823.7502
Once again. Bridges, *Mrs. Col.* —.
in 823.5040
Once and forever. Grant, M. M.   823.641
One fair woman, The. Miller, C. H.
823.7403
One in a thousand. James, G: P. R.
823.873
One maid's mischief. Fenn, G: M.
823.5568
One night's mystery. Fleming, *Mrs.* M. A.
(E.)   823.580
One of his inventions. Gibbon, C:
in 823.4993
One of our conquerors. Meredith, G:
823.7553
One of the Duanes. Hamilton, A. K.
823.4887
One of the family. Payn, J.   823.6064
Same.   823.7181

English Fiction. *Contin.*

One of "The six hundred." Grant, J.
823.642
One of the thirty. Jennings, H., *ed.*
823.4589
One of the thirty pieces. 40 pp. Bishop,
W: H: p. 81, *in* 823.4702
One of the 28th. Henty, G: A.   808.1668
One of them. Lever, C: J.   823.990
"One of three." Fothergill, J.   823.1848
One summer. Teufel, *Mrs.* B. W. (H.)
823.827
One thing needful. Maxwell, *Mrs.* M.. E..
(B.)   823.5131
One woman's two lovers. Townsend, V. F..
823.1597
One year. Peard, F.. M..   823.6095
Only a clod. Maxwell, *Mrs.* M.. E.. (B.)
in 823.2408
Same.   *in* 823.5061
Only a fiddler. Andersen, H. C.   823.4219
Only a girl. Hillern, *Mrs.* W. (B.) von.
823.5548
Same.   823.5617
Only a girl's love. Fleming, G.   823.4778
Only a woman. Maxwell, *Mrs.* M.. E.. (B.)
in 823.5126
Same.   *in* 823.6695
Only an ensign. Grant, J.   823.643
Only girls. Townsend, V. F..   823.216
Same.   823.1598
Only one, The. French, H. W.   823.7450
Open door, The. 54 pp. Oliphant, *Mrs.* M.
O. (W.)   823.4951
Same.   823.5026
Open door, The. Teufel, *Mrs.* B. W. (H.)
823.6209
Open question, An. De Mille, J.   823.5850
Open verdict, An. Maxwell, *Mrs.* M.. E.. (B.)
823.6077
Opening a chestnut burr. Roe, E. P.   823.1360
Opening the oyster. Marsh, C: L.   823.6322
Operation in money. 30 pp. Webster, A. F.
p. 146, *in* 823.4702
Opie, *Mrs.* Amelia (Alderson). Works. 3
vols.   823.6134-36
Contents:—Adeline Mowbray; or, the mother and
daughter. v. 1.—After the ball; or, the 2 Sir Williams. v. 3.—Appearance is against her. v. 2.—Austin and his wife. v. 2.—Biographical sketch. v. 1.—
The black velvet pelisse. v. 1.—The brother and sister. v. 1.—The confessions of an odd-tempered man.
v. 3.—The deathbed. v. 1.—False or true; or, the
journey to London. v. 3.—The fashionable wife, and
unfashionable husband. v. 1.—The father and
daughter. v. 1.—Happy faces; or, benevolence and
selfishness. v. 1.—Henry Woodville. v. 2.—Lady
Ann and Lady Jane. v. 2.—Love and duty. v. 1.—
Love, mystery, and superstition. v. 3.—Illustrations
of lying, in all its branches. v. 3.—Madeline. v. 1.—
The mother and son. v. 2.—Mrs. Arlington; or, all
is not gold that glitters. v. 2.—Murder will out. v. 1.
—The mysterious stranger. v. 2.—The opposite
neighbor. v. 3.—The orphan. v. 1.—Proposals of
marriage. v. 2.—The Quaker, and the young man of
the world. v. 2.—The revenge. v. 1.—The robber. v. 1.
—The ruffian boy. v. 2.—The soldier's return. v. 1.—
Tale of trials, told to my children. v. 2.—New tales.
v. 2.—Simple tales. v. 1.—Tales of real life. v. 2.—
Temper. v. 3.—The two sons. v. 3.—The uncle
and nephew. v. 1.—Valentine's eve. v. 2.—The wel-
come home; or, the ball. v. 2.—White lies. v. 2.—
A wife's duty: being a continuation of a woman's
love. v. 3.—A woman's love. v. 3.

Opportunity. Seemüller, *Mrs.* A.. M. (C.)
823.344

English Fiction. *Contin.*
Opposite neighbour, The. 21 pp. Opie, *Mrs.*
A. (A.) p. 300, *in* 823.6136
Optic, Oliver, *pseud. See* Adams, W: T.
Orange and green. Henty, G: A. 808.1457
Orange blossoms. Arthur, T. S. 823.5688
Oraquill, *pseud. See* Bornemann, *Mrs.* M..
Ordeal of Richard Feverel. Meredith, G:
823.6619
O'Reilly, *Rev.* A. J. Alvira; the heroine of
Vesuvius: a remarkable sensation of the
17th century. 823.1222
O'Reilly, Bernard. The two brides.
823.1224
O'Reilly, J: Boyle. Moondyne; a story from
the under-world. 3d ed. 823.1223
——, *joint author. See* Grant, R.
Oriental pearl, The. Dorsey, *Mrs.* A.. H.
823.474
Oriental tales. 91 pp. (Weber, H:, *comp.*
Tales of the East, v. 2.)
p. 599, *in* ** 823.6231
Original belle, An. Roe, E: P. 823.4858
Orley farm. Trollope, A. 823.1618
Ormond. Brown, C: B. 823.141
Same. * 823.6205
Ormond. Edgeworth, M. 823.7439
Same. 2 vols. p. 285, *in* ** 823.4658-9
Orphan of Moscow. Woillez, *Mme.* N.
823.6919
Orphan sisters, The. Hoffman, M.. J.
823.773
Orphan's trials, The. Bennett, E. 823.74
Orthodox. Gerard, D. 823.7078
Osborne, S: Duffield. The spell of Ashtaroth.
823.5215
Osbourne, Lloyd, *joint author. See* Steven-
son, Robert L:
Osego chronicles. Sleight, M.. B. 823.1942
Osgood's predicament. 36 pp. Stoddard,
Mrs. E.. D. (B.) p. 170, *in* 823.4709
Oswald, E. J. The dragon of the north: a
tale of the Normans in Italy. 823.7086
Oswald Cray. Wood, *Mrs.* E. (P.) 823.6006
Othello the second. Robinson, F: W:
823.4383
Other girls, The. Whitney, *Mrs.* A. D. (T.)
823.1696
Other people's money. Gaboriau, É.
in 823.3014
Same. *in* 823.5057
Othmar. La Ramée, L. de. 823.4956
Ought we to visit her? Edwardes, *Mrs.* A.
823.3233
Same. 823.5869
Ouida, *pseud. See* La Ramée, Louise de.
Our boys in India. French, H. W. 808.1872
Our children: how shall we save them? Ar-
thur, T. S. p. 110, *in* 823.5911
Our Christmas in a palace. Hale, E: E.
823.4741
Our forefathers. *See* Freytag, G.
Our Helen. Clarke, R.. S. 823.1915
Our little lady. Holt, E. S.. 808.1524
Our mutual friend. Dickens, C: J: H.
823.1858
Same. 823.5171; 823.5552
Same. 2 vols. 823.5319-20; 823.6342-3
Same. 4 vols. 823.427-30

English Fiction. *Contin.*
Our new crusade. Hale, E: E. 823.683
Our old home. Hawthorne, N. 823.731
Our own set. Kirschner, L. 823.7416
Our refugee household. Clack, *Mrs.* L.
823.1852
Our sensation novel. McCarthy, J. H.
823.5040
Our standard-bearer. Adams, W: T.
808.1555
Our village. 2 vols. Mitford, M.. R.
823.2148-9
Our young folks in Africa. McCabe, J. D.,
Jr. 808.1874
Out in the forty-five. Holt, E. S.. 823.5609
Out of the foam. Cooke, J: E. 823.5526
Out of the wreck. Douglas, A. M.
823.4871
Out on the pampas. Henty, G: A. 808.1611
Out west. Adams, W: T. 808.502
Outcast, The. Reade, W: W. 823.1296
Outsider, The. Smart, H. *in* 823.5100
Outward bound. Adams, W: T. 808.490
Over the Rocky mountains. Ballantyne, R.
M. 808.1280
Overland. De Forest, J: W: 823.5854
Overland tales. Clifford, J. 823.2155
Ovingdean Grange. Ainsworth, W: H.
823.25
Owen, Ashford, *pseud. See* Ogle, Annie.
Owen, G: W. Leech club; or, the mysteries
of the Catskills. 823.1226
Owen, *Mrs.* J. A. After shipwreck.
823.6945
Owen, Robert Dale. Beyond the breakers.
(Village life in the west.) 823.5954
Owen Tudor. Robinson, J.. 823.1345
Oxenford, J: The enthusiast in anatomy. 7
pp. (*In* Half-hours with great story tellers.)
p. 100, *in* 823.5478
——, *and* Feiling, C. A., *trs.* Tales from the
German; comprising specimens from the
most celebrated authors. 823.6276
Contents.—Introduction.—Göthe, J. W. von. The
new Paris.—Hauff, W. The cold heart;—Nose, the
dwarf;—The severed hand.—Hoffmann, E. T. W.
The elementary spirit;—The Jesuits' church in G—;—
The sandman.—Immermann, K. L. The wonders
in the Spessart.—Kleist, H. v. Michael Kohlhass;
—St. Cecilia; or, the power of music.—Musæus, J.
K: A. Libussa.—Oehlenschläger, A. G. Ali and
Gulhyndi.—Richter, J. P. F. The moon.—Schiller,
J. C. F. v. The criminal from lost honour.—Tieck,
L. The Klausenburg.—Velde, C. F. van der. Axel.
—Zschokke, H. Alamontade.
Oxonians, The: sequel to The roué.
823.6472
Attributed to E: G: E. L. Bulwer-Lytton.
Ozollo, *Inca* Pancho. The lost inca.
823.7293
P—, *Count* Paul. The conspirator: a ro-
mance of real life. Ed. by F. Harkut. 2
vols. 823.7327-8
Paalzow, *Mrs.* Henriette (Wach) von.
—— The citizen of Prague. Tr. by Mrs. M..
Howitt. 823.6073
Pabke, Marie, *and* Pitman, *Mrs.* Marie J.
(Davis) [*Margery Deane*], *trs.*
—— Wonder-world stories from the Chinese,
French, German, Hebrew, Hindoostanee,
Hungarian, Irish, Italian, Japanese, Rus-
sian, Swedish, and Turkish. 808.393

English Fiction. *Contin.*
Pacha of many tales. Marryat, *Capt.* F:
                823.1108
   Same.   ** 823.6667
Pacific ocean.
—— Ballantyne, R. M. The coral island.
                808.817
—— — Gascoyne, the sandal-wood trader.
                808.210
—— — Sunk at sea.   808.1282
—— Collingwood, H. The pirate island: a
story of the south Pacific.   808.1707
—— Cooper, J. F. The crater.   823.292
—— Gill, W: W. Myths and songs from the
south Pacific. 1876.   291.21
—— Hearn, L. The fountain maiden: a leg-
end of the south Pacific. 8 pp. (*In his*
Stray leaves, etc.)   p. 33, *in* 823.4791
—— Henty, G: A. Under Drake's flag. (Dis-
covery of the Pacific ocean.)   808.1487
—— Melville, H. White-Jacket.   823.1149
—— Reade, C:, *and* Boucicault, D. Foul
play.   823.1288
—— Willis the pilot: a sequel to the Swiss
family Robinson. (Anon.)   808.373
NEW GUINEA. Kingston, W: H: G. In the
eastern seas.   808.350
PITCAIRN ISLAND. Ballantyne, R. M. The
lonely island; or, the refuge of the muti-
neers.   808.1263
SOUTH SEA ISLANDS.
—— Ballantyne, R. M. The cannibal islands;
or, Captain Cook's adventures in the south
seas. (*In his* Tales of adventure, etc.)
              in 808.1266
—— — *Same.* (*With his* Hunting the lions.)
              in 808.1284
—— White, C. E. Love in the tropics..
              823.6997
—— Wilkinson, J. A. A real Robinson
Crusoe.   808.1698
Note.—See **Burney,** J. Chronological history of
the discoveries in the South sea, or Pacific ocean.
6 vols. 1803-17. ** 9191.31-6.—**Herbert and Kings-**
ley. South-sea bubbles. 1872. 919.124.—**Réclus,** J.
J. E. The earth and its inhabitants: Oceanica.
Maps. Illus. * 919.123.—**Winsor,** J., *ed.* Narra-
tive and critical hist. of America. 8 vols. (*See*
Index, v. 8.) * 970.127-127⁵.
See also **Catalogues** of this Library.
   No. 2, 1880, p. 173.   No. 4, 1884, p. 213.
   No. 3, 1882, p. 141.   No. 5, 1888, p. 275.
See also **Poole's Index** (to 1882). p. 956, *in* ** 50.
1;—*Same.* Jan. 1, 1882-Jan. 1, 1887. p. 326, *in* **
50.1².
   See also Journal of the **Royal Geographical
Society** (Index). vols. i-xxx. ** 910.47.
   See also under heading "**Océanie**" *In* Décennale
du "**Tour du monde.**" 1860-1870. p. 20, *in* **
913.138¹.
Pactolus Prime. Tourgée, A. W.   823.7065
Paddock, *Mrs.* A. G. In the toils; or, mar-
tyrs of the latter days.   823.1228
Paddy Finn. Kingston, W: H: G. 808.1614
Paeon, *Dr.* Jupiter. The dead man's secret;
or, the adventures of a medical student.
              in 823.5141
—— *Same.*   *in* 823.5188
Pagans, The. Bates, A.   823.5533
Page, T: Nelson. In ole Virginia; or, Marse
Chan and other stories.   823.5363
—— Marse Chan: a tale of old Virginia. 36
pp. (*In* Stories by Amer. authors, v. 9.)
            p. 5, *in* 823.4710

English Fiction. *Contin.*
Page, T: Nelson. *Contin.*
—— Two little confederates.   823.5929
Paget, Violet. [*Vernon Lee.*]
—— Hauntings: fantastic stories.   823.7021
Painter, The. Galt, J: *in* 823.702
Painter of Parma. Dunlap, W. D.
              823.7011
Pair of blue eyes. Hardy, T: 823.699
   Same.   823.4991
Palace and cottage. Adams, W: T:
              808.491
Palaces and prisons. Stephens, *Mrs.* A. S.
(W.)   823.1976
Paladin of finance, A. Jenkins, E:
              823.4559
Palestine. *See notes under* Crusades.—Jews.
—Syria.
—— Butterworth, H. Zigzag journeys in
the Levant with a Talmudist story-teller.
              808.1812
—— Knox, T: W. The boy travellers in the
far East. Pt. 4.   808.1838
Palgrave, W: Gifford. Hermann Agha: an
eastern narrative.   823.1229
Palmetto-leaves. Stowe, *Mrs.* H. E.. (B.)
              823.5600
Paltock, Robert. [*R. S.*] The life and ad-
ventures of Peter Wilkins.   823.4062
Pamela. 3 vols. Richardson, S:
            ** 823.6161-3
   Same. 4 vols.   * 823.1317-20
Pancha. 39 pp. Janvier, T: A.
          p. 5, *in* 823.4711
Pandora. 78 pp. James, H:, *Jr.*
          p. 81, *in* 823.4894
Pandour and his princess, The: a Hungarian
sketch. 64 pp. (*In* Tales from Blackwood,
v. 9.)   ** *in* 823.6655
Pansy, *pseud. See* Alden, *Mrs.* I.. (McD.)
Paper city. Locke, D: R.   823.1008
Papers for thoughtful girls. Keddie, H:
              808.325
Paragreens on a visit to the Paris Universal
Exhibition. Ruffini, G. D.   823.1374
Pardoe, Julia. Life-struggle.   823.1230
—— The will. 52 pp. (*With* Fortunes of
the Colville family. By F. E: Smedley.)
         p. 186, *in* 823.1443
Parents' assistant, The. Edgeworth, M.
         p. 317, *in* 808.292
Paris, J: Ayrton. Philosophy in sport made
science in earnest.   808.991
Paris. *See also* France: *Life in Paris,* p. 94.
—— Abbott, J. Rollo in Paris.   808.922
Paris, An attic philosopher in. Souvestre,
É.   823.5644
Paris in America. Laboulaye, É. R. L.
              823.6870
Parisians, The. 2 vols. Lytton, E: G: E.
L. Bulwer-   823.1041-2
Parker, F.. Talbot, *Countess of Morley.*
—— Dacre: a novel. 2 vols. (in 1).
          ** 823.6731
Parr, *Mrs.* L.. (Taylor).
—— Adam and Eve.   823.6092
—— The Bluebell of Red-neap; or, Shingle
cord: a Christmas story.   823.1231
—— Dorothy Fox.   823.5942

English Fiction. *Contin.*
Parr, *Mrs.* L.. (Taylor). *Contin.*
—— John Thompson, and other stories.
                                823.1233
—— Robin.   823.3711
—— *Same.*   823.6686
Parson o' Dumford. Fenn, G: M. 823.2261
Same.   *in* 823.5047; *in* 823.5083
Parsonage of Mora. Bremer, F.   823.6106
Parsons, *Mrs.* Gertrude (Hext).
—— Edith Mortimer; or, the trials of life at
Mortimer Manor.   823.1234
Parson's daughter, The. Hook, T. E:
                                823.822
Part of the property. Whitby, B.. 823.7358
Partisan, The. Simms, W: G.   823.1435
Partisan leader, The. Sydney, E: W:
                             ** 823.6003
Partners, The. Daudet, A.   823.5580
Parton, James. Captains of industry; or,
men of business who did something besides
making money: a book for young Ameri-
cans.   808.1548
Pascarel. La Ramée, L. de.   823.1824
Passages from the diary of a late physician.
Warren, S: 823.6974
Passages from the journal of a social wreck.
23 pp. Crosby, M.   p. 80, *in* 823.4708
Passages in the life of Mrs. Margaret Mait-
land of Sunnyside. Oliphant, *Mrs.* M. O.
(W.)   823.4821
—— *Same.*   *in* 823.5044
Passages in the life of the faire gospeller.
Rathbone, *Mrs.* M.. A. (M.)   823.4079
Passe Rose. Hardy, A. S.   823.5452
Passion and principle. Grey, *Mrs.* M. G. (S.)
                                823.6208
Passion and principle. Hook, T. E:
                                823.5182
Passion flower, A. Brame, *Mrs.* C.. M. (L.)
                                823.4772
Passion in tatters, A. Cudlip, *Mrs.* A. H. (T.)
                            in 823.6263
Passion in the desert, A. 20 pp. Balzac, H.
de.   p. 275, *in* 823.5211
Passionate pilgrim, and other tales. James,
H:, *Jr.*   823.885
Passion's slave. King, R: A.   823.7050
Past forgiveness. Majendie, *Lady* M.
                                823.6984
Patagonia, The. 82 pp. James, H:, *Jr.*
                         p. 159, *in* 823.6536
Pater, Walter Horatio.
—— Imaginary portraits.   823.5426
    Contents:—A prince of court painters.—Denys
    l'Auxerrois.—Sebastian van Storck.—Duke Carl of
    Rosenmold.
—— Marius the epicurean: his sensations and
ideas. 2d ed. 2 vols.   823.6197-8
Path of duty, The. 60 pp. James, H:, *Jr.*
                         p. 261, *in* 823.4894
Pathfinder, The. Cooper, J. F. 823.304
Same.   823.7462
Patience Strong's outings. Whitney, *Mrs.* A.
D. (T.)   823.1697
Patmore, P: G: Chatsworth; or, the romance
of a week. Ed. by (R. P. Ward). 823.6074
Paton, *Sir* Joseph Noel. [*Elsie Strivelyne.*]
The princess of Silverland, and other tales.
                                808.1329

English Fiction. *Contin.*
Patricia, *pseud.* Blanche Carey; or, scenes in
many lands.   823 1235
Patricia Kemball. Linton, *Mrs.* E. (L.)
                                823.1005
Patriot and tory. Wright, *Mrs.* J. (McN.)
                                823.6021
Patronage. 2 vols. Edgeworth, M.
                             ** 823.4656-7
Same. 3 vols.   823.7435-7
Patty. Macquoid, *Mrs.* K.. S. 823.1077
Patty's perversities. Bates, A. 823.1866
Same.   823.5701
Paul, *Mrs.* Margaret Agues (Colville). Kiu-
tail Place: a tale of revolution. 823.7200
Paul and Christina. Barr, *Mrs.* A. E. (H.)
                                823.5226
Paul and Virginia. Saint-Pierre, J. H. B. de.
                                823.217
Same.   *in* 823.4206
Same.   p. 629, *in* * 823.6215
Paul Clifford. Lytton, E: G: E. L. Bulwer-
                                823.1044
Paul Crew's story. Carr, A. C. *in* 823.4981
Same.   *in* 823.4982
Paul Faber, surgeon. MacDonald, G:
                                823.2016
Same.   823.6041
Paul Massie. McCarthy, J.   823.1058
Paul Patoff. Crawford, F. M.   823.5230
Paul Vargas, and other tales. Fargus, F. J.
                            in 823.4981
Same.   *in* 823.4982
Paulding, James Kirke. The Dutchman's
fireside. 2 vols. (in 1).   823.7014
—— Merry tales of the three wise men of
Gotham.   ** 823.7528
—— The old continental; or, the price of
liberty. 2 vols. (in 1).   823.7408
—— The puritan and his daughter. 2 vols.
(in 1).   ** 823.7527
—— Tales of the good woman. By a doubtful
gentleman. Ed. by W: I. Paulding.
                                823.1238
——, *joint author. See* Irving, W.
Pauline. Dumas, A. D.   823.5565
Pauline. Walford, *Mrs.* L. B. (C.)
                                823.1812
Pausanias, the Spartan. Lytton, E: G: E.
L. Bulwer-   823.1045
Same. 823.5729; *in* 823.5863; *in* 823.5975
Pawnee hero stories and folk-tales. Grin-
nell, G: B.   808.1717
Payn, James. At her mercy.   823.5952
—— A beggar on horseback; or, a county
family. .   823.5988
—— *Same.*   823.6057
—— The best of husbands.   823.6063
—— Bitter reckoning.   *in* 823.4994
—— Bred in the bone; or, like father, like
son.   823.6052
Issued also as Like father, like son.
—— The burnt million.   823.7088
—— By proxy.   823.6059
—— The canon's ward. (*Also*) Thicker than
water.   823.6588
—— Carlyon's year.   823.6065
—— Cecil's tryst.   823.6053
—— The eavesdropper. 69 pp. *in* 823.6691

English Fiction. *Contin.*
Phantasmion. Coleridge, *Mrs.* S. H. (C.)
823.4124
Phantastes. MacDonald, G: 823.1065
Same. *in* 823.5054; 823.7010
Phantom fortune. Maxwell, *Mrs.* M.. E.. (B.)
in 823.5116
Phantom regiment, The. Grant, J. 823.644
Phantom 'rickshaw, The, and other tales.
Kipling, R. 823.7345
Phantom ship. Marryat, *Capt.* F: 823.1111
Same. ** 823.6670
Phantom wedding, The. 81 pp. Southworth,
Mrs. E. D. E. (N.) 823.1504
Phaulcon the adventurer. Dalton, W:
823.6082
Phelps, E.. Stuart, *now* Ward, *Mrs.* E.. S.
(P.)
Phemie Keller. Riddell, *Mrs.* C.. E. L. (C.)
823.1333
Phemie Millar. 3 vols. (in 2). Keddie, H.
823.7312–13
Phemie's temptation. Terhune, *Mrs.* M.. V.
(H.) 823.1562
Philip II., of France. *See* Philip Augustus.
Philip. Cutler, *Mrs.* M.. C. 823.7248
Philip, Adventures of. Thackeray, W: M.
823.1571
Same. 2 vols. 823.5002–3
Philip Augustus, *called* Philip II., *King of
France.* James, G: P. R. Philip Augustus; or, the brothers in arms. 823.874
Philip Earnscliffe. Edwardes, *Mrs.* A.
in 823.3233
Philip Nolan's friends. Hale, E: E.
823.684
Philip Rollo. Grant, J. 823.645
Philistines, The. Bates, A. 823.5489
Philosopher's baby, The. (*In* Tales from
Blackwood. 2d ser., v. 1.) *in* 823.7485
Philosophical novels. *See also* Psychological
novels.—Spiritualism in story.
—— Balzac, H. de. Louis Lambert.—Facino
Cane.—Gambara. 823.5428
—— — Seraphita,—with Jesus Christ in
Flanders, and, The exiles. 823.7335
—— Bellamy, E. Miss Ludington's sister: a
romance of immortality. 823.7338
—— Fawcett, E. Confessions of Claud.
(Study in heredity.) 823.5743
Philothea. Child, *Mrs.* L. M. (F.)
823.7084
Philosophy in sport made science in earnest.
Paris, J: A. 808.991
Phineas Finn. Trollope, A. 823.1619
Phineas Redux. Trollope, A. 823.5995
Phœbe. Harris, *Mrs.* M. (C.) 823.4753
Phœbe, junior. Oliphaut, *Mrs.* M. O. (W.)
823.5966
Phœnicia. Cahun, L. Adventures of Captain Mago; or, a Phœnician expedition, B.
C. 1000. 823.6392
Note.—See Duncker, M. W. Hist. of antiquity,
v. 2. 930.146.—Rawlinson, G: The story of Phœnicia. 939.33.
See also Catalogues of this Library.
No. 2, 1880, p. 180. No. 5, 1888, p. 287.
Phyllis. Hungerford, *Mrs.* M. 823.745
Phyllis of the Sierras, A. Harte, F. B.
823.5281

English Fiction. *Contin.*
Physiology.
—— Benedict, A. K. My wonder-story.
808.1900
Note.—See Foster, M., *and* M'Kendrick, J. G.
Article "Physiology," Ency. Brit., v. 19. p. 8, *in* **
32.27l.
See also Catalogues of this Library.
No. 2, 1880, p. 181. No. 4, 1884, p. 227.
No. 3, 1882, p. 150. No. 5, 1888, p. 288.
See also Poole's Index (to 1882). p. 1,007, *in* ** 50.
1;—*Same.* Jan. 1, 1882–Jan. 1, 1887. p. 341, *in* **
50.1².
Piazzi, *Mme.* Adrienne (Delcambre.) [*Leila-Hanoum.*] A tragedy in the imperial
harem at Coustantinople. Tr. by Gen. R.
E. Colston. 823.4565
Picciola. 86 pp. Boniface, J. X.
p. 755, *in* ** 823.6215
Same. 823.6294
Picked up in the streets. Schobert, H.
823.5271
Picken, Andrew. The deer-stalkers of Glenskiach: a Highland legend. (Picken, A., *ed.*
The club-book, v. 2.) *in* 823.702
—— Eisenbach; or, the adventures of a
stranger: a metropolitan story. (Picken,
A., *ed. The club-book*, v. 1.)
p. 119, *in* 823.702
—— Mary Ogilvie: a tale of the squire's experience. 823.7235
—— The three Kearneys: a tale of the dominie. (Picken, A., *ed. The club-book*, v.
2.) *in* 823.702
——, *ed.* The club-book: being original tales
by James, Galt, Power, and others. 2 vols.
(in 1). 823.702
Pickering, Ellen. The grandfather.
823.6071
—— The grumbler. 823.6070
Pickwick club, Posthumous papers of the.
Dickens, C: J: H. 823.5556
Same. 823.5677
Same. 2 vols. 823.449–9²
Pickwick papers. Dickens, C: J: H.
823.5173
Same. 2 vols. 823.5296–7
Same. 4 vols. 823.445–8
Picture, The. Reade, C: *in* 823.6686
Same. *in* 823.6697
Pictures from Italy. Dickens, C: J: H.
p. 431, *in* 823.4968
Same. *in* 823.5331
Pictures of country life. Cary, A. 823.182
Pictures of Hellas. Mariager, P. 823.5279
Piedouche, a French detective. Du Boisgobey, F. *in* 823.5094
Pierce, *Mrs.* H.. Corwin. Curse of Everleigh; or, purified by fire. 823.1261
Pierre. Melville, H. 823.1147
Pierre and Jean. Maupassant, H. R. A. G.
de. 823.6936
Pierre's soul. Ohnet, G. 823.7326
Pierson, Ernest Delancey. A vagabond's
honor. 823.6395
Pigeon pie: a tale of Roundhead times.
Yonge, C.. M.. 823.1771
Pilgrim and the shrine. Maitland, E:
823.1081
Pilgrims and puritans. Moore, N.
808.1720

English Fiction. *Contin.*
Poland. *Contin.*
Note. Contin.
Röpell, *Dr.* R: Geschichte Polens (850-1300). *Contin.* by Dr. J. Caro to 1506. 5 vols. 949.106-10.—
Saxton, L. C. Fall of Poland. 2 vols. 1852. 949.1-2.
See also Catalogues of this Library.
No. 2, 1880, p. 183. No. 4, 1884, p. 231.
No. 3, 1882, p. 153.
See also Poole's Index (to 1882). pp. 1,023-24, *in* ** 50.1;—*Same.* Jan. 1, 1882-Jan. 1, 1887. p. 347, *in* ** 50.1².

Polikouchka. 70 pp. Tolstoï, *Count* L. N.
823.6589
Polish Jew, The. 49 pp. Erckmann, É., and Chatrian, P. A. 823.5089
Same, and others tales. Erckmann, É., and Chatrian, P. A. 823.6858
Political economy. Martineau, H. Illustratious of political economy. (Stories with applications to questions of political economy.) 9 vols. ** 823.6706-14
For contents, *see* Martineau, H.
Note.—See Atkinson, E: The industrial progress of the nation. 1890. 330.177.—Bibliography:
Bowker, R: R., *and* Iles, G., *eds.* The reader's guide in economic science. 1891. 16.235.—Laughlin, J. L. Elements of political economy. 1887. (A teacher's library, pp. xxii-xxiv.) 330.171.—Marx, K. Capital. 2 vols. 1887. (Works and authors quoted. v. 2, pp. 801-816.) 331.278-9.—Sumner, W. G. A selected list of books. (*Library journal.* 1880. v. 5.) p. 17, *in* 19.20.—Clark, J. B., *and* Giddings, F. H. The modern distributive press. 1888. 331.283.—Denslow, Van B. Principles of the economic philosophy of society, gov't, and industry. 1888. 330.165.—Economic monographs: essays, etc. 330.170.—Ingram, J: K. A hist. of political economy. 1888. 330.187.—Lalor, J: J. Cyclopædia of political science, etc. 3 vols. v. 1: A-D; v. 2: E-N; v. 3: O-Z. ** 320.115-17.—Lunt, E: C. The present condition of economic science. 1888. 330.182.—Mill, J. S. Principles of political economy. 1886. 330.42.—Nicol, D: The political life of our time. 2 vols. 1889. 329.48-9.—Rand, B:, *comp.* Selections illus. economic hist. since the Seven years' war. 1889. 330.184.—Wells, D: A. Recent economic changes. 1890. 330.179.
See also Catalogues of this Library.
No. 2, 1880, p. 183. No. 4, 1884, p. 232.
No. 3, 1882, p. 153. No. 5, 1888, p. 290.
See also Poole's Index (to 1882). p. 1,025, *in* ** 50.1;—*Same,* to Jan. 1, 1887. p. 347, *in* ** 50.1².

Polko, *Mrs.* Elise (Vogel). Musical sketches. Tr. by F. Fuller. 823.6452
Pollok, Robert. Tales of the covenanters. With life of the author by J. L. Watson.
823.1270
Pompey the little, History of. Coventry, F. ** 823.2084
Poor gentleman, A. 2 pts. Oliphant, *Mrs.* M. O. (W.) *in* 823.5100
Poor gentleman, The. Conscience, H.
823.5707
Poor Jack. Marryat, *Capt.* F: 823.1114
Poor Miss Finch. Collins, W: W. 823.264
Poor Ogla-Moga. 35 pp. Lloyd, D: D.
p. 99, *in* 823.4704
Poor scholar, and other tales of Irish life. Carleton, W: 823.174
Popanilla. Disraeli, B: *in* 823.458
Popular romances of the middle ages. Cox, *Sir* G: W:, *and* Jones, E. H. 823.7193
Popular tales. *See* Edgeworth, M.
Popular tales for children. Andersen, H. C.
808.1729
Popular tales from the Norse. 3d ed. Dasent, *Sir* G: W. 808.1801

English Fiction. *Contin.*
Port Tarascon. Daudet, A. 823.6449
Portent, The. MacDonald, G: 823.1066
Same. *in* 823.4995 ; *in* 823.5141
Same. *in* 823.7010
Porter, D: Dixon, *Admiral U. S. N.* The adventures of Harry Marline; or, notes from an American midshipman's lucky bag. 823.6142
—— Arthur Merton. 823.6503
Porter, J.. Scottish chiefs. 823.1271
—— Thaddeus of Warsaw. 823.1272
Porter, Linn Boyd. [*Albert Ross.*] Speaking of Ellen. 823.6989
Porter, W: Ogilvie. [*Sir E: Seaward.*] Sir Edward Seaward's narrative of his shipwreck, and consequent discovery of certain islands in the Caribbean sea, etc. Ed. by Miss J.. Porter. 823.4047
Portia. Hungerford, *Mrs.* M. 823.5787
Portrait, The. 45 pp. Oliphant, *Mrs.* M. O. (W.) *in* 823.4951
Same. *in* 823.5026
Portrait of a lady. James, H:, *Jr.* 823.5251
Portugal. *See* Spain, and *note under* Spain.
—— Adams, W: T. Vine and olive; or, Young America in Spain and Portugal.
808.499
—— Harding, V. E., *and* Braga, T. Twelve Portuguese legends. 12 pp. (Henderson, *Mrs.* F.. C. *Dunderviksborg, etc.*) 1881.
p. 305, *in* 823.6534
—— Longfellow, H: W. Poems of places.
p. 57, *in* 821.220
—— Monteiro, H. Portuguese stories. 19 pp. (*Folk-lore record,* v. 4.) 1881.
p.141, *in* * 293.22
Post haste. Ballantyne, R. M. 808.1271
Postel, K: [*C: Sealsfield.*] Adventures in Texas. Abr. and tr. by F: Hardman. (*In* Tales from Blackwood, v. 5.) ** *in* 823.6651
Posthumous papers of the Pickwick club. Dickens, C: J: H. 823.5173
Same. 823.5556; 823.5677
Same. 2 vols. 823.449-9
Potter, Frank H., *tr.* Near to happiness. (*A coté du bonheur.*) 823.5504
Pottleton legacy. Smith, A. 823.1452
Poushkin, A. S. *See* Pushkin, A. S.
Pouvillon, Émile. Césette: a story of peasant life in the south of France. Tr. by C: W: Woolsey. 823.4484
Poverty corner. Fenn, G: M. 823.4906
Same. *in* 823.5047; *in* 823.5083
Powell, Mary, Maiden & married life of. Rathbone. *Mrs.* M.. A. (M.) 823.4763
Power, Tyrone. The gipsy of the Abruzzo. (Picken, A., *ed.* The club-book, v. 1.)
p. 77, *in* 823.702
Powers, Stephen. Muskingum legends, with other sketches and papers descriptive of the young men of Germany and the old boys of America. 823.4145
Poynter, Eleanor F.. Among the hills.
823.1857
—— Ersilia. 823.1273
—— Madame de Presnel. 823.4907
—— *Same.* *in* 823.5055; *in* 823.5068
—— My little lady. 823.6977

English Fiction. *Contin.*
Prose tales. 1st ser., v. 1. Poe, E. A.
823.5796
Same. 1st and 2d ser. 2 vols.
823.1920–21
Prosper. Cherbuliez, V. 823.6841
Prothero, H: The misogynist. 11 pp. (*In*
Tales from Blackwood. 3d ser., v. 1.)
in 823.7497
Provence rose, A. 27 pp. La Ramée, L. de.
in 823.7056
Provost and other tales. Galt, J: 823.4192
Prudence Palfrey. Aldrich, T: B. 823.37
Prudence Winterburn. Douduey, S..
808.1631
Prue and I. Curtis, G: W: 823.358
Prusias. 2 vols. Eckstein, E. 823.4731–2
Prussia. *See also* Germany: *Prussia*, p. 102.
—— Adams, W: T. Northern lands; or,
Young America in Russia and Prussia.
808.495
Psyche of to-day. Jenkins, *Mrs.* H. C. (J.)
823.4240
Psychological novels.
—— Cobban, J. M. Julius Courtney; or,
master of his fate. 823.7246
—— Darnell, H: F. Craze of Christian En-
gelhart. 823.7001
——— *Same.* 823.7037
—— Flammarion, C. Uranie. 823.7257
—— Howells, W: D. Shadow of a dream.
823.7166
—— Lytton, E: R. Bulwer- Ring of Amasis:
a romance. 823.7053
See also Tales by C: B. Brown.
Note.—See Catalogues of this Library.
No. 2, 1880, p. 187. No. 4, 1884, p. 240.
No. 3, 1882, pp. 156–7. No. 5, 1888, p. 296.
Publicans and sinners. Pt. 1. Maxwell,
Mrs. M.. E.. (B.) *in* 823.5135
Same. Pt. 2. *in* 823.5186
Same. 2 pts. (in 1). 823.2401; *in* 823.5140
Puck. La Ramée, L. de. 823.1825
Pulszky, Francis Aurelius, *and* Pulszky,
Theresa. Tales and traditions of Hungary.
3 vols. 823.5731–3
Puritan and his daughter, The. 2 vols. (in 1).
Paulding, J. K. ** 823.7527
Purse, The. Balzac, H. de. *in* 823.4255
Pushkin, Aleksandr Sergeïevitch.
—— The captain's daughter. 823.5023
—— Marie: a story of Russian love. Tr. by
M. H. de Zielinska. 823.4225
—— Russian romance. Tr. by Mrs. J. B.
Telfer. 823.4196
—— The snow-storm. Tr. by Mrs. F.. C.
Henderson. (Henderson, *Mrs.* F.. C.
Dunderviksborg, etc.) p. 125, *in* 823.6534
Puss-cat Mew, and other stories for my chil-
dren. Hugessen, E: H. Knatchbull-
808.1679
Put asunder. Brame, *Mrs.* C.. M. (L.)
in 823.4980
Put to the test. Maxwell, *Mrs.* M.. E.. (B.)
823.5106
Same. *in* 823.6604
Put yourself in his place. Reade, C:
823.1294

English Fiction. *Contin.*
Pyle, Howard. The Rose of Paradise: ac-
count of adventures that happened to Capt.
J: Mackra, in connection with the famous
pirate, Edward England, in 1720, etc.
823.5288
—— Within the capes. 823.4882
Q., *pseud. See* Crouch, Arthur T: Quilter.
Quadroon, The. Reid, T: M. 823.1297
Quaker girl of Nantucket, A. Lee, M.. C.
823.6961
Queechy. 2 vols. (in 1). Warner, S.
823.1681
Same. 2 vols. 823.6582–3
Queen among queens. MacDowall, C.
823.7188
Queen amongst women, A. Brame, *Mrs.* C..
M. (L.) *in* 823.5080
Queen Hildegarde. Richards, *Mrs.* L. E..
(H.) 808.1539
Queen Mab. 3 vols. (in 1). Kavanagh, J.
823.918
Queen Money. Kirk, *Mrs.* E. W. (O.)
823.5260
Queen of Bohemia. Hatton, J. 823.719
Queen of hearts. Collins, W: W. 823.265
Queen of Sheba. Aldrich, T: B. 823.38
Queen Titania. Boyesen, H. H. 823.1865
Queenhoo-Hall. 4 vols. Strutt, J.
* 823.4675–8
Queenie Hetherton. Holmes, *Mrs.* M.. J..
(H.) 823.4847
Queenie's whim. Carey, R. N. 823.3376
Same. 823.4815
Queens. Emery, *Mrs.* E. B. 823.533
Queen's cadet. 26 pp. Grant, J. 823.646
Queen's favorite, The; or, the price of a
crown: an historical romance of the 15th
century. 823.1254
Queen's Maries. Melville, G: J: Whyte-
** 823.4663
Same. 823.7283
Queen's necklace. Dumas, A. D. 823.3481
Same. 823.6519
Queer folk. Hugessen, E: H. Knatchbull-
808.1049
Queer stories for boys and girls. Eggleston,
E: 808.1418
Queiros, Eça de. Dragon's teeth: a novel
from the Portuguese by M.. J. Serrano.
823.5471
Quentin Durward. Scott, *Sir* W. 823.1409
Same. *in* 823.5157; ** 823.6030
Question, A. Ebers, G. M. 823.4200
Question of honor, A. Tiernan, *Mrs.* F.. C.
(F.) 823.6358
Quicksands. Streckfuss, A. 823.4782
Quicksilver. Fenn, G: M. 808.1497
Quiet heart, The. Oliphant, *Mrs.* M. O. (W.)
823.5967
Quiet life, A. Burnett, *Mrs.* F.. E. (H.)
823.5630
Quiet Miss Godolphin. 53 pp. Mayo, *Mrs.*
I.. (F.) 823.4050
Quillinan, E: Rangers of Connaught. (*In*
Standard tales, etc. Ed. by Mrs. C. I. John-
stone.) *in* * 823.6194
—— *Same.* (Tieck, L. *The elves, etc.*) 1864.
p. 68, *in* 823.6328

English Fiction. *Contin.*

Quinton, M. A. The money-god; or, the empire and the papacy: a tale of the third century.   823.1279

Quintus Claudius. 2 vols. Eckstein, E.   823.6982–3

Quisisana. Spielhagen, F.   *in* 823.6688

Quits. Tautphoeus, J. (M.), *Freiherrin* von.   823.1798

Quixstar. Taylor, E..   823.4112

Quod, J:, *pseud. See* Irving, J: T.

Quodlibet. Kennedy, J: P.   823.930

Rabbi's spell, The. Cumberland, S. C.   *in* 823.5097

Rachel Gray. Kavanagh, J.   823.919

Rachel Noble's experience. Edwards, B.   823.7073

Racowitza, Helene von. The evil that women do. Tr. by A. Howard.   823.7025

Radcliffe, *Mrs.* Anne (Ward). The mysteries of Udolpho: a romance.   823.1280

—— *Same.* Interspersed with pieces of poetry. 3 vols. (Barbauld, *Mrs.* A. L. (A.), *ed. The British novelists*, vols. 45–47.)   ** 823.2106–8

—— Romance of the forest.   823.1281

—— *Same.* Interspersed with some pieces of poetry. 2 vols. (Barbauld, *Mrs.* A. L. (A.), *ed. The British novelists*, vols. 43–44.)   ** 823.2104–5

Radical, The. Galt, J: ** 823.6721

Railroad and the churchyard, etc. 54 pp. Björnsou, B.   p. 89, *in* 823.7545

Railway junction, A; or, the romance of Ladybank. 59 pp. (*In* Tales from Blackwood. 2d ser., v. 4.)   *in* 823.7488

Raimund, Golo, *pseud. See* Friedrich, *Mrs.* Bertha Heyn.

Rainbow gold. Murray, D: C.   823.4948

Same.   *in* 823.5081

Rainy June, A. 32 pp. La Ramée, L. de.   *in* 823.4994

Same.   p. 321, *in* 823.5747

Rajah's heir, The. (Anon.)   823.7182

Raleigh Westgate. Johnson, *Mrs.* H.. (K.)   823.5502

Ralph the heir. Trollope, A.   823.1623

Ralph Wilton's weird. Hector, *Mrs.* A. (F.)   823.746

Same.   *in* 823.5015

Ralston, W: Ralston Shedden. Russian folktales.   823.1282

Rambles among the Alps. Abbott, J.   *in* 808.586

Rambling story. Clarke, *Mrs.* M.. V. (N.) Cowden-   823.4110

Ramona. Jackson, *Mrs.* H.. M. (F.)   823.4865

Randolph Gordon. 68 pp. La Ramée, L. de.   823.1826

Randolph, J. Thornton. Heiress of Sweetwater. (Anon.)   823.1283

Rangers, The. 2 vols. (in 1). Thompson, D. P.   823.4170

Rangers of Connaught. Quillinan, E: *in* * 823.6194

Ranthorpe. Lewes, G: H: 823.5053

Raphael. Lamartine, A. M. L: de P. de.   823.6875

English Fiction. *Contin.*

Raphaela. Monniot, *M'lle.* —.   823.6876

Rarahu. Viaud, L: M. J.   823.7194

Rask, *Dr.* E. C. The storm-bride. 4 pp. Tr. by Mrs. F.. C. Henderson. (Henderson, *Mrs.* F.. C. *Dunderviksborg, etc.*) 1881.   p. 350, *in* 823.6534

Raspe, Rudolph Erich. The adventures of Baron Münchausen. 4th ed. Illus. by G. Doré.   823.6101

—— The travels and surprising adventures of Baron Münchausen. (Anon.)   808.379

—— Travels of Baron Münchausen. 10 pp. (Scudder, H. E., *comp. The children's book.*) 1881.   p. 393, *in* 808.1882

Rasselas, History of. Johnson, S: 823.903

Same.   ** 823.2087; *in* 823.4489

Same.   823.4964

Rathbone, *Mrs.* M.. Anne (Manning). [*Nicholas Moldwarp, B. A.*] Cherry and Violet: a tale of the great plague.   823.1093

—— Heroes of the desert: the story of the lives of Moffat and Livingstone.   823.5583

—— Jacques Bonneval; or, the days of the dragonnades.   823.4103

—— Lady Willoughby; or, passages from the diary of a wife and mother in the seventeenth century. (Anon.)   823.7394

—— Lord Harry Bellair: a tale of the last century. 2 vols.   823.7112–3

—— Maiden & married life of Mary Powell, afterwards Mistress Milton. (Anon.)   823.4763

—— The old Chelsea bun-house: a tale of the last century.   ** 823.6715

—— Passages in the life of the faire gospeller, Mistress Anne Askew.   823.4079

—— The sower's reward.   823.5901

—— The Spanish barber: a tale.   823.5581

Rattlin, the reefer. Marryat, *Capt.* F: 823.1116

Same.   ** 823.6673

Rau, Heribert. Mozart: a biographical romance. Tr. by E: R. Sill.   823.7350

Ravellings from the web of life. Cannon, C: J.   823.166

Ravenshoe. Kingsley, H: 823.943

Raymond, Grace. How they kept the faith: a tale of the Huguenots of Languedoc.   823.6367

Raymond, Rossiter Worthington. No laggards we.   823.1843

Raymonde. Theuriet, A.   823.5592

Raymond's atonement: Bürstenbinder, E..   823.4995

Same.   823.5202

Read, Emily, *joint author. See* Reeves, M. C. L.

Read, Opie P. A Kentucky colonel. 823.6465

—— Len Gausett.   823.5500

Reade, C: The box tunnel. 10 pp. (Johnson, R., *ed. Little classics*, v. 9.   p. 217, *in* 829.132

—— Christie Johnstone.   *in* 823.5420

—— *Same.*   *in* 823.5429; 823.7410

—— *Same,* and other stories.   823.1285

Contents:—Christie Johnstone.—Clouds and sunshine.—Art: a dramatic tale.—Propria quæ maribus. A jeu d'esprit.—The box tunnel: a fact.—Jack of all trades: a matter-of-fact romance.

English Fiction. *Contin.*
Reformation of the 16th century. *Contin.*
In Germany. Charles, *Mrs.* E.. (R.) Chronicles of the Schönberg-Cotta family.
823.204
In Italy. Cross, *Mrs.* M.. A. (E.) Romola.
(Savonarola.) 823.1003
In Scotland. Oliphant, *Mrs.* M. O. (W.)
Magdalen Hepburn. *in* 823.5084
In Spain. Charles, *Mrs.* E.. (R.) The martyrs of Spain. 823.6598

Note.—For bibliography, *see* **Cornell University**. Catalogue of the historical library of A. D. White (compiled by G: L. Burr). Pt. 1. The Protestant Reformation and its forerunners. 1889. **
16.220.—**Eamaus,** J. Reading notes on Luther. 16 pp. (*From* Mercantile Lib. bulletin.) 1883. ** 16. 219.—**Fisher,** *Dr.* G. P. History of the Reformation. 1883. (Bibliography, pp. 567-591.) 274.28.—**Hurst,** J. F. Bibliotheca theologica. 1883. ** 16. 8a.—**Malcolm,** H. Theological index. 1868. ** 16.237.—**Schaff,** P. History of the Christian church. v. 6: The German Reformation, 1517-1530. 1888. (General literature, pp. 89-93; literature of the German Reform, p. 94; with additional ref. in each chapter.) 270.160.—**Seebohm,** F. The era of the Protestant revolution. 2d ed. 1875. (Notes on books in English relating to the Reformation. pp. 239-246.) 274.13.
In general. **Coxe,** W. House of Austria. 4 vols. 1864. 943.17-20.—**Hallam,** H: Europe during the middle ages. 3 vols. 1872. 940.2-4.—**Hardwi k,** C: History of the Christian church during the Reformation, 3d ed., by W. Stubbs. 1886. 274.58.—**Lindsay,** *Prof.* T. M. The Reformation. (Handb. ser., conc. and admir. arrng.) 1884. 274.66.—**Merle d'Aubigné,** J. H. History of the Reformation in the 16th century. 1872. *274.6.—**Ranke.** L. von. History of the popes, and their conflicts with Protestantism in xvi-xviith centuries. 3 vols. 1878. 282.55-7.—**Robertson,** W: History of Emperor Charles V. 3 vols. 1878. 923.121-3.—**Roscoe,** W: Life and pontificate of Leo X. 2 vols. 1846. 922.7.—**Schlegel,** K. W. F. Lectures on modern history (12th lecture). 1878. p. 158, *in* 901.11.—**Smyth,** W. Lectures on modern history. v. 1 (9th and 10th lectures). 1854. p. 245, *in* 901.9.—**Stebbing,** W. History of the Reformation. 2 vols. 1833. 274.69-70.—**Villers,** C. F. D. Spirit and influence of the Reformation. 1836. 274.71.—**Waddington,** G: Reformation on the continent. 3 vols. 1841. 274.72-4.
For Reformation in *Bohemia, see* **Loserth,** *Dr.* J. Wyclif and Hus. 1884. 274.65.
In England. **Blunt,** J. H. Reformation of the Church of England (1514-1547). (High Church view.) 1869. 283.57.—**Burnet,** G. History of the Reformation of the Church of England. 7 vols. 1865. 270.1-7.—**Hume,** D. History of England. 6 vols. (Protestant.) 942.65-70.—**Lingard,** J: History of England. 10 vols. (Catholic.) 942.87-96.—**Neal,** D. History of the Puritans. 2 vols. 1856. (Puritan view.) 277.12-13.
In France. **Caldwell,** *Mrs.* A. Marsh- Protestant Reformation in France. 2 vols. 1851. 274.14-15.—**Capefigue,** J. B. H. R. Histoire de la réforme et la ligne. 8 vols. 1834-5. (Roman Catholic view.) 274.75-82.—**Froude** J. A. Calvinism. (*In his* Short studies, etc., v. 2.) 824.33.—**Ranke,** *Prof.* L. von. Civil wars and monarchy in France (16th and 17th centuries). 2 vols. 1852. 944.788-9.—**White,** H: Massacre of St. Bartholomew (1500-1574). 1871. 944.40.
In Germany. **Bayne,** P: Martin Luther: his life and work. 2 vols. 1887. 922.348-9.—**Carlyle,** T: Martin Luther. (Ferris, G. T. *Great leaders.*) 1889. p. 222, *in* 920.329.—**Häusser,** L. The period of the Reformation, 1517-1648. 1885. 274.67.—**Köstlin,** J: Life of Luther. 1883. 922.263.—**Hallam,** H. Luther, Martin. (*In his* Literature of Europe, v. 2.) 1871. *in* 809.4.—**Schmidt,** C. Philipp Melanchton, 1861. 922.352.—**Ranke,** L. von. History of the Reformation in Germany. 3 vols. 1845-47. 274.59-61.
In Italy. **Villari,** *Prof.* P. Life and times of Savonarola. 2 vols. 1889. 922.327-8.
In the Netherlands. **Motley,** J. L. Dutch Republic. 3 vols. 1879. 949.10-12.

English Fiction. *Contin.*
Reformation of the 16th century. *Contin.*
Note. Contin.
In Poland. **Krasiński,** *Count* P. Historical sketch . . of the Reformation in Poland. 2 vols. 1838-40. 274.83-4.
In Scotland. **Burton,** J: H. History of Scotland. 9 vols. 1873. 941.121-9.
See also **Catalogues** of this Library.
No. 2, 1880, p. 191. No. 5, 1888, p. 300.
No. 3, 1882, p. 160.
See also **Poole's Index** (to 1882). pp. 1,089-90, *in* ** 50.1:—*Same,* Jan. 1, 1882, to Jan. 1, 1887. p. 367, *in* ** 50.1².

Refugee, The. Melville, H. 823.1148
Regent's daughter. Dumas, A. D. 823.2739
Same. 823.6517
Regimental legends. Stannard, *Mrs.* H. E.
V. (P.) *in* 823.6607
Reginald Archer. Seemuller, *Mrs.* A.. M.
(C.) 823.4264
Reginald Dalton. Lockhart, J: G. 823.4511
Reichenbach, Moritz von, *pseud.* *See* Bethusy-Huc, Valeska, *Gräfin.*
Reid, Christian, *pseud.* *See* Tiernan, *Mrs.* F.. C. (Fisher).
Reid, Mayne. *See* Reid, T: Mayne.
Note.—Captain Reid was christened T: Mayne, but in after life was known only as Mayne. Lib. jl., p. 253; Aug., 1890.
Reid, *Capt.* T: Mayne. Afloat in the forest; or, a voyage among the tree-tops.
808.436
—— The boy hunters; or, adventures in search of a white buffalo. 808.758
—— The boy slaves. 808.422
—— Bruin: the grand bear hunt. 808.426
—— The bush-boys; or, the history and adventures of a cape farmer and his family in the wild karoos of southern Africa.
808.756
—— The child wife. 823.6334
—— The cliff-climbers. (A sequel to The plant-hunters.) 808.757
—— The desert home; or, the adventures of a lost family in the wilderness. 808.431
Issued also as English family Robinson.
—— The English family Robinson. 808.431
—— Finger of fate. 823.5018
—— The forest exiles; or, the perils of a Peruvian family amid the wilds of the Amazon. 808.434
—— The Free Lances: a romance of the Mexican valley. 823.6335
—— Gaspar, the gaucho: a tale of the Gran Chaco. 808.1579
—— Giraffe-hunters. 808.432
—— No quarter! 823.6336
—— Plant hunters; or, adventures among the Himalaya mountains. 808.430
—— The quadroon; or, adventures in the far west. 823.1297
Issued also as Love's vengeance.
—— The scalp hunters; or, adventures among the trappers. 808.437
—— The vee-boers: a tale of adventure in southern Africa. 808.1463
—— Wild life; or, adventures on the frontier: a tale of the early days of the Texan republic. 808.429
—— The wood-rangers; or, the trappers of Sonora. 823.7145

English Fiction. *Contin.*

Reid, *Capt.* T: Mayne. *Contin.*
—— The young voyageurs; or, the boy hunters in the north: with a memoir by R: H: Stoddard. 808.1681
—— The young yägers; or, a narrative of hunting adventures in southern Africa. 808.1466
Reid, T: Wemyss. Mauleverer's millions: a Yorkshire romance. *in* 823.5090
Reigning belle, The. Stephens, *Mrs.* A. S. (W.) 823.1974
Rejected wife. Stephens, *Mrs.* A. S. (W.) 823.1975
Remarkable history and daring exploits of Valentine and Orson, the two sons of the emperor of Greece. 823.1900
Remarkable history of Sir Thomas Upmore. Blackmore, R: D. 823.4761
Remember the Alamo. Barr, *Mrs.* A. E. (H.) 823.5702
Remorse. Blanc, *Mme.* M. T. (de S.) 823.2329
Rena. Hentz, *Mrs.* C. L. (W.) 823.762
Rent in a cloud, A. Lever, C: J: *in* 823.971
Repented at leisure. Braine, *Mrs.* C.. M. (L.) *in* 823.5036
Repository tales. More, H. 823.1168
Reprinted pieces. Dickens, C: J: H. 823.394
Same. *in* 823.412; *in* 823.414
Same. *in* 823.4750; *in* 823.4957
Same. *in* 823.5302; *in* 823.6585
Reproach of Annesley. Uttiet, M. G. 823.5475
Residuary legatee, The. Stimson, F: J. *in* 823.5457
Resolution. Roe, A. S. 823.2021
Retribution. Southworth, *Mrs.* E. D. E. (N.) 823.1506
Return of the native, The. Hardy, T: 823.700
Reuben: a prince in disguise. Holding, C. B. 823.7259
Reuben Davidger, The adventures of. Greenwood, J. 823.6018
Reuter, Fritz. An old story of my farming days. Tr. by M. W. MacDowall. 2 pts. *in* 823.5030
Revenge. 8 pp. Pfleger, G. p. 269, *in* 823.6534
Reverberator, The. James, H:, *Jr.* 823.5412
Reverend idol, A. Noble, L. G. 823.4546
Reveries of a bachelor. Mitchell, D. G. 823.5289
Revolution in Tanner's lane. White, W. H. 823.5272
Reybaud, *Mrs.* Henriette Étiennette Fanny (Arnaud). Claude Stocq. (*With* Cousin Geoffry. By T. E: Hook.) *in* 823.812
Reynolds, Beatrice, *pseud.* *See* Sheppard, E.. S..
Reynolds, G: W. M. The necromancer; or, the mysteries of the court of Henry the Eighth. 823.6339
Rheil, Marie. The farm of Muiceron. Tr. by Mrs. A. B. Storrs. (*With* Madame Agnes. By C: Dubois.) *in* 823.6285

English Fiction. *Contin.*

Rhine, The. *See also* Germany: *The Rhine,* p. 102.
—— Abbott, J. Rollo on the Rhine. 808.920
—— Champney, *Mrs.* E.. (W.) Three Vassar girls on the Rhine. 808.1827
Rhoda Fleming. Meredith, G: 823.5381
Rhode Island. *See* New England.
Rhodes, *City and island.*
—— James, G: P. R. Bertrand de la Croix; or, the siege of Rhodes. 19 pp. (*In his* Eva St. Clair, and other tales.) p. 45, *in* 823.5892
—— *Same.* (*In* Club-book; ed. by A. Picken.) p. 15, *in* 823.702
Note.—See Torr, C. Rhodes in ancient times. 1885. 938.94;—Rhodes in modern times. 1887. 915. 383.
Rhona. Bridges, *Mrs. Col.* —. 823.3513
Same. *in* 823.5120
Rice, James, *joint author.* *See* Besant, W.
Rice, M. Spring. A king and not a king. 808.1724
Rich husband. Riddell, *Mrs.* C.. E. L. (C.) 823.1335
Richard Coer de Lion. 2 pts. Weber, H: W: p. 1, *in* * 821.1240
Richard Edney and the governor's family. Judd, S. 823.2340
Richard Feverel, The ordeal of. Meredith, G: 823.6619
Richard Hurdis. Simms, W: G. 823.1442
Richard Vandermarck. Harris, *Mrs.* M. (C.) 823.706
Richards, *Mrs.* Laura E.. (Howe). Queen Hildegarde: a story for girls. 808.1539
Richardson, *Mrs.* Abby (Sage). Stories from old English poetry. 808.1690
Contents:—Chaucer, G. The two noble kinsmen; —The pious Constance;—The knight's dilemma.— Three unknown poets. Patient Griselda.—Story of Candace. (From Chaucer and Spenser.)—Greene, R. Friar Bacon's brass head;—Margaret, the fair maid of Fresingfield.—Lyly, J: Campaspe and the painter.—Shakespeare, W: The story of Perdita; —Story of Lear and his three daughters;—The witty Portia; or, the three caskets;—Story of Rosalind; or, as you like it;—Macbeth, king of Scotland;—The wonderful adventures of Pericles, prince of Tyre;— The tempest;—Sketch of Shakespeare.—Spenser, E. Adventures of the fair Florimel.
Richardson, B: Ward. The son of a star: a romance of the second century. 823.6943
Richardson, S: Clarissa [Harlowe]; or, the history of a young lady. Condensed by C. H. Jones. 823.1316
—— *Same.* 8 vols. (Barbauld, *Mrs.* A. L. (A.), *ed. The British novelists,* vols. 1-8.) ** 823.2062-9
—— Pamela; or, virtue rewarded. 14th ed. 4 vols. * 823.1317-20
—— Sir Charles Grandison, History of. 7 vols. (Barbauld, *Mrs.* A. L. (A.), *ed. The British novelists,* vols. 9-15.) ** 823.2070-6
—— Works; with a prefatory chapter of biographical criticism by Leslie Stephen. Port. 12 vols. ** 823.6161-72
vols. 1-3: Pamela; or, virtue rewarded. ** 823.6161-3
vols. 4-8: History of Clarissa Harlowe. ** 823.6164-8
vols. 9-12: History of Sir Charles Grandison. ** 823.6169-72

English Fiction. *Contin.*

Richelieu. James, G: P. R. 823.875

Richter, Johann Paul Friedrich. Campaner Thal, and other writings. 823.6818
Contents:—Campaner Thal. Tr. by Julliette Bauer.—Life of Quintus Fixlein. Tr. by T: Carlyle. —Schmelzle's journey to Flätz. Tr. by T: Carlyle. —Analects from Richter. Tr. by T: De Quincey.— Miscellaneous pieces.

—— Flower, fruit, and thorn pieces; or, the wedded life, death, and marriage of Firmian Stanislaus Siebenkæs, parish advocate in the burgh of Kuhschnappel. Tr. by A. Ewing. With a memoir of the author by T: Carlyle. 823.2144

—— *Same.* Tr. E: H: Noel. 2 vols. 823.6816–17

—— Hesperus; or, forty-five dog-post-days: a biography. Tr. by C: T. Brooks. 2 vols. 823.6814–15

—— The invisible lodge. Tr. by C: T. Brooks. 823.4613

—— Schmelzle's journey to Flætz. (*Also*) Life of Quintus Fixlein. (Carlyle, T:, *tr. Tales, etc.,* v. 2.) *in* 823.6831

—— Titan: a romance. Tr. by C: T. Brooks, 2 vols. 823.6810–11

Ricketicketack. Conscience, H. p. 145, *in* 823.5704

Riddell, *Mrs.* C.. Eliza Lawson (Cowan). [*G. F. Trafford.*]

—— Austin Friars. 823.1321
—— City and suburb. 823.1322
—— The earl's promise. 823.1323
—— Far above rubies. 823.1324
—— Frank Sinclair's wife, and Forewarned, forearmed. 823.1325
—— Forewarned, forearmed. (*With her* Frank Sinclair's wife.) 823.1325
—— George Geith of Fen Court. 823.1326
—— Home, sweet home. 823.1327
—— Joy after sorrow. 823.1328
—— A life's assize. 823.1329
—— *Same.* *in* 823.6213
—— Miss Gascoigne: a novel. 823.5593
—— Mortomley's estate. 823.1331
—— My first love, and My last love. 823.1332
—— The nun's curse. 823.5368
—— Phemie Keller. 823.1333
—— The rich husband. 823.1335
—— The ruling passion. 823.1336
—— Susan Drummond. 823.7062
—— Too much alone. 823.5203
—— *Same.* 823.5963
—— The world in the church. 823.1338

Riddell, *Mrs.* J. H. *See* Riddell, *Mrs.* C.. E. L. (C.)

Riddle, Albert Gallatin. The house of Ross, and other tales. 823.7144

Ride for life. 30 pp. (*In* Tales from Blackwood. 2d ser., v. 11.) *in* 823.7495

Rideing, W: H: Young folks' history of London. 942.1309

——, *joint author. See* Lathrop, G: P.

Rideout, *Mrs.* J. B. Early western life. 808.1596

Ridgely, James Lot, *and* Donaldson, Paschal, *eds.* The Odd-fellows' offering, for 1848. Illus. ** 823.6220

English Fiction. *Contin.*

Ridley, James. Tales of the genii. (Weber, H: *Tales of the east,* v. 3.) p. 417, *in* ** 823.6232

Rienzi. Lytton, E: G: E. L. Bulwer- 823.1039
—— *Same.* ** 823.6762

Rifle, rod, and gun in California. Van Dyke, T. S. 823.4157

Right at last, and other tales. Gaskell, *Mrs.* E.. C. (S.) 823.605

Right Honourable, The. McCarthy, J., *and* Praed, *Mrs.* R. (M.-P.) C. 823.5488

Right one, The. Schwartz, *Mrs.* M. S. (B.) 823.6048

Ring, Ivar, *pseud. See* Mecklenburg, *Mrs.* A. (S.)

Ring, Max. John Milton and his times. Tr. by F. Jordan. 823.5964

Ring of Amasis, The. Lytton, E: R. Bulwer- 823.7053

Righted wrong, A. Yates, E. H. 823.1755

Ripley, Eliza McHatton- From flag to flag: a woman's adventures and experiences in the south during the war, in Mexico, and in Cuba. 823.5439

Rise of Iskander. Disraeli, B: *in* 823.460

Rise of Silas Lapham, The. Howells, W: D. 823.4867

"Rita," *pseud. See* Booth, *Mrs.* E. M. J. (G.) von.

Ritchie, *Mrs.* A.. Cora (Ogden). Mimic life; or, before and behind the curtain: a series of narratives. (Theatrical experiences.) 823.7516

Ritchie, *Mrs.* A.. I.. (Thackeray). Bluebeard's keys, and other stories. 823.5984

—— Miss Angel. (Angelica Kauffman.) 823.5986
—— Mrs. Dymond. *in* 823.5138
—— Old Kensington. 823.5985
—— *Same.* *in* 823.6261
—— The story of Elizabeth. 823.1569
—— Village on the cliff, and other stories and sketches. 823.1570

Ritchie, Leitch. The cheaterie packman. (Picken, A., *ed.* The club-book, v. 2.) *in* 823.702
—— Romance of history: France. 823.1278

Rival belles, The. Jones, J: B. 823.905

Rivals, The. Griffin, G. 823.676

Rivers of ice. Ballantyne, R. M. 808.814

Rives, Amélie. *See* Chanler, *Mrs.* A. (R.)

Roanoke of Roanoke Hall. Bell, M. 823.6344

Rob of the bowl. Kennedy, J: P. 823.928
—— *Same.* 2 vols. ** 823.6630–31

Rob Roy. Scott, *Sir* W. 823.1408
—— *Same.* 823.5161; ** 823.6025

Rob Roy, Adventures of. Grant, J. 823.647

Robb, J: S. ["*Madison Tensas*" *M. D. and* . "*Solitaire.*"] Swamp doctor's adventures in the south-west. 823.1340

Robbery under arms. Boldrewood, R. 823.7168

Robbing Peter to pay Paul. Saunders, J: 823.4816

English Fiction. *Contin.*
Robert; or, the influence of a good mother, and other stories, original and translated.
823.5811
Robert Elsmere. Ward, *Mrs.* M.. A. (A.)
823.5342
Robert Falconer. MacDonald, G: 823.1067
Robert Graham. Hentz, *Mrs.* C. L. (W.)
823.763
Robert Greathouse. Swift, J: F.   823.1536
Robert Helmont. Daudet, A.   823.6331
Roberts, Margaret. A child of the revolution.   *in* 823.5033
—— In the olden time.   823.5792
—— Noblesse oblige.   823.1342
—— *Same.*   823.5789
    Note.—Published in London under the title, "The atelier du Lys; or, an art student in the reign of terror."
—— On the edge of the storm.   823.1341
Roberts, Morley. In low relief: a Bohemian transcript.   823.7411
Robertson, Margaret M. By a way she knew not: a story of Allison Bain.
823.7087
—— The two Miss Jean Dawsons.   823.2335
Robertson, Muirhead. A Lombard street mystery: a detective story.   823.5457
Robin. Parr, *Mrs.* L.. (T.)   823.3711
Same.   823.6686
Robin Tremayne. Holt, E. S..   823.5724
Robinson, *Mrs.* Annie Douglas (Green). [*Marian Douglas.*] Peter and Polly.
823.4072
Robinson, E: A., *and* Wall, G: A. The disk: a tale of two passions.   823.4727
Robinson, F.. Mabel. [*F. Stephenson Griggs.*]
—— Mr. Butler's ward.   *in* 823.4987
—— The plan of campaign: a story of the fortune of war. 2 vols.   823.7224-5
—— A woman of the world: an every-day story. 3 vols.   823.7329-31
Robinson, F: W: Anne Judge, spinster. 3 vols.   823.4128-30
—— A fair maid.   823.7063
—— Jenny's girl. 11 pp. (*In* Twenty novelettes, etc.)   p. 241, *in* 823.7183
—— Othello the second.   823.4383
—— A woman's ransom.   823.4693
Robinson, J.. Cæsar Borgia.   823.2027
—— The gold-worshippers.   823.1343
—— Madeleine Graham.   823.1344
—— The maid of Orleans.   823.2025
—— Owen Tudor: an historical romance.
823.1345
—— Westminster Abbey; or, the days of the reformation.   823.2026
—— Whitefriars; or, the days of Charles the Second: an historical romance. (Anon.)
823.1346
—— Whitehall; or, the days of Charles the First: an historical romance.   823.1347
Robinson, *Dr.* J. H. Nick Whiffles, the trapper guide: a tale of the north-west.
823.1353
Robinson, *Mrs.* Therese Albertine Luise (von Jakob). [*Talvj.*] Heloise; or, the unrevealed secret.   823.1542

English Fiction. *Contin.*
Robinson Crusoe. De Foe, D.   808.368
Same.   823.2128; 823.2147
Same. p. 163, *in* ** 823.6215; ** 823.6627
Same. 2 vols.   ** 823.2077-8
Robur the conqueror. Verne, J. *in* 823.5127
Roche, Regina Maria. Children of the abbey.
823.1354
Rochefort, Henri. *See* Rochefort, V. H.
Rochefort, Victor Henri, *marquis de Roche-fort-Luçay.* Mademoiselle Bismarck. Tr. by V. Champlin.   823.4187
Rock ahead, The. Yates, E.   823.1756
Roderick Hudson. James, H:, *Jr.*   823.886
Roderick Hume. Bardeen, C. W.   823.4144
Roderick Random, Adventures of. Smollett, T. G: 823.1473
Rodman the keeper. Woolson, C. F.
823.2039
Rodney the partisan. Fosdick, C: A.
808.1704
Roe, Azel Stevens. How could he help it? or, the heart triumphant.   823.1362
   Issued also as Give me thine heart.
—— James Montjoy; or, I've been thinking.
823.2022
   Issued also as I've been thinking.
—— Resolution; or, the soul of power.
823.2021
—— The star and the cloud; or, a daughter's love.   823.1365
—— To love and to be loved, and The minister's story.   823.1366
—— True to the last; or, alone on a wide, wide sea.   823.1367
   Issued also as Faithful to the end.
Roe, E: Payson.
—— Barriers burned away.   823.1355
—— A day of fate.   823.2341
—— Driven back to Eden.   823.4859
—— The earth trembled.   823.5270
—— A face illumined.   823.1356
—— Found, yet lost.   823.5481
—— From jest to earnest.   823.1357
—— He fell in love with his wife.   823.5540
—— His sombre rivals.   823.4609
—— The hornet's nest: a story of love and war.   823.6971
—— A knight of the nineteenth century.
823.1358
—— "Miss Lou."   823.5523
—— Nature's serial story.   823.5524
—— Near to nature's heart.   823.1359
—— Opening a chestnut burr.   823.1360
—— An original belle.   823.4858
—— Taken alive, and other stories. With an autobiography.   823.6549
—— An unexpected result, and other stories.
823.4506
—— What can she do?   823.1361
—— Without a home.   823.7443
—— A young girl's wooing.   823.4870
Roe, E: Reynolds. Dr. Caldwell; or, the trail of the serpent.   823.7412
Roe, *Mrs.* J. Harcourt. Bachelor vicar of Newforth.   *in* 823.5108
Roe, M.. Abigail. [*C. M. Cornwall.*] Free, yet forging their own chains.   823.1368
Roger Berkeley's probation. Campbell, H.. S.   823.5250

English Fiction. *Contin.*

Roger Willoughby. Kingston, W: H: G.
808.1578
Rogue, The. Norris, W: E: 823.5582
Rogue's life, A. Collins, W: W. 823.266
Rohlfs, *Mrs.* A.. K.. (Green).
—— Behind closed doors. 823.7147
—— The forsaken inn. 823.7241
—— Hand and ring. 823.4696
—— The Leavenworth case: a lawyer's story.
823.663
—— A matter of millions. 823.7512
—— The mill mystery. 823.7148
—— A strange disappearance. 823.664
—— The sword of Damocles: a story of New
York life. 823.7149
Roland, The story of. Baldwin, J. 823.5624
Roland Blake. Mitchell, S. W. 823.5245
Roland Cashel. Lever, C: J. 823.991
Same. 2 vols. 823.5714-15; 823.6927-8
Roland Yorke. Wood, *Mrs.* E. (P.)
823.6005
Rollins, *Mrs.* Ellen Chapman (Hobbs). [*E.
H. Arr.*] Old-time child-life. 808.1530
Roman singer. Crawford, F. M. 823.4737
Roman traitor, The. Herbert, H: W:
823.5620
Romance at the antipodes. Douglass, *Mrs.*
R. Dun. 823.7038
Romance of a black veil. Brame, *Mrs.* C..
M. (L.) *in* 823.5013
Romance of a mummy. Gautier, T.
823.4544
Romance of a poor young man. Feuillet, O.
823.2495
Same. *in* 823.4986; *in* 823.5021; 823.6864
Same. 823.6887
Romance of a shop. Levy, A. 823.7142
Romance of an honest woman. Cherbuliez,
V. 823.7119
Romance of Beauseincourt. Warfield, *Mrs.*
C. A. (W.) 823.1840
Romance of Dollard. Catherwood, *Mrs.* M..
(H.) 823.6555
Romance of history: England. Neele, H:
823.1182
——: France. Ritchie, L. 823.1278
——: India. Caunter, H. 823.194
——: Italy. MacFarlane, C: 823.1072
——: Spain. Trueba y Cosio, T. de. 823.1639
Romance of Jenny Harlowe. Russell, W: C.
823.6546
Romance of old court-life in France. Elliot,
F.. 823.6050
Romance of perfume lands, A. Clifford, F.
S. 823.7539
Romances of real life. 2 vols. Huut, J. H:
L. 823.5461-2
Romance of student life abroad. Kimball,
R: B. 823.5734
Romance of the canoness, The. Heyse, J.
L. P. 823.5618
Romance of the forest. Radcliffe, *Mrs.* A.
(W.) 823.1281
Same. 2 vols. ** 823.2104-5
Romance of the nineteenth century, A.
Mallock, W: H. 823.5585
Romance of the revolution. Bunce, O. B.
823.157

English Fiction. *Contin.*

Romance of war, The. Grant, J. 823.648
Romances of the east. Gobineau, J. A.,
comte de. 823.2323
Romantic adventures of a milkmaid. Hardy,
T: *in* 823.4999
Romantic tales. Lewis, M. G. 823.4275
Romany rye, The. Borrow, G: 823.4586
Rome.
—— Abbott, J. Rollo in Rome. 808.925
—— Beesly, *Mrs.* —. Stories from the history
of Rome. 808.841
—— Berens, E. M. Myths and legends of
ancient . . . Rome. 292.42
—— Bonner, J: A child's history of Rome.
2 vols. 808.623-4
v. 1: B. C. 282-B. C. 61.
v. 2: B. C. 57-A. D. 476.
—— Busk, R. H. Roman legends: a collec-
tion of the fables and folk-lore of Rome.
829.31
—— Butterworth, H. Zigzag journeys in
classic lands. 808.1816
—— Hanson, C: H: Wanderings of Æneas
and the founding of Rome. 808.1494
—— Lander, S.. W. Rome. 808.102
—— Yonge, C.. M.. Young folks' history of
Rome. 808.749
ANCIENT HISTORY.
8TH CENTURY B. C. Metastasio, P. A. D. B.
T. Romulus and Hersilia; drama.
in 822.1127
7TH CENTURY B. C. Marmontel, J. F. Aris-
tomène; trag. *in* 894.41
Horatii and Curiatii, B. C. 669.
—— Corneille, P. Horace; trag. ** 842.105
—— *Same.* ** 842.121
—— Whitehead, W: The Roman father;
trag. *in* ** 822.1019
Note.—For Regal period, B. C. 753-508, *see* Bibliography. Adams, C. K. Histories of Rome. (*In
his* Man. of hist. lit., 3d ed.) 1889. pp. 121-61, *in* * 907.
4³.—Middleton, J. H: Ancient Rome 1885.
(Sources of information, pp. xi-xxvi.) 945.74.—
Gilman, A. The story of Rome from the earliest
times (to B. C. 44). (Story of the nations.) 1890.
937.162.—Ihne, W. Early Rome. (B. C. 753-343) 1886.
937.133.—Lewis, *Sir* G. C. Inquiry into the credi-
bility of the early Roman history. 2 vols. 1855.
937.100-1.—Livius Patavinus, T. History of
Rome. 4 vols. 1877. 937.74-7.—Merivale, C: Gen
eral history of Rome. B. C. 753-A. D. 476. 1881.
937.42.—Plutarch's Lives of Romulus, Numa, and
Puplicola. 920.10.—Smith, P. Ancient history.
(Earliest record to A. D. 476.) 3 vols. 930.30-2.
6TH CENTURY B. C.
Brutus.
—— Alfieri, V. Brutus (first); trag. 852.2
—— Payne, J: H. Brutus; trag.
in * 928.104
—— Voltaire, F. M. A. de. Brutus; trag.
in 842.215
5TH CENTURY B. C. Macaulay, T: B. The
battle of Lake Regillus; poem. (*In his*
Lays of ancient Rome.) p. 171, *in* 824.137
Coriolanus, B. C. 491-488, etc. Drama by
W: Shakespeare. *in* 822.1026
Note.—For other editions, *see under* Shake-
speare *in* Catalogues of this Library.
No. 2, 1880, p. 207. No. 4, 1884, p. 265.
No. 3, 1882, p. 173. No. 5, 1888, p. 318.
Horatius Cocles. Poem by T: B. Macaulay.
(*In his* Lays of ancient Rome.)
p. 149, *in* 824.137

English Fiction. *Contin.*
Rome. *Contin.*
ANCIENT HISTORY. *Contin.*
5TH CENTURY B. C. *Contin.*
Virginia, B. C. 449.
—— Alfieri, V. Virginia; trag. 852.1
—— Chaucer, G. The doctoures tales. (*In his* Canterbury tales.) p. 323, *in* 821.87
—— Macaulay, T: B. Virginia. (*In his* Lays of ancient Rome.) p. 201, *in* 824.137
Appius Claudius. Appius and Virginia. (*Dodsley's Old Eng. plays*, v. 4.)
p. 105, *in* ** 822.295
Note.—For period B. C. 508–340 (Commonwealth), *see* Arnold, T. History of Rome. 3 vols. (in 1). 1851. 937.27.—Duruy, J. V. History of Rome. (v. 1: 753–216 B. C.) 1883. 937.153.—Livius Patavinus, T. History of Rome. (Books ii to vii.) 4 vols. 1877. 937.74-7.—Michelet, J. History of the Roman republic. 937.163.—Mommsen, C. M. T. History of Rome. 4 vols. 1875. 937.4-7.—Napoleon III. History of Julius Cæsar. 2 vols. 1865. 923.517-8.—Niebuhr, B. G: History of Rome, epitomised. 1845. 937.1.—Plutarch's Lives (of Publicola, Coriolanus, and Camillus). 920.10.
4TH CENTURY B. C. Marmontel, J. F. Denys-le-tyran; trag. p. 13, *in* 849.41
Note.—For period B. C. 340–264, *see* Arnold, T. History of Rome. 3 vols. (in 1). 1851. 937.27.—Duruy, J. V. History of Rome. (v. 1: 753–216 B. C.) 1883. 937.153.—Ihne, J. A. F. W. History of Rome. 5 vols. 1871–1882. 937.146-150. —Livius Patavinus, T. History of Rome. 4 vols. 1872. 937.44-7.—Mommsen, C. M. T. History of Rome. 4 vols. 1877. 937.4-7.—Plutarch's Lives (of Pyrrhus). 920.10.
3D CENTURY B. C.
First Punic war, 264–241. Flaubert, G. Salammbô. 843.848
Regulus. Tragedy by Metastasio. (*Dramas*, v. 3.) *in* 822.1127
Hannibal, 247–183.
—— Grillparzer, F. Hannibal; play. (*Sämmtl. Werke*, v. 5.) p. 319, *in* 832.13
—— Henty, G: A. The young Carthaginian. 808.1436
Sophonisba, Numidia, *d.* 203 B. C.
——; trag. Alfieri, V. p. 219, *in* 852.2
——; trag. Corneille, P. (French.) 842.106
2D CENTURY B. C.
Caius Gracchus, 154–121. Tragedy by J. S. Knowles. 822.1114
Numantine war, 133 B. C. Cervantes Saavedra, M. de. Numancia; trag. (Spanish.) p. 353, *in* 861.8
Note.—For period B. C. 264–133, *see* Arnold, T. History of Rome. 3 vols. 1851. 937.27.—Duruy, J. V. History of Rome. vols. 1 and 2. (v. 1: 753–216 B. C.; 2: 83–30 B. C.) 937.153-4.—Ihne, J. A. F. W. History of Rome. 5 vols. 1871–1882. 938.146-50.—Livius Patavinus, T. History of Rome. 4 vols. 1872. 937.44-7.—Mommsen, C. M. T. History of Rome. (v. 2: Book iii, chapters 11–12.) 937.5.—Nepos, C. Hannibal. (*In his* Vitæ.) 923.6.—Plutarch's Lives. (Fabius Maximus, Paulus Æmilius, Marcellus, Marcus Cato, and Flaminius.) 920.10.—Polybius. History of the wars of the Romans. 1812. 937.106.
1ST CENTURY, B. C. Corneille, P. Sertorius (In Spain B. C. 72); trag. (French.) 842.106
Sylla and Marius, 82, etc.
—— Caux, G. de. Marius; trag. (French.) p. 215, *in* 842.65
—— Otway, T: Caius Marius; trag. (*Works*, v. 2.) p. 109, *in* 822.454

English Fiction. *Contin.*
Rome. *Contin.*
ANCIENT HISTORY. *Contin.*
1ST CENTURY B. C. *Contin.*
Spartacus, 73–71.
—— Eckstein, E. Prusias: a romance of ancient Rome under the republic. 2 vols. 823.4731-2
—— Saurin, J. B. Spartacus; trag. (French.) (Petitot, C. B., *and* A. *Répert. théât. fr.*, v. 4.) p. 28, *in* 842.67
Catiline, 63 B. C.
—— Crébillon, P. J. de. Catiline; trag. (*Œuvres*, v. 2.) *in* 842.160
—— Herbert, H: W: Roman traitor; or, the days of Cicero, Cato and Cataline (*sic.*): a true tale of the republic. 823.5620
—— Jonson, B. Catiline; trag. (*Works*.) p. 272, *in* 822.121
—— Voltaire, F. M. A. de. Catiline (French); trag. (*Œuvres*, v.4.) p. 191, *in* 842.18
Cato the younger, Utica, kills himself, 46 B. C. Metastasio, P. A. D. B. T. Catone in Utica. (*Opere*, v. 1.) p. 179, *in* 822.1125
First triumvirate (Cæsar, Pompey, Crassus), 60 B. C.
—— Crébillon, P. J. de. Le triumvirat (French); trag. (*Œuvres*, v. 2.) p. 341, *in* 842.160
—— Voltaire, F. M. A. de. Le triumvirat (French); trag. (*Œuvres*, v. 4.) p. 105, *in* 842.19
Cæsar and Pompey's war, 50 B. C.
—— Beaumont, *and* Fletcher. The false one. (Cæsar at Alexandria); trag. p. 388, *in* 822.118
—— Chapman, G: Cæsar and Pompey; trag. (*Works*, v. 3.) p. 123, *in* 822.887
—— Corneille, P. Pompée (French); trag. p. 1, *in* 842.105
—— Lucan, M. A. Pharsalia; poem. 871.6
Cæsar killed, 44 B. C.
—— Alfieri, V. Bruto secondo. p. 365, *in* 852.2
—— Voltaire, F. M. A. de. La mort de César (French). (*Œuvres*, v. 2.) p. 325, *in* 842.16
See also Tragedies by W: Shakespeare.
Second triumvirate (Octavius, Antony, Lepidus), 43 B. C. Beaumont, *and* Fletcher. The false one; trag. p. 388, *in* 822.118
Cleopatra.
—— Alfieri, V. Antony and Cleopatra; trag. p. 419, *in* 852.2
—— Corneille, P. Pompée, altered by C. Cibber as "Cæsar in Egypt." 842.105
—— Dryden, J. All for love. (*Works*, v. 4.) p. 172, *in* ** 822.138
—— Hemans, *Mrs.* F. D. The last banquet of Antony and Cleopatra; poem. (*Works*, v. 2.) p. 97, *in* 821.154
—— Kotzebue, A. F. F. von. Cleopatra. (*Theater*, v. 14.) p. 193, *in* 832.72
—— Marmontel, J. F. Cléopâtre; trag. 849.41
—— Shakespeare, W: Antony and Cleopatra. 822.735

English Fiction. *Contin.*
Rome. *Contin.*
ANCIENT HISTORY. *Contin.*
1ST CENTURY B. C. *Contin.*

Note.—For other editions, *see under* Shakespeare *in* Catalogues of this Library.
No. 2, 1880, p. 207.　　No. 4, 1884, p, 265.
No. 3, 1882, p. 173.　　No. 5, 1688, p. 86.
Note.—For period B. C. 133-30, *see* Cæsar, C. J.
Commentaries. 937.53.—Cicero, M. T. Orations.
5 vols. 875.1-5.—Duruy, J. V. History of Rome.
v. 2. 937.154.—Forsyth, W: Life of Cicero. 2
vols. 928.4-5.—Ihne, W. History of Rome. 5 vols.
1882. 937.146-50.—Inge, W: R. Society in Rome
under the Cæsars. 1888. 937.151.—Judson, H. P.
Cæsar's army. 1888. 937.143.—Merivale, C: The
Roman triumvirates. 937.57.—Michelet, J. History of the Roman republic. 1863. 973.163.—
Mommsen, C. M. T. History of Rome. 4 vols.
1877. 937.4-7.—Napoleon III. Life of Cæsar. 2
vols. 923.517-18.—Paterculus, C. V. Compendium
of Roman history to the reign of Tiberius. 1876.
p. 425, *in* *937.18.—Plutarch's lives. (Gracchi,
Marius, Sylla, Lucullus, Crassus, and Sertorius,
Cicero, Pompey, Cæsar, Cato the Younger, Brutus,
and Antonius.) 920.10.—Reed, J. E. Lives of the
Roman emperors. (B. C. 100-A. D. 476.) 5 vols. **
920.335-9.—Sallustius Crispus, C. Conspiracy of
Catiline. p. 1, *in* 937.109;—The Jugurthine war.
937.18.—Smith, P. Ancient history. (*History of
the world*, v. 3.) 930.32.—Suetonius Tranquillus,
C. Lives of the twelve Cæsars. (Julius and Octavius.) 937.70.

ROMAN EMPIRE, B. C. 31-A. D. 192.
AUGUSTUS, B. C. 31-A. D. 14.
—— Becker, W. A. Gallus, manners and
customs. 1876.　　　　　　390.5
—— Corneille, P. Cinna; drama. (French.)
842.105
—— Jonson, B. The poetaster; drama.
p. 105, *in* 822.121
—— Tieck, L. Kaiser Octavianus; drama.
(*Schriften*, v. 1.)　　　　830.62
Octavia, sister of Augustus, d. B. C. 11.
——. Alfieri, V.　　　p. 365, *in* 852.1
——; *tr.* Kotzebue, A. F. F. von. (*The-
ater*, v. 12.)　　　p. 29, *in* 832.71
TIBERIUS, A. D. 14-37.
—— Graham, J: W. Neæra: a tale of an-
cient Rome.　　　　　823.6904
—— Jonson, B. Sejanus; trag.
p. 137, *in* 822.121
CLAUDIUS, A. D. 41-54. Kotzebue, A. A.
F. von. (*Theater*, v. 21.) p. 67, *in* 832.76
Britannicus. Trag. Racine, J. (*Œuvres*,
v. 2.)　　　　　　　842.124
Messalina (executed A. D. 48); trag. Logan,
A. S.　　　　　　　822.1100
NERO, A. D. 54-68.
—— Berry, E: P. Leah of Jerusalem: a
story of the times of Paul.　　823.6396
—— Baillie, J. The martyr; trag. (*Works*.)
p. 508, *in* 822.897
—— Eckstein, E. Nero. 2 vols. 823.7150-1
—— Story, W: W. Nero; hist. play.
822.282
Note.—For manners, *see* Martial's epigrams. **
871.7.

OTHO, A. D. 69. Corneille, P. Othon;
trag. (French.)　　　p. 132, *in* 842.106
VITELLIUS, A. D. 69.
—— Melville, G: J: Whyte- The gladiators:
a tale of Rome and Judæa.　** 823.4670
—— *Same.*　　　　　823.7402
VESPASIAN, A. D. 70-79. Alfieri, V. Otta-
via; trag.　　　　p. 365, *in* 852.1

English Fiction. *Contin.*
Rome. *Contin.*
ROMAN EMPIRE, B. C. 31-A. D. 192. *Con-
tin.*
TITUS, A. D. 79-81.
Corneille, P. Tite et Bérénice; drama.
(French.)　　　　p. 212, *in* 842.106
—— Metastasio, P. A. D. B. T. Titus;
drama.　　　　　　*in* 822.1125
—— Otway, T., *tr.* Titus and Bérénice;
drama. (*Works*, v. 1.) p. 169, *in* 822.453
—— Racine, J. Bérénice; trag. (French.\
in 842.124
Pompeii and Herculaneum, 79.
—— Holt, E. S. Slave girl of Pompeii.
808.1515
—— Lytton, E: G: E. L. Bulwer- Last days
of Pompeii.　　　　　823.1033
—— —— *Same.*　　　　823.6308
—— —— *Same.* 2 vols.　** 823.6734-5
—— Vestal, The; or, a tale of Pompeii.
(Anon.)　　　　　** 823.6252
DOMITIAN, A. D. 81-96.
—— Eckstein, E. Quintus Claudius: a ro-
mance of imperial Rome. 2 vols.
823.6982-3
—— Marks, *Mrs.* M.. A. M. (H.) Masters
of the world. 3 vols. 823.7203-5
—— Massinger, P. The Roman actor; play.
p. 172, *in* 822.124
EARLY CHRISTIANS.
—— Charles, *Mrs.* E.. (R.) Victory of the
vanquished.　　　　　823.211
—— Chateaubriand, F. A., *vicomte* de. Les
martyrs. 3 vols.　　　843.686-8
See also under names of emperors.
NERVA, A. D. 96-98. Eckstein, E. Quintus
Claudius: a romance of imperial Rome. 2
vols.　　　　　　　823.6982-3
TRAJAN, A. D. 98-117.
—— Lockhart, J: G. Valerius: a Roman
story. (Persecution of Christians.)
823.4513
—— —— *Same.* 2 vols.　** 823.6718-19
HADRIAN, A. D. 117-138.
—— Metastasio, P. A. D. B. T. Adriano in
Siria; play.　　　　*in* 822.1126
—— Pellico, S. Ester d'Engaddi; trag.
(*Opere*.)　　　p. 119, *in* 852.35
—— Richardson, B: W. The son of a star: a
romance of the second century. 823.6943
Note.—For manners, *see* Juvenalis, D. J. Sat-
ires. 874.2.
THE CHURCH IN THE SECOND CENTURY A.
D. Church, A. J: To the lions: a tale of
the early Christians.　　　823.6545
EXPOSITION OF EPICUREANISM. Pater, W. H.
Marius the epicurean: his sensations and
ideas. 2 vols.　　　　823.6197-8
Note.—For the period B. C. 31-A. D. 192 (the empire), *see* Capes, W. W. Roman empire of the 2d
century. 1887. 937.138.—De Quincey, T: The
Cæsars. *in* 829.87;—Duruy, J. V. History of Rome.
(v. 4: B. C. 30-A. D. 54; v. 5: A. D. 54-180.) * 937.
156-7;—Gibbon, E. Decline and fall of the Roman
empire. 6 vols. 937.8-13;—*Same.* 7 vols. 937.63-9.
—Josephus. Antiquities and wars of the Jews.
933.1.—Lecky, W. E. H. History of morals. (Account of persecution of Christians.) 177.55-6.—
Merivale, C. Romans under the empire. 7 vols.
937.34-40.—Milman, H. H. History of Christianity.

English Fiction. *Contin.*
Rome. *Contin.*
ROMAN EMPIRE, B. C. 31–A. D. 192. *Contin.*
  Note. Contin.
3 vols. 1871. 270.30-2.—**Paterculus, C. V.** Compendium of Roman history to the reign of Tiberius. 1876. p. 425, *in* * 937.18.—**Plutarch's Lives.** (Galba and Otho.) 920.10.—**Reed, J. E.** Lives of the Roman emperors. (B. C. 100–A. D. 476.) 5 vols. ** 920.335-9.—**Smith, P.** Ancient history. v. 3. 930.32.—**Suetonius Tranquillus, C.** Lives of the twelve Cæsars. 937.70.—**Tacitus, C. C.** Works. (v. 1: Annals; v. 2: History.) 2 vols. 937.14-15;—*Same.* 937.71-2.
  For illustration of the period, *see also* Lives of Augustus. (Encyclop. Britann., v. 23.) p. 534, *in* ** 32.293.—**Hadrian.** (Encyclop. Britann., v. 3.) p. 68, *in* ** 32.273.—**Nero.** (Encyclop. Britann., v. 17.) p. 357, *in* ** 32.287.—**Trajan.** (Encyclop. Britann., v. 23.) p. 534, *in* ** 32.293.
MAXIMIN, *d.* 238. Dryden, J: Tyrannic love; drama.   p. 380, *in* ** 822.136
VALERIAN, 253–260. Moore, T. The epicurean. (Worship of Isis in Egypt.)
                            187.2
CHRISTIANS PERSECUTED. *See names of emperors.*
—— Charles, *Mrs.* E.. (R.) Lapsed, but not lost.   823.2158
—— Corneille, P. Polyeucte in A. D. 250 (French); trag.   842.105
—— Dryden, J: Tyrannic love; trag.
              p. 380, *in* ** 822.136
—— Newman, J: H: Callista: a sketch of the third century.   823.1188
—— Quinton, M. A. The money-god; or, the empire and the papacy. 823.1279
ZENOBIA. (*Palmyra*, 266–273.)
——; trag. Metastasio, P. A. D. B. T.
                 in 822.1127
——; trag. Murphy, A. (*Works*, v. 1.)
           p. 107, *in* ** 822.32
AURELIAN, 276–282.
—— Milman, H. H. The martyr of Antioch; drama.   p. 115, *in* 821.1327
—— Ware, W: Aurelian; or, Rome in the third century. In letters of Lucius M. Piso, from Rome, to Fausta, the daughter of Gracchus, at Palmyra. 2 vols. 823.1648-9
  Note.—For period A. D. 193–284, *see* **De Quincey, T:** The Cæsars. *in* 829.87.—**Duruy, J. V.** History of Rome. (v. 6: A. D. 180–211; v. 7: A. D. 211–337.) 937.158-9.—**Gibbon, E.** Decline and fall of the Roman empire. 6 vols. 937.8-13;—*Same.* 7 vols. 937.63-9.—**Rawlinson, G:** Manual of ancient history. 1875. 930.21.—**Reed, J. E.** Lives of the Roman emperors. (B. C. 100–A. D. 476.) 5 vols. ** 920.335-39.
DIOCLETIAN, 284–305.
—— Crake, A. D. The victor's laurel: school-life during the tenth persecution in Italy.
                   823.7121
—— Eckstein, E. Chaldean magician: an adventure in Rome in the reign of the emperor Diocletian.   823.7125
—— Massinger, P. The virgin-martyr, Dorothea, 284; drama.   *in* 822.123
CONSTANTINE THE GREAT, 306–337.
—— Bayle, A. Thalia; or, Arianism and the council of Nice.   823.62
—— Kouns, N. C. Arius the Libyan: a romance of the primitive church. 823.7239
—— Lytton, E: R. Bulwer- Licinius; poem.
           p. 109, *in* 821.569

English Fiction. *Contin.*
Rome. *Contin.*
JULIAN THE APOSTATE, 361–363. Franco, J: J. Tigranes.   823.6891
VALENTINIAN, 364–375. Trag. Beaumont, and Fletcher.   p. 438, *in* 822.118
CHRISTIANS AT ALEXANDRIA. Kingsley, C: Hypatia (murdered 415).   823.933
  Note.—For period A. D. 284–395, *see* **Ammianus Marcellinus.** Roman history. 1862. 937.41.—**Duruy, J. V.** History of Rome. 8 vols. 1883. * 937.153-60.—**Eusebius Pamphilus.** Life of Constantine from A. D. 306–337. 1845. 270.88.—**Gibbon, E.** Decline and fall of the Roman empire. 6 vols. 937.8-13;—*Same.* 7 vols. 937.63-9.—**Reed, J. E.** Lives of the Roman emperors. (B. C. 100–A. D. 476.) 5 vols. ** 920.335-39.
HONORIUS. *Western empire*, 395–423. Wiseman, N. The hidden gem; drama. 822.649
CHRISTIANS. Charles, *Mrs.* E.. (R.) Conquering and to conquer.   823.205
THEODOSIUS. *Eastern empire*, 402–450.
—— Claudianus; poems (social aspects).
                 ** 871.29
—— Massinger, P. The emperor of the east.   p. 240, *in* 822.123
ALARIC, 410. Hemans, *Mrs.* F. D. Alaric in Italy; poem. (*Works*, v. 2.)
           p. 104, *in* 821.154
ATTILA, 450–451.
—— Corneille, P. Attila; drama. (French.) (*Œuvres*, v. 9.)   p. 188, *in* 842.106
—— James, G: P. R. Attila.   823.848
—— — *Same.*   823.7020
—— Niebelungenlied.   830.50
HERACLIUS, *Emperor of the East*, 610–641.
—— Collins, W: W: Antonina.   823.250
—— Wiseman, N. Fabiola; or, the church of the catacombs.   823.4615
  Note.—For period A. D. 395–476 (fall of the empire). *see* **Bury, J. B.** History of the later Roman empire. 395–800 A. D. 2 vols. 1889. 937.144-5.—**Döllinger, J. J. I. von.** First age of Christianity, and the church. 2 vols. 1862. 270.163-4.—**Duruy, J. V.** History of Rome. 8 vols. 937.153-60.—**Freeman, E: A.** Flavian Cæsars. (*In his* Hist. essays, 2d ser.) p. 307, *in* 904.17.—**Gibbon, E.** Decline and fall of the Roman empire. 6 vols. 937.8-13;—*Same.* 7 vols. 937.63-9.—**Merivale, C.** History of Rome. B. C. 753–A. D. 476. 937.42.—**Milman, H. H.** Latin Christianity. 8 vols. 270.41-8;—*Same.* 9 vols. 270. 50-8.—**Mommsen, C. M. T.** History of Rome. 4 vols. 937.4-7.—**Pressensé, E. D. de.** History of the early years of Christianity. 4 vols. 270.165-8.—**Reed, J. E.** Lives of the Roman emperors and their associates. (B. C. 100–A. D. 476.) 5 vols. ** 920.335-9.—**Renan, J, E.** The apostles. 1871. 209.24.—**Smith, P.** Ancient history. (Book 9.) 1866. 930.22.
  Note.—For later periods, *see under* Italy.

  For bibliography of Rome, *see* **Adams, C. K.** Histories of Rome. (*In his* Manual of hist. lit., 3d ed., 1889.) pp. 121-61, *in* * 907.4².—**Middleton, J. H.** Ancient Rome in 1885. (Sources of information, pp. xi-xxvi.) 945.74.
  For antiquities, etc., *see* **Lanciani, R.** Ancient Rome in the light of recent discoveries. 1889. 937.152.—**Smith, W.** Dictionary of Greek and Roman antiquities; rev. by C. Anthon. 1861. 930.27.
  See also **Catalogues** of this Library.
    No. 2, 1880, p. 197.   No. 5, 1888, p. 305.
    No. 3, 1882, p. 165.
  For description of the catacombs, *see* **Kip, W. J.** The catacombs of Rome, as illus. the Church of the first three centuries. 6th ed. 1890. 719.5.—**Northcote, J. S.** Epitaphs of the catacombs. 1878. (Christian inscriptions in Rome during the first four centuries.) 719.2.—**Parker, J. H.** Archæology of Rome. Pt. 9: Tombs in and near Rome. Pt. 10: Sculpture. 1877. 914.479.—**Rossi, G. B. de.** Roma

English Fiction. *Contin.*
Rome. *Contin.*

Note. Contin.
sotterranea; or, an account of the Roman catacombs, esp. of the cemetery of St. Callixtus. 3 vols.
(in 2). New ed. Plates. 1879. * 719.3-4.
See also Wiseman, N. Fabiola. 823.4615
On the religion of Rome, *see* Clarke, J. F. Ten
great religions. 2 vols. 1878-1883. (Sources of information. v. 2: pp. x-xx.) 208.2-2¹.—Coulanges,
F. de. Ancient city: religion, laws, etc. 1874.
930.58.—Merivale, C. Conversion of the Roman
empire. 1879. 258.10.
For a concise account of early Christian art and
antiquities, *see* Jameson, *Mrs.* A. M. Sacred and
legendary art. 2 vols. 1875. 700.2-3.
For manners and customs, *see* Becker, W. A.
Gallus: or, Roman scenes of the time of Augustus.
390.5.—Falke, J. von. Greece and Rome, their life
and art. 1882. * 930.235.—Guhl, E. K., *and* Koner,
W. Life of the Greeks and Romans. 1876. 930.48.
—Inge, W: R. Society in Rome under the Cæsars.
(1st cent.) 1888. 937.151.
For general histories, *see* Allen, W: F., *and*
Myers, P. V. N. Ancient history, pt. 2. Short history of the Roman people. (B. C. 332-A. D. 476.)
By W: F. Allen. 1890. 930.223.—Arnold, T. History of Rome. 937.27.—Cicero, M. T. Life and
letters. 923.516;—Orations. 4 vols. 875.6-9.—
Duruy, J. V. History of Rome. (B. C. 753-A. D.
395.) 8 vols. * 937.153-60.—Dyer, T: H. History of
the kings of Rome. 1868. 937.24.—Eliot, S: Liberty of Rome. 2 vols. 1849. 937.58-9.—Froude, J.
A. Cæsar: a sketch. 1880. 937.1048.—Gibbon, E.
Decline and fall of the Roman empire. 6 vols.
937.8-13.—Ihne, W. The history of Rome. 5 vols.
1871-82. 937.146-50.—Long, G: The decline of the
Roman republic. 5 vols. 1874. (Authorities
given.) 937.164-8.—Macaulay, T: B. Lays of ancient Rome. p. 747, *in* 824.69. *Note.*—The preface
is devoted to the ballad-poetry of Rome.—Merivale, C: General history of Rome. (B. C. 753-
A. D. 476.) 1881. 937.42;—History of the Romans
under the empire. (B. C. 100-A. D. 180.) 7 vols.
(Gives authorities.) 937.34-40.—Michelet, J. History of the Roman republic. (B. C. 809-30.) 1863.
937.163.—Mommsen, C. M. T. History of Rome.
4 vols. 937.4-7.—Niebuhr, B. G. History of Rome,
epitomized. 937.1²;—Lectures on the history of
Rome. 3 vols. 1853. 937.169-71.—Rawlinson, G:
Manual of ancient history. 1875. (Book v. gives
sources of information.) 930.21.—Reed, J. E. The
lives of the Roman emperors. (B. C. 100-A. D. 476.)
5 vols. ** 920.335-9.—Trollope, A. Life of Cicero.
2 vols. 928.311-12.—Vollgraff, J. C. Greek writers
of Roman history. 1880. 937.161.
For a rapid review of the progress and fall of the
empire, *see* Seeley, J. F. Roman imperialism.
1871. 824.81.
For military history, *see* Cæsar, C. J. Commentaries. 937.53.—Judson, H. P. Cæsar's army.
1888. 937.143.—Livius Patavinus, T. History of
Rome (to B. C. 166). 4 vols. 937.74-7.—Napoleon III. History of Julius Cæsar. 2 vols. 923.
517-18.—Polybius. History of the wars of the
Romans. 1812. ** 937.106.—Viollet-le-Duc, E.
Annals of a fortress. 1876. (Military engineering.)
623.2.
See also Catalogues of this Library.
No. 2, 1880, p. 197. No. 4, 1884, p. 253.
No. 3, 1882, p. 165. No. 5, 1888, p. 305.
See also Poole's Index (to 1882). p. 1,123-4, *in* **
50.1;—*Same,* Jan. 1, 1882-Jan. 1, 1887. p. 377, *in* **
50.1².
For general history of the city, *see* Dyer, T: H:
History of the city of Rome. 1865. 937.2.—Gre-
gorovius, F. Geschichte der Stadt Rom im Mittel-
alter vom V. bis zum xvi. Jahrhundert. 7 vols.
1869-73. * 945.117-23.—Hübner, J. A., *Freiherr*
von. Life of Sixtus V. (*see* pt. 3: pp. 149-180). 922.11.
For maps of the city, *see* Middleton, J. H. Ancient Rome in 1885. 945.74.
See also Catalogues of this Library. No. 2, 1880.
p. 197.
See also Ency. Brit., v. xx. ** 32.27K.
See also Poole's Index (to 1882). p. 1,124, *in* **
50.1;—*Same,* to Jan. 1, 1887. p. 377, *in* ** 50.1².

Romeo and Juliet. 54 pp. Black, W:
in 823.5131

English Fiction. *Contin.*

Romer, Jonathan. Kaloolah; or, journey-
ings to the Djébel Kumri; ed. by W. S.
Mayo. 823.1144
Romola. Cross, *Mrs.* M.. A. (E.) 823.1003
Rookstone. Macquoid, K.. S. 823.5979
Rookwood. Ainsworth, W: H. 823.26
Same. 823.5625
Rory O'More. Lover, S: 823.1017
Rosamond. Holmes, *Mrs.* M.. J.. (H.)
in 823.787
Rosaura: a tale of Madrid. 70 pp. (*In* Tales
from Blackwood, v. 9.) *in* ** 823.6655
Roscoe, T:, *tr.* German novelists: tales se-
lected from ancient and modern authors in
that language . . . Tr. from the originals;
with critical and biographical notices. 4
vols. ** 823.6826-9
Contents.—Düsching, J. G. G. Local popular
traditions. v. 2.—Eberhardt, (—). The Bet;—
Treachery its own betrayer. v. 2.—Engel, M. E.
Tales. v. 4.—Doctor Faustus. v. 1.—Gottschalck,
C. F. Popular traditions and tales of the Germans.
v. 2.—Grimm, J. L. K., and Grimm, W. K. Specimens from the Kinder und Haus Märchen, collected
from oral tradition. v. 2.—Howleglass, the merry
jester. v. 1.—La Motte-Fouqué, F. H. K., *Freiherr* de. The field of terror; or, the haunted field;—
The mandrake;—Head master Rhenfried and his
family. v. 2.—Laughein, A. F. R. Albert Lim-
bach; or, a martyr to the fair;—An hour's instruction
in political economy;—The irreconcileable man;—
The lady's palfrey;—Marianne Richards;—Seven
marriages, and never a husband. v. 4.—Lothar
(*pseud.*) The archrogue;—Castle Christburg. v. 2.—
Musæus, J. K. A. The dumb lover. v. 3.—Nachti-
gal, O. Popular traditions. v. 2.—Reineke Fuchs,
(Reynard the Fox), numerous authors and eds. of
it. v. 1.—Schiller, J. C. F. von. The apparitionist:
a fragment;—The criminal; or, martyr to lost honour: a true story:—Fraternal magnanimity;—Sport
of destiny;—Walk among the linden trees. v. 3.—
Tieck, L. Auburn Egbert;—Faithful Eckart and
the Tannenhäuser, pt. 1;—Tannenhäuser, pt. 2. v. 4.

Rose Budd. *Same as* Jack Tier. Cooper, J..
F. 823.298
Rose d'Albret. James, G: P. R. 823.7234
Rose Fleming. Russell, D. *in* 823.5041
Rose Mather. Holmes, *Mrs.* M.. J.. (H.)
823.801
Rose of disentis. Zschokke, J. H. D. 823.6929
Rose of Paradise, The. Pyle, H. 823.5288
Rose-bush of Hildesheim, The. Waller, M.
E. * 823.6140
Rosecroft. Round, W: M. F. 823.1834
Rose-garden. Peard, F.. M.. 823.1245
Rosery folk, The. Fenn, G: M. 823.4808
Same. *in* 823.4993
Rosine. Melville, G: J: Whyte-
in ** 823.4669
Same. 823.7284
Ross, Albert, *pseud. See* Porter, L. B.
Rossetti, Christina Georgina. Commonplace,
and other short stories. 2d ed. 823.1370
Ross-shire Buffs. Grant, J. 823.649
Roua pass, The. 3 vols. Grogan, *Mrs.* M.
823.7308-10
Roué, The. 823.6473
Note.—Attributed to E: G: E. L. Bulwer-Lytton.
Rouge et noir. About, E. F. V. 823.6282
Round, W: Marshall Fitz. [*Rev. P: Pennot.*]
Achsah: a New England life-study.
823.1371
—— Rosecroft: a story of common places
and common people. 823.1834

English Fiction. *Contin.*
Round a posada fire. Middlemore, *Mrs.* S.
G. C. 823.4745
Round the moon. Verne, J. 823.2855
Same. 823.5487
Round the world. Kingston, W: H: G.
808.346
Round-about rambles in lands of fact and
fancy. Stockton, F. R: 808.1886
Rousselet, L: The serpent-charmer. Tr. by
M.. de Hauteville. 823.6036
  Issued later as A tale of the Indian mutiny; or,
  the serpent charmer.
Routledge's picture book of animals. Wood,
J: G: 808.1883
Routledge's picture book of birds. Wood, J:
G: 808.1884
Routledge's picture book of fishes, insects,
etc. Wood, J: G: 808.1885
Rover's secret, The. Collingwood, H.
808.1708
Rowcroft, C: Australian Crusoes; or, the
adventures of an English settler and his
family in the wilds of Australia. 823.1373
Rowe, Nicholas. Macauley, E. Tales of the
drama founded on the tragedies of . . .
Rowe, etc. 823.1051
Rowson, *Mrs.* Susanna (Haswell). Char-
lotte Temple: a tale of truth. *in* 823.5022
Roxy. Eggleston, E: 823.4029
Roy, Gordon. For her sake: a tale of life in
Ireland. 823.6369
Roy, Just Jeanne Étienne. [*Théophile Mé-
nard.*] The adventures of a casket: an epi-
sode of the invasion of 1814. 823.6292
Roy and Viola. Bridges, *Mrs. Col.* —
823.4053
Same. 823.4996; *in* 823.5422
Royal Highlanders. Grant, J. 823.5678
Same. 823.6530; *in* 823.6699
Royal regiment, and other novelettes. Grant,
J. 823.650
Royalist's daughter and the rebels. Mur-
doch, *Rev.* D: 823.1177
Royce, Josiah. The feud of Oakfield creek:
a novel of California life. 823.6506
Roy's wife. Melville, G: J: Whyte-
in ** 823.4666
Same. 823.7285
Ruby Gray's strategy. Stephens, *Mrs.* A. S.
(W.) 823.1971
Ruby Grey. 3 vols. Dixon, W: H.
823.4552-4
Ruby's husband. Terhune, *Mrs.* M..V. (H.)
823.1563
Rudder Grange. Stockton, F. R: 823.1521
Ruffini, Giovanni Domenico.
—— Lavinia. 3 vols. (in 1). 823.7128
—— Lorenzo Benoni; or, passages in the life
of an Italian. 823.7413
—— The Paragreens on a visit to the Paris
Universal Exhibition. 823.1374
  Issued also as Dear experience.
Ruggiero and Bradamante, Story of. (*In*
Tales from Ariosto.) p. 69, *in* 808.777
Ruling passion. Riddell, *Mrs.* C.. E. L. (C.)
823.1336
Rumor. Sheppard, E.. S.. 823.6043
Running the gauntlet. Yates, E. H.
823.1757

English Fiction. *Contin.*
Rupert Godwin. Maxwell, *Mrs.* M.. E.. (B.)
in 823.2415
Same. *in* 823.5114
Ruskin, J: The king of the Golden river.
32 pp. (Johnson, R., *ed. Little classics,*
v. 10.) p. 56, *in* 829.133
Russell, *Col.* —. Coincidences?? 49 pp.
(*In* Tales from Blackwood. 3d ser., v. 5.)
p. 47, *in* 823.7501
Russell, C: Wells. Fall of Damascus: an
historical novel. 823.1375
Russell, Dora. Rose Fleming: the story of
an heiress. *in* 823.5041
—— A secret diary. 14 pp. (*In* Twenty
novelettes, etc.) p. 129, *in* 823.7183
Russell, W: Clark.
—— Flying Dutchman; or, the death ship.
(*With his* A sailor's sweetheart.)
in 823.2510
—— The Golden Hope: a romance of the
deep. *in* 823.5074
—— In the middle watch: sea stories.
in 823.5065
—— Jack's courtship. 823.4947
—— *Same.* *in* 823.5092
—— John Holdsworth, chief mate.
in 823.5128
—— Little Loo. 823 4776
—— *Same.* *in* 823.4977
—— Marooned. 823.6319
—— My shipmate Louise: a romance of a
wreck. 823.6466
—— The mystery of the "Ocean Star:" a
collection of maritime sketches. 823.5588
—— The romance of Jenny Harlowe, and
sketches of maritime life. 823.6546
—— Sailor's sweetheart. *in* 823.5111
—— *Same.* (*Also*) The Flying Dutchman;
or, the death ship. 823.2510
—— A sea queen. 823.4507
—— *Same.* 823.4986; 823.5021
—— A strange voyage. *in* 823.5013
—— A voyage to the Cape. 823.4985
—— *Same.* 823.5020
—— Wreck of the "Grosvenor."
in 823.6702
Russell. James, G: P. R. 823.877
Russia. *See also* Caucasus.—Poland.
—— Adams, W: T. Northern lands; or,
Young America in Russia and Prussia.
808.495
—— Champney, *Mrs.* E.. (W.) Three Vas-
sar girls in Russia, etc. 808.1823
—— Dole, N. H. Young folks' history of
Russia. 947.46
—— Greey, E: The bear-worshippers of Yezo
and the island of Karafuto* (Saghalin); or,
the adventures of the Jewett family and
their friend Oto Nambo. Illus. 808.1892
  (*Ceded to Russia in 1875.)
—— Gueullette, T: S. Tartarian tales.
(Weber, H: *Tales of the east,* v. 3.)
p. 221, *in* ** 823.6232
—— Hetzel, P. J. Maroussia: a maid of
Ukraine. 808.1725
—— Knox, T: W. The boy travellers in the
Russian empire. 808.1844

English Fiction. *Contin.*
Russia. *Contin.*
—— Lander, S.. W. Moscow.   808.99
—— — St. Petersburg.   808.103
—— Longfellow, H: W. Poems of places.
                                    821.226
—— Ralston, W: R. S. Russian folk-tales.
                                    823.1282
—— Wratislaw, A. H., *tr.* Great Russian
stories.—Little Russian Stories (*and*) White
Russian stories. (*In his* Sixty folk-tales,
etc.)   *in* 823.6946
16TH CENTURY A. D. Gogol, N. V. Taras
Bulba.   823.5259
17TH CENTURY A. D.
—— Byron, *Lord.*   Mazeppa (Ukraine);
poem.   pp. 391–424, *in* * 821.70
—— Hasselt, A. H. C. van. Menshikoff; or,
the peasant prince.   823.7172
—— Immermann, K. L. Alexis.
             p. 161, *in* 832.86
—— Pushkin, A. S. The moor of Peter the
Great. (*In his* Russian romance.)
             p. 247, *in* 823.4196
—— Sienkiewicz, H. With fire and sword:
an historical novel of Poland and Russia.
                                    823.6338
Demetrius (murdered 1610).
—— Bain, F. W. Dmitri. (Claimed to be
the son of Ivan IV.)   823.7355
18TH CENTURY A. D.
—— Grant, J. The secret dispatch; or, the
adventures of Captain Balgonie.   823.653
—— Helps, *Sir* A. Ivan de Biron; or, the
Russian court in the middle of last century.
                                    823.750
—— Mundt, *Mme.* C. (M.) Daughter of an
empress.   823.5800
—— Pushkin, A. S. The captain's daughter.
                                    823.5023
—— — *Same.* (*In his* Russian romance.)
                              in 823.4196
—— Taylor, B. Beauty and the beast.
                                    823.1543
19TH CENTURY A. D.
French invasion, 1812.
—— Alcock, D. The czar: a tale of the time
of the first Napoleon.   · 823.5909
—— Tolstoï, *Count* L. N. War and peace.
3 pts. in 6 vols.   823.4928–33
  Pt. 1: Before Tilsit. 1805-1807. 2 vols.
  Pt. 2: The invasion. 1807-1812. 2 vols.
  Pt. 3: Borodino, the French at Moscow. 1812-
  1820. 2 vols.
Crimean war, 1854. Melville, G: J: Whyte-
The interpreter.   823.1853
See also England, *Crimean war*, p. 74.
Poland. See Poland, p. 206.
Siberia.
—— Bowman, A. The young exiles; or, the
wild tribes of the north.   808.203
—— Cottin, *Mme.* S. (R.) Elizabeth; or,
the exiles of Siberia.   823.4965
—— — *Same.* (*In* Libr. of famous fiction.)
             p. 701, *in* 823.6215
—— Tissot, V:, *and* Améro, C. Escaped from
Siberia: the adventures of three distressed
fugitives.   823.6332

English Fiction. *Contin.*
Russia. *Contin.*
19TH CENTURY A. D. *Contin.*
Nihilism.
—— Dostoyevsky, F. M. Crime and punish-
ment.   823.5476
—— Dragomonov, M. A female nihilist.
24 pp.   823.6188
—— Gagneur, *Mme.* L. (M.) Nihilist prin-
cess.   823.1846
—— O'Meara, K. Narka, the nihilist.
                                    823.5214
Woman question.
—— Tchernuishevsky, N. G. A vital ques-
tion; or, what is to be done?   823.7143
MANNERS AND CUSTOMS.
—— Campbell, *Sir* G. Wild and weird; or,
remarkable stories of Russian life.
                                    823.7244
—— Dumas, A. D. Louisa; or, the adven-
tures of a French milliner.   823.5881
—— Durand, *Mme.* A. M. C. (H.) Pretty
little countess Zina: a Russian story.
                                    823.7101
—— Gogol, N. V. St. John's eve. 823.5258
—— — Tchitchikoff's journeys; or, dead
souls.   823.5344-5
—— Hooper, *Mrs.* L. (H.) The tzar's win-
dow.   823.4153
—— MacGahan, *Mrs.* B. (E.) Xenia Rep-
nína: a story of the Russia of to-day.
                                    823.7267
—— Pushkin, A. S. Marie: A story of Rus-
sian love. (Garrison life on the Russian
plains.)   823.4225
—— Tolstoï, *Count* L. N. Anna Karénina.
                                    823.5241
—— — Iván Ilyitch, and other stories.
                                    823.5243
—— — Long exile, and other stories for
children.   808.1348
—— — Polikouchka. 70 pp.   823.6589
—— — A Russian proprietor.   823.5239
—— — Two generations. (*With his* Poli-
kouchka.)   *in* 823.6589
—— Turguenef, I. S. Diary of a superfluous
man. 68 pp. (*With his* Mumu.)
             p. 63, *in* 823.4740
—— — Dimitri Roudine.   823.7066
—— — Fathers and sons.   823.4211
—— — A Lear of the steppe. 71 pp. (*With
his* Spring floods.)   p. 149, *in* 823.7131
—— — Liza; or, "a nest of nobles." 823.4212
—— — Mumu.   823.4740
—— — On the eve.   823.4213
—— — Smoke: a Russian novel.   823.4214
—— — Spring floods.   823.7131
—— Verne, J. Michael Strogoff, the courier
of the czar.   823.3283
—— — *Same.*   823.6112
—— Woillez, *Mme.* N. Orphan of Moscow;
or, the young governess.   823.6919
Peasant life.
—— Tolstoï, *Count* L. N. In pursuit of hap-
piness.   823.5378
—— — Where love is, there God is also. 17
pp.   823.6531
—— Turguenef, I. S. Annals of a sportsman.
                                    823.4910

English Fiction. *Contin.*
Russia. *Contin.*
MANNERS AND CUSTOMS. *Contin.*
Peasant life. Contin.
—— — An unfortunate woman. (*Also*)
Ass'ya. 823.5763
Note.—See Bibliography. Adams, C. K. Histories of Russia and Poland. (*In his Manual of hist. lit.*, 3d ed.) 1889. pp. 407-429, *in* * 907.4².
For general history and description, *see* Armstrong, W: J. Siberia and the nihilists. 1890. 947.55.—Bond, E: A., *ed.* Russia at the close of the 16th century. (*Hakl. Soc.*) 1856. *in* ** 947.14.—Brandes, G. Impressions of Russia. (1889.) 914.43b.—Dragomonov, M. Russia under the tsars. (Social.) 1885. 947.39;—The Russian peasantry: their agrarian condition, social life and religion. 1888. 947.43;—The Russian storm cloud: Russia in her relations to neighbouring states. 1886. 947.64;—Underground Russia. 1883. (Nihilists. Tr. fr. French MSS.) 947.37.—Edwards, H. S. The Romanoffs: tsars of Moscow and emperors of Russia. 1890. 947.47.—Froude, J. A. The eastern question. 34 pp. (*In his* Short studies, etc., 2d ser.) p. 410, *in* 824.33.—Gibbon, D. Decline and fall of the Roman empire. v. 5., chap. 55. (Origiu of Russian monarchy.) pp. 404-439, *in* 937.12;—Gowing, L. F. Five thousand miles in a sledge; a mid-winter journey across Siberia. 1890. 914.433.—Guild, C. Britons and Muscovites. 1888. 914.467.—Kelly,W. K. History of Russia (to 1854). 2 vols. 1878. 947. 17-18.—Kennan, G: [Papers on Russia and Siberia.] (*Century mag.*, n. s.,vols. 13-14, 1887-8.) *in* * 51.1243⁴·⁴ —Klaczko, J. Gortchakof. (*In his* Two chancellors.) 1877. 940.198.—Morfill, W: R. The story of Russia. 1890. 947.48.—Rambaud, A. History of Russia (to 1882). 3 vols. 1879-82. 947.52-4.—Réclus, J. J. E. The earth and its inhabitants—Asia. v. 1: Asiatic Russia, Caucasia, Aralo-Caspian basin, Siberia. Map. Illus. 1884. * 915.375.—Schuyler, E. Peter the Great. 2 vols. 1884. * 923.1577-8.—Shearwood, J. A. A short history of Russia. 1888. 947.51.—Stead, W. T. Truth about Russia. 1888. 947.45.—Vogüé, E. M., *vicomte* de, *and* Child, T. The tsar and his people; or, social life in Russia. Illus. 1891. 947.56.—Voltaire, F. M. A. de. History of Charles XII. (Time of Peter the Great.) 923. 221.—Wallace, D. M. Russia. (Picture of modern Russia.) 1883. 914.117.—Weir, A. St. Petersburg and Moscow. 50 pp. (Galton, F. *Vacation tourists.* 1861.) p. 1, *in* 910.230.
Note.—See Catalogues of this Library.
No. 2, 1880, p. 199. No. 4, 1884, p. 255.
No. 3, 1882, p. 167. No. 5, 1888, p. 308.
See also Index to Consular reports. 1880-1885; 1886-1889. 2 vols. (U. S. Pub. Docs. *Dept. of State.*) ** 350.5496¹·³.
See also Poole's Index (to 1882). pp. 1,133-37, *in* ** 50.1;—*Same.* Jan. 1, 1882-Jan. 1, 1887. pp. 380-81, *in* ** 50.1³.

Russian folk-tales. Ralston, W: R. S.
823.1282
Russian proprietor, A, and other stories.
Tolstoi, *Count* L. N. 823.5239
Russian romance. Pushkin, A. S. 823.4196
Rutherford, M:, *pseud. See* White, W. Hale.
Rutledge. Harris, *Mrs.* M. (C.) 823.707
Ruy Blas. Williams, H. L., *ed.* 823.7261
S., E. L. *See* Saxon, *Mrs.* E. Lydell.
S., H. Carl. Who painted the great Murillo de la Merced? 88 pp. (*In* Tales from Blackwood. 2d ser., v. 3.) *in* 823.7487
S., J. *of Dale, pseud. See* Stimson, F: Jesup.
S., R. *See* Paltock, Robert.
S., V. Dr. Goethe's courtship: a tale of domestic life. 823.4249
Sabina Zembra. Black, W: 823.5543
Sable cloud, The. Adams, N. 823.6980
Sacher-Masoch, Leopold von. 1836- . The sledge-ride. (Zimmern H.., *and* A. *Half-hours with foreign novelists.*)
in ** 823.6613

English Fiction. *Contin.*
Sacred nugget, The. Farjeon, B: L.
in 823.6587
Sacrifice. Green, W. S. 823.6244
Sacristan's household. Trollope, *Mrs.* F.. E. (T.) 823.6001
Saddle and sabre. Smart, H. 823.5777
Sadlier, *Mrs.* J. *See* Sadlier, *Mrs.* M.. A. (M.)
Sadlier, *Mrs.* M.. Anne (Madden). The confederate chieftains. 823.1377
—— Con O'Regan; or, emigrant life in the new world. 823.1378
—— The heiress of Kilorgan; or, evenings with the old Geraldines. 823.1379
—— MacCarthy More; or, the fortunes of an Irish chief in the reign of Queen Elizabeth. 823.1380
—— Maureen Dhu, the admiral's daughter: a tale of the Claddagh of Galway.
823.1381
—— New lights; or, life in Galway. 823.1382
—— Old and new; or, taste versus fashion.
823.1383
Safar-Hadgi. Lubomirski, S. H., *prince.*
823.2330
Sailor boy, The. Adams, W: T. 808.512
Sailor boys of '61. Soley, J. R. 808.1911
Sailor's sweetheart, A. Russell, W: C.
823.2510
Same. *in* 823.5111
St. Clair of the isles. Helme, *Mrs.* E..
823.6437
St. Elmo. Wilson, *Mrs.* A. J.. (E.)
823.1709
St. George and St. Michael. MacDonald, G:
823.1068
St. George for England. Henty, G: A.
808.1479
Saint James's. Ainsworth, W: H. 823.28
St. John, Percy Bolingbroke. Arctic Crusoe: a tale of the polar sea. 808.374
St. John's eve and other stories. Gogol-Janovskij, N. W. 823.5258
St. Leon. 4 vols. Godwin, W:
* 823.6779-82
St. Martin's eve. Wood, *Mrs.* E. (P.)
823.6016
Saint Michael. Bürstenbinder, E.. 823.5762
St. Patrick's eve. Lever, C: J. *in* 823.971
St. Petersburg. *See also* Russia.
—— Lander, S.. W. St. Petersburg.
808.103
St. Philip's. Harris, *Mrs.* M. (C.) 823.708
Saint-Pierre, Jacques Henri Bernardin de.
—— Paul and Virginia. 823.217
—— *Same.* (*In* Lib. of famous fiction, etc.)
in ** 823.6215
—— *Same.* (*With* Vicar of Wakefield. By O. Goldsmith.) *in* 823.4206
St. Ronan's well. Scott, *Sir* W: 823.1411
Same. 823.5326; p. 297, *in* ** 823.6030
St. Simon's niece. Benedict, F. L. 823.6039
Same. 823.6131
Saintine, Joseph Xavier Boniface, *pseud. See* Boniface, J. X.
Saints and sinners. Cherbuliez, V. 823.6384
Same. 823.6435

English Fiction. *Contin.*

Sala, G: A: Dead men tell no tales but live men do.   823.7303
— The seven sons of mammon.   823.5958
— Strange adventures of Capt. Dangerous.
    in 823.5026
Salardo. 10 pp. Straparola, G. F.
    p. 115, *in* 823.6534
Salathiel. 3 vols. Croly, *Rev.* G: 823.345-7
Salathiel, the immortal. Croly, *Rev.* G:
    823.5558
Salem. Castleton, D. R.   823.183
Salem Chapel. Oliphant, *Mrs.* M. O. (W.)
    in 823.5093
Salamagundi. Irving, W:, Paulding, J. K.,
   and Irving, W.   823.1811
Salt master of Lüneburg. Wolff, J. 823.7185
Salter, Edith. Assunta Howard, and other stories and sketches.   823.5961
Saltus, Edgar Evertson. The truth about Tristrem Varick.   823.5273
Salvage. Latimer, *Mrs.* E.. (W.)   823.2339
Sam Lawson's Oldtown fireside stories.
  Stowe, *Mrs.* H. E.. (B.)   823.1936
Samaria. Eddy, D. C. Walter in Samaria.
    808.1648
Samuel Brohl and Company. Cherbuliez, V.
    823.2322
   Same.   823.6688
Samuel Titmarsh, History of. Thackeray,
  W: M.   *in* 823.2537
Sanctuary. Nichols, G: W.   823.1189
Sand, G:, *pseud. See* Dudevant, *Mme.* A. L. A. (D.)
Sand. Gally, J. W.   823.4162
Sandeau, Jules. *See* Sandeau, L. S. J.
Sandeau, Léonard Lylvain Jules. 1811- . The last of an old family. (Zimmern, H.., *and* A. *Half-hours with foreign novelists,* v. 2.)
    in ** 823.6614
— Madeleine: a story of French love. Tr. by F. Charlot.   823.6832
Sand-hills of Jutland. Andersen, H. C.
    808.1730
   Same.   823.4182
Sandra Belloni. Meredith, G: 823.5382
   Issued also as Emilia in England.
Sandwich islands. *See* Hawaiian islands.
Sanford, *Mrs.* M. Malonia (Ray). A visit to El-fay-guo-land.   808.768
San Rosario ranch. Elliott, *Mrs.* M. (H.)
    823.4751
Sans merci. Lawrence, G: A.   823.962
Sant' Ilario. Crawford, F. M.   823.6548
Sappho. Daudet, A.   * 823.5423
Sappho of Green Springs, A. Harte, F. B.
    823.6394
Saracen. 4 vols. (in 2). Cottin, *Mme.* S. (R.)   * 823.2364-5
Saracinesca. Crawford, F. M.   823.4970
Sarah de Berenger. Ingelow, J.   823.5791
   Same. 3 vols.   823.7385-7
Sarchedon. Melville, G: J: Whyte-
    in ** 823.4662
   Same.   823.7286
Sartaroe. Maitland, J. A.   823.1085
Satanella. Melville, G: J: Whyte-
    ** 823.4668
   Same.   823.7287

English Fiction. *Contin.*

Satanstoe. Cooper, J. F.   823.311
   Same.   *in* 823.7461
Saucy Arethusa. Chamier, *Capt.* F:
    823.6347
Saunders, J: Guy Waterman. 2d ed. 3 vols.   823.5153, 3²-3³
— A noble wife.   *in* 823.5073
— Robbing Peter to pay Paul.   823.4816
Saunders, K.. *See* Cooper, *Mrs.* K.. (S.)
Savage, Marmion W. The bachelor of the Albany.   ** 823.4674
— *Same.*   823.4832; *in* 823.4988
— The Falcon family; or, young Ireland.
    * 823.6144
— My uncle, the curate.   823.5916
Saved by the life-boat. Ballantyne, R. M.
    in 808.1269
   Same.   *in* 808.1282
Saved from the sea. Kingston, W: H: G.
    808.349
Saxe Holm's stories. 2 vols. Jackson, *Mrs.* H.. M. (F.)   823.891-2
Saxon, *Mrs.* E. Lydell, *ed.* [*E. L. S.*] Belt and spur: stories of the knights of the middle ages from the old chroniclers.
    808.1610
— The city in the sea: stories of the deeds of the old Venetians from the chronicles.
    823.7173
Say and seal. 2 vols. (in 1). Warner, S.,
  and Warner, A.. B.   823.1682
Scalp hunters, The. Reid, T: M.   808.437
Scandinavia. *See also* Denmark, Iceland, Norway, Sweden.
— Boyesen, H. H. Modern vikings: stories of life and sport in the Norseland.
    808.1464
— Buchanan, R. Scandinavian ballad stories.   898.4
— Corbett, J. The fall of Asgard.
    823.5648
— Dasent, *Sir* G: W. Popular tales from the Norse. With an introductory essay on the origin and diffusion of popular tales.
    808.1801
— Keary, A., *and* E. Heroes of Asgard: tales from Scandinavian mythology. 293.8
— Thorpe, B:, *ed.* Yule-tide stories: a collection of Scandinavian . . . popular tales and traditions.   823.4231
   Note.—See Mallet, P. H. Northern antiquities. 1878. 293.5.—Otté, *Miss* E. C. Scandinavian history. 1874. 948.16.—Thorpe, B. Northern mythology. 3 vols. 1851. 293.32-4.—Wheaton, H. History of the Northmen. 1831. 948.3.
   See also Catalogues of this Library.
    No. 2, 1880, p. 203.   No. 4, 1884, p. 260.
    No. 3, 1882, p. 169.   No. 5, 1888, p. 313.
   See also Poole's Index to (1882). p. 1,155, *in* ** 50.1;—*Same.* Jan. 1, 1882-Jan. 1, 1887. p. 387, *in* ** 50.1².
   For late descriptive accounts, *see* Brown, J. Land of Thor. 1870. 914.141.—Du Chaillu, P. B. Land of the midnight sun. 2 vols. 914.284-5.—Kimball, E. C. Midnight sunbeams; or, bits of travel through the land of the Norseman. (1888.) 914.445.
Scapegrace Dick. Peard, F.. M..   808.1513
Scarlet letter. Hawthorne, N.   823.733
   Same.   823.7509
Scenes and legends of the north of Scotland. Miller, H.   823.1157

English Fiction. *Contin.*
Scotland. *Contin.*
—— Cunningham, A. Traditional tales of the English and Scottish peasantry. 2 vols.
* 291.52-3
—— Historical and traditional tales, south of Scotland. 1843.   941.87
3D CENTURY A. D. Macpherson, J. Poems of Ossian. 2 vols.   * 898.1-2
11TH CENTURY A. D. Shakespeare, W: Macbeth (traditional); trag.   ** 822.669
Note.—For other editions, *see under* Shakespeare *in* Catalogues of this Library.
No. 2, 1880, p. 207.   No. 4, 1884, p. 265.
No. 3, 1882, p. 173.   No. 5, 1888, pp. 317-318.
WALLACE (*executed* 1305).
—— Baillie, J. William Wallace; poem.
p. 710, *in* 822.897
—— Henty, G: A. In freedom's cause: a story of Wallace and Bruce.   808.1478
—— Porter, J.. The Scottish chiefs.   823.1271
BRUCE (*crowned* 1306, *d.* 1329).
—— Aguilar, G. Days of Bruce: a story from Scottish history. 2 vols. (in 1).
823.5398
—— — *Same.* 2 vols.   823.5-6
—— Barbour, J. Bruce; poem. (*Early Eng. Text Soc.* Extra Nos. 11, 21, 29, 55.)
** 806.2¹¹; ²¹, ²⁹, ⁵⁵
—— Henty, G: A. In freedom's cause: a story of Wallace and Bruce.   808.1478
—— Porter, J.. Bannockburn: sequel to the Scottish chiefs. 2 vols.   823.6743-4
—— Scott, *Sir* W. Castle Dangerous.
823.1410
—— — *Same.*   *in* 823.5329; *in* 823.6034
14TH CENTURY A. D.
—— Battle of Otterbourne; Chevy-Chase; ballads. (Child, F. J., *ed. Eng. and Scottish ballads*, v. 4.)   821.92
15TH CENTURY A. D.
—— Grant, J. Captain of the guard. 823.621
—— — Sir Andrew Wood of Largo.
p. 187, *in* 823.623
—— — The Yellow Frigate.   823.658
—— Helme, *Mrs.* E.. St. Clair of the isles; or, the outlaws of Barra: a Scottish tradition.   823.6437
—— Holt, E. S.. Margery's son; or, "until he find it:" a tale of the court of Scotland.
823.809
—— Scott, *Sir* W. Fair maid of Perth. 2 vols. (in 1). (Time of Robert III.)
823.1397
—— — *Same.*   823.5155; ** 823.6033
—— — Halidon Hill; dramatic sketch. (*Works*, v. 9.)   821.360
—— Yonge, C.. M.. The caged lion. (James I. imprisoned in England.)   823.1761
16TH CENTURY A. D.
—— Ainsworth, W: H. Crichton.   823.16
—— Baillie, J. The family legend; trag.
p. 462, *in* 822.128
—— Grant, J. Jane Seton; or, the king's advocate. (Witchcraft, 1537.)   823.632
—— — Mary of Lorraine. (Lowlands, 1547.)
823.638
—— Hogg, J. The Laidlaws and the Scotts: a border tradition. (Picken, A., *ed. The club-book*, v. 2.)   *in* 823.702

English Fiction. *Contin.*
Scotland. *Contin.*
16TH CENTURY A. D. *Contin.*
—— Maclaren, *Miss.* Thrust out: an old legend.   823.1185
—— Scott, *Sir* W. Auchindrane; drama. (*Works*, v. 9.)   p. 117, *in* 821.360
—— — The lady of the lake; poem. (About A. D. 1540.)   821.357
—— — *Same;* drama.   *in* 822.693
—— — The lay of the last minstrel; poem. (A. D. 1550.)   *in* 821.356
—— — The monastery. (A. D. 1559-1568.)
823.1403
—— — *Same.*   *in* ** 823.6027
Flodden field, 1513.
—— Ainsworth, W: H. Crichton.   823.16
—— Aytoun, W: E. Edinburgh after Flodden. (*In his* Lays of the Scottish cavaliers.)   p. 12, *in* 821.15
—— Green, R. James the Fourth; trag.
p. 183, *in* 822.120
—— Scott, *Sir* W. Marmion; poem. (*Works*, v. 2.)   821.356
Gowrie conspiracy, 1600. James, G: P. R. Gowrie; or, the king's plot.   823.861
Reformation.
—— Alcock, D. The dark year of Dundee.
823.7532
—— Oliphant, *Mrs.* M. O. (W.) Magdalen Hepburn: a story of the Scottish reformation.   *in* 823.5084
See note under Reformation, p. 212.
MARY, QUEEN OF SCOTS (*beheaded* 1587).
—— Alfieri, V. Mary Stuart; drama.
p. 531, *in* 852.1
—— Aytoun, W: E. Bothwell; poem: with historical notes.   821.1382
—— Banks, J: The Albion queens (Elizabeth and Mary).   822.22
—— Grant, J. Bothwell; or, the days of Mary, Queen of Scots.   823.620
—— — Mary, of Lorraine. (Mary as a child.)   823.638
—— Melville, G: J: Whyte- The queens Maries: a romance of Holyrood. ** 823.4663
—— — *Same.*   823.7283
—— Motherwell, W: Cruxtoun castle; poem.
p. 219, *in* 821.518
—— Murray, W. Mary, Queen of Scots; drama.   822.664
—— St. John, J: Mary, Queen of Scots; trag.   822.103
—— Schiller, J. C. F. von. Mary Stuart; trag.   p. 205, *in* 832.36
—— Scott, *Sir* W. The abbot . . . sequel to The monastery.   823.1391
—— — *Same.*   823.4803; *in* 823.5159
—— — *Same.*   *in* ** 823.6027
—— — The monastery. (Mary's escape from Lochleven.)   823.5159
—— Swinburne, A. C. Mary, Queen of Scots; trag.   822.658
—— — (Trilogy.) *viz.:*
I. Chastelard; trag.   822.495
II. Bothwell; trag.   822.793
III. Fotheringay.   822.1128

English Fiction. *Contin.*
Scotland. *Contin.*
17TH CENTURY A. D.
—— Aytoun, W: E. Lays of the Scottish cavaliers. 821.15
—— Grant, J. The Scottish cavalier; or, the First Royal Scots. 823.651
—— Mackay, C. Jacobite songs and ballads of Scotland from 1688 to 1746. 821.254
—— Pollok, R. Tales of the covenanters. (*viz.:* Helen of Glen.—The persecuted family.—Ralph Gemmell.) 823.1270
—— Scott, *Sir* W. Legend of Montrose. *in* 823.1395
—— — *Same.* *in* 823.5326; *in* 823.5337
—— — *Same.* *in* 823.5797; *in* ** 823.6026
—— — *Same.* *in* ** 823.6724
—— — Old Mortality. 823.1404
—— — *Same.* *in* 823.5157; *in* 823.5161
—— — *Same.* ** 823.6024
—— — Rokeby; poem. (1644.) (*Works,* v. 4.) 821.357
—— Talfourd, T. N. Glencoe; trag. (1689.) p. 162, *in* 822.522
18TH CENTURY A. D.
1700. Scott, *Sir* W. The pirate. 823.1406
—— — *Same.* *in* 823.5156; *in* 823.5158
—— — *Same.* ** 823.6028
1708. — The black dwarf. 823.5797
—— — *Same.* (*With his* St. Ronan's well.) *in* 823.5326
1711. — The bride of Lammermoor. 823.1396
—— — *Same.* 823.4437; *in* 823.5326
—— — *Same.* *in* 823.5337; *in* 823.5797
—— — *Same.* ** 823.6026; ** 823.6724
—— — *Same.* Dramatised by J: W: Calcraft. 822.688
Old Pretender's rebellion.
—— Grant, J. Adventures of Rob Roy. 823.647
1715-16. Scott, *Sir* W. Rob Roy. 823.1408
—— — *Same.* 823.5161; *in* ** 823.6025
—— Wordsworth, W: Rob Roy's grave; poem. p. 460, *in* 821.737
Porteous riots.
1736-51. Scott, *Sir* W. Heart of Mid-Lothian. 823.1400
—— — *Same.* *in* ** 823.6025
Young Pretender's rebellion.
—— Grant, J. White cockade. 823.657
—— Henty, G: A. Bonnie Prince Charlie: a tale of Fontenoy and Culloden. 808.1443
1745. Scott, *Sir* W. Waverley. 823.1413
—— — *Same.* *in* ** 823.6023
1755. — The Highland widow. 96 pp. p. 273, *in* 823.1394
—— — *Same.* *in* 823.5328
1760-82. — Guy Mannering; or, the astrologer. 823.1399
—— — *Same.* 823.5327; *in* ** 823.6023
1765. — The two drovers. p. 183, *in* 823.1412
—— — *Same.* ** 823.6032
1766. — Redgauntlet: a tale of the 18th century. 823.1407
—— — *Same.* 823.5156; *in* 823.5327
—— — *Same.* ** 823.6031

English Fiction. *Contin.*
Scotland. *Contin.*
18TH CENTURY A. D. *Contin.*
1798. — The antiquary. 823.1393
—— — *Same.* *in* ** 823.6024
—— Sullivan, *Mrs.* A. (B.) Winifred, countess of Nithsdale. v. 1: (of) Tales of the peerage and of the peasantry. ** 823.6761
SCOTTISH CHARACTER.
—— Barrie, J. M. When a man's single. (A tale of literary life.) 823.6371
—— Ferrier, S. E. Destiny; or, the chief's daughter. 823.2051
—— — The inheritancy. 823.2052
—— — Marriage. 823.1991
—— Galt, J: Annals of the parish. 823.4191
—— — Ayrshire legatees. p. 167, *in* 823.4191
—— — The entail. 823.4193
—— — The provost. 823.4192
—— — Sir Andrew Wylie of that ilk. 823.4194
—— — The steam-boat. *in* 823.4192
—— Leys, J: K. The Lindsays: a romance of Scottish life. 3 vols. 823.7214-16
—— MacDonald, G: David Elginbrod. 823.1062
—— — Malcolm. 823.5962
—— — *Same.* 823.5981
—— Mason, T: Adam Dickson. 823.7187
—— Miller, H. Scenes and legends of the north of Scotland; or, the traditional history of Cromarty. 823.1157
—— — A true story of a Scotch merchant (W: Forsyth) of the 18th century. p. 293, *in* 823.1158
—— Oliphant, *Mrs.* M. O. (W.) Adam Graeme of Mossgray. *in* 823.5089
—— — Harry Muir: a story of Scottish life. *in* 823.5108
—— — Magdalen Hepburn. *in* 823.5084
—— — Passages in the life of Mrs. Margaret Maitland of Sunnyside. 823.4821
—— Reade, C: Christie Johnstone. 823.5420
—— Taylor, E.. Blindpits: a story of Scottish life. 823.4107
—— Walford, *Mrs.* L. B. (C.) Dick Netherby. 823.4320
—— Wilson, J: Lights and shadows of Scottish life. 823.7067
—— Wilson, J: M. Tales of the borders. 24 vols. (in 12.) 823.1711-22
See also novels by A. Cunningham.—*Sir* T. D. Lauder.
In the islands.
—— Barr, *Mrs.* A. E. (H.) Jan Vedder's wife. 823.5703
—— — Paul and Christina. 823.5226
—— Black, W: Princess of Thule. 823.87
—— Gordonhaven: scenes and sketches of fisher life in the north. By an old fisherman. 823.7202
—— Martineau, H. Ella of Garveloch. *in* 823.6707
—— Maxwell, W: H. Sports . . . in the Highlands and islands of Scotland. 823.1130

English Fiction. *Contin.*
Scotland. *Contin.*
SCOTTISH CHARACTER. *Contin.*
Highland life.
—— Barr, *Mrs.* A. E. (H.) Last of the
Macallisters.   823.5513
—— Black, W: In far Lochaber.   823.6550
—— Butler, *Lady* R. Jessie Cameron: a
Highland story.   823.7319
—— Grogan, *Mrs.* M. The Roua pass; or,
Englishmen in the Highlands. 3 vols.
                                   823.7308-10
—— Maxwell, W: H. Sports . . . in the
Highlands . . . of Scotland.   823.1130
—— Oliphant, *Mrs.* M. O. (W.) Kirsteen:
the story of a 'Scotch family seventy years
ago.   823.6464
—— Picken, A. The deer-stalkers of Glens-
kiach.   *in* 823.702
—— Verne, J. The green·ray.   843.7420
Lowland and shepherds' life. Hogg, J. Tales
and sketches. 5 vols.   823.774-8
Middle classes.
—— Craik, *Mrs.* D. M. (M.) Head of the
family.   823.329
—— —— A noble life.   823.4285
—— Robertson, M. M. By a way she knew
not.   823.7087
—— Smith, J. The Dalbroom folks. 2 vols.
                                   823.6397-8
Military life.
—— Grant, J. The "Black Watch."
                                   823.619
—— —— The constable of France (and other
stories).   823.623
—— —— The Scots Fusilier Guards. (Their
origin and services.)   p. 261, *in* 823.623
—— —— Second to none.   823.652
Sporting life. Melville, G: J: Whyte- Scot-
land and the moors. 40 pp.
                           p. 323, *in* 823.7289
Village life. Fife, M. B. In Glenoran.
                                   823.7191
Religious movements.
—— MacDonald, G: Robert Falconer.
                                   823.1067
—— Macleod, N. The starling.
                               in 823.4999
—— Oliphant, *Mrs.* M. O. (W.) The minis-
ter's wife.   823.1209
—— *Same.*   *in* 823.6208
Second sight.
—— MacDonald, G: The portent. 823.1066
—— *Same.*   *in* 823.4995; *in* 823.7010
Superstition. Linton, E. L., *ed.* Witch stories
(of England and Scotland).   133.8
Temperance.
—— Balfour, *Mrs.* C. L. The Burnish fam-
ily.   823.7311
—— Edwards, B. Rachel Noble's experi-
ence.   823.7073
University life. Sime, W: Haco the dream-
er.   *in* 823.5108

IN POEMS, SONGS AND BALLADS.
—— Aitkin, M.. C., *comp.* Scottish song.
                                   821.1220
—— Aytoun, W: E. Lays of the Scottish
cavaliers.   821.15

English Fiction. *Contin.*
Scotland. *Contin.*
IN POEMS, SONGS AND BALLADS. *Contin.*
—— Burns, R. Works.   821.54
—— Longfellow, H: W. Poems of places.
3 vols.   821.212-14
—— Murray, J. C. Ballads and songs of
Scotland.   821.294
—— Ramsay, A. Ever green. 2 vols.
                               * 821.465-6
—— —— Poems. 3 vols.   821.437-9
—— —— The tea-table miscellany. (Scotch
and English songs.) 2 vols. * 821.467-8
—— Roberts, J: S. Legendary ballads of
England and Scotland.   821.340
—— Scott, *Sir* W., *ed.* Minstrelsy of the
Scottish border. 2 vols.   821.843-4
—— Whitelaw, A. The book of Scottish
ballads.   821.749
—— Wilson, J. G. Poets and poetry of
Scotland. 2 vols.   821.439-40

Note.—See Blackie, J: S. Language and literature of the Scottish Highlands. 1876. 829.698.—
Burton, J: H. The history of Scotland; from Agricola's invasion to the extinction of the last Jacobite insurrection. 8 vols. and index. (9vols.) (1873.)
941.121-9.—Carlyle, T: War with Scotland, 1650-51.
(*Works,* v. 2.) p. 81, *in* 923.1843.—Freeman, E: A.
History of the Norman conquest in England. 6
vols. (v. 6, index.) 942.107-11A.—Hume, D. History of England (to 1688). 6 vols. 1872. 942.65-70.
—Macaulay, T· B. History of England. 5 vols.
942.97-101.—Mackenzie, J. The story of Scotland.
(Earliest times to A. D. 1707.) 1888. 941.132.—
Mackintosh, J. The story of Scotland, from the
earliest times to the present century. Map. 1890.
941.136.—Robertson, W: History of Scotland (to
1603). 3 vols. 1812. 942.155-7.—Scott, *Sir* W.
Tales of a grandfather. 6 vols. 1865. 942.158-63.—
Smyth, W. Union of England and Scotland. (*In
his* Modern history, v. 2, Lecture XXV.) p. 175, *in*
901.10.—Strickland, A. Lives of the queens of
Scotland, and English princesses connected with
the regal succession of Great Britain. 8 vols. 920.
342-9.

See also Brown, T. Craig- History of Selkirk-
shire; or, chronicles of Ettrick Forest. (Border
war.) 2 vols. 1886. ** 942.1286-7.—Buckle, H: T:
History of civilization in England. 2 vols. 1878.
313.35-6.—Burnet, G. History of his own time.
942.250.

For church history, *see* Cunningham, *Rev.* J:
Church history of Scotland. 2 vols. 1859. (Pres-
byterian.) 274.85-6.—Spottiswood, J: History of
the church of Scotland. 3 vols. (in 2). 1851. (Epis-
copalian.) 274.87-9.

For the Reformation period, *see* Fisher, G. P.
The Reformation. 1873. (Bibliography, pp. 567-
591.) 274.28.

See also note under Reformation, p. 212.

For manners and customs, *see* Logan, J. Manners, customs and antiquities of Scotland. 1855.
942.195.—Ramsay, E. B. Scottish life and character. 1861. 914.45.—Ramsay, J: Scotland and
Scotsmen in the eighteenth century. 2 vols. 1888.
941.130-1.—Stewart, *Col.* D. Sketches of the Highlanders. 2 vols. 1822. 941.84-5.

See also Catalogues of this Library.
No. 2, 1880, p. 204.   No. 4, 1884, p. 261.
No. 3, 1882, p. 170.   No. 5, 1888, p. 315.
See also Index to Consular reports. 1880-1885;
1886-1889. 2 vols. (U. S. Pub. Docs. *Dept. of State.*)
** 350.5496¹·².

See also Poole's Index (to 1882). pp. 1,165-8, *in*
** 50.1;—*Same.* Jan. 1, 1882-Jan. 1, 1887, p. 391, *in*
** 50.1².

Scotland and the moors. 40 pp. Melville,
G: J: Whyte-   p. 323, *in* 823.7289

Scots Brigade, The. Grant, J.   823.4795

Scotsman's tale, The. 48 pp. Lee, H.
                           p. 300, *in* 823.1778

English Fiction. *Contin.*

Scott, *Lady* C.. Harriet J.. (Lockhart) Hope-
The pride of life. 823.1388

Scott, Michael. The cruise of the Midge.
(Anon.) 823.1389
—— Tom Cringle's log. 823.1390

Scott, *Sir* Walter. (1771–1832.)
—— The abbot: sequel to the monastery.
823.1391
—— *Same.* *in* 823.4803; *in* 823.5159
—— Anne of Geierstein. 823.1392
—— The antiquary. 823.1393
—— The betrothed: a tale of the crusaders.
823.7471
—— *Same.* (*With his* The bride of Lam-
mermoor.) *in* 823.4803
—— *Same.* (*With his* Count Robert of
Paris.) *in* 823.5328
—— *Same.* 2 vols. (in 1). (*Also*) Chron-
icles of the Canongate. (*viz.:* The High-
land widow. 96 pp.) 823.1394
—— The black dwarf. (*With his* St. Ro-
nan's well.) *in* 823.5326
—— *Same.* (*Also*) Legend of Montrose.
823.1395
—— *Same.* (*Also*) The bride of Lammer-
moor. 823.5797
—— *Same.* (*Also*) Old Mortality. 823.7472
—— *Same.* *in* ** 823.6024
—— *Same.* (*Also*) Quentin Durward. (With
notes and glossary.) 823.5157
—— The bride of Lammermoor. 823.1396
—— *Same.* 823.4437; *in* 823.5326
—— *Same.* *in* 823.5797
—— *Same.* (*Also*) The abbot (sequel to The
monastery).—The betrothed.—The High-
land widow.—(*And*) Peveril of the Peak.
823.4803
—— *Same.* (*And*) Legend of Montrose.
** 823.6724
—— Castle Dangerous. (*With his* Peveril of
the Peak.) *in* 823.5329
—— *Same.* (*With his* The surgeon's daugh-
ter.) *in* 823.1410
—— Chronicles of the Canongate. 823.4826
(*viz.:*) Two drovers.—My aunt Margaret's mirror.
—Tapestried chamber; or, the lady in the sacque.—
Death of the laird's Jock.
—— *Same.* *in* 823.1412; *in* 823.5160
—— *Same.* 823.7473
—— Count Robert of Paris. 823.1781
—— *Same.* (*Also*) The betrothed: a tale of
the Crusades, *and* The Highland widow.
(All with notes.) 823.5328
—— The fair maid of Perth. 2 vols. (in 1).
823.1397
—— *Same.* *in* 823.5155
—— Fortunes of Nigel. 823.1398
—— *Same.* 2 vols. 823.7474-5
—— *Same* (with notes). (*Also*) The pirate
(with notes). 823.5158
—— Guy Mannering; or, the astrologer.
823.1399
—— *Same.* (With notes and fragment of
Thomas the rhymer, and The lord of En-
nerdale. (*Also*) Redgauntlet (with notes).
823.5327
—— Heart of Mid-Lothian. 823.1400

English Fiction. *Contin.*

Scott, *Sir* Walter. (1771–1832.) *Contin.*
—— The Highland widow. (*With his* The
betrothed.) *in* 823.1394
—— *Same.* (*With his* The bride of Lam-
mermoor.) *in* 823.4803
—— *Same.* (*With his* Count Robert of
Paris.) *in* 823.5328
—— Ivanhoe. 823.1401
—— *Same* (with notes). (*Also*) The talis-
man: a tale of the crusaders (with notes).
(*And*) Chronicles of the Canongate (with
notes). 823.5160
—— The keepsake stories. (*With his* Chron-
icles of the Canongate.) *in* 823.7473
For contents, see under Chronicles of the Canongate.
—— Kenilworth. 2 vols. (in 1). 823.1402
—— *Same* (with notes). (*Also*) Fair maid
of Perth; or, Saint Valentine's day (with
notes). 823.5155
—— Legend of Montrose. (*With his* The
black dwarf.) *in* 823.1395
—— *Same.* *in* 823.5326; *in* ** 823.6724
—— *Same.* *in* 823.5797
—— The monastery. 823.1403
—— *Same* (with notes). (*Also*) The abbot
(with notes). 823.5159
—— Old Mortality. 823.1404
—— *Same.* *in* 823.5157; *in* 823.5161
—— *Same.* *in* 823.7472
—— Peveril of the Peak. 823.1405
—— *Same.* *in* 823.4803
—— *Same.* (*Also*) The surgeon's daugh-
ter.—(*And*) Castle Dangerous, and glossary.
(All with notes.) 823.5329
—— The pirate. 823.1406
—— *Same.* *in* 823.5156; *in* 823.5158
—— Quentin Durward. 823.1409
—— *Same.* *in*. 823.5157
—— Redgauntlet. 823.1407
—— *Same.* *in* 823.5327
—— *Same* (with notes, glossary, and index).
(*Also*) The pirate (with notes, etc.)
823.5156
—— Rob Roy. 823.1408
—— *Same.* (*Also*) Old Mortality. 823.5161
—— St. Ronan's well. 823.1411
—— *Same.* (*Also*) The black dwarf.—A
legend of Montrose.—(*And*) The bride of
Lammermoor. (All with notes.) 823.5326
—— The surgeon's daughter. (*With his*
Peveril of the Peak.) *in* 823.5329
—— *Same.* (*Also*) Castle Dangerous, and
glossary. 823.1410
—— Tales of my landlord. 3d ser.: The
bride of Lammermoor;—A legend of Mon-
trose. 2 vols. (in 1). 823.5337
—— The talisman: a tale of the crusaders.
823.7476
—— *Same.* (*With his* Ivanhoe.)
in 823.5160
—— *Same.* (*Also*) Chronicles of the Canon-
gate. 823.1412
—— Waverley. 823.1413
—— Waverly novels. Abbotsford ed. 12
vols. ** 823.6023-34
Contents:—
v. 1: Waverley.—Guy Mannering.
v. 2: The antiquary.— The black dwarf.— Old
Mortality.

English Fiction. *Contin.*

Scott, *Sir* Walter. (1771–1832.) *Contin.*
—— Waverley novels. Abbotsford ed. 12
vols. *Contin.*
　　Contents. Contin.
　　v. 3: Rob Roy.—The heart of Mid-Lothian.
　　v. 4: The bride of Lammermoor.—A legend of
　　Montrose.—Ivanhoe.
　　v. 5: The monastery.—The abbot.
　　v. 6: Kenilworth.—The pirate.
　　v. 7: The fortunes of Nigel.—Peveril of the Peak.
　　v. 8: Quentin Durward.—St. Ronan's well.
　　v. 9: Redgauntlet.—The betrothed.—The talis-
　　man.
　　v. 10: Woodstock.—Chronicles of the Canongate.
　　(*viz.:*) The Highland widow.—The two drovers.—
　　The surgeon's daughter.
　　v. 11: The fair maid of Perth.—Anne of Geier-
　　stein.
　　v. 12: Count Robert of Paris.—Castle Dangerous.
　　—My aunt Margaret's mirror.—The tapestried
　　chamber.—Death of the laird's Jock.

—— Woodstock.　　　　　　　823.1414
—— *Same.*　　　　　　　　　823.7477
　　Note.—For his life and writings, *see* Bagehot,
　　W. The Waverley novels. 42 pp. (*Works,* v. 2.)
　　p. 197, *in* 814.23.—Carlyle, T: Sir W. Scott. (*In
　　his* Crit. and misc. essays, v. 3.) pp. 167–223, *in* 824.
　　401.—Drake, S: A. Our great benefactors. 1884.
　　p. 74, *in* * 920.312.—Hale, E: E. Lights of two cen-
　　turies. 1887. p. 205, *in* * 920.314.—Harris, A. B.
　　Little biographies. (1887.) p. 7, *in* 928.692.—Hodg-
　　kins, L. M. Scott. (*In her* A guide to the study of
　　19th cent. authors.) *in* 820.155.—Hood, T: Ode
　　to the great unknown. 11 pp. (*Poetical works,* v.
　　2.) p. 193, *in* 821.185.—Howitt, W: *In his* Homes
　　and haunts of the English poets. p. 446, *in* 914.10.
　　—Hutton, R. H. Scott. 928.284.—Irving, W. Ab-
　　botsford. (*In his* Crayon miscellany.) p. 241, *in*
　　829.668.—Jeaffreson, J: C. Walter Scott. 53 pp.
　　(*In his* Novels, etc., v. 2.) p. 31, *in* 820.187.—Lock-
　　hart, J. G. Life of Sir Walter Scott. 1851. 928.
　　496.—Lodge, E. Sir W. Scott. 11 pp. (*In his* Por-
　　traits, etc., v. 8.) p. 263, *in* * 920.192.—Minto, *Prof.* W.
　　Article "Scott, Sir W.," *in* Encyclop. Brit., v. 21. **
　　32.291.—Mitchell, D. G. A Scotch magician. 32
　　pp. (*In his* About old story tellers.) p. 166, *in* 813.
　　33.—Prescott, W: H. *In his* Biographical and crit-
　　ical miscellanies. 1873. p. 176, *in* 829.221.—Sainte-
　　Beuve, C. A. Sir W. Scott. (*In his* Premiers lundis,
　　vols. 1 and 2.) 824.443-4.—Scott, Sir W. The journal
　　of. (1825–1832.) 2 vols. 1890. 928.796-7.—Stephen,
　　L. Some words about Sir W. Scott. 30 pp. (*In his*
　　Hours in a library.) p. 174, *in* 824.86.
　　For brief sketches of the historical novels, *see*
　　Grey, H: Key to the Waverley novels. 1884. **
　　823.6776.
　　For an index and glossary, *see* Waverley novels.
　　** 823.6777.
　　See also Allibone's Dic. of Eng. lit., v. 2. pp.
　　1,964–1,979. *in* ** 803.7.
　　See also Poole's Index (to 1882). pp. 1,168–9, *in*
　　** 50.1;—*Same.* Jan. 1, 1882–Jan. 1, 1887. p. 391, *in*
　　** 50.1¹.

—— Blaisdell, A. F. Sir Walter Scott for
young people: readings from the Waverley
novels. Ed. for school and home use.
　　　　　　　　　　　　　　808.1667
Scottish cavalier, The. Grant, J.　823.651
Scottish chiefs. Porter, J..　　　823.1271
Scottish orphans. Blackford, *Mrs.* —.
　　　　　　　　　　　　　　823.6584
Scottish soldiers of fortune. Grant, J.
　　　　　　　　　　　　　　823.5932
Scouring of the White Horse. Hughes, T:
　　　　　　　　　　　　　　823.836
Scout, The. Simms, W: G.　　　823.1436
Scribner, J. P. [*An old mountaineer.*] La-
conia; or, legends of the White mountains
and Merry Meeting bay.　　　823.1782
Scripture club of Valley Rest. Habberton,
J:　　　　　　　　　　　　　823.4091

English Fiction. *Contin.*

Scrope. Perkins, F: B.　　　　823.5953
Scudder, Horace Elisha. The Bodley grand-
childern and their journey in Holland.
　　　　　　　　　　　　　　808.1852
—— The Bodleys afoot.　　　808.1850
—— The Bodleys on wheels　808.1849
—— The Bodleys telling stories.　808.1848
—— Doings of the Bodley family in town
and country.　　　　　　　808.1855
—— Dream children.　　　　808.1560
—— The English Bodley family.　808.1853
—— Mr. Bodley abroad.　　　808.1851
—— Seven little people and their friends.
　　　　　　　　　　　　　　808.1559
—— Stories and romances.　823.4005
—— The Viking Bodleys: an excursion into
Norway and Denmark.　　　808.1854
——, *comp.* The children's book: a collection
of the best and most famous stories and
poems in the English language. Illus.
　　　　　　　　　　　　　　808.1882
Sculptor's daughter. 2 pts. (in 1). Du
Boisgobey, F.　　　　　　*in* 823.5025
Sea and its wonders, The. Kirby, M.., *and*
Kirby, E..　　　　　　　　808.1875
Sea and shore. Warfield, *Mrs.* C.. A. (W.)
　　　　　　　　　　　　　　823.1663
Sea chauge, A. Shaw, F. L.　*in* 823.5053
Sea lions, The. Cooper, J. F.　823.312
Same.　　　　　　　　　　823.7466
Sea queen, A. Russell, W: C.　823.4507
Same.　　　　　　823.4986; 823.5021
Sea stories. *See also* Arctic regions.—Notes
under England, United States.—Life-boat.
—Mutinies.—Whale fishery.
—— Adams, W: T. Lake breezes; or, the
cruise of the Sylvania.　　　808.503
—— —— Outward bound; or, Young America
afloat.　　　　　　　　　　808.490
—— —— Up the river; or, yachting on the
Mississippi.　　　　　　　808.963
—— Baker, *Sir* S: B. Cast up by the sea.
　　　　　　　　　　　　　　823.2301
—— Ballantyne, R. M. The battery and the
boiler; or, adventures in the laying of sub-
marine electric cables.　　808.1262
—— —— Red Eric; or, the whaler's last cruise.
　　　　　　　　　　　　　　823.6908
—— —— Saved by the life-boat.　*in* 823.1282
—— Clarke, *Mrs.* M..V.. (N.) Cowden- Yarns
of an old mariner.　　　　823.4248
—— Cobb, J. F. Martin the skipper.
　　　　　　　　　　　　　　808.1627
—— Collingwood, H. Pirate island: a story
of the southern Pacific.　833.7036
—— Cupples, G: The green hand: adven-
tures of a naval lieutenant.　808.345
—— Dixon, R. B. Fore and aft: a story of
actual sea-life.　　　　　　823.1512
—— Doyle, A. C. The captain of the Pole-
star.　　　　　　　　　　　823.6410
—— Edgar, J: G: Sea-kings and naval he-
roes.　　　　　　　　　　　808.802
—— Eggleston, G: C. Wreck of the Red
Bird: a story of the Carolina coast.
　　　　　　　　　　　　　　808.1142

English Fiction. *Contin.*
Sea stories. *Contin.*

—— Fenn, G: M. In the king's name; or, the cruise of the "Kestrel." 808.1714

—— —— Mother Carey's chicken; her voyage to the unknown isle. 808.1438

—— —— "Ship ahoy!" 823.5922

—— Grant, J. Derval Hampton. 823.5680

—— —— *Same.* 823.6524

—— —— Jack Manly: his adventures by sea and land. 823.631

—— Habberton, J: The crew of the "Sam Weller." 823.7401

—— Hale, E: E. Stories of the sea. 808.1368

—— —— *Same.* 910.201

—— Hall, C: W. Adrift in the ice-fields. 808.1321

—— —— Drifting round the world: a boy's adventures by land and sea. 808.1869

—— Harley, *Dr.* The young Crusoe. 808.375

—— Hayes, I: I. Cast away in the cold. 808.367

—— Heldmann, B. Mutiny on board the Leander. 808.1637

—— Kingston, W: H: G. Hurricane Hurry; or, the adventures of a naval officer afloat and ashore. 808.1613

—— Ker, D: Into unknown seas; or, the cruise of two sailor-boys. 808.1360

—— Manning, E. Six months on a slaver. 823.6959

—— Nordhoff, C: The merchant vessel: a sailor boy's voyages to see the world. 808.166

—— Porter, W: O. Sir Edward Seaward's narrative of his ship-wreck and consequent discovery of certain islands in the Caribbean sea. 823.4047

—— Pultock, R. Life and adventures of Peter Wilkins, containing an account of his visit to the flying islanders, etc. 823.4062

—— Scott, M. Cruise of the Midge. 823.1389

—— —— Tom Cringle's log. 823.1390

—— Shand, A. I. Wrecked off the Riff coast. (*In* Tales from Blackwood. 2d ser., v. 6.) *in* 823.7490

—— Shillaber, B: P. Cruises with Capt. Bob on sea and land. 808.1604

—— Shippen, E. Thirty years at sea. 823.7296

—— Sleeper, J: S. Tales of the ocean, and essays for the forecastle. 823.1838

—— Smith, H. Crew of the Dolphin. 823.1455

—— Smith, L. A. The music of the waters: a coll. of the sailors' chanties . . . and water legends. 784.40

—— Stables, G. On special service. 808.1423

—— Stearns, W. A. Wrecked on Labrador. 808.1672

—— Stephens, C: A. On the Amazons; or, the cruise of "The Rambler." 808.242

—— Stockton, F. R: Casting away of Mrs. Lecks and Mrs. Aleshine. 823.6906

English Fiction. *Contin.*
Sea stories. *Contin.*

—— Verne, J. Twenty thousand leagues under the sea. 823.2713

—— —— Wreck of the Chancellor: diary of J. R. Kazallon, passenger. 823.5162

—— W., F. Wreck of the Strathmore. 64 pp. (*In* Tales from Blackwood. 2d ser., v. 8.) *in* 823.7492

—— Williams, A. B. Who saved the ship? 808.1640

See also Novels by W: H: G. **Kingston.**—Capt. F: **Marryat.**—W. C. **Russell.**

Note.—For voyages and travels, *see* under "Shipwrecks," *in* Catalogues of this Library.
No. 2, 1880, p. 209. No. 4, 1884, p. 267.
No. 3, 1882, p. 174. No. 5, 1888, p. 320.

See also "Shipwrecks" *in* Poole's Index (to 1882). p. 1,192, *in* ** 50¹.

See also "Voyages around the world" *in* Catalogues of this Library.
No. 2, 1880, p. 244. No. 4, 1884, p. 308.
No. 3, 1882, p. 201. No. 5, 1888, p. 380-1.

See also "Voyages" *in* Poole's Index (to 1882). pp. 1,378-9, *in* ** 50¹.

See also **Griswold**, W. M., *comp.* Travel: a series of narratives of personal visits to places famous for natural beauty and historical association. 1890. * 910.643.—Le tour du monde. 1860-1882. 23 vols. ** 913.128-49.

Seaboard parish. MacDonald, G: 823.2043

Seaforth. Montgomery, F. 823.1166

Sea-kings and naval heroes. Edgar, J: G: 808.802

Sealed lips. Du Boisgobey, F. 823.5096

Sealed orders. Ward, *Mrs.* E.. S. (P.) 823.1258

Sealsfield, C:, *pseud. See* **Postel,** K:

Seamy side, The. Besant, W., *and* Rice, J. 823.6086

Seaside library. [*Pocket ed.*]
Hay, M.. C. Lester's secret. 823.4973
Harrison, *Mrs.* R. G. (K.) Colonel Enderby's wife.
Hausrath, *Mrs.* A. Klytia.
Tennyson, A. Locksley Hall sixty years after, etc.

Armitt, A. In shallow waters. 823.4975
Hardy, E. J. How to be happy though married.
Lawless, E. Hurrish.
O'Donoghue, *Mrs.* N. (L.) P. Unfairly won.

Hector, *Mrs.* A. (F.) The Freres. 823.4976
Verne, J. Great voyages and great navigators.

Hector, *Mrs.* A. (F.) Executor. 823.4977
Maxwell, *Mrs.* M.. E.. (B.) Doctor's wife.
Russell, W: C. Little Loo.

Court Royal. 823.4978
Craik, *Mrs.* D. M. (M.) King Arthur.
Fargus, F: J: Living or dead.
Hector, *Mrs.* A. (F.) Beaton's bargain.

Hector, *Mrs.* A. (F.) Second life. 823.4979
Maxwell, *Mrs.* M.. E.. (B.) Mount Royal.

Brame, *Mrs.* C.. M. (L.) Put asunder. 823.4980
Hector, *Mrs.* A. (F.) Heritage of Langdale.
Verne, J. 20,000 leagues under the sea.

Besant, W. Uncle Jack. 823.4981
Carr, A. C. Paul Crew's story.
Fargus, F: J: Paul Vargas, and other tales.
Guthrie, F: A. Toy tragedy.
Hector, *Mrs.* A. (F.) At bay.
Hungerford, *Mrs.* M. As it fell upon a day.
Mad love.
Oliphant, *Mrs.* M. O. (W.) Perpetual curate.

English Fiction. *Contin.*
Seaside library. [*Pocket ed.*] *Contin.*
Murray, D: C. Hearts, queen, knave, and deuce.   823.5024
—— Life's atonement.
Oliphant, *Mrs.* M. O. (W.) Ombra.

Du Boisgobey, F. Pretty jailer. 2 pts.   823.5025
—— Sculptor's daughter.
O'Hanlon, A. Unforeseen.

Lang, A. Mark of Cain.   823.5026
Oliphant, *Mrs.* M. O. (W.) Open door.
—— Portrait.
Sala, G: A: Strange adventures of Captain Dangerous.
Tadema, L. A. Love's martyr.

Brown, F.. Hidden sin.   823.5027
Oliphant, *Mrs.* M. O. (W.) Days of my life.
Waters of Hercules.

Oliphant, *Mrs.* M. O. (W.) Innocent. 2 parts.   823.5028
Verne, J. Mathias Sandorf. 3 parts.

Gaboriau, É. Widow Lerouge.   823.5029
Maxwell, *Mrs.* M.. E.. (B.) Octoroon.
—— Under the red flag.

Oliphant, *Mrs.* M. O. (W.) Agnes. 2 parts.   823.5030
Reuter, F. Old story of my farming days.

Gaskell, *Mrs.* E.. C. (S.) Cranford.   823.5033
Girl's heart.
Roberts, M. Child of the revolution.
Shaw, G: B. Cashel Byron's profession.

Bridges, *Mrs. Col.* —. From Olympus to Hades.   823.5034
Gaboriau, É. Mystery of Orcival.
Hector, *Mrs.* A. (F.) Admiral's ward.

Brame, *Mrs.* C.. M. (L.) That beautiful lady.   823.5035
—— Unnatural bondage.
Gaboriau, É. Marriage at a venture.
Gray, A. Periwinkle.

Beale, A. Idonea.   823.5036
Brame, *Mrs.* C.. M. (L.) Repented at leisure.
Edwards, M. B. B.- Love and mirage.
Maxwell, *Mrs.* M.. E.. (B.) Barbara.
Miller, *Mrs.* A. McV. Lancaster's choice.
Norris, W: E: Man of his word.
Wood, *Mrs.* E. (P.) Surgeon's daughters.

Majendie, *Lady* M. E.. Dita.   823.5037
Marks, *Mrs.* M.. A. M. (H.) Great treason.
Muir, A. "Golden girls."

Alexander, F. Story of Ida, ed. by J. Ruskin.   823.5038
Gaboriau, É. Monsieur Lecocq.
Murray, D: C. By the gates of the sea.
Oliphant, *Mrs.* M. O. (W.) A little pilgrim.

Besant, W. Dorothy Forster.   823.5039
Buchanan, R. God and the man.
McCarthy, J. Maid of Athens.

Blagden, I. Woman I loved and the woman who loved me.   823.5040
Bridges, *Mrs. Col.* —. Once again.
McCarthy, J. H. Our sensation novel.
Oliphant, *Mrs.* M. O. (W.) House divided against itself.
Stannard, *Mrs.* H. E. V. (P.) Army society.

Caddy, *Mrs.* —. Adrian Bright.   823.5041
Martin, *Mrs.* M.. E. For a dream's sake.
Mixed motives.
Russell, D. Rose Fleming.

English Fiction. *Contin.*
Seaside library. [*Pocket ed.*] *Contin.*
Brame, *Mrs.* C.. M. (L.) Fair mystery.   823.5042
MacNabb, *Mrs.* M. (L.) Singer's story, A.
Molesworth, *Mrs.* M.. L.. (S.) Us.
Wedded hands.

D'Ennery, A. P. The two orphans.   823.5043
John Bull's neighbor in her true light. By a "Brutal Saxon."
MacDonald, G: Donal Grant.
Miller, *Mrs.* A. M. Lady Gay's pride.
—— Laurel Vane.
Ohnet, G. Master of the forges.

Burton, J. B. Silent shore.   823.5044
Miller, *Mrs.* A. McV. Sworn to silence.
Oliphant, *Mrs.* M. O. (W.) House on the moor.
—— Passages in the life of Mrs. Margaret Maitland.

Clifford, *Mrs.* L. (L.) Mrs. Keith's crime.   823.5045
Maxwell, *Mrs.* M.. E.. (B.) Asphodel.
—— John Marchmont's legacy.

Besant, W. Self or bearer.   823.5046
Broughton, R. Mrs. Smith of Longmains.
Fargus, F: J: Slings and arrows, and other stories.
Fenn, G: M. Dark house.
Hardy, T: Mere interlude.
My wife's niece.
Oliphant, *Mrs.* M. O. (W.) Oliver's bride.
Stannard, *Mrs.* H. E. V. (P.) Houp-la.
—— Man of honor.

Fenn, G: M. Parson o' Dumford.   823.5047
—— Poverty corner.
Hunter, H., *and* White, W. My ducats and my daughter.
Norris, W: E: Adrian Vidal.

Manzoni, A. Betrothed.   823.5048
Maxwell, *Mrs.* M..E.. (B.) Charlotte's inheritance.

Bridges, *Mrs. Col.* —. Although he was a lord, and other tales.   823.5049
James Gordon's wife.
Lang, *Mrs.* A. Dissolving views.
Maxwell, *Mrs.* M.. E.. (B.) Hostages to fortune.
Vida's story.

James Gordon's wife.   823.5050
Lang, *Mrs.* A. Dissolving views.'
Maxwell, *Mrs.* M.. E.. (B.) Hostages to fortune.
Vida's story.

Grey, *Mrs.* E.. C. Gambler's wife.   823.5051
Maxwell, *Mrs.* M.. E.. (B.) Ishmaelite.
Stahr, *Mrs.* F. (L.) Stella.
Stevenson, R. L: Kidnapped.

Allen, G. For Maimie's sake.   823.5052
Bayly, A. E. In the golden days.
Society's verdict.

Coleridge, C. R. English squire.   823.5053
Lewes, G: H: Ranthorpe.
Shaw, F. L. Sea change.
Taylor, I. A. Venus's doves.

Brame, *Mrs.* C.. M. (L.) Golden dawn.   823.5054
—— Love for a day.
French, C.. Secret of the cliffs.
Halsey, H. George Christy.
Lee, M. May Blossom.
MacDonald, G: Phantastes.

Edwards, M. B. B. Doctor Jacob.   823.5055
Oliphant, *Mrs.* M. O. (W.) Perpetual curate.
Poynter, E. F.. Madame de Presnel.
Stahr, *Mrs.* F. (L.) Stella. Tr. by B. Marshall.

Craik, *Mrs.* D. M. (M.) King Arthur.   823.5056
Fargus, F: J: Living or dead.
Gould, S. Baring- Court Royal.
Hector, *Mrs.* A. (F.) Beaton's bargain.

English Fiction. *Contin.*
Seaside library. [*Pocket ed.*] *Contin.*
Gaboriau, É. Other people's money.   823.5057
Hay, M.. C. For her dear sake.
Irving, W. Sketch book of Geoffrey Crayon, Gent.

Grey, *Mrs.* E.. C. Gambler's wife.   823.5058
James, G: P. R. Agnes Sorel.
Maxwell, *Mrs.* M.. E.. (B.) Ishmaelite.

James, G: P. R. Agnes Sorel.   823.5059
Maxwell, *Mrs.* M.. E.. (B.) Mistletoe bough.
Oliphant, *Mrs.* M. O. (W.) Son of his father.

Buchanan, *Mrs.* H. (J.) Marriage of convenience.
  823.5060
Elliot, F.. Red cardinal.
Keeling, E. D'E. Three sisters.
Meredith, G: Diana of the crossways.
Murray, D: C. Bit of human nature.
Oliphant, *Mrs.* M. O. (W.) Prodigals and their inheritance.
Ward, *Mrs.* M.. A. (A.) Miss Bretherton.

Brame, *Mrs.* C.. M. (L.) Bitter atonement. 823.5061
Jenkins, E: Week of passion.
Maxwell, *Mrs.* M.. E.. (B.) Only a clod.

Coleman, J. Curly: an actor's story.   823.5062
King, R: A. Coquette's conquest.
—— Drawn game.
My poor wife.
Sime, W: Red route.

Brame, *Mrs.* C.. M. (L.) Dora Thorne.   823.5063
Dumas, A. D. Beau Tancrede.
Hay, M.. C. Dorothy's venture.

Brame, *Mrs.* C.. M. (L.) Dead heart.   823.5064
—— In Cupid's net.
—— Lady Gwendoline's dream.
Fargus, F: J. Blatchford bequest, and other stories.
Feuillet, O. Led astray.
Godfrey, *Mrs.* G. W. Mrs. Forrester's secret.
Muir, A. Tumbledown farm.
Oliphant, *Mrs.* M. O. (W.) Lucy Crofton.
Verne, J. Archipelago on fire.

Colquhoun, M. J. Primus in Indis.   823.5065
Half way.
Murray, D: C. Valentine Strange.
Russell, W: C. In the middle watch.

Fargus, F: J. Living or dead.   823.5066
Maxwell, *Mrs.* M.. E.. (B.) Aurora Floyd.
Oliphant, *Mrs.* M. O. (W.) Minister's wife.

Fargus, F: J. Bound by a spell.   823.5067
Maxwell, *Mrs.* M.. E.. (B.) Mistletoe bough.
Oliphant, *Mrs.* M. O. (W.) Son of his father.
Stevenson, R. L: Kidnapped.

Edwards, M. B. Betham- Doctor Jacob.   823.5068
Fargus, F: J. Bound by a spell.
Griffith, C. Victory Deane.
Poynter, E. F.. Madame de Presnel.

Archer, E. M. Betwixt my love and me.   823.5069
Du Boisgobey, F. Zig-zag, the clown.
Fargus, F: J. Family affair.

Gaboriau, É. Within an inch of his life.   823.5070
Hector, *Mrs.* A. (F.) Wooing o't.

Haggard, H: R. King Solomon's mines.   823.5071
—— She.
—— Witch's head.

Haggard, H: R. Allan Quatermain.   823.5072
—— Dawn.

Darrell, J. Winifred Power.   823.5073
Hill, J: Waters of Marah.
Saunders, J: Noble wife.
Trollope, T: A. Diamond cut diamond.

English Fiction. *Contin.*
Seaside library. [*Pocket ed.*] *Contin.*
Edwards, H: S. Case of Reuben Malachi. 823.5074
Haggard, H: R. Jess.
Mulholland, R. Late Miss Hollingford.
Russell, W: C. Golden Hope.

Bridges, *Mrs.* Col. —. Although he was a lord, and
other tales.   823.5075
Haggard, H: R. Jess.
Needell, *Mrs.* J: H. Lucia, Hugh, and another.
Tennyson, A., *Lord.* Locksley Hall sixty years after, etc.

Brame, *Mrs.* C.. M. (L.) Prince Charlie's daughter.
  823.5076
—— Thorns and orange blossoms.
Lang, A., *and* Latimer, D. He.
Stannard, *Mrs.* H. E. V. (P.) Childhood's memories.
—— Siege baby.

Dumas, A. D. Twenty years after.   823.5077
Hay, M.. C. Old Myddelton's money.

Du Boisgobey, F. Cry of blood. Tr. by L. E. Kendall. 2 parts.   823.5078
Hay, M.. C. Wicked girl.
Sergeant, A. No saint.
Stevenson, R. L:, *and* Stevenson, F. Van de G. The dynamiter.

Brame, *Mrs.* C.. M. (L.) For another's sin. 823.5079
—— Squire's darling.
Hay, M.. C. Victor and vanquished.

Brame, *Mrs.* C.. M. (L.) Duke's secret.   823.5080
—— Queen amongst women.
Hay, M.. C. Arundel motto.

Hardy, T: Far from the madding crowd.   823.5081
Murray, D: C. Rainbow gold.
Sime, W: Cradle and spade.

Bridges, *Mrs.* Col. —. I have lived and loved.
  823.5082
MacDonald, G: What's mine's mine.

Fenn, G: M. Parson o' Dumford.   823.5083
—— Poverty corner.
Hunter, H., *and* White, W. My ducats and my daughter.
Norris, W: E: Adrian Vidal.

Brougham, J. Lottery of life.   823.5084
Felbermann, H. Princess Dagomar of Poland.
Gross, F. Not dead.
Hunter, H., *and* White, W. Crime of Christmas day.
Mackay, W. Devil's ward.
Norris, W: E: That terrible man.
Oliphant, *Mrs.* M. O. (W.) Magdalen Hepburn.
Pettitt, H: Poet's ghost.
Vince, H: S. As Avon flows.

Du Boisgobey, F. Condemned door.   823.5086
Edwards, A. B. Miss Carew.
Society's verdict.

Brame, *Mrs.* C.. M. (L.) Earl's atonement.
  823.5088
Dumas, A. D. Three guardsmen.
Ebers, G. M. Serapis.

Erckmann, É., *and* Chatrian, P. A. Polish Jew.
  823.5089
Felbermann, H. Princess Dagomar of Poland.
Gross, F. Not dead.
Hector, *Mrs.* A. (F.) Mrs. Vereker's courier maid.
Landor, O. Three sisters of the Briars.
Mackay, W. Devil's ward.
Norris, W: E: That terrible man.
Oliphant, *Mrs.* M. O. (W.) Memoirs and resolutions of Adam Graeme of Mossgray.
Pettitt, H: Poet's ghost.
Verne, J. Southern star.
Vosmaer, C. Amazon.

English Fiction. *Contin.*
Seaside library. [*Pocket ed.*] *Contin.*
Bradshaw, A. Crimson stain. 823.5090
Byron, *Lord.* Childe Harold's pilgrimage; poem.
Ewing, Mrs. J. H. (G.) Jackanapes, and other stories.
King, K.. Ethel Mildmay's follies.
Reid, T: W. Mauleverer's millions.

Blatherwick, C. Ducie diamonds.   823.5091
Eiloart, *Mrs.* C. J. Some of our girls.
Jennings, L: J. The millionaire.
Norris, W: E: Thirlby Hall.

Du Boisgobey, F. Closed door.   823.5092
Russell, W: C. Jack's courtship.

Du Boisgobey, F. Coral pin. 2 parts.   823.5093
Middlemass, J. Lady Muriel's secret.
Oliphant, *Mrs.* M. O. (W.) Salem Chapel.

Brame, *Mrs.* C.. M. (L.) Hilda.   823.5094
Du Boisgobey, F. Piedouche; a French detective.
Fargus, F: J. Called back.
—— Daughter of the stars, and other tales.
James, *Mrs.* F. A. (P.) House on the marsh.
Kingsley, C: Water-babies: a fairy tale for a land baby.

Du Boisgobey, F. Lottery ticket.   823.5095
Libbey, L. J. Madolin Rivers.
Willful maid.

Du Boisgobey, F. Sealed lips.   823.5096
Maxwell, *Mrs.* M.. E.. (B.) Lady's mile.
—— Wyllard's weird.

Cumberland, S. C. Rabbi's spell.   823.5097
Du Boisgobey, F. Angel of the bells.
Murray, D: C. First person singular.
Oliphant, *Mrs.* M. O. (W.) Country gentleman.

Du Boisgobey, F. Consequences of a duel.
                                          823.5098
Hector, *Mrs.* A. (F.) Which shall it be?
McCarthy, J. Camiola.

Brame, *Mrs.* C.. M. (L.) Fair but false.   823.5099
—— Wedded and parted.
—— Wife in name only.
—— Wife's secret.

Brame, *Mrs.* C.. M. (L.) At war with herself.
                                          823.5100
Oliphant, *Mrs.* M. O. (W.) Poor gentleman.
Smart, H. Outsider.

Brame, *Mrs.* C.. M. (L.) Like no other love.
                                          823.5101
—— Sin of a life time.
—— Two kisses.
Hayden, *Mrs.* S. Little Goldie.

Brame, *Mrs.* C.. M. (L.) Her martyrdom. 823.5103
James, *Mrs.* F. A. (P.) Prince of darkness.
Maxwell, *Mrs.* M.. E.. (B.) To the bitter end.

Brame, *Mrs.* C.. M. (L.) From gloom to sunlight.
                                          823.5104
Bride of Monte-Cristo. Sequel to "Count of Monte-Cristo."
Maxwell, *Mrs.* M.. E.. (B.) Lady Audley's secret.

Balzac, H. de. Père Goriot.   823.5105
Hardy, T: Mayor of Casterbridge.
McCarthy, J. H. Doom!
Murray, D: C. Aunt Rachel.
Stevenson, R. L: Prince Otto.

Brame, *Mrs.* C.. M. (L.) Love's warfare.   823.5106
Fargus, F: J: Dark days.
Maxwell, *Mrs.* M.. E.. (B.) Put to the test.

English Fiction. *Contin.*
Seaside library. [*Pocket ed.*] *Contin.*
Hector, *Mrs.* A. (F.) Her dearest foe. 2 parts.
                                          823.5107
Maxwell, *Mrs.* M.. E.. (B.) Mohawks.

Edwards, M. B. B. Flower of doom, and other stories.   823.5108
Maxwell, *Mrs.* M.. E.. (B.) Cut by the county.
—— Fatal marriage, *and* The shadow in the corner.
Oliphant, *Mrs.* M. O. (W.) Harry Muir.
Roe, *Mrs.* A. (F.) Bachelor vicar of Newforth.
Sime, W: Haco the dreamer.

Boyle, F. Good hater.   823.5109
King, R. A. Wearing of the green.
Oliphant, *Mrs.* M. O.(W.) John: a love story.

Brame, *Mrs.* C.. M. (L.) Between two sins.
                                          823.5111
—— True Magdalen.
Russell, W: C. Sailor's sweetheart.

Maxwell, *Mrs.* M.. E.. (B.) Just as I am. 823.5112
—— Taken at the flood.

Hood, T: Tylney Hall.   823.5114
Maxwell, *Mrs.* M.. E.. (B.) Cloven foot.
—— Rupert Godwin.

Brame, *Mrs.* C.. M. (L.) Which loved him best?
                                          823.5115
Gaboriau, É. File No. 113.
Walsh, M. Hazel Kirke.

Buchanan, R. W: Annan water.   823.5116
Maxwell, *Mrs.* M.. E.. (B.) Phantom fortune.
Smart, H. From post to finish.

Brame, *Mrs.* C.. M. (L.) Between two loves.
                                          823.5117
—— Lady Damer's secret.
Maxwell, *Mrs.* M.. E.. (B.) Married in haste.

Brame, *Mrs.* C.. M. (L.) Shadow of a sin. 823.5118
—— Woman's error.
Bridges, *Mrs.* Col. —. Dolores.

Brame, *Mrs.* C.. M. (L.) Sunshine and roses.
                                          823.5119
Hector, *Mrs.* A. (F.) Valerie's fate.
Maxwell, *Mrs.* M.. E.. (B.) Diavola. 2 parts.

Brame, *Mrs.* C.. M. (L.) Dark marriage morn.
                                          823.5120
Bridges, *Mrs.* Col. —. Rhona.
Norris, W: E: Bachelor's blunder.

Blossom and fruit.   823.5123
Brame, *Mrs.* C.. M. (L.) Arnold's promise.
—— Earl's error.
—— Letty Leigh.
—— Shattered idol.

Brame, *Mrs.* C.. M. (L.) Shadow of a sin. 823.5124
—— 'Twixt smile and tear.
Maxwell, *Mrs.* M.. E.. (B.) Vixen.

Fargus, F: J: Cardinal sin.   823.5125
Hector, *Mrs.* A. (F.) Look before you leap.
Maxwell, *Mrs.* M.. E.. (B.) Dead men's shoes.

Brame, *Mrs.* C.. M. (L.) Evelyn's folly.   823.5126
—— Woman's temptation.
Du Boisgobey, F. Prima donna's husband.
Maxwell, *Mrs.* M.. E.. (B.) Only a woman.

Brame, *Mrs.* C.. M. (L.) Her second love. 823.5127
Gaboriau, É. Count's secret. 2 parts.
Verne, J. Robur the conqueror.

English Fiction. *Contin.*
Seaside library. [*Pocket ed.*] *Contin.*

Brame, *Mrs.* C.. M. (L.) At war with herself.
           823.5128
   Hay, M.. C. Squire's legacy.
   Hector, *Mrs.* A. (F.) Maid, wife, or widow.
   Russell, W: C. John Holdsworth, chief mate.
   Sergeant, A. Beyond recall.

Brame, *Mrs.* C. M. (L.) Broken wedding-ring.
           823.5129
   Verne, J. Dick Sand.

Du Boisgobey, F. Red band. 2 parts.   823.5130
Maxwell, *Mrs.* M.. E.. (B.) Joshua Haggard's
   daughter.

Black, W: Romeo and Juliet.   823.5131
Maxwell, *Mrs.* M.. E.. (B.) One thing needful.
Murray, D: C. Bulldog and butterfly.
—— Cynic fortune.
Oliphant, *Mrs.* M. O. (W.) Effie Ogilvie.
Stevenson, R. L: New Arabian nights.

Brame, *Mrs.* C.. M. (L.) Ingledew House. 823.5132
—— More bitter than death.
—— Set in diamonds.
—— Thrown on the world.

Brame, *Mrs.* C.. M. (L.) From gloom to sunlight.
           823.5133
—— Mystery of the holly-tree.
—— On her wedding morn.
Whyte, V. Her Johnnie.

Brame, *Mrs.* C.. M. (L.) Madolin's lover. 823.5134
—— Redeemed by love.
—— Woman's war.

Besant, W. Holy rose.   823.5135
Du Boisgobey, F. Cash on delivery.
Hardy, T: Trumpet-major.
Maxwell, *Mrs.* M.. E.. (B.) Publicans and sinners.
   2 parts.

Besant, W. Holy rose.   823.5136
Du Boisgobey, F. Cash on delivery.
Hardy, T: Trumpet-major.
—— Woodlanders.

Brame, *Mrs.* C.. M. (L.) Under a shadow. 823.5137
—— World between them.
Woman's love story.

Buchanan, R. W: Master of the mine.   823.5138
Mayo, *Mrs.* I.. (F.) Mystery of Allan Grale.
Ritchie, *Mrs.* A.. I.. (T.) Mrs. Dymond.
Stannard, *Mrs.* H. E. V. (F.) In quarters with the
   25th (the Black Horse) Dragoons.

Brame, *Mrs.* C.. M. (L.) Marjorie. 2 parts.
           823.5140
Maxwell, *Mrs.* M.. E.. (B.) Publicans and sinners.
   2 parts.

Aïdé, H. Introduced to society.   823.5145
Besant, W. World went very well then.
Hunt, *Mrs.* M. (R.) That other person. (1st part.)
Willful young woman.

Brame, *Mrs.* C.. M. (L.) A struggle for a ring.
           823.5180
—— Sweet Cymbeline.

Brame, *Mrs.* C.. M. (L.) Marjorie. 2 pts. 823.5186
Hardy, T: The woodlanders.
Maxwell, *Mrs.* M.. E.. (B.) Publicans and sinners.
   2d half.

Aïdé, H. Introduced to society.   823.5187
Besant, W. The world went very well then.
Hunt, *Mrs.* M. (R.) That other person. 1st hf.
Willful young woman, A.

English Fiction. *Contin.*
Seaside library. [*Pocket ed.*] *Contin.*

Besant, W. In luck at last.   823.5188
Buchanan, R. W: Matt: a tale of a caravan.
Carleton, L. C. Mysterious hunter.
Du Boisgobey, F. Bablole, the pretty milliner.
Paeon, J. Dead man's secret.
Thomas, B. Ichabod: a portrait.

Bürstenbinder, E. Raymond's atonement.
           823.5202
James, *Mrs.* F. A. (P.) Deldee; or, the iron hand.
Mayo, *Mrs.* I. (F.) At any cost.
Smart, H. Tie and trick.

Bridges, *Mrs.* Col. —. Roy and Viola.   823.5422
—— Viva.
Hector, *Mrs.* A. (F.) Beaton's bargain.
Walpole, H. The castle of Otranto.

John, E. In the counselor's house.   823.6693
Yonge, C.. M.. Under the storm.

Edwardes, *Mrs.* A. A vagabond heroine. 823.6694
Hay, M.. C. A dark inheritance.
Hector, *Mrs.* A. (F.) Forging the fetters, and The
   Australian aunt.

Maxwell, *Mrs.* M.. E.. (B.) Only a woman.
           823.6695
Oliphant, *Mrs.* M. O. (W.) A little pilgrim.

Collins, W: W. Love's random shot, and other
   stories.   823.6696

Pellico, S. My ten years' imprisonment. 823.6697
Reade, C: The picture.
—— Jack of all trades.

Fenn, G: M. Commodore Junk.   823.6698
Hughes, T: Tom Brown's school days at Rugby.

Gaboriau, É. A thousand francs reward. 823.6699
Grant, J. The Royal Highlanders; or, the Black
   Watch in Egypt.
Mérimée, P. Carmen: the power of love.

Sturgis, J. R. Dick's wanderings.   823.6700
Walford, *Mrs.* L. B. (C.) Mr. Smith.

Besant, W., *and* Rice, J. Love finds the way, and
   other stories.   823.6701
Maxwell, *Mrs.* M.. E.. (B.) The golden calf.

Du Boisgobey, F. The mystery of an omnibus.
           823.6702
Russell, W: C. The wreck of the Grosvenor.
Tolstoi, *Count* L. N. My husband and I.

Season-ticket, The. Haliburton, T: C.
           823.690
Seaward, *Sir* E:, *pseud. See* Porter, W: O.
Seawell, Molly Elliot. Throckmorton.
           823.7447
Sebastian Strome. Hawthorne, J. C.
           823.6390
Second life, A. Hector, *Mrs.* A. (F.)
           823.4909
Same.   823.4979
Second son, The. Oliphant, *Mrs.* M. O.
   (W.), *and* Aldrich, T: B.   823.5216
Second to none. Grant, J.   823.652
Second wife, The. John, E.   823.2455
Secondthoughts, Solomon, *Schoolmaster,*
   pseud. See Kennedy, J: P.
Secret dispatch. Grant, J.   823.653
Secret inheritance, A. Farjeon, B: L.
          in 823.6587

English Fiction. *Contin.*
Secret of a birth, The.´ McKenna, C.. M. S.
823.4811
Secret of Fontaine-la-Croix. Field, M.
823.7079
Secret of the cliffs. French, C.. *in* 823.5054
Secret of the island, The. Verne, J.
823.5784
Secret of the Lamas, The: a tale of Thibet.
823.7076
Secret of the sea, &c. Matthews, J. B.
823.5366
Secret passion, The. Williams, R. F.
in ** 823.6260
Section 558. From the diary of Inspector
Byrnes. Hawthorne, J. C. 823.5269
Sedgwick, Catherine Maria. (1789–1867.) The
Linwoods; or, "sixty years since" in Amer-
ica. 2 vols. ** 823.6754-5
Note.—For her life and writings, *see* **Griswold,**
R. W. Prose writers of America. 1870. p. 357, *in*
* 829.110.—**Homes** of Amer. authors. 1853. p. 159,
in 917.37.
See also **Allibone's** Dict. of Eng. lit., v. 2. pp.
1,987-8, *in* ** 803.7.
See also **Poole's** Index (to 1882). p. 1,175, *in* **
50.1.
Seeley, Richmond, *joint author. See* Church,
A. J:
Seelye, *Mrs.* Lillie (Eggleston), *joint author.*
See Eggleston, E:
Seemüller, *Mrs.* A.. Moncure (Crane). Op-
portunity: a novel. 823.344
—— Reginald Archer. 823.4264
Segrave, Adolphus, *pseud. See* Hamerton,
P. G.
Ségur, Sophie (Rostopchine), *comtesse* de.
Fairy tales. Tr. by Mrs. C. Coleman and
daughters. 808.1326
"Self or bearer." Besant, W. *in* 823.5046
Self-raised. Southworth, *Mrs.* E. D. E. (N.)
823.1507
Semi-detached house. Eden, E. 823.4183
Sense and sensibility. Austen, J.. 823.47
Same. 823.5536
Sentimental journey. Sterne, L.
p. 555, *in* 823.4489
Septimius Felton. Hawthorne, N.
in 823.731
Same. 823.5166
Seraphita. Balzac, H. de. 823.7335
Serapis. Ebers, G. M. 823.4926
Same. *in* 823.5088
Serbia. Wratislaw, A. H., *tr.* Serbian sto-
ries. (*In his* Sixty folk-tales, etc.)
p. 204, *in* 823.6946
Sergeant, Adeline.
—— Beyond recall. *in* 823.5128
—— A fatal choice. 15 pp. (*In* Twenty
novelettes, etc.) p. 39, *in* 823.7183
—— A life sentence. 823.7064
—— The luck of the house. 823.6967
—— No saint: a study. *in* 823.5078
Serpent-charmer, The. Rousselet, L:
823.6036
Serrao, Teodoro. Brushes and chisels.
823.7514
Set in diamonds. Brame, *Mrs.* C.. M. (L.)
in 823.5132
Settler and the savage, The. Ballantyne, R.
M. 808.206

English Fiction. *Contin.*
Settlers in Canada. Marryat, *Capt.* F:
808.776
Same. 823.1118
Seuyn sages, Proces of. Weber, H: W:
p. 1, *in* 821.1241
Seven champions of Christendom. King-
ston, W: H: G. 808.617
Seven daughters. Douglas, A. M. 823.483
Seven little people and their friends. Scud-
der, H. E. 808.1559
Seven little sisters. Andrews, J.. 808.1428
Seven sons of mammon. Sala, G: A:
823.5958
Seven stories, with basement and attic. Mit-
chell, D. G. 823.5291
Seven years, and other tales. Kavanagh, J.
823.920
Sevenoaks. Holland, J. G. 823.783
1791: a tale of San Domingo. Gilliam, E.
W. 823.7174
Severa. Hartner, E. 823.4271
Severance, M: Sibley. Hammersmith: his
Harvard days. 823.1415
Severed hand. Du Boisgobey, F. 823.3393
Sewell, A.. Black Beauty: his grooms and
companions. 808.1697
Sewell, E.. Missing. A glimpse of the
world. 823.5207
—— Margaret Percival. 823.4177
Seymour, Robert, *and* Cruikshank, G: The
odd volume. Illus. 823.350
Sforza. Astor, W: W. 823.7015
Shabby genteel story. Thackeray, W: M.
in 823.1571
Same. *in* 823.5002
Shadow in the corner. 20 pp. Maxwell,
Mrs. M.. E.. (B.) *in* 823.5108
Same. *in* 823.6604
Shadow of a dream. Howells, W: D.
823.7166
Shadow of a sin, The. Brame, *Mrs.* C.. M.
(L.) *in* 823.5118
Same. *in* 823.5124
Shadow of Hampton Mead. Van Loon, *Mrs.*
E.. 823.1787
Shadow of Moloch mountain. Austin, J.. G.
823.5835
Shadow of the door. 60 pp. (*In* Tales from
Blackwood. 2d ser., v. 8.) *in* 823.7492
Shadow of the sword. Buchanan, R. W.
823.4166
Shadows on the snow. Farjeon, B: L.
823.5866
Shady side, The. Hubbell, *Mrs.* M. (S.)
823.4639
Shakespeare, W: 1564-1616.
—— Clarke, *Mrs.* M..V. (N.) Cowden- Girl-
hood of Shakespeare's heroines: in a ser.
of tales. 2 vols. 823.5821-2
—— Hamley, *Sir* E: B. Shakespeare's fu-
neral. 65 pp. (*In* Tales from Blackwood.
2d ser., v. 1.) *in* 823.7485
—— Lamb, C:, *and* Lamb, M.. Tales from
Shakespeare. 823.953
—— —— *Same.* 808.783
—— Macauley, E. Tales of the drama
founded on the tragedies of Shakespeare,
etc. 823.1051

English Fiction. *Contin.*
Shakespeare, W: 1564–1616. *Contin.*
—— Ribson, J. Fairy tales, legends and romances, illustrating Shakespeare, etc.
822.309
—— Williams, R. F. Shakespeare and his friends; or, the golden age of merrie England.—Secret passion; sequel to "Youth of Shakespeare."—Youth of Shakespeare.
** 823.6260

Note.—For life and bibliographies of his works, *see* **Bagehot, W.** Shakespeare—the man. (*Works*, v. 1.) p. 254, *in* 814.22.—**Baynes,** *Prof.* T. S. Article "Shakespeare" in Encyclop. Brit., v. 21. ** 32. 291.—**Bryant, W: C.** Orations and addresses. 1878. p. 369, *in* 825.12.—**Carlyle, T:** Shakespeare. 10 pp. (*In his* On heroes and hero-worship.) p. 84, *in* 829.662.—**Clarke, J. F.** Shakspeare. 38 pp. (*In his* Mem. . . . sketches.) 1878. p. 301, *in* 923.915.—**De Quincey, T:** Shakespeare. 92 pp. (*In his* Biog. essays.) p. 9, *in* 824.122.—**Dowden,** *Prof.* E: Critical study of mind and art (of S.) 1880. 824.138. —**Drake, S: A.** Our great benefactors. 1884. p. 12, *in* * 920.312.—**Emerson, R. W.** Shakespeare; or, the poet. 32 pp. (*In his* Representative men.) p. 187, *in* 920.73.—**Gervinus,** *Prof.* G. G. Commentaries on Shakespeare. 1877. * 822.546.—**Hallam, H.** Literature of Europe, v. 2. 1871. 809.4.—**Halliwell-Phillips, J. O.** Outlines of the life of Shakespeare. 1882. 928.466.—**Lowell, J. R.** Shakespeare once more. 77 pp. (*In his* Among my books, 1st ser.) p. 151, *in* 824.102.—**Lowndes, W: T:** Bibliography of Shakespeare. (*Bibliographer's manual*, v. 8.) p. 2,252, *in* ** 15.8.

See also **Allibone's** Dict. of Eng. lit., v. 2. p. 2,006, *in* ** 803.7.
See also **Catalogues** of this Library.
No. 2, 1880, pp. 207–8. No. 4, 1884, p. 265.
No. 3, 1882, p. 173. No. 5, 1888, pp. 317–19.
See also **Poole's** Index (to 1882). pp. 1,183–7, *in* ** 50.1;—*Same.* Jan. 1, 1882–Jan. 1, 1887. pp. 397–8, *in* ** 50.1³.
See also **England,** *note,* under reign of Elizabeth, p. 68.

Shakespeare and his friends. Williams, R. F. ** 823.6260
Shall I win her? Grant, J: 823.654
Shamrock and rose. 3 vols. Lunn, *Mrs.* J. C. 823.7218–20
Shamrock and thistle. Adams, W: T. 808.492
Shand, Alexander Innes. Mr. Cox's protégé. (*In* Tales from Blackwood. 3d ser., v. 5.)
p. 209, *in* 823.7501
—— Wrecked off the Riff coast. (*In* Tales from Blackwood. 2d ser., v. 6.)
in 823.7490
Shandon bells. Black, W: 823.6539
Shandy McGuire. Boyce, J: 823.114
Shapley, Rufus R. Solid for Mulhooly: a sketch of municipal politics under the leaders, the ring, and the boss. 823.4351
Sharkey, T. K. Mate to mate. 823.1416
Sharp, W: Children of to-morrow. 823.7295
Shattered idol, The. Brame, *Mrs.* C. M. (L.)
in 823.5123
Shaving of Shagpat. Meredith, G: 823.5274
Shaw, Flora L. A sea change. *in* 823.5053
Shaw, G: Bernard. Cashel Byron's profession.
in 823.5033
Shaw, W. J. Solomon's story. 823.6049
She. Haggard, H: R. 823.5071
Same. 823.7158
Shedlock, Emma L. A trip to music-land: a fairy tale. Illus. 808.1933
Sheldon, Louise Vescelius- An I. D. B. in south Africa. 823.6580

English Fiction. *Contin.*
Shelley, *Mrs.* M.. Wollstonecraft (Godwin). Frankenstein; or, the modern Prometheus.
823.1421
Shepherd of Salisbury plain, and other tales. More, H. 823.1172
Shepherds all and maidens fair. Besant, W., and Rice, J. *in* 823.6084
Sheppard, E.. Sara. [*E.. Berger, Mme. Kinkel, B.. Reynolds.*]
—— Charles Auchester. 823.5960
—— *Same.* 3 vols. ** 823.6233–5
—— Counterparts; or, the cross of love.
823.6127
—— The matchmaker. 823.1420
—— Rumor. 823.6043
Sheppard, F. H. Love afloat: a story of the American navy. 823.1419
Sheridan, *Mrs.* F.. (Chamberlaine). History of Nourjahad. 34 pp. (Weber, H., *Tales of the east,* v. 2.) p. 691, *in* ** 823.6231
Sheridan, *Gen.* Philip H:
—— Headley, P. C. Fighting Phil: the life . . . of Philip Henry Sheridan, etc.
808.1600
Sherman, Frank Dempster, *joint author.* See Bangs, J: K.
Sherwood, *Mrs.* M.. E.. (Wilson). A transplanted rose: a story of New York society. (Anon.) 823.4486
Shifting winds. Ballantyne, R. M. 808.212
Shiftless folks. Smith, J. P. 823.614
Shigemi, Shiukichi. A Japanese boy.
808.1742
Shillaber, B: Penhallow. Cruises with Captain Bob on sea and land. 808.1604
Shinn, Milicent Washburn. Young Strong of "The Clarion:" 46 pp. (*In* Stories by Amer. authors, v. 9.) p. 93, *in* 823.4710
"Ship ahoy!" Fenn, G: M. 823.5922
Shipley, M.. E.. Looking back: a memory of two lives. 823.1423
Shippen, E:, U. S. N. Thirty years at sea: the story of a sailor's life. 823.7296
Shirley, James. Macauley, E. Tales of the drama founded on the tragedies of . . . Shirley, etc. 823.1051
Shirley, Philip, (*pseud.?*) On the verge: a romance of the centennial. 823.1424
Shirley. Nicholls, *Mrs.* C.. (B.) 823.128
Shorter stories. Balzac, H. de. 823.7353
Shorthouse, Joseph H:
—— The countess Eve. 823.5766
—— John Inglesant. 823.4531
—— The little schoolmaster Mark: a spiritual romance. 823.4881
—— *Same.* *in* 823.4993; 823.5413
—— Sir Percival: a story of the past and of the present. 823.5767
—— *Same.* *in* 823.6690
—— A teacher of the violin, and other tales.
823.5438
Shreve, T: H. Drayton: a story of American life. 823.4266
Siam.
—— Butterworth, H. Zigzag journeys in the antipodes. 808.1815
—— Knox, T: W. The boy travellers in the far East. Pt. 2. 808.1836

English Fiction. *Contin.*
Siam. *Contin.*

Note.—*See* **Bacon**, G: B. Siam: the land of the white elephant. 1887. 915.356.

See also **Catalogues** of this Library.
No. 2, 1880, p. 209.   No. 5, 1888, p. 320.
No. 4, 1884, p. 267.

See also **Index** to **Consular reports.** 1880–1885; 1886–1889. 2 vols. (U. S. Pub. Docs. *Dept. of State.*) *in* ** 350.5496¹·².

See also **Poole's Index** (to 1882). pp. 1,193–4, *in* ** 50.1;—*Same.* Jan. 1, 1882–Jan. 1, 1887. p. 401, *in* ** 50.1².

Sibyl Huntington. Dorr, *Mrs.* J. C. (R.)
823.472
Sidney, *Sir* Philip. The countess of Pembroke's Arcadia. 823.6639
—— *Same.* (Ed. of 1638.)   ** 823.6467
Sidney. Deland, *Mrs.* M. W. (C.) 823.7337
Sidonie. Daudet, A. 823.2827
Same. 823.6922
Siege baby, A. 44 pp. Stannard, *Mrs.* H. E. V. (P.) *in* 823.5076
Siege of Damascus. 3 vols. Nisbet, J.
** 823.6947–9
Siege of London. James, H:, *Jr.* 823.4524
Siege of Troy. Hanson, C: H: 808.1492
Siege of Washington, D. C. Adams, F. C.
808.1700
Siegfried, The story of. Baldwin, J.
823.5623
Sienkiewicz, Henryk. With fire and sword: an historical novel of Poland and Russia. Tr. by J. Curtin. 823.6338
Sierras, First fam'lies of the. Miller, C. H.
823.1159
Sights and insights. 2 vols. Whitney, *Mrs.* A. D. (T.) 823.1699–1700
Sigismund Fatello. 87 pp. (*In* Tales from Blackwood, v. 8.) *in* ** 823.6654
Sign of four. Doyle, A. C. 823.7520
Signa. La Ramée, L. de. 823.1827
Signing the contract. Finley, M. 823.561
Signor Monaldini's niece. Tincker, M.. A.
823.2000
Sigourney, *Mrs.* Lydia (Huntley). Lucy Howard's journal. 823.1425
Sigrid. Thoroddsen, J. T. 823.7136
Sikes, *Mrs.* Olive (Logan). Château Frissac; or, home scenes in France. 823.6116
Silas Marner. Cross, *Mrs.* M.. A. (E.)
823.1004
Silcote of Silcotes. Kingsley, H: 823.2033
Silent and true. Fleming, *Mrs.* M. A. (E.)
823.577
Silent partner, The. Ward, *Mrs.* E.. S. (P.)
823.1259
Silent shore, The. Burton, J: B.-
in 823.5044
Silent struggles. Stephens, *Mrs.* A. S. (W.)
823.1970
Silver caves, The. Ingersoll, E. 808.1719
Silver city, The. Ober, F: A. 808.1878
Silver pitchers, and other stories. Alcott, L.. M. 823.34
Silverado squatters, The. Stevenson, R. L:
808.1344
Silvermead. Middlemass, J. *in* 823.4987
Silverpen, *pseud.* *See* Meteyard, E.
Silvia. Kavanagh, J. 823.5920

English Fiction. *Contin.*
Sime, W: Boulderstone. *in* 823.4994
—— Cradle and spade. *in* 823.5081
—— Haco the dreamer: a tale of Scotch university life. *in* 823.5108
—— King Capital. 823.4503
—— The red route. *in* 823.5062
Simms, W: Gilmore. (1806–1870.)
—— Beauchampe; or, the Kentucky tragedy: a sequel to Charlemont. 823.1426
—— Border beagles: a tale of Mississippi.
823.1427
—— Charlemont; or, the pride of the village: a tale of Kentucky. 823.1428
—— Confession; or, the blind heart: a domestic story. 823.1429
—— The damsel of Darien. 2 vols. (in 1).
** 823.6729
—— Eutaw. 823.1430
—— The forayers; or, the raid of the dogdays. 823.1431
—— Guy Rivers: a tale of Georgia.
823.1432
—— Katharine Walton; or, the rebel of Dorchester. 823.1433
—— Mellichampe: a legend of the Santee.
823.1434
—— The partisan: a romance of the revolution. 823.1435
—— Richard Hurdis: a tale of Alabama.
823.1442
—— The scout; or, the black riders of Congaree. 823.1436
—— Southward ho! a spell of sunshine.
823.1437
—— Vasconselos: a romance of the new world. 823.1438
—— The wigwam and the cabin. 823.1439
Issued also as Life in America.
—— Woodcraft; or, hawks about the dovecote: a story of the south at the close of the revolution. 823.1440
Issued also as The sword and the distaff; or, "fair, fat, and forty."
—— The Yemasee: a romance of Carolina.
823.1441

Note.—For his life and writings, *see* **Griswold**, R. W. Prose writers of America. 1870. p. 503, *in* * 829.110.—**Homes** of Amer. authors. 1853. p. 257, *in* 917.37.—**Writings.** (Lit. world, Oct. 21, 1882, xiii.) p. 351, *in* ** 805.661.

See also **Allibone's** Dict. of Eng. lit., v. 2. pp. 2,104–6, *in* ** 803.7.—**Appleton's** Cyclop. of Amer. biog., v. 5. pp. 533–4, *in* ** 920.324.

See also **Poole's** Index (to 1882). p. 1,199, *in* ** 50.1;—*Same.* Jan. 1, 1882–Jan. 1, 1887. p. 403, *in* ** 50.1².

Simple story. Inchbald, *Mrs.* E.. (S.)
** 823.2089
Simple tales. Opie, *Mrs.* A. (A.)
p. 228, *in* 823.6134
Simpleton, *Maj.* —, *pseud.* Civil-service reform; or, the postmaster's revenge.
823.4593
Simpleton, A. Reade, C: 823.1983
Sims, G: R. Where is Mrs. Smith? 11 pp. (*In* Twenty novelettes, etc.)
p. 215, *in* 823.7183
Sin of a lifetime. Brame, *Mrs.* C.. M. (L.)
in 823.5101
Sinfire. Hawthorne, J. C. 823.5571

English Fiction. *Contin.*
Singer's story, A. MacNabb, *Mrs.* M. (L.)
 823.4954
Same.   *in* 823.5042
Singleheart and Doubleface. Reade, C:
  in 823.6677
Singleton, *Mrs.* M.. (Montgomerie Lamb).
[*Violet Fane.*] The story of Helen Davenant. 823.7254
Singleton, M.., *pseud. See* Brooke, *Mrs.* F..
(M.)
Sinnett, Alfred Percy. Karma. 823.4937
Sintram and his companions. La Motte-Fouqué, F. H. K: de. 823.3892
Same. p. 219, *in* 823.4762; *in* 823.5196
Sir Amadas. Weber, H: W:
 p. 241, *in* 821.1241
Sir Andrew Wylie of that ilk. Galt, J:
 823.4194
Sir Brooke Fosbrooke. Lever, C: J. 823.992
Sir Charles Grandison, History of. 4 vols.
Richardson, S: ** 823.6169–72
Same. 7 vols. ** 823.2070–6
Sir Cleges. Weber, H: W:
 p. 329, *in* * 821.1239
Sir Edward Seaward's narrative of his shipwreck. Porter, W: O. 823.4047
Sir Gervase Grey. 3 vols. (in 2). Gordon,
Mrs. —. 823.7314–15
Sir Gibbie. MacDonald, G: 823.1950
Same. 823.6042
Sir Harry Hotspur of Humblethwaite. Trollope, A. 823.1624
Same. 823.5997
Sir Hugues de Coucy. Herbert, H: W:
 p. 7, *in* 823.4253
Sir Jasper Carew. Lever, C: J. 823.993
Sir Jasper's tenant. Maxwell, *Mrs.* M.. E..
(B.) 823.2399
Same. 823.4955
Sir Noel's heir. Fleming, *Mrs.* M. A. (E.)
  in 823.578
Sir Percival. Shorthouse, J: H: 823.5767
Same.   *in* 823.6690
Sir Rohan's ghost. Spofford, *Mrs.* H. E..
(P.) 823.1516
Sir Tom. Oliphant, *Mrs.* M. O. (W.)
  in 823.6593
Sister Louise. Melville, G: J: Whyte-
 ** 823.4665
Same. 823.7288
Sister Rose. Holt, E. S.. 823.7232
Sister Saint Sulpice. Valdés, A. P.
 823.6426
Sister Silvia. 32 pp. Tincker, M.. A.
 p. 166, *in* 823.4703
Sisters, The. Ebers, G. M. 823.2578
Sister's story, A. Craven, *Mme.* P. (de la F.)
 823.6844
Six months at the Cape. Ballantyne, R. M.
 808.1550
Six months on a slaver. Manning, E:
 823.6959
Six of one by half a dozen of the other.
Stowe, *Mrs.* H. E.. (B.), *and others.*
 823.1531
Six to one. Bellamy, E: 823.7162
Six to sixteen. Ewing, *Mrs.* J. H. (G.)
 823.537

English Fiction. *Contin.*
Six years ago. Grant, J. 823.655
Six years later. Dumas, A. D. 823.6286
Sixty folk-tales from exclusively Slavonic
sources. Wratislaw, A. H:, *tr.* 823.6946
Sketch-book, The. Irving, W. 823.843
Same. 823.5057
Same. 2 vols. ** 823.6722–3
Sketches by Boz. (Pt. 1.) Dickens, C: J: H.
  in 823.4957
Same. Pt. 2.   *in* 823.385
Same. (Complete.) 823.5324
Sketches of Irish character. Hall, *Mrs.* A..
M. (F.) 823.691
Sketches of the women of Christendom.
Charles, *Mrs.* E.. (R.) 823.5696
Sketches of young couples. 49 pp. Dickens, C: J: H. p. 481, *in* 808.686
Same. p. 479, *in* 942.1259
Skirmishing. Jenkin, *Mrs.* H. C. (J.)
 823.896
Slave girl of Pompeii. Holt, E. S.. 808.1515
Slaves of the ring. Fleming, G. 823.7042
Sleeper, J: Sherburne. [*Hawser Martingale.*] Tales of the ocean and essays for
the forecastle. 823.1838
Sleepless woman, The. Jerdan, W:
 p. 198, *in* 823.702
Sleight, M.. B. The flag on the mill.
 823.5406
—— Osego chronicles; or, the Kuylers and
their friends. 823.1942
Slick, Sam, *pseud. See* Haliburton, T: C.
Slings and arrows. Fargus, F: J:
  in 823.5046
Slip in the fens, A.   . 823.807
Smallchange family, The. 17 pp. (*In* Famous Stories. By De Quincey, and others.)
 p. 283, *in* 823.1778
Smart, Hawley. At fault. 823.7129
—— Bad to beat.   *in* 823.4985
—— *Same.*   *in* 823.5020
—— Belles and ringers. 823.4030
—— Breezie Langton: a story of 'fifty-two to
'fifty-five. 823.7524
—— Courtship in 1720 and in 1860. Romances of two centuries. 823.4331
—— From post to finish: a racing romance.
  in 823.5116
—— The master of Rathkelly: a novel.
 823.5589
—— The outsider.   *in* 823.5100
—— Saddle and sabre. 823.5777
—— Struck down.   *in* 823.5012
—— Tie and trick.   *in* 823.4995
—— *Same.*   *in* 823.5202
—— Two kisses. 823.5590
Smedley, Francis E: The fortunes and misfortunes of Harry Racket Scapegrace.
 823.6387
—— The fortunes of the Colville family; or,
a cloud and its silver lining. (*Also*) Seven
tales,* ed. by F. E: Smedley. 823.1443
Contents:—"The trust." By Mrs. Burbury.—The
last in the lease. By Mrs. A. M. (F.) Hall.—Norfolk and Hereford. By G: P. R. James.—The will.
By Miss Pardoe.—The mysteries of Redgrave
Court. By F. E: Smedley.—A very woman. By
Miss M. B. Smedley.—King Veric: a scene of the
Romans in Britain. By M. F. Tupper.

English Fiction. *Contin.*
Smedley, Francis E: *Contin.*
—— Frank Fairlegh; or, scenes from the life of a private pupil.   823.1444
—— Harry Coverdale's courtship and marriage and what came of it.   823.1445
—— Lewis Arundel; or, the railroad of life.
                             823.1446
—— *Same.*   823.5987
—— Lorrimer Littlegood.   823.1447
—— The mysteries of Redgrave Court. 34 pp.   p. 115, *in* 823.1443
—— Tom Racquet, and his three maiden aunts.   823.5940
Smedley, Menella Bute. A very woman. 32 pp. (*With* Fortunes of the Colville family. By F. E: Smedley).   p. 272, *in* 823.1443
Smike. Dickens, C: J: H.   *in* 808.1569
Smith, Albert. Adventures of Mr. Ledbury and his friend Jack Johnson.   823.1451
—— The fortunes of the Scattergood family. (*Also*) The armourer of Paris: a romance of the 15th century.   823.1449
—— The ·marchioness of Brinvilliers; the poisoner of the seventeenth century: a romance of old Paris.   823.1450
—— The Pottleton legacy: a story of town and country life.   823.1452
—— Struggles and adventures of Christopher Tadpole at home and abroad.   823.1448
Smith, Alexander. Dreamthorp.   17 pp. (Johnson, R., *ed. Little classics*, v. 4.)
                          p. 108, *in* 829.127
—— Miss Oona McQuarrie. Sequel to Alfred Hagart's household.   823.4104
Smith, Mrs. C.. (Turner). The old manor house. 2 vols. (Barbauld, *Mrs.* A. L. (A.), *ed. The British novelists*, vols. 36–37.)
                            ** 823.2097–8
Smith, Mrs. E.. Thomas (Meade). Vaughan of Balliol. 14 pp. (*In* Twenty novelettes, etc.)   p. 13, *in* 823.7183
Smith, Hannah. [*Hesba Stretton.*]
—— Bede's charity.   823.2028
—— Brought home.   823.1453
—— Cassy.   823.1454
—— The crew of the "Dolphin."   823.1455
—— David Lloyd's last will.   823.1456
—— Hester Morley's promise.   823.1457
—— In prison and out.   823.1458
—— *Same.*   *in* 823.6687
—— The king's servants.   823.1459
—— The lord's pursebearers.   823.3860
—— Lost Gip, and Michel Lorio's cross.
                             823.1460
—— Max Kromer: a story of the siege of Strasburg, 1870.   823.1461
—— Nelly's dark days.   823.1462
—— Through a needle's eye.   823.2036
Smith, Horace. The picnic party. 29 pp. (Johnson, R., *ed. Little classics*, v. 9.)
                          p. 102, *in* 829.132
Smith, Rev. J. The Dalbroom folks. 2 vols.
                             823.6397–8
Smith, J. Moyr, *comp.* Tales of old Thule.
                             808.753
Smith, Joseph Emerson. Oakridge: an old-time story.   823.1463

English Fiction. *Contin.*
Smith, Mrs. Julie P. [*Christabel Goldsmith.*]
—— Blossom-bud and her genteel friends.
                             823.4537
—— Chris and Otho: the pansies and orange-blossoms they found in Roaring river and Rosenbloom. A sequel to "Widow Goldsmith's daughter."   823.1464
—— Courting and farming; or, which is the gentleman?   823.1465
—— His young wife.   823.1466
—— Kiss, and be friends.   823.2029
—— Lucy.   823.1941
—— The married belle; or, our red cottage at Merry Bank.   823.1467
—— Peace Pelican, spinster: a love story.
                             823.4180
—— Shiftless folks: an undiluted love story.
                             823.614
—— Ten old maids; and five of them were wise, and five of them were foolish: a novel.
                             823.1468
—— Widow Goldsmith's daughter.
                             823.1469
—— The widower: also, a true account of some brave frolics at Craigenfels. 823.1470
Smith, Mrs. M.. Prudence (Wells.) [*P. Thorne.*] The great match, and other matches.   823.5615
—— Jolly good times; or, child-life on a farm.   808.1004
Smith, Rev. Rowland, *tr.* The Greek romances of Heliodorus, Longus, and Achilles Tatius, comprising The Ethiopics; or, adventures of Theagenes and Chariclea; The pastoral amours of Daphnis and Chloe; and The loves of Clitopho and Leucippe.
                             823.2134
Smithson, Isabel, *and* Barnes, G: Foster. About giants and other wonder people.
                             808.1598
Smoke. Turgenef, I. S.   823.4214
Smollett, Tobias G: The adventures of Peregrine Pickle, in which are included memoirs of a lady of quality.   823.1472
—— The adventures of Roderick Random. With a memoir of the author.   823.1473
—— Humphry Clinker.   823.1471
—— *Same.* 2 vols. (Barbauld, *Mrs.* A. L. (A.), *ed. The British novelists*, vols. 30–31.)   ** 823.2091–2
Smyth, Patrick G. King and viking; or, the ravens of Lochlan: a tale of the Danish invasion of Ireland.   823.7305
—— The wild rose .of Lough Gill: a tale of the Irish war in the seventeenth century.
                             823.7306
Snarleyyow. Marryat, *Capt.* F:
                          in ** 823.6674
Snob papers. Welcker, A.   823.4888
Snow man, The. Dudevant, *Mme.* A. L. A. (D.)   823.6853
Snow-bound at Eagle's. Harte, F. B.
                             823.5280
Snow-image, and other twice-told tales. Hawthorne, N.   823.734
Same.   *in* 823.5878
Snow-shoes and canoes. Kingston, W: H: G.   808.1590

English Fiction. *Contin.*
Snow-storm. 12 pp. Pushkin, A. S.
    p. 125, *in* 823.6534
Snowing-up of Strath Lugas. 24 pp. (*In*
Tales from Blackwood, v. 12.)
    in ** 823.6658
Society in search of truth. Clark, J. F.
    823.4512
Society's verdict. By the author of "My
marriage." *in* 823.5052
Same. *in* 823.5086
Soldier's orphans, The. Stephens, *Mrs.* A.
S. (W.) 823.1969
Soldiers three. Kipling, R. 823.7344
Soley, James Russell. The sailor boys of '61.
    808.1911
Solid for Mulhooly. Shapley, R. R. 823.4351
Solitary of Juan Fernandez, The. Boniface,
J. X. 823.6838
Solomon's story. Shaw, W. J. 823.6049
Some of our girls. Eiloart, *Mrs.* C. J.
    823.5091
Some one else. Croker, B. M. 823.4822
Some women's hearts. Moulton, *Mrs.* E. L.
(C.) 823.1176
Somebody else. Lathrop, G: P. 823.4108
Somebody's Ned. Freeman, *Mrs.* A. M.
    823.589
Somebody's neighbors. Cooke, *Mrs.* R. (T.)
    823.4169
Somers, Felix, *pseud.* *See* Chambers, J.
Somnambulism in story. *See also* Hypno-
tism.
—— Cockton, H: Sylvester Sound: the
somnambulist. 823.242
—— *Same.* 823.5843
—— Howitt, M. Stories of dreams, second
sight, etc. (Ennemoser, J. *In his* History
of magic, v. 2.) p. 410, *in* 133.15
—— Immermann, K. L. Der Carneval und
die Somnambule. p. 61, *in* 830.57
    Note.—See Hammond, W: A. Sleep and its de-
rangements. 1878. 613.40.—M'Kendrick, J. G.
Article "Sleep" in Encyclop. Brit. v. 22. ** 32.292.
Macnish, R. Physiology of sleep. *in* 829.467.
    See also Poole's Index (to 1882). p. 1,219, *in* **
50.1:—*Same.* Jan. 1, 1882–Jan. 1, 1887. p. 409, *in* **
50.1².
Son of a star, The. Richardson, B: W.
    823.6943
Son of Hagar, A. Caine, H. 823.5519
Son of his father, The. Oliphant, *Mrs.* M.
O. (W.) *in* 823.5059
Same. *in* 823.5067
Son of Issachar. Brooks, E. S. 823.7164
Son of the organgrinder. Schwartz, *Mme.*
M. S. (B.) 823.1933
Son of the soil, A. Oliphant, *Mrs.* M. O.
(W.) 823.5968
Sonora.
—— Marryat, *Capt.* F: Travels . . . of Mon-
sieur Violet in . . . Sonora, etc. 823.1104
—— Reid, *Capt.* T: M. The wood-rangers.
    823.7145
    Note.—See Bancroft, H. H. Works. v. 15.
970.79.
    See also Catalogue of this Library. No. 2, 1880,
p. 213.
    See also Index to Consular reports. 1880–1885;
1886–1889. 2 vols. (U. S. Pub. Docs. *Dept. of State.*)
** 350.5496¹·².
    See also Décennale du "Tour du monde."
1860–1870. ** 913.138¹.

English Fiction. *Contin.*
Sons and daughters. Kirk, *Mrs.* E. W. (O.)
    823.5610
Sons of the soil. Balzac, H. de. 823.6942
Sooner or later. Brooks, C: W: S. 823.6346
Soprano, The. Barnard, C: 823.6632
Sorrows of Werther. Göthe, J. W. von.
    in 823.2183
Same. ** 823.6646
South America. *See also* Brazil.
—— Ballantyne, R. M. Lost in the forest.
    808.1279
—— Champney, *Mrs.* E.. (W.) Three Vassar
girls in South America. 808.1822
—— Henty, G: A. Out on the pampas; or,
the young settlers. 808.1611
—— Isaacs, J. Maria: a South American ro-
mance. 823.6941
—— Kingston, W: H: G. On the banks of
the Amazon; or, adventures in the tropical
wilds of South America. 808.364
—— — The wanderers; or, adventures in the
wilds of Trinidad and up the Orinoco.
    808.353
—— — The young llanero: a story of war
and wild life in Venezuela. 808.354
—— Knox, T: W. The boy travellers in
South America. 808.1840
—— Reid, *Capt.* T: M. Afloat in the forest;
or, a voyage among the tree-tops. 808.436
—— — Gaspar the gaucho: a tale of the
Gran Chaco. 808.1579
—— Verne, J. Giant raft. Pt. 1: Eight
hundred leagues on the Amazon. Pt. 2:
The cryptogram. 823.6310
—— — Voyage round the world: South
America. 823.5547
    *Note.—*For bibliography, *see* Soldanha da
Gama, J. de. Works on South America. (*In* Cata-
logo de Exposicao de bibliotheca nacional.) 1885.
** 15.83.—Trübner, N. Bibliotheca Hispano-Ameri-
cano. 1878. ** 15.84.
    For history, *see* Markham, C. R. Colonial his-
tory of South America, and the wars of indepen-
dence. (Winsor, J., *ed. Narr. and crit. hist. of Amer.,*
v. 8.) 1889. p. 295, *in* * 970.127².—Wilkes, C. *In* U.
S. Explor. Exped., v. 1. 1856. *in* 910.70.
    See also Cieza de Leon, P. Travels. 1532–1559.
(*Hakl. Soc.*) 1864. ** 980.4.
    See also Catalogues of this Library.
  No. 2, 1880, p. 8.   No. 5, 1888, p. 338.
  No. 4, 1884, pp. 273-4.
    See also Poole's Index (to 1882). pp. 1,224-5, *in* **
50.1:—*Same.* Jan. 1, 1882–Jan. 1, 1887. p. 411, *in* **
50.1².
South pole. *See* Antarctic regions, p. 8.
South sea islands. *See* Pacific ocean, p. 201.
South sea whaler, The. Kingston, W: H: G.
    808.352
Southern star, The. Verne, J. *in* 823.5089
Southern woman's story. Pember, *Mrs.* P.
Y. (L.) 823.1250
Southey, *Mrs.* Caroline Anne (Bowles). Dev-
ereux Hall. 56 pp. (*In* Tales from Black-
wood, v. 2.) *in* ** 823.6648
—— La petite Madelaine. 69 pp. (*In* Tales
from Blackwood, v. 3.) ** *in* 823.6649
Southlanders, The: expedition to the interior
of New Holland. 3d ed. rev. (Anon.)
    823.4095
Southward ho! Simms, W: G. 823.1437

English Fiction. *Contin.*
Southworth, *Mrs.* Emma Dorothy Eliza
(Nevitte).
—— Allworth Abbey; or, Eudora. 823.1474
—— The artist's love, and stories by Mrs. F..
(H.) Baden. 823.1475
—— A beautiful fiend; or, through the fire.
823.1476
—— The bridal eve; or, Rose Elmer.
823.1477
—— The bride's fate. Sequel to "The
changed brides." 823.1479
—— The changed brides; or, winning her
way. 823.1480
—— The Christmas guest; or, the crime and
the curse. And stories by Mrs. F.. (H.)
Baden. 823.1481
—— Cruel as the grave. 823.1482
—— Curse of Clifton; or, the widowed bride.
823.1483
—— The deserted wife. 823.1484
—— The discarded daughter; or, the children
of the isle. 823.1485
—— Fair play; or, the test of the lone isle.
823.1486
—— Fallen pride; or, the mountain girl's
love. 823.1487
Issued also as Curse of Clifton.
—— The family doom; or, the sin of a count-
ess. 823.1488
—— The fatal marriage; or, Orville Deville.
823.1489
—— The fatal secret, and other stories by
Mrs F.. (H.) Baden. 823.1490
—— The fortune seeker; or, the bridal day.
823.1491
—— The gipsy's prophecy; or, the bride of
an evening. 823.1492
Issued also as Bride of an evening.
—— The haunted homestead, and other nov-
elettes. With an autobiography of the
author. 823.1493
—— The hidden hand; or, Capitola the mad-
cap. 823.5176
—— How he won her. A sequel to "Fair
play." 823.1982
—— *Same.* 823.4061; 823.5174
—— India; or, the pearl of Pearl river.
823.1494
—— Ishmael; or, in the depths. 823.1495
—— The lady of the isle; or, the island prin-
cess. 823.1496
—— The lost heir of Liulithgow. 823.1497
—— The lost heiress. 823.1498
—— Love's labor won. 823.1499
—— The maiden widow. A sequel to "The
family doom." 823.1980
—— The missing bride; or, Miriam, the
avenger. 823.1500
Issued also as Miriam the avenger.
—— The mother-in-law; or, married in haste.
823.1501
—— The mystery of Dark Hollow. 823.1502
—— A noble lord. The sequel to "The lost
heir of Linlithgow." 823.1503
—— The phantom wedding, and other stories
by Mrs. F.. (H.) Baden. 823.1504
—— The prince of darkness: a romance of
the Blue Ridge. 823.1505
Issued also as Hickory Hall; or, the outcast.

English Fiction. *Contin.*
Southworth, *Mrs.* Emma Dorothy Eliza
(Nevitte). *Contin.*
—— Retribution: a tale of passion. 823.1506
—— Self-raised; or, from the depths. Sequel
to "Ishmael." 823.1507
—— The spectre lover, and other stories by
Mrs. F.. (H.) Baden. 823.1508
—— The three beauties; or, Shannoudale.
823.1509
—— Tried for her life. 823.1510
—— The two sisters; or, Virginia and Mag-
dalene. 823.1511
Issued also as Virginia and Magdalene.
·—— Victor's triumph. The sequel to "The
beautiful fiend." 823.1512
—— Vivia; or, the secret of power. 823.1513
—— The widow's son; or, left alone.
823.1981
—— The wife's victory, and other novelettes.
823.1514
Souvestre, Émile. Brittany and La Vendée:
tales and sketches. With life of author.
823.6878
—— The chamois-hunter. 823.5941
—— Pleasures of old age. 823.1874
Sowers not reapers. Martineau, H.
823.6602
Same. *in* ** 823.6712
Sower's reward, The. Rathbone, *Mrs.* M..
A. (M.) 823.5901
Spaewife. Boyce, J: 823.115
Same. 2 vols. 823.6931-2
Spain.
—— Abbott, J: S. C. Romance of Spanish
history. 946.19
—— Adams, W: T. Vine and olive; or,
Young America in Spain and Portugal.
808.499
·—— Champney, *Mrs.* E.. (W.) Three Vas-
sar girls abroad. Rambles . . . through
. . . Spain. 808.1821
—— Longfellow, H: W. Poems of places.
2 vols. 821.219-20
—— Trueba y Cosio, T. de. The romance of
history. 823.1639
Spain and Portugal.
8TH CENTURY, A. D.
—— Irving, W. Crayon miscellany, No. 3:
Legends of the conquest of Spain.
** 823.6739
—— Southey, R. Roderick (*killed* 711), the
last of the Goths; poem. 821.378
Charlemagne invades Spain, 777-8. *See*
Charlemagne cycle of romances, p. 37.
11TH CENTURY, A. D.
The Cid, 1040-1099.
—— Corneille, P. Le Cid; trag.
p. 219, *in* 842.105
—— Hemans, *Mrs.* F. Songs of the Cid.
p. 111, *in* 821.157
—— Herder, J. G. F. Der Cid (ballads).
p. 335, *in* 831.16
—— Lockhart, J. G., *tr.* Spanish ballads.
821.854
12TH CENTURY, A. D. Fernandez y Gonzalez,
M. Hermesenda; or, bishop, husband, and
king. 823.7211

English Fiction. *Contin.*
Spain and Portugal. *Contin.*
13TH CENTURY, A. D. Baillie, J. Henriquez;
trag. p. 361, *in* 822.897
14TH CENTURY, A. D.
—— Baillie, J. Romiero; trag.
p. 312, *in* 822.897
—— Dumas, A. D. The half brothers; or,
the head and the hand. 823.7085
Peter the Cruel, 1319–1369. Calderon de la
Barca, P. El médico de su honra (play).
p. 97, *in* 862.15
Agnes or Inez de Castro, 1355.
—— Camoëns, L. de. Lusiad; poem. 861.1
—— La Motte, A. H. de. Inéz de Castro;
trag. (French.) 842.65
15TH CENTURY, A. D.
—— Aguilar, G. The edict: a tale of 1492.
(Jews expelled.) p. 118, *in* 823.8
—— — Vale of cedars. (Jews expelled.)
823.10
—— Camoëns, L. de. The Lusiad; poem.
(Vasco da Gama, and discov. of passage to
the Indies.) 861.1
—— — *Same.* 861.13
FERDINAND AND ISABELLA, 1474, etc. Coop-
er, J. F. Mercedes of Castile. 823.300
Columbus, C. *See* Colombo, C., p. 42.
Abencerrages, 1480–1492.
—— Hemans, *Mrs.* F. The Abencerrage;
poem. * 821.154
Fall of Granada, 1492.
—— Irving, W. The Alhambra. 823.1807
—— — The conquest of Granada. 946.12
—— — *Same.* *in* 946.36
—— Lytton, E: G: E. L. Bulwer- Leila; or,
the siege of Granada. 823.1035
—— — *Same.* 823.5957
Gonzalvo de Córdova. Ticknor's History of
Spanish literature. v. 1, pp. 211–17, *in* 860.4
Inquisition. Weiss, M., *ed.* The Marannos:
a tale of the inquisition. *in* 823.6123
CHARLES I., 1516–1556, became, 1519, *Em-
peror Charles V. of Germany, which see* p.
100.
—— Godwin, W: St. Leon. 4 vols. (In-
quisition and battle of Pavia, 1525.)
** 823.6779–82
—— Hugo, V. Hernani; drama.
in * 822.737
—— — *Same.* (French.) 840.47
Inquisition.
—— Alcock, D. The Spanish brothers.
823.1184
—— — *Same.* 823.5910
Insurrection in Castile, 1520–21. Talfourd,
—. The Castillian; trag. 822.522
PHILIP II., 1556–1598 (*married Mary of Eng-
land*).
—— Alfieri, V. Filippo II.; trag. 852.1
—— Coleridge, S: T. Remorse; trag.
p. 345, *in* 829.60
—— Delavigne, C. Don Juan d'Autriche;
com. 842.98
—— Sheil, R. L. The apostate; trag.
p. 83, *in* 822.24
Persecution of Protestants, 1561.
—— Charles, *Mrs.* E.. (R.) The martyrs of
Spain. 823.6598

English Fiction. *Contin.*
Spain and Portugal. *Contin.*
PHILIP II., 1556–1598. *Contin.*
Persecution of Protestants, 1561. *Contin.*
—— Hemans, *Mrs.* F. The forest sanctuary;
poem. p. 76, *in* 821.156
Don Carlos.
—— Alfieri, V. Philip II.; trag. 852.1
—— Le Fevre. Don Carlos; trag. 842.69
—— Otway, T. Don Carlos; trag.
p. 75, *in* 822.453
—— Schiller, F. von. Don Carlos; trag.
** 832.5
—— — *Same.* (German.) 832.16
Don Sebastian (defeated 1578). Trag. Dry-
den, J: p. 1, *in* ** 822.140
17TH CENTURY, A. D. Williams, H. L., *ed.*
Ruy Blas; or, the king's rival. Founded on
the drama by Victor Hugo. . 823.7261
PHILIP III., 1598–1621.
—— Lytton, E: G: E. L. Bulwer- Calderon
the courtier. *in* 823.1035
—— — *Same.* *in* 823.5957
PHILIP IV., 1621–1665. Lost Portugal in
1640.
18TH CENTURY, A. D.
—— Aguilar, G. The escape: a tale of 1755.
p. 156, *in* 823.8
—— Great earthquake at Lisbon. (1755.) 38
pp. (*In* Tales from Blackwood. 2d ser.,
v. 12.) *in* 823.7496
—— Henty, G: A. The bravest of the brave;
or, with Peterborough in Spain. 808.1473
—— Peck, W: H: The stone-cutter of Lis-
bon. 823.7294
PHILIP V., 1700–1746.
CHARLES IV., 1788–1808. Perez Galdos, B.
Court of Charles IV.: a romance of the Es-
corial. 823.7074
FERDINAND VII., 1808.
JOSEPH BONAPARTE, 1808–1814. (*See note on*
French history, p. 92.)
Peninsular war.
—— Grant, J. The romance of war; or, the
Highlanders in Spain. 823.648
—— Henty, G: A. The young buglers: a
tale of the Peninsular war. 808.1471
—— Maxwell, W: H. Stories of the Penin-
sular war. 823.1131
FERDINAND VII. RESTORED, 1814–1833. Ros-
aura: a tale of Madrid. (Death of Ferdi-
nand VII.) 70 pp. (*In* Tales from Black-
wood, v. 9.) *in* ** 823.6655
ISABELLA II., 1833–1868.
LIFE AND MANNERS.
—— Arrom, *Mrs.* C. (B. de F.) La Gaviota—
the sea-gull. 823.6892
—— Bowring, J: Ancient poetry and ro-
mances of Spain. 861.2
—— Byron, *Lord.* Childe Harold.
in * 821.69
—— Griffiths, A. Lola: a tale of Gibraltar.
823.678
—— Hemans, *Mrs.* F. The siege of Valen-
cia; drama. p. 284, *in* 821.155
—— Hugo, V. M., *vicomte.* Les orientales;
poem. (Moorish life in Spain.) 849.85
—— Lockhart, J. G., *tr.* Spanish ballads.
821.854

English Fiction. *Contin.*
Spain and Portugal. *Contin.*
LIFE AND MANNERS. *Contin.*
—— Middlemore, *Mrs.* S. G. C. Round a posada fire. Spanish legends. 823.4745
—— Perez, Galdós, B. Leon Roch. 2 vols. (Influence of the Roman Catholic Church upon social relations in Spain.)
823.6969-70
—— Scott, *Sir* W. The vision of Don Roderick. (Moorish invasion, Height of Spanish power, and Peninsular war.)
p. 269, in 821.355
—— — *Same.* p. 357, in 821.357
—— Valdés, A. P. Sister Saint Sulpice.
823.6426
Gypsy life. See Gypsies, p. 111.
CUBA.
—— Collingwood, H. The rover's secret.
808.1708
—— Ripley, E. McH. From flag to flag: a woman's adventures and experiences . . . in Cuba. 823.5439
LISBON. Queiros, E. de. Dragon's teeth. (The humbler class of Spaniards.) 823.5471
MADRID. Burnett, *Mrs.* F.. E. (H.) Pretty sister of José. 823.7033
Note.—For Spain under the Arabs and Moors, *see* Condé, J. A. History of the dominion of Arabs in Spain. 3 vols. 1854. 946.7-9.—Gibbon, E. Decline and fall of the Roman empire, v. 5 (51st chap.) p. 170, *in* 937.12.—Irving, W. Spanish papers. 1868. 829.667.—Poole, S. Lane- The story of the Moors in Spain. (Story of the nations.) Map. Illus. 1889. 946.87.—Yonge, C. M.. Christians and Moors in Spain. 946.51.
Granada, 1238-1492.—Hallam, H: Europe during the middle ages. 3 vols. 1872. 940.2-4.—Irving, W. Conquest of Granada. 946.12;—Spanish paper. 1868. 829.667.—Prescott, W: H. Ferdinand and Isabella. 3 vols. 1879. 946.4-5.
Discoveries and conquests in America.—Bancroft, H. H. History of Mexico. (1516-1861.) 5 vols. 1885. * 970.73-7.—Columbus, C. Select letters of, and other documents. (*Hakluyt Soc.*) 1870. ** 917.24.—Helps, *Sir* A. Life of H. Cortes and the conquest of Mexico. 2 vols. 1871. 923.203-4;—Spanish conquest in America. 4 vols. 1856. 970. 37-40.—Irving, W. Life and voyages of Columbus and his companions. 3 vols. 1868. 920.207-9.—Prescott, W: H. Conquest of Peru. 2 vols. 1879. 985. 1-2.—Winsor, J. Narrative and critical history of America. 8 vols. 1887-9. 970.127-127*.
Peninsular war, 1807-1814.—Guizot, F. P.G. History of France. 6 vols. 944.4-9.—Jones, J. T. Journals of sieges carried on by the army under the Duke of Wellington in Spain, 1811-14. 3 vols. 1846. 946.3-5.—Napier, *Sir* W. F. P. History of the war in the peninsula. 5 vols. 1877. 946.14-18.—Wellington, *Lord.* Dispatches, 1799-1818. 13 vols. (v. 13, index.) 1837-9. 923.1334-46.
History of Spain in general, and for long periods.—Alison, *Sir* A. The Carlist struggle in Spain. 21 pp. (*In his* Misc. essays.) p. 325, *in* 824.90;—History of Europe. (1789-1815.) 12 vols. (v. 12, index.) 940.36-47;—Spanish revolution of 1820. 11 pp. (*In his* Misc. essays.) p. 279, *in* 824.90.—Buckle, H: T. History of civilization. 2 vols. 1878. 313.35-6.—Froude, J. A. History of England (reigns of Henry VIII. and Elizabeth). 12 vols. 1871. 942. 44-55.—Hale, E: E., *and* Hale, S. The story of Spain. (Story of the nations.) Maps. Illus. 1890. 946.88.—Harrison, J.. H. (History of) Spain. 1881. 946.68.—Lembke, F. W. Schäfer, H., *and* Schirrmacher, F. W. Geschichte von Spanien. (1-1387.) 5 vols. (Heeren, A. H. L., *and* Ukert, F. A. Gesch. der europ. Staaten.) 1831. 946.89-93.—Maxwell, J: Stirling- Cloister life of the Emperor Charles V. 1891. 923.2088.— Maxwell, *Sir* W: Stirling- Annals of the artists of Spain. (1516-1880.) Illus. 4 vols. 1891. ** 709.45-8.—Motley, J: L. History of the United Netherlands. 4 vols. 1879. 949.4-7;—*Same.* 949.27-30.—Prescott, W: H.

English Fiction. *Contin.*
Spain and Portugal. *Contin.*
Note. Contin.
Philip II. 3 vols. 1871. 923.195-7.—Robertson, W: History of Charles V. 3 vols. 1878. 923.121-3.—Smyth, W. Modern history. (8th lecture.) 1856. p. 134, *in* 904.1;—*Same.* p. 220, *in* 901.9.—Stanhope, *Earl.* History of war of succession in Spain (1701-14.) 1832. 946.82. *Note.— See also* Macaulay's article on this book in his Essays, v. 3. pp. 75-142, *in* 824.135.—Wellington, *Duke of.* Despatches. vols. 4-9. (Consult index, ** 923.1346.) ** 923.1337-42.
See also **Catalogues** of this Library.
(Portugal, p. 185.) No. 2, 1880, pp. 214-15. (Portugal, p. 154.) No. 3, 1882, p. 177. (Portugal, p. 235.) No. 4, 1884, p. 274. (Portugal, p. 293.) No. 5, 1888, p. 339.
See also **Index to Consular reports.** 1880-1885; 1886-1889. 2 vols. (U. S. Pub. Docs. *Dept. of State.*) ** 350.5496¹·².
See also **Poole's** Index (to 1882). Spain, pp. 1,228-31, Portugal, pp. 1,036-7, *in* ** 50.1;—*Same.* Jan. 1, 1882-Jan. 1, 1887. Spain, pp. 412-13, Portugal, p. 350, *in* ** 50.1².
For studies of Spanish life and character, *see* **Borrow, G.** The Zincali; or, the gypsies of Spain. 1872. 949.50.—Byrne, *Mrs.* W: P. Cosas de España, illustrative of Spain and the Spaniards as they are. 2 vols. 1866. 946.84-5.—Harrison, J. A. Spain in profile. 1879. 914.435.—Hay, J: Castilian days. 1871. 914.107.—Patch, O. (*pseud.*) Sunny Spain, its people and places, with glimpses of its history. 1884. 946.86.—Thiéblin, N. L. Spain and Spaniards. 1875. 914.109.

Spanish barber, The. Rathbone, *Mrs.* M.. A. (M.) 823.5581
Spanish brothers, The. Alcock, D. 823.1184
—— *Same.* 823.5910
Sparhawk, F.. Campbell. A lazy man's work. 823.4178
Speaking of Ellen. Porter, L. B. 823.6989
Spectacles for young eyes. *See* Lander, S.. West.
Spectre lover, The. Southworth, *Mrs.* E. D. E. (N.) 823.1508
Spectre of Milaggio. By the author of 'The abode of snow.' 46 pp. (*In* Tales from Blackwood. 2d ser., v. 4.) *in* 823.7488
Spell of Ashtaroth, The. Osborne, S: D.
823.5215
Spell-bound fiddler. Janson, K. N. 823.2020
Spender, Emily. Until the day breaks.
823.5016
Spendthrift, The. Ainsworth, W: H. 823.29
Sphynx in Aubrey parish, The. Chamberlain, N. H: 823.7140
Spicer, H: Madonna. 19 pp. (*In* Famous stories. By De Quincey, and others.)
p. 182, *in* 823.1778
Spider's eye. 24 pp. O'Brien, F. J.
p. 1, *in* 823.4704
Spielhagen, Friedrich. Hammer and anvil. Tr. by W: II. Browne. 823.6821
—— The Hohensteins. Tr. by Prof. Schele de Vere. 823.4281
—— Quisisana; or, rest at last. Tr. by H. E. Goldsmith. *in* 823.6688
—— The storm. (Zimmern, H.., *and* A. *Half-hours with foreign novelists.*)
in ** 823.6613
—— Through night to light. Tr. by Prof. Schele de Vere. 823.6822
—— What the swallow sang. 823.6823
Spinoza. Auerbach, B. 823.4576
Spiridion (tr.) Dudevant, *Mme.* A. L.. A. (D.) ** 823.6640

English Fiction. *Contin.*
Spirite. Gautier, T. 823.2316
Same. 823.6454
Spirit-rapper. Brownson, O. A: 823.1867
Spiritual Quixote. 2 vols. Graves, *Rev.* R:
** 823.2093-4
Spiritualism in story. *See also* Ghost stories.
—Strange tales. — Supernatural, The, in
story.—Theosophy in story.
—— Besant, W. Herr Paulus. 823.5885
—— Brownson, O. A: Spirit-rapper: an auto-
biography. 823.1867
—— Flammarion, C. Stories of infinity.
523.5
—— Hamley, W: G. A medium of last cen-
tury. (*In* Tales from Blackwood. 3d ser.,
v. 4.) p. 1, *in* 823.7500
—— Howitt, M. Stories of spirit rappings,
etc. (Ennemoser, J. *In his* History of
magic, v. 2.) 1854. 133.15
—— Stockton, F. R: Amos Kilbright: his
adscititious experiences. 823.5764
—— Ward, *Mrs.* E.. S. (P.) Beyond the
gates. 823.4620
—— — Gates ajar. 823.1255
—— — The gates between. 823.5224
Note.—See **Bibliography.** Abbot, R. Mod. spiritualism: ghosts, etc. 3 pp. (*In his* The lit. of the
doctrine of a future life. *With* Alger, W: R. *Doctrine of a future life.*) 1878. p. 866, *in* 237.1.—
Fiske, J: Modern witchcraft. 10 pp. (*In his* Dar-
winism, etc.) p. 120, *in* 824.377.—**James**, H: Spiritual rappings. 18 pp. (*In his* Lectures and miscel.)
p. 407, *in* 824.223.—**Jastrow**, J. The psychology of
spiritualism. 12 pp. (*Pop. sci. mo.*, v. 34. 1889.)
p. 721, *in* 505.469².—**Savage**, M. J. Experiences
with spiritualism. 15 pp. (*Forum*, v. 8. 1889.) p.
449, *in* * 51.4701⁴.—**Tyndall**, J: Science and the
"spirits." 8 pp. (*In his* Fragment of science.) p.
314, *in* 504.9.
For works favoring spiritualism, *see* **Hare**, R.
Experimental investigation of the spirit manifesta-
tions. 1855. * 133.101.—**Home**, D. D. Lights and
shadows of spiritualism. (*See* Browning, R. *Mr.
Sludge, the medium;* poem.) (*Works*, v. 7. p.
162, *in* 821.1259.) 133.11.—**Kardec**, A. Book of
mediums. 1874. 133.29;—The spirit's book. 1880. 133.
9¹.—**Newton**, A. E. Why I am a spiritualist. 15
pp. (*N. Amer. rev.*, v. 147. 1888.) p. 654, *in* * 51.
625².—**Sargent**, E. Planchette. 1874. 133.30.—
Wallace, A. R. Miracles and modern spiritualism.
1881. 133.307.
See also periodicals, **Banner of Light.** vols. 18-
21, 1866-7 (in 2 vols.) ** 133.224⁴-5¹ vols. 24-41,
1869-77 (in 9 vols.) ** 133.227-35. — **Religio-
philos. Journal.** vols. 13-23, 1873-77 (in 5 vols.)
** 133.120-4; vols. 29-41, 1887 (in 9 vols.) ** 133.130-8;
vols. 42-48, 1887-90 (in 7 vols.) ** 133.138¹-138².
For works opposing, *see* **Davenport**, R. B. The
death-blow to spiritualism: being the true story of
the Fox sisters. 1888. 133.315.—Preliminary report
of the commission appointed by the University of
Pennsylvania to investigate modern spiritualism in
accordance with the request of the late Henry Sey-
bert. 1887. 133.310.
See also **Catalogues** of this Library.
No. 2, 1860, p. 216. No. 4, 1884, p. 276.
No. 3, 1882, p. 178. No. 5, 1888, p. 340.
See also **Poole's Index** (to 1882). pp. 1,237-8, *in* **
50.1;—*Same.* Jan. 1, 1882-Jan. 1, 1887. p. 415, *in* **
50.1³.
Splendid spur, The. Crouch, A. T: Q.
823.7061
Split zephyr. 53 pp. Beers, H: A.
p. 48, *in* 823.4709
Spofford, *Mrs.* Harriet E.. (Prescott). The
amber gods, and other stories. 823.4199
—— Azarian: an episode. 823.5165
—— *Same.* 823.5759

English Fiction. *Contin.*
Spofford, *Mrs.* Harriet E.. (Prescott). *Contin.*
—— D'outre mort. 31 pp. (Johnson, R., *ed.
Little classics*, v. 2.) p. 60, *in* 829.125
—— Hester Stanley at St. Marks. 823.5756
—— Marquis of Carabas. 823.4463
—— The mount of sorrow. 24 pp. (*In* Sto-
ries by Amer. authors, v. 2.)
p. 141, *in* 823.4703
—— Ray. 52 pp. (*In* Johnson, R., *ed.
Little classics*, v. 11.) p. 51, *in* 829.134
—— Sir Rohan's ghost. 823.1516
—— The south breaker. 69 pp. (Johnson,
R., *ed. Little classics*, v. 7.)
p. 115, *in* 829.130
—— The thief in the night. 823.1517
Sporting adventures. *See* Hunting, etc.
Sporting scenes and characters. 2 vols.
Herbert, H: W. 823.5754-5
Sports . . . in the Highlands . . . of Scot-
land. Maxwell, W: H. 823.1130
Sprague, M.. Aplin. Earnest trifler. (Anon.)
823.2005
Sprees and splashes. Morford, H: 823.1173
Spring floods. Turgenef, I. S. 823.7131
Springfield armory. Abbott, J. Marco Paul
at Springfield armory. 808.724
Springhaven. Blackmore, R: D. 823.5151
Same. 823.5514
Spurr, G: G. The land of gold: a tale of '49.
Illustrative of early pioneer life in Califor-
nia, and founded upon fact. 823.4336
Spy, The. Cooper, J. F. 823.319
Same. *in* 823.7464
Square, A., *pseud. See* Abbott, E. A.
Squatter and the don. Loyal, C. 823.4813
Squire Arden. Oliphant, *Mrs.* M. O. (W.)
823.5959
Squire of low degree, A. Long, L. A.
823.7396
Squire of Sandal-Side, The. Barr, *Mrs.* A.
E. (H.) 823.5359
Squire Trevlyn's heir. Wood, *Mrs.* E. (P.)
823.6017
Squire's darling, The. Brame, *Mrs.* C.. M.
(L.) *in* 823.5079
Squire's legacy. Hay, M.. C. 823.3394
Same. *in* 823.5128
Stables, Gordon. On special service: a tale
of life at sea. 808.1423
——, Hicks, C. Stansfeld, *and others.* The
boy's own book of indoor games and recre-
ations. Ed. by G. A. Hutchison. 808.1906
Staël-Holstein, Anne Louise Germaine
(Necker), *baronne* de.
—— Corinne; or, Italy. *in* 823.6261
—— *Same:* a story of Italy. 823.6297
—— *Same.* Tr. by I. Hill; with metrical
versions of the odes by L. E. Landon.
823.4258
Stage-struck. Macchetta, *Mrs.* B. R. (T.)
823.4780
Stahl, P. J., *pseud. See* Hetzel, P. J.
Stahr, *Mrs.* Fanny (Lewald). The aristo-
cratic world. 87 pp. (*Also*) The maid of
Oyas. 16 pp. (*In* Masterpieces of Ger-
man fict.) *in* 823.7552
—— Stella. Tr. by B.. Marshall. 823.5051
—— *Same.* 823.5055

English Fiction. *Contin.*
Stories from the Greek tragedians. Church, A. J: 808.1378
Stories from the history of Rome. Beesly, *Mrs. —.* 808.841
Stories from the Italian poets. 2 vols. Hunt, J. H: L. 823.7081-2
Stories from Virgil. Church, A. J: 808.1413
Stories of adventure. Hale, E: E. 808.1367
Stories of American history. Dodge, N. S. 808.1675
Stories of discovery. Hale, E: E. 808.1369
Stories of English and foreign life. Howitt, W:, *and* Howitt, *Mrs.* M.. (B.) 823.2135
Stories of invention. Hale, E: E. 808.1426
Stories of old renown. Moncrieff, R. H. 808.1686
Stories of Provence. Daudet, A. 823.4958
Stories of the east from Herodotus. Church, A. J: 808.1546
Stories of the gorilla country. Du Chaillu, P. B. 808.799
Stories of the island world. Nordhoff, C: 808.165
Stories of the magicians. Church, A. J: 823.5663
Stories of the Old Dominion. Cooke, J: E. 808.1468
Stories of the Peninsular war. Maxwell, W: H. 823.1131
Stories of the prairie. Cooper, J. F. 808.1127
Stories of the sagacity of animals. Kingston, W: H: G. 808.1445
Stories of the sea. Hale, E: E. 808.1368
Stories of the sea. Marryat, *Capt.* F: ** 823.6730
Stories of the three burglars. Stockton, F. R: 823.7003
Stories of war. Hale, E: E. 808.1370
Same. 823.5164
Stories of Waterloo. Maxwell, W: H. 823.1133
Stork's nest, A. Vicary, J: F., *comp.* 823.5415
Storm, E. Herr Sinclair (poem). 6 pp. (Bushby, *Mrs. —, tr. The Danes, etc.,* v. 3.) p. 137, *in* 823.6446
Storm-bride. 4 pp. Rask, E. C. p. 350, *in* 823.6534
Storm-driven. Bigot, *Mrs.* M.. (H.) 823.738
Stormy waters. Buchanan, R. W. 823.6594
Same. 823.7009
Story, W: Wetmore. A modern magician. 66 pp. (*In* Tales from Blackwood. 2d ser., v. 7.) *in* 823.7491
Story book of science, A. Farmer, *Mrs.* L. H. 808.1712
Story of a bad boy. Aldrich, T: B. 808.283
Story of a country town. Howe, E. W. 823.4868
Story of a feather. Jerrold, D. W: *in* 823.4828
Story of a mine. Harte, F. B. 823.2041
Story of a mountain. Lawrence, *Uncle.* 808.1894
Story of a short life. 67 pp. Ewing, *Mrs.* J. H. (G.) *in* 823.5090

English Fiction. *Contin.*
Story of an honest man. About, E. F. V. 823.6051
Story of ancient history. Abbott, J. 808.584
Story of Antony Grace. Fenn, G: M. 823.5569
Story of Avis. Ward, *Mrs.* E.. S. (P.) 823.1260
Story of carnival. Marks, *Mrs.* M.. A. M. (H.) 823.4572
Story of Elizabeth. Ritchie, *Mrs.* A.. I.. (T.) 823.1569
Story of Farquharson of Inverey. Lauder, *Sir* T: D. *in* * 823.6194
Story of Gisli the outlaw. From the Icelandic by G: W. Dasent. 823.6448
Story of Helen Davenant. Singleton, *Mrs.* M.. (M. L.) 823.7254
Story of Ida. 45 pp. Alexander, F. *in* 823.5038
Story of John Marbeck, The. Marshall, *Mrs.* E. (M.) 823.5578
Story of Kennett. Taylor, B. 823.1547
Story of liberty. Coffin, C: C. 808.1858
Story of Margaret Kent. Kirk, *Mrs.* E. W. (O.) 823.5527
Story of Martha Guinnis and her son. Crowe, *Mrs.* C. (S.) *in* * 823.6194
Story of music and musicians for young readers. Lillie, *Mrs.* L. C. (W.) 808.1459
Story of my uncle Toby, The. Sterne, L. 823.5599
Story of Roland, The. Baldwin, J. 823.5624
Story of Ruth, from the Bible. 9 pp. (Johnson, R., *ed. Little classics,* v. 6.) p. 128, *in* 829.129
Story of Sibylle. Feuillet, O. 823.6287
Story of Siegfried, The. Baldwin, J. 823.5623
Story of three sisters. Maxwell, C. 823.1132
Story of Touty, The. Catherwood, *Mrs.* M.. (H.) 823.6994
Story of the golden age. Baldwin, J. 823.5515
Story of the Latin quarter. 30 pp. Burnett, *Mrs.* F.. E. (H.) p. 30, *in* 823.4704
Story of the man who didn't know much. Murray, W: H: H. p. 111, *in* 823.6326
Story of the Persian war. Church, *Rev.* A. J: 823.5671
Story of the rock. Ballantyne, R. M. *in* 808.1269
Story of two lives. 32 pp. Schayer, J. p. 154, *in* 823.4711
Story of Valentine and his brother. Oliphant, *Mrs.* M. O. (W.) 823.5969
Story of Viteau. Stockton, F. R: 808.1411
Story or two from an old Dutch town. Lowell, R. T. S. 823.1019
Story that the keg told me. Murray, W: H: H. 823.6326
Stowe, *Mrs.* Harriet E.. (Beecher). (1812- .)
—— Agnes of Sorrento. 823.2038
—— Betty's bright idea, and other stories. *in* 823.6678

English Fiction. *Contin.*
Stowe, *Mrs.* Harriet E.. (Beecher). (1812– .) *Contin.*

—— Dred: a tale of the great dismal swamp.
    823.1526

Issued also as Nina Gordon.

—— The Mayflower, and miscellaneous writings.   823.2037

—— The minister's wooing.   823.1524

—— My wife and I; or, Harry Henderson's history.   823.1525

—— Oldtown folks.   823.1527

—— Palmetto-leaves.   823.5600

—— The pearl of Orr's island: a story of the coast of Maine.   823.1528

—— Pink and white tyranny.   823.1529

—— Poganuc people: their loves and lives.
    823.1530

—— Sam Lawson's Oldtown fireside stories.
    823.1936

Issued also as Oldtown fireside stories.

—— Uncle Tom's cabin; or, life among the lowly. With account of the work by the author.   823.1532

—— *Same.*   823.6037

—— We and our neighbors; or, the records of an unfashionable street. (Sequel to "My wife and I.")   823.1533

Note.—For her life and writings, *see* **Bullen,** G: Bibliography of Uncle Tom's cabin. 1880. *in* ** 16.81.—**Drake,** S: A. *In his* Our great benefactors. 1884. p. 131, *in* *920.312.—**Gilder,** J. L., *and* J. B. *In their* Authors at home. p. 313, *in* 820.159.— **Stowe,** C: E: Life of H. B. Stowe. 1889. 928.685.
See also Appleton's Cyclop. of Amer. biog., v. 5. *in* ** 920.324.
See also Poole's Index (to 1882). p. 1,258, *in* ** 50. 1;—*Same.* Jan. 1, 1882–Jan. 1, 1887. p. 422, *in* ** 50.1².

——, *and others.* Six of one by half a dozen of the other: an every day novel.   823.1531
Strait gate, The. Abbott, J.   *in* 808.580
Stranded ship, A. Davis, L. C.   823.360
Strange adventures of a phaeton. Black, W: 823.88
Strange adventures of Capt. Dangerous. Sala, G: A: *in* 823.5026
Strange case of Dr. Jekyll and Mr. Hyde. Stevenson, R. L: 823.4952
Same.   823.5013
Strange disappearance, A. Rohlfs, *Mrs.* A. K.. (G.)   823.664
Strange friend, A. Hawthorne, J. C.
    p. 138, *in* 823.7383
Strange infatuation, A. Harrison, L.
    823.7077
Strange stories. Erckmann, É., *and* Chatrian, P. A.   823.4003
Strange stories. Hoffmann, E. T. W.
    823.6807
Strange stories from history for young people. Eggleston, G: C.   808.1432
Strange story. Lytton, E: G: E. L. Bulwer-
    823.1043
Strange surprising adventures of the venerable Gooroo Simple, and his five disciples, Noodle, Doodle, Wiseacre, Zany and Foozle. With fifty illustrations by A. H. Forrester. [*Alfred Crowquill.*]
    ** 823.1855

English Fiction. *Contin.*
Strange tales.

—— Ainsworth, W: H. Auriol; or, the elixir of life.   823.27

—— Beckford, W: Vathek: an Arabian tale.
    823.4232

—— *Same.* (*In* Lib. of famous fiction.)
    p. 841, *in* 823.6215

—— Cobban, J. M. Julius Courtney; or, master of his fate.   823.7246

—— Hauff, W. The mysterious manuscript.
    in ** 1000.106

—— Hawthorne, N. Ethan Brand. 23 pp. (Johnson, R., *ed. Little classics,* v. 1.)
    p. 7, *in* 829.124

—— Hoffmann, E. T. W. Strange stories.
    823.6807

—— Howitt, *Mrs.* M.. (B.) Apparitions.— Haunted houses.—Second sight. (Eunemoser, J. *In his* History of magic, v. 2.)
    133.15

—— Irving, W. The money-diggers.—Strange stories by a nervous gentleman. (*In his* Tales of a traveller.)   823.844

—— Johnson, R., *ed.* Little classics. v. 8: Mystery.   829.131

—— Kipling, R. The phantom 'rickshaw, and other tales.   823.7345

—— Lynton, E. L., *ed.* Witch stories. (Scotland and England.)   133.8

—— Lytton, E: G: E. L. Bulwer- A strange story.   823.1043

—— Marryat, *Capt.* F: The phantom ship.
    823.1111

—— *Same.*   ** 823.6670

—— Paget, V. Hauntings: fantastic stories.
    823.7021

—— Paltock, R. Life and adventures of Peter Wilkins.   823.4062

—— Radcliffe, *Mrs.* A. (W.) Mysteries of Udolpho.   823.1280

—— — *Same.* 3 vols.   ** 823.2106-8

—— — Romance of the forest. 2 vols.
    ** 823.2104-5

—— Reeve, C. The old English baron. (Barbauld, *Mrs.* A. L. (A.), *ed. The Brit. novelists,* v. 22.)   ** 823.2083

—— Scott, *Sir* W. The bride of Lammermoor.   823.1396

—— — *Same.*   823.4437; 823.4803

—— — *Same.*   *in* 823.5326; *in* 823.5337

—— — *Same.*   *in* 823.5797; ** 823.6026

—— — *Same.*   ** 823.6724

—— — The monastery.   823.1403

—— — *Same.*   823.5159; ** 823.6027

—— — My aunt Margaret's mirror.
    in 823.1412

—— — *Same.*   *in* 823.4826; *in* 823.5160

—— — *Same.*   *in* ** 823.6034

—— — The tapestried chamber. *in* 823.1412

—— — *Same.*   *in* 823.4826; *in* 823.5160

—— — *Same.*   *in* ** 823.6034

—— — Wandering Willie's tale.
    p. 164, *in* 823.1407

—— Shelley, *Mrs.* M.. W. (G.) Frankenstein.   823.1421

—— Timbs, J: Oddities of hist., and strange stories.   829.533

English Fiction. *Contin.*
Sue, Marie Joseph, *called* Eugène. *Contin.*
—— Wandering Jew. 2 vols. (in 1).
823.2864
—— *Same.* 823.5014; 823.5799
Sue-sand, Alexander, *fils, pseud.* See Hamley, *Sir* E: B.
Sullivan, *Mrs.* Arabella (Wilmot). Tales of the peerage and the peasantry. Ed. by Lady Dacre. 2 vols. (v. 1 only): Winifred, countess of Nithsdale. ** 823.6761
Sullivan, T: Russell. Day and night stories.
823.7026
Summer idyl, A. Tiernan, *Mrs.* F.. C. (F.)
823.568
Summer in a cañon, A. Wiggin, *Mrs.* K.. D. (S.) 823.6189
Summer in Leslie Goldthwaite's life. Whitney, *Mrs.* A. D. (T.) 823.1701
Summer legends. Baumbach, R. 808.1660
Sun, To the. Verne, J. 823.7127
Sunk at sea. Ballantyne, R. M. 823.1282
Sun-maid. Grant, M.. M. 823.661
Sunny shores. Adams, W: T. 808.497
Sunnybank. Terhune, *Mrs.* M.. V. (H.)
823.1564
Sunrise. Black, W: 823.4016
Sunshine and roses. Brame, *Mrs.* C.. M. (L.)
823.5119
Superior to circumstances. Blackall, E. L.
823.7340
Supernatural, The, in story. *See also* Spiritualism in story.—Strange tales.
—— Besant, W., *and* Rice, J. The case of Mr. Lucraft, etc. Pt. 1. 823.6330
—— Campbell, *Sir* G. Mysteries of the unseen; or, supernatural stories of English life. 823.7243
—— Dahlgren, *Mrs.* M. (V.) South-mountain magic. 133.316
—— Grant, J. Apparitions and wonders. 63 pp. p. 233, *in* 823.646
—— —— The veiled portrait. 16 pp.
p. 250, *in* 823.649
—— Hawthorne, J. C. Constance, and Calbot's rival. 823.5507
—— Hubbell, W. The great Amherst mystery: a true narrative of the supernatural.
823.6199
—— Oliphant, *Mrs.* M. O. (W.) A beleaguered city. 823.5640
—— —— Old lady Mary: a story of the seen and the unseen. 823.4723
—— —— *Same.* *in* 823.4988
—— —— The open door and The portrait: two stories of the seen and unseen.
823.4951

Note.—Argyll, *Duke of.* The supernatural. 52 pp. (*In his* The reign of law.) p. 1, *in* 340.14.—De Quincey, T: Modern superstition. 60 pp. (*In his* Narr. and miscel. papers, v. 2.) p. 55, *in* 829.551.— Howitt, W. History of the supernatural. 2 vols. 1863. 133.318-19.—Mather, I. Remarkable providences. 1856. * 133.35.—Parker, H. W. Contemporary supernaturalism. 10 pp. (*Forum*, v. 1, 1887.) p. 284, *in* * 51.4700.—Smedley, *and others.* Glimpses of the supernatural. 133.5.—Taylor, B. My supernatural experiences. (*In his* At home and abroad.) 1862. pp. 140-164, *in* 910.149.
See also Poole's Index (to 1882). p. 1,271, *in* ** 50.1:—*Same.* Jan. 1, 1882–Jan. 1, 1887. p. 427, *in* ** 50.1¹.

English Fiction. *Contin.*
Surgeon's daughter. Scott, *Sir* W. 823.1410
Same. *in* 823.5329
Surgeon's daughters. 35 pp. Wood, *Mrs.* E. (P.) *in* 823.5036
Surgeon's stories, The. See Topelius, Z.
Surly Tim, and other stories. Burnett, *Mrs.* F.. E. (H.) 823.5362
Surry of Eagle's Nest. Cooke, J: E.
823.281
Susan Drummond. Riddell, *Mrs.* C.. E. L. (C.) 823.7062
Susan Fielding. Edwardes, *Mrs.* A.
823.5856
Sutherlands, The. Harris, *Mrs.* M. (C.)
823.709
Suttner, A. G. von. Djambek the Georgian: a tale of modern Turkey. Tr. by H. M. Jewett, with an introd. by M. M. Mangasarian. 823.7049
Suwanee river tales. McDowall, *Mrs.* K.. S. (B.) 823.4891
Suzanne de l'Orme. G., H. 808.1659
Swallow Barn. Kennedy, J: P. 823.929
Swamp doctor's adventures in the south-west. Robb, J: S. 823.1340
Swan, *Rev.* C:, *tr.* Gesta Romanorum; or, entertaining moral stories. Rev. and corrected by W. Hooper. 823.2132
Sweden. *See also* Scandinavia.
—— Adams, W: T. Up the Baltic. 808.498
GUSTAVUS VASA, 1523–1560.
—— Drama. Brooke, H: 822.77
—— Drama. Kotzebue, A. F. F. von. (German.) 832.72
—— Drama. Piron, A. (French.) 842.65
GUSTAVUS ADOLPHUS, 1611–1632.
—— De Foe, D. Memoirs of a cavalier.
in 823.2123
—— Topelius, Z. Times of Gustaf Adolf.
823.4476
See also Germany, *Thirty years' war*, p. 100.
CHARLES XII., 1697–1718.
—— Planché, J. R. Charles XII.; drama.
822.727
—— Tegnér, E. Axel; poem. 821.895
—— Topelius, Z. Times of Charles XII.
823.4637
18TH CENTURY A. D.
—— Topelius, Z. Times of alchemy.
823.4972
—— —— Times of battle and rest. 823.4558
—— —— Times of Linnæus. 823.4734
FREDERICK I., 1720–1751.
—— Topelius, Z. Times of Frederick I.
823.4701
LIFE AND MANNERS.
—— Bremer, F. The four sisters. 823 1919
—— —— The home. 823.2119
—— —— The neighbors. 823.2175
—— —— The president's daughter. Pt. 2: Nina. 823.6129
—— Dudevant, *Mme.* A. L. A. (D.) The snow man. 823.6853
—— Janson, K. N. The spell-bound fiddler: a Norse romance. 823.2020
—— Kuorring, *Freifrau* S. M. (Z.) The peasant and his landlord. 823.952
See also Novels by Mrs. M. S. (B.) Schwartz.

English Fiction. *Contin.*
Sweden. *Contin.*

Note.—See Dunham, S. A. History of Denmark, Sweden and Norway. 3 vols. 1839. 948.12-14.—**Fletcher,** C. R. L. Gustavus Adolphus and the struggle of Protestantism for existence. 1890. 923.2050.—**Geijer,** E. G., **and** Carlson, F. F. Geschichte Schwedens (to 1706). 6 vols. (Heeren, A. H. L., *und* Ukert, F. A., *eds. Gesch. der europ. Staaten.*) 1832-75. 948.42-7.—History of **Gustavus Vasa,** King of Sweden. 1852. 923.2089.—**Keen,** G. B. New Sweden; or, the Swedes on the Delaware. (Winsor, J., *ed. Narr. and crit. hist. of Amer.,* v. iv., chap. ix.) p. 443, *in* * 970.127⁴.—**Meredith,** W. C. Memorials of Charles John, King of Sweden and Norway. 1829. 923.222.—**Otté,** *Miss* F. C. Scandinavian history. 1874. 948.16.—**Taylor,** B. *In his* Northern travel. 1878. 914.126.—**Voltaire,** F. M. A. de. L'histoire de Charles XII. (*Œuvres compl.,* v. 26.) 948.4.—**Watson,** P. B. Swedish revolution under Gustavus Vasa. 1889. (Bibliography, pp. 277-291.) 948.28.
For literature, *see* Howitt, W., *and* Howitt, *Mrs.* M.. B. Literature and romance of northern Europe. 2 vols. 1852. 804.13-14.—**Longfellow,** H: W. Poems of places. p. 251, *in* 821.214.—**Svensk bibliographie.** 1847-64. * 15.86.
For folk-lore, *see* Hofberg, H. Swedish folklore. 1888. 291.89.
See also under "Scandinavia" *in* **Catalogues of** this Library.
   No. 2, 1880, p. 202.   No. 4, 1884, p. 260.
   No. 3, 1882, p. 169.   No. 5, 1888, p. 313.
See also Index to Consular reports. 1880-1885; 1886-1889. 2 vols. (U. S. Pub. Docs. *Dept. of State.*) ** 350.5496¹·².
See also Poole's Index (to 1882). p. 1,274, *in* ** 50.1;—*Same.* Jan. 1, 1882-Jan. 1, 1887. pp. 427-428, *in* ** 50.1³.

Swedenborgianism. Amid the corn. By the author of " The evening and the morning." 3 vols.   823.1987-9
Note.—See Dasa, P. Swedenborg, the Buddhist. 1887. 289.107.—**De Quincey,** T: A Manchester Swedenborgian and a Liverpool literary coterie. 25 pp. (Masson, D:, *ed. Coll. writings,* v. 2.) p. 113, *in* 829.680.—**Ellis,** J: The new Christianity. 1887. 289.195.—**Potts,** J: F., *comp.* The Swedenborg concordance. 4 vols. v. 1: A-C. 289.108.
See also **Catalogues** of this Library.
   No. 2, 1880, p. 221.   No. 4, 1884, p. 284.
   No. 3, 1882, p. 182.   No. 5, 1888, p. 347.
Sweet and twenty. Collins, M., *and* Collins, *Mrs.* F.. (C.)   823.248
Sweet Cymbeline. Brame, *Mrs.* C.. M. (L.)   *in* 823.5180
Sweet Dorothy Capell. (Anon.)
   p. 20, *in* 923.862
Sweet Mace. Fenn, G: M.   823.7117
Swift, J. Franklin. Robert Greathouse.
   823.1536
Swift, Jonathan. (1667-1745.) Gulliver's travels. 89 pp. (*In* Lib. of famous fiction, etc.)   p. 539, *in* ** 823.6215
—— *Same.* (*In* Classic tales.) 1885.
   p. 279, *in* 823.4489
—— *Same.* With life of the author by W. C. Taylor.   808.397
—— *Same.* With notes, and life of the author by W. C. Taylor.   823.2966
—— A voyage to Lilliput. 30 pp. (Scudder, H. E. *The children's book.*)
   p. 362, *in* 808.1882
Note.—For his life and writings, *see* Garnett, R: Article " Swift, J.," *in* Encyclop. Brit., v. 22. ** 32. 292.—**Hale,** E: E. *In his* Lights of two centuries. 1887. p. 135, *in* * 920.314.—**Howitt,** W: Dean Swift. 24 pp. (*In his* Home and haunts of British poets.) p. 116, *in* 914.10.—**Hunt,** T. W. The prose style of J. Swift. 22 pp. (*In his* Represent. Eng. prose.) p. 265, *in* 820.120.—**Johnson,** S: *In his* Lives of the poets. 1881. p. 235, *in* * 928.291.—**Lecky,** W: E. H.

English Fiction. *Contin.*
Swift, Jonathan. (1667-1745.) *Contin.*
Note. Contin.
In his Leaders of public opinion in Ireland. 1872. pp. 1-62, *in* 923.20.—**Mahon,** *Lord.* Character of Swift. 2 pp. (*In his* Hist. of Eng. v. 1.) p. 69, *in* * 942.330.—**Masson,** D: *In his* Three devils, etc. 1874. p. 235, *in* 824.71.—**Mitchell,** D. G. Gulliver Swift. 19 pp. (*In his* About old story tellers.) p. 96, *in* 813.33.—**Russell,** W: Jonathan Swift, D. D., and dean of St. Patrick. 11 pp. (*In his* Eccentric personages.) p. 168, *in* 920.369.—**Stephen,** L. Memoir of Swift. 1882. 928.402.—**Taine,** H. A. *In his* History of English literature, v. 2. pp. 352-92, *in* 820.57.—**Thackeray,** W: M. Swift. 54 pp. (*In his* The Eng. humorists of the 18th cent.) p. 1, *in* 820.180.—**Timbs,** J. *In his* Anecdote lives of wits and humorists, v. 1. 1872. p. 1, *in* 828.129.
See also Allibone's Dict. of Eng. lit., v. 2. pp. 2,311-18, *in* ** 803.7.
See also Poole's Index (to 1882). p. 1,275, *in* ** 50.1;—*Same.* Jan. 1, 1882-Jan. 1, 1887. p. 428, *in* ** 50.1³.

Swiss family Robinson. Wyss, J. D:
   808.376
Switzerland.
—— Abbott, J. Rollo in Switzerland.
   808.924
—— Adams, W: T. Palace and cottage; or, Young America in France and Switzerland.
   808.491
—— Champney, *Mrs.* E.. (W.) Three Vassar girls in Switzerland.   808.1919
—— Hale, E: E., *and* Hale, S. A family flight through . . . Switzerland, etc.
   808.1831
—— Longfellow, H: W. Poems of places.
   821.221
—— *Same.*   *in* * 821.231
14TH CENTURY A. D. Baillie, J. Orra; trag.
   822.128
William Tell (1306).
—— Knowles, J. S. William Tell.
   p. 113, *in* 822.147
—— —— *Same.* (*In* Lacy's plays.)
   in * 822.743
—— Schiller, F. von. William Tell. (German.)   p. 230, *in* 832.18
—— Strickland, A. William Tell. 27 pp. (*In her* Stories from history.)
   p. 276, *in* 808.294

Hemans, *Mrs.* F. The league of the Alps. (1307-8.)   p. 102, *in* 821.159
Battle of Morgarten, 1315. Poem by *Mrs.* F. Hemans. (*Works,* v. 3.)
   p. 252, *in* 821.155
15TH CENTURY A. D.
—— Scott, *Sir* W. Anne of Geierstein.
   823.1392
—— —— *Same.*   ** 823.6033
—— Zschokke, J. H. D. Der Freihof von Aarau. 2 vols. (War.)
   p. 178, *in* 833.1044-5
REFORMATION. Byron, *Lord.* The prisoner of Chillon; poem.   p. 363, *in* 821.61
Note.—See also Reformation, *note,* p. 212.

17TH CENTURY A. D. Zschokke, J. H. D. Addrich im Moos. (Life and manners.)
   p. 190, *in* 833.1045
HELVETIAN REPUBLIC. Zschokke, J. H. D. The rose of Disentis.   823.6929
—— *Same.*   *in* 833.1052

English Fiction. *Contin.*

Tachypomp, The. 24 pp. Mitchell, E: P.
p. 142, *in* 823.4706

Tadema, Laurence Alma. Love's martyr.
in 823.5026

Taken alive. Roe, E: P. 823.6549

Taken at the flood. Maxwell, *Mrs.* M.. E..
(B.) *in* 823.2412

Same. 823.5112

Taken by the enemy. Adams, W: T.
808.1680

Taking the Bastile. Dumas, A. D.
823.6520

Tale of a lonely parish, A. Crawford, F. M.
823.4921

Tale of the house of the Wolfings, A. Morris, W: 829.697

Tale of the Tyne, A. Martineau, H.
** 823.6712

Tale of three lions, A. 58 pp. Haggard, H:
R. 823.6606

Tale of two cities. Dickens, C: J: H.
823.414

Same. 823.5317; *in* 823.5557

Tales and legends from the land of the tzar.
Hodgetts, E. M. S., *tr.* 808.1734

Tales and novels. 18 vols. Edgeworth, M.
823.7422–39

Tales and romances. De Quincey, T:
829.690

Tales and sketches. 5 vols. Hogg, J.
823.774–8

Tales and sketches. Miller, H. 823.1158

Tales and traditions of Hungary. 3 vols.
Pulzsky, F. A., *and* Pulzsky, T. 823.5731–3

Tales at tea-time. Hugessen, E: H. Knatchbull- 808.886

Tales before supper. Gautier, T., *and* Mérimée, P. 823.5737

Tales from Ariosto. Retold by a lady.
808.777

Tales from Blackwood. 12 vols. (in 6).
823.7479–84

Same. 12 vols. 823.98–109

Same. ** 823.6647–58

Same. 2d ser. 12 vols. 823.7485–96

Same. 3d ser. vols. 1–6. 6 vols.
823.7497–502

Tales from English history for children.
Strickland, A. 808.293

Tales from Shakespeare. Lamb, C:, *and*
Lamb, M.. 808.783

Same. 823.953

Tales from the Arabian nights' entertainments. Forster, E:, *tr.* (*In* Lib. of famous fiction, etc.) p. 953, *in* * 823.6215

Tales from the German. Heyse, J. L. P.
823.2332

Tales from the German. Tr. by J: Oxenford
and C. A. Feiling. 823.6276

Tales from two hemispheres. Boyesen, H.
H. 823.4237

Tales of a traveller. Irving, W. 823.844

Tales of adventure. Ballantyne, R. M.
808.1268

Tales of adventure on the coast. Ballantyne,
R. M. 808.1269

Tales of adventure on the sea. Ballantyne,
R. M. 808.1266

English Fiction. *Contin.*

Tales of all countries. Trollope, A.
823.1627

Tales of ancient Greece. Cox, *Sir* G: W:
808.837

Tales of daring and danger. Henty, G: A.
808.1669

Tales of fashionable life. *See* Edgeworth, M.

Tales of Flemish life. Conscience, H.
823.4235

Tales of my landlord. 3d ser. 2 vols. (in
1). Scott, *Sir* W. 823.5337

Tales of New England. Jewett, S.. O.
823.7175

Tales of old Thule. Smith, J. M., *comp.*
808.753

Tales of other days. Akerman, J: Y. 823.1

Tales of real life. Opie, *Mrs.* A. (A.)
p. 5, *in* 823.6135

Tales of the Argonauts, and other sketches.
Harte, F. B. 823.714

Tales of the borders. 24 vols. (in 12). Wilson, J: M. 823.1711–22

Tales of the covenanters. Pollok, R.
823.1270

Tales of the drama. Macauley, E. 823.1051

Tales of the east. 3 vols. Weber, H: W.
** 823.6230–2

Tales of the French revolution. Martineau,
H. 823.6602

Tales of the genii. Ridley, J.
p. 417, *in* ** 823.6232

Tales of the good woman. Paulding, J. K.
823.1238

Tales of the kings and queens of England.
Percy, S. 808.1603

Tales of the Munster festivals. Griffin, G.
823.667

Same. 2d ser. 823.668

Tales of the ocean and essays for the forecastle. Sleeper, J: S. 823.1838

Tales of the peerage and the peasantry. v. 1
(only). Sullivan, *Mrs.* A. (W.)
** 823.6761

Tales of the southern border. Webber, C:
W. 823.5804

Tales of the woods and fields. Marsh, *Mrs.*
A. (C.) ** 823.6732

Tales out of school. Stockton, F. R:
808.1887

Talis qualis: tales of the jury-room. Griffin,
G. 823.677

Talisman, The. Scott, *Sir* W. 823.1412

Same. 823.5160; p. 485, *in* ** 823.6031

Same. 823.7476

Talking leaves, The. Stoddard, W: O.
808.1359

Tallants of Barton, The. Hatton, J.
.823.720

Talmud. Hearn, L. Traditions from the
Talmud. 34 pp. (*In his* Stray leaves,
etc.) p. 191, *in* 823.4791

Note.–See Deutsch, E. The Talmud. (*In his*
Literary remains.) 1874. 814.1.–Kalisch, I. A
sketch of the Talmud. 1877. *in* ** 204.80.–McClintock & Strong's Cyclopædia of Biblical . . .
literature, v. 10. Article "Talmud." pp.166–90, *in* **
203.11C.–Polano, H. Selections from the Talmud.
(5636.) 296.21.–Well, G. Bible, Koran and the
Talmud; or, Biblical legends of the Mussulmans.
1878. 297.5.

English Fiction. *Contin.*
Talmud. *Contin.*
   See also Poole's Index (to 1882). pp. 1,281-2, *in*
   ** 50.1;—*Same.* Jan. 1, 1882-Jan. 1, 1887. p. 430, *in*
   ** 50.1³.
Talvj, *pseud. See* Robinson, *Mrs.* T. A. L.
   (von Jakob).
Tamenaga Shunsui. The loyal Ronins: an
   historical romance. Tr. by S. Saito and E:
   Greey.   823.6083
Tancred. Disraeli, B: 823.467
Tangled paths. Dorsey, *Mrs.* A. (H.)
   823.475
Tangled tale, A. Dodgson, *Rev.* C: L.
   823.4925
Tangled web, A. Holt, E. S..   823.7105
Tanglewood tales. Hawthorne, N. 808.549
Same.   *in* 808.1890
Tanner boy, The. Denison, C: W. 808.224
Taras Bulba. Gogol-Janovskij, N. W.
   823.5259
Tartarian tales. Gueullette, T: S.
   p. 221, *in* ** 823.6232
Tartarin of Tarascon. Daudet, A.
   823.5253
Tartarin on the Alps. Daudet, A. 823.5347
Tasma, *pseud. See* Fraser, J.
Tautphœus, Jemima (Montgomery), *Frei-*
   herrin von.
   —— At odds.   823.1797
   —— Cyrilla.   823.6439
   —— The initials.   823.1796
   —— Quits. 2 vols. (in 1).   823.1798
Tavernicus, The. Gore, *Mrs.* C. F.. G. (M.)
   p. 59, *in* ** 823.6568
Taylor, *Miss* —. Known too late. 823.1548
Taylor, Bayard. (1825-1878.) Beauty and
   the beast, and tales of home. 823.1543
   —— Hannah Thurston: a story of American
   life.   823.1544
   —— John Godfrey's fortunes, related by him-
   self.   823.1545
   —— Joseph and his friends: a story of Penn-
   sylvania.   823.1546
   —— The story of Kennett.   823.1547
   —— Who was she? 45 pp. (*In* Stories by
   Amer. authors, v. 1.)   p. 5, *in* 823.4702
   Note.—For his life and writings, *see* Conwell, R.
   H. Life, travels and literary career of Taylor, 1881.
   928.342.—**Harris,** A. B. B. Taylor. 22 pp. (*In her*
   Amer. authors for young folks.) p. 141, *in* 820.157.
   —**Shepard,** W: Pen pictures of modern authors.
   1886. p. 178, *in* 820.163.—**Stoddard,** R: H: Bayard
   Taylor. 15 pp. (*Lippincott's mag.,* v. 43, 1889.) p.
   571, *in* * 51.692².—**Taylor,** M. Hansen, *and* Scudder, II. E., *eds.* Life and letters of Taylor. 2 vols.
   1884. 928.548-9.
   See also **Allibone's** Dict. of Eng. lit., v. 3. p.
   2,340, *in* ** 803.8.—**Appleton's** Cyclop. of Amer.
   biog., v. 6. p. 40, *in* ** 920.325.—**Stedman,** E. C.,
   and Hutchinson, E. M. Lib. of Amer. lit., v. 8. p.
   208, *in* ** 820.129.
   See also **Poole's** Index (to 1882). p. 1,286, *in* ** 50.
   1;—*Same.* Jan. 1, 1882-Jan. 1, 1887. p. 431, *in* **
   50.1².
Taylor, B: Franklin. Three November days.
   37 pp. (Johnson, R., *ed. Little classics,*
   v. 11.)   p. 103, *in* 829.134
Taylor, E.. Blindpits: a story of Scottish
   life. (Anon.)   823.4107
   —— Quixstar.   823.4112
Taylor, G:, *pseud. See* Hausrath, A.
Taylor, Ida Ashworth. Venus's doves.
   in 823.5053

English Fiction. *Contin.*
Taylor, Jefferys. Boy Crusoes; or, the young
   islanders: a tale of the last century.
   808.1658
Taylor, Meadows. Confessions of a Thug.
   823.4276
   —— *Same.* 3 vols.   * 823.4629-31
Taylor, *Gen.* Zachary. Life of Z. T., the
   hero of Okee Chobee, Palo Alto, Resaca de
   la Palma, Monterey and Buena Vista; containing numerous anecdotes. 808.728
Tchernuishevsky, Nikolaï Gavrilovitch. A
   vital question; or, what is to be done.
   823.7143
Tchitchikoff's journeys. 2 vols. Gogol-
   Janovskij, N. W.   823.5344-5
Teacher of the violin, and other tales. Short-
   house, J. H: 823.5438
Tecumseh and the Shawnee prophet. Eggle-
   ston, E:, *and* Seelye, *Mrs.* L. (E.)
   808.1589
Telemachus. Fénelon, F. de S. de la M.
   823.6211
Same.   823.6916
Temper. Opie, *Mrs.* A. (A.)
   p. 5, *in* 823.6136
Tempest and sunshine. Holmes, *Mrs.* M..
   J.. (H.)   823.802
Temple, G: Lancelot Ward, M. P.
   in 823.4987
Temple house. Stoddard, *Mrs.* E.. D. (B.)
   823.5449
Temptation, The. Sue, M. J.   823.5895
Tempting of Pescara. Meyer, K. F.
   823.7351
Ten old maids. Smith, J. P.   823.1468
Ten tales. Coppée, F. E. J.   823.7540
Ten thousand a year. Warren, S: 823.1689
Ten times one is ten. Hale, E: E. 823.685
Same.   823.4540
Tenant of Wildfell Hall. Brontë, A.
   823.125
Tenants of Malory. Le Fanu, J. S.
   823.6175
Tender recollections of Irene Magillicuddy.
   Oliphant, L.   823.4059
Tenney, E. P. Agamenticus.   823.1549
Terhune, *Mrs.* M.. Virginia (Hawes). [*Ma-*
   rion Harland.]
   —— Alone.   823.1550
   —— At last.   823.1551
   —— A battle summer. (*With her* Helen
   Gardner's wedding-day.)   *in* 823.1554
   —— The empty heart; or, husks. 823.1552
   Issued also as Husks.
   —— From my youth up.   823.1553
   —— Helen Gardner's wedding-day; or, Colo-
   nel Floyd's wards. (*Also*) A battle sum-
   mer.   823.1554
   Issued also as Colonel Floyd's wards.
   —— The hidden path.   823.1555
   —— Husbands and homes.   823.1556
   —— Jessamine.   823.1557
   —— Judith: a chronicle of old Virginia.
   823.4698
   —— Miriam.   823.1558
   —— Moss-side.   823.1559
   —— My little love.   823.1560
   —— Nemesis.   823.1561

English Fiction. *Contin.*

Terhune, *Mrs.* M.. Virginia (Hawes). [*Marion Harland.*] *Contin.*
— Phemie's temptation. 823.1562
— Ruby's husband. 823.1563
— Sunnybank. 823.1564
— True as steel. 823.1565
— With the best intentions: a midsummer episode. 823.7195
Terrible secret, A. Fleming, *Mrs.* M. A. (E.) 823.581
Terrible temptation. Reade, C: 823.1295
Teufel, *Mrs.* Blanche Willis (Howard).
— Aulnay Tower. 823.4898
— Aunt Serena. 823.1863
— Guenn: a wave on the Breton coast. 823.4672
— One summer. 823.827
— The open door. 823.6209
Thackeray, Aune I.. *See* Ritchie, *Mrs.* A. I.. (Thackeray).

Thackeray, W: Makepeace. [*Mr. M. A. Titmarsh.*] (1811-1863.)
— The adventures of Philip. (*Prefixed,*) A shabby genteel story. 823.1571
— Complete works. vols. 5 and 7. (Illus. lib. ed.) 823.6323-4
   v. 5: The memoirs of Mr. C. J. Yellowplush.—The Fitzboodle papers.—The wolves and the lamb.—Stories. (*viz.:* The Bedford-row conspiracy.—A little dinner at Timmins's.—The fatal boots.)—Little travels and roadside sketches. (*viz.:* From Richmond in Surrey to Brussels in Belgium.—Ghent.—Bruges.—Waterloo.
   v. 7: The history of Samuel Titmarsh and the great Hoggarty diamond.—Men's wives.—The book of snobs.
— Denis Duval. (*Also*) The history of Samuel Titmarsh and the great Hoggarty diamond. 823.2537
— Henry Esmond, and Lovel the widower. 823.2242
— The history of Pendennis. 823.1576
— The history of Samuel Titmarsh and the great Hoggarty diamond. (*With his* Denis Duval.) *in* 823.2537
— Lovel the widower. *in* 823.2242
— *Same.* *in* 823.5338
— Luck of Barry Lyndon: a romance of the last century. 2 vols. 823.4642-3
— Miscellanies. 823.6552
   Contents:—The memoirs of Barry Lyndon, Esq.—The history of Samuel Titmarsh and the great Hoggarty diamond.—Burlesques. (*viz.:* Novels by eminent hands.—A plan for a prize novel.—The diary of C. Jeames de la Pluche, Esq., with his letters.—The tremendous adventures of Major Gahagan.—A legend of the Rhine.—Rebecca and Rowena: a romance upon romance.—The history of the next French revolution.)
— Pendennis, History of. 823.1576
— A shabby genteel story. (*Prefixed to his* The adventures of Philip.) *in* 823.1571
— Vanity fair: a novel without a hero. 823.1580
— *Same.* (*Also*) Lovel the widower. 823.5338
— The Virginians: a tale of the last century. 823.1581
— Works. 12 vols. vols. 3, 4, 8, 9, 11, 12.
   v. 3: The Newcomes. 823.1578
   v. 4: History of Henry Esmond.—Memoirs of Barry Lyndon. 823.1575

English Fiction. *Contin.*

Thackeray, W: Makepeace. [*Mr. M. A. Titmarsh.*] (1811-1863.) *Contin.*
— Works. 12 vols. vols. 3, 4, 8, 9, 11, 12. *Contin.*
   v. 8: History of Samuel Titmarsh and the great Hoggarty diamond.—Memoirs of Mr. C. J. Yellowplush and Burlesques. (*viz.:* Novels by eminent hands.—Plan for a prize novel.—Diary of C. Jeames de la Pluche.—Tremendous adventures of Major Gahagan.—A legend of the Rhine.—Rebecca and Rowena.—History of the next French revolution.—Cox's diary.—The fatal boots.)
   v. 9: The book of snobs.—Sketches of life and character.—Men's wives.—The Fitzboodle papers.—The Bedford-row conspiracy.—A little dinner at Timmins's. 823.1572
   v. 11: Catherine.*—Lovel the widower.—Denis Duval.—Ballads.—The wolves and the lamb.—Critical reviews. (*viz.:* George Cruikshank.—John Leech's pictures of life and character.)—Little travels and road-side sketches. I: From Richmond in Surrey to Brussels in Belgium. II: Ghent (1840) to Bruges. III: Waterloo. 823.1573
   Note.—Intended "to counteract the injurious influence of some popular fictions of that day, which made heroes of highwaymen and burglars, and created a false sympathy for the vicious and criminal."
   v. 12: The Christmas books of Mr. M. A. Titmarsh. (*viz.:* Mrs. Perkins's ball.—Our street.—Dr. Birch, and his young friends.—The Kickleburys on the Rhine.—The rose and the ring; or, the history of prince Giglio and prince Bulbo.) 823.1574
— Works. 26 vols. vols. 1-7, 10, 11, 15.
   vols. 1-2: Vanity fair: a novel without a hero. 2 vols. 823.5004-5
   vols. 3-4: History of Pendennis. 2 vols. 823.5006-7
   vols. 5-6: The Newcomes: memoirs of a most respectable family. 2 vols. 823.5001-2
   v. 7: The history of Henry Esmond, etc. 823.5008
   vols. 10-11: The adventures of Philip. Prefixed, A shabby genteel story. 2 vols. 823.5002-3
   v. 15: Burlesques. (*viz.:* Novels by eminent hands.—Plan for a prize novel.—Diary of C. Jeames de la Pluche, Esq.—History of the next French revolution.—A legend of the Rhine.—Adventures of Major Gahagan.) 823.5010
— The Yellowplush papers. 823.7419
   Contents:—Miss Shum's husband.—The amours of Mr. Deuceace.—Skimmings from "The diary of George IV."—Foring parts.—Mr. Deuceace at Paris.—Mr. Yellowplush's ajew.—Epistles to the literati.
   Note.—For his life and writings, *see* Bagehot, W: Sterne and Thackeray. 43 pp. (*Works,* v. 2.) p. 154, *in* 814.23 —Bayne, P, The modern novel: . . .—Thackeray. 30 pp. (*In his* Essays in biog. and crit.) p. 363, *in* 824.185.—Brown, J; M. D. Thackeray's lit. career. 58 pp;—Thackeray's death. 10 pp. (*In his* Spare hours, 2d ser.) pp. 239, 227, *in* 824.362.—Fields, J. T. Thackeray. 24 pp. (*In his* Yesterdays with authors.) p. 11, *in* 928.76.—Hale, E: E. Thackeray. 11 pp. (*In his* Lights of two centuries.) p. 257, *in* ⁕920.314.—Hodgkins, L. M. Thackeray. (*In her* A guide to the study of 19th cent. authors.) pp. 41-44, *in* 820.155.—Jeaffreson, J: C. William Makepeace Thackeray. 20 pp. (*In his* Novels, etc., v. 2.) p. 262, *in* 820.167.—Johnson, C: P. The early writings of William Makepeace Thackeray. Illus. 1888. ⁕824.450.—A collection of (his) letters, 1847-1855. 1890. 816.61.—Shepard, W: Pen portraits of modern authors. p. 294, *in* 820.163.—Smith, G: B. *In his* Poets and novelists. 1876. p. 3, *in* 829.237.—Stoddard, R: H., *ed.* Anecdote biog. of Thackeray, etc. 1875. 928.53.—Taine, H. A. Hist. of Eng. lit., v. 3. 820.58;—Thackeray: son talent et ses œuvres. 36 pp. (*Rev. d. d. Mondes,* 1857. 2e sér., v. 7.) p. 165, *in* ⁕54.212.—Trollope, A. Account of Thackeray. 928.284.—Whipple, E. P. Thackeray. 21 pp. (*In his* Character and characteristic men.) p. 197, *in* 824.195.
   See also Allibone's Dict. of Eng. lit., v. 3. p. 2,377, *in* ⁕⁕ 803.8.—Johnson, C: P. Hints to collectors of original eds. of the works of T. 1885. ⁕⁕ 10.11.
   See also Poole's Index (to 1882). p. 1,298, *in* ⁕⁕ 50.1;—*Same.* Jan. 1, 1882–Jan. 1, 1887. p. 436, *in* ⁕⁕ 50.1².

English Fiction. *Contin.*
Three ages, The. Martineau, H.
    in ** 823.6713
Three beauties, The. Southworth, *Mrs.* E.
  D. E. (N.) 823.1509
Three brides, The. Yonge, C.. M.. 823.1774
Three clerks, The. Trollope, A. 823.1628
Three courses and a dessert. Illus. by G:
  Cruikshank. Clarke, C: 823.352
Three cousins, The. Maitland, J. A.
  823.1086
Three cutters, The. Marryat, *Capt.* F:
  in 823.1112
Same. *in* ** 823.6671; *in* 823.6730
Three days. Cooper, S: W. 823.7000
Three Englishmen and three Russians in
  southern Africa, Adventures of. Verne, J.
  823.6973
Three feathers. Black, W: 823.89
Three generations. Emery, S.. A. 823.5858
Three gold dollars, The. Abbott, J.
  in 808.586
Three Greek children. Church, A. J:
  808.1705
Three guardsmen. Dumas, A. D.
  in 823.3229
Same. *in* 823.5088; 823.6930
Three guardsmen ser. *See* Dumas, A. D.
Three hundred years ago. Kingston, W: H:
  G. 808.1615
Three Kearneys, The. Picken, A.
  in 823.702
Three lieutenants. Kingston, W: H: G.
  808.1616
Three men in a boat. Jerome, J. K.
  823.6939
Three musketeers, The. Dumas, A. D.
  823.6509
Three scouts, The. Trowbridge, J: T.
  823.1638
Three sisters. Keeling, E. d'E. *in* 823.5060
Three sisters of the Briars, The. Landor,
  O. *in* 823.5089
Three Spaniards, The. Walker, G: 823.1667
Three Vassar girls abroad. Champney, *Mrs.*
  E.. (W.) 808.1821
Three Vassar girls at home. Champney, *Mrs.*
  E.. (W.) 808.1825
Three Vassar girls in England. Champney,
  Mrs. E.. (W.) 808.1824
Three Vassar girls in France. Champney,
  Mrs. E.. (W.) 808.1826
Three Vassar girls in Italy. Champney, *Mrs.*
  E.. (W.) 808.1828
Three Vassar girls in Russia and Turkey.
  Champney, *Mrs.* E.. (W.) 808.1823
Three Vassar girls in south Africa. Champ-
  ney, *Mrs.* E.. (W.) 808.1822
Three Vassar girls in Switzerland. Champ-
  ney, *Mrs.* E.. (W.) 808.1919
Three Vassar girls on the Rhine. Champ-
  ney, *Mrs.* E.. (W.) 808.1827
Throckmorton. Seawell, M. E. 823.7447
Throne of David. Ingraham, J. H.
  823.7441
Through a needle's eye. Smith, H.
  823.2036
Through night to light. Spielhagen, F.
  823.6822

English Fiction. *Contin.*
Through one administration. Burnett, *Mrs.*
  F.. E. (H.) 823.4579
Through the fray. Henty, G: A. 808.1484
Same. 808.1612
Through the looking-glass. Dodgson, C: L.
  808.687
Through winding ways. Kirk, *Mrs.* E. W.
  (O.) 823.6055
Thrown on the world. Brame, *Mrs.* C.. M.
  (L.) 823.5132
"Thrust out:" an old legend. Maclaren,
  Miss —. 823.1185
Thurlston tales. 2 vols. Gillies, R. P.
  ** 823.6250-1
Thwarted. Montgomery, F. 823.1167
Tibbles, T. H. Hidden power: a secret his-
  tory of the Indian ring . . . revealing the
  manner in which it controls three impor-
  tant departments of the United States gov-
  ernment. A defense of the U. S. army,
  and a solution of the Indian problem.
  823.1844
Ticket No. "9672." Verne, J. 823.4997
Tickler among the thieves. 96 pp. (*In*
  Tales from Blackwood, v. 12.)
  ** *in* 823.6658
Ticonderoga. James, G: P. R. 823.6385
Tie and trick. Smart, H. *in* 823.4995
Same. *in* 823.5202
Tieck, Ludwig. The elves. Tr. by T: Carlyle.
  With other stories and sketches. 823.6328
—— The fair-haired Eckbert. (*Also*) The
  trusty Eckart, — The Runenburg, — The
  elves, (*and*) The goblet. (Carlyle, T:, *tr.*
  Tales, etc.) 2 vols. *in* 823.6830-1
—— Love magic. (*Also*) Faithful Eckart
  and the Tannenhäuser, (*and*) Auburn Eg-
  bert. (Roscoe, T:, *tr.* *The German novel-*
  ists, v. 4.) ** 823.6829
Tiernan, *Mrs.* F.. C. (Fisher). [*Christian*
  Reid.] After many days. 823.5928
—— Bonny Kate. 823.6360
—— A daughter of Bohemia. 823.6359
—— Ebb-tide, and other stories. 823.6226
—— A gentle belle: a novel. 823.5897
—— Heart of steel: a novel. 823.4475
—— Hearts and hands. 823.5896
—— "The land of the sky;" or, adventures
  in mountain by-ways. 823.6044
—— Mabel Lee: a novel. 823.6035
—— Miss Churchill: a study. 823.7130
—— Nina's atonement, and other stories.
  823.5805
—— A question of honor. 823.6358
—— A summer idyl. 823.1568
—— Valerie Aylmer. 823.6045
Tiernan, *Mrs.* M.. Spear (Nicholas). Jack
  Horner. 823.6944
Tiger prince. Dalton, W: 808.870
Tiger-lilies. Lanier, S. 823.7110
Tigers and traitors. Verne, J. 823.4235
Tigranes. Franco, J: J. 823.6891
Tilbury Nogo. Melville, G: J: Whyte-
  in ** 823.4664
Same. 823.7289
Timboo and Fanny. Abbott, J. *in* 808.582
Timboo and Joliba. Abbott, J. *in* 808.582
Times of alchemy. Topelius, Z. 823.4972

English Fiction. *Contin.*
Times of battle and of rest. Topelius, Z.
  823.4558
Times of Charles XII. Topelius, Z.
  823.4637
Times of Frederick I. Topelius, Z.
  823.4701
Times of Gustaf Adolf. Topelius, Z.
  823.4476
Times of Linnæus. Topelius, Z. 823.4734
Tincker, M.. Agnes.
—— Aurora. 823.4905
—— By the Tiber. 823.4152
—— Grapes and thorns. 823.6307
—— The house of Yorke. 823.5993
—— The jewel in the lotos. Illus. 823.4743
—— Signor Monaldini's niece. 823.2000
—— Sister Sylvia. 32 pp. (*In* Stories by Amer. authors, v. 2.) p. 166, *in* 823.4703
—— Two coronets. 823.6327
—— A winged word, and other sketches and stories. 823.6279
Ting-a-ling. Stockton, F. R: 808.1137
Same. 808.1410
Tinkling cymbals. Fawcett, E. 823.5742
Tinted vapors. Cobban, J. M. *in* 823.4988
Tinted Venus, The. Guthrie, F: A. 823.4872
Tiny Tim. Dickens, C: J: H. *in* 808.1571
Tissot, V:, *and* Améro, Constant. Escaped from Siberia: the adventures of three distressed fugitives. Tr. by H: Frith.
  823.6332
Titan. 2 vols. Richter, J. P. F. 823.6810–11
Tithe-proctor, The. Carleton, W: 823.175
Titmarsh, *Mr.* M. A., *pseud. See* Thackeray, W: Makepiece.
To call her mine. Besant, W. *in* 823.4983
To horse and away. Peard, F.. M.. 808.1509
To leeward. Crawford, F. M. 823.4634
To love and to be loved. Roe, A. S.
  823.1366
To the bitter end. Maxwell, *Mrs.* M.. E.. (B.) 823.2405
Same. 823.5103; *in* 823.6208
To the lions. Church, A. J: 823.6545
To the sun? Verne, J. 823.7127
Todkill, Anas, *pseud. See* Cooke, J: E.
Toilers of Babylon. Farjeon, B: L. 823.6320
Toilers of the sea, The. Hugo, V: M. 823.5908
Same. 823.6054; 823.6421
Toinette. Tourgée, A. W. 823.1594
Same. 823.2357
Told after supper. Jerome, Jerome K.
  823.6469
Tolstoï, *Count* Leo Nikolaievitch. Anna Karénina. Tr. by N. H. Dole. 823.5241
—— Childhood, boyhood, youth. Tr. by I. F. Hapgood. 823.6366
—— The cossacks: a tale of the Caucasus in 1852. Tr. by E. Schuyler. 823.1871
—— In pursuit of happiness. Tr. by Mrs. A. Delano. 823.5378
—— The invaders, and other stories. Tr. by N. H. Dole. 823.5242
—— Iváu Ilyitch, and other stories. Tr. by N. H. Dole. 823.5243
—— Katia. 823.5240
—— The long exile, and other stories for children. Tr. by N. H. Dole. 808.1348

English Fiction. *Contin.*
Tolstoï, *Count* Leo Nikolaievitch. *Contin.*
—— My husband and I. *in* 823.6702
—— Polikouchka. (*Also*) Two generations, and other stories. 823.6589
—— A Russian proprietor, and other stories. Tr. by N. H. Dole. 823.5239
—— War and peace. Tr. from French by C. Bell. 3 pts., in 6 vols. 823.4928–33
Contents:—
Pt. I: Before Tilsit. 1805-1807. 2 vols. 823.4928–9
Pt. II: The invasion. 1807-1812. 2 vols. 823.4930–1
Pt. III: Borodino, the French at Moscow,—Epilogue. 1812-1820. 2 vols. 823.4932–3
—— Where love is, there God is also. 17 pp.
  823.6531
Note.—For his life and writings, *see* **Farrar, F.** W. Count Leo Tolstoï. 16 pp.;—Count Tolstoï's religious views. 13 pp. (*The forum,* v. 6, 1888–9.) pp. 109, 337, *in* * 51.4701⁴.—**Hapgood, I. F.** Count Tolstoï and the public censor. 10 pp. (*Atlantic mo.,* v. 40, 1887.) p. 57, in * 51.933³.—**Schuyler, E.** Count Leo Tolstoy twenty years ago. (*Scribner's mag.,* v. 5, 1889.) pp. 536, 733, *in* * 51.5102³.—**Turner, C: E.** Count Tolstoï as novelist and thinker: lectures. 1888. 824.449.—**Vogüé, E. M. de.** Nihilism and mysticism.—Tolstoï. 60 pp. (*In his* The Russian novelists.) p. 290, *in* 890.6.—**Wedgwood, J.** Count Leo Tolstoï. 15 pp. (*Contemp. rev.,* v. 52, 1887.) p. 249, *in* * 52.5402.
Tom Bowling. Chamier, *Capt.* F: 823.6348
Tom Brown at Oxford. Hughes, T: 823.837
Same. *in* 823.5955
Tom Brown's schooldays. Hughes, T:
  823.5167
Same. 823.5955; *in* 823.6677; *in* 823.6698
Tom Burke of "Ours." Lever, C: J. 823.994
Same. 2 vols. 823.5720–1; ** 823.6224–5
Tom Cringle's log. Scott, M. 823.1390
Tom Jones, History of. Fielding, H:
  823.556
Same. 2 vols. 823.6149–50; 823.7071–2
Same. 3 vols. ** 823.2080–2
Tom Racquet. Smedley, F. E. 823.5940
"Tommy Upmore." *See under* Blackmore, R: D.
To-morrow. Edgeworth, M.
  p. 141, *in* ** 823.4651
Tone masters, The. *See* Barnard, C:
Tonty, Henri de. Catherwood, *Mrs.* M.. H. The story of Tonty. 823.6994
Tony Butler. Lever, C: J. 823.995
Too curious. Goodman, E: J. 823.5360
Too much alone. Riddell, *Mrs.* C:. E. L. (C.) 823.5203
Same. 823.5963
Too rich. Streckfuss, A. F. K. 823.6824
Too soon. Macquoid, *Mrs.* K.. S. 823.5918
Topankalon. 31 pp. Underwood, F. H:
  p. 79, *in* 823.4174
Topelius, Zacharias. The surgeon's stories. 6 cycles.
1st cycle: Times of Gustaf Adolf. 823.4476
  Issued also as Gustav Adolf and the Thirty years' war.
2d cycle: Times of battle and of rest. 823.4558
3d cycle: Times of Charles XII. 823.4637
4th cycle: Times of Frederick I. 823.4701
5th cycle: Times of Linnæus. 823.4734
6th cycle: Times of alchemy. 823.4972
Tour of the world in eighty days. Verne, J.
  in 823.5401
Tourgée, Albion Winegar. [*H: Churton.*]
—— Black ice. 823.5294
—— Bricks without straw. 823.2312
—— Button's inn. 823.5295

English Fiction. *Contin.*
Tourgée, Albion Winegar. [*H: Churton.*] *Contin.*
—— Figs and thistles. 823.1593
—— A fool's errand, by one of the fools.
823.4283
—— *Same.* Together with part II. The invisible empire: an historical review of the epoch on which this tale is based. 823.4176
—— Hot plowshares. 823.4538
—— The invisible empire. Part I: A new ed. of "A fool's errand, by one of the fools." Part II: A concise review of recent events showing the elements on which the tale is based, etc. 2 pts. (in 1). 823.2189
—— John Eax, and Mamelon; or, the south without the shadow. 823.4303
—— Pactolus Prime. 823.7065
—— Toinette: a tale of transition. 823.1594
—— *Same.* 823.2357
Issued also as A royal gentleman.
—— With Gauge & Swallow, attorneys.
823.7555
Note.—In chronological order the novels would stand as follows:—
1. Hot plowshares.   4. A fool's errand.
2. Figs and thistles.   5. Bricks without straw.
3. A royal gentleman.   6. John Eax.
Toussaint, A. L. G. *See* Bosboom, *Mrs.* A.. L. G. (T.)
Tower of London. Ainsworth, W: H.
823.5825
Tower of Percemont. Dudevant, *Mme.* A. L. A. (D.) 823.2317
Towhead. Greene, *Mrs.* S.. P. (McL.)
823.4473
Towle, G: Makepeace. Young folks' heroes of history.
Voyages and adventures of Vasco da Gama.
808.740
Pizarro: his adventures and conquests. 808.739
Magellan; or, the first voyage round the world.
808.738
Drake, the sea-king of Devon. 808.1144
—— Young people's history of England.
942.1310
—— Young people's history of Ireland.
941.133
Town and country. Adams, J: S. 823.2
Townsend, G: Alfred. [*Gath.*]
—— The entailed hat; or, Patty Cannon's times. 823.4729
—— Katy of Catoctin; or, the chain-breakers: a national romance. 823.7446
Townsend, Virginia F..
—— But a Philistine. 823.4752
—— Darryll Gap; or, whether it paid.
823.1595
—— Lenox Dare. 823.4167
—— The mills of Tuxbury. 823.1596
—— One woman's two lovers; or, Jacqueline Thayne's choice. 823.1597
—— Only girls. 823.216
—— *Same.* 823.1598
—— That queer girl. 823.1599
—— A woman's word, and how she kept it.
823.1600
Toy tragedy, A. 20 pp. Guthrie, F: A.
in 823.4981
Same. *in* 823.4982; *in* 823.4999
Tracy's ambition. Griffin, G. *in* 823.676
Same. 823.4960

English Fiction. *Contin.*
Trafton, Adeline. *See* Knox, *Mrs.* A. (T.)
Tragedy in the imperial harem at Constantinople. Piazzi, *Mme.* A. (D.) 823.4565
Tragic comedians. 2 vols. Meredith, G:
* 823.4682-3
Tragic muse. 2 vols. James, H:
823.7332-3
Tragic mystery, A. Hawthorne, J. C.
823.5400
Tragic tales. 2 vols. Brydges, *Sir* S. E.
* 823.144-5
Traits and stories of the Irish peasantry. Carleton, W: 823.7363
Same. 2 vols. 823.5819-20
Same. 5 vols. ** 823.6641-5
Transferred ghost. 19 pp. Stockton, F. R:
p. 5, *in* 823.4703
Transplanted. Newberry, F. E. 823.7324
Transplanted rose, A. Sherwood, *Mrs.* M.. E.. (W.) 823.4486
Travel, war, and shipwreck. Gillmore, P.
823.2165
Travels and adventures of little Baron Trump and his wonderful dog Bulger. Lockwood, I. 808.1895
Travels and adventures of Monsieur Violet. Marryat, *Capt.* F: 823.1104
Same. ** 823.6664
Travels and surprising adventures of Baron Münchausen. Raspe, R. E. 808.379
Travels into several remote nations of the world. Swift, J. 808.397
Treasure hunters, The. Fenn, G: M.
823.5919
Treasure island. Stevenson, R. L:
823.4694
Same. 823.5015
Treasure of pearls, The. Aimard, L.
in 823.7008
Trebor, *pseud. See* Davis, R. S.
Tremaine. 3 vols. (in 1). Ward, R. P.
** 823.6733
Tressilian and his friends. Mackenzie, R. S.
823.1074
Trial, The. 2 vols. (in 1). Yonge, C.. M..
823.1775
Trial of Gideon. Hawthorne, J. C.
823.5683
Trials of life, The. 2 vols. Grey, *Mrs.* E.. C. ** 823.6255-6
Trials of Raïssa. Durand, *Mme.* A. M. C. (H.) 823.4001
Tribulations of a Chinaman in China. Verne, J. 823.4342
Tricotrin. La Ramée, L. de. 823.1829
Tried for her life. Southworth, *Mrs.* E. D. E. (N.) 823.1510
Trip to music-land. Shedlock, E. L.
808.1933
Tristram Shandy, Life . . . of. Sterne, L.
823.1518
Tristrem Varick, The truth about. Saltus, E. E. 823.5273
Tritons. Bynner, E. L. 823.4033
Trois-Etoiles, *pseud. See* Murray, E. C. G.
Trollope, Anthony. (1815-1882.)
—— The Belton estate. 823.1603
—— *Same.* *in* 823.6262

English Fiction. *Contin.*
Trollope, Anthony. (1815-1882.) *Contin.*
—— The Bertrams. 823.1604
—— Can you forgive her? 823.1605
—— Castle Richmond. 823.1606
—— Diamond cut diamond: a story of Tuscan life. *in* 823.5073
—— Doctor Thorne. 823.1607
—— *Same.* *in* 823.6262
—— An editor's tales: Mary Gresley, and other tales. 823.1616
—— The Eustace diamonds. 823.1608
—— The Golden Lion of Granpere. 823.1610
—— *Same.* 823.5994
—— Harry Heathcote of Gangoil: a tale of Australian bush-life. 823.5889
—— He knew he was right. 823.1611
—— Is he Popenjoy? 823.2009
—— The Kellys and the O'Kellys. 823.1612
—— The land leaguers. (*With his* An old man's love.) *in* 823.6590
—— The last chronicle of Barset. *in* 823.6262
—— Lotta Schmidt, and other stories. 823.1614
—— The Macdermots of Ballycloran. 823.1615
—— Miss Mackenzie. 823.1617
—— Mr. Scarborough's family. 2 vols. (in 1). 823.6596
—— An old man's love. (*Also*) The land leaguers. 823.6590
—— Orley farm. 823.1618
—— Phineas Finn, the Irish member. 823.1619
—— Phineas Redux. 823.5995
—— The prime minister. 823.1621
—— *Same.* 823.5996
—— Ralph the heir. 823.1623
—— Sir Harry Hotspur of Humblethwaite. 823.1624
—— *Same.* 823.5997
—— The struggles of Brown, Jones and Robinson. By one of them. 823.5998
—— Tales of all countries. 823.1627
—— The three clerks. 823.1628
—— La Vendée. 823.2007
—— The vicar of Bullhampton. 823.1629
—— *Same.* 823.5999
—— The warden. 823.1630
—— The way we live now. 823.6088

Note.—For his life and writings, *see* Autobiography. 928.522.—English character and manners as portrayed by A. Trollope. 17 pp. (*Liv. age*, 1884, v. 161.) p. 195, *in* ** 51.1103.—James, H: A. Trollope. 36 pp. (*In his* Partial portraits.) 1888. p. 97, *in* 824.390.—Last reminiscences of A. Trollope. 5 pp. (*Temple bar*, 1884, v. 70.) p. 129, *in* ** 52.1169.
See also Allibone's Dict. of Eng. lit., v. 3. p. 2,454, *in* ** 803.8.
See also Poole's Index (to 1882.) p. 1,326, *in* ** 50.1.

Trollope, *Mrs. F.*. Eleanor (Ternan).
—— Anne Furness. 823.6002
—— Mabel's progress. 823.6130
—— The sacristan's household: a story of Lippe-Detmold. 823.6001

Trollope, *Mrs. F.*. (Milton). The life and adventures of Michael Armstrong, the factory boy. Illus. ** 823.6222

English Fiction. *Contin.*
Troublesome daughters. Walford, *Mrs. L. B.* (C.) 823.4044
Trowbridge, J: Townsend. Coupon bonds, and other stories. 823.5234
—— Cudjo's cave. 823.1635
—— The kelp-gatherers: a story of the Maine coast. 808.1728
—— Lawrence's adventures among the ice-cutters, glass-makers, coal-miners, iron-men, and ship-builders. 808.238
—— A start in life: a story of the Genesee country. 808.1505
—— The three scouts. 823.1638
Trowel, or the cross, The. 26 pp. Bischoff, J. E. K. 823.6275
True as steel. Terhune, *Mrs. M.. V.* (H.) 823.1565
True Blue. Kingston, W: H: G. 808.365
True history of Joshua Davidson, communist. Linton, *Mrs. E.* (L.) 823.4814
True Magdalen, A. Brame, *Mrs. C.. M.* (L.) *in* 823.5111
True stories from ancient history: chronologically arranged, from the creation of the world to the death of Charlemagne. By a mother. 808.296
True stories from modern history: chronologically arranged, from the death of Charlemagne to the battle of Waterloo. By the author of "True stories from ancient history." 808.295
True to the last. Roe, A. S. 823.1367
True to the old flag. Henty, G: A. 808.1434
Trueba y Cosio, Telesforo de. Romance of history: Spain. 823.1639
Truman, Ben C. Occidental sketches. 823.5185
Trumpet major. Hardy, T: 823.4041
—— *Same.* 823.5135; *in* 823.5136
Trumps. Curtis, G: W: 823.359
Trust, The. 24 pp. Burbury, *Mrs. E. J.* p. 310, *in* 823.1443
Truth about Tristrem Varick. Saltus, E. E. 823.5273
Tsar's window, The. Hooper, *Mrs. L. H.* (J.) 823.4153
Tubber Derg, and other tales. Carleton, W: 823.178
Tucker, N. B., *pseud. See* Sydney, E: W:
Tulloch, W. W. The story of the life of queen Victoria told for boys and girls. Rev. by her majesty. 808.1674
Tumbledown farm. Muir, A. *in* 823.5064
Tupper, Martin Farquhar. King Veric: a scene of the Romans in Britain. 12 pp. (*With* Fortunes of the Colville family. By F. E. Smedley.) p. 239, *in* 823.1443
—— The twins, and Heart. 823.6090
Turgenef, Ivan Sergheïevitch. (1818- .) Annals of a sportsman. Tr. by F. P. Abbott. 823.4910
—— Annouchka. Tr. by F. P. Abbott. 823.4901
—— Ass'ya. (*With his* An unfortunate woman.) *in* 823.5763
—— The diary of a superfluous man. (*With his* Mumu.) *in* 823.4740

English Fiction. *Contin.*
Turgenef, Ivan Serghéievitch. (1818– .)
Contin.
—— Dimitri Roudine. (Repr. from *Every Saturday.*) 823.7066
—— Fathers and sons. Tr. by E. Schuyler. 823.4211
Issued also as Fathers and children.
—— A Lear of the steppe. Tr. by W. H. Browne. (*With his* Spring floods.)
in 823.7131
—— Liza; or, "a nest of nobles." Tr. by W. R. S. Ralston. 823.4212
—— Mumu; and, The diary of a superfluous man. Tr. by H: Gersoni. 823 4740
—— The nihilist. (Zimmern, H.., *and* A. *Half-hours with foreign novelists*, v. 2.)
in ** 823.6614
—— On the eve. Tr. by C. E. Turner.
823.4213
—— Smoke: a Russian novel. Tr. by W: F. West. 823.4214
—— Spring floods. Tr. by Mrs. S. M. Butts. (*Also*) A Lear of the steppe. Tr. by W: H. Browne. 823.7131
—— An unfortunate woman, and Ass'ya. Tr. by H: Gersoni. 823.5763
—— Virgin soil. Tr. by T. S. Perry.
823.4216
Note.—For his life and writings, *see* Daudet, A. Tourguéneff. 21 pp. (*In his* Trente ans de Paris.) p.323, *in* 840.74.—Dupuy, E. Turgéníef. 96 pp. (*In his* Great masters of Russian lit., etc.) p. 117, *in* 890.4.—James, H: Turgéníeff. 36 pp. (*In his* Partial portraits.) 1888. p. 291, *in* 824.390.—Moore, G: Turgueneff. 26 pp. (*Fortnightly rev.*, v. 49, 1888.) p. 237, *in* ⁵ 52.1226⁴.—Vogüé, E. M. de. Turgenef. 52 pp. (*In his* The Russian novelists.) p. 88, *in* 890.6; —34 pp. (*Rev. d. d. Mondes*, 1883, 3e pér., v. 59.) p. 786, *in* ** 54.374.
See also under "Tourgénieff" *in* Poole's Index (to 1882). p. 1,317, *in* ** 50.1; —*and* "Turgenief." *Same.* Jan. 1, 1882–Jan. 1, 1887. p. 448, *in* ** 50.1².
Turgénieff, Ivan Serghéievitch. *See* Turgenef, I. S.
Turkestan. *See also* Asia.
—— Longfellow, H: W. Poems of places.
p. 245, *in* 821.228
Turkey. *See also* Rhodes.
—— Adams, W: T. Cross and crescent; or, Young America in Turkey and Greece.
808.496
—— Champney, *Mrs.* E.. (W.) Three Vassar girls in . . . Turkey. 808.1823
—— Longfellow, H: W. Poems of places.
p. 205, *in* 821.225
15TH CENTURY A. D. Hemans, *Mrs.* F. The last Constantine; poem. p. 178, *in* 821.155
Scanderbeg, Albania, 1443. Ludlow, J. M. Captain of the Janizaries. 823.7022
Constantinople, Fall of, 1453. Baillie, J. Constantine Paleologus; drama. 822.128
SOLIMAN II., 1520–66. Marmontel, J. T. Soliman II. (tale). (French.) 849.35
Rhodes, Siege of, 1522. James, G: P. R. Bertrand de la Croix. 823.702
LIFE AND MANNERS.
—— Cameron, V. L. Among the Turks.
808.1585
—— Crawford, F. M. Paul Patoff. 823.5230
—— Morier, J. Adventures of Hajji Baba in Turkey, Persia and Russia. 823.4280

English Fiction. *Contin.*
Turkey. *Contin.*
LIFE AND MANNERS. *Contin.*
—— Piazzi, *Mme.* A. (D.) Tragedy in the imperial harem at Constantinople.
823.4565
—— Suttner, A. G. von. Djambek the Georgian: a tale of modern Turkey.
823.7049
—— Turkish tales. 58 pp. (Weber, H:, *comp. Tales of the east*, v. 3.)
p. 163, *in* 823.6232
Note.—*See* Bibliography. Eastern question. Bost. Pub. Lib. Bulletins, Nos. 42, 46. pp. 247, 379, *in* ** 17.135.—Church, R. W. The early Ottomans. (*In his* Misc. essays.) p. 261, *in* 824.391.—Finlay, G: Greece under Ottoman and Venetian domination. (1453-1831.) 1856. 949.104:—Greek revolution. 2 vols. 1861. 949.102-3.—Kennin Bey, (*pseud?*) The evil of the east; or, truths about Turkey. 1888. 956. 37.—Kinglake, A. W. Invasion of the Crimea. 6 vols. 1875-80. 947.1-3².—Newman, Cardinal J: H: Lectures on the history of the Turks, in their relation to Europe. 1853. (*In his* Hist. sketches, v. 1.) 1888. p. 1, *in* 904.36.—Poole, S. Lane- The story of Turkey. (1250-1880.) Maps. Illns. 1888. 949. 87.—Salmoné, H. A. The Ottoman empire. 8 pp. (*Also*) "Why does not the sick man die?" By C. D. Collet. (*In* National life and thought.) p. 311, *in* 904.50.—Zinkeisen, J. W. Geschichte des osmanischen Reiches in Europa (to 1812). 7 vols. (Heeren, A. H. L., *and* Ukert, F. A., *eds.* Gesch. der europ. Staaten.) 1843-63. 949.94-100.
For diplomatic history, *see* Bulwer, *Sir* H. Palmerston. 2 vols. 1871. 923.833-4.—Forster, C: T., *and* Daniell, F. H. B. The life and letters of Ogier Ghiselin de Busbecq. (1554-90.) 2 vols. 1881. 923. 2058-9.—Wellington, *Lord*. Despatches. (New ser.) 8 vols. 1867-71. 923.2091-98.
For life and manners, *see* Cox, S: S. Diversions of a diplomat in Turkey. 1887. ⁴ 949.82.—Dwight, H. O. Turkish life in war time. (1876-79.) 1881. 949.54.
See also Catalogues of this Library.
No. 2, 1880, p. 231. No. 4, 1884, p. 295.
No. 3, 1882, p. 190. No. 5, 1888, p. 357.
See also Index to Consular reports. 1880-1885; 1886-1889. 2 vols. (U. S. Pub. Docs. *Dept. of State.*) ** 350.5496¹⁻².
See also Poole's Index (to 1882). pp. 1,330-3, *in* ** 50.1;—*Same.* Jan. 1, 1882-Jan. 1, 1887. pp. 448-9, *in* ** 50.1².
Turkish tales. 58 pp. (Weber, H: *Tales of the east*, v. 3.) p. 163, *in* ** 823.6232
'Twas in Trafalgar's bay. Besant, W., *and* Rice, J. 823.6084
Twells, *Mrs.* Julia H.. Mills of the gods.
823.1642
Twelve noble men. Wright, *Mrs.* J. (McN.)
808.1540
Twelve Portuguese legends. 12 pp. Harding, V. E., *and* Braga, T.
p. 305, *in* 823.6534
Twenty novelettes by twenty prominent novelists. 823.7183
Finding his fate. By R. M. Ballantyne.—Bordone girl, The. By F: Boyle.—For money or for love. By Mrs. M. (A.) Caird.—Miss Tweed's ghost story. By S.. Doudney.—Murderer's confession. By B: L. Farjeon.—The fanfare. By G: M. Fenn. —To Paris for pleasure. By Mrs. A. (F.) Hector. —A shark's fin. By G: A. Henty.—Where the chain galls. By Mrs. F. (M.) Lean.—Lucy. By Mrs. K.. S. Macquoid.—The Duffer. By W: E: Norris.—Two brothers. By Mrs. H. B. (M.) Reeves.—Jenny's girl. By F: W: Robinson.—A secret diary. By D. Russell.—A fatal choice. By A. Sergeant.—Where is Mrs. Smith? By G: R. Sims.—Vaughan of Balliol. By Mrs. E. T. (M.) Smith.—Hunks. By Mrs. H. E. V. (P.) Stannard. —Susan: a winter scene. By Mrs. L. B. (C.) Walford.—Love and war. By W: Westall.

English Fiction. *Contin.*

Twenty years after. Dumas, A. D.
823.2748
Same. *in* 823.5077; 823.6500; 823.6510
20,000 leagues under the sea. Verne, J.
823.2713
Same. *in* 823.4980
Twice lost. Kingston, W: H: G. 808.348
Twice taken. Hall, C: W. 823.7523
Twice-told tales. 2 vols. (in 1). Hawthorne,
N. 823.5561
Same. 823.6195
Same. 2 vols. 823.735-6
Twilight thoughts. Claude, M.. S. 808.1467
Twin captains, The. Dumas, A. D.
823.5564
Twins, The. Tupper, M. F. 823.6090
Twins of Table mountain, and other stories.
Harte, F. B. 823.715
'Twixt love and law. Miller, *Mrs.* A. (J.)
823.5506
'Twixt smile and tear. Brame, *Mrs.* C.. M.
(L.) 823.5124
Two admirals. Cooper, J. F. 823.313
Same. *in* 823.7467
Two Arrows. Stoddard, W: O. 808.1429
Two baronesses. Andersen, H. C. 823.4006
Same. 823.6635
Two brides, The. O'Reilly, B. 823.1224
Two brothers, The. Balzac, H. de. 823.5213
Two buckets in a well. 25 pp. Willis, N.
P. p. 57, *in* 823.4705
Two, by tricks. Yates, E. H. 823.5614
Two captains, The. 50 pp. La Motte-
Fouqué, F. H. K: de. p. 107, *in* 823.4762
Same. p. 97, *in* 823.5196
Two chiefs of Dunboy. Froude, J. A.
823.5512
Two coronets. Tincker, M.. A. 823.6327
Two daughters, The. Dickens, C: J: H.
in 808.1569
Two destinies, The. Collins, W: W.
823.267
Two Dianas, The. Dumas, A. D. 823.7347
Two Elsies, The. Finley, M. 823.4904
Two family mothers. Schwartz, *Mrs.* M. S.
(B.) 823.6114
Two generations. Tolstoï, *Count* L. N.
in 823.6589
Two guardians, The. Yonge, C.. M..
823.1776
Two kisses. 62 pp. Brame, *Mrs.* C.. M.
(L.) 823.5101
Two kisses. Smart, H. 823.5590
Two life-paths. Mundt, *Mrs.* C. (M.)
823.5899
Two lilies. Kavanagh, J. 823.5745
Two little confederates. Page, T: N.
823.5929
Two marriages. Craik, *Mrs.* D. M. (M.)
823.340
Two Miss Jean Dawsons. Robertson, M. M.
823.2335
Two Mrs. Scudamores, The. 98 pp. (*In*
Tales from Blackwood. 2d ser., v. 7.)
in 823.7491
Two modern women. Wells, *Mrs.* K. (G.)
823.7515
Two of us. Halsey, C. 823.692

English Fiction. *Contin.*

Two on a tower. Hardy, T: 823.3747
Two orphans, The. D'Ennery, A. P.
in 823.5043
Two pictures. McIntosh, M. J.. 823.4078
Two purse-companions. 38 pp. Lathrop,
G: P. p. 62, *in* 823.4704
Two runaways, and other stories. Edwards,
H. S. 823.6325
Two sides of the shield. Yonge, C.. M..
in 823.3347
Two sisters, The. Southworth, *Mrs.* E. D.
E. (N.) 823.1511
Two sons, The. 31 pp. Opie, *Mrs.* A. (A.)
p. 269, *in* 823.6136
Two years ago. Kingsley, C: 823.934
Tylney Hall. Hood, T: *in* 823.5114
Typhaines Abbey. Gobineau, J. A., *comte*
de. 823.7044
Tytler, Margaret Fraser. The deformed. 10
pp. (Tieck, L. *The elves, etc.*)
p. 117, *in* 823.6328
Tytler, S., *pseud.* See Keddie, H.
Tzigány, The. 58 pp. Gore, *Mrs.* C. F.. G.
(M.) p. 1, *in* ** 823.6668
Uarda. 2 vols. Ebers, G. M. 823.2161-2
Ubaldo and Irene. 2 vols. Bresciani, A.
823.6888-9
Ulbach, L: For fifteen years. Sequel to
"The steel hammer." Tr. by E. W. Lati-
mer. 823.5410
—— Madame Gosselin. 823.2320
—— The steel hammer: a novel. Tr. by E.
W. Latimer. 823.5440
Ulysses, Adventures of. Lamb, C:
in 823.5562
Ulysses, The wanderings of. Hanson, C: H:
p. 194, *in* 808.1492
Unawares. Peard, F.. M.. 823.1244
Uncle Chesterton's heir. Colomb, *Mme.*
823.6913
Uncle Jack. 74 pp. Besant, W.
in 823.4981
Same. *in* 823.4982; *in* 823.4999
Uncle John. Melville, G: J: Whyte-
** 823.4660
Same. 823.7290
Uncle Piper of Piper's Hill. Fraser, J.
823.6370
Uncle Tom's cabin. Stowe, *Mrs.* H. E.. (B.)
823.1532
Same. 823.6037
Uncloseted skeleton, An. Hale, L. P., *and*
Bynner, E. L. 823.6960
Uncommercial traveller. Dickens, C: J: H.
823.426
Same. 823.5321; *in* 823.5333
Same. *in* 823.5555
Under a ban. Lodge, *Mrs.* —. 823.4767
Same. *in* 823.5023
Under a shadow. Brame, *Mrs.* C.. M. (L.)
823.5137
Under Bayard's banner. Frith, H: 808.1606
Under Drake's flag. Henty, G: A. 808.1487
Under Salisbury spire in the days of George
Herbert. Marshall, *Mrs.* E. (M.)
823.7269
Under Slieve-Ban. Francillon, R. E:
823.1897

English Fiction. *Contin.*
United States. *Contin.*
COLONIAL PERIOD. *Contin.*
NEW YORK. *Contin.*

—— Paulding, J. K.   The Dutchman's fireside.   2 vols. (in 1).   823.7014
—— Spielhagen, F.   Deutsche Pioniere.
                                                    833.403

PENNSYLVANIA.
—— Stephens, *Mrs.* A. S. (W.)   Mary Derwent.   823.1959
—— Whittier, J: G.   The Pennsylvania pilgrim; poem.   p. 360, *in* 821.431
RHODE ISLAND.   *See* New England, p. 192.
TEXAS.   *War for independence.*
—— De Forest, J: W: Overland.   823.5854
—— Wilson, *Mrs.* A. J.. (E.)   Inez.
                                                    823.4009
VERMONT.   *See* New England, p. 192.
VIRGINIA.
—— Bowyer, J. T.   The witch of Jamestown.
                                                    823.7561
—— Cooke, J: E.   Doctor Vandyke.   (1750.)
                                                    823.5830
—— — Fairfax.   823.5509
—— — Henry St. John, Gentleman. (1774-5.)
                                                    823.2017
—— — Justin Harley.   823.276
—— — Leather stocking and silk.   823.277
—— — My Lady Pokahontas.   823.5690
—— — Stories of the Old Dominion.
                                                    808.1468
—— — The Virginia comedians.   823.5662
—— Eggleston, G: C.   A man of honor.
                                                    823.7560
—— Hopkins, S: Youth of the Old Dominion. (Jamestown and Pocahontas, 1607-1676.)   823.826
—— Kennedy, J: P.   Swallow Barn.   823.929
—— Thackeray, W: M.   The Virginians.
                                                    823.1581
OLD FRENCH WAR, 1755-1762.
—— Cooper, J. F.   Last of the Mohicans.
                                                    823.320
—— James, G: P. R.   Ticonderoga; or, the Black Eagle.   823.6385
—— McKnight, C: Captain Jack the scout; or, the Indian wars about old Fort Duquesne.   823.1075
Note.—See **Bancroft,** G: History of the U. S. (1492-1782.) 10 vols. 973.32-41;—*Same.* 6 vols. 973.196-201.—**Bibliography.** Adams, C: K. Manual of hist. lit. 3d ed. 1889. ** 907.4².—American colonies. (*Lib. Jl.,* Nov., 1880. v. 5.) p. 229, *in* ** 19.20. —Boston Pub. Lib. *Bulletin,* No. 36. p. 31, *in* ** 17. 135.—**Brooks,** E. S. The story of the American sailor. (Best hundred books on the Amer. sailor, pp. 324-331.) 1888. 359.53;—Story of the American soldier. 1889. (Best hundred books on the Amer. soldier, pp. 338-343.) 973.658.—**Brown,** A., *comp.* The genesis of the U. S. (1485-1616.) 2 vols. 1890. * 973.726-7.—**Doyle,** J. A. The American colonies previous to the declaration of independence. 1869. (Characteristic of the colonies and colonial life.) 973.741.—**Fiske,** J: The beginnings of New England. 1890. 974.147.—**Frothingham,** R. The rise of the republic. 1873. 324.10;—*Same.* 973.181. —**Hildreth,** R: History of the U. S. (1497-1821.) 6 vols. 973.20-5;—*Same.* 973.240-5.—**Jay,** J: Correspondence and public papers. 1763-1781. 2 vols. 826.118-8².—**Lodge,** H: C. Short history of English colonies in America. (1606-1782.) 1881. 973.717.— **Mackay,** C: Founders of the Amer. republic. 1885. 920.373.—**Palfrey,** J: G. History of New England. v. 1. 974.1.—**Ridpath,** J: C. Popular history of U. S. of America. 1881. 973.173.—**Robertson,** W:

English Fiction. *Contin.*
United States. *Contin.*
COLONIAL PERIOD. *Contin.*
Note. *Contin.*
History of discovery and settlement of America. 1856. 970.61.—**Smith,** G. On the foundation of the American colonies. (Lectures on the study of history.) 1866. p. 185, *in* 907.2.—**Taylor,** W: W. England's struggle with the American colonies. (*Mag. Amer. hist.,* v. 22, Aug. 1889.) p. 120, *in* 905.20⁴.— **Washington,** G: Writings. vols. 1 and 2. 1748-1775. ** 923.1889-90.—**Winsor,** J., *ed.* Narrative and critical history of America. 8 vols. 1887-89. ** 970.127¹-127⁸.
See also Catalogues of this Library.
      No. 2, 1880, p. 238.   No. 4, 1884, p. 301.
      No. 3, 1882, p. 196.   No. 5, 1888, p. 359.
For accounts of the rise and fall of French power in North America, *see* **Parkman,** F., *Jr.* France and England in North America. 10 vols.
    (*viz.:* Pioneers of France in the new world. 1878. 923.154.—The Jesuits in North America. 1879. 271. 6.—La Salle and the discovery of the great west. 1879. 973.177.—The Oregon trail. 1879. 973.176.— The old régime in Canada (under Louis XIV.) 1878. 972.1.—Count Frontenac and New France (under Louis XIV.) 970.35.—Montcalm and Wolfe. 2 vols. 1885. 972.25-6.—The conspiracy of Pontiac. 1851. 973.318.—The discovery of the great west. (1643-1689.) 1869. 977.177.)
Old French war, 1755-1762, *see* **Bancroft,** G: History of the U. S., v. 3. 973.198.—**Barry,** J: S. History of Massachusetts. 3 vols. 1855. 974.17-19.— **Haliburton,** T: C. Hist. account of Nova Scotia. (1497-1829.) 2 vols. ** 972.7-8.—**Hildreth,** R: History of the U. S. v. 2. 973.21;—*Same.* 973.241.— **Irving,** W. Life of Washington. 5 vols. 923.285-9.—**Scharf,** J. T: Hist of Maryland. (1600-1880.) 3 vols. * 9176.21-3.—**Stanhope,** P. H., *Earl.* History of England. 1713-1783. 7 vols. (English accounts.) 1851-54. 942.330-6.
    See also references in **Poole's** Index (to 1882). pp. 1,341-55, *in* ** 50.1;—*Same.* Jan. 1, 1882-Jan. 1, 1887. pp. 451-5, *in* ** 50.1³.
    See also references in Catalogue of the gov't pubs. of the U. S. 1774-1881. ** 15.202.

REVOLUTIONARY WAR (and preceding troubles).

IN NEW ENGLAND.
—— Cooper, J. F.   Lionel Lincoln. (Siege of Boston, 1775.)   823.299
—— Hawthorne, N.   Septimius Felton. (Concord, 1775.)   823.5166
—— Longfellow, H: W.   Paul Revere's ride. (Night before Lexington fight.)
                              pp. 235-7, *in* 821.888
—— Scudder, H. E.   A story of the siege of Boston.   30 pp.   (*In his* Stories and romances.)   p. 199, *in* 823.4005
—— Tiffany, N. M.   From colony to commonwealth: stories of the revolutionary days in Boston.   973.731
IN NEW YORK.
—— Burdett, C: Margaret Moncrieffe: the first love of Aaron Burr.   (N. Y. city.)
                                                    823.2061
—— Cooper, J. F.   The spy.   823.319
—— Roe, E: P.   Near to nature's heart.
                                                    823.1359
André.   Grant, J.   The traitor and his victim; or, the story of the unfortunate Major André.   p. 69, *in* 823.623
Saratoga campaign, 1777.   Thompson, D. P. The rangers; or, the Tory's daughter.
                                                    823.4170
BATTLE OF TRENTON.   Ballad. (Stedman, *and* Hutchinson.   *Lib. of Amer. lit.,* v. 3.)
                              p. 349, *in* ** 820.124

Note.—*See* Adams, J: Familiar letters of. 1876. 923.1887:—Life and writings of A. By C: F. Adams. 10 vols. 923.294-302A.—Adolphus, J. History of England. (1760-1804.) 7 vols. (English account.) 942.441-7.—Allen, J. Battles of the British navy. 2 vols. (English side.) 942.338-9.—Arnold, Benedict, Life and treason of. By J. Sparks. *in* 920.104. —Bancroft, G: History of the U. S. 10 vols. vols. 7-8. 973.38-9.—Baxter, J. P. British invasion from the north: campaigns of Generals Carleton and Burgoyne from Canada. 1776-77. With journal of Lieut. W: Digby. 1887. * 973.683.—Bibliography. Bost. Pub. Lib. Bulletins: No. 34. pp. 382-389, *in* ** 17.134; No. 36. pp. 31-34; No. 40. pp. 172-76, *in* ** 17.135.—Winsor, J. Reader's handbook of the Amer. revolution, 1761-1783. 1880. 973.247.—Hotta, C: History of the war of the independence of the U. S. 2 vols. 1820. 973.66-7.—Brooks, E. S. The story of the American sailor. 1888. (Best hundred books on the Amer. sailor, pp. 324-31.) 359.53;—Story of the American soldier. 1889. (Best hundred books on the Amer. soldier, pp. 338-43.) 973.658.—Carrington, H. B. Battles of the revolution. (Plans.) 1878. 973.264.—Clinton, *Sir* H: The campaign in Virginia, 1781. 2 vols. 1888. * 973.681-2.—Cooper, J. F. History of the navy. 2 vols. 1839. (Amer. side.) 973.143-4.—Franklin, B: Life and writings of. 2 vols. 1852. 829.94-5;—Life and times of F. By J. Parton. 2 vols. 1884. 925.92-3.—Greene, G: W. Historical view of the American revolution. 1876. 973.729.—Hamilton, A. (An account of) by W: G. Sumner. 923.2072.—Hartley, C. B. . . . Lives of Generals Moultrie and Pickens and Gov. Rutledge. 1860. *in* 920.375.—Henry, Patrick, Life of. By W: Wirt. 923.913.—Hildreth, R. History of the U. S. 6 vols. v. 3. 973.22;—*Same.* 973.242.—Jay, J: Correspondence and public papers, 1763-

English Fiction. *Contin.*
United States. *Contin.*
REVOLUTIONARY WAR (and preceding troubles). *Contin.*

Note. Contin.
1781. 1890. v. I. 826.118;—Life and times of J. (1745-1829.) By W: Whitelock. 1887. 923.1944.—**Lafayette**, *Gen.* Life of. By B. Tuckermann. 2 vols. 1889. 923.1942-3.—**Loasing**, B. J: Field book of the revolution. 2 vols. 1855. 973.59-60;—Hours with the living men and women of the revolution: a pilgrimage. 1889. 973.678.—**Marion**, *Gen.* Francis. Life of. By C. B. Hartley. 1890. 920.375.—**Montgomery**, R: Life of. By J. Sparks. *in* * 920.102.—**Niles**, H. Principles and acts of the revolution. 1876. 973.161.—**Otis**, James, Life of. By W. Tudor. 923.2100.—**Paine**, T: The political writings. 2 vols. * 324.1-2.—**Quincy**, Josiah, Life of. By his son, E. Quincy. 923.346.—**Ramsay**, D. History of the U. S. (1607-1808.) 3 vols. 1818. 973.222-4.—**Sabine**, L. American loyalists. (Tory.) 923.248.—**Smyth**, W: Lectures on modern history. (*See* Index, "Revolution, etc.") p. 736, *in* 904.1.—**Stanhope**, P: H., *Earl.* History of England, 1713-1783. 7 vols. 1861-64. * 942.330-6.—**Stedman**, C: History of the origin, progress, and termination of the American war, 1763-82. 2 vols. 1794. * 973.744-5.—**Stedman**, F. C., *and* Hutchinson, E. M. Library of American literature. (Gen. index, v. 11.) p. 647, *in* ** 820.131[1].—**Warren**, Joseph, Life and times of. By R: Frothingham. 923.249;—Life of W. By J. Sparks. *in* * 920.111.—**Washington**, G: Writings. 14 vols. vols. 1-7. (1748-1779.) ** 923.1889-95;—Life of W. By W. Irving. 5 vols. 923.285-9;—Life of W. By J: Marshall. 2 vols. 1854. 923.533-4;—Life of W. By J. Sparks. 12 vols. 923.260-71.—**Watson**, H: C. The Boston tea party and other stories of the American revolution. 1889. 973.705.—**Winsor**, J., *ed.* Narrative and critical history of America. 8 vols. 1887-9. (*See* Index, v. 8, pp. 597-8.) * 970.127[1]-127".

See also **Catalogues** of this Library.
  No. 2, 1880, p. 238.   No. 4, 1884, p. 301.
  No. 3, 1882, p. 197.   No. 5, 1888, p. 359.
See also references in Index to **Harper's** monthly. p. 703, *in* ** 51.475.
See also **Poole's** Index (to 1882). pp. 1,341-55, *in* ** 50.1;—*Same.* Jan. 1, 1882, 1887. pp. 451-5, *in* ** 50.1[2].
See also references in Catalogue of the gov't pubs. of the U. S. 1774-1881. ** 15.202.
For history of the United States flag, *see* **Preble**, G: H. History of the flag of the U. S. 1880. * 929.22.

POST-REVOLUTIONARY PERIOD.
UNDER THE CONFEDERATION.
—— **Brown**, C: B. Arthur Mervyn; or, memoirs of 1793. 2 vols.   823.137-8
—— *Same.*   * 823.6201-2
—— **Gayarré**, C: É. F. Aubert Dubayet; or, the two sister republics. Sequel to "Fernando de Lemos."   823.4624
—— **Sheppard**, F. H. Love afloat: a story of the American navy. (Buccaneers.)
    823.1419
—— **Simms**, W: G. Woodcraft. (Border life.)   823.1440
ALABAMA. **Simms**, W: G. Richard Hurdis. (Border life.)   823.1442
CONNECTICUT. **Mitchell**, D. G. Doctor Johns.   823.1161-2
GEORGIA. **Simms**, W: G. Guy Rivers.
    823.1432
KENTUCKY.
—— **Bird**, R. M. Nick of the woods. (Indians and settlers.)   823.79
· —— **Simms**, W: G. Beauchampe. Sequel to Charlemont.   823.1426
—— —— Charlemont; or, the pride of the village.   823.1428
MISSISSIPPI. **Simms**, W: G. Border beagles.
    823.1427

English Fiction. *Contin.*
United States. *Contin.*
POST-REVOLUTIONARY PERIOD. *Contin.*

PENNSYLVANIA:
—— **Brown**, C: B. Arthur Mervin. 2 vols.
    823.137-8
—— *Same.*   * 823.6201-2

JEFFERSON'S ADMINISTRATION. (1801-1809.)
Hale, E: E. Philip Nolan's friends: a story of the change of western empire. 823.684
WAR OF 1812-15.
—— **Eggleston**, G: C. Captain Sam; or, the boy scouts of 1814.   808.1057
—— , *ed.* American war ballads and lyrics. 2 vols. 1889.   * 821.1271-2
VIRGINIA. **James**, G: P. R. The Old Dominion. (Southampton insurrection, 1831.)
    823.5427

Note.—See **Adams**, H: History of the U. S. during the administrations of Thomas Jefferson. 4 vols. 1889. 973.663-66;—History of the U. S. during the first administration of James Madison. (1809-13.) 2 vols. 1890. 973.666[1-4].—**Alison**, *Sir* A. History of Europe. (1789-1815.) 12 vols. Index, v. 12. 940. 36-47.—**Barry**, J: S. Hist. of Massachusetts, v. 3. 974.19.—**Brooks**, E. S. The story of the American sailor. 1888. (Best hundred books on the Amer. sailor, pp. 324-331.) 359.53;—Story of the American soldier in war and peace. 1889. (Best hundred books on the Amer. soldier, pp. 338-43.) 973.658.—**Canning**, G: The war with America; address Feb. 18, 1813. (*Speeches*, v. 3.) p. 376, *in* 825.18.—**Conway**, M. D. Omitted chapters of history disclosed in the life and papers of E. Randolph. 1888. 923.1864.—**Fiske**, J: Critical period of American history, 1783-1789. (Bibliographical note, pp. 351-56.) 973.638.—**Gallatin**, A. Writings of. 3 vols. 923.1137-9.—**Hildreth**, R. History of the U. S. 2d ser. (1789-1821.) 3 vols. 973.23-5.—**Jackson**, Andrew, Life of. By J. Parton. 3 vols. 923.312-14.—**Johnson**, R. A history of the war of 1812-15, betw. the U. S. and Gr. Britain. (1882.) 973.723.—**Lossing**, B. J: Field book of the revolutionary war. 2 vols. 1873. 59-60.—**McMaster**, J: B. History of the people of the U. S. v. I: 1784-1790; v. 2: 1790-1803. 2 vols. 1885. 973.440-1.—**Palmer**, T. H. Historical register, 1812-1814. 4 vols. 973.216-19.—**Porter**, *Commodore* D: Memoir of. By D. D. Porter. 1875. 923.2090.—**Roosevelt**, T. The winning of the west. 2 vols. (1769-1783.) 1889. * 973.653-4.—**Scharf**, J: T: Hist. of Maryland. vols. 2-3. 9176. 22-3.—**Scott**, *Gen.* Winfield. Autobiography. 2 vols. 923.376-7.—**Washington**, G: The writings of. 14 vols. vols. 1-7. (1748- .) ** 923.1889-1902.—**Winsor**, J. Narrative and critical history of America. 8 vols. (*See* Index, v. 8, p. 597.) * 970.127[1]-127".
For naval histories of the war, *see* **Cooper**, J. F. History of the American navy. 2 vols. 973.143-4.—**Cullum**, G. W. Campaigns of the war of 1812-15. 1879. 973.735.—**Roosevelt**, T. The naval war of 1812. 1882. * 973.447.

See also **Catalogues** of this Library.
  No. 2, 1880, p. 238.   No. 4, 1884, p. 301.
  No. 3, 1882, p. 197.   No. 5, 1888, p. 359.
See also **Poole's** Index (to 1882). pp. 1,341-55, *in* ** 50.1;—*Same.* Jan. 1, 1882-Jau. 1, 1887. pp. 451-5, *in* ** 50.1[2].
See also references in Catalogue of the gov't pubs. of the U. S. 1774-1881. ** 15.202.

VAN BUREN'S ADMINISTRATION. (1837-41.)
Kennedy, J: P. Quodlibet: containing some annals thereof, with au authentic account of the origin . . . of the borough, and the sayings . . . of the townspeople. 3d ed.
    823.930

MEXICAN WAR, 1846-1847.
—— **Clemens**, J. Bernard Lile. 823.7100
—— **Lowell**, J. R. The Biglow papers. 1st ser.   821.243

English Fiction. *Contin.*
United States. *Contin.*
THE CIVIL WAR, 1861–1865.
— Adams, W: T. Fighting Joe; or, the fortunes of a staff-officer. 808.511
— — Ou the blockade. 808.1701
— — The sailor boy. 808.512
— — Taken by the enemy. 808.1680
— — Within the enemy's lines. 808.1536
— — The Yankee middy. 808.514
— — The young lieutenant. 808.515
— Baker, W: M. Inside: a chronicle of secession. 823.5927
— Boylston, P: John Charáxes. 823.7032
— Brooks, N. Abraham Lincoln: a biography for young people. 923.1821
— Cable, G: W. War diary of a Union woman in the south. (*In his* Strange, true stories of Louisiana.) p. 261, *in* 823.6507
— Coffin, C: C. Freedom triumphant. (Sept., 1864, to its close.) 808.1862
— — Winning his way. 823.245
— Collingwood, H. W. Andersonville violets: a tale of northern and southern life. 823.7320
— Cooke, J: E. Hilt to hilt. (Shenandoah valley, 1864.) 823.5525
— — Surry of Eagle's Nest. 823.281
— — Wearing of the gray, comprising personal portraits . . . of the late war. 973.657
— Davis, *Mrs.* R. B. (H.) Waiting for the verdict. 823.5857
— Earl of Mayfair. (Anon.) (Louisiana, 1862.) 823.1253
— Fosdick, C: A. Rodney the partisan. 808.1704
— French, A. Expiation. (Arkansas.) 823.6950
— Fuller, J., G. The Brownings. (Georgia and Florida.) 808.1580
— Gilmore, J. R. Mountain-White heroine. (Southern Alleghanies.) 823.6364
— — My southern friends. 823.611
— Goss, W. L. Jed: a boy's adventures in the army of '61-'65: a story of battle and prison, of peril and escape. 808.1561
— Greene, C. S. Thrilling stories of the great rebellion. 973.108
— Hague, P. A. A blockaded family: life iu southern Alabama during the civil war. 9176.66
— Hale, E: E. Stories of war told by soldiers. 808.1370
— — *Same.* 823.5164
— Halpine, C. G. Life and adventures, . . . of Private Miles O'Reilly. 823.7083
— Headley, P. C. Fighting Phil: the life . . . of Philip Henry Sheridan. 808.1600
— Henty, G: A. With Lee in Virginia. 808.1670
— Holmes, *Mrs.* M.. J.. (H.) Rose Mather. 823.801
— King, *Capt.* C: Between the lines. 823.6544
— — The colonel's daughter. 823.7392
— Lanier, S. Tiger-lilies. 823.7110

English Fiction. *Contin.*
United States. *Contin.*
THE CIVIL WAR, 1861–1865. *Contin.*
— Mitchell, S. W. In war time. 4th ed. 823.5399
— — Roland Blake. 823.5245
— Nichols, G: W. The sanctuary. (Sherman's march.) 823.1189
— Page, T: N. In ole Virginia; Marse Chan, and other stories. (Life in Virginia before, during and after the rebellion.) 823.5363
— — Two little confederates. 823.5929
— Pember, *Mrs.* P. Y. (L.) Southern woman's story. 823.1250
— Ripley, E. McH. From flag to flag: a woman's adventures and experiences in the south during the war, in Mexico, and in Cuba. 823.5439
— Roe, E: P. His sombre rivals. (Bull Run.) 823.4609
— — "Miss Lou." (Virginia.) 823.5523
— — An original belle. (N. Y. draft riots of 1863.) 823.4858
— Rogers, J. H. The California hundred (poem). 821.500
— Soley, J. R. Sailor boys of '61. 808.1911
— Terhune, *Mrs.* M.. V. (H.) Sunnybank. 823.1564
— Tiernan, M.. S. Jack Horner. (Richmond.) 823.6944
— Tourgée, A. W. With Gauge & Swallow, attorneys. (Before and after the civil war.) 823.7555
— Trowbridge, J: T. Cudjo's cave. (Tennessee.) 823.1635
— — The three scouts. 823.1638
— Verne, J. The blockade runners. (*With his* A floating city.) *in* 823.7091
— Woolson, C. F. East Angels. (Florida before and during the rebellion.) 823.4966
IN POETRY.
— Boker, G. H. Poems of the war. *in* 822.131
— Browne, F. F., *ed.* Battle-echoes. (*In his* Golden poems.) 1886. 821.853
— Eggleston, G: C., *ed.* American war ballads and lyrics. 2 vols. 1889.
   * 821.1271-2
— Jack Morgan songster; by a captain in Lee's army. 1865. * 821.1394
— Lowell, J. R. The Biglow papers. 2d ser. *in* 821.1396
— Mason, E. V. Southern poems of the war. 821.258
— Melville, H. Battle pieces. 821.260
— Moore, F. Anecdotes, poetry and incidents of the war, 1860–65. 973.564
— — Lyrics of loyalty. 1864. 821.1375
— — Personal and political ballads. 1864. 821.462
— — Rebel rhymes and rhapsodies. 821.276
— — Songs of the (Union) soldiers. 821.460
—, *ed.* The civil war in song and story, 1860–65. 1889. 973.686

English Fiction. *Contin.*
United States. *Contin.*
THE CIVIL WAR, 1861-1865. *Contin.*
IN POETRY. *Contin.*
—— Preston, *Mrs.* M. J. Beechenbrook.
1866.   821.1353
—— Read, T: B. Sheridan's ride. (*Poetical
works.*) 1881.   p. 227, *in* 821.1375
—— Redden, L. C. Idyls of battle. 821.327
—— —— *Same.*   821.328
—— Schreiner, H. L. The Gen. Lee song-
ster. 1865.   821.1393
—— Stedman, E. C. Alice of Monmouth.
1869.   821.629
—— —, *and* Hutchinson, E. M., *comps.* Pop-
ular songs and ballads of the civil war. (*In
their* Lib. of Amer. lit., v. 8.)
                          pp. 361-371, *in* ** 820.129
—— Whittier, J: G. Barbara Frietchie.
                          p. 269, *in* 821.431
—— —— In war time. 1864.   821.1142
—— —— National lyrics. Illus.   821.436
—— Woolson, C. F. Two women, 1862.
1885.   821.1318
See also Poems of Howe, Ryan, Stoddard,
Thompson, Whitman, Work, and others.
Note.—See Bibliography. Bartlett, J. R. Litera-
ture of the rebellion. 1866. ** 16.4.—Bowen, J. L.
Massachusetts in the war, 1861-65. 1889. 973.743.—
Campaigns of the civil war.—I. The outbreak of
the rebellion. (Opening of the war, covering the
period from the election of Lincoln to the end of the
first battle of Bull Run.) By J: G. Nicolay. 973.329.
—II. From Fort Henry to Corinth. (Events in the
west from summer of 1861 to May, 1862,—covering
capture of Fts. Henry and Donelson, battle of
Shiloh, etc.) By M. F. Force. 973.330.—III. The
peninsula. (McClellan's peninsular campaign from
his appointment to end of Seven Days' fight.) By
A. S. Webb. 973.390.—IV. The army under Pope.
(From appointment of Pope to command the Army
of Virginia to appointment of McClellan to general
command, Sept., 1862.) By J. C. Ropes. 973.389.—
V. The Antietam and Fredericksburg. (From appointment of McClellan, Sept., 1862, to end of battle
of Fredericksburg.) By F. W. Palfrey. 973.407.—VI.
Chancellorsville and Gettysburg. (From appointment of Hooker to retreat of Lee after Gettysburg.)
By A. Doubleday. 973.410.—VII. The army of the
Cumberland. (Formation of the army of the Cumberland to end of battles at Chattanooga, Nov., 1863.)
By H: M. Cist. 973.421.—VIII. The Mississippi.
(Account of the operations—especially at Vicksburg
and Port Hudson—by which the Miss. river and its
shores were restored to the control of the Union.)
By F. V. Greene. 973.439.—IX. Atlanta. (Sher-
man's first advance into Georgia in May, 1864, to
beginning of the march to the sea.) By J. D. Cox.
973.422.—X. March to the sea—Franklin and Nashville. (From beginning of march to the sea to
surrender of Johnston,—including operations of
Thomas in Tennessee.) By J. D. Cox. 973.438.—
XI. Shenandoah valley in 1864. The campaign of
Sheridan. By G: E. Pond. 973.437.—XII. Virginia campaign of '64 and '65. The army of the
Potomac and the armies of the James. By A. A.
Humphreys. 973.559.—XVII. Gettysburg to Rapidan. By A. A. Humphreys. 1883. 973.513.—The civil
war. (1861-65.) (Stedman, *and* Hutchinson. *Lib.
of Amer. lit.*) (Gen. index, v. 11.) p. 646, *in* ** 820.
131¹.—Conway, M. D. Omitted chapters of history
disclosed in the life and papers of Edmund Randolph. 1888. 923.1864.—Crawford, S: W. The
genesis of civil war: the story of Sumter. 1860-1.
973.706.—Dodge, T. A. A bird's-eye view of our
civil war. Maps. 1884. 973.722.—Draper, J: W:
History of the civil war. 3 vols. 973.232-4.—Giddings, J. R. Hist. of the rebellion: its authors and
causes. 1864. 973.718.—Guernsey, *and* Alden.
Harper's pictorial history of the rebellion. 2 vols.
** 973.257-8.—Herr, G: W. Nine campaigns in nine
states. (1861-1865.) 1890. 973.702.—Johnson, R.
Short history of the war of secession, 1861-1865.
Maps. 1888. 973.670.—Johnson, R. U., *and* Buel,

English Fiction. *Contin.*
United States. *Contin.*
THE CIVIL WAR, 1861-1865. *Contin.*
Note. Contin.
C. C., *eds.* Battles and leaders of the civil war.
4 vols. 1888. 973.630-3.—Lossing, B. J. Pictorial
history of the civil war. 3 vols. 1868. 973.94-6.—
Moore, F., *ed.* Rebellion record. 8 vols. 1861-69.
973.570-81.—Parls, *comte* de. History of the civil
war in America. 4 vols. 973.255-256⁴.—Parton, J.
General Butler in New Orleans. (1862.) 1882. 973.
698.—Phisterer, *Capt.* F. New York in the war of
the rebellion, 1861-65. 1890. 973.742.—Pictorial battles of the civil war. 2 vols. 1885. ** 973.668-9.
—Raymond, H. J. History of the administration
of President Lincoln. (1861-64.) 1864. 973.738.—
Swinton, W: The twelve decisive battles of the
war of the rebellion. 1867. 973.276.—U. S. 37th
Congress. 3d sess. Report of joint committee
on the conduct of the war. (1861-63.) 3 vols. *Contents:* v. 1: Army of the Potomac; v. 2: Bull Run.
—Ball's Bluff; v. 3: Western dept. — Misc. ** 350.
707¹·⁴.—U. S. 38th Congress. 2d sess. Report
of joint committee on the conduct of the war.
(1864-65.) 3 vols. *Contents:* v. 1: Army of the
Potomac.—Battle of Petersburg; v. 2: Red river expedition. — Fort Fisher expedition. — Heavy ord-
nance; v. 3: Sherman, Johnston.— Light-draught
monitors.—Massacre of the Cheyenne Indians.—Ice
contracts.—Rosecrans's campaign.—Misc. ** 350.
762-4.—U. S. 39th Congress. 1st session. Sup-
plemental report. 2 vols. (Senate reps.) *Contents:*
v. 1: Report by Maj.-Gen. Sherman.—Thomas; v. 2:
Pope.—Foster.— Pleasanton.— Hitchcock.— Sheridan.— Ricketts. — Communication of Wiard.—Memorial of Wiard. ** 350.764²·³.—U. S. War Dep't.
War of the rebellion. Compilation of the official
records of the Union and Confederate armies, (ed.)
by R. N. Scott. 35 vols. (in 62). 1880-91. 973.347-
72; 973.612-612²⁴.—Wilson, H. History of the slave
power. 3 vols. 326.26-8.

See also Catalogues of this Library.
   No. 2, 1880, p. 239.   No. 4, 1884, pp. 301-2.
   No. 3, 1882, pp. 197-8.   No. 5, 1888, pp. 359-60.
See also Poole's Index (to 1882). pp. 1,341-55, *in*
** 50.1;—*Same,* Jan. 1, 1882-Jan. 1, 1887. p. 451-5,
in ** 50.1².
See also Catalogue of the gov't pubs. of the U.
S. (1774-1881.) ** 15.202.

For Battles, *see:*—
Bull Run, July 21, 1861.—Fry, J. B. McDowell
and Tyler in the campaign of Bull Run. 63 pp.
1884. 923.1782.—Johnson, *and* Buel. Battles and
leaders of the civil war. (*See* v. 4, Index.) 973.633.
—Nicolay, J: G. The outbreak of the rebellion.
1881. 973.329.
Fort Donelson, Tenn., Feb. 14, 1862.—Force, M.
F. From Fort Henry to Corinth. 1881. 973.330.—
Johnson, *and* Buel. Battles and leaders of the
civil war. (*See* v. 4, Index.) 973.633.
Shiloh, Tenn., Apr. 6-7, 1862.—Force, M. F.
From Fort Henry to Corinth. 1881. 973.330.—
Johnson, *and* Buel. Battles and leaders of the
civil war. (*See* v. 4, Index.) 973.633.
2d Battle of Bull Run, Aug. 30, 1862.—Cox, J. D.
Second battle of Bull Run, as connected with the
Fitz-John Porter case. 1882. 973.474.—Johnson,
and Buel. Battles and leaders of the civil war. (*See*
v. 4, Index.) 973.633.—Ropes, J: C. Roster of the
Federal and Confederate armies, Aug. 30, 1862. (*In
his* The army under Pope.) pp. 204-15, *in* 973.389.
Antietam, Md. (also Sharpsburg), Sept. 16-17,
1862.—Johnson, *and* Buel. Battles and leaders of
the civil war. (*See* v. 4, Index.) 973.633.—Palfrey,
F. W. The Antietam and Fredericksburg. 1882.
973.407.
Stone's River, Tenn., Dec. 31, 1862-Jan. 3, 1863.—
Cist, H. M. The army of the Cumberland. 1882.
973.421.—Johnson, *and* Buel. Battles and leaders of
the civil war. (*See* v. 4, Index.) 973.633.—Stevenson, A. F. Battle of Stone's river. 1884. 973.583.
Gettysburg, July 1-3, 1863.—Bates, S. P. Battle
of Gettysburg. 1875. 973.305.—Doubleday, A.
Chancellorsville and Gettysburg. 1882. 973.410.—
Humphreys, A. A. Gettysburg to the Rapidan.
1883. 973.513. Johnson, *and* Buel. Battles and
leaders of the civil war. (*See* v. 4, Index.) 973.633.
—Lee, A. E. The battle of Gettysburg. 1888. 973.
680.—Paris, L: P., *comte* de. The battle of Gettysburg. 973.648.

English Fiction. *Contin.*
United States. *Contin.*
THE CIVIL WAR, 1861–1865. *Contin.*
Note. Contin.

Vicksburg, Miss. (surrender, July 4, 1863).—Greene, F. V. The Mississippi. 1882. 973.439.—Johnson, *and* Buel. Battles and leaders of the civil war. (*See* v. 4, Index.) 973.633.—Reed, S. R. Vicksburg campaign and Chattanooga under Grant. 1883. 973.473.

Chickamauga, Ga., Sept. 19–20, 1863.—Johnson, *and* Buel. Battles and leaders of the civil war. (*See* v. 4, Index.) 973.633.—Turchin, J: B. Chickamauga. Maps. 1888. * 973.674.

Wilderness, Va., May 5–7, 1864.—Johnson, *and* Buel. Battles and leaders of the civil war. (*See* v. 4, Index.) 973.633.

Nashville, Tenn., Dec. 15–16, 1864.—Cox, J. D. The march to the sea; Franklin and Nashville. 1882. 973.438.—Johnson, *and* Buel. Battles and leaders of the civil war. (*See* v. 4, Index.) 973.633.

Battles of Atlanta, Ga., July 20–22, 1864; Nov. 12–Dec. 21, 1864.—Cox, J. D. Atlanta. 1882. 973.422.—Johnson, *and* Buel. Battles and leaders of the civil war. (*See* v. 4, Index.) 973.633.

Five Forks, Va., Apr. 1, 1865.—Johnson, *and* Buel. Battles and leaders of the civil war. (*See* v. 4, Index.) 973.633.

For biography, *see* Chesney, C. C. Military biographies. 923.395.—Fitch, J. Annals of the army of the Cumberland. 1864. 973.117.—Grant, U. S. Personal memoirs. 2 vols. 923.1761-2.—Johnson, *and* Buel. Battles and leaders of the civil war. 4 vols. (*See* Index, v. 4.) 1884–88. 973.630-33.—Lincoln, Abraham, Life of. By Herndon and Weik. 3 vols. 923.1855-7;—Life of L. By W. H. Lamon. 923.321.—Scott, *Gen.* Winfield, Life of. By E. D. Mansfield. 928.104.

See also forward under Military history.

For Confederate biography, *see* Davis, Jefferson, Life of. By R. E. Pollard. 923.360.—Lee, Robert E:, Life, campaigns, and public services of. By E. A. Pollard. 923.2005;—Memoirs of L. By A. L. Long. 1886. 923.1802.

See also Leo, *Gen.* R. E:, *note*, p. 152.

See also Lives of Beauregard.—N. B. Forrest.—Albert Sidney Johnston.—J. E. Johnston.—J. Morgan.—J. E. B. Stuart, and others.

For hospital and sanitary service, etc., *see* Ellis, T. T. Leaves from the diary of an army surgeon. 1863. 973.740.—Hanaford, *Mrs.* P. A. Field, gunboat, hospital and prison. 1886. 973.739.—Letterman, J. Medical recollections of the army of the Potomac. 1866. 973.260.—U. S. War Dept. Medical and surgical history of the rebellion. Med. pt. 2 vols. ** 610.99-100. Surg. pt. 2 vols. ** 617.2-3.

For military history, *see* Badeau, *Gen.* A. Military history of U. S. Grant. 3 vols. 923.1024-6.—Borcke, H. von. Memoirs of the Confederate war for independence. (*Blackwood's mag.*, vols. 98, 99.) ** 52.196-7.—Brooks, E. S. Story of the American soldier in war and peace. 1622–1889. (Best hundred books on the Amer. soldier, pp. 338–343.) 973.658.—Grant, *Gen.* U. S. Personal memoirs. 2 vols. 923.1761-2.—Johnson, *and* Buel. Battles and leaders of the civil war. 4 vols. 973.630-3.—McClellan, C. The personal memoirs and military history of U. S. Grant *versus* the record of the army of the Potomac. 1887. 973.701.—Paris, *comte* de. History of the civil war. 4 vols. 973.255-256ᵃ.—Sheridan, *Gen.* P. H. Personal memoirs of. 2 vols. 1888. * 923.1808-9.—Sherman, *Gen.* W: T. Personal memoirs. 2 vols. 1875. 923.388-9;—*Same.* Rev. ed. 1886. 923.437-8.

See also Catalogue of the gov't pubs. of the U. S. (1774–1881.) ** 15.202.

For accounts of negro troops, *see* Brown, W. W. The negro in the American rebellion. (1812–1867.) 973.624.—Williams, G. W. History of the negro troops in the war of the rebellion. 1861–65. 1888. 973.716.—Wilson, J. T. The black phalanx. 1888. 326.21.

For personal narratives, *see* Coffin, C: C. Four years of fighting. (*Same as* Boys of '61.) 973.423;—My days and nights on the battle-field. 1887. 973.643.—Hosmer, J. K. Color-guard: being a corporal's notes of military service in the 19th army corps. 1864. 973.409.—Kieffer, H. M. Recollections of a drummer boy. 1883. 923.1506.—Livermore, *Mrs.* M..A. R. My story of the war: . . . personal experience during the war of the rebel-

English Fiction. *Contin.*
United States. *Contin.*
THE CIVIL WAR, 1861–1865. *Contin.*
Note. Contin.

lion. Plates. 1890. 973.724.—Nichols. *Brev. Maj.* G: W. The story of the great march. Illus. 1865. 973.725.—Watson, W: Life in the Confederate army: being observations and experiences of an alien in the south during the Amer. civil war. 1887. 973.720.—Williams, G. F. Bullet and shell. 973.434.

For Confederate narratives, *see* Eggleston, G: C. Rebel's recollection. 973.138.—Gilmor, H. Four years in the saddle. 1866. 973.293.—Jones, J. B. Rebel war clerk's diary. 2 vols. 973.1-2.—Mosby, J: S. War reminiscences, and Stuart's cavalry campaigns. (Cop. 1887.) 973.679.—Taylor, W. H. Four years with General Lee. 1877. 973.132.

For prison experience, *see* Abbott, A. O. Prison life in the south. (1864–65.) 973.165.—Drake, J. M. Fast and loose in Dixie. 973.269.—Isham, A. B., *and others*. Prisoners of war and military prisons. 1890. 973.737.—Oats, *Sergeant*. Prison life in Dixie. 973.312.—Pittenger, W. Capturing a locomotive. 1882. 973.413.—Spencer, A. Narrative of Andersonville. 973.281.

For secret service, *see* Pittenger, W. Capturing a locomotive. 1882. 973.413.—Richardson, A. D. The secret service, the field, the dungeon, and the escape. 1865. 973.225.

For history of the navy, *see* Boynton, C: B. History of the navy during the rebellion. 2 vols. 973.141-2.—Brooks, E. S. Story of the American sailor in active service on merchant vessel and man-of-war. (Best hundred books on the Amer. sailor, pp. 324–331.) 359.53.—Hamersly, T: H. S. Army and navy register of the U. S. 1776–1887. ** 973.616;—Records of living officers of the U. S. navy and marine corps. 4th ed. 1890. ** 359.55.—Lossing, B. J. Story of the U. S. navy for boys. (1880.) 973.261.—Navy in the civil war. 3 vols. (*viz.*: I. The blockade and the cruisers. By J. R. Soley. 973.491.—II. The Atlantic coast. By D. Ammen. 973.511.—III. The gulf and inland waters. By A. T. Mahan. 973.510.)—Porter, D: D. Naval history of the civil war. 1886. 973.609.

For Confederate navy, *see* Semmes, R. Cruise of the Alabama. 1887. 973.125;—Service afloat; "Sumter" and "Alabama" during the war between the states. 1887. 973.119.

For political history, *see* Draper, J: W. History of the civil war. 3 vols. 973.232-4.—Greeley, H. The American conflict. 1860–64. 2 vols. 1864–67. 973.207-8.—Helper, H. R. Impending crisis of the south. 1857. 326.19.—Julian, G. W. Political recollections. (1840–1872.) 923.1590.—Lincoln, Abraham, Life of. By Herndon and Weik. 3 vols. 923.1855-7;—Life of L. By W. H. Lamon. 923.321.—Lowell, J. R. Political essays. 1888. 329.45.—McPherson, E. Political history of the U. S. during the great rebellion. 1860–64. 973.97.—Mill, J: S. The contest in America. 28 pp. (*In his* Dissertations, etc., v. 1.) p. 1, *in* 829.165.—Phillips, Wendell. Speeches, etc. 845.48.—Soward, W: H. Works. vols. 4, 5. * 320.111-12.

See also Catalogues of this Library.

No. 2, 1880, p. 239.   No. 4, 1884, pp. 301-2.
No. 3, 1882, pp. 197-8.   No. 5, 1888, pp. 359-60.

For southern side, *see* Davis, J. Rise and fall of the Confederate government. 2 vols. 1881. 973.321-2;—Life of Jeff. Davis. By E: A. Pollard. 923.360.—Southern Hist. Soc. Papers. vols. 1–13 (in 10 vols.) 1876–85. ** 976.95-104;—*Same.* vols. 15, 17. 1887; 1889. 2 vols. ** 976.106; 108.—Stephens, A. H. Constitutional view of the war between the states. 2 vols. 1868. 973.106-7.

For foreign views, *see* Gasparin, *comte* A. E. de. The uprising of a great people. Tr. by M. L. Booth. 1861. 973.567.—Mill, J: S. The contest in America. (*In his* Dissertations and discussions, v. 1.) 829.165.—Paris, *comte* de. History of the civil war in America. Tr. by L. F. Tasistro. Ed. by H: Coppee. 4 vols. 973.255-256ᵃ.—Trobriand, R, de. Four years with the army of the Potomac. 1889. 973.688.

For statistics, *see* Fox, W: F. Regimental losses in the American civil war. 1861–1865. 1889. * 973.700.—Phisterer, F. Statistical record of the armies of the U. S. 1890. 973.728.

See also Catalogue of gov't pubs. of the U. S., 1774–1881. ** 15.202.

English Fiction. *Contin.*
United States. *Contin.*
THE CIVIL WAR, 1861-1865. *Contin.*
Note. Contin.
For anecdotes, *see* **Kirkland**, F. Pictorial book of anecdotes of the rebellion. (1830-1865.) (Cop. 1889.) 973.734.—**Moore,** F., *ed.* Anecdotes, poetry, and incidents of the war of the rebellion. 1867. 975.564.—**Porter,** D; D. Incidents and anecdotes of the civil war. 1885. 973.596.—**Townsend,** E. D. Anecdotes of the civil war in the U. S. 973.544.
For humorous illustrations, *see* **Adams,** F. C. Siege of Washington, D. C. 808.1700.—**Hinman,** W. F. Corporal S. Klegg and his pard. 1887. 828. 228.—**Newell,** R. H. Orpheus C. Kerr papers. 1871. 828.71.—**Peck,** G: W. How private Geo. W. Peck put down the rebellion. 823.7409.
RECONSTRUCTION.
—— Baker, W: M. Colonel Dunwoddie, millionaire. (South. life since the war.)
823.6372
—— Claytor, G. Pleasant Waters: a story of southern life and character. 823.7170
—— De Forest, J: W: The bloody chasm.
823.1891
—— Finley, M. Elsie's motherhood. (Ku-Klux.) 823.560
—— Hale, E: E. Mrs. Merriam's scholars: a story of the "original ten." (Schools among the freedmen.) 823.2342
—— Henderson, *Mrs.* F.. C. Priscilla Baker, the freedwoman. 22 pp.
p. 9, *in* 823.6534
—— Murfree, M.. N. Where the battle was fought. (Tennessee.) 823.4893
—— Page, T: N. In ole Virginia; or, Marse Chan, and other stories. 823.5363
—— Tiernan, *Mrs.* F.. C. (F.) Valerie Aylmer. 823.6045
—— Tourgée, A. W. Bricks without straw.
823.2312
—— — Figs and thistles. 823.1593
—— — Fool's errand. (A northern man's experiences in the south since the war.)
823.4176
—— — Same. 823.4283
—— — Hot plowshares. 823.4538
—— — Invisible empire. (Pt. 2 of A fool's errand.) (Ku Klux Klan.) 823.2189
—— — Same. *in* 823.4176
—— — John Eax. 823.4303
—— — Mamelon. (*With his* John Eax.)
823.4303
—— — Toinette. (Relations betw. freed people and the whites.) 823.2357
Note.—In chronological order the novels would stand as follows:
1: Hot plowshares.   4: A fool's errand. (Pt.
2: Figs and thistles.   2: Invisible empire.)
3: A royal gentleman.   5: Bricks without straw.
                              6: John Eax.
Note.—See **King,** E. The great south. 1875. 9176.2.—**Lowell,** J. R. The Seward-Johnson reaction. 44 pp. (*In his* Political essays.) p. 250, *in* 329.45.—**McPherson,** E. Political history of the U. S. during reconstruction. 1865-70. 973.418.—**Pike,** J. S. The prostrate state. 1874. 326.1.—**Taylor,** R. Destruction and reconstruction. 1879. 973.124.
See also reference "Reconstruction of the seceded states" *in* Catalogue of the gov't pubs. of the U. S. 1774-1881. p. 1,354, *in* ** 15.202.

AMERICAN LIFE AND CHARACTER.
California. See California, pp. 32-3.
Colorado.
—— Biguey, T. O. Colorado tales and legends (poems). 821.29

English Fiction. *Contin.*
United States. *Contin.*
AMERICAN LIFE AND CHARACTER. *Contin.*
Colorado. Contin.
—— Hammond, W: A. Lal. 823.7017
—— Ingersoll, E. The silver caves: a mining story. 808.1719
Connecticut. See New England, p. 191.
Florida.
—— Munroe, K. The flamingo feather. (Expedition sent out by Adm. Ribault.)
808.1371
—— — Wakulla. 808.1372
—— Stowe, *Mrs.* H. E.. (B.) Palmetto-leaves. 823.5600
Note.—See **Norton,** C: L. A handbook of Florida. Maps. 1891. 9176.70.
Georgia.
—— Harris, J. C. Free Joe, and other Georgian sketches. 823.5255
—— Johnston, R: M. Mr. Absalom Billingslea and other Georgian folk. 823.5267
—— — Ogeechee cross-firings. (Before the civil war.) 823.6558
—— — The Primes and their neighbors. (Dialect tales of middle Georgia.) 823.7549
—— — Widow Guthrie. (Before the civil war.) 823.7390
—— Longstreet, A: B. Georgia scenes, characters, incidents, &c., in the first half century of the republic. 823.1012
—— Pendleton, L: In the wire-grass. (Southern life to-day.) 823.6529
Illinois.
—— Eggleston, E: The Graysons. 823.5516
—— Kirkland, J. Zury: the meanest man in Spring county. (2d quarter of 19th cent.)
823.4962
Indiana.
—— Eggleston, E: The Hoosier schoolmaster. 823.522
Kentucky.
—— Dodd, *Mrs.* A.. B. (B.) Glorinda.
823.5456
—— McGlasson, E. Diana's livery.
823.7397
—— Read, O. P. A Kentucky colonel.
823.6465
—— Underwood, F. H: Lord of himself.
823.1646
Note.—See **Shaler,** N. S. Kentucky. (*Amer. commonwealths.*) 9176.58.
Lake states.
—— Campbell, W: W. Lake lyrics and other poems. 821.1332
—— Hamlin, *Mrs.* M. C. W. Legends of le Détroit. 823.4756
—— Woolson, C. F. Castle Nowhere, and other stories. (Lake country sketches.)
823.4085
Louisiana.
—— Cable, G: W. Bonaventure: a prose pastoral of Acadian Louisiana. 823.5248
—— — Strange, true stories of Louisiana.
823.6317
Maine. See New England, p. 192.
Maryland.
—— Townsend, G: A. Katy of Catoctin; or, the chain-breakers. 823.7446
Note.—See **Browne,** W: H. Maryland. (*Amer. commonwealths.*) 9176.59.

English Fiction. *Contin.*
United States. *Contin.*
AMERICAN LIFE AND CHARACTER. *Contin.*
Massachusetts. See New England, p. 192.
Michigan.
— Littlejohn, F. J. Legends of Michigan. (1800–11.) 970.41
— Trowbridge, J: T. A start in life: a story of the Genesee country. 808.1505
  Note.—See Cooley, T. M. Michigan. (*Amer. commonwealths.*) 9177.599.
Minnesota. Eggleston, E: Mystery of Metropolisville. 823.523
New England. See New England, p. 191.
New Hampshire. See New England, p. 192.
New Jersey. Allen, R: Miss Eaton's romance. (Boarding house life.) 823.7028
New Orleans.
— Cable, G: W. Dr. Sevier. 823.4863
— — The Grandissimes: a story of creole life. 823.2442
— — Madame Delphine. 823.1895
— — Old creole days. 823.162
— — *Same.* 823.5247
  Note.—See Howe, W: W. Municipal hist. of New Orleans. 33 pp. (*In* Johns Hopkins Univ. Studies, etc., v. 7.) *in* 973.582⁷.
New York.
— Brown, C: B. Ormond. (*Novels*, v. 6.) (Scenes in N. Y. and Phila.) 823.141
— Chambers, J. Mad world and its inhabitants. (Dr. Baltric's Asylum on Bloomingdale Road.) 823.196
— Cooper, J. F. The redskins. (Antirentism in N. Y.) 823.310
— Fay, T. M. Norman Leslie: a tale of the present times. 2 vols. (1835.) ** 823.6759-60
— Frederic, H. The Lawton girl. 823.6996
— Paulding, J. K. The Dutchman's fireside. 2 vols. (in 1). (Dutch life.) 823.7014
— Young, J. D. Adrift: a story of Niagara. 823.6576
  Note.—See Roberts, E. H. New York. (*Amer. commonwealths.*) 2 vols. 974.137-8.
New York city.
— Bishop, W: H: House of a merchant prince. 823.4480
— Champney, *Mrs.* E.. (W.) Witch Winnie: the story of a "King's daughter." 808.1913
— Curtis, G: W: Potiphar papers. (Satire.) 828.16
— — Prue and I. 823.358
— — Trumps. 823.359
— Fawcett, E. An ambitious woman. (N. Y. society.) 823.6560
— — The evil that men do. (Life in tenements of N. Y. city.) 823.6411
— — A man's will. (Intemperance among the business men.) 823.5419
— Harland, H: The yoke of the Thorah. (Jewish life.) 823.5198
— Howells, W: D. Hazard of new fortunes. 2 vols. 823.7018-19
— Hume, J. F. Five hundred majority; or, the days of Tammany. 823.6097
— Irving, J: T. The attorney; or, the correspondence of John Quod. 823.4025
— — Harry Harson. 823.4026

English Fiction. *Contin.*
United States. *Contin.*
AMERICAN LIFE AND CHARACTER. *Contin.*
New York city. *Contin.*
— Miller, C. H. The destruction of Gotham. (Poor and rich in N. Y.) 823.5388
— — *Same.* 823.5769
— Rohlfs, *Mrs.* A.. K.. (G.) The sword of Damocles. 823.7149
— Sherwood, *Mrs.* M.. E.. (W.) Transplanted rose. 823.4486
— Stoddard, W: O. Chuck Purdy. 808.1726
— Taylor, B. John Godfrey's fortunes. (Literary life.) 823.1545
— Thébaud, A. J. Louisa Kirkbride. 823.5991
  Note.—See Riis, J. A. How the other half lives. Studies among the tenemeuts of New York. Illus. 1890. 9175.56.
North Carolina. Daniel, J. W. The girl in checks; or, the mystery of the mountain cabin. 823.7249
Ohio. Bennett, E. Kate Clarendon. 823.72
  Note.—See King, R. Ohio: first fruits of the ordinance of 1787. (*Amer. commonwealths.*) 977.164.
Pennsylvania.
— Taylor, B. Joseph and his friend. 823.1546
— — Story of Kennett. (Friends in Penn.) 823.1547
  Note.—See McVeagh, W. Pennsylvania. (*Amer. commonwealths.*) 975.142.
Philadelphia.
— Brown, C: B. Ormond. (*Novels*, v. 6.) (Scenes in N. Y. and Phila.) 823.141
— Mitchell, S. W. In war time. 823.5399
Rhode Island. See New England, p. 192.
South Carolina. Schoolcraft, *Mrs.* M.. (H.) The black gauntlet. (Plantation life before the war.) 823.7414
Southern.
— Baker, W: M. Mose Evans. 823.50
— Dahlgren, *Mrs.* M. (V.) Lights and shadows of a life. 823.5666
— Roe, E: P. The earth trembled. 823.5270
— Tiernan, *Mrs.* F.. C. (F.) Hearts and hands. 823.5896
— Webber, C: W. Tales of the southern border. 823.5804
— Woolson, C. F. Rodman the keeper: southern sketches. 823.2039
Tennessee.
— Murfree, M.. N. The despot of Broomsedge cove. 823.5469
— — Down the ravine. 808.1343
— — In the Tennessee mountains. 823.5232
— — The prophet of the Great Smoky mountains. 823.4880
— — Where the battle was fought. 823.4893
  Note.—See Phelan, J. Tennessee. (*Amer. commonwealths.*) 976.139.
Texas.
— Baker, W: M. The Virginians in Texas. 823.5923
— Barr, *Mrs.* A. E. (H.) Christopher. 75 pp. 823.5418
— — Remember the Alamo. (Revolution in Texas, 1835.) 823.5702

English Fiction. *Contin.*
United States. *Contin.*
AMERICAN LIFE AND CHARACTER. *Contin.*
Texas. *Contin.*
—— Clemens, J. Bernard Lile: an historical romance . . . of the Texas revolution and the Mexican war. 823.7100
—— Marryat, *Capt.* F: Travels . . . of Monsieur Violet in . . . western Texas. 823.1104
—— Paxton, P. A stray Yankee in Texas 9176.16
—— Postel, K: Adventures in Texas. (*In* Tales from Blackwood, v. 5.) *in* ** 823.6651
—— Reid, *Capt.* T: M. Wild life; or, adventures on the frontier: a tale of the early days of the Texan republic. 808.429
—— Webber, C: W. Old Hicks the guide. 823.1691
Vermont. *See* New England, p. 192.
Virginia.
—— Bradley, A. G. The doctor: an old Virginia fox-hunter. 47 pp. (*In* Tales from Blackwood. 3d ser., v. 4.) p. 365, *in* 823.7500
—— — Mar'se Dab after the war. 39 pp. (*In* Tales from Blackwood. 3d ser., v. 6.) p. 119, *in* 823.7502
—— Cooke, J: E. The Virginia Bohemians. 823.5902
—— — The Virginia comedians; or, old days in the Old Dominion. 823.5662
—— Hopkins. S:, *of Northampton.* Youth of the Old Dominion. 823.826
—— Page, T: N. In ole Virginia; or, Marse Chan, and other stories. 823.5363
—— — Marse Chan: a tale of old Virginia. 36 pp. (*In* Stories by Amer. authors, v. 9.) p. 5, *in* 823.4710
—— Pendleton, F. A Virginia inheritance. 823.5229
—— Seawell, M. E. Throckmorton. (After the civ. war.) 823.7447
—— Terhune, *Mrs.* M., V. (H.) Judith: a chronicle of old Virginia. 823.4698
Note.—See Cooke, J: E. Virginia: a history of the people. (*American commonwealths.*) 976.119.
—Trent, W: P. English culture in Virginia. (*In* Johns Hopkins Univ. Studies, etc., v. 7.) *in* 973.582¹.
Washington city.
—— Benedict, F. L. My daughter Elinor. 823.5834
—— Burnett, *Mrs.* F., E. (H.) Through one administration. 823.4579
—— Clemens, S: L., *and* Warner, C: D. The gilded age. 823.5809
—— Townsend, G: A. Katy of Catoctin; or, the chain-breakers. 823.7446
Western.
—— Adams, W: T. Going west. 808.965
—— — Out west. 808.502
—— Ballantyne, R. M. Dog Crusoe. 808.207
—— — The pioneers. 808.1280
—— — Wild man of the west. 808.703
—— Beecher, *Mrs.* E. W. (B.) From dawn to daylight; or, story of a western home. 823.7375

English Fiction. *Contin.*
United States. *Contin.*
AMERICAN LIFE AND CHARACTER. *Contin.*
Western. *Contin.*
—— Bishop, W: H: The golden justice. 823.5785
—— Bright, *Mrs.* M. A. Margaret: . . . life in a prairie home. 823.1248
—— — *Same.* 823.2047
—— Brooks, N. The boy emigrants. (Overland travel to Calif.) 808.1416
—— Cary, A. Clovernook; or, recollections of our neighborhood in the far west. 823.181
—— Clifford, J. Overland tales. 823.2155
—— Cozzens, S: W. Crossing the quicksands. 808.1629
—— Derby, G. H. [*John Phœnix.*] Phœnixiana; sketches. ·828.17
—— Dickens, C: J: H. Life and adventures of Martin Chuzzlewit. 2 vols. (in 1). 823.424
—— — *Same.* 823.5848
—— Eggleston, E: The circuit rider. 823.520
—— Habberton, J: The Jericho road. 823.679
—— Hall, J. Legends of the west. 823.6316
—— Hammond, W: A. Lal. 823.4781
—— Harte, F. B. Tales of the Argonauts, and other sketches. 823.714
—— — A waif of the plains. (Crossing the plains in 1852.) 823.6999
—— Kirkland, *Mrs.* C. M. (S.) Forest life. 2 vols. 823.7529-30
—— — New home—who'll follow? 823.7108
—— — Western clearings. 823.7109
—— McCabe, J. D., *Jr.* Planting the wilderness; or, the pioneer boys. 808.1655
—— Marryat, *Capt.* F: Travels . . . of Monsieur Violet in California, Sonora, and western Texas. 823.1104
—— — *Same.* *in* ** 823.6664
—— — Valerie. 823.1119
—— — *Same.* ** 823.6675
—— Miller, C. H. First fam'lies of the Sierras. 823.1159
—— — Songs of the Sierras. 821.1317
—— Owen, R. D. Beyond the breakers. (Village life in the west.) 823.5954
—— Pearson, C: H. Cabin on the prairie. 808.1654
—— Powers, S. In the great west. p. 204, *in* 823.4145
—— Reid, M. The quadroon; or, adventures in the far west. 823.1297
—— Riddle, A. G. The house of Ross. (1830-40.) 823.7144
—— Rideout, *Mrs.* J. B. Early western life. 808.1596
—— Riley, H. H. Puddleford papers. 828.80
—— Roe, E: P. Barriers burned away. 823.1355
—— Truman, B. C. Occidental sketches. 823.5185
—— Victor, *Mrs.* F., A. (F.) The new Penelope. 823.6126

English Fiction. *Contin.*
United States. *Contin.*
AMERICAN LIFE AND CHARACTER. *Contin.*
Western. Contin.
—— Winthrop, T. John Brent.   823.1725
See also California, p. 33.

North-western.
—— Ballantyne, R. M. The big otter.
823.1531
—— Pearson, C: H. Young pioneers of the
great north-west.   808.1656
—— Robinson, *Dr.* J. H. Nick Whiffles.
823.1353

South-western.
—— Bennett, E. Viola.   823.77
—— Robb, J: S. Swamp doctor's adventures
in the south-west.   823.1340

Army life. King, C: Starlight ranch and
other stories of army life on the frontier.
823.7176
Domestic economy. Cruger, M.. How she
did it; or, comfort on $150 a year.
823.5498
Emigrant life. Sadlier, *Mrs.* M.. A. (M.)
Con O'Regan.   823.1378
Games and songs. Newell, W: W., *comp.*
Games and songs of American children.
808.1876
The Indian question.
—— Harsha, *Judge* —. Ploughed under:
the story of an Indian chief told by him-
self.   823.4158
—— Jackson, *Mrs.* H.. M. (F.) Ramona.
823.4865
—— Tibbles, T. H. Hidden power. (Hist.
of the Indian ring.)   823.1844
See also Indians, p. 130.

Industrial life.
—— Adams, W: T. Living too fast; or, the
confessions of a bank officer.   823.5339
—— Hale, E: E. How they lived in Hampton: a study of practical Christianity applied in the manufacture of woollens.
823.5693
—— Johnston, J. P. Twenty years of hus'-
ling: portraying the peculiar incidents . . .
of a man who tried almost every kind of
business and finally wins.   923.1970
—— Keenan, H: F. The money-makers: a
social parable.   823.4856
—— Kimball, R: B. Henry Powers (banker).
823.4097

Labor question.
—— Bellamy, C: J. Breton mills.   823.5700
—— Elliott, S.. B. Jerry.   823.7533
—— Porter, L. B. Speaking of Ellen. (Cap-
ital against labor.)   823.6989
—— White slaves of monopolies. (Anon.)
823.4806

Mining life.
—— Greene, H. Blind brother: a story of
the Pennsylvania coal mines.   808.1357
—— Ingersoll, E. The silver caves: a mining story. (Colorado.)   808.1719
—— Munroe, K. Derrick Stirling: a story of
the mines (in Pennsylvania).   808.1440
—— White slaves of monopolies. (Anon.)
823.4806

English Fiction. *Contin.*
United States. *Contin.*
AMERICAN LIFE AND CHARACTER. *Contin.*
The opium habit. Noble, A. L. In a coun-
try town.   823.7325
Political life.
—— Cooper, J. F. The ways of the hour.
(Evils of the jury system.)   823.315
—— Crawford, F. M. An American politi-
cian.   823.4873
—— Henry, E. '89. Ed. from the original
manuscript. (South and north in 1889.)
823.5441
—— Hume, J. F. Five hundred majority;
or, the days of Tammany. (N. Y. city.)
823.6097
—— Jackson, *Mrs.* H.. M. (F.) Ramona.
(Indian question.)   823.4865
—— King, C. Democracy.   823.4577
—— Shapley, R. R. Solid for Mulhooly:
sketch of municipal politics under the
leaders, the ring, and the boss.   823.4351
—— Simpleton, *Maj.* —. Civil-service reform; or, the postmaster's revenge.
823.4593
—— Tibbles, T. H. Hidden power. (The
Indian ring.)   823.1844
—— Townsend, G: A. Katy of Catoctin; or,
the chain-breakers. (Election of Pres.
Lincoln; civ. war; conspiracy of Booth.)
823.7446

Religious movement.
—— Alden, *Mrs.* L. (McD.) Chautauqua
girls at home.   808.1511
—— Deland, *Mrs.* M. W. (C.) John Ward,
preacher.   823.5278
—— Eggleston, E: The circuit rider: a tale
of the heroic age.   823.520
—— Father Oswald: a genuine Catholic
story. (Anon.)   823.1178
—— Hale, E: E. Ten times one is ten: the
possible reformation.   823.685
—— — *Same.*   823.4540
—— Hoffman, M.. I. Agnes Hilton; or,
practical views of Catholicity.   823.769
—— Hubbell, *Mrs.* M. (S.) The shady side;
or, life in a country parsonage.   823.4639
Mormonism.
—— Paddock, *Mrs.* A. G. In the toils; or,
martyrs of the latter days. (Against.)
823.1226
—— Tourgée, A. W. Button's inn. (Mor-
monism in N. Y., Ohio and Vermont.)
823.5295
School life.
—— Bardeen, C. W. Roderick Hume: the
story of a New York teacher.   823.4144
—— Grant, R. Jack Hall.   808.1716
—— Lowell, R. T. S. Antony Brade.
823'.1018
—— Severance, M: S. Hammersmith: his
Harvard days.   823.1415
—— Thomas, C. Frontier schoolmaster.
823.1842
—— Washburn, W: T. Fair Harvard: a story
of American college life.   823.7115
Sea life.
—— Clark, H. H. Joe Bently, naval cadet.
823.7035

English Fiction. *Contin.*
United States. *Contin.*
AMERICAN LIFE AND CHARACTER. *Contin.*
Sea life. *Contin.*

—— Dana, R: H:, *Jr.* Two years before the mast. *in* 823.6696
—— Hart, *Col.* J. C. Miriam Coffin; or, the whale-fisherman. 823.6110
—— —— *Same.* 2 vols. (in 1). 823.6210
—— Melville, H. White-Jacket; or, the world in a man-of-war. 823.1149
—— Nordhoff, C: Man-of-war life. 808.167
—— —— *Same.* 808.1898
—— Porter, D: D. Adventures of Harry Marline; or, notes from an American midshipman's lucky bag. 823.6142
—— Shippen, E:, *U. S. N.* Thirty years at sea. 823.7296
See also Sea stories, p. 230.

Social studies.

—— Bellamy, E: Looking backward 2000–1887. 823.5495
—— Brown, C: B. Edgar Huntley; or, memoirs of a sleep-walker. 823.139
—— —— Wieland; or, the transformation. 823.142
—— Hale, E: E. My friend the boss. 823.5692
—— Hawthorne, J. C. An American penman. 823.5444
—— —— Another's crime. 823.5752
—— —— The great bank robbery. 823.5446
—— —— Section 558. 823.5269
—— —— A tragic mystery. 823.5400
—— Hay, J: The bread-winners. (Anon.) 823.4692
—— Holland, J. G. Nicholas Minturn. 823.782
—— Tourgée, A. W. Pactolus Prime. (The negro question.) 823.7065
—— Townsend, G: A. The entailed hat. 823.4729
—— Woods, K:. P. Metzerott, shoemaker. 823.6995
See also Laboulaye, E. R. L:. Paris in America. (Social and political criticisms.) 823.6870.

Sporting life. Herbert, H: W: Frank Forester's sporting scenes and characters. 2 vols. 823.5754-5

Temperance movement.

—— Arthur, T. S. All's for the best. 823.6975
—— —— The Latimer family . . . and other temperance stories. 823.5911
—— —— The mill and the tavern. 823.5758
—— —— Orange blossoms fresh and faded. 823.5688
—— —— The strike at Tivoli mills. 823.5622
—— —— The wife's engagement ring. 823.5757
—— Bolton, *Mrs.* S.. (K.) The present problem. 823.110
—— Hale, E: E. Our new crusade. 823.683

Woman question.

—— Stowe, *Mrs.* H. E.. (B.) My wife and I. 823.1525
—— Taylor, B. Hannah Thurston. 823.1544

Note.—*See* Bibliographies. Adams, C. K. Histories of the U. S. (*In his* Man. of hist. lit. 3d ed. pp. 566–672.) 1889. ** 907.4². —American colonies.

English Fiction. *Contin.*
United States. *Contin.*

Note. Contin.

(*Lib. jl.* Nov., 1880, v. 5.) p. 329, *in* ** 19.20.—Griffin, A. P. C. Bibliographies of special subjects. No. 3: Index of articles on Amer. local history in hist. coll. in Boston Public Lib. 1889. ** 15.278.—Hildreth, R. History of the U. S. 1849. (Authorities, v. 3, pp. 548–564; v. 6, pp. 715–720.) 973.20-5.—Rev. ed. 973.240-5.—U. S. Catalogue of the gov't pubs. of the U. S., Sept. 5, 1774–Mar. 4, 1881. 1885. ** 15.202.—Winsor, J., *ed.* Narrative and critical history of America. vols. 6–8. (Bibliographical notes and essays on sources of information. v. 6: The Amer. revolution; v. 7: The United States, 1775–1782, the loyalists, the confederation, the constitution, the hist. of political parties, the wars of the U. S., 1789–1850; the diplomacy of the U. S., territorial acquisitions, etc.; v. 8: Comprehensive printed authorities upon the general and upon some special phases of the history of the U. S., 1776–1850; the manuscript sources of the history of the U. S. of A., with particular reference to the American revolution.) 970.127⁶-127⁹.

For comprehensive works, *see* Bancroft, G: History of the U. S. from the discovery of the American continent to the close of the revolution. 6 vols. 973.196-201;—*Same.* 10 vols. 973.32-41.—Boynton, H: The world's greatest conflict. (Cop. 1890.) 940.201.—Brown, E. The national standard history of the U. S. for popular use. 1888. 973.699.—Bryant, W: C., *and* Gay, S. H. Popular history of the U. S. from the first discovery of the western hemisphere to the end of the first century. 4 vols. 973.11-13².—Doyle, J. A. History of the U. S. With maps illustrative of the acquisition of territory and the increase of population, by F. A. Walker. 1876. 973.259.—Hathaway, B. A. 1001 questions and answers in U. S. history. (1882.) 973.687.—Hildreth, R: History of the U. S. from the discovery of America to the end of the 16th Congress. 6 vols. 1879. 973.20-5;—*Same.* Rev. ed. 973.240-5.—Holmes, A. Annals of America (1492–1826), with list of authorities. 2 vols. 970.136-7.—Howland, E: Annals of North America. (1492–1877.) 970.130.—Johnston, A. The U. S.: its history and constitution. 1889. 973.709.—Leeds, J. W. A history of the U. S. of A. (A. D. 875–1876.) 1881. 973.703.—McMaster, J: B. History of the people of the U. S. from the revolution to the civil war. 5 vols. vols. 1-2. (vols. 3-5 in prep.) 973.440-1.—Magazine of American history, Jan., 1877–June, 1891. 2 vols. pr. yr. 27 vols. 905.1-20⁷.—Montgomery, D. H. The leading facts of Amer. history (to 1890). 973.730.—Patton, J. H. Nat. resources of the U. S. 1888. 973.699;—Red letter life of the republic: concise history of the American people. (1492–1882.) 2 vols. 1888. * 973.676-77.—Preble, G. H. History of the flag of the U. S. * 929.22.—Ramsay, D: History of the U. S. (1607–1808.) 3 vols. 973.222-4.—Ridpath, J: C. A popular history of the U. S. of A., from the aboriginal times to the present day. Illus. with maps, charts, portrs. and diagrams. 1881. 973.172.—Schouler, J. Hist. of U. S. of Amer. under the constitution. (1783–1847.) 4 vols. 1880-89. 973.505, 6, 6¹·². —Thayer, W. M. Marvels of the new west. Illus. 1888. 9177.627.—Townsend, J., *comp.* An index to the U. S. of America, hist., geog. and political; a handbook of . . the "curious" in U. S. history. (Cop. 1890.) 973.733.—Whitney, J. D. The U. S.: facts and figures illus. the physical geography of the country and its material resources. 1889. 973.261.—Winsor, J., *ed.* Narrative and critical history of America. 8 vols. ** 970.127-127⁹.

See also Catalogues of this Library.
No. 2, 1880, pp. 237–40. No. 4, 1884, pp. 301–4.
No. 3, 1882, pp. 196–98. No. 5, 1888, pp. 358–74.

See also references in Poole's Index (to 1882). pp. 1,341–55, *in* ** 50.1;—*Same*, to Jan. 1, 1887. pp. 451–55, *in* ** 50.1³.

For constitutional history, *see* Adams, J: Works. 10 vols. vols. 4–6. (*See* index, v. 10.) * 923.294-303.—Alden, J. Science of government. 1842. 921;—*Same*, 320.30.—Benton, T: H. Thirty years' view. (1820-50.) 2 vols. 328.8-9.—Brownson, O. A. American republic. 1866. 324.4.—Cooley, T. M., *and others*. Constitutional history of the U. S. as seen in the development of American law. 1888. 324.90.—Curtis, G: T. Constitutional history of the U. S. as seen in the development of American law. 2 vols.

English Fiction. *Contin.*
United States. *Contin.*
Note. Contin.

v. 1: 1774–1788. 324.93;—History of the constitution. 2 vols. 342.3-4.—Elliot, J. Debates on adoption of federal constitution. 5 vols. * 328.3-7.—Federalist on the new constitution in 1788. By Hamilton, Jay, and Madison. 1818. 324.14.—Frothingham, R. Rise of the republic. (U. S.) 973.181.—Hart, A. B. Topical outline of the courses in constitutional and political hist. of the U. S. at Harvard Coll. 1889-1891. 2 pts. (in 1). 1783-1829. * 973.715.—Hildreth, R. History of the U. S. v. 4. 973.23; —Same. 973.243.—Holst, E. H. von. Constitutional and political history of the U. S. 4 vols. 342.1-2².—Hosmer, J. K. Hist. of Anglo-Saxon freedom. 1890. (Polity of Eng.-speaking race.) 323.17.—Jennings, L. J. 80 years of republican government in the U. S. 1868. 324.21.—Johnston, A. The history of political parties. (Winsor, J., ed. Narr. and crit. hist. of Amer., v. 7.) (With crit. essay on the sources of information.) pp. 267-356, in 970.127';—The U. S.: its history and constitution. (Bibliography, pp. 273-6.) 973.719.—Justice and jurisprudence: an inquiry concerning the constitutional limitations of the 13th, 14th and 15th amendments. 1889. 326.24.—Landon, J. S. The constitutional history and government of the U. S. (Lectures.) 1889. 324.94.—McKee, T. H., comp. Index to Senate reports 14th to 49th Cong. 1815-1887. ** 350.5572;—Index to the House of Representatives' reports, 14th to 49th Cong. 1815-1887. ** 350.5571.— Madison, James, Life of. By Rives. 3 vols. 923. 308-10.—Monroe, J. The people the sovereign. 1867. 324.56.—Mulford, E. The nation. 1887. D1. 49.—Rupert, W: W. A guide to the study of the history and constitution of the U. S. 1888. (With references to authorities.) 973.707.—Story, J. Commentaries on the constitution of the U. S. 2 vols. * 342.103-4.—Tocqueville, A. de. Democracy in America. 2 vols. 1864. 323.74-4.—Van Buren, Martin, Life of. By E: M. Shepard. 923.1870.— Webster, D. Speeches. 825.54.

For political history, 1789-1890, *see* American annual register, 1825-33. 8 vols. (Gives a selection of public documents, political speeches, letters, etc.) ** 902.19-26.—American state papers. 38 vols. (broken set). For docs. before 1823. (Documents are classified by subject.) *Contents:* Commerce and navigation. v. 1 (of 2). ** 350.5468;— Finance. vols. 4-5. 2 vols. ** 350.5466-7;—Foreign relations. vols. 5-6. 2 vols. ** 350.5459-60;—Military affairs. v. 1. ** 350.5472;—Same. vols. 3-7. 5 vols. ** 350.5472-6;—Naval affairs. vols. 2-4. 3 vols. ** 350.5478-80;—Public lands. vols. 1-8 (all). 8 vols. ** 350.5482-9.—American statesmen . . . men conspicuous in the political history of the U. S. Ed. by J: T. Morse, Jr. (viz.: Adams, J: By J: T. Morse, Jr. 923.1771;—Adams, J: Quincy. By J: T. Morse, Jr. 923.1236;—Adams, S: By J. K. Hosmer. 923.1773;—Benton, T: H. By T. Roosevelt. 923.1804; —Calhoun, J: C. By Dr. H. von Holst. 923.1408;— Clay, H: By C. Schurz. 2 vols. 923.1867-8;—Gallatin, Albert. By J: A. Stevens. 923.1505;—Hamilton, Alexander. By H: C. Lodge. 923.1406.—Henry, Patrick. By M. C. Tyler. 923.1869;—Jackson, Andrew. By W. G. Sumner. 923.1407;—Jefferson, T: By J: T. Morse, Jr. 923.1410;—Madison, James. By S. H. Gay. 923.1773;—Marshall, J: By A. B. Magruder. 923.1769;—Monroe, James. By D. C. Gilman. 923.1411;—Morris, Gouverneur. By T. Roosevelt. 923.1930;—Randolph, J: By H: Adams. 923. 1770;—Van Buren, Martin. By E: M. Shepard. 923. 1870;—Washington, G: By H: C. Lodge. 2 vols. 923.1871-2;—Webster, Daniel. By H: C. Lodge. 923.1491.) (Index to each v.) ** 328.33-74.—Benton, T: H. Thirty years' view (1820-50). 2 vols. 328.8-9. —Blaine, J. G. Twenty years of congress, from Lincoln to Garfield. 2 vols. 923.1582-3.—Blanchard, R. Rise of political parties in the U. S. 1888. 324.100.—Boston Public Library. Catalogue. (A convenient index of public interest from 1823-1863.) p. 815. in ** 17.46; Supplement, p. 647, in ** 17.47.—Brown, E., and Strauss, A. Dict. of American politics. 1888. ** 324.96.—Brownson, O. A. American republic. 1865. 324.4.—Bryce, J. The American commonwealth. 2 vols. 1889. 320.128-9. —Burr, Aaron, Life and times of. By J. Parton. 2 vols. 923.333-4.—Congressional debates. 1824-37. 13 vols. (Index to each v.) 1825-37. ** 328.703-

English Fiction. *Contin.*
United States. *Contin.*
Note. Contin.

29.—Congressional globe. 1833-73. (For continuation, *see* Congressional record. Each session is indexed.) ** 328.75-118; ** 328.434-89.—Congressional record, 1873- . (For debates previous to 1873, *see* Congressional debates.—Congressional globe. Each session is indexed.) ** 328.120-47.—Cooper, H. T., and Fenton, T. V. American politics; political laws; federal blue book, etc. * 973.543.—Crittenden, J: J., Life of. Ed. by his daughter, Mrs. Chapman Coleman. 2 vols. 1878. 923.876.—Fiske, J: Civil government in the U. S. considered with some reference to its origin. 1890. 324.99.—Forces. P. American archives. 1774-1783. . 9 vols. (Gives documents, letters, etc., both Amer. and Eng., for the period.) (1774-1776.) ** 973.481-8.—Greeley, H. Recollections. 923.405.—Hart, A. B. Topical outline of the courses in constitutional and political hist. of the U. S. at Harvard Coll. in 1889-91. 2 pts. (in 1). 1783-1861. * 973.715.—Howard, G: E. An introduction to the local constitutional history of the U. S. v. 1: Development of the township, hundred and shire. 1889. (Authorities cited, pp. 476-498.) 324.97.—Hudson, F: History of journalism in the U. S. (1690-1872.) 1873. 820.39.—Johnston, A. History of American politics. 1882. 973.412;— Representative American orations. 3 vols. 825. 204-6.—Lalor, J: J., ed. Cyclopædia of political science and political history of U. S. 3 vols. 1881-4. v. 1: A-D; v. 2, E-N; v. 3: O-Z. ** 320.115-17.— Lanman, C: Dictionary of the U. S. Congress. 1866. * 303.5.—Livingston, E. C. By C. H. Hunt. 923.807.—Long, J: D. The Republican party. 1888. 324.102.—Lowell, J. R. Political essays. 1888. 329.45.—McCulloch. H. Men and measures of half a century. 1889. 973.652.—McKinley, C. An appeal to Pharaoh. The negro problem and its radical solution. 1889. 326.22.—Mulford, E. The nation: the foundations of civil order and political life in the U. S. 1887. 324.104.—Niles, H. Weekly register, 1811-July, 1849. 75 vols. (Contains, besides public documents, many political speeches, letters, etc.) ** 51.124-199.—Pinkney, W., Life of. By H. Wheaton. in ** 920.107.—Poore, B: P. Congressional directory. 1776-1878. * 328.1.— Taney, R. B., Memoir of. By S. Tyler. 923.923.— Townsend, V. F.. Our presidents; or, the lives of the twenty-three presidents of the U. S. 1889. * 923.1947.—Tucker, G: P. Monroe doctrine: its origin and growth. 1885. 973.606.—Wilson, H. History of the slave power in America. 3 vols. 1874-77. 326.26-8.—Wirt, W:, Life of. By J: P. Kennedy. 2 vols. 923.344-5.

For military and naval history, *see* Allen, J. Battles of the British navy. 2 vols. 1858. (Eng. side.) 942.338-9.—Boynton, C: B. History of the navy during the rebellion. 2 vols. 1867-8. 973. 141-2.—Brackett, A. G. History of the U. S. cavalry to 1863. 1865. 973.195.—Brooks, E. S. The story of the American sailor in active service on merchant vessel and man-of-war. 1888. (Best hundred books on the Amer. sailor, pp. 324-331.) 359. 53;—Story of the American soldier in war and peace. 1622-1889. (Best hundred books on the American soldier, pp. 338-343.) 973.658.—Cooper, J. F. History of the navy of the U. S. of A. 2 vols. 1839. 973.143-4.—Cullum, Bvt. Maj.-Gen. G: W. Biog. register of the officers and graduates of the U. S. Mil. Acad. at West Point, N. Y., 1802-1890. 3 vols. 1891. ** 920.376-8.—Hamersley, T: H. S., comp. Complete army and navy register, 1776-1887. 1888. ** 973.616.—Johnson, and Buel. Battles and leaders of the civil war. 4 vols. 973.630-3.—Porter, D: D. Naval history of the civil war. 1886. 973.609.— Powell, W: H:, comp. Records of the living officers of the U. S. army. 1890. ** 355.518.

See also before under general histories, and also histories of periods.

For ecclesiastical history, *see* Parkman, F. Jesuits in North America in the 17th century. 271. 6.—Sprague, W: B. Annals of the American pulpit. (vols. 1-2. Trinitarian Congregationalists. * 922.273-4.—vols. 3-4. Presbyterians. * 922.275-6.— v. 5. Episcopalians. * 922.277.—v. 6. Baptists. * 922.278.—v. 7. Methodists. * 922.279.—v. 8. Unitarians. 922.280.—v. 9. Lutheran. 922.281.)—Whitefield, G:, Life of. By J: Gillies. (Rise of Methodism.) 922.59.

English Fiction. *Contin.*
United States. *Contin.*
Note. Contin.
For communistic societies in the U. S., *see* Dixon, W. H. New America. 2 vols. 9173.129-30;—Spiritual wives. 2 vols. 289.96-7.—Greeley, H. Recollections of a busy life. (Some chapters.) 923.405.—Hinds, W: A. Amer. communities. 289.113.—Nordhoff, C: Communistic societies of the U. S. 1875. 369.2.—Shakers, The. (*Harper's mag.*, v. 15.) p. 164, *in* ** 51.410.

For life and manners, *see* Blouët, P., *and* Allyn, J: Jonathan and his continent. 1889. 917.52.—Brydges, H. Uncle Sam at home. 1888. 9173.481.—Campbell, *Sir* G: White and black in the U. S. 1879. 9173.11.—Chevalier, M. Society, manners, and politics in the U. S. 1839. 973.103.—Delano, A. Life on the plains. 1854. 9173.99.—Farnham, E. W. Life in prairie land. 1855. 9173.95.—Freeman, E. A. Some impressions of the U. S. 1883. 9173.420.—Glazier, *Capt.* W. Peculiarities of American cities. 1886. 917.53.—Grund, F. J. Aristocracy in America. 2 vols. 1839. * 9173.470-1.—Hall, J. Sketches in the west. 2 vols. 9173.120-1.—Hardman, F. Frontier life in the south-west, 1857. 9173.85.—Hobbs, —. Wild life in the far west. 9173.64.—Howe, *Mrs.* J. (W.) Modern society; changes in American society. 1881. D1.9.—Kip, L. Army life on the Pacific. 1859. 977.14.—Marcy, R. B. Border reminiscences. 1872. 9177.167;—Thirty years of army life on the border. 1874. 9177.166.—Martineau, H. Society in America. 1837. * 9173.449.—Poore, B: P. Perley's reminiscences of sixty years in the national metropolis. 2 vols. 1886. 973.613-14.—Pulszky, F., *and* M. White, red, and black. 2 vols. 1853. 9173.8-9.—Raymond, R. W. Camp and cabin: life and travel in the west. 9173.113.—Reminiscences of America, by two Englishmen. 9171.70.—Rideing, W: H. A-saddle in the wild west. 1879. 9173.35.—Scudder, H. E., *ed.* Men and manners in America one hundred years ago. 1876. 397.1.—Stedman, E. C., *and* Hutchinson, E. M., *comps.* Library of American literature. (*Gen. index*, v. 11.) p. 628, *in* ** 820.131¹.—Steele, J. W. Frontier army sketches. 1883. 9177.562.—Trollope, *Mrs.* F. Domestic manners of the Americans. (1828-30.) 2 vols. 9173.416-17.—Valrose, *Viscount, pseud.* Hon. Uncle Sam. 1888. 9173.485.—Views of society, etc. 1818-19-20. By an Englishman. 9173.152.—Warner, C: D. Studies in the south and west, with comments on Canada. 1889. 9173.479.

Unkind word, and other stories. Craik, *Mrs.* D. M. (M.)   823.341
Unnatural bondage, An. Brame, *Mrs.* C.. M. (L.)   *in* 823.5035
Until the day breaks. Spender, E.   823.5016
Unto the third and fourth generation. Campbell, *Mrs.* H.. (S.)   823.1909
Up in the clouds. Ballantyne, R. M.   *in* 808.1268
Same.   808.1281
Up the Baltic. Adams, W: T.   808.498
Up the river. Adams, W: T.   808.963
Upmore, Sir Thomas, Remarkable history of. Blackmore, R: D.   823.4761
Upon the waters. 26 pp. Hay, M.. C.   *in* 823.4998
Ups and downs. Hale, E: E.   823.686
Uranie. Flammarion, C.   823.7257
Urith. Gould, S. Baring-   823.7546
Ursula. Balzac, H. de.   823.7535
"Us." Molesworth, *Mrs.* M.. L.. (S.)   823.5042

Useful arts.
—— Abbott, J. The engineer; or, how to travel in the woods. (*In his* Harper's story books, v. 7.)   808.586
—— The Harper establishment; or, how the story books are made. (*In his* Harper's story books, v. 4.)   808.583

English Fiction. *Contin.*
Useful arts. *Contin.*
—— Boy's workshop, with plans and designs for in-door and out-door work. By a boy and his friends. (1884.)   808.1552
—— Davidson, E. A. The boy joiner and model-maker. Containing practical directions . . . with descriptions of various tools, and the method of using them.   808.1867
—— Emery, M. S. Every-day business notes in its practical details: arranged for young people.   808.1586
—— Griffith, R. Boys' useful pastimes.   808.1645
—— Lukin, J. The amateur mechanic's workshop. 1888.   680.1
—— Amongst machines: a description of various mechanical appliances used in the manufacture of wood, metal and other substances.   808.630
—— The boy engineers: what they did and how they did it.   808.1662
—— Manson, G: J. Ready for business; or, choosing an occupation: ser. of practical papers for boys. 1889.   658.36
—— Morris, E. Farming for boys: what they have done . . . how to begin . . . what to aim at.   808.1547
—— Trowbridge, J: T. Lawrence's adventures among the ice-cutters, glass-makers, coal-miners, iron-men, and ship-builders.   808.238

Note.—See also Inventions.—Science.
Also American Institute of Mining Engineers. Transactions. Contents and index. vols. 1-15 incl. 1888. ** 628.155.—Annals of scientific discovery, 1850-1869. 19 vols. ** 605.1-19.—Annual record of science and industry, 1871-7. 7 vols. ** 605.20-6.—Barlow, P., *and* Barbage, C. Encyclopædia of arts, manufactures and machinery. D3.46.—Barnard, F. A. P. Machinery and processes of the industrial arts, etc. (*In* U. S. Comm. for the Paris Exposition. 1867. *Reports*, v. 3.) 06.3.—Beeton's dictionary of industries and commerce. ** 603.35.—Byrne, O. Hand-book for the artisan, mechanic and engineer. 1870. 600.1.—Dodd, G. Dictionary of manufactures, mining and industrial arts. 1869. ** 603.34.—Galloupe, F. E. Index to engineering periodicals, 1883-1887 inclusive. Comprising engineering, railroads, science, manufactures, and trade. 1888. ** 620.536.—Hazen, E. Popular technology. 2 vols. 1842. 600.37-8.—Lock, C. G. W. Workshop receipts. 2-4 ser. 3 vols. 1883-5. 680.21-2; 25.—Lossing, B. J. History of American industries. 1878. D3.1.—Muspratt, S. Chemistry applied to arts and manufactures. 2 vols. v. 1: A-Eth; v. 2: Fuel-Z. ** 540. 9-10.—Ronalds, E., *and* Richardson, T: Chemical technology. 5 pts. (*viz.*: Pts. 1-2. Fuel and its applications.—Pts. 3-5. Acids, alkalies, and salts: their manufacture, etc.) 53.57-61.—Simmonds, P. L. Animal products: their preparation, commercial uses, and value. 1877. 670.19;—Waste products and undeveloped substances. 670.20.—Thorpe, T: E. A dict. of applied chemistry. 3 vols. v. 1: A-Dy. (vols. 2 and 3 in preparation.) ** 540.90-2.—Ure, A. Dictionary of arts, manufactures, and mines. 4 vols. ** 603.10-13.—Vegetable substances used in the arts, domestic economy, etc. 1830. 633.15.—Whitehill, J. C. Cyclopedia of things worth knowing. ** 603.3.—Year-book of facts in science and art. By [J. Timbs] 1861-97. 6 vols. 500.49-54.

See also Industrial arts *in* Catalogues of this Library.
   No. 2, 1880, p. 117.   No. 4, 1884, p. 143.
   No. 3, 1882, p. 98.   No. 5, 1888, p. 213.
See also Index to Consular reports. 1880-1885; 1886-1889. 2 vols. (U. S. Pub. Docs. *Dept. of State.*) ** 350.5496¹˙².

English Fiction. *Contin.*
Useful arts. *Contin.*
Note. Contin.
See also Paris. Universal Exposition, 1867. Reports of the U. S. Commissioners. 5 vols. ** 06.1-5.—Vienna Exhibition, 1873. Reports of the U. S. Commissioners. 4 vols. ** 350.352-5.—U. S. International Exhibition, Phil. 1876. Reports. 9 vols. * 600.16-24.—Paris. Universal Exhibition. 1878. Reports of U. S. Commissioners. 5 vols. * 500.31-5.— Paris, L'exposition de. 1889. * 600.52.

List of periodicals on useful arts, current numbers of which may be had in the reading room: American agriculturist.—American architect and building news.—American machinist.—California architect and building news.—Electrical review.—Engineering.—Engineering and building record.—English mechanic.—Journal of the Iron and Steel Institute.—Manufacturer and builder.—Metal worker.—Official patent gazette (U. S.).—Pacific lumberman and contractor.—Pacific rural press.—Railroad and engineering journal.—Scientific American.—Scientific American architect and builder.—Scientific American supplement.—Van Nostrand's eclectic engineering magazine.—Wilson's photographic magazine.

See also, in **Catalogues** of this library, Architecture, Carpentry, Drawing, Engineering, Mining, Patents, etc.

For periodicals in bound volumes, *see* **Catalogues** of this Library.
No. 2, 1880, p. 178. No. 4, 1884, p. 219.
No. 3, 1882, p. 145. No. 5, 1888, p. 280.

Usurper, The. Mendès, *Mme.* J. (G.)
823.4785
Uttiet, M. G. [*Maxwell Grey.*] The reproach of Annesley. 823.5475
—— An unexpected fare. 47 pp. (*In* Tales from Blackwood. 3d ser., v. 4.)
p. 148, *in* 823.7500
Vagabond heroine, A. Edwardes, *Mrs.* A.
823.517
Same. *in* 823.6694
Vagabondia. Burnett, *Mrs.* F.. E. (H.)
823.4697
Vagabond's honor, A. Pierson, E. D.
823.6395
Vagrant wife, A. James, *Mrs.* F. A. (P.)
in 823.4988
Valdés, Armando Palacio. Sister Saint Sulpice. Tr. by N. H. Dole. Port. 823.6426
Vale of cedars. Aguilar, G. 823.10
Valentin. Kingsley, H: 823.946
Valentine, *Mrs.* —, *ed.* Eastern tales by many story-tellers. 808.389
Valentine and Orson, The remarkable history and daring exploits of. 823.1900
Valentine M'Clutchy. Carleton, W:
823.179
Valentine Strange. Murray, D: C.
in 823.3712
Same. *in* 823.5065
Valentine, the countess. Bauer, K. 823.6795
Valentine Vox, Life and adventures of. Cockton, H: * 823.243
Same. 823.5818
Valerie. Marryat, *Capt.* F: 823.1119
Same. ** 823.6675
Valerie Aylmer. Tiernan, *Mrs.* F.. C. (F.)
823.6045
Valerie's fate. Hector, *Mrs.* A. (F.)
in 823.5119
Valerius. Lockhart, J: G. 823.4513
Same. 2 vols. ** 823.6718-19
Vance, Elmer E. Nellie Harland: a romance of rail and wire. 823.5175

English Fiction. *Contin.*
Vanderdecken's message home; or, the tenacity of natural affection. 13 pp. (*In* Tales from Blackwood, v. 1.) p. 45, *in* ** 823.6647
Van Dyke, Theodore Strong. Flirtation camp; or, the rifle, rod, and gun in California: a sporting romance. 823.7137
Issued also as Rifle, rod, and gun in California.
—— Rifle, rod, and gun in California: a sporting romance. 823.4157
Vanity fair. Thackeray, W: M. 823.1550
Same. 823.5338
Same. 2 vols. 823.5004-5
Van Loon, *Mrs.* E.. Shadow of Hampton mead. 823.1787
Van Zile, E: S. A magnetic man and other stories. 823.7298
Vasconselos. Simms, W: G. 823.1438
Vashti. Wilson, *Mrs.* A. J.. (E.) 823.1710
Same. 823.4012
Vathek. Beckford, W: 823.4232
Same. p. 841, *in* ** 823.6215
Vaughan, Herbert. Coldstream. 13 pp. (*In* Famous stories by De Quincey, and others.)
p. 169, *in* 823.1778
Vee-boers, The. Reid, *Capt.* T: M.
808.1463
Veil withdrawn, The. Craven, *Mme.* P.. (de la F.) 823.6284
Veitch, Sophie F. F. The dean's daughter.
823.7445
Veley, Margaret. "For Percival." 823.4844
—— Milly's first love. 79 pp. (*In* Tales from Blackwood. 2d ser., v. 11.)
in 823.7495
Vendée, La. Trollope, A. 823.2007
Vendetta, The. Balzac, H. de.
p. 153, *in* 823.4254
Same. 823.7118
Venetia. Disraeli, B: 823.469
Same. *in* 823.3230
Venetian glass. 26 pp. Matthews, J. B.
in 823.4704
Vengeance of a Jew. Guenot, C. 823.616
Venice. *See also* Italy.
—— De Mille, J. The winged lion; or, stories of Venice. 808.172
Venus of Ille, The. Mérimée, P.
in 823.5737
Venus's doves. Taylor, I. A. *in* 823.5053
Verdant Green. Bradley, E: 823.117
Vere of "Ours." Grant, J. 823.4800
Verena. Holt, E. S.. 808.1521
Verga, Giovanni. The house by the medlar-tree. Tr. by M.. A. Craig. (*With*) introd. by W: D. Howells. 823.7186
Vermont. *See* New England, p. 192.
Vernaleken, Theodor. In the land of marvels: folk-tales from Austria and Bohemia. With preface by E. Johnson. 808.1691
Verne, Jules. Adventures in the land of the behemoth. 823.5486
Issued also as Adventures of three Englishmen and three Russians in south Africa. (*Also*) Meridiana.
—— Adventures of a Chinaman in China. Tr. by V. Champlin. 823.5178
—— The adventures of Captain Hatteras. (2 pts.) I: The English at the north pole. II: The field of ice. 823.7126

English Fiction. *Contin.*
Verne, Jules. *Contin.*
—— The adventures of three Englishmen and three Russians in southern Africa. Tr. by H: Frith. 823.6973
—— The archipelago on fire. *in* 823.5064
—— Around the world in eighty days. Tr. by G: M. Towle. 823.3105
Issued also as Tour of the world in eighty days.
—— *Same.* 823.6918
—— At the north pole; or, the adventures of Captain Hatteras. 823.5537
—— Blockade runners. 823.5181
—— *Same. in* 823.6243; *in* 823.7091
—— The cryptogram. Pt. 2 of The giant raft. 823.4491
—— *Same.* 823.6310
—— The desert of ice; or, the further adventures of Captain Hatteras. 823.6879
—— Dick Sand; or, a captain at fifteen. *in* 823.2855
—— *Same. in* 823.5129
Issued also as Dick Sands, the boy captain.
—— Dick Sands, the boy captain. 823.6300
—— Eight hundred leagues on the Amazon. Pt. 1 of The giant raft. 823.4350
—— *Same.* 823.6310
—— The English at the north pole. 823.6880
Issued also as Adventures of Captain Hatteras.—Journey to the north pole.—Voyages and adventures of Captain Hatteras.
—— The field of ice. 823.4343
—— Five weeks in a balloon. 823.6924
—— A floating city, and, The blockade runners. 823.6243
—— *Same.* Tr. by H: Frith. 823.7091
—— From the earth to the moon direct in 97 hours 20 minutes. Tr. by L: Mercier and E. E. King. 823.5485
—— *Same.* 823.6305
—— *Same.* (*Also*) Tour of the world in eighty days. 823.2541
—— The fur country. Tr. by H: Frith. 2 pts. 823.6881-2
—— The giant raft. Pt. 1: Eight hundred leagues on the Amazon. Tr. by W. J. Gordon. 823.4350
—— *Same.* Part 2: The cryptogram. 823.4491
—— *Same.* 2 pts. (in 1). 823.6310
—— Godfrey Morgan: a Californian mystery. Tr. by W. J. Gordon. 823.4608
—— The green ray: a romance of the Scottish highlands. Tr. by M.. de Hauteville. 823.7420
—— Hector Servadac. 823.6111
—— The ice desert. (*Voyages . . . of Capt. Hatteras.*) 823.7114
—— In search of the castaways. 823.6381
Issued also as A voyage round the world.
—— A journey to the centre of the earth. 823.6160
—— Martin Paz. p. 265, *in* 823.5162
—— *Same.* p. 219, *in* 823.5204; 823.5380
—— Mathias Sandorf. 3 parts (in 1). *in* 823.5028
—— Michael Strogoff, the courier of the czar. 823.6112

English Fiction. *Contin.*
Verne, Jules. *Contin.*
—— The mysterious island; containing "Dropped from the clouds," "Abandoned," "The secret of the island." 823.5784
—— *Same.* 823.6306
—— Off on a comet! A journey through planetary space. (A sequel to "To the sun.") Tr. by E: Roth. 823.6925
—— Robur the conqueror; or, a trip round the world in a flying machine. *in* 823.5127
—— Round the moon. A sequel to "From the earth to the moon." Tr. by L: Mercier and E. E. King. 823.5487
—— *Same.* (*Also*) Dick Sand. 823.2855
—— The steam house. Pt. 1: The demon of Cawnpore. Tr. by A. D. Kingston. 823.4024
—— *Same.* Pt. 2: Tigers and traitors. Tr. A. D. Kingston. 823.4235
—— *Same.* 2 pts. 823.6193
—— Three Englishmen and three Russians in southern Africa, Adventures of. 823.6973
—— Ticket No. "9672." Tr. by L. E. Kendall. 2 pts. 823.4997
—— To the sun? A journey through planetary space. Tr. by E: Roth. 823.7127
Constitutes pt. 1 of Hector Servadac.
—— Tour of the world in eighty days. (*With his* From the earth to the moon.) *in* 823.2541
—— Tribulations of a Chinaman in China. Tr. by V. Champlin. 823.4342
—— 20,000 leagues under the sea. 823.2713
—— *Same.* 823.4980
—— Underground city; or, the child of the cavern. Tr. by W: H: G. Kingston. 823.4638
Issued also as Child of the cavern; or, strange doings underground.
—— A voyage round the world. 823.6381
—— *Same.* (3 parts):
Pt. 1: South America. 823.5547
Pt. 2: Australia. 823.5546
Pt. 3: New Zealand. 823.5545
Issued also as In search of the castaways.
—— Voyages and adventures of Captain Hatteras. The ice desert. 823.7114
—— The waif of the "Cynthia." *in* 823.4997
—— A winter in the ice, and other stories. Tr. by G: M. Towle. 823.6972
Issued also as Dr. Ox, and other stories.—From the clouds to the mountains.
—— The wreck of the Chancellor. Diary of J. R. Kazallon, passenger. (*Also*) Martin Paz. Tr. by E. Frewer. 823.5162
—— *Same.* Tr. by G: M. Towle. 823.5204
Note.—Jules Verne is by birth a Pole, and his family name is Olchewitz. "The Author," May, 1890.

Verner's pride. Wood, *Mrs.* E. (P.) 823.6015
Veronica. Zschokke, J. H. D. 823.6274
Very woman, A. 32 pp. Smedley, M. B. p. 272, *in* 823.1443
Vestal, The; or, a tale of Pompeii. Gray, T. ** 823.6252
Vestigia. Fletcher, J. C. 823.4739
Veva. Conscience, H. 823.5660

English Fiction. *Contin.*
Voyages, Imaginary. *See* Imaginary countries, voyages and travels, p. 128.
W. A sketch from Babylon. 97 pp. (*In*
Tales from Blackwood. 2d ser., v. 11.)
in 823.7495
W., A. B. *See* Wood, A. B.
W., F. The wreck of the Strathmore. 64
pp. (*In* Tales from Blackwood. 2d ser., v.
8.) *in* 823.7492
W., H. D. A feuilleton. 18 pp. (*In* Tales
from Blackwood. 2d ser., v. 8.)
in 823.7492
W., T. P. Reminiscence of a march. 14
pp. (*In* Tales from Blackwood. 3d ser.,
v. 4.) p. 195, *in* 823.7500
Wagner, Harr, *and* Bunyan, E. T. The
street and the flower. With introd. essay
by Rev. R. Mackenzie. 823.4736
Wagner, Hermann. Entdeckungsreisen in
der Wohnstube. 808.1879
Wägner, *Dr.* W. Epics and romances of the
middle ages. Adapted from the work of
Dr. W. Wägner by M. W. MacDowall, and
ed. by W. S. W. Anson. * 823.6146
Contents:—
Pt. I: The Amelung, and kindred legends. (*viz.:*
Langobardian legends. The Amelungs.—Dietrich
of Bern.)
Pt. II: The Nibelung, and kindred legends.
(*viz.:* The Nibelungs' hero.—The Nibelungs' woe.—
The Hegeling legend.—Beowulf.)
Pt. III: The Carolingian legends.—Legends of
King Arthur and the Holy Grail.—Tannhäuser.
Wags, The. 31 pp. (*In* Tales from Black-
wood, v. 7.) *in* 823.6653
Waif of the "Cynthia." Verne, J.
in 823.4997
Waif of the plains, A. Harte, F. B.
823.6999
Waiting for the verdict. Davis, *Mrs.* R.. B.
(H.) 823.5857
Waiting heart, A. Hammond, *Mrs.* —.
823.4810
Waiting race. Yates, E. H. 823.2010
Waking dream, A. 10 pp. (Bushby, *Mrs.*
—., *tr.* The Danes, *etc.*, v. 1.)
p. 263, *in* 823.6444
Wakulla. Munroe, K. 808.1372
Waldfried. Auerbach, B. 823.6628
Same. 823.6794
Wales. *See also* England.
—— Lanier, S., *ed.* Knightly legends of
Wales; or, the boy's Mabinogion, etc.
808.1899
Walford, *Mrs.* Lucy Bethia (Colquhon).
—— Bee or Beatrix. 63 pp. (*In* Tales from
Blackwood. 2d ser., v. 5.) *in* 823.7489
—— Cousins. 823.1664
—— Dick Netherby. 823.4320
—— Her great idea, and other stories.
823.5499
—— The history of a week. 823.4935
—— Lady Adelaide: a study. 33 pp. (*In*
Tales from Blackwood. 2d ser., v. 10.)
in 823.7494
—— Mr. Smith: a part of his life. 823.1665
—— *Same.* 823.6700
—— Nan: a summer scene. 65 pp. (*In*
Tales from Blackwood. 2d ser., v. 1.)
in 823.7485

English Fiction. *Contin.*
Walford, *Mrs.* Lucy Bethia (Colquhon).
Contin.
—— Pauline. 823.1812
—— Susan: a winter scene. 17 pp. (*In*
Twenty novelettes, etc.)
p. 55, *in* 823.7183
—— Troublesome daughters. 823.4044
Walford. Kirk, *Mrs.* E. W. (O.) 823.7393
Walker, Annie L. In life and in death: a
page of family history. 30 pp. (*In* Tales
from Blackwood. 2d ser., v. 10.)
in 823.7494
Walker, G: Three Spaniards. 823.1667
Wall, G: A., *joint author. See* Robinson, E:
A.
Wallace, *Mrs.* E. D. Strife: a romance of
Germany and Italy. 823.2358
Wallace, *Gen.* Lewis. Ben-Hur: a tale of
the Christ. 823.4860
—— Fair god; or, the last of the 'Tzins: a
tale of the conquest of Mexico. 823.1668
Waller, M. E. Giotto's sheep: a cathedral
story. 808.1907
—— The rose-bush of Hildesheim: a cathe-
dral story. * 823.6140
Walloth, Wilhelm. The king's treasure
house: a romance of ancient Egypt. Tr.
by M.: J. Safford. 823.6986
Walmsley, Hugh Mulleneux. Branksome
Dene: a sea tale. 823.1669
—— The chasseur d'Afrique, and The brig
and the lugger. 823.1670
Walpole, Horace, 4 *Earl of Orford.* Cas-
tle of Otranto: a Gothic story. 823.1671
—— *Same.* 823.4996; 823.5422
—— *Same.* (Barbauld, *Mrs.* A. L. (A.), *ed.*
The British novelists, v. 22.)
p. 175, *in* ** 823.2083
Walrée, *Mrs.* E. C. W. (Gobie) van. [*Chris-
tine Müller.*] The burgomaster's family;
or, weal and woe in a little world. Tr. by
Sir J: S. Lefevre. 823.6272
Walsh, Marie. Hazel Kirke. 823.4843
—— *Same.* 823.5115
Walter. Dixon, *Mrs.* —. 808.1187
Walter Goring. Cudlip, *Mrs.* A. H. (T.)
823.1584
Walter in Athens. Eddy, D. C. 808.1651
Walter in Constantinople. Eddy, D. C.
808.1650
Walter in Damascus. Eddy, D. C. 808.1649
Walter in Egypt. Eddy, D. C. 808.1646
Walter in Jerusalem. Eddy, D. C. 808.1647
Walter in Samaria. Eddy, D. C. 808.1648
Walter's tour in the east. 6 vols. Eddy, D.
C. 808.1646-51
Wanda, Countess von Szalras. La Ramée,
L. de. 823.5484
Wanderer, The. Maitland, J. A. 823.1087
Wanderers, The. Kingston, W: H: G.
808.353
Wandering heir, The. Reade, C: (*With his*
A simpleton.) *in* 823.1983
Wandering Jew. Sue, M. J. 823.2864
Same. 823.5014; 823.5799
Note.—See Reddall, H: F. Fact, fancy and
fable. pp. 517-22, *in* ** 803.34.
See also Jews.

English Fiction. *Contin.*

Wandering Willie's tale, and others. Cruik-
shank, G: 823.353
Wanderings of Æneas. Hanson, C: H:
808.1494
Wanderings of Persiles and Sigismuuda.
Cervantes Saavedra, M. de. 823.6903
Wanderings of Ulysses. Hanson, C: H:
p. 194, *in* 808.1492
Wanneta, the Sioux. Moorehead, W. K.
823.6470
Wanted—a pedigree. Finley, M. 823.562
War and peace. 3 pts. (in 6 vols.) *See* Tol-
stoï, *Count* L. N.
War ser. *See* Fosdick, C: A.
Warburton, Eliot Bartholomew G: Darien;
or, the merchant prince: a historical ro-
mance. 3 vols. 823.2048-50
Ward, *Mrs.* E.. Stuart (Phelps).
—— Beyond the gates. 823.4620
—— Doctor Zay. 823.4487
—— Friends: a duet. 823.5244
—— The gates ajar. 823.1255
—— The gates between. 823.5224
—— Hedged in. 823.1256
—— Jack the fisherman. Illus. by C. W.
Reed. 823.6196
—— The lady of Shalott. 19 pp. (Johnson,
R., *ed. Little classics*, v. 10.)
p. 89, *in* 829.133
—— The madonna of the tubs. 823.6212
—— Men, women, and ghosts. 823.1257
—— Old maids, and burglars in paradise.
823.5544
—— Sealed orders. 823.1258
—— The silent partner. 823.1259
—— The story of Avis. 823.1260
—— Zerviah Hope. 36 pp. (*In* Stories by
Amer. authors, v. 8.) p. 102, *in* 823.4709
——, *and* Ward, Herbert Dickinson. The
master of the magicians. 823.7342
Ward, Herbert Dickinson, *joint author. See*
Ward, *Mrs.* E.. S. (P.)
Ward, *Mrs.* Humphry. *See* Ward, *Mrs.* M..
A. (A.)
Ward, *Mrs.* M.. Augusta (Arnold).
—— Miss Bretherton. *in* 823.5060
—— *Same.* 823.5496
—— Robert Elsmere. 823.5342
Ward, Robert Plumer. 823.6074
—— De Vere; or, the man of independence.
2 vols. (in 1). 823.4054
—— Tremaine; or, the man of refinement.
(Anon.) ** 823.6733
Ward of the Golden Gate, A. Harte, F. B.
823.7382
Warden, Florence, *pseud. See* James, *Mrs.*
F. A. (P.)
Warden, The. Trollope, A. 823.1630
Ware, W: Aurelian; or, Rome in the third
century. 2 vols. (Sequel to Zenobia.)
823.1648-9
Issued also as Probus.
—— Julian; or, scenes in Judea. 2 vols.
823.1650-1
Warfield, *Mrs.* Catherine Ann (Ware).
—— The cardinal's daughter. A sequel to
"Ferne Fleming." 823.1654

English Fiction. *Contin.*

Warfield, *Mrs.* Catherine Ann (Ware). *Con-
tin.*
—— A double wedding; or, how she was won.
823.1655
—— Ferne Fleming. 823.1656
—— Hester Howard's temptation; a soul's
story. 823.1657
—— The household of Bouverie; or, the
elixir of gold. 2 vols. (in 1). 823.1658
—— Lady Ernestine; or, the absent Lord of
Rocheforte. 823.1659
—— Miriam's memoirs. A sequel to "Mon-
fort Hall." Being a romance of Beausein-
court. 823.1662
Issued also as Romance of Beauseincourt.
—— Monfort Hall. 823.1661
Issued also as Miriam Monfort.
—— Romance of Beauseincourt. 823.1840
Issued also as Miriam's memoirs.
—— Sea and shore. A sequel to "Miriam's
memoirs." 823.1663
Warlock o' Glenwarlock. MacDonald, G:
823.5374
Same. 823.6538
Warner, A.. Bartlett. [*Amy Lothrop.*]
—— Dollars and cents. 823.1672
—— My brother's keeper. 823.1673
——, *joint author. See* Warner, S.
Warner, C: Dudley. A little journey in the
world. 823.6579
——, *joint author. See* Clemens, S: L.
Warner, Susan. [*E.. Wetherell.*]
—— Daisy. Continued from "Melbourne
house." 2 vols. (in 1). 823.1674
—— Diana. 823.1675
—— The hills of the Shatemuc. 823.1677
—— The letter of credit. 823.1862
—— Melbourne house. 2 vols. (in 1).
823.1678
—— My desire. 823.1679
—— The old helmet. 823.1929
—— Pine needles. 823.1680
—— Queechy. 2 vols. (in 1). 823.1681
—— *Same.* 2 vols. 823.6582-3
—— The wide, wide world. 823.1683
——, *and* Warner, A.. Bartlett. [*Amy Loth-
rop.*] The gold of Chickaree. (Sequel to
Wych Hazel.) 823.1676
—— Say and seal. 2 vols. (in 1). 823.1682
—— Wych Hazel. 823.1684
Warren, S: Merchant's clerk. 823.4994
—— Now and then. 823.1685
—— Passages from the diary of a late physi-
cian. 823.6974
—— Ten thousand a year. 823.1689
Warriner, E: A. Victor La Tourette. By a
broad churchman. 823.1690
Wars of the Roses. Edgar, J: G: 808.801
Was he guilty? Dupuy, E. A. 823.501
Washburn, K.. Sedgwick. Perfect love cast-
eth out fear. 823.4081
Washburn, W: Tucker. Fair Harvard: a
story of American college life. 823.7115
Washington, G:, *President of the U. S.*
(1732-1799.) Abbott, J: S. C. George
Washington; or, life in America one hun-
dred years ago. 808.543
—— Brown, E. E. Young folks' life of W.
808.1652

English Fiction. *Contin.*
Webster, Albert Falvey.
—— Miss Eunice's glove. 27 pp. (*In* Stories by Amer. authors, v. 6.)
p. 117, *in* 823.4707
—— An operation in money. 30 pp. (*In* Stories by Amer. authors, v. 1.)
p. 146, *in* 823.4702
Wedded and parted. Braine, *Mrs.* C.. M. (L.)   *in* 823.5099
Wedded hands. (Anon.)   823.4834
Same.   *in* 823.5042
Wee Willie Winkie, and other child stories. Kipling, R.   p. 207, *in* 823.7345
Week of passion, A. Jenkins, E: 823.5061
Weighed and wanting. MacDonald, G:
823.4561
Weird tales. 2 vols. Hoffmann, E. T. W.
823.4884-5
Welcker, Adair. Snob papers: a humorous novel.   823.4888
Well in the desert. Holt, E. S..   823.5768
Wellfields, The. Fothergill, J.   823.2336
Wells, H: P. City boys in the woods; or, a trapping venture in Maine.   808.1802
Wells, Mrs. Kate (Gannett). Two modern women.   823.7515
Wenderholme. Hamerton, P. G.   823.693
Wentworth, Walter, *pseud.* See Gilman, J: B.
Wept of Wish-Ton-Wish. Cooper, J. F.
823.316
Same.   *in* 823.7460
Werner, Ernst, *pseud.* See Bürstenbinder, E..
Wesselhoeft, Mrs. E.. Foster (Pope). The winds, the woods, and the wanderer: a fable for children.   808.1692
Wessex tales. Hardy, T: 823.6190
West, B: 1738–1820. Hawthorne, N. Biographical stories. 13 pp. (*In his* Tales and sketches.) 1889.   p. 144, *in* 824.414
West Lawn. Holmes, *Mrs.* M.. J.. (H.)
823.803
Westall, W: Love and war. 8 pp. (*In* Twenty novelettes, etc.)
p. 197, *in* 823.7183
Westbury, Hugh. "Acte."   823.7556
Western clearings. Kirkland, *Mrs.* C. M. (S.)   823.7109
West Indies.
—— Fenn, G: M. Commodore Junk.
in 823.6698
—— Hearn, L. Youma: the story of a West-Indian slave.   823.6354
—— Kingsley, C: At last: a Christmas in the West Indies.   823.5746
—— Scott, M. Cruise of the Midge.
823.1389
—— Tom Cringle's log.   823.1390
San Domingo.
—— Fresneau, *Mrs.* A. Theresa at San Domingo: a tale of the negro insurrection of 1791.   823.6938
—— Gilliam, E. W. 1791: a tale of San Domingo.   823.7174
Trinidad. Allen, G. In all shades.
823.5447

English Fiction. *Contin.*
West Indies. *Contin.*
Note.—See Froude, J. A. English in the West Indies. 1888. 9179.48.—Hearn, L. A midsummer trip to the W. I. (*Harper's mag.*, v. 77, 1888.) *in* * 51.469*;—Two years in the French West Indies. 1890. 9179.51.—St. John, *Sir* S. Hayti. 1889. 979. 21. (*See also* Froude on the West Indies. *Saturday review*, v. 68, p. 336.) * 52.4850.—Winsor, J., *ed.* Narrative and critical history of America. 8 vols. (*See* index, v. 8.) * 970.127-127*.
See also **Catalogues** of this Library.
No. 2, 1880, p. 248.   No. 4, 1884, p. 313.
No. 3, 1882, p. 204.   No. 5, 1888, p. 385.
See also Index to **Appleton's** Ann. cyclop., 1876–1887. ** 31.36[11].
See also Index to **Consular reports.** 1880–1885; 1886–1889. 2 vols. (U. S. Pub. Docs. *Dept. of State.*) ** 350.5496[1.2].
See also references *in* Index to **Harper's** monthly. *in* ** 51.475.
See also **Poole's** Index to (1882). p. 1,401, *in* ** 50.1;—*Same.* Jan. 1, 1882–Jan. 1, 1887. p. 470, *in* ** 50.1².
See also **United States.** Catalogue of the government publications. 1774–1881. p. 1,387, *in* ** 15. 202.
Westminster Abbey. Robinson, J.. 823.2026
Westward ho! Kingsley, C: 823.935
Wetherel affair, The. De Forest, J: W: .
823.5853
Wetherell, E.., *pseud.* See Warner, S.
Wetterbergh, Carl Anton. [*Uncle Adam.*] The fatal chain. From the Swedish. 40 pp. (Bushby, *Mrs.* —., *tr.* The Danes, etc., v. 2.)   p. 263, *in* 823.6445
—— The hereditary goblet. From the Swedish. 26 pp. (Bushby, *Mrs.* —., *tr.* The Danes, etc., v. 3.)   p. 229, *in* 823.6446
Weyman, Stanley J. The house of the wolf.   823.7299
Whale fishery.
—— Ballantyne, R. M. Fighting the whales.
808.674
—— —— *Same.*   *in* 808.1266 ; *in* 808.1284
—— —— World of ice; or, whaling cruise of "The Dolphin," and the adventures of her crew in the polar regions.   808.265
—— Hart, *Col.* J. C. Miriam Coffin.
823.6110
—— —— *Same.*   823.6210
—— Kingston, W: H: G. Peter Trawl; or, the adventures of a whaler.   808.1014
—— South sea whaler: story of the loss of the "Champion," etc.   808.352
—— Melville, H. Moby-Dick; or, the whale.
823.1146
—— Nordhoff, C: Whaling and fishing.
808.168
Note.—See **Aldrich,** H. L. Arctic Alaska and Siberia. 1889. 9177.617.—**Beale,** T: Sketch of a south sea whaling voyage. 1839. p. 193, *in* ** 599. 14.—**Cheever,** H: T. The whale and his captors. 910.131.—**Leslie,** *Sir* J:, *and others. In their* Discov. . . . in polar seas, etc. p. 297, *in* 808.12.—**Markham,** A. H. A whaling cruise to Baffin's bay. 1874. 9191.92.—**Scammon,** C: M. The marine mammals, with account of the American whale-fishery. 1874. * 599.33.—**U. S. Fish Commission.** Fisheries and fishing industries of the U. S. By G. B. Goode. 2 vols. v. 1: Text. v. 2: Plates. 1884. * 639.28-9. — **U. S. Fish Comm'r** (Starbuck). Report. 1875-6. ** 350.306.—**Weeden,** W: B. The whale fishery. 1713-1745. 17 pp. (*In his* Econ. . . . hist. of New England, v. 1.) 1890. p. 430, *in* 974.149.
See also Index to **Consular reports.** 1880–1885; 1886–1889. 2 vols. (U. S. Pub. Docs. *Dept. of State.*) ** 350.5496[1.2].
See also references in **Encyc. Brit.** index. ** 32. 395.

English Fiction. *Contin.*
Whaling and fishing. Nordhoff, C: 808.168
. **Wharton**, T: [*Ethel Jones.*] A latter-day saint: being the story of the conversion of Ethel Jones, related by herself. 823.4635
What came of it. Stitzel, *Mrs.* H. V.
823.1520
What can she do? Roe, E: P. 823.1361
What dreams may come. Atherton, *Mrs.* G. F. (H.) 823.7359
What might have been expected. Stockton, F. R: 823.6541
What the swallow sang. Spielhagen, F.
823.6823
What will he do with it? 2 pts. (in 1). Lytton, E: G: E. L. Bulwer- 823.6679
Same. 2 vols. 823.1047-8; 823.5973-4
What's his offence? (Anon.) 823.4837
What's mine's mine. MacDonald, G:
in 823.5082
Wheel of fire. Bates, A. 823.4874
Wheelwright, J: Tyler. A child of the century. 823.5430
——, *joint author. See* Grant, R.
When a man's single. Barrie, J. M. 823.6371
When we were boys. O'Brien, W: 823.7023
Where love is, there God is also. 17 pp. Tolstoi, L. N. 823.6531
Where the battle was fought. Murfree, M.. N. 823.4893
Which loved him best? Brame, *Mrs.* C.. M. (L.) 823.5115
Which shall it be? Hector, *Mrs.* A. (F.)
823.747
Same. *in* 823.5098
Whim, A, and its consequences. James, G: P. R. 823.881
Whimsical wooing, A. Barrili, A. G.
823.4481
Whist at our club. 22 pp. (*In* Tales from Blackwood. 2d ser., v. 12.) *in* 823.7496
Whitby, B.. The awakening of Mary Fenwick. 823.7357
—— Part of the property. 823.7358
White, Alfred Ludlow. Doctor Hildreth.
823.1940
White, C. H., *pseud. See* Chaplin, H. W.
White, Caroline Earle. Love in the tropics: a romance of the south seas. 823.6997
White, Eliza Orne. Miss Brooks. 823.7184
White, J: Silas, *ed.* The boys' and girls' Herodotus: being parts of the history of Herodotus. 808.1880
—— The boys' and girls' Plutarch: being parts of the "lives" of Plutarch. 808.1881
White, R: Grant. Fate of Mansfield Humphreys, with the episode of Mr. Washington Adams in England and an apology—
823.4783
White, W. Hale. [*Mark Rutherford.*] Revolution in Tanner's lane. By M: Rutherford. Ed. by his friend Reuben Shapcott.
823.5272
White as snow. Mayo, *Mrs.* L. (F.)
823.5723
White cockade. Grant, J. 823.657
White elephant. Dalton, W: 808.872
White fawn, The. Johnson, *Col.* —.
in * 823.6194

English Fiction. *Contin.*
White heather. Black, W: 823.4841
White heron, and other stories. Jewett, S.. O.
823.5262
White lies. Reade, C: 823.1985
White Marie. Harben, W. N. 823.7258
White rose, The. Melville, G: J: Whyte-
823.1153
Same. *in* ** 823.4663
White rose of Langley. Holt, E. S.
808.1528
White slaves of monopolies, The; or, John Fitz Patrick, the miner, soldier and workingman's friend. (Anon.) 823.4806
White Wings. Black, W: 823.2350
White witch, The. (Anon.) 823.4989
Whitefriars. Robinson, J.. 823.1346
Whitehall. Robinson, J.. 823.1347
White-Jacket. Melville, H. 823.1149
Whiteladies. Oliphant, *Mrs.* M. O. (W.)
823.1219
Whitney, *Mrs.* Adeline Dutton (Train).
—— Bonnyborough. 823.4883
—— Faith Gartney's girlhood. 823.1693
—— The Gayworthys: a story of threads and thrums. 823.1694
—— Hitherto: a story of yesterdays.
823.1695
—— Odd, or even? 823.2024
—— The other girls. 823.1696
—— Patience Strong's outings. 823.1697
—— Real folks. 823.1698
—— Sights and insights: Patience Strong's story of over the way. 2 vols.
823.1699-1700
—— A summer in Leslie Goldthwaite's life.
823.1701
—— We girls: a home story. (Sequel to "A summer in Leslie Goldthwaite's life.")
823.1702
—— Zerub Throop's experiment. 823.1703
——, *and others.* The New England storybook. Stories by famous New England authors. 808.1864
Whittlebridge. 53 pp. (*In* Tales from Blackwood. 2d ser., v. 12.) *in* 823.7496
Whittlesey, Elsie Leigh. The hemlock swamp, and a season at the White Sulphur Springs. 823.4764
Whitty, E: Michael. Friends of Bohemia; or, phases of London life. 2 vols.
823.6155-6
"Who breaks—pays." Jenkin, *Mrs.* H. C. (J.) 823.897
Who saved the ship? Williams, A. B.
808.1640
Who shall be victor? Dupuy, E. A. 823.502
Who was Philip? Adams, H: C. 808.1609
Who was she? 45 pp. Taylor, B.
p. 5, *in* 823.4702
Whole history of Grandfather's chair. Hawthorne, N. *in* 808.548
Whom Kathie married. Douglas, A. M.
823.4502
Whose fault? Harrison, J. 823.7381
Why did he marry her? Dupuy, E. A.
823.503
Why did he not die? Volckhausen, A. v.
823.6820

English Fiction. *Contin.*
Why I did not become a sailor. Ballantyne, R. M.   p. 263, *in* 808.213
Why Thomas was discharged. 25 pp. Arnold, G: *in* 823.4706
Whyte, Violet. Her Johnnie.   *in* 823.5133
Wichert, Ernst Auguste August Georg. The green gate. Tr. by Mrs. A. L. Wister.
823.6819
Wicked girl, A. Hay, M.. C.   823.5078
Wide, wide world. Warner, S.   823.1683
Widow and the marquess. Hook, T. E:
823.825
Widow Goldsmith's daughter. Smith, J. P.
823.1469
Widow Guthrie. Johnston, R: M. 823.7390
Widow Lerouge. Gaboriau, É.   823.2463
Same.   *in* 823.5029
Widower, The. Smith, J. P.   823.1470
Widow's son, The. Arthur, T. S.
p. 149, *in* 823.5911
Widow's son, The. Southworth, *Mrs.* E. D. E. (N.)   823.1981
Wieland. Brown, C: B.   823.142
Same.   * 823.6200
Wife, The. Maxwell, *Lady* C. E.. S.. (S.)
Stirling-   p. 97, *in* ** 823.6747
Wife in name only. Brame, *Mrs.* C.. M. (L.)   823.5099
Wife of a vain man. Schwartz, *Mrs.* M. S. (B.)   823.6091
Wife's duty, A. Opie, *Mrs.* A. (A.)
p. 209, *in* 823.6136
Wife's engagement ring, The. Arthur, T. S.
823.5757
Wife's secret, The. Brame, *Mrs.* C.. M. (L.)
in 823.5099
Wife's secret, The. Stephens, *Mrs.* A. S. (W.)   823.1973
Wife's tragedy, A. Fleming, *Mrs.* M. A. (E.)
823.4205
Wife's victory, The, and other novelettes. Southworth, *Mrs.* E. D. E. (N.) 823.1514
Wiggin, *Mrs.* Kate Douglas (Smith). A summer in a cañon: a California story.
823.6189
Wightman, M. G. Mrs. Carr's companion.
823.4993
Wigwam and the cabin. Simms, W: G.
823.1439
Wilbrandt, Adolf von. Fridolin's mystical marriage: a study of an original founded on reminiscences of a friend. Tr. by C. Bell.   823.4759
—— The pilot captain. 69 pp. (*In* Masterpieces of Germ. fiction.)   *in* 823.7552
Wild and weird. Campbell, *Sir* G.
823.7244
Wild Irish girl. 3 vols. Morgan, *Lady* S. (O.)   * 823.2361-3
Wild life. Reid, *Capt.* T: M.   808.429
Wild life under the equator. Du Chaillu, P. B.   808.694
Wild man of the west. Ballantyne, R. M.
808.703
Wild men and wild beasts. Cumming, *Lt.-Col.* W: G.   823.6581
Wild rose of Lough Gill. Smyth, P. G.
823.7306

English Fiction. *Contin.*
Wild times. ;Caddell, C. M..   823.164
Wild western scenes. Jones, J: B. 823.906
Wilde, Oscar O'Flahertie Fingal Wills. The happy prince, and other tales. 808.1643
Wilfrid Cumbermede. MacDonald, G:
823.5370
Wilhelm Meister's apprenticeship. Göthe, J. W.   823.2133
Same. 2 vols.   823.6799-6800
Wilkins, *Rev.* G: Body and soul. 2 vols. (in 1). (Anon.)   ** 823.6736
Wilkins, M.. Eleanor.
—— The adventures of Ann: stories of colonial times from original documents and family traditions.   808.1932
—— A humble romance and other stories.
823.7336
—— A New England nun, and other stories.
823.7557
Wilkins, W. A. The Cleverdale mystery; or, the machine and its wheels: a story of American life.   823.4485
Wilkinson, J. A. A real Robinson Crusoe . . . story of . . . a company of castaways on a Pacific island.   808.1698
Will, The. 52 pp. Pardoe, J.
p. 186, *in* 823.1443
Will Denbigh, Nobleman. Craik, *Mrs.* D. M. (M.)   823.2003
Wille, E.. de. Johannes Olaf. Tr. by F. E. Bunnètt.   823.4088
Willful maid, A.   *in* 823.5095
Willful young woman.   *in* 823.5145
Same.   *in* 823.5187
Williams, Annie Bowles [*Jak.*]
—— The giant dwarf.   808.1639
—— The man of the family. (*With her* Who saved the ship?) *in* 808.1640
—— Professor Johnny.   808.1641
—— Who saved the ship; and, The man of the family.   808.1640
Williams, C:, *joint author. See* Forbes, A.
Williams, H. L., *ed.* Ruy Blas; or, the king's rival: a historical romance. Founded on the drama by V. Hugo.   823.7261
Williams, *Dr.,* and Williams, *Mrs.* Harold. Mr. and Mrs. Morton. (Anon.) 823.4550
Williams, Robert Folkestone. Shakespeare and his friends; or, the golden age of merrie England. (*Also*) The secret passion. (A sequel to ''Youth of Shakespeare.'') (*And*) The youth of Shakespeare.   ** 823.6260
Williamson, *Mrs.* Emma S.. (Carmichael). Her own sister.   *in* 823.4983
Willie and the mortgage. Abbott, J.
in 808.580
Willis, Nathaniel Parker.
—— Beauty and the beast. 14 pp. (Johnson, R., *ed. Little classics,* v. 4.)
p. 85, *in* 829.127
—— Two buckets in a well. 25 pp. (*In* Stories by Amer. authors, v. 4.)
p. 57, *in* 823.4705
Willis the pilot: a sequel to the Swiss family Robinson; or, adventures of an emigrant family wrecked on an unknown coast of the Pacific ocean. (Anon.)   808.373

English Fiction. *Contin.*
Willoughby, F. Fairy guardians. 808.1693
Willy Reilly, and his dear Coleen bawn.
Carleton, W: 823.180
Wilson, *Mrs.* Augusta J.. (Evans).
—— Beulah. 823.4013
—— Inez: a tale of the Alamo. 823.4009
—— Infelice. 823.1707
—— Macaria. 823.1708
—— St. Elmo. 823.1709
—— Vashti; or, "until death us do part."
823.1710
—— *Same.* 823.4012
Wilson, J: Lights and shadows of Scottish
life. 823.7067
—— The snow-storm. 22 pp. (Johnson,
R., *ed. Little classics*, v. 7.)
p. 184, *in* 829.130
Wilson, John Mackay, *and others.* Tales of
the borders and of Scotland: historical, tra-
ditionary, and imaginative. 24 vols. (in 12).
823.1711-1722
Winds, the woods, and the wanderer. Wes-
selhoeft, *Mrs.* E.. F. (P.) 808.1692
Windsor Castle. Ainsworth, W: H. 823.32
Wing of Azrael. Caird, *Mrs.* M. (A.)
823.7199
Wing-and-Wing. Cooper, J. F. 823.317
Same. 823.6173; 823.7468
Winged lion, The. De Mille, J. 808.172
Winged word, A. Tincker, M.. A. 823.6279
Wingfield, Lewis. The curse of Koshiu: a
chronicle of old Japan. 823.7192
Winifred Bertram. Charles, *Mrs.* E.. (R.)
823.212
Winifred, countess of Nithsdale. 2d ed.
Sullivan, *Mrs.* A. (W.) ** 823.6761
Winifred Power. Darrell, J. *in* 823.5073
Winning his way. Coffin, C: C. 823.245
Winter, J: Strange, *pseud. See* Stannard,
Mrs. H. E. V. (P.)
Winter in the ice, and other stories. Verne, J.
823.6972
Winter story, A. Peard, F.. M.. 823.1247
Winther, Christian. *See* Winther, R. W. C.
F.
Winther, Rasmus Willads Christian Ferdi-
nand. The confessional. 12 pp. (Bushby,
Mrs. —., *tr. The Danes, etc.*, v. 1.)
p. 273, *in* 823.6444
Winthrop, Theodore.
—— Cecil Dreeme. With a biog. sketch of
the author by G: W: Curtis. 823.1723
—— Edwin Brothertoft. 823.1724
—— John Brent. 823.1725
—— Life in the open air, and other papers.
823.5612
—— Love and skates. 66 pp. (*In* Famous
stories. By De Quincey, and others.)
p. 85, *in* 823.1778
—— *Same.* (Johnson, R., *ed. Little classics,*
v. 6.) p. 7, *in* 829.129
Wiseman, N: Patrick Stephen, *Cardinal.*
Fabiola; or, the church of the catacombs.
823.4615
Wister, *Mrs.* Annis Lee (Furness), *tr.*
Bethusy-Huc, V., *Gräfin.* The Eichhofs. 823.4345
Bürstenbinder, E.. Banned and blessed. 823.4614
—— Saint Michael. 823.5762

English Fiction. *Contin.*
Wister, *Mrs.* Annis Lee (Furness), *tr. Con-
tin.*
Friedrich, *Mrs.* B. (H.) From hand to hand.
823.4548
Glumer, C. von. A noble name. 823.4549
Hackländer, F. W. Enchanting and enchanted.
808.1493
Harder, L. A family feud. 823.6802
Hartner, E. Severa. 823.4271
Hillern, *Mrs.* W. (B.) von. Only a girl.
823.5548; 823.5617
John, E. At the councillor's. 823.2775
—— The bailiff's maid. 823.4060
—— Countess Gisela. 823.2654
—— Gold Elsie. 823.6601
—— In the Schillingscourt. 823.2023; 823.2444
—— The little moorland princess. 823.3052
—— The old mam'selle's secret. 823.5781
—— The second wife. 823.2455
Kirschner, L. Erlach court. 823.6578
—— "O thou, my Austria !" 823.7415
Schmieden, *Mrs.* E. (J.) Margarethe. 823.6808
Schobert, H. Picked up in the streets. 823.5271
Streckfuss, A. F. K: Castle Hohenwald. 823.5549
—— Quicksands. 823.4762
—— Too rich. 823.6824
Volckhausen, A. von. Why did he not die?
823.6820
Wichert, E. The green gate. 823.6819
Witch of Melton hill. By the author of
"Mount St. Lawrence." 823.1384
Witch Winnie. Champney, *Mrs.* E.. (W.)
808.1913
Witcherley ways: a Christmas tale. 47 pp.
(*In* Tales from Blackwood. 2d ser., v. 10.)
in 823.7494
Witch-hampton Hall: five scenes in the life
of its last lady. 87 pp. (*In* Tales from
Blackwood. 2d ser., v. 3.) *in* 823.7487
Witch's head. Haggard, H: R. *in* 823.5071
Same. 823.7159
With Clive in India. Henty, G: A. 808.1474
With fire and sword. Sienkiewicz, H.
823.6338
With Gauge & Swallow, attorneys. Tour-
gée, A. W. 823.7555
With harp and crown. Besant, W., *and*
Rice, J. 823.6409
With Lee in Virginia. Henty, G: A.
808.1670
With the best intentions. Terhune, *Mrs.* M..
V. (H.) 823.7195
With the immortals. 2 vols. (in 1). Craw-
ford, F. M. 823.5542
With Wolfe in Canada. Henty, G: A.
808.1477
Within an ace. Jenkin, *Mrs.* H. C. (J.)
823.898
Within an inch of his life. Gaboriau, É.
823.5070
Same. 823.6080
Within iron walls. Lucas, A.
p. 190, *in* 823.1020
Within the capes. Pyle, H. 823.4882
Within the enemy's line. Adams, W: T.
808.1536
Without a home. Roe, E: P. 823.7443
Wives and widows. Stephens, *Mrs.* A. S.
(W.) 823.1977
Wives of men of genius. Daudet, A.
823.6340
Wizard's son, The. Oliphant, *Mrs.* M. O.
(W.) 823.5466
Woffington, Margaret. Reade, C: Peg Wof-
fington. 823.1293

English Fiction. *Contin.*
Woillez, *Mme.* Natalie. The orphan of
Moscow; or, the young governess. Tr. by
Mrs. J. Sadlier. 823.6919
Wolf at the door. 823.2002
Wolf boy of China. Dalton, W: 808.871
Wolfe, *Gen.* James. (1726–1759.)
—— Henty, G: A. With Wolfe in Canada.
808.1477
Note.—For life and character, *see* Grant, J.
Memoir of Wolfe. (*With his* Constable of France.)
p. 69, *in* 823.623.—Irving, W. Wolfe and Montcalm
at Quebec. 13 pp. p. 355, *in* 973.625.—Parkman,
F. Montcalm and Wolfe. 2 vols. 1885. 972.25-6.—
Walpole, H. Letters. (*See* index, * 816.27.) 9 vols.
* 816.19-27.—Winsor, J. Narrative and critical his-
tory of America. v. 5, p. 541; v. 8, p. 131. * 970.
127²; 127ᵇ.
See also references *in* Alllbone's Dict. of Eng.
lit. v. 3. p. 2,812, *in* ** 803.8.
Wolfert's Roost, and other papers. Irving,
W. 823.1808
Wolff, Julius. The salt master of Lüneburg.
Tr. by W. H: Winslow and E.. R. Winslow.
823.7185
Wolfings, A tale of the house of. Morris,
W: 829.697
Woman I loved and the woman who loved
me. Blagden, I. *in* 823.5040
Woman in white. Collins, W: W. 823.268
Woman of fire. Belot, A. 823.7526
Woman of honor, A. Bunner, H: C.
823.4595
Woman of the world. 3 vols. Robinson, F..
M. 823.7329-31
Woman the stronger. Hagg, W: J. 823.1804
Woman-hater, A. Reade, C: 823.1984
Woman's error, A. Brame, *Mrs.* C.. M. (L.)
823.5118
Woman's friendship. Aguilar, G. 823.11
Woman's kingdom. Craik, *Mrs.* D. M. (M.)
823.342
Woman's love, A. 34 pp. Opie, *Mrs.* A. (A.)
p. 175, *in* 823.6136
Woman's love story, A. *in* 823.5137
Woman's ransom, A. Robinson, F: W:
823.4693
Woman's reason, A. Howells, W: D.
823.4625
Woman's reward. 2 vols. Maxwell, *Lady*
C. E.. S.. (S.) Stirling- ** 823.6746-7
Woman's temptation, A. Brame, *Mrs.* C..
M. (L.) *in* 823.5126
Woman's vengeance, A. Payn, J. 823.6060
Woman's war, A. Brame, *Mrs.* C.. M. (L.)
823.5134
Woman's word, and how she kept it. Town-
send, V. F.. 823.1600
Won by waiting. Bayly, A. E. 823.6563
Won, not wooed. Payn, J. 823.6061
Wonder-book, A. Hawthorne, N. 808.548
Same. 808.1890
Wonderful woman, A. Fleming, *Mrs.* M. A.
(E.) 823.582
Wonder-world stories. Pabke, M., *and* Pit-
man, *Mrs.* M. J. (D.) 808.393
Wondrous strange. Newby, *Mrs.* C. J.
823.5913
Wood, A. B. Cupid on crutches; or, one
summer at Narragansett Pier. 823.1647
Wood, C.. Dunning. A step aside. 823.6559

English Fiction. *Contin.*
Wood, *Mrs.* Ellen (Price).
—— Bessy Rane. 823.6011
—— The castle's heir; or, Lady Adelaide's
oath. 823.6010
Issued also as Lady Adelaide's oath, *and* Out of
the deep.
—— The Channings. 823.6388
—— Clara Lake's dream. (*With her* The
Red Court farm.) *in* 823.6227
—— Dene Hollow. 823.6009
—— East Lynne. 823.1731
—— Edina; or, missing since midnight.
823.6361
—— Elster's folly. 823.6008
—— A life's secret. (*With her* The mystery.)
in 823.2921
—— Mail-cart robbery. *in* 823.4994
—— The master of Greylands. 823.6007
—— Mystery: a love story. 823.6229
Issued also as Anne Hereford.
—— *Same.* (*Also*) A life's secret. 823.2921
—— The nobleman's wife. (*With her* The
Red Court farm.) *in* 823.6227
—— Oswald Cray. 823.6006
—— The Red Court farm. 823.1739
—— *Same.* (*Also*) The nobleman's wife,
(*and*) Clara Lake's dream. 823.6227
—— Roland Yorke. A sequel to "The Chan-
nings." 823.6005
—— St. Martin's eve. 823.6016
—— Squire Trevlyn's heir; or, Trevlyn Hold.
823.6017
Issued also as Trevlyn Hold.
—— The surgeon's daughters. 35 pp.
in 823.5036
—— Verner's pride: a tale of domestic life.
823.6015
Wood, *Mrs.* H: *See* Wood, *Mrs.* E. (P.)
Wood, J: G: Routledge's picture book of
animals. 808.1883
—— Routledge's picture book of birds.
808.1884
—— Routledge's picture book of fishes, in-
sects, etc. 808.1885
Wood, Roland A. [*Paul Cushing.*] A bud
that lived. 30 pp. (*In* Tales from Black-
wood. 3d ser., v. 5.) p. 361, *in* 823.7501
Wood magic: a fable. Jefferies, R:
823.1595
Woodburn Grange. Howitt, W: 823.833
Woodcraft. Simms, W: G. 823.1440
Wooden Clara. Conscience, H. *in* 823.5704
Woodlanders, The. Hardy, T: *in* 823.5136
Same. *in* 823.5186
Woodman, The. James, G: P. R. 823.882
Wood-rangers, The. Reid, T: M. 823.7145
Woods, K.. Pearson. Metzerott, shoemaker.
823.6995
Woods, *Mrs.* Margaret L. (Bradley). A vil-
lage tragedy. 823.5454
Woodstock. Scott, *Sir* W. 823.1414
Same. ** 823.6032; 823.7477
Wooed and married. Carey, R. N.
823.2993
Wooing o't. Hector, *Mrs.* A. (F.) 823.748
Same. *in* 823.5070
Woolsey, S.. Chauncey. [*Susan Coolidge.*]
—— For summer afternoons. 823.4105
—— Just sixteen. 808.1534

English Fiction. *Contin:*
Woolson, Constance Fenimore.
—— Anne. 823.4468
—— Castle Nowhere: lake-country sketches.
823.4085
—— East Angels. 823.4966
—— For the major. 823.4539
—— Miss Grief. 35 pp. (*In* Stories by
Amer. authors, v. 4.) p. 5, *in* 823.4705
—— Rodman the keeper: southern sketches.
823.2039
Word only a word, A. Ebers, G. M. 823.7452
Work. Alcott, L.. M. 823.35
Working and waiting. Brock, *Mrs.* F.. E..
G. (R.) Carey- 823.4337
World between them. Brame, *Mrs.* C.. M.
(L.) 823.4768
Same. *in* 823.5137
World by the fireside, The. Kirby, M.., *and*
Kirby, E.. 808.1891
World in the church. Riddell, *Mrs.* C.. E.
L. (C.) 823.1338
World of ice. Ballantyne, R. M. 808.265
World we live in, The. Crawford, O. J: F:
823.4793
World went very well then. Besant, W.
823.5145
Same. 823.5187
World's desire, The. Haggard, H: R., *and*
Lang, A. 823.7380
World's verdict, The. Hopkins, M:, *Jr.*
823.5453
Wratislaw, Albert H:, *tr.* Sixty folk-tales
from exclusively Slavonic sources. With
introd. and notes. 823.6946
Wraxall, F: C: Lascelles. Golden-hair.
823.1745
Wreck of the Chancellor. Verne, J.
823.5162
Same. 823.5204
Wreck of the "Copeland." 14 pp. Haggard,
H: R. *in* 823.6606
Wreck of the "Grosvenor." Russell, W: C.
in 823.6702
Wreck of the Red Bird. Eggleston, G: C.
808.1142
Wrecked but not ruined. Ballantyne, R. M.
808.1265
Same. *in* 808.1269
Wrecked in port. Yates, E. H. 823.5891
Wrecked on Labrador. Stearns, W. A.
808.1672
Wright, D. Thew. Mrs. Armington's ward;
or, the inferior sex. 823.4092
Wright, Henrietta Christian.
—— Children's stories in American history.
808.1581
Contents:—Ancient America.—The mound-build-
ers.—The red men.—The Northmen.—Columbus
and the discovery of America.—The Cabots.—Amer-
icus Vespucius.—Ponce de Leon.—Vasco Nunez de
Balboa, the discoverer of the Pacific ocean.—Cabeca
de Vaca.—Hernando Cortez and the conquest of
Mexico.—Pizarro and the conquest of Peru.—Fer-
dinand de Soto, the discoverer of the Mississippi.—
Verrazano.—Jacques Cartier.—The Huguenots.—Sir
Walter Raleigh.—Story of Pocahontas, the Indian
princess.—Settlement of Maine, and discovery of
Lake Champlain.—Henry Hudson and the Knicker-
bockers.—The Pilgrims and the settlement of New
England.—La Salle.—Story of Acadia.—Story of
Pontiac.—The revolution.
—— *Same.* 808.1695

English Fiction. *Contin.*
Wright, Henrietta Christian. *Contin.*
—— Children's stories in English literature.
From Taliesin to Shakespeare. 808.1533
Contents:—The old British songs.—The old Saxon
songs.—Caedmon.—The venerable Bede.—King Al-
fred.—The romance of King Arthur.—Robin Hood:
the hero of the people.—Langlande.—Gower.—Sir
John Mandeville.—Geoffrey Chaucer.—Wickliffe.—
Caxton.—Edmund Spenser and The faëry queene.—
Sir Philip Sidney.—The rise of the drama.
—— Children's stories of American progress.
808.1696
Contents:—Beginning of western settlement.—
The Barbary pirates.—Purchase of Louisiana.—Ex-
pedition of Lewis and Clarke to the Pacific ocean.—
First steamboat.—Battle of Tippecanoe.—War of
1812.—Purchase of Florida.—Story of slavery.—
Story of the railroad.—Indian troubles in Florida.—
Story of the telegraph.—Annexation of Texas.—
Mexican war.—Settlement of the northwest bound-
ary.—Discovery of gold.—The rebellion.—The south
after the war.
—— Children's stories of the great scientists.
Ports. 808.1644
Contents:—Galileo and the wonders of the tele-
scope, 1564-1642.—Kepler and the pathways of the
planets, 1571-1635.—Newton and the finding of the
world secret, 1642-1727.—Franklin and the identity
of lightning and electricity, 1706-1790. — Charles
Linnæus and the story of the flowers, 1707-1778.—
Herschel and the story of the stars, 1738-1822.—
Rumford and the relations of motion and heat,
1753-1814.—Cuvier and the animals of the past, 1769-
1832.—Humboldt and nature in the new world, 1769-
1859.—Davy and nature's magicians, 1778-1829.—Faraday and the production of electricity by magnet-
ism, 1791-1867.—Charles Lyell and the story of the
rocks, 1797-1875.—Agassiz and the story of the animal kingdom, 1807-1874.—Tyndall and diamagnet-
ism and radiant heat, 1825.—Kirchoff and the story
told by sunbeam and starbeam, 1824-1887.—Darwin
and Huxley.
—— The princess Liliwinkins, and other stories. 808.1558
Wright, *Mrs.* Julia (McNair).
—— Patriot and Tory; one hundred years
ago: a tale of the revolution. 823.6021
—— (Stories of) Twelve noble men. 808.1540
Contents:—Booz, Martin.—Howard, J:—King,
Rev. Jonas.—Krummacher, F: W.—Lyman, H:—
Miller, Roger.—Newton, J:—Sanctis, Luigi de.—
Savonarola, Girolamo.—Wesley, J: and C:—
Whitefield, G:—Wilberforce, W:
Wright, *Mrs.* S.. A. The crimson star; or,
the midnight vision: a romance founded on
facts. 823.1746
Wrong box, The. Stevenson, R. L:, *and*
Osbourne, L. 823.6985
Wuthering heights. Brontë, E. 823.130
Wyandotté. Cooper, J. F. 823.318
Same. 823.7469
Wyatt, T: The cottage by the river. 56 pp.
(*In* Tales from Blackwood. 2d ser., v. 11.)
in 823.7495
Wych Hazel. Warner, S., *and* Warner, A..
B. 823.1684
Wylde, K.. A dreamer. 823.4043
Wyllard's weird. Maxwell, *Mrs.* M.. E.. (B.)
in 823.5096
Wyncote. Erskine, *Mrs.* T: 823.535
Wyss, Johann D: The Swiss family Robin-
son; or, adventures of a shipwrecked fam-
ily on a desolate island. With introd. of
C: Nodier. (Anon.) 808.376
Xenia Repninà. MacGahan, *Mrs.* B. (E.)
823.7267
Xénie's inheritance. Durand, *Mme.* A. M.
C. (H.) 823.4209

English Fiction. *Contin.*
Zoroaster. Crawford, F. M.   823.4886
Zschokke, Heinrich. *See* Zschokke, J. H. D.
Zschokke, Johann Heinrich Daniel.
—— The broken pitcher. 23 pp. (*With*
Betty's bright idea. By Mrs. H. (B.)
Stowe.)   *in* 823.6678
—— The goldmakers' village; or, a history
of the manner in which two and thirty
men sold themselves to the devil. 823.6834
—— Labour stands on golden feet: a holiday
story. Tr. by J: Yeats.   823.6833
—— The princess of Brunswick-Wolfenbüt-
tel, and other tales. Tr. by M. A. Faber.
                                     823.6835
—— The rose of Disentis. Tr. by J. J. D.
Trenor.   823.6929
—— A Sylvester night's adventure. Tr. by
M. B. W.   823.4746

English Fiction. *Contin.*
Zschokke, Johann Heinrich Daniel. *Contin.*
—— Veronica; or, the free court of Aarau.
Tr. by S: Spring.   823.6274
Zululand. *See also note under* Africa.
—— Adams, H: C. Perils in the Transvaal
and Zululand.   808.1618
—— Haggard, H: R. The witch's head.
(Adventures in Zululand.)   823.7159
Note.—See Du Val, C: With a show through
southern Africa. 1884. 916.201.—Haggard, H: R.
Cetywayo and his white neighbours. 1890. 968.5.—
Little, J. S. South Africa: men, manners, and
facts. 2 vols. 1884. 916.202.—Müller, F. M. Nur-
sery tales. (*Chips from a German workshop*, v. 2.)
290.7.—Sheldon, I.. V. Yankee girls in Zululand.
1888. 916.205.
Zürich. Lander, S.. W.   808.104
See also Switzerland.
Zury: the meanest man in Spring county.
Kirkland, J.   823.4962

APPENDIX.

English Fiction. *Contin.*

Bradley, A. G. *Contin.*
—— Mar'se Dab after the war: a Virginia reminiscence. 39 pp. (*In* Tales from Blackwood. 3d ser., v. 6.)
p. 119, *in* 823.7502
Bradley, Marian. Pentock. 84 pp. (*In* Tales from Blackwood. 3d ser., v. 3.)
p. 135, *in* 823.7499
Bravo, The. Cooper, J. F. 823.7454
Breezie Langton. Smart, H. 823.7524
Bresciani, *Rev.* Antonio, *S. J.* Lorenzo; or, the conscript. 823.7531
Brewster, A.. H. M. Compensation.
823.7559
Bride from the bush, A. Hornung, E. W:
823.7522
Britton, J. J. Flight. 823.7521
Brushes and chisels. Serrao, T. 823.7514
Buckland, C. T. A pickle of salt: a tale of the Indian monopoly. 16 pp. (*In* Tales from Blackwood. 3d ser., v. 6.)
p. 314, *in* 823.7502
Bunner, H: Cuyler. Zadoc Pine, and other stories. 823.7565
Burkhardt, C. B. Fairy tales and legends of many nations; selected, . . . translated.
808.1744
Burton, *Mrs.* M. E. Don Angelo's stray sheep. (*In* Tales from Blackwood. 3d ser., v. 4.) p. 209, *in* 823.7500
—— Fiddlers three. 41 pp. (*In* Tales from Blackwood. 3d ser., v. 3.)
p. 349, *in* 823.7499
California. Jenner, G. A philanthropist: a tale of the vigilance committee at San Francisco. 40 pp. (*In* Tales from Blackwood. 3d ser., v. 6.) p. 193, *in* 823.7502
Campbell, J: G: E: H: Douglas Sutherland, *Marquis of Lorne.* From shadow to sunlight. 823.7578
—— Who were they? a Maltese apparition. 36 pp. (*In* Tales from Blackwood. 3d ser., v. 2.) p. 247, *in* 823.7498
Cause worth trying, A. 49 pp. (*In* Tales from Blackwood. 2d ser., v. 10.)
in 823.7494
Chainbearer, The. Cooper, J. F. 823.7455
Charles, C. Mitchell. Arvon; or, the trials: a legend. 2 vols. 823.7537-8
Cheadle, Walter B. My hunt of the silver fox. 29 pp. (*In* Tales from Blackwood. 2d ser., v. 10.) *in* 823.7494
Chesney, C: Cornwallis. The battle of Dorking: reminiscences of a volunteer. 83 pp. (*In* Tales from Blackwood. 2d ser., v. 2.)
in 823.7486
Child, *Mrs.* Lydia Maria (Francis), *ed.* Rainbows for children. 808.1745
Christmas stories. Dickens, C: J: H., *and others.* 823.452
Chronicles of the Canongate. Scott, *Sir* W.
823.7473
Church, Alfred J: Stories from the Bible. Illus. 808.1733
Clifford, Frank S. A romance of perfume lands; or, the search for Capt. Jacob Cole; with interesting facts about perfumes and articles used in the toilet. 823.7539

English Fiction. *Contin.*

Clifford, *Mrs.* Lucy (Lane). Thomas. 28 pp. (*In* Tales from Blackwood. 3d ser., v. 1.) *in* 823.7497
Clifford, *Mrs.* W. K. *See* Clifford, *Mrs.* L. (L.)
Collins, W: Wilkie, *joint author. See* Dickens, C: J: H.
Compensation. Brewster, A. H. M. 823.7559
Condensed novels and stories. Harte, F. B.
823.6477
Cooley, *Mrs.* Alice (Kingsbury). Asaph: au historical novel. 823.7478
Cooper, James Fenimore. Afloat and ashore. (*With his* The sea lions.) *in* 823.7466
—— The bravo. (*Also*) Mercedes of Castile; or, the voyage to Cathay. 823.7454
—— The chainbearer; or, the Littlepage manuscripts. (*Also*) The redskins; or, Indian and injin: being the conclusion of the Littlepage manuscripts. 823.7455
—— The crater; or, Vulcan's peak: a tale of the Pacific. (*Also*) Miles Wallingford. Sequel to "Afloat and ashore." 823.7456
—— The deerslayer; or, the first war-path. (*Also*) The last of the Mohicans. 823.7457
—— The headsman; or, the abbaye des Vignerons. (*With his* Heidenmauer.)
in 823.7458
—— The Heidenmauer; or, the Benedictines: a legend of the Rhine. (*Also*) The headsman; or, the abbaye des Vignerons.
823.7458
—— Home as found. Sequel to Homeward bound. (*With his* Homeward bound.)
in 823.7459
—— Homeward bound; or, the chase: a tale of the sea. (*Also*) Home as found. Sequel to Homeward bound. 823.7459
—— Jack Tier; or, the Florida reef. (*With his* Wing and Wing.) *in* 823.7468
—— The last of the Mohicans. (*With his* The deerslayer.) *in* 823.7457
—— Lionel Lincoln; or, the leaguer of Boston. (*Also*) The wept of Wish-Ton-Wish.
823.7460
—— Mercedes of Castile; or, the voyage to Cathay. (*With his* The bravo.) *in* 823.7454
—— Miles Wallingford. Sequel to "Afloat and ashore." (*With his* The crater.)
in 823.7456
—— The monikins. (*With his* Wyandotté.)
in 823.7469
—— The oak-openings; or, the bee-hunter. (*Also*) Satanstoe; or, the Littlepage manuscripts: a tale of the colony. 823.7461
—— The pathfinder; or, the inland sea. (*Also*) The pioneers; or, the sources of the Susquehanna. 823.7462
—— The pilot: a tale of the sea. (*Also*) The Red Rover: a tale of the sea. 823.7463
—— The pioneers; or, the sources of the Susquehanna. (*With his* The pathfinder.)
in 823.7462
—— The prairie. (*Also*) The spy. 823.7464
—— Precaution. (*Also*) The ways of the hour. 823.7465
—— The Red Rover: a tale of the sea. (*With his* The pilot.) *in* 823.7463

English Fiction. *Contin.*
Cooper, James Fenimore. *Contin.*
— The redskins; or, Indian and injin: being the conclusion of the Littlepage manuscripts. (*With his* The chainbearer.)
in 823.7455
— Satanstoe; or, the Littlepage manuscripts: a tale of the colony. (*With his* The oak-openings.) *in* 823.7461
— The sea lions; or, the lost sealers. (*Also*) Afloat and ashore. 823.7466
— The spy. (*With his* The prairie.)
in 823.7464
— The two admirals: a tale of the sea. (*With his* The Water-Witch.) *in* 823.7467
— The Water-Witch. (*Also*) The two admirals: a tale of the sea. 823.7467
— The ways of the hour. (*With his* Precaution.) *in* 823.7465
— The wept of Wish-Ton-Wish. (*With his* Lionel Lincoln.) *in* 823.7460
— Wing and Wing. (*Also*) Jack Tier; or, the Florida reef. 823.7468
— Wyandotté; or, the hutted knoll. (*Also*) The monikins. 823.7469
Coppée, François Edouard Joachim. Ten tales, tr. by W. Learned, with introd. by B. Matthews. Illus. with fifty pen-and-ink drawings by A. E. Sterner. 823.7540
Count Lucanor. Manuel, J. 823.7513
Cousin John's property. 58 pp. (*In* Tales from Blackwood. 2d ser., v. 7.)
in 823.7491
Cowper, Frank. Christmas eve on a haunted hulk. 34 pp. (*In* Tales from Blackwood. 3d ser., v. 6.) p. 1, *in* 823.7502
Crater, The. Cooper, J. F. 823.7456
Crosby, Margaret. A violin obligato, and other stories. 823.7569
Cruger, *Mrs.* Julie Grinnell (Storrow). [*Julien Gordon.*] A diplomat's diary.
823.7510
— A successful man. 823.7511
Cumming, Constance Frederika Gordon. "Unfathomed mysteries." 45 pp. (*In* Tales from Blackwood. 3d ser., v. 6.)
p. 158, *in* 823.7502
Cushing, Paul, *pseud. See* Wood, Roland A.
Dark year of Dundee, The. Alcock, D.
823.7532
Dean's daughter, The. Veitch, S. F. F.
823.7445
Deerslayer, The. Cooper, J. F. 823.7457
Dellenbaugh, F. S. A singular case. (*In* Tales from Blackwood.) 3d ser., v. 3.
p. 1, *in* 823.7499
De Quincey, T: Tales and romances. (*Coll. writings*, v. 12.) Ed. by D: Masson.
829.690
Contents:—Editor's preface.—Klosterheim; or, the masque.—The household wreck.—The avenger.—The fatal marksman.—Mr. Schnackenberger; or, the two masters for one dog.—The dice.—The king of Hayti.—The incognito; or, Count Fitz-Hum.—The love-charm; tr. fr. Tieck.
Devil's frills, The: a Dutch illustration of the water cure. 29 pp. (*In* Tales from Blackwood. 2d ser., v. 8.) *in* 823.7492
Dickens, C: J: Huffam. Life and adventures of Nicholas Nickleby. 2 vols. (*Comp. works.* Cambr. ed.) 823.6474-5

English Fiction. *Contin.*
Diplomat's diary, A. Cruger, *Mrs.* J. G. (S.)
823.7510
Dodge, *Mrs.* M.. E.. (Mapes). A few friends and how they amused themselves.
823.7525
Douglas, Robert Kennaway.
— A matrimonial fraud; adapted from a chapter of a Chinese novel. 31 pp. (*In* Tales from Blackwood. 3d ser., v. 1.)
p. 361, *in* 823.7497
— The twins. p. 319, *in* 823.7500
— Within his danger: a tale from the Chinese. 51 pp. (*In* Tales from Blackwood. 3d ser., v. 2.) p. 273, *in* 823.7498
Doyle, A. Conan. The sign of four. (*Also*) The siege of Sunda Gunge. 823.7520
Doyle, R: (1824-1883.) Green, F. G. (Memoir of) D. 19 pp. (*In* The Doyle fairy book.) p. 27, *in* 808.1737
Doyle fairy book, The. Twenty-nine fairy tales tr. from various languages by A. R. Montalba. With a memoir of Doyle and an introd. by a member of the Folk Lore Society. Illus. by R: Doyle. 808.1737
Dreams. Schreiner, O. 823.7518
Same. 823.7519
Duncan, Sara Jeannette. An American girl in London. 823.7541
— A social departure: how Orthodocia and I went round the world by ourselves. Illus.
823.7542
Dziewicki, M. H. Airy nothing. 42 pp. (*In* Tales from Blackwood. 3d ser., v. 6.)
p. 51, *in* 823.7502
Easter trip of two ochlophobists, by one of themselves. (*In* Tales from Blackwood. 2d ser., v. 9.) *in* 823.7493
Eckstein, Ernst. Against the stream. 29 pp. (*Also*) The boarding school girls. 28 pp. (*And*) The visit to the lockup. 26 pp. (*In* Masterpieces of Germ. fict.)
in 823.7552
Edgeworth, Maria. Tales of fashionable life: the absentee. 823.504
Egerton, *Lord* Francis Leveson Gower. *Earl of Ellesmere. Viscount Brackley.*
For works, *see* Bulletin No. 5 of this Library.
Eggleston, G: Cary. A man of honor. Illus.
823.7560
—, *and* Marbourg, Dolores. Juggernaut: a veiled record. 823.7543
Elliott, S.. Barnwell. Jerry: a novel.
823.7533
Emilie de Coulanges. Edgeworth, M.
p. 143, *in* 823.7431
England.
— Duncan, S. J. An American girl in London. (London life.) 823.7541
— Gould, S. Baring- Urith: a tale of Dartmoor. (Country parish life after the close of civil war. 17th cent.) 823.7546
— James, G: P. R. Agincourt. (Battle of Agincourt, 1415.) 823.6478
Fairy tales.
— Burkhardt, C. B. Fairy tales and legends of many nations. 808.1744

English Fiction. *Contin.*
Fairy tales. *Contin.*
—— Child, Mrs. L. M. (F.) Rainbows for children. 808 1745
—— Doyle fairy book, The. . . . Tr. from various languages by A. R. Montalba. Illus. by R: Doyle. 808.1737
—— Grimm, J. L. K., *and* Grimm, W. K: Grimm's goblins. 808.1743
—— — Household stories. Tr. by L. Crane. 808.1738
—— Hamilton, *Count* A. Fairy tales and romances. ** 808.1739
—— Maguire, J: F. Young Prince Marigold, and other fairy stories. 808.1740
—— Shedlock, E. L. A trip to music-land: a fairy tale forming an allegorical . . . exposition of the elements of music. Illus. 808.1933
Fairy tales and legends of many nations. Burkhardt, C. B. 808.1744
Fairy tales and romances. Hamilton, *Count* A. ** 808.1739
Farrington, Margaret Vere. Fra Lippo Lippi: a romance. Port. Illus. 823.6476
Felicia. Murfree, F. N. D. 823.7581
Few friends, A, and how they amused themselves. Dodge, *Mrs.* M.. E.. (M.) 823.7525
Flight. Britton, J. J. 823.7521
Flute and violin, and other Kentucky tales, etc. Allen, J. L. 823.7551
Flying mail, The. 36 pp. Goldschmidt, M. A. p. 7, *in* 823.7545
Forest life. 2 vols. Kirkland, *Mrs.* C. M. (S.) 823.7529–30
Fortunes of Nigel. 2 vols. Scott, *Sir* W. 823.7474–5
Fourteen to one. Ward, *Mrs.* E.. S. (P.) 823.7583
Fra Lippo Lippi. Farrington, M. V. 823.6476
France.
—— Balzac, H. de. Ursula. Tr. by K.. P. Wormeley. (Scene in Nemours; provincial life.) 823.7535
—— Genlis, S.-F. (D. de S.-A.), *comtesse* de. Mademoiselle de La Fayette: an hist. novel . . . of the court of Louis XIII. (1610–1643.) ** 823.7544
—— Hope, A. Alive and yet dead. Some passages in the life of a French convict. 47 pp. (*In* Tales from Blackwood. 3d ser., v. 4.) p. 101, *in* 823.7500
—— Metamorphoses: a tale. (*In* Tales from Blackwood. 2d ser., v. 4.) (French revolution.) *in* 823.7488
Francis, Francis. Mosquito: a tale of the Mexican frontier. 823.7517
French, Alice. [*Octave Thanet.*] Otto the knight, and other trans-Mississippi stories. 823.7588
From shadow to sunlight. Campbell, J: G: E: H: D. S. 823.7578
Games. Dodge, *Mrs.* M.. E.. (M.) A few friends, and how they amused themselves. 823.7525

English Fiction. *Contin.*
Genlis, Stéphanie-Félicité (Ducrest de Saint-Aubin), *comtesse* de. Mademoiselle de La Fayette, an hist. novel illustrating the character . . . of the court of Louis XIII. 2 vols. (in 1). ** 823.7544
Geographical novel. Duncan, S. J. A social departure: how Orthodocia and I went round the world by ourselves. 823.7542
German fiction, Masterpieces of. 823.7552
For contents, *see* Masterpieces of German fiction.
Ghost stories. Jerome, J. K. Told after supper. 823.6469
Goldschmidt, Meier Aaron. The flying mail. (From the Danish.) 36 pp. (*Also*) Old Olaf, by M. Thoresen. 46 pp. (*And*) The railroad and the churchyard (etc.), by B. Björnson. 54 pp. (All) tr. by C. Larsen. 823.7545
Gordon, Julien, *pseud.* See Cruger, *Mrs.* J. G. (S.)
Gould, Sabine Baring- Urith: a tale of Dartmoor. 823.7546
Grant, Robert. Mrs. Harold Stagg. 823.7547
Gray, T. The vestal; or, a tale of Pompeii. (Anon.) ** 823.6252
Grimm, Jakob Ludwig K:, *and* Grimm, Wilhelm K: Grimm's goblins. 808.1743
—— Household stories. Tr. from the German by L. Crane, and (illus.) by W. Crane. 808.1738
Grimm's goblins. Grimm, J. L. K:, *and* W. K: 808.1743
Hall, C: W. Twice taken: an historical romance of the maritime British provinces. 823.7523
Hamilton, *Count* Anthony. (1646–1720.) Fairy tales and romances. Tr. from the French by M. Lewis, H. T. Ryde and C. Kenney. ** 808.1739
Hamley, *Sir* E: Bruce. [*Alexander Sue-Sand, fils.*] The last French hero: being some chapters of a very French novel not yet published. 55 pp. (*In* Tales from Blackwood. 2d ser., v. 4.) *in* 823.7488
—— A recent confession of an opium-eater. 23 pp. (*In* Tales from Blackwood. 2d ser., v. 1.) *in* 823.7485
Hamley, W: G. A magnetic mystery. 58 pp. (*In* Tales from Blackwood. 3d ser., v. 2.) p. 353, *in* 823.7498
—— A medium of last century. (*In* Tales from Blackwood. 3d ser., v. 4.) p. 1, *in* 823.7500
Hans of Iceland. Hugo, V. M., *vicomte.* ** 823.6471
Harcourt, Alfred. Jack and Minory: a tale of Christmas-tide. 55 pp. (*In* Tales from Blackwood. 3d ser., v. 2.) p. 144, *in* 823.7498
Hardman, F: The great unknown: a jest from the German. 41 pp. (*In* Tales from Blackwood. 2d ser., v. 9.) *in* 823.7493
Häring, Georg Wilhelm Heinrich. [*Wilibald Alexis.*] Hans Preller: a legend of the Rhine falls. Tr. by C. L. Lewes. 26 pp. (*In* Tales from Blackwood. 3d ser., v. 2.) p. 90, *in* 823.7498

English Fiction. *Contin.*

Harris, Joel Chandler. Balaam and his master, and other sketches and stories.
823.7572

Harte, Francis Bret. Condensed novels and stories. 823.6477

Hartley, Gilfrid W. The factor's shooting. 29 pp. (*In* Tales from Blackwood. 3d ser., v. 2.) p. 324, *in* 823.7498

—— Master Tommy's experiment: a heather-burning story. 24 pp. (*In* Tales from Blackwood. 3d ser., v. 1.)
p. 337, *in* 823.7497

Heyse, Johann Ludwig Paul. L'Arrabiata. 28 pp. (*Also*) Beppe, the star gazer. 50 pp. (*And*) Maria Francisca. 64 pp. (*In* Masterpieces of Germ. fict.) *in* 823.7552

Hodgetts, Edith M. S., *tr.* Tales and legends from the land of the tzar: a collection of Russian stories. 808.1734

Homo sum. Ebers, G. M. 823.4525

Honor May. Bartol, M. 823.7558

Hope, Andrée. Alive and yet dead: some passages in the life of a French convict. 47 pp. (*In* Tales from Blackwood. 3d ser., v. 4.) p. 101, *in* 823.7500

Hopfen, Haus. Trudel's ball. 70 pp. (*Also*) The fortunes and fate of little Spangle. 53 pp. (*In* Masterpieces of Germ. fict.) *in* 823.7552

Hornung, Ernest W: A bride from the bush. 823.7522

Household stories. Grimm, J. L. K., *and* Grimm, W. K: 808.1738

Hugessen, *Hon.* Eva Knatchbull- A dramatic effect. 46 pp. (*In* Tales from Blackwood. 3d ser., v. 5.) p. 315, *in* 823.7501

Hugo, Victor Marie, *viconte.* Hans of Iceland. Tr. by A. L. Alger. Illus.
** 823.6471

Iermola. Kraszewski, J. I. 823.7577

Imaginary countries and travels.

—— Clifford, F. S. A romance of perfume lands . . . with interesting facts about perfumes . . . used in the toilet. 823.7539

Infidel, The. 2 vols. Bird, R. M.
823.7562-3

Iron, Ralph, *pseud. See* Schreiner, O.

Iron game, The. Keenan, H: F. 823.7575

Italy.

—— Farrington, M. V. Fra Lippo Lippi: a romance. (Florence, 15th cent.) 823.6476

James, G: Payne Rainsford. Agincourt.
823.6478

Jamestown, The witch of. Bowyer, J. T.
823.7561

Jerome, Jerome K. Three men in a boat (to say nothing of the dog). 823.6939

—— Told after supper. Illus. 823.6469

Jerry. Elliott, S.. B. 823 7533

Johnston, R: Malcolm. The Primes and their neighbors: ten tales of middle Georgia.
823.7549

Juggernaut. Eggleston, G: C., *and* Marbourg, D. 823.7543

Keenan, H: F. The iron game: a tale of the war. 823.7575

Kirkland, *Mrs.* Caroline Matilda (Stansbury). Forest life. 2 vols. 823.7529-30

English Fiction. *Contin.*

Knickerbocker nuggets. Stories from the Italian poets. 2 vols. 823.7081-2

Korolenko, Vladimir. The blind musician. Tr. from the Russian by A. Delano, with an introd. by G: Kennan. Illus.
823.7550

Kraszewski, Joseph Ignatius. Iermola. Tr. by Mrs. M. Carey. 823.7577

Last days of Pompeii. Lytton, E: G: E. L. Bulwer- 823.1033

Life . . . of Nicholas Nickleby. 2 vols. Dickens, C: J: H. 823.6474-5

Lily of the valley, The. Balzac, H. de.
823.7534

Lindau, Rudolf. All in vain. 42 pp. (*Also*) First love. 10 pp. (*And*) Haus the dreamer. 94 pp. (*In* Masterpieces of Germ. fict.) *in* 823.7552

Lippi, Filippo, *called* Fra Filippo del Carmine. Farrington, M. V. Fra Lippo Lippi: a romance. 823.6476

Literature. German literature. *Coll. and selections.* Masterpieces of German fiction. 823.7552

Lorenzo. Bresciani, A. 823.7531

Lorne, *Marquis of. See* Campbell, J: G: E: H: D. S.

Lytton, E: G: Earle Lytton Bulwer-, *Baron Lytton.* The last days of Pompeii.
823.1033

McLeod, Grace Dean. Stories of the land of Evangeline. 823.7580

Mademoiselle de La Fayette. Genlis, S.-F. (D. de S.-A.), *comtesse* de. ** 823.7544

Maguire, J: Francis. Young Prince Marigold, and other fairy stories. 808.1740

Man of honor, A. Eggleston, G: C.
823.7560

Marbourg, Dolores, *joint author. See* Eggleston, G: C.

Mark Twain, *pseud. See* Clemens, S: L.

Masterpieces of German fiction. 823.7552
Contents:—Eckstein, E. The visit to the lockup;—The boarding school girls;—Against the stream. —Heyse, P. L'Arrabiata;—Beppe, the star gazer;—Maria Francisca.—Hopfen, H. Trudel's ball;—The fortunes and the fate of little Spangle.—Lewald, F. The aristocratic world;—The maid of Oyas.—Lindau, R. Haus the dreamer;—All in vain;—First love.—Wilbrandt, A. The pilot captain.

Meredith, G: One of our conquerors.
823.7553

Merry tales of the three wise men of Gotham. Paulding, J. K. ** 823.7528

Mexico. Bird, R. M. The infidel; or, the fall of Mexico. 2 vols. 823.7562-3

Mrs. Harold Stagg. Grant, R. 823.7547

Murfree, Fanny N. D. Felicia. 823.7581

Musical novel. Stephenson, *Mrs.* E. (T.) St. Olave's. 823.7554

Noble deeds of our forefathers. Watson, H: C. 808.1741

Nova Scotia. McLeod, G. D. Stories from the land of Evangeline. 823.7580

Oliphant, L. Dollie and the two Smiths. 35 pp. Anon. (*In* Tales from Blackwood. 2d ser., v. 6.) *in* 823.7490

On Newfound river. Page, T: N. 823.7582

Otto the knight, and other trans-Mississippi stories. French, A. 823.7588

English Fiction. *Contin.*
Page, T: Nelson. On Newfound river.
                823.7582
Picken, Andrew, *ed.* The club-book: being
  original tales by James, Picken, Galt,
  Power, and others. 2 vols. (in 1). 823.702
Psychological novel. Korolenko, V. The
  blind musician. (The mind of the blind.)
                823.7550
Rainbows for children. Child, *Mrs.* L. M.
  (F.)   808.1745
Rudder Grangers abroad, and other stories.
  Stockton, F. R: 823.7587
Russia. Kraszewski, J. I. Iermola. (Peas-
  ant life in Wolhynia, Poland.) 823.7577
St. Olave's. Stephenson, *Mrs.* E. (T.)
                823.7554
Schick, L:, *pub.* Masterpieces of German
  fiction.   823.7552
  For contents, *see* Masterpieces of German fiction.
Social departure, A. Duncan, S. J. 823.7542
Stockton, Francis R: The Rudder Grangers
  abroad, and other stories.   823.7587

English Fiction. *Contin.*
Stories of the land of Evangeline. McLeod,
  G. D.   823.7580
United States.
—— Allen, J. L. Flute and violin, and other
  Kentucky tales and romances. 823.7551
—— Bunner, H: C. Zadoc Pine. (New Jer-
· sey. Labor and labor union.) 823.7565
—— French, A. Otto the knight, and other
  trans-Mississippi stories. (Arkansas, life
  and manners.)   823.7588
—— Keenan, H: F. The iron game. (1st yr.
  of civil war.)   823.7575
—— Page, T: N. On Newfound river. (Vir-
  ginia. Life before the war.) 823.7582
—— Ward, *Mrs.* E.. S. (P.) Fourteen to one.
  (Ku Klux Klan.)   823.7583
Violin obligato, and other stories. Crosby, M.
                823.7569
Ward, *Mrs.* E.. Stuart (Phelps). Fourteen
  to one.   823.7583
Zadoc Pine, and other stories. Bunner, H: C.
                823.7565

INDEX.

www.ingramcontent.com/pod-product-compliance
Lightning Source LLC
Chambersburg PA
CBHW031357270326
41929CB00010BA/1225